Index

to the

Australian Dictionary of Biography

Volumes 1 & 2
(A to Z — 1788-1850)

Editors

Malcolm R. Sainty

Michael C. Flynn

Library of Australian History

Sydney

1991

LIBRARY OF AUSTRALIAN HISTORY
17 Mitchell Street, North Sydney, NSW 2060
First published 1991
ISBN 0 908120 81 8
© Library of Australian History

Neither this Index nor the Library of Australian History has any connection with the Australian Dictionary of Biography or Melbourne University Press. This Index is published by the Library of Australian History to assist readers of the *Australian Dictionary of Biography* and further information regarding that publication should be addressed to Melbourne University Press.

Data entry by Library of Australian History
Typeset by Photoset Computer Service Pty Limited, Sydney NSW 2000
Printed in Australia by Star Printery, Erskineville NSW 2043

Contents

Introduction 6
Personal Names Index 8
Personal Names Addenda 64
Occupations Index 65
Placenames Index and Explanation 75
General Index and Explanation 102
Abbreviations . . . .

Acknowledgements

We acknowledge with thanks the vast amount of time and effort devoted by Keith Johnson to checking the material selected for inclusion and for proof reading the index. Jill Baxter also selected material for inclusion and did much of the initial data entry. Also acknowledged is the editorial work of Carol Baxter as well as data entry by her and by Allison Allen. Philip Graham prepared the data for typesetting and assisted with design and layout.

Introduction

The *Australian Dictionary of Biography* was first published in 1966. Two volumes covering the period 1788-1850 were the first to appear. Four more volumes were later produced for the years 1851-1890, followed by another six for the years 1891-1939. The last of these, volume twelve, was published in November 1990.

This index aims to provide a comprehensive guide to the contents of volumes one and two. These volumes comprise 1116 biographies of men and women who played a role in the formative period of colonial Australia, beginning with the arrival of the First Fleet in 1788 and ending in 1850, the year before the Gold Rush brought great social, economic and political change. Early explorers and others associated with Australia prior to European settlement are also included.

The subjects of biographies were chosen mainly on the basis of their having been widely regarded as being significant figures in the course of Australian history. Those who lived and worked beyond 1850 were included if their most important contributions or the greater part of their working life fell before 1850. A small number of less well known persons and a sprinkling of women and Aboriginal men were also included as "samples of the Australian experience". Quotas were allocated to the six states and the larger number dealing with New South Wales and Tasmania (Van Diemen's Land) reflects the earlier foundation of those colonies.

In the quarter-century which has elapsed since the 1788-1850 volumes were published a number of errors and omissions have been detected. These have been printed in a series of corrigenda sheets which are annotated in the index with a (C) for volume one and (2C) for volume two. The biographies of a number of relevant persons were omitted in error or owing to lack of material. For example Thomas Townshend, Lord Sydney, the Home Secretary at the time of the despatch of the First Fleet and after whom the city of Sydney was named, finds no place in these volumes; other omissions include the Irish rebel Michael Dwyer (1772-1825), the prominent lay Catholic James Dempsey (1768-1838), the Master Attendant at Sydney Captain John Nicholson, R.N. (1787-1863), the early businesswoman Elizabeth Needham (c1761-1825) and Samuel Thorley (1769-1821) and Philip Thorley (1799-1883).

Since the 1960s there has been an increase in interest in social history and the role of the ordinary person. A variety of more specialised biographical dictionaries have apppeared in this new field of study. Examples include *The Founders of Australia: a Biographical Dictionary of the First Fleet, Biographical Index of South Australians, 1836-1885, Dictionary of Western Australians, 1829-1914*, and the Australian Biographical and Genealogical Record (biographies of miscellaneous Australians for the years 1788-1899).

In spite of the length of time since its first publication, the *Australian Dictionary of Biography* remains a standard work of historical reference. This index aims to provide greater access to the vast amount of data contained in the work. All personal names, place names and occupations are indexed separately. These include parents, spouses, children, some grandchildren and other relatives as well as business associates, professional colleagues or other persons not included as principal biographies and not previously indexed in any way. In addition, a

comprehensive general subject index lists references to areas as diverse as Aborigines, armies, books, churches, companies, convicts, courts, education, exploration, industries, newspapers, organisations, politics, shipping, religion, schools and universities. They enable the researcher to trace the connections of particular individuals with a subject area or organisation, allowing links and associations between different historical figures and organisations to be explored more fully than has been possible in the past.

Personal Names

a'Beckett, (Judge) 252(2)
a'Beckett, William 520
A'Gutta, Margaret 552
A'Gutta, Mary 552
A'Gutta, Sarah Rout 552
Aaron, Isaac 1
Abbot, James 610(2)
Abbott, Edward 2, 39, 49, 61, 469, 550, 163(2), 170(2), 436(2)
Abbott, Edward (Dep. Judge Advocate) 459(2), 461(2)
Abbott, Edward (Jun) 2
Abbott, John 2, 110
Abercrombie, Andrew 449(2)
Abercrombie, Rachel 449(2)
Abercromby, 443(2)
Abercromby, (General) 188(2)
Abercromby, (Mrs) 558(2)
Abercromby, Helen 558(2)
Abercromby, Madeleine 558(2)
Aberdeen, (Earl of) 532
Abingdon, (Earl of) 105
Abinger, (Judge) 558(2)
Abrahams, Esther 19(2)
Abrahams, Rosanna 283(2)
Achin (King of) 555
Ackermann, 592(2)
Ackermann, Rudolph 467
Acland, (Colonel) 13
Adams, (Archdeacon) 207(2)
Adams, Elizabeth 401(2)
Adams, John 288(2), 289(2)
Adams, John (Rev) 268
Adams, Maria Ann 247(2)
Adams, Robert 14(2)
Adams, Selina Anne 207(2)
Adamson, John 544
Adamson, Margaret 544
Adcock, Sarah 86
Addenbroke, Emily 50(2)
Addenbroke, Henry 50(2)
Addison, 224
Adey, Stephen 3, 270, 457, 500(2)
Adkins, James 133(2)
Adkins, Sophia Rebecca 133(2)
Adolphus, John 21(2)
Adye, Susan 151
Adye, William 151
Agnew, Edward 66
Agnew, James (Dr) 59, 298(2)
Agnew, James (Sir) 308(2)
Agnew, Janet Mary 304
Aikenhead, James 3, 590(2)
Aikenhead, William 3, 4
Ainslie, Elizabeth 171
Ainsworth, Mary (Mrs) 121(2)
Ainsworth, Oliver Dixon (Maj) 121(2)
Airy, George Biddell (Sir) 404(2)
Aitken, 14
Aitken, John 4, 70

Aiton, William T. 265, 267
Aiton, W.T. 268
Albrecht, August 421(2)
Alexander, George 150
Alexander, James 370(2)
Alexander, John 442
Alexander, Sarah (Mrs) 370(2)
Alford, John 553(2)
Alford, Mary 553(2)
Ali, Mohammed 116(2)
Allan, 25
Allan, (Commissary) 22(2), 307(2)
Allan, Andrew 323, 358
Allan, David 5, 157, 322, 549
Allan, David (Commissary Gen) 19(2)
Allan, Maxwell Rennie 5
Allen, 280
Allen, A.G. 559(2)
Allen, Andrew 5
Allen, David 158
Allen, Elizabeth 7
Allen, Elizabeth 5
Allen, George 5, 6, 204(2), 554(2)
Allen, George Wigram 6
Allen, Harriet 105(2)
Allen, James 377
Allen, John 230
Allen, John (Rev) 625(2)
Allen, Martha 87(2)
Allen, Mary 32
Allen, Nathaniel Paul 7
Allen, Patience 314(2)
Allen, Richard 5, 235
Allen, Robert 5
Allen, Sophia 5
Allen, Thomas 7, 87(2)
Allen, William 5, 7
Allin, C.D. 591(2)
Allison, Frances (Mrs) 7
Allison, Francis 7
Allison, William 7
Allison, William Race 7
Allman, Francis 8, 102
Allman, George 9
Allman, Harriet 8
Allman, Harriet (Mrs) 8
Allman, John 8, 9
Allman, Sarah (Mrs) 8
Allport, Hannah (Mrs) 9
Allport, Joseph 9
Allport, Mary Morton 9
Allport, Morton 9
Allport, William 9
Alltree, (Dr) 453(2)
Allwood, Anna Rebecca 10
Allwood, Anne Rocke 530
Allwood, R. (Rev) 425(2)
Allwood, Robert 10, 150, 163, 336, 530
Allwood, Robert (Rev) 530
Alphonsine, Maria 185

Alt, (Surveyor Gen) 487
Alt, Augustus 183
Alt, Augustus Theodore Henry 11
Alt, Henry George 12
Alt, Jeanetta (Mrs) 11
Alt, Jost Heinrich 11
Alt, Lucy 12
Alt, Matthew Bowles 12
Althorp, (Lord) 609(2)
Altree, (Surgeon) 4(2)
Amerydeth family 224(2)
Amos family 225(2)
Amos, Adam 12
Amos, Helen (Mrs) 12
Amos, James 12
Amos, John 12
Amos, Mary (Mrs) 12
Amos, T.S. 263, 373
Anacreon, (author) 612(2)
Anderson, (Colonel) 9(2)
Anderson, (Major) 40
Anderson, Elizabeth Ann 14
Anderson, Fairlie Gordon 14
Anderson, General John 14
Anderson, Hugh 14
Anderson, James 13, 589(2)
Anderson, Janet (Mrs) 13, 14
Anderson, John 13
Anderson, John (Prof) 520
Anderson, John (Rev) 192, 428, 144(2)
Anderson, Joseph 13
Anderson, Juliet Vivion 14
Anderson, Mary 15
Anderson, Mary (Mrs) 14
Anderson, Mary Walkman 14
Anderson, Samuel 14
Anderson, Thomas 14
Anderson, William Acland Douglas 14
Andrada, Jose Bonifacio 94(2)
Andrew, Helen Warden 442
Andrew, Thomas 442
Andrews, H.C. 120(2)
Andrews, Sarah 358
Angas, Caleb 15
Angas, George Fife 15, 18, 166, 443, 540, 33(2), 176(2), 290(2), 356(2), 440(2), 480(2), 481(2)
Angas, George French 17, 18, 38, 444, 478
Angas, John Howard 17, 18
Angas, Joseph 17
Angas, Rosetta (Mrs) 18
Angas, Sarah (Mrs) 15
Angas, William Henry 15
Angel, 565
Anglesea, Marquis of 271(2)
Anglesey, (Lord) 149
Anley, Charlotte 334
Ansdell, R. 562(2)
Anstey, Arthur Oliphant 21

Anstey, Clara 20
Anstey, Elizabeth (Mrs) 19
Anstey, Ellen Lucy 20
Anstey, G.A. 443
Anstey, George Alexander 20
Anstey, Henry Frampton 21
Anstey, John 19
Anstey, Julia Capper 20
Anstey, Thomas 19, 27(2)
Anstey, Thomas Chisholm 20
Antill, (Captain) 520(2)
Antill, Edward 21
Antill, Eliza (Mrs) 21, 558
Antill, Elizabeth (Mrs) 605(2)
Antill, H.C. 199, 558
Antill, Henry Colden 21
Antill, Henry Colden (Maj)
    605(2)
Antill, John 21
Appleby, Mary 625(2)
Appleton, Charles 23(2), 600(2)
Arabanoo 22, 50
Archer, Ann 26
Archer, Alexander 23
Archer, Archibald 22, 23
Archer, Charles 22
Archer, Charlotte (Mrs) 23
Archer, Colin 22
Archer, David 22, 566(2)
Archer, Edward 24, 25
Archer, Edward Walker 23
Archer, Elinor (Mrs) 225
Archer, Ellen 26, 469(2)
Archer, Grace (Mrs) 23
Archer, J.L. 41
Archer, John 22, 23
Archer, John Lee 23, 73(2),
    38(2), 527(2), 595(2)
Archer, Joseph 24, 25, 511,
    94(2), 143(2), 225(2)
Archer, Joseph (Mrs) 225
Archer, Julia (Mrs) 22, 566(2)
Archer, Lee 110
Archer, Martha 50(2)
Archer, Martha (Mrs) 24, 25
Archer, Martha Elizabeth
    Henrietta 26
Archer, Susan Ann 26
Archer, Susannah 26
Archer, Thomas 22, 24, 25,
    50(2), 94(2), 469(2), 566(2)
Archer, Thomas William 26
Archer, William 22, 23, 24, 25,
    333, 143(2), 566(2)
Arden, (Lady) 111(2)
Arden, (Lord) 291
Arden, George 26, 216, 603(2)
Arden, Samuel 26
Argyll, (Duke of) 197, 118(2),
    187(2), 194(2)
Ariola, Martena 573
Armstrong, (Captain) 305,
    214(2)
Armstrong, Francis 439(2)
Armytage, George 27
Armytage, George Stephen 27
Armytage, Elizabeth (Mrs) 27
Armytage, Thomas 27
Arndell, Anthony 27(C)
Arndell, Elizabeth (Mrs) 27(C)
Arndell, Elizabeth Emily 458
Arndell, Esther 27(C), 556

Arndell, Esther (Mrs) 556
Arndell, Francess Hannah 494
Arndell, John 27(C)
Arndell, Mary Louisa 72(2)
Arndell, Sarah 529(2)
Arndell, Thomas 27, 242, 556
Arndell, Thomas (Dr) 458, 494,
    570, 529(2)
Arndell, Thomas (Surgeon)
    4(2), 72(2), 208(2)
Arnold, (Dr) 411, 412
Arnold, Edward 29
Arnold, Joseph 29
Arnold, Joseph (Dr) 444(2)
Arnold, Julia Frances 31
Arnold, Julia (Mrs) 30, 462(2)
Arnold, Mary (Mrs) 29
Arnold, Mary Augusta 31
Arnold, Samuel 172, 143(2)
Arnold, Thomas 29, 251, 436,
    462(2), 608(2)
Arnold, Thomas (Rev) 29
Arnold, William Thomas 31
Arrot, Andrew 169
Arrot, Christina 169
Arscott, Catherine (Mrs) 31
Arscott, John 31
Arthur, 2, 41, 172
Arthur, Catherine (Mrs) 32
Arthur, Charles 32, 38, 214(2)
Arthur, Elizabeth 139
Arthur, Frederick 36
Arthur, George 32, 323
Arthur, George (Col) 404, 413,
    474, 475
Arthur, George (Gov) 170(2),
    563(2), 593(2)
Arthur, George (Lt. Gov) 15,
    19, 23, 45, 106, 147, 332, 339,
    356, 360, 361, 372, 394, 400,
    410, 428, 429, 429, 430, 437,
    439, 467, 486, 494, 507, 559,
    37(2), 40(2), 44(2), 49(2),
    67(2), 71(2), 72(2), 73(2),
    94(2), 121(2), 126(2), 128(2),
    132(2), 133(2), 143(2), 164(2),
    176(2), 204(2), 205(2), 214(2),
    225(2), 229(2), 246(2), 248(2),
    260(2), 267(2), 273(2), 278(2),
    296(2), 302(2), 311(2), 315(2),
    317(2), 319(2), 366(2), 371(2),
    384(2), 382(2), 385(2), 396(2),
    396(2), 421(2), 423(2), 427(2),
    429(2), 434(2), 447(2), 452(2),
    454(2), 457(2), 461(2), 462(2),
    466(2), 500(2), 502(2), 504(2),
    515(2), 517(2), 522(2), 534(2),
    541(2), 564(2), 576(2), 577(2),
    604(2), 622(2), 633(2)
Arthur, George (Sir) 182, 191,
    194, 213, 219, 225, 241, 242,
    250, 270, 301, 302, 407, 457
Arthur, Henry 38, 355, 475,
    49(2)
Arthur, John 32
Arthur, John Lake Allen 32
Arthur, Mary (Mrs) 32
Ascough, Barbara (Mrs) 283(2)
Ascough, James 284(2)
Ascough, James (Capt) 284(2)
Ascough, Miss 284(2)
Ashe, J.J. 451(2)

Ashley, (Lord) 222
Aspinall, Richard 461
Asprey, Martha Sarah 191
Astley, Anne 196(2)
Astley, Jacob (Sir) 196(2)
Astley, William 352(2)
Atholl, (Duke of) 349, 49(2)
Atholl, (Dutchess of) 49(2)
Atkins (Bowyer), Richard 38
Atkins, (Judge Advocate) 209(2)
Atkins, Anne (Mrs) 38
Atkins, Richard 39, 51, 87, 121,
    157, 218, 263, 469, 550, 571,
    39(2), 154(2), 388(2)
Atkins, Richard (Sir) 39
Atkins, Sophia 3(2)
Atkins, Thomas 40
Atkins, Thomas (Rev) 13, 78(2),
    508(2)
Atkinson, Caroline Louisa
    Waring 42
Atkinson, Cassandra 488
Atkinson, Charles 41
Atkinson, Charlotte 557(2)
Atkinson, Charlotte Elizabeth
    42
Atkinson, Elizabeth 515
Atkinson, George 602(2)
Atkinson, James 42, 486
Atkinson, James John Oldbury
    42
Atkinson, Rhoda (Mrs) 602(2)
Auchinleck, Alison 218(2)
Auckland, (Lord) 541, 446
Aufrere, George 498(2)
Austin, (Dr) 381
Austin, (Lieut) 186(2)
Austin, Amelia 356(2)
Austin, Anna 43
Austin, James 42, 43
Austin, John 43
Austin, Josiah 43
Austin, Lucy 381
Austin, Solomon 43
Austin, Thomas 43
Austin, William 43
Austria, (Francis Archduke of)
    71
Axford, Rose 106
Axford, Thomas 106
Ayrton, Mary Charlotte
    Dorking 321(2)
Backas, (Backhouse), Eliza
    458(2)
Backhouse, 429, 441(2)
Backhouse, Deborah 46
Backhouse, Deborah (Mrs) 45
Backhouse, (Backas), Eliza
    458(2)
Backhouse, J. 529(2)
Backhouse, James 45, 69, 103,
    177, 192, 225, 249, 262, 334,
    492, 523, 185(2), 216(2),
    229(2), 442(2), 491(2), 562(2),
    563(2)
Backhouse, John 289(2)
Backhouse, Marian 289(2)
Backhouse, Mary 45
Backler, (artist) 562
Bacon, Anthony 462, 560(2)
Bacon, Anthony (Jun) 46
Bacon, Anthony (Sen) 46

Bacon, Charlotte (Mrs) 46
Bacon, Mary Ann (Mrs) 163(2)
Bacon, Matthew 163(2)
Baffen, John 74
Bagot, C.H. 341
Bagot, Charles 48
Bagot, Charles Harvey 47
Bagot, Charles Hervey 47(C)
Bagot, Charles Samuel 47
Bagot, Charlotte 48
Bagot, Christopher 47
Bagot, Edward 48
Bagot, Elizabeth (Mrs) 47
Bagot, Mary 48
Bailey, Mary 48, 601(2)
Bailey, Mary (Mrs) 48
Bailey, Robert 48
Bailey, William 48
Bailey, William (Dr) 49
Bain, James 49
Bain, James (Rev) 351, 17(2)
Baines (Barnes), Elizabeth
  574(2)
Baird, (General) 188(2)
Baird, David 451(2)
Baird, David (Sir) 21(2)
Baker, 497
Baker, Mary 499
Baker, William 32(2)
Balch, (Captain) 313(2)
Balfour, 2
Balfour, Charlotte 49
Balfour, W. 147
Balfour, W. (Col) 596(2)
Balfour, William 49, 282
Ball, (Lieut) 453(2)
Ball, Ann 590(2)
Ball, Ann Maria 50, 50(C)
Ball, George 50(C), 64
Ball, Henry Lidgbird 50
Ball, Lucy 50(C)
Ballasis, George 59(2)
Ballow, David Keith 51
Ballow, D.K. (Dr) 448(2)
Ballow, John 51
Balmain, Alexander 51
Balmain, Jane (Mrs) 51
Balmain, William (Surgeon) 49,
  51, 54, 242, 519, 12(2), 58(2),
  154(2), 310(2), 594(2)
Banks, Annie Eliza 193
Banks, Deborah 212
Banks, Jabez (Rev) 440(2)
Banks, Joseph 243, 276, 314(2),
  456(2)
Banks, Joseph (Sir) 50, 52, 62,
  73, 83, 115, 118, 138, 166,
  183, 194, 195, 203, 242, 265,
  266, 320, 374, 403, 468, 566,
  571, 17(2), 46(2), 56(2), 69(2),
  72(2), 88(2), 155(2), 190(2),
  208(2), 231(2), 272(2), 317(2),
  437(2), 498(2), 537(2), 574(2),
  592(2), 610(2)
Banks, Sarah (Mrs) 52
Banks, Sarah Sophia 54
Bannister, (Attorney Gen)
  477(2)
Bannister, Harriet Catherine
  73(2)
Bannister, Saxe 55, 153, 286,
  393, 73(2), 256(2), 570(2),

572(2)
Barangaroo (Aborigine) 85
Barber, George 564
Barber, W.H. 220
Barber, William Henry 393(2)
Barclay, Andrew 56
Barclay, Elizabeth 178(2)
Barclay, James 178(2)
Barclay, Marjory 227
Barclay, Mary 57
Barff, Charles 599(2)
Barff, Henry Ebenezer 600(2)
Barfould, Benjamin 66
Baring, 350, 151(2)
Barker, (Bishop) 11, 198, 212,
  2(2), 484(2)
Barker, (Mrs) 212
Barker, Collet 57, 148, 285,
  372(2)
Barker, Collet (Capt) 117(2),
  612(2)
Barker, Edward 515(2)
Barker, Ellen (Mrs) 424(2)
Barker, Frederic (Bishop)
  570(2)
Barker, Frederic 255
Barker, George 563
Barker, Isabella (Mrs) 563
Barker, James 57, 58, 424(2)
Barker, Mary (Mrs) 57
Barker, Richard 40(2)
Barker, Sarah Elizabeth 524
Barker, Thomas 57, 306, 493(2)
Barker, Thomas Charles 58
Barker, William 57(C), 289(2)
Barnard, (Bishop) 421
Barnard, G. W. 391
Barnard, James 58
Barnard, John George 58
Barnard, Margaret 280(2)
Barnes, Anne (Mrs) 436(2)
Barnes (Baines), Elizabeth
  574(2)
Barnes, J. 227
Barnes, Joseph 365
Barnes, Maria 574(2)
Barnes, Mary 199(2)
Barnes, William 59, 32(2),
  436(2), 534(2)
Barney, (Colonel) 325(2)
Barney, (Lt. Col) 326(2)
Barney, George 60, 189
Barney, Jane (Mrs) 60
Barney, Joseph 60
Barney, Maria Jane 428(2)
Barracks, 610(2)
Barrallier, 519, 272(2)
Barrallier, (Ensign) 54, 213(2)
Barrallier, F.L. 195, 219(2),
  597(2)
Barrallier, Francis 83, 469, 487,
  59(2)
Barrallier, Francis Luis 61
Barrell, Ann 254
Barrett, Mary 353(2)
Barrington, (Captain) 62
Barrington, (Viscount) 299
Barrington, Daines 403
Barrington, George 62, 521
Barron, Esther 373
Barrow, Judith 250(2)
Barry, (Judge) 518(2)

Barry, Redmond (Sir) 116(2)
Barthelemon, Cecilia Maria 530
Barthelemon, Francois
  Hippolyte 530
Bartlett, Ann (Mrs) 394(2)
Bartlett, Elizabeth 394(2)
Bartlett, Louisa 2(2)
Bartlett, Thomas 394(2)
Bartley, Elizabeth (Mrs) 63
Bartley, Hannah (Mrs) 63
Bartley, Onesiphorus Windle 63
Bartley, Theodore 304
Bartley, Theodore Bryant 63
Bartley, William 63
Barton, Elizabeth 66(2)
Barton, George Bruce 42
Barton, Maria 497
Bass, George 54, 107, 127, 172,
  389, 438, 527, 571, 443(2),
  450(2), 574(2)
Bass, George (Sen) 64
Bass, George (Surgeon) 312(2)
Bass, Sarah (Mrs) 64
Bassett, (Dr) 535
Bate, Samuel 66
Bate, Sarah 52
Bateman, Charles 66
Bateman, Eleanor 553(2)
Bateman, John 66
Bateman, John Wesley 67
Bateman, Mary 67, 491
Bateman, Mary (Mrs) 66
Bateman, Walter 66
Bateman, William 67
Bath, Edward 183(2)
Bathurst, 99, 241, 289, 460,
  341(2)
Bathurst, (Earl) 67, 457, 76(2),
  178(2), 194(2), 365(2), 399(2),
  461(2), 462(2), 476(2), 633(2)
Bathurst, (Lord) 374, 375,
  128(2), 192(2), 193(2), 267(2)
Bathurst, Henry 67
Bathurst, Henry (Earl) 212,
  219, 393
Bathurst, Henry (Lord) 394
Batman, Adelaide 70
Batman, Eliza 70
Batman, Elizabeth Mary 70
Batman, Ellen 70
Batman, Henry 5, 68, 372(2)
Batman, John 4, 38, 67, 148,
  174, 176, 369, 532, 125(2),
  371(2), 372(2), 409(2), 458(2),
  501(2), 576(2)
Batman, John Charles 69
Batman, Lucy 70
Batman, Maria 67, 70
Batman, Mary 67
Batman, Pelonamena 70, 176
Batman, Robert 67
Batman, William 67
Batt, Harriett 291
Batts, Elizabeth 243
Baudin, N. 323(2)
Baudin, Nicholas 65, 123, 218,
  233(2), 318(2)
Baudin, Nicholas (Capt) 390,
  39(2)
Baudin, Nicholas Thomas 71,
  123
Bauer, Ferdinand 54, 223(2)

Bauer, Ferdinand Lukas 73
Bauer, Franz 73
Bauer, Lukas 73
Baughan, John 51, 74, 571
Baughan, Mary (Mrs) 74
Bavaria, King of 114(2)
Baxter, 629(2)
Baxter, (Attorney Gen) 572(2)
Baxter, Alexander Macduff 74
Baxter, A.M. 286, 51(2), 247(2)
Baxter, Andrew 296
Baxter, Annie Maria (Mrs) 296
Baxter, Benjamin 411(2)
Baxter, Benjamin (Capt) 547
Baxter, Colin (Rev) 74
Baxter, Fanny Agnes 547
Baxter, Jacobina (Mrs) 74
Baxter, John 362
Baxter, William 167
Baylee, (Major) 75
Baylee, Pery 75
Bayley, 310(2)
Bayly, 283(2)
Bayly, Nicholas 5, 76, 139, 353, 39(2), 97(2), 130(2), 171(2), 210(2), 361(2)
Bayly, Sarah (Mrs) 76, 97(2)
Bayne, Alexander 219
Bayne, Cecilia 219
Bayne, Henry 514(2)
Bayne, Susan(na) 541(2)
Baynes, Henry 375
Beamish, Peter Teulon 406(2)
Beamont, John 76
Bean, Elizabeth 438(2)
Beare, Charlotte Hudson 481(2)
Beatty, Mary 359(2)
Beaufort, (Duke of) 201(2)
Beautemps-Beaupre 172
Beazley, Charles 23
Beazley, Joseph (Rev) 317(2)
Beazley, Sarah Tice (Mrs) 317(2)
Becker, Ludwig 175
Bedford, (Captain) 506(2)
Bedford, (Duke of) 196(2)
Bedford, (Sixth Duke of) 407(2)
Bedford, (Surgeon) 351(2)
Bedford, Edward 78
Bedford, Eleanor 78
Bedford, Eleanor Martha (Mrs) 77
Bedford, William 77, 78
Bedford, William (Dr) 207(2)
Bedford, William (Rev) 35, 292, 356, 267(2), 286(2), 311(2)
Beechey, (Captain) 236
Beechey, William 316(2)
Belbin, James 78
Belcher, Catherine (Mrs) 420
Belcher, Edward (Capt) 446(2)
Belcher, T.L. 420
Bell, (Dr) 267(2)
Bell, (Major) 73(2), 278(2), 316(2), 461(2)
Bell, Archibald 28, 78, 367, 63(2)
Bell, Archibald (Jun) 80
Bell, Charles 85
Bell, Edward

Bell, Elizabeth 100(2)
Bell, Elliot Margaret 82
Bell, Frederic 300(2)
Bell, Henrie 82
Bell, James (Rev) 192
Bell, James Thomas 80
Bell, Jane (Mrs) 100(2)
Bell, Janet (Mrs) 81
Bell, Jessie M. 82
Bell, John 80, 81, 263(2)
Bell, Louisa (Mrs) 81
Bell, Lorraine Wilson 82
Bell, Maria 367
Bell, Maria (Mrs) 78
Bell, Mary Caroline 82
Bell, T. (Major) 71(2)
Bell, Thomas 81
Bell, William 81, 362, 100(2)
Bell, William Montgomerie 82
Bell, William Sims 80
Bellamy, Sarah 122
Bellasis, George Bridges 83
Bellingshausen, F.F. (Capt) 99(2)
Bellingshausen, Faddei Faddeevich 83, 105
Belmore, (Lady) 334
Belmore, James 446(2)
Bendemeer 325(2)
Benison, James 31
Benison, Josephine 31
Benjamin, Judah 84
Benjamin, Lyon Judah 84
Benjamin, Mary Ann (Mrs) 550(2)
Benjamin, Samuel 84
Bennelong (Aborigine) 84, 145, 234, 331(2), 566(2)
Bennet, 275
Bennet, (convict) 215(2)
Bennet, George 529(2)
Bennet, Henry Grey 66, 359, 550(2)
Bennet, H.G. 192(2), 584(2)
Bennet, Mary 116(2)
Bennett, Catherine 502, 217(2)
Bennett, George 85, 197
Bennett, Julian (Mrs) 197
Bennett, Mary 214
Bennett, Matilda 391(2)
Bennyfield, Mary Ann 66
Bensley, Benjamin 490
Bensley, Thomas 490
Benson, Ann 216(2)
Benson, Joseph (Rev) 216(2)
Benson, Sarah (Mrs) 216(2)
Benstead, James 466
Bent, Andrew 37, 43, 86, 561, 385(2), 397(2), 515(2), 577(2)
Bent, E. 16(2)
Bent, E. (Judge) 581(2)
Bent, Ellis 87, 101, 121, 199, 219, 263, 426, 460, 159(2), 190(2), 210(2), 305(2), 520(2), 552(2), 627(2), 628(2)
Bent, Ellis (Jun) 87
Bent, Jeffery 460, 282(2), 550(2)
Bent, Jeffery Hart 87
Bent, J.H. 115, 158, 199, 211, 219, 263, 343, 373, 426, 192(2), 255(2), 307(2), 371(2), 395(2)

Bent, Robert 87
Bentham, G. 325
Bentham, George 168(2), 245(2)
Bentham, Jeremy 211, 94(2), 247(2), 280(2), 376(2)
Bentham, Samuel (Sir) 568
Bentley, Sarah 570(2)
Beresford, John Poo (Capt) 545
Bernal, Clara Christiana (Mrs) 595(2)
Bernal, Ralph 595(2)
Berners, Bridget 550(2)
Berners, William 550(2)
Berrie, Isabel 94
Berrie, James 92
Berry, Alexander 92, 305, 564, 81(2), 213(2), 620(2), 621(2)
Berry, David 93
Berry, Elizabeth (Mrs) 621(2)
Berry, Emma Mary Ann Catherine (Mrs) 64(2)
Berry, Isabel (Mrs) 92
Berry, Sarah 549
Bertram, William 70
Bertrand, (l'abbe) 172
Best, Charles 95, 356
Best, Douglas 95
Best, Francis 95
Best, Henry 95, 356, 597(2)
Best, Jane (Mrs) 95, 597(2)
Best, John 95
Best, John (Jun) 95
Best, Mary 553(2)
Betham, Elizabeth 118
Betham, Jane 311
Bethune, F.P. (Rev) 96
Bethune, John (Rev) 95
Bethune, J.W. (Rev) 96
Bethune, W.A. 365(2)
Bethune, Walter 176(2)
Bethune, Walter Angus 95
Beveridge, Grace 268(2)
Beveridge, James 268(2)
Bibb, John 96, 554(2)
Bibb, Phoebe (Mrs) 96
Bibb, Samuel 96
Bibb, Sarah (Mrs) 96
Bicheno, Ann 97
Bicheno, Ann (Mrs) 97
Bicheno, James (Rev) 97
Bicheno, James Ebenezer 97
Bicknell, Henry 253
Biddlecombe, Janet (Mrs) 409(2)
Biddlecombe, John 409(2)
Biddulph, Frances Maria 464(2)
Bidwill, John Carne 98, 407(2)
Bigge, Charlotte (Mrs) 431(2)
Bigge, John Thomas 2, 99
Bigge, J.T. 66, 67, 79, 116, 137, 138, 151, 158, 162, 188, 207, 223, 247, 255, 257, 259, 263, 264, 284, 289, 325, 343, 359, 373, 374, 375, 383, 392, 393, 416, 427, 429, 471, 474, 496, 506, 537, 562, 566, 528, 561, 575, 11(2), 32(2), 37(2), 40(2), 45(2), 134(2), 102(2), 113(2), 147(2), 157(2), 192(2), 195(2), 210(2), 215(2), 217(2), 260(2), 306(2), 336(2), 359(2), 368(2),

370(2), 393(2), 399(2), 401(2),
427(2), 431(2), 459(2), 461(2),
462(2), 468(2), 508(2), 510(2),
520(2), 547(2), 584(2), 585(2),
628(2)
Bigge, Thomas Charles 99
Bigge, Thomas Hanway 431(2)
Bigger, Frances 320
Biggs, Anne 228
Bignell, Sophia 217(2)
Bignell, William (Lt) 217(2)
Billyard, W.W. 61
Binfield, Elinor 24, 225
Bingham, George 46
Bingham, John 74
Bingle, John 101, 226(2), 479(2)
Bingle, John Rayden 101, 102
Bingle, Mary (Mrs) 102
Binks, Louisa 540(2)
Binney, Thomas (Rev) 165
Binns, Frances 589(2)
Biraban 102, 529(2)
Birch, Sarah (Mrs) 104, 491
Birch, T.A. 491
Birch, T.W. 227
Birch, T.W. (Dr) 36(2)
Birch, Thomas William 104
Bird, Ann 558
Bird, Sarah 559
Birnie, Alexander 104
Birnie, James 92, 104, 522
Birnie, Martha Matilda 104
Birnie, Richard 160(2)
Biscoe, Anne (Mrs) 105
Biscoe, John 105
Biscoe, S. 357
Biscoe, Thomas 105
Bisdee, Alfred Henry 106
Bisdee, Edward 106
Bisdee, Edward (Sir) 248
Bisdee, Edward Oldmixon 106
Bisdee, Elizabeth (Mrs) 106
Bisdee, Henrietta Charlotte
  (Mrs) 107
Bisdee, Isaac 106
Bisdee, John 106, 416
Bisdee, John Hutton 107
Bisdee, Mary 416
Bisdee, Rose (Mrs) 106
Bisdee, Thomas 106
Bishop, Charles 65, 107, 527
Bishop, Elizabeth 106
Bishop, Julia (Mrs) 108
Bishop, Peter 108
Bishton, J. (Rev) 32(2)
Black, John 130(2)
Black, Mary Ann 305
Blackburn, 35(2)
Blackburn, Ann (Mrs) 109
Blackburn, James 109, 219, 220,
  100(2), 528(2)
Blackburn, John 109
Blacker, Anne (Mrs) 557(2)
Blacker, George 557(2)
Blacker, Hester Anna 557(2)
Blacket, Edmund 284(2)
Blacket, E.T. 151
Blackman, Elizabeth (Mrs) 110
Blackman, James 110, 96(2)
Blackman, James (Sen) 110
Blackman, John 110
Blackman, William 110

Black Mary (Aborigine) 561
Blackwood (Capt) 212(2)
Blackwood, F.P. (Capt) 167(2)
Blackwood, Francis Price 111
Blackwood, Harriet (Mrs) 111
Blackwood, Henry (Sir) 111
Blair, James 111, 43(2)
Blair, William 101
Blake, Ursula 311(2)
Bland, 617(2)
Bland, (Dr) 367(2)
Bland, Eliza (Mrs) 114
Bland, Robert 112
Bland, Sarah (Mrs) 112, 252,
  522
Bland, W. 148(2)
Bland, William 112, 118, 534,
  556, 152(2), 521(2), 586(2),
  587(2)
Bland, William (Dr) 252, 397,
  495, 520, 522, 142(2)
Blandford, Henrietta 137(2)
Blaxcell, Ann (Mrs) 115
Blaxcell, G. 627(2)
Blaxcell, Garnham 115, 207,
  208, 290, 459, 13(2), 15(2),
  156(2), 201(2), 307(2), 310(2),
  438(2), 531(2), 581(2)
Blaxcell, John 115
Blaxland family 205(2)
Blaxland, (Mrs) 348
Blaxland, Anna Elizabeth
  564(2)
Blaxland, G. 359
Blaxland, Gregory 54, 115,
  96(2), 130(2), 169(2), 538(2),
  583(2), 623(2)
Blaxland, Harriet 319
Blaxland, Harriet (Mrs) 117
Blaxland, John 6, 115, 117, 127,
  157, 319, 130(2), 310(2),
  564(2)
Blaxland, John (Jun) 226(2)
Blaxland, Mary (Mrs) 115, 117
Blaxland, Sarah (Mrs) 117
Blenkinsop, 497
Blessington, (Earl of) 348(2)
Bligh, Elizabeth 50
Bligh, Elizabeth (Mrs) 118
Bligh, J.W. 388
Bligh, Mary 295(2)
Bligh, Rodney (Admiral) 506(2)
Bligh, W. 558
Bligh, William 2, 76, 79, 115,
  116, 117, 118, 156, 195, 196,
  203, 204, 227, 239, 240, 242,
  259, 260, 263, 264, 290, 308,
  380, 381, 383, 389, 542
Bligh, William (Capt) 72(2),
  231(2), 398(2)
Bligh, William (Gov) 365, 408,
  409, 422, 459, 487, 491, 519,
  542, 551, 553, 573, 10(2),
  13(2), 19(2), 20(2), 25(2),
  31(2), 39(2), 45(2), 47(2),
  53(2), 96(2), 98(2), 111(2),
  121(2), 145(2), 147(2), 156(2),
  189(2), 202(2), 213(2), 218(2),
  220(2), 233(2), 255(2), 291(2),
  295(2), 306(2), 310(2), 318(2),
  348(2), 371(2), 374(2), 380(2),
  388(2), 401(2), 419(2), 461(2),

499(2), 508(2), 520(2), 537(2),
  538(2), 570(2), 580(2), 598(2),
  602(2), 609(2)
Blitz, A. 624(2)
Blomfield, (Bishop) 401, 483(2),
  521(2), 569(2)
Blomfield, Thomas Valentine
  157
Bloodsworth, James 122, 101(2)
Bloodsworth, Maria (Mrs)
  101(2)
Bloodworth, James 122
Blosset, Harriet 54
Blosseville, Jules Poret De 122
Blount, Edward M.P. 513(2)
Blunt, Mary 238(2)
Blunt, Richard (Gen) 238(2)
Boardman, Mary 211
Boccius, Norbert 73
Bock, 339
Bock, Alfred 124, 215
Bock, Thomas 123
Bock, William 124
Boggis, Elizabeth 533(2)
Bogle, John 339
Bogle, Sarah Jane (Mrs) 339
Bogue, Adam 141
Bogue, David (Dr) 491(2)
Bohan, William 369(2)
Bolden, Armyne 124
Bolden brothers 200(2)
Bolden, John Satterthwaite 124
Bolden, Lemuel 124
Bolden, Samuel Edward 124
Bolden, Sandford George 124
Bolden, William 124
Boldrewood, Rolf 573
Bolivar, Simon 402(2), 516(2)
Bolton, Dorothy 320(2)
Bolton, Duke of 349(2)
Bonaparte, Napoleon 264, 390,
  417, 364(2)
Bonar, Elliot Margaret 82
Bonar, J.A. 82
Bond, Elizabeth 25(2)
Bond, Ensign 76
Bongaree 177
Bonham-Carter family 151(2)
Boni 337
Boniface, Charles 532
Boniface, Susan 532
Bonisky, Count 11
Bonney, Charles 350, 524
Bonstein, James (Sir) 430(2)
Bonwick, James 369, 462(2),
  505(2)
Booker, Letitia 218
Boorong 234
Booth, Charles O'Hara 125,
  213
Booth, E.C. 354(2)
Booth, Richard 125
Booth, William (Gen) 373(2)
Boothby, (Judge) 17, 262(2)
Boothby, Benjamin 244
Boothman, John Broadhurst
  126
Boscawen, 442(2)
Bostadia, Magdalena 456(2)
Bostock, Eliza Anne 572
Boston, John 126, 438, 97(2),
  170(2), 312(2)

Boswell, Annabella 4(2)
Boswell, James 174
Botany Bay Colebe 234
Boucher, Charles 127
Boucher, F. 216
Boucher, Frederick 127
Bougainville, 85(2)
Boughton, Samuel 79
Boulger, 245(2)
Boungaree 177
Bourbon family 573
Bourke, 4
Bourke, Anne 133
Bourke, Anne Maria 523(2)
Bourke, Elizabeth 128
Bourke, Frances 133
Bourke, John 128, 133
Bourke, John Conway 524
Bourke, Mary Jane 133
Bourke, Richard 13, 202, 318,
   450(2)
Bourke, Richard (Gov) 231,
   397, 398, 422, 450, 531, 532,
   545, 547, 556, 25(2), 46(2),
   72(2), 77(2), 86(2), 119(2),
   120(2), 125(2), 204(2), 239(2),
   256(2), 265(2), 274(2), 304(2),
   335(2), 341(2), 367(2), 377(2),
   378(2), 395(2), 447(2), 450(2),
   464(2), 471(2), 477(2), 479(2),
   511(2), 522(2), 523(2), 586(2),
   609(2), 615(2), 567(2)
Bourke, Richard (Jun) 133
Bourke, Richard (Sir) 128, 160,
   187, 205, 207, 211, 310, 367,
   368, 398, 402, 453, 481,
   179(2), 544(2)
Bourne, 600(2)
Bourne, Anne 51(2)
Bourne, George 600(2)
Bourne, Harriet 600(2)
Bourne, Mary Caroline 82
Bourne, Robert 23(2), 599(2)
Bourne, Robert (Rev) 529(2)
Boutcher, Mary 506(C)
Bowden, Ambrose 134
Bowden, Amelia Gilbert 134
Bowden, Edmund 134
Bowden, Jane 6
Bowden, Matthew 134, 553
Bowden, Thomas 6, 135
Bowen, (Gov) 263(2), 597(2)
Bowen, Elizabeth 136
Bowen, George 9
Bowen, George Meares
   Countess 135
Bowen, George (Sir) 284(2)
Bowen, G.M.C. 80
Bowen, Henrietta 137
Bowen, James 136
Bowen, John 136, 238, 491,
   272(2)
Bowen, John (Lt) 59(2), 264(2)
Bowen, Martha Charlotte 137
Bowen, W.H.H. 135
Bowes, Arthur 453(2)
Bowes-Lyon, Mary Isabella
   604(2)
Bowes-Lyon, Thomas 604(2)
Bowie, James 54, 265
Bowie, Kate 335
Bowie, William (Dr) 335

Bowles, Catherine 553(2)
Bowles, Mary (Mrs) 456
Bowman, 151(2)
Bowman, (Dr) 62(2)
Bowman, Ann 137
Bowman, Edward 137
Bowman, George 139, 214
Bowman, James 137, 324,
   370(2), 425(2), 554(2)
Bowman, John 138, 86(2)
Bowman, Mary (Mrs) 145(2)
Bowman, William 138, 139
Bowyer, George (Admiral Sir)
   39
Bowyer, Henry (Lt. Gen) 39
Bowyer, William (Sir) 38, 39
Boxell, Jane 427(2)
Boyce, W.B. 293, 172(2)
Boyd, 565
Boyd family 360(2)
Boyd, Archibald 139, 141
Boyd, Benjamin 4, 139, 140,
   160(2), 387(2), 521(2)
Boyd, Edward 140, 142, 467(2)
Boyd, Edward (Capt) 429(2)
Boyd, James 141
Boyd, Jane 142
Boyd, John 139
Boyd, William Sprott 142
Boyes, George 217
Boyes, George Lukin 143
Boyes, George Thomas 143,
   416
Boyes, George Thomas William
   Blamey 24, 78, 143, 191, 347,
   411, 416, 530, 551, 354(2)
Boyle, Anne 41(2)
Boyle, Janet 338
Brabyn, Jennifer Ann 232(2)
Brabyn, John 144
Brabyn, John (Capt) 232(2)
Brabyn, Mary 144(C)
Bracefell, David 144
Bracefield, David 144
Bracewell, 313(2), 448(2)
Bracewell, David 144, 326(2)
Bracewell, James 407(2)
Brackenbury, Jane 212(2)
Bradbourne, (Lord) 54
Bradbury, Charles 564(2)
Bradbury, Julia Speke (Mrs)
   564(2)
Braddick, John 519(2)
Bradford, Mary 289(2)
Bradish, Lily 32(2)
Bradley, (Lt. Col) 33
Bradley, (Mr) 132(2)
Bradley, Henry Burton 184
Bradley, James 145, 146
Bradley, William 101, 145, 234
Brady, (Bishop) 278(2)
Brady, (Dr) 416(2)
Brady, Elizabeth 39
Brady, John 146
Brady, John (Bishop) 6(2)
Brady, M. 575(2)
Brady, Matthew 68, 95, 147,
   282, 328, 428, 566, 225(2),
   504(2), 596(2)
Bragg, Sarah Jane 303(2)
Brain, (Dr) 217
Bramston, (Bishop) 341(2)

Brandard, Thomas 123
Brander, Gustavus 456(2)
Brander, Louise Eleonore 85(2)
Branham, Alicia 226
Branham, Mary 226
Brannon, John 602(2)
Branscombe, Elizabeth 19
Bransgrove, William 369
Braund, Charlotte Spence 173
Braund, Mary 173 (see also
   Bryant, Mary Mrs)
Braxfield, (Lord Justice) 266(2)
Breach, (Captain) 326(2)
Breach, Elizabeth 326(2)
Breach, Mary Ann 569(2)
Breadalbane, (Earl of) 186(2),
   194(2)
Bready, Matthew 147
Brecknock, (Earl of) 196
Breillat, Robert 306
Bremer, Ann 148
Bremer, (Captain) 542(2)
Bremer, Jacob 503(2)
Bremer, James 148
Bremer, J.G. 391(2)
Bremer, James John Gordon
   (Sir) 148
Brenan, John 149
Brenan, John O'Neill 149
Brenan, John Ryan 149
Brennan, (poet) 515
Brereton, Le Gay (Dr) 515
Brewer, Bede 340(2)
Brewer, Henry 149
Brewer, Susanna 573(2)
Brewer, W.V. 396(2)
Bridgman, Orlando (Sir) 55
Bridport, (Viscount) 83(2)
Brierly, Oswald (Sir) 160(2)
Brierly, Oswald Walters 141
Brietyche, Charles 233
Brietyche, Eliza 233
Briggs, (Captain) 229
Briggs, (Lady) 262
Briggs, J.G. 80
Briggs, J.P. 271(2)
Brigstocke, Charles Ferdinand
   150
Brigstocke, Susan 151
Brigstocke, Thomas 150
Brine, James 132(2)
Brisbane, Anna Maria (Mrs)
   151
Brisbane, Thomas (Brig. Gen)
   305(2)
Brisbane, Thomas Makdougall
   (Sir & Gov) 101, 151, 200,
   209, 224, 250, 259, 266, 280,
   283, 284, 301, 314, 315, 320,
   323, 324, 348, 331, 338, 373,
   374, 375, 383, 393, 394, 460,
   463, 472, 503, 513, 523, 547,
   556, 561, 11(2), 62(2), 102(2),
   119(2), 123(2), 124(2), 128(2),
   131(2), 147(2), 157(2), 172(2),
   178(2), 211(2), 220(2), 256(2),
   259(2), 269(2), 291(2), 305(2),
   306(2), 307(2), 308(2), 311(2),
   337(2), 388(2), 403(2), 404(2),
   477(2), 483(2), 499(2), 510(2),
   515(2), 529(2), 566(2), 567(2),
   571(2), 578(2), 580(2), 585(2),

628(2), 629(2)
Briscoe, Peter 53
Bristor, (Captain) 357
Bristow, Elizabeth 534(2)
Bristow, Sarah 311
Britten, 245(2)
Britten, James 54, 456(2)
Broad, Mary 173 (see also
  Bryant, Mary Mrs)
Broadhurst, Susan 550
Brockman, E. 190
Brockman, Edmund Ralph 155
Brockman, Elizabeth 155
Brockman, William Locke 155
Brodie, Louisa 250
Brodie, W. 250
Brodribb, Kenneth E. 164(2)
Brodribb, Mary Ann (Mrs)
  164(2)
Brogden, Catherine 350(2)
Brogden, Catherine (Mrs)
  350(2)
Brogden, John 350(2)
Bromley, (Dr) 170(2), 517(2)
Bromley, E.F. 36, 77, 123, 250
Bromley, Edward Foord 155
Bromley, Elizabeth 354
Bromley, Robert Howe (Sir)
  354
Bromley, Sarah (Mrs) 155
Bronte, Charlotte 516
Brook, (Rajah) 15(2)
Brooke, Agnes 348(2C)
Brooke, Elizabeth 564(2)
Brooke, G.V. 161(2)
Brookes, Sophia 390(2)
Brooks, (Captain) 405(2)
Brooks, Christiana 157
Brooks, George (Dr) 254,
  337(2)
Brooks, Henry 157
Brooks, Honoria 157
Brooks, Mary Stephena (Mrs)
  254
Brooks, Richard 90, 156, 12(2),
  554(2)
Brooks, Robert 275
Brougham, (Lord) 203(2)
Brougham, Henry 317
Broughton, (Acting
  Commissary) 128(2)
Broughton, Bartholomew 156
Broughton, Betsey 531(2C)
Broughton, Emily 159
Broughton, Grant 158
Broughton, Phoebe 159
Broughton, Rebecca 292(2)
Broughton, Sarah 159
Broughton, W.H. 564
Broughton, William 25, 89, 91,
  105, 157, 211, 263, 323, 536,
  97(2), 292(2), 531(2C)
Broughton, William Grant
  (Archdeacon) 34, 401, 537,
  76(2), 211(2), 311(2), 433(2)
Broughton, William Grant
  (Bishop) 10, 40, 77, 103, 131,
  136, 150, 158, 205, 231, 254,
  255, 446, 450, 452, 473, 523,
  557, 574, 2(2), 160(2), 198(2),
  236(2), 255(2), 280(2), 341(2),
  350(2), 374(2), 406(2), 414(2),

424(2), 484(2), 513(2), 521(2),
  533(2), 554(2), 569(2), 619(2)
Broun, Anne Elizabeth (Mrs)
  99(2)
Broun, Peter 228, 236, 253(2),
  486(2)
Broun, Peter Nicholas 164
Broun, Richard McBride 99(2)
Broun, William (Sir) 164
Brouwer, Hendrick (Admiral)
  322(2)
Brown, Alexander 345, 236(2)
Brown, Barclay 269(2)
Brown, G.A. 4
Brown, George (Rev) 373(2)
Brown, Harry 103
Brown, Jacob (Gnl) 233
Brown, James 345, 63(2), 236(2)
Brown, James (Rev) 166
Brown, John 4, 165, 379, 540,
  201(2), 482(2)
Brown, Maria Josepha 165,
  201(2)
Brown, Peter Nicholas 164
Brown, Robert 54, 73, 166, 194,
  265, 266, 269, 566, 120(2),
  178(2), 597(2)
Brown, Samuel 165
Browne, (convict artist) 103
Browne, Catherine 292(2)
Browne, Fielding 168, 393(2)
Browne, Gordon D. 275
Browne, Henry 168
Browne, J.H. 498(2)
Browne, John 292(2)
Browne, Sarah 256
Browne, T.A. 124
Browne, Thomas 210
Browne, W.H. (Dr) 291
Browne, W.H. (Rev) 418
Browne, William 292(2)
Browne, William Henry 168
Browning, (Dr) 411
Browning, Colin Arrott 169
Browning, Elizabeth 169
Browning, John 169
Browning, Robert 169
Bruce, George 170
Brumby, James 171
Brumby, John 171
Brumby, Rebecca 171
Brumby, William 171
Brunswick, Duke of 301, 294(2)
Bruny D'Entrecasteaux 72, 305,
  527, 69(2), 85(2)
Bruny D'Entrecasteaux, Joseph
  Antoine Raymond 171
Bruny, Jean Baptiste 171
Bruun, Anna 26(2)
Bryan, Mary 389(2)
Bryan, R. 221(2)
Bryan, Robert 172, 173
Bryan, Robert Butler 172
Bryan, Samuel 172, 532
Bryan, William 37, 172, 372,
  143(2)
Bryant, Edmund 4
Bryant, Elizabeth 63
Bryant, Emanuel 173
Bryant, Francis 4
Bryant, Maria Wilhelmina
  223(2)

Bryant, Mary 173, 443(2)
Bryant, Mary (Mrs) 31
Bryant, Robert (Dr) 223(2)
Bryant, William 173, 443(2)
Buchan, Alexander 53, 314(2)
Buchanan, Alexander 341
Buchanan, Isaac 82
Buchanan, John 253
Buchanan, Walter 72(2)
Buchanan, William 72(2)
Buckingham, (Marquis of) 573
Buckland, J.R. 436
Buckle, Henry 372(2)
Buckley, (Captain) 514(2)
Buckley, Henrietta 279(2)
Buckley, William 174, 114(2),
  125(2), 372(2), 540(2), 576(2)
Bucknall, Caroline 28(2)
Bucknall, E.G. 28(2)
Bucknell, Georgina Lindsay 529
Bucknell, Martha 582(2)
Buckner, Richard 589(2)
Buffett, John 288(2)
Bulger, James 333(2)
Bull, H.E. 134
Bull, John (Rev) 175
Bull, John Wrathall 175, 379(2)
Buller, Charles 113, 343, 151(2),
  586(2)
Bullock, 374
Bulman, Thomas 46
Bulow, (Baron) 114(2)
Bulteel, Catherine 471(2)
Bulwer, E. Lytton 68(2)
Bulwer, Edward Lytton (Sir)
  113
Bulwer, Henry Lytton 481,
  482(2)
Bulwer, Lytton 343, 586(2)
Bunbury, (Major) 546
Bunbury, Amelia (Mrs) 245(2)
Bunbury, H.W. (Lt) 99(2)
Bunbury, Henry (Sir) 76, 175
Bunbury, Henry William St
  Pierre 175·
Bunbury, Richard (Capt) 424(2)
Bunbury, Sarah Susanna (Mrs)
  424(2)
Bunbury, William Richardson
  245(2)
Bunbury, William St Pierre 176
Bunce, Daniel 70, 176
Bund, Ann Susanna Kent
  604(2)
Bundell (Aborigine) 62(2)
Bungaree (Aborigine) 177,
  61(2)
Bunker, Ann (Mrs) 234(2)
Bunker, Eber 120, 178, 98(2),
  234(2)
Bunker, Hannah (Mrs) 178(C)
Bunker, James 178(C)
Bunker, Noah 288(2)
Bunn, Anna Maria (Mrs) 274(2)
Bunn, George (Capt) 274(2)
Bunting, Jabez (Rev) 540(2)
Burbury, Alfred 308(2)
Burbury, Arthur James 179
Burbury, Mary 178
Burbury, Thomas 178
Burbury, William 178
Burdekin, Thomas 611(2)

Burder, (Dr) 229(2)
Burder, George (Rev) 521
Burdett, Algernon 144(2)
Burdett, Louisa Jean 144(2)
Burdett-Coutts, (Baroness) 7, 222
Burdett-Coutts, Angela 186(2)
Burford, Anne 179
Burford, Benjamin 179
Burford, Robert 348, 349
Burford, S. (Rev) 61(2)
Burford, William 179
Burford, William Henville 179
Burges, Isabella 180
Burges, L.C. 75(2)
Burges, Lockier 180
Burges, Samuel 180
Burges, William 180
Burgess, Amelia 181
Burgess, Amelia (Mrs) 181
Burgess, Ellen 181
Burgess, Francis 180, 219
Burgess, Gordon Walter Haines 181
Burgess, Mary 538(2)
Burgess, Murray 181
Burke, Edmund 128, 133, 586(2)
Burke, James Lester 214
Burleigh, Elizabeth 28
Burn, 182, 373, 427
Burn, David 181, 505(2)
Burn, Jacobina (Mrs) 181
Burn, Jemima 182
Burn, Jemima Frances 181
Burn, Simon 5(2)
Burn, William 409(2)
Burnett, Alexander 540(2)
Burnett, J. 517(2)
Burnett, James 182
Burnett, John 36, 182, 508, 118(2), 249(2), 622(2)
Burnett, Mary Gascoigne 118(2)
Burnett, William 93(2)
Burney, Charles (Dr) 377, 566, 558(2)
Burns, Robert 233, 268
Burns, Terence 324
Burrard, Harry (Sir) 631(2)
Burrell, Marianne 516(2)
Burrow, James 373(2)
Burrowes, Mary Ann 162(2)
Burt, 175(2)
Burtchell, James 81(2)
Burton, David 12, 54, 183, 355
Burton, Edmond 184
Burton, Elizabeth (Mrs) 184
Burton, J.C. 178, 45(2)
Burton, John Campbell 374(2)
Burton, Margaret (Mrs) 184
Burton, Maria Alphonsine (Mrs) 185
Burton, W. 342(2)
Burton, William 242(2), 478(2)
Burton, William Westbrooke (Sir, Judge) 103, 184, 318, 319, 397, 398, 402, 17(2), 66(2), 236(2), 338(2)
Busby, Alexander 188, 189
Busby, George 188, 189
Busby, James 186, 189, 269,

545, 546, 494(2), 554(2)
Busby, John 186, 188, 333, 554(2)
Busby, Margaret (Mrs) 188
Busby, William 189
Buscall, Martha 433(2)
Bush, Anna Rebecca 10
Bush, Constance (Mrs) 122(2)
Bush, Joseph 10
Bush, Robert Edward 122(2)
Bushelle, Elisabeth (Mrs) 568(2)
Bushelle, John 568(2)
Bussell, Bessie 189
Bussell, Capel 190
Bussell, Caroline 190
Bussell, Elizabeth 539(2)
Bussell, Emily 190
Bussell, Fanny 189
Bussell, John Garrett 189
Bussell, Josephine 190
Bussell, Lenox 189
Bussell, Mary 189
Bussell, William Marchant (Rev) 189
Bute, (Marquess of) 217
Butler, (Captain) 316(2)
Butler, (Dr) 256
Butler, Charles 489(2)
Butler, Francis 191
Butler, Gamaliel 190
Butler, Henry 191, 194
Butler, James 191
Butler, John 210(2)
Butler, John George 190
Butler, Mary Sarah (Mrs) 191
Butler, Mary 489(2)
Butler, Sarah (Mrs) 191
Butler, Sarah Elizabeth 172
Butler, Weeden (Rev) 462(2)
Butler-Danvers, Augustus 334
Butler-Danvers, Eliza Bizarre (Mrs) 334
Butler-Danvers, Elizabeth Sophia 334
Button, Henry 493(2)
Buttrey, Eliza 357(2)
Buxton, Fanny Agnes (Mrs) 547
Buxton, Fowell 166
Buxton, Mary 357
Buxton, Richard Buckhurst 547
Byng, 442(2)
Byrne, Thomas 259(2)
Byron, 46
Byron, (Lord) 264, 279(2)
Byron, Harriet 303(2)
Byron, Juliana Elizabeth 554
Cabone Johnny (Aborigine) 183(2)
Cadell family 614(2)
Cadell, Francis 352(2)
Cadman, Elizabeth (Mrs) 192
Cadman, John 192
Cairncross, Jane 373
Cairnduff, Alexander 192
Cairnduff, Annie Eliza 193
Cairnduff, Margaret 193
Cairnduff, Rachel 193
Cairnduff, Sarah Ann 193
Cairns, Adam (Dr) 399
Calder, Elizabeth Margaret (Mrs) 194

Calder, J.E. 251, 411, 170(2)
Calder, James 467(2)
Calder, James Erskine 193
Caledon, (Earl of) 199
Caley, George 54, 167, 194, 215, 59(2), 210(2), 223(2), 453(2)
Callaghan, Eliza (Mrs) 196
Callaghan, Elizabeth 68, 325(2)
Callaghan, Malachi 195
Callaghan, Thomas 195
Calvert, John 81
Cambridge, (Duke of) 341
Camden, (Earl) 196
Camden, (Lord) 155(2), 158(2)
Cameron, (General) 479
Cameron, Alan 183(2)
Cameron, Catherine (Mrs) 196
Cameron, Charles 49, 196, 224
Cameron, Charles (Col) 377
Cameron, Charles Duncan 197
Cameron, Charles (Lt. Col) 341, 64(2)
Cameron, Charlotte 197, 341
Cameron, Charlotte (Mrs) 201(C)
Cameron, Donald 196
Cameron, Donald Meeut 197
Cameron, Ewen Wallace 197
Cameron, Julian 197
Cameron, Luduvina 197
Cameron, Luduvina Catherina da Silva 64(2)
Cameron, Luduvina Rosa (Mrs) 197
Cameron, Luduvina Rosa da Silva (Mrs) 377
Cameron, Mary (Mrs) 197
Camfield, Maria 616(2)
Camfield, Susannah Matilda 532
Campbell, (Captain) 226, 312(2), 449(2)
Campbell, (Lord) 247(2)
Campbell, Agnes (Mrs) 203
Campbell, Alexander 197, 195(2)
Campbell, Alexander (Col) 14
Campbell, Annie Sophia (Mrs) 206
Campbell, Barbara Isabella (Mrs) 202, 180(2)
Campbell, Catherine Irene (Mrs) 198
Campbell, Charles 141, 198, 206
Campbell, Charlotte (Mrs) 201
Campbell, Colin 187(2)
Campbell, Donald 118, 197, 516(2)
Campbell, Duncan 4(2)
Campbell, Elizabeth 189(2)
Campbell, Elizabeth (Mrs) 371
Campbell, Frederick 206
Campbell, Frederick Foster 201
Campbell, George 206, 232
Campbell, Isabella Hamilton Dundas 187(2)
Campbell, James 218
Campbell, James (Capt) 397(2)
Campbell, Janet 426(2)
Campbell, Jean (Mrs) 206

Campbell, J.T. 323, 427, 463, 500, 17(2), 62(2), 211(2), 282(2), 510(2), 628(2)
Campbell, John 199, 202, 203, 206, 231, 186(2)
Campbell, John Edwin 201
Campbell, John Thomas 199, 148(2)
Campbell, John "Tinker" 201
Campbell, Lyon 410(2)
Campbell, Margaret 208
Campbell, Margaret (Mrs) 207, 208
Campbell, Margaretta 377(2)
Campbell, Marrianne Collinson (Mrs) 232
Campbell, Mary 14
Campbell, Mary (Mrs) 199
Campbell, Neil 371
Campbell, Pieter Laurentz 201
Campbell, P.L. 180(2)
Campbell, R. 178
Campbell, Robert 74, 156, 198, 199, 202, 206, 252, 290, 290, 362, 388, 402, 409, 439, 472, 492, 522, 551, 11(2), 13(2), 31(2), 58(2), 129(2), 227(2), 232(2), 307(2), 309(2), 373(2), 566(2), 573(2)
Campbell, Robert (Jun) 79, 121, 206, 218, 38(2), 548(2)
Campbell, Robert (Sen) 254(2), 373(2), 548(2)
Campbell, Robert Perkins 201
Campbell, Robert "Tertius" 207
Campbell, Ronald 201, 201(C)
Campbell, Sarah 206
Campbell, Sophia Ives 206
Campbell, Sophia (Mrs) 198, 199, 206, 309(2)
Campbell, Temperance (Mrs) 201
Campbell, W. 306
Campbell, William 107, 199, 206, 208, 463
Campbell, William Douglas 208
Cane, Elizabeth Alice 423
Cankrein, Charlotte (Mrs) 341
Cankrein, Richard 341
Canning, 470(2)
Canterbury, (Viscount) 348(2)
Cantey, Eliza (Mrs) 233
Capalti, 527(2)
Cape, Eliza 209
Cape, Eliza Jane 210
Cape, Elizabeth Jane 76(2)
Cape, Emily 209
Cape, Francis Henry 210
Cape, Henry 209
Cape, Jane (Mrs) 210
Cape, John 209
Cape, Mary Ann 209
Cape, Mary Ann (Mrs) 209
Cape, Richard 209
Cape, Rollo Albert 209
Cape, William 209, 530, 76(2)
Cape, William Timothy 209
Cape, W.T. 397
Capon, Thomas 458(2)
Cargill, David 308
Carlow, Alexander 193
Carmichael, Andrew 271(2)

Carmichael, Gavin Thomas 211
Carmichael, George Graham 211
Carmichael, Henry 210
Carmichael, Jean 271(2)
Carmichael, Jeremy Bentham 211
Carmichael, John 230, 242(2)
Carmichael, Lillias 271(2)
Carnegie, Clementine 435(2)
Carnegie, James 435(2)
Carr, Ann 224
Carr, John 224
Carr, Robert 515
Carr, Ursula 515
Carr-Harris, Grant 516
Carroll, Sarah 229
Carstairs, Anne 408(2)
Carstairs, Euphemia 409(2)
Carter, Charles 537
Carter, Charlotte 531
Carter, Elizabeth 282
Carter, Helen Sarah Burrington 418
Carter, Jane Brackenbury 212(2)
Carter, W. 420
Carter, William 418, 212(2)
Carter, William (Jun) 134
Cartier, George 353(2)
Cartwright, Ann 414(2)
Cartwright, George 9, 395(2)
Cartwright, Isabella (Mrs) 212
Cartwright, James 212
Cartwright, John 625(2)
Cartwright, Mary (Mrs) 211
Cartwright, Richard 343
Cartwright, Robert 150, 211, 343(C), 212(2)
Cartwright, Robert (Rev) 213, 414(2)
Cartwright, Thomas 211
Carvosso, Benjamin 212
Carvosso, Deborah (Mrs) 212
Carvosso, William 212
Casabianca, (Captain) 538
Case, Robert 112
Casey, Bartholomew 213
Casey, Cornelius Gavin 213, 434(2)
Casey, Letitia (Mrs) 213
Casey, Richard Gardiner 214
Cash, George 214
Cash, Margaret (Mrs) 214
Cash, Martin 214, 164(2)
Cassell, J.H.N. 197, 545, 91(2)
Castlereagh, (Lord) 308, 156(2), 189(2)
Castlereagh, (Viscount) 190(2), 550(2), 580(2)
Catchpole, Elizabeth 215
Catchpole, Margaret 215, 374(2), 401(2)
Catherine (Empress of Russia) 403 Cato, Sarah Ann 193
Caulfield, (Dr) 309
Cavanough, Owen 521, 220(2)
Cavenagh, George 216, 367, 376, 48(2), 50(2)
Cavenagh, Jemima Caroline (Mrs) 216
Cavenagh, P. (Major) 216

Cavenagh, Philip 216
Cavendish-Bentinck family 151(2)
Cayley, (Caley) George 223(2)
Cecil, Arabella 296
Chace, Samuel Rodman 31(2)
Chacon, Dona Ana 358(2)
Chaffey, Anne 84(2)
Challis, John Henry 415(2)
Chalmers, Thomas (Dr) 291, 76(2)
Chalmers, William (Dr) 468
Chambers, Hugh John 251(2)
Champ, W.T.N. 220, 476
Champion, Alexander 357
Champion, A.R. (Rev) 335
Champion, Charles 533(2)
Champion, Maria Celia (Mrs) 335
Chandler, Jane 60
Chapman, 201(2)
Chapman, Catherine (Mrs) 217
Chapman, Christina (Mrs) 218
Chapman, Elizabeth 511
Chapman, Henry 218
Chapman, Henry Samuel 542(2)
Chapman, Israel 217
Chapman, Mary 575
Chapman, Mary Morton 9
Chapman, Montague (Sir) 47
Chapman, T.D. 330
Chapman, Thomas Evans 217
Chapman, W.N. 157, 366, 53(2), 56(2), 171(2), 608(2)
Chapman, William Neate 218
Chappell, Ann 389
Charlemont, (Lord) 579(2)
Charles II. (King) 223(2), 579(2)
Charles XIII (King of Sweden) 10(2)
Charlotte, (Princess) 279(2)
Chartres, George 218, 263
Chartres, Letitia (Mrs) 218
Chase, (Captain) 129(2)
Chatfield, Laetitia 485
Chatfield, Samuel 485
Chatham, (Earl of) 97(2)
Chauner, Mary 599(2)
Cherry, Elizabeth Curtis 460
Cherry, George 460
Cheshire, George 110
Chester, Elizabeth 345
Chester, W. 420
Chetwynd, (Viscount) 463, 464, 471(2)
Chetwynd, Susannah 463
Chevalier, Nicholas 175, 160(2)
Cheyne, (Captain) 214(2)
Cheyne, Alexander 109, 219, 35(2)
Cheyne, George 236
Cheyne, John 219
Chidley, Sarah 514
Child, William Knox 38(2)
Childs, Joseph 220, 392(2)
Childs, Joseph (Major) 351(2)
Chipperton, John 334(2)
Chipperton, Sibyl Herlock 334(2)
Chisholm, 525

Chisholm, A.H. 516
Chisholm, Archibald 221
Chisholm, Caroline 221, 420, 450, 534, 338(2), 343(2), 445(2), 511(2)
Chisholm, James 306
Chitty, Robert 294
Christian, Fletcher 288(2)
Christian, Sarah 288(2)
Christie, 345
Christie, (Major) 609(2)
Christie, Stella 41(2)
Chute, Charity 536(2)
Chute, Richard 536(2)
Cimitiere, 25
Cimitiere, (Colonel) 459(2)
Cimitiere, (Lt. Col) 393(2), 564(2)
Cimitiere, G. 171
Cimitiere, Gilbert 223
Claiborne, Richard B. (Rev) 355
Clapperton, Hugh 268
Clark, (Lieut) 17(2)
Clark, Agnes (Mrs) 224
Clark, Alexander Russell 224
Clark, Alicia 226
Clark, Andrew 224
Clark, Andrew (Dr) 228
Clark, Andrew Inglis 224
Clark, Ann 536
Clark, Ann Elphinstone 593(2)
Clark, Ann (Mrs) 224
Clark, Betsy Alicia (Mrs) 226
Clark, Charles 227, 434(2)
Clark, G.C. 7(2), 8(2)
Clark, G.C. (Mrs) 24, 339
Clark, George 86
Clark, George Carr 224, 434(2), 563(2)
Clark, Hannah Maria (Mrs) 225
Clark, John 224
Clark, John 224, 421(2)
Clark, Marcus 352(2)
Clark, Marjory (Mrs) 227
Clark, Phillis (Mrs) 434(2)
Clark, Ralph 225, 319(2), 398(2), 444(2)
Clark, Ralph (Lt) 4(2), 328(2)
Clark, Ralph Stuart 226
Clark, Thomas 224, 226, 70(2), 71(2)
Clark, William (Capt) 593(2)
Clark, William Nairne 227
Clark, William Nairne (Sir) 227
Clark, Z. 218
Clark, Zachariah 361 536, 229(2)
Clarke brothers 181(2)
Clarke, (Mrs) 161(2)
Clarke, A. (Lt. Col) 253(2)
Clarke, Andrew 228, 547
Clarke, Andrew (Gov) 5(2)
Clarke, Andrew (Lt. Col) 381
Clarke, Anne (Mrs) 228
Clarke, Catherine 273(2)
Clarke, Elizabeth (Mrs) 228
Clarke, Frances (Mrs) 228
Clarke, George 552, 553
Clarke, George (Rev) 553
Clarke, James Langton 228

Clarke, James (Sir) 284(2)
Clarke, Janet Marion (Mrs) 455(2)
Clarke, John 229
Clarke, Joseph 228, 229
Clarke, Louisa (Mrs) 228
Clarke, Marcus 228, 27(2), 393(2), 397(2)
Clarke, Martha (Mrs) 552, 553
Clarke, Mary Ann 87(2)
Clarke, Richard 442(2)
Clarke, Sarah (Mrs) 228
Clarke, Thomas 226
Clarke, Thomas Bigges 229
Clarke, W.B. 494(2), 495(2)
Clarke, W.B. (Rev) 94, 279, 287, 29(2)
Clarke, William 228, 229
Clarke, William (Sir) 455(2)
Clarke, William Hislop 228
Clarke, William John Turner 228
Clarke, W.J.T. 4, 182, 9(2)
Clarkson, James 510
Clarkson, Michael 510
Claude, (landscape painter) 213(2)
Claxton, Marshall 402
Clayton, 496(2)
Cleaver, Mary 74
Cleburne, Harriet Beauvais 230
Cleburne, Micajah 229
Cleburne, Richard 229
Cleburne, Sarah 229
Clement VIII (Pope) 357(2)
Clementine, Mary 634(2)
Clements, Elizabeth 112(2)
Clements, John 108(C)
Clerke, Alexander 329
Clermont, (Viscount) 66(2)
Clermont-Tonnerre 123
Clewes, Catherine 105(2)
Clibborn, Elizabeth 47
Clifford, Bessie 214
Clifton, Elizabeth (Mrs) 372
Clifton, Marshall Waller 576
Clifton, W. 372
Clint, George 230
Clint, Mary Ann 230
Clint, Raphael 230
Clive, 277
Clive, George 290
Clode, Samuel 252
Clode, Samuel High 251
Cloete, Charlotte 201, 201(C)
Clooes, Elizabeth Lindley 137
Close, E.C. 449(2)
Close, Edward 231, 311(2)
Close, Edward Charles 231, 337(2)
Close, George Thomas Palmer 232
Close, Marrianne (Mrs) 231
Close, Marrianne Collinson 232
Close, Robert Campbell 232
Close, Sophia Susannah (Mrs) 231, 311(2)
Clough, Arthur Hugh 436
Clow, Helen 232
Clow, Helen (Mrs) 232
Clow, Helena Johanna 400
Clow, James 232

Clow, James (Rev) 399
Clow, Margaret 232
Clow, Mary (Mrs) 232
Clowes, Elizabeth Lindley 137
Clowes, Henry 28(2)
Clowes, Robert 28(2)
Clowes, Thomas 28(2)
Clunie, James Oliphant 233
Clunie, John (Rev) 233
Coalby, 234
Cobb, Eliza 369
Cobbett (Corbett), Catherine (Mrs) 27(2)
Cobbett (Corbett), Norah 27(2)
Cobbett (Corbett), Patrick 27(2)
Cobbold, John 215
Cobbold, John (Mrs) 215
Cobbold, Richard 215
Cobbold, Richard (Rev) 374(2)
Cobden, 225
Cochrane, (Lord) 288(2)
Cock, Ann (Mrs) 252
Cock, John 251, 252
Cockburn, (Lord) 438
Cockburn, Anne Frances 207(2)
Cockerell, S.P. 34(2)
Coke, Thomas 171(2)
Coke, Thomas Walker 85
Cole, Eliza (Mrs) 233
Cole, George Ward 233, 252(2)
Cole, John 233
Cole, Lowry (Sir) 377
Cole, Thomas Anne (Mrs) 233
Colebe (Aborigine) 145, 234, 331(2)
Colebrooke, William 101
Colenso, (Bishop) 256
Colenso, J.W. 437
Coleridge, Edward 163, 347
Coleridge, Edward (Rev) 424(2)
Coleridge, Samuel 374
Collet, Samuel 57(C)
Collicott, John Thomas 234
Collicott, Mary 6
Collicott, Thomas 5, 234
Collie, Alexander 235
Collie, Christina (Mrs) 235
Collie, George 235
Collie, James 235
Collie, John 235
Collie, John (Sir) 235
Collie, Norman (Prof.) 235
Collingwood, Cuthbert (Admiral) 178, 178(C)
Collingwood, Isabella 178(C)
Collins, Arthur 236
Collins, Arthur Tooker 236
Collins, Charity (Mrs) 240
Collins, David 39, 54, 121, 134, 226, 227, 236, 240, 257, 260, 288, 313, 355, 405, 409, 435, 439, 491, 497, 516, 536, 542, 565, 3(2), 67(2), 120(2), 229(2), 264(2), 336(2), 394(2), 397(2), 506(2), 574(2), 610(2)
Collins, David (Lt. Col) 490, 127(2)
Collins, David (Lt. Gov) 553, 97(2), 217(2)
Collins, David (Judge Advocate) 517, 568

Collins, E.J. 562(2)
Collins, George 239
Collins, Henrietta Caroline (Mrs) 236, 236(C)
Collins, Mary (Mrs) 236
Collins, Patrick 570(2)
Collins, R.J. 602(2)
Collins, William 226, 240, 407, 491, 566, 36(2), 127(2)
Collinson, Marrianne 231
Collinson, Michael 231
Collinson, Peter 456(2)
Collison, Marcus 505(2)
Collits, Mary (Mrs) 240
Collits, Pierce 240
Collits, Sophia 241
Collyer, John 70
Collyer, William 70
Colman, G. 161(2)
Colman, W.A. 505(2)
Colnett, (Captain) 218
Colnett, James 357
Colonicus 74(2)
Colp, Ann 252
Colpits, Robert 498
Colquhoun, Mary 57
Colquhoun, Walter 57
Colquhoun, Peter 253
Colston, Elizabeth 123(2)
Coltish, Robson 69
Colville, (Earl of) 410
Colville, Catherine 339
Combe, 211
Combermere, (Lord) 268(2)
Combermere, (Viscount) 250
Condamine, Thomas 241
Condell, Henry 271, 442(2)
Conn, Rum John 504(2)
Connel, Mary 257
Connell, John 98(2)
Connell, Margaret 98(2)
Connolly, Catherine (Mrs) 535
Connolly, Eliza 509(2)
Connolly, Harriet 49
Connolly, Matthew 49
Connolly, Michael 197, 486
Connolly, Nathaniel 535
Connor, Philip 91
Conolly, (Father) 528
Conolly, John 134
Conolly, P. 544(2)
Conolly, Philip 241, 341(2)
Conolly, Philip (Fr) 509(2)
Considen, (Surgeon) 4(2)
Considen, Constance 242
Considen, Constantine 242
Considen, Dennis 54, 242
Cook, Elizabeth (Mrs) 243
Cook, J. (Capt) 323(2)
Cook, James 52, 105, 107, 118, 243, 276, 357(2), 419(2)
Cook, James (Capt) 266, 402-3, 57(2), 85(2), 314(2), 390(2), 550(2)
Cook, James (Sir) 374
Cook, Mary 201(2)
Cook, Samuel Wellington 281
Cooke, 295
Cooke, Matilda Jordan 202(2)
Cooke, Nichola Anne 69
Cookney, Charles 581(2), 583(2)

Cookworthy, Charlotte 190
Cooley, Sarah 171(2), 327
Cooling, (Captain) 80
Coombe, Anna Josepha 52(2), 56(2), 61(2)
Cooper, (& Levey) 246
Cooper, (Judge) 20, 473(2), 624(2)
Cooper, (Mr) 67(2)
Cooper, Charles (Sir) 244, 434
Cooper, Daniel 75, 245, 246, 110(2), 322(2), 613(2)
Cooper, Daniel (Sir) 246
Cooper, Eleanor 444(2)
Cooper, Eliza (Mrs) 246
Cooper, Elizabeth (Mrs) 246
Cooper, Emily Grace (Mrs) 244
Cooper, Frederick Augustus 246
Cooper, Hannah (Mrs) 245
Cooper, James 253
Cooper, John 88(2)
Cooper, Mary 575, 198(2)
Cooper, Robert 207, 246, 141(2), 547(2)
Cooper, Sarah (Mrs) 246
Cooper, Thomas 244, 245
Coote, Eyre (Sir) 32
Copley, Josiah (Sir) 480
Copley, Maria 480
Coppin, George Selth 98(2)
Corcoran, (Father) 341(2)
Cordeaux, Ann (Mrs) 247, 257(2)
Cordeaux, Richard 246
Cordeaux, William 246, 257(2)
Corley, Ann 512(2)
Cornelisz, Agnes (Mrs) 555
Cornelisz, Pieter 555
Corney, Robert 430
Cornish, Catherine 32
Cornwallis, 538
Corri, Domenico 279(2)
Corrigan, J. (Dr) 322
Corsnip, Janet 81
Cortis, Florence (Mrs) 423
Cory, Edward Gostwyck 247
Cory, Frances (Mrs) 247
Cory, John 247
Cory, John Johnson 247
Cory, Mary (Mrs) 247
Cotter, Barry 272
Cotter, Jane (Mrs) 248
Cotter, Richard 248
Cotter, Thomas Young 248
Cottingham, Jane 324
Cotton, 352
Cotton, (Major) 346, 555(2)
Cotton, Anna Maria (Mrs) 248
Cotton, Caroline 250
Cotton, Catherine (Mrs) 249
Cotton, Charlotte 250
Cotton, Charlotte Agnes 455(2)
Cotton, Edward 249
Cotton, Francis 248, 490(2), 491(2)
Cotton, H.C. 49(2), 348(2)
Cotton, Henry Calveley 250
Cotton, Hugh Calveley 250
Cotton, John 249
Cotton, Louisa (Mrs) 250
Cotton, Marian 250

Cotton, Marianne (Mrs) 250
Cotton, Matilda (Mrs) 250
Cotton, Michael Cullen 439
Cotton, S.J. 303
Cotton, Sidney (Sir) 224
Cotton, Susannah (Mrs) 249
Cotton, Sydney John (Sir) 250
Cotton, William 249
Cottrell, Anthony 458(2)
Cottrell, Frances (Mrs) 458(2)
Coulson, Elizabeth 123(2)
Counsel, E.A. 194
Court, Francis 302
Courthope, Elizabeth 5(2)
Cousins, Ann Catherina 440(2)
Cousins, John 440(2)
Coutart, Elizabeth 303
Coutts, Alfreda (Mrs) 29(2)
Coutts, David 29(2)
Coventry, Andrew 426
Cover, J. 259
Cover, James Fleet 251, 253
Cover, J.F. 518
Cover, J.F. (Rev) 521, 523, 290(2), 438(2)
Coverdale, 412
Coverdale, (Dr) 249(2)
Coverdale, Anne (Mrs) 253
Coverdale, Edith (Mrs) 254
Coverdale, John 181, 253
Coverdale, Julia (Mrs) 253
Coverdale, Julia Speke 564(2)
Covington, 287
Cowe, Hudson (Sir) 631(2)
Cowell, John 559
Cowell, Mary Ann Risdon (Mrs) 559
Cowie, Emma 557(2)
Cowie, George 290(2), 557(2)
Cowie, Georgina 290(2)
Cowley, Ann 242
Cowper, Ann (Mrs) 254
Cowper, Charles 254, 388, 389, 152(2), 181(2), 276(2) 339(2), 512(2)
Cowper, Charles (Sir) 367, 633(2)
Cowper, Hannah (Mrs) 254
Cowper, Harriet (Mrs) 254
Cowper, Henry 369(2)
Cowper, Mary Stephena 254
Cowper, W. (Archdeacon) 570(2)
Cowper, William 162, 254, 260, 334, 523, 212(2), 550(2)
Cowper, William (Rev) 365, 537, 105(2), 194(2), 226(2), 369(2), 255(2)
Cowper, William Macquarie 254
Cox, (Lt. Gen) 459(2)
Cox, Alexander Temple 258
Cox, Anna Maria 258
Cox, Eliza (Mrs) 257
Cox, Francis 351, 589(2)
Cox, Frederick (Rev) 256
Cox, Frederick Holdship 256
Cox, George 258, 523, 96(2), 401(2)
Cox, Henry 401(2)
Cox, James 256, 257, 511
Cox, James C. (Dr) 168(2)

Cox, John 257, 431
Cox, John Edward 257, 308(2)
Cox, Louisa Matilda 459(2)
Cox, Maria 431
Cox, Mary Ann 41(2)
Cox, Mary (Mrs) 257, 431
Cox, Rebecca (Mrs) 258
Cox, Richard 258
Cox, Samuel Emanuel 258
Cox, Sarah 589(2)
Cox, Sarah (Mrs) 256, 351
Cox, William 205, 256, 258,
    259, 262, 359, 18(2), 101(2),
    111(2), 130(2), 573(2)
Cox, William (Capt) 550
Coxen, Charles 465
Coxen, Elizabeth 465
Coxen, Henry 465
Coxen, Nicholas 465
Coxen, Stephen 465
Cozens, Samuel 316
Craike, Marianne 440(2)
Crash, Susanna 559(2)
Craven, (Earl of) 439
Crawford, George John 244
Crawford, James 504(2)
Crear, (Captain) 59
Creek Jimmy (Aborigine) 234
Cressy, Charles 223(2)
Crockford, Mary Ann 404(2)
Croft, John 453(2)
Cromarty, (Earl of) 270(2)
Crombie, Alexander (Dr)
    583(2)
Crone, E.A. 187(2)
Crone, Mary Anne 431(2)
Crook, Hannah (Mrs) 260
Crook, Maria (Mrs) 259
Crook, Mary 509
Crook, Stephen 259
Crook, W. 291(2)
Crook, William Pascoe 259
Crook, W.P. 252, 253, 353, 509,
    518, 521, 439(2), 529(2),
    600(2)
Crooke, Emmeline Anne (Mrs)
    93(2)
Crooke, Warren (Sir) 93(2)
Crooke, William 559(2)
Crookes, Charlotte Elizabeth
    Margaret (Mrs) 261
Crookes, John 261, 373(2)
Cropper, Thirza 315(2)
Cross, Ann 336(2)
Cross, Ann Mary 262
Cross, Ann (Mrs) 262
Cross, Ben 424
Cross, George 102
Cross, John 261
Cross, John (Rev) 253
Cross, Lillias 271(2)
Cross, Louisa 262
Cross, Mary 102
Cross, Mary Ann (Mrs) 262
Cross, Mary (Mrs) 253
Cross, William 262
Crossley, Anna Maria (Mrs)
    262
Crossley, George 39, 89, 121,
    218, 262, 308, 373, 374, 564,
    21(2), 597(2)
Crotty, F.C. 496(2)

Crow, Margaret 243(2)
Crowder, Sarah (Mrs) 264
Crowder, Thomas 264
Crowder, Thomas Ristol 264
Crowder, T.R. 71(2)
Crowe, Emma 105
Crowley, Catherine 582(2)
Crowther, William (Dr) 420(2)
Crozier, (Captain) 492
Crozier, (Commander) 34(2)
Crozier family 151(2)
Cruden, Elizabeth Sadlier
    293(2)
Cruden, William 293(2)
Crummer, Augusta Louisa 265
Crummer, Henry Samuel
    Walker 265
Crummer, James Henry 264
Crummer, Katerina Georgia
    (Mrs) 264
Crummer, Samuel 264
Crump, (Dr) 260(2)
Crump, Aphra 260(2)
Crump, Sylverius 260(2)
Cruttenden, Sarah Browne 256
Cruttenden, Thomas 256
Cullen, 199(2)
Cullen, (Archbishop) 346(2)
Cullen, Patrick 371(2)
Culley, James (Major) 436(2)
Culley, Mary Jane 436(2)
Cumberland, (Duke of) 573(2)
Cummins, 64(2)
Cunningham, A. 69(2), 124(2)
Cunningham, Allan 54, 97, 167,
    247, 265, 267, 268, 269, 276,
    280, 284, 304, 416, 61(2),
    108(2), 119(2), 168(2), 238(2),
    316(2), 495(2)
Cunningham, Elizabeth (Mrs)
    267
Cunningham, John 267
Cunningham, Peter 468(2)
Cunningham, Peter Miller 267
Cunningham, Richard 267, 268,
    239(2), 360(2)
Cunningham, Thomas
    Mounsey 268
Curling, Jane (Mrs) 402(2)
Curling, Jonathan 559(2)
Curling, Mary 417
Curling, Thomas Oakley 402(2)
Curling, William 417
Curr, 170(2)
Curr, E. 429(2)
Curr, Edward 3, 241, 269, 406,
    440, 457, 528
Curr, Elizabeth (Mrs) 269
Curr, John 269
Curr, Joseph 269
Currey, Sophia Browell 3(2)
Currie, (Captain) 305(2), 598(2)
Currie, J.L. 438(2)
Currie, Raikes 557
Currison, Anne 330
Curtis, Anthony 272
Curtis, John 377
Curtis, Roger (Sir) 136, 568
Curtis, Suzannah (Mrs) 272
Curzon, Hannah 9
Cussen, Patrick Edward 272
Cuthbert, Sophia 401(2)

Cuthbertson, J.L. 43
Cuthbertson, John 273
Cuthbertson, Mary 326(2C)
Cutter, James 49
Cutts, Isaac 529
Cuvier, Georges 182(2)
D'Arcy, (surveyor) 547
D'Arcy, Frederick Robert
    409(2)
D'Arcy, Mary 165(2)
d'Aribeau 172
D'Emden, James 164(2)
D'Entrecasteaux; see Bruny
    D'Entrecasteaux
d'Hericourt, Rochet 103(2)
D'Hotman, (Madame) 121(2C)
D'Oyly, Thomas 320
d'Urville, Dumont 72, 172, 266,
    85(2), 123(2)
Da Silva, Luduvina Rosa 197
Dacre, George 275
Dacre, Julia (Mrs) 275
Dacre, Margaret (Mrs) 275
Dacre, Ranulph 275, 25(2)
Dainglia, Trimbackjee 500(2)
Dale, (Ensign) 253(2)
Daley, Bernard 141(2)
Dalrymple, (Captain) 170
Dalrymple, Alexander 65, 146,
    243, 275
Dalrymple, Barbara 522(2)
Dalrymple, Ernest 108(2)
Dalrymple, Ernest George Beck
    Elphinstone 276
Dalrymple, G.E. 263(2)
Dalrymple, Graeme (Mrs) 276
Dalrymple, James (Sir) 275
Dalrymple, Robert (Horn
    Elphinstone) 276
Dalziel, James 107(2)
Dampier, William 277
Dana, Harriet (Mrs) 278, 279
Dana, Henry Edward Pulteney
    278
Dana, James 278
Dana, James Dwight 278
Dana, J.D. 494(2)
Dana, William Augustus
    Pulteney 278
Dana, William Pulteney 278
Dance, (Commander) 236
Dandridge, J.S. 354(2)
Dandridge, Matilda (Mrs)
    354(2)
Dangar, Albert Augustus 281
Dangar, Charles Cary 281
Dangar, Florence 281
Dangar, Francis Richard 281
Dangar, Frederick Holkham
    281
Dangar, Grace (Mrs) 280
Dangar, Henry 247, 280, 285,
    300, 86(2), 168(2), 316(2)
Dangar, Henry Cary 281
Dangar, Judith (Mrs) 280
Dangar, Margaret 281
Dangar, Richard Cary 281
Dangar, Thomas 281, 294
Dangar, William 247, 280, 281
Dangar, William John 281
Danger, John Hooper 282
Daniel, George 270

D'Arcy, 547
D'Arcy, Frederick Robert 409(2)
D'Arcy, Mary 165(2)
Dare, Hannah 260
Dargin, Mary 102(2)
Dargin, Thomas 102(2)
d'Aribeau, 172
Darke, (surveyor) 547
Darke, Elizabeth 316
Darke, Elizabeth (Mrs) 282
Darke, John 282
Darke, John Charles 282
Darke, Susanna (Mrs) 316
Darke, William Wedge 282, 409(2)
Darling, (Lady) 505(2)
Darling, Charles 283
Darling, Charles (Sir) 474(2)
Darling, Christopher 282
Darling, David 599(2)
Darling, Eliza (Mrs) 283, 285, 286, 333
Darling, R. 348
Darling, R. (Lt. Gov) 567(2)
Darling, Ralph 56, 74, 191, 207, 217, 241, 248, 254, 280, 315, 417
Darling, Ralph (Gov) 9, 113, 231, 332, 333, 394, 395, 396, 410, 501, 507, 512, 556, 7(2), 46(2), 70(2), 76(2), 109(2), 119(2), 119(2), 124(2), 131(2), 148(2), 158(2), 169(2), 178(2), 202(2), 204(2), 235(2), 238(2), 256(2), 265(2), 307(2), 309(2), 319(2), 324(2), 335(2), 365(2), 389(2), 400(2), 404(2), 426(2), 429(2), 430(2), 432(2), 477(2), 478(2), 483(2), 485(2), 495(2), 510(2), 511(2), 513(2), 523(2), 529(2), 549(2), 553(2), 567(2), 570(2), 578(2), 585(2), 609(2), 614(2), 615(2), 630(2)
Darling, Ralph (Sir) 200, 204, 205, 282, 299, 303, 304, 317, 318, 325, 497(2)
Darvall, 616(2)
Darwin, Charles 22, 279, 349, 212(2), 416(2), 489(2), 597(2)
Darwin, Charles Robert 286
Darwin, Emma (Mrs) 287
Darwin, Erasmus 286
Darwin, Robert 286
Darwin, Susannah (Mrs) 286
Dashwood, George Frederick 287
Dashwood, James 287
Dashwood, Sarah Rebecca (Mrs) 288
Da Silva, Luduvina Rosa 197
Davey, John 288
Davey, Lucy 427(2)
Davey, Lucy Margaretta 289
Davey, Margaret (Mrs) 289
Davey, Temperance (Mrs) 288
Davey, Thomas 2, 135, 240, 288, 328, 140(2)
Davey, Thomas (Lt. Gov) 76, 368, 435, 436, 560, 40(2), 45(2), 87(2), 127(2), 159(2), 279(2), 295(2), 427(2), 459(2)

Davice, Hannah Maria 24, 225
Davidson, (Dr) 236
Davidson, Anna Jocelyn 516(2)
Davidson, Gilbert 290
Davidson, Henry 224
Davidson, Jane 108(2)
Davidson, Martha (Mrs) 290
Davidson, Patrick (Rev) 290
Davidson, Walter 196, 157(2), 306(2), 307(2)
Davidson, Walter Stevenson 290
Davidson, W.S. 277, 24(2), 108(2), 155(2), 380(2)
Davies, Arthur 290
Davies, Catherine Elizabeth 291
Davies, Elizabeth (Mrs) 291
Davies, Harriett (Mrs) 291
Davies, John 353
Davies, Maria (Mrs) 291
Davies, Robert 291
Davies, Robert Rowland 291
Davies, Rowland (Dean) 291
Davies, R.R. (Rev) 143(2), 468(2), 593(2)
Davies, Sarah 117, 264
Davis, 313(2), 448(2)
Davis, (Bishop) 425(2)
Davis, Ann 262
Davis, C.H. (Bishop) 199(2), 607(2)
Davis, Charles Henry 292, 344(2)
Davis, Edward 293, 300
Davis, Edwin 292
Davis, Elizabeth 439
Davis, Frances Harriet 426(2)
Davis, James 145, 294, 407(2)
Davis, James (Duramboi) 326(2)
Davis, Jefferson 235(2)
Davis, Richard 292
Davis, Sarah 264, 600(2), 601(2)
Davoren, Laurence 388(2)
Davy, Arabella (Mrs) 296
Davy, Edward 295
Davy, George Boutflower 296
Davy, Mary (Mrs) 296
Davy, Rebecca (Mrs) 296
Davy, Thomas 295
Dawbin, Annie Maria (Mrs) 296
Dawbin, Robert 296, 297
Dawes, Benjamin 297
Dawes, Frederick 437
Dawes, Grace (Mrs) 298
Dawes, Judith 298
Dawes, Macauley 298
Dawes, William 12, 297
Dawes, William (Lt) 506(2)
Dawes, William Rutter 298
Dawson, Anna Eliza 450(2)
Dawson, Anne (Mrs) 299
Dawson, John 299
Dawson, Joseph 298
Dawson, Margaret 52
Dawson, Robert 138, 298
Dawson, Robert Barrington 300
Day, 300
Day, E.D. 265
Day, Edward 294
Day, Edward Denny 300

Day, John 300(C)
Day, Margaret (Mrs) 300
Dayes, Edward 238
de Blosseville; see Blosseville 301
de Caen, (General) 390, 391
de Castella, Paul 14
de Eredia; see Eredia 301
de Freycinet; see under Baudin 301
de Gillern, Harriet (Mrs) 301
de Gillern, William 301
de Houtman; see Houtman 303
de Kerilleau; see Huon de Kerilleau 303
de Kermadec, Huon 171
de la Condamine, Elizabeth (Mrs) 303
de la Condamine, Janet Mary (Mrs) 304
de la Condamine, Jean 303
de la Condamine, Thomas 241, 303
de Lacy, (Sister) 346(2)
de Langle, (Commandant) 85(2)
de Lestang-Parade, Dorothee 171
de Little, Caroline (Mrs) 304
de Little, John 304
de Little, Joseph 304
de Little, Robert 304
de Ly, Dorothea Agatha 123(2C)
de Marquett, Harriet 117
de Marquett, Jean Louis 117
de Mestre, 374
de Mestre, Etienne Livingstone 305
de Mestre, Mary Ann (Mrs) 305
de Mestre, Prosper 305
de Mirgy, Annie 164
de Mirgy, Peter 164
de Mole, E.V. 482(2)
de Quincy, 558(2)
de Quiros; see Quiros 305
de Riveau; see Duriault
de Rossel 172
de Strzelecki; see Strzelecki 306
de Thierry, Baron 187
de Torres; see Torres 306
de Villiers, C. 278
de Vlamingh; see Vlamingh 306
de Wesselow; see Simpkinson de Wesselow
Deane, Edward 301
Deane, John 301
Deane, John Philip 301
Deane, J.P. 32
Deane, Morris (Charles Muzio) 301
Deane, Rosalie 301
Deane, Rosalie (Mrs) 301
Deas Thomson; see Thomson 301
Deasey, Joanna 261(2)
Deaton, Irene 490(C)
Deaton, Mary Ann 490(C)
Dedel, Jacob 555
Deering, Ellen 597(2)
Degraves, 338
Degraves, Peter 302

Degraves, Sophia (Mrs) 303
Dejether, D. Geary (Rev) 439
Delane, John 136(2)
D'Emden, Henri James 164(2)
Dendy, Henry 590(2C)
Denham, H.M. (Capt) 167(2)
Deniehy, Daniel 535, 276(2)
Deniehy, D.H. 339(2), 514, 515
Denison, 483
Denison, (Gov) 30, 229, 251, 484
Denison, John 326(2)
Denison, Margaret (Mrs) 326(2)
Denison, Sarah 144
Denison, William (Gov) 288(2), 463(2), 524(2), 525(2), 526(2)
Denison, William (Lt. Gov) 8, 29, 220, 253, 324, 361, 371, 416, 505, 35(2), 50(2), 118(2), 128(2), 230(2), 241(2), 247(2), 296(2), 297(2), 320(2), 336(2), 348(2), 351(2), 375(2), 393(2), 490(2), 503(2), 511(2), 542(2), 563(2), 594(2), 607(2)
Denison, William (Sir) 329, 388, 100(2), 183(2), 291(2), 454(2)
Denmark (King of) 541
Dennis, Alexander 539(2)
Dennis, Emma (Mrs) 539(2)
Dennys, C.J. 88(2)
Denton, Elizabeth 533(2)
Denton, James 534(2)
D'Entrecasteaux; see Bruny D'Entrecasteaux
Derby, (Earl of) 442, 466, 167(2), 342(2), 470(2)
Derby, (Earl of) see Stanley, Edward 306
Derby, Caroline 112(2)
Desailly, Francis 225(2)
Despointes, M. 332
Devereaux, Catherine 36(2)
d'Hericourt, Rochet 103(2)
Dick, Alexander (Col. Sir) 131(2)
Dick, Alexander (Sir) 449(2)
Dick, Charles Edwin 540(2)
Dick, Isabella 176(2)
Dickens, Charles 222, 186(2), 558(2), 559(2)
Dickin, (Miss) 265, 268
Dickinson, John Nodes 513(2)
Dickson, Helen 58
Dickson, James 58
Dickson, Joanna 58
Dickson, John 57, 58, 306, 282(2)
Dickson, Lily 306
Dickson, Martha 579(2)
Dicky, 634(2)
Dieffenbach, (Dr) 98
Diggins, Ann 217(2)
Dight family 215
Dight, Elizabeth 564
Dight, John Hannah 564
Dighton, Robert 54(2)
Dilboong (Aborigine) 85
Dillon, Martha 308
Dillon, Mary (Mrs) 307
Dillon, Peter 306, 42(2)

Dillon, Robert Coram 101
Dillon, Wentworth 579(2)
Disney, John (Rev) 312(2)
Disney, Moore (Sir) 631(2)
Disraeli, (politician) 364
Divine, Amie (Mrs) 308
Divine, Anna Maria 262
Divine, John 309
Divine, Margaret (Mrs) 308
Divine, Nicholas 262, 308, 283(2)
Divine, Patrick 308
Divine, Philip 308
Divine, Sarah 516(2)
Dixon, Eleanor 273(2)
Dixon, Elizabeth (Mrs) 309
Dixon, Esther 216(2)
Dixon, George 309
Dixon, Henry (Capt) 46, 462
Dixon, J. (Rev) 287(2)
Dixon, James 309
Dixon, James (Capt) 216(2)
Dixon, James (Fr) 513, 59(2), 340(2)
Dixon, John 309
Dixon, Margaret (Mrs) 310
Dixon, Nicholas 309
Dixon, Robert 281, 309, 472(2)
Dixon, Sarah (Mrs) 273(2)
Dixon, Thomas 273(2)
Dobie, John 310, 418(2)
Dobinson, Sarah Maria 498(2)
Dobson, James (Rev) 144(2)
Dobson, Jane Jeffreys 452(2)
Dobson, Lambert (Sir) 542(2)
Dobson, Martha 144(2)
Dobson, Michael 452(2)
Dobson, William Lambert 330
Docker, Jane (Mrs) 311
Docker, Joseph 311, 334
Docker, Mary Jane 311
Docker, Sarah (Mrs) 311
Docker, William 311
Dodd, 615(2)
Dodd, Hannah (Mrs) 245
Dodd, Henry Edward 311
Dodds, 374
Dodgson, James Davy 331
Doge, Ludwig 421(2)
Dolman, William 535
Don, George (Sir) 33
Donaldson, 526(2)
Donaldson, Alexander 236(2)
Donaldson, S.A. 24(2)
Donaldson, Stuart 108(2), 152(2), 241(2), 494(2)
Donaldson, William 236(2)
Donaldson, W.S. 290
Donnolan, Joseph 625(2)
Donohoe, John 312
Donovan, Thomas 294(2)
Dore, Maria (Mrs) 313
Dore, Richard 39, 313, 571
Dore, Richard 388(2)
Dore, Richard (Judge Advocate) 46(2), 283(2)
Dore, William 313
Dorlton (Dollin), George 53
Dorr, Ebenezer (Capt) 266(2)
Doswell, Maria 333(2)
Doughty, Charles 116(2)
Doughty, John (Dr) 20

Douglas, Adye 329
Douglas, James (Sir) 124(2)
Douglass, Adam 314
Douglass, Ann (Mrs) 314
Douglass, Henry Grattan (Dr) 153, 286, 314, 324, 374, 394, 463, 503, 69(2), 148(2), 211(2), 256(2), 308(2), 311(2), 477(2), 499(2), 571(2), 628(2)
Douglass, Hester (Mrs) 315
Dow, Agnes 187
Dowbiggin, Jane 407
Dowling, (Chief Justice) 553(2)
Dowling, (Father) 511(2)
Dowling, Cecilia (Mrs) 316
Dowling, Eliza 371(2)
Dowling, Elizabeth 228
Dowling, Elizabeth (Mrs) 316
Dowling, George 575
Dowling, George Pyke 228
Dowling, Hannah Maria 316
Dowling, Hannah Read (Mrs) 316
Dowling, Harriet (Mrs) 319
Dowling, Henry 316, 458, 7(2), 355(2)
Dowling, Henry (Rev) 224, 225
Dowling, James Sheen 319
Dowling, James (Sir, Judge) 184, 210, 294, 306, 317, 397, 398, 495, 66(2), 478(2), 512(2), 553(2), 603(2), 615(2)
Dowling, John 230, 316
Dowling, John Leonard 316
Dowling, Leonard Thomas 316
Dowling, Lily (Mrs) 306
Dowling, Maria (Mrs) 319
Dowling, Mary 316
Dowling, Mary Jane (Mrs) 316
Dowling, Robert 330, 493(2)
Dowling, Robert H. 594(2)
Dowling, Robert Hawker 225, 316
Dowling, Thomas 316
Dowling, Vincent 317, 318
Dowling, Vincent George 306
Dowling, Willoughby James 306
Dowling, Winifred 371(2)
Downing, Louisa 228
Downshire, (Marquess of) 188
Dowse, Thomas 201
Doyle, Andrew 320, 321
Doyle, Bartholomew 321
Doyle, Catharine 377(2)
Doyle, Catherine Broughton (Mrs) 321
Doyle, Cyrus Matthew 320
Doyle, Elizabeth Maria (Mrs) 320
Doyle, Emily Agnes (Mrs) 321
Doyle, Mary 514
Doyle, Sophia Isabella (Mrs) 320
Doyle, Thomas 320
D'Oyly, Thomas 320
Draffen, (Ensign) 530(2)
Drake, (Captain) 199
Drake, F.L. 80(2)
Drake, Richard 112
Drake-Brockman, Julius 155
Draper, Daniel James 321

Draper, Elizabeth (Mrs) 321
Draper, James 321
Draper, Mary (Mrs) 321
Dredge, James 520
Drennan, F. 5, 153, 223, 247, 358
Drennan, Frederick 158, 322, 324, 393(2), 577(2)
Drennan, Frederick (Commissary) 562, 628(2)
Dresser, Aaron 430
Drewry, Jane 500
Driscoll, Cornelius 323
Driver, Elizabeth 319(2), 366(2)
Drought, (Dr) 428
Druce, Joseph 170
Druce, William 170
Druitt, Edward 324
Druitt, George 324
Druitt, George (Major) 575, 578(2)
Druitt, Jane (Mrs) 324
Drummond, Duncan 327
Drummond, Elizabeth (Mrs) 327, 328
Drummond, Francis Pinkerton 327
Drummond, Helen 566
Drummond, James 325, 326, 349(2)
Drummond, John 77, 326, 327, 513
Drummond, John Duncan Wellington 327
Drummond, John Francis (Sir) 327
Drummond, John Nicol 326
Drummond, Johnston 325, 349(2)
Drummond, Martha (Mrs) 326
Drummond, Mary (Mrs) 326
Drummond, Ralph 327
Drummond, Samuel 316(2)
Drummond, Sarah (Mrs) 325
Drummond, Thomas 325
Drummond, William 327
Drury, 112(2)
Drury, Dru 111(2)
Drury, Elizabeth 598(2)
Dry, Anne (Mrs) 328, 329
Dry, Clara (Mrs) 329, 225(2)
Dry, Harriett 329, 74(2)
Dry, Richard 50, 147, 296, 328, 329, 371, 74(2), 225(2), 590(2)
Dry, Richard (Sir) 64, 329
Dry, William 329
Dryander, Jonas 54, 166
Drysdale, (Miss) 71(2)
Drysdale, Anne 330
Drysdale, Anne (Mrs) 330
Drysdale, George Russell 330
Drysdale, John 330
Drysdale, William 330
Du Cane, Edmund 245(2)
Du Cane, Mary (Mrs) 245(2)
Du Faur, Augusta Louisa (Mrs) 265
Du Faur, Eccleston 265
Ducharme, Leon 353(2)
Duckworth, John (Admiral Sir) 424(2)
Duddingstone, (Rear Admiral) 140

Duddingstone, Elizabeth 140
Dudgeon, Peter 300(2)
Dudley and Ward (Lord) 469
Dudley, W.H. 250
Duffy, Charles Gavan 376, 234(2)
Duffy, Gavan 351
Dulhunty, Alfred 332
Dulhunty, Eliza Julia (Mrs) 331
Dulhunty, Hubert 332
Dulhunty, Jane (Mrs) 331
Dulhunty, John 331, 332
Dulhunty, John (Dr) 331
Dulhunty, Lawrence 331, 332
Dulhunty, Marcus 332
Dulhunty, Robert (Jun) 332
Dulhunty, Robert Venour 331
Dumaresq, 362, 426
Dumaresq, Anne (Mrs) 333
Dumaresq, Charlotte (Mrs) 333
Dumaresq, Christiana Susan (Mrs) 334, 180(2)(C)
Dumaresq, (Colonel) 109(2), 477(2)
Dumaresq, E. 436(2)
Dumaresq, Edward 193, 332, 333, 410, 508, 429(2)
Dumaresq, Edward John 333
Dumaresq, Eliza 283, 333
Dumaresq, Elizabeth Sophia (Mrs) 334
Dumaresq, Frances Blance (Mrs) 332
Dumaresq, Helen (Mrs) 334
Dumaresq, Henry 283
Dumaresq, Henry 332
Dumaresq, Henry 333
Dumaresq, Henry 377(2)
Dumaresq, Henry (Col) 316(2)
Dumaresq, Henry (Col) 571(2)
Dumaresq, Henry (Col) 572(2)
Dumaresq, John 332, 333
Dumaresq, John (Col) 332
Dumaresq, John Saumarex (Rear Adm) 334
Dumaresq, Susan 334
Dumaresq, William 188, 281, 283, 332
Dumaresq, William (Col) 180(2)
Dumaresq, William Alexander 334
Dumaresq, William John 333
Dumas, Dorothea Jessie 336(2)
Dumas, J.C. (Capt) 336(2)
Duncan, 515, 535, 345(2)
Duncan, (Gov) 188(2)
Duncan, Andrew 335
Duncan, Andrew Henry 335
Duncan, Anne (Mrs) 335
Duncan, Annie 335
Duncan, Dandasyde 335
Duncan, Emily Susan (Mrs) 335
Duncan, Jane (Mrs) 335
Duncan, Kate (Mrs) 335
Duncan, Lewis 337
Duncan, Mary 337
Duncan, Mary Celia 335
Duncan, Mary (Mrs) 335, 337
Duncan, Peter 335
Duncan, W.A. 87, 514, 534,

342(2), 513(2), 545(2)
Duncan, William Augustine 335
Dundas, Charles 240
Dundas, David (Sir) 190(2)
Dundas, Henry 337, 266(2)
Dunlop, David 337
Dunlop, Eliza Hamilton 337
Dunlop, Helen Buchanan 258(2)
Dunlop, James 338, 348, 403(2), 404(2)
Dunlop, Janet (Mrs) 338
Dunlop, Jean (Mrs) 338
Dunlop, John 338
Dunlop, Rachel 337
Dunmore, Mary 76(2)
Dunn, (bushranger) 367
Dunn, Catherine 420
Dunn, Catherine (Mrs) 339
Dunn, John 212, 338, 339, 347, 371, 420, 563(2)
Dunn, William 338
Dunsford, Sophia Mullet 589(2)
Dunwich, (Viscount) 400(2)
Duperrey, L.J. 123
Duramboi (Aborigine) 145, 294, 326(2)
Durham, (Lord) 561(2)
Durham, Joseph 562(2)
Duriault, Francois 371(2)
Duriault, Winifred (Mrs) 371(2)
Durrell, (Admiral) 567
d'Urville, Dumont 72, 172, 266, 85(2), 123(2)
Duterrau, Benjamin 339
Duterrau, Sarah Jane 339
Dutton, (brothers) 47
Dutton, Caroline (Mrs) 341
Dutton, Charlotte (Mrs) 197, 341
Dutton, Francis S. 47
Dutton, Francis Stacker 341
Dutton, Frederick Hansborough 341
Dutton, Frederick Hugh Hampden 341
Dutton, Henry 340, 341
Dutton, Margaret 340
Dutton, Mary (Mrs) 340
Dutton, Pelham John Richard 341
Dutton, Roseanne 337(2)
Dutton, Thomas (Lt) 517(2)
Dutton, W.H. 197, 340, 377. 497
Dutton, William 340, 341, 486, 231(2), 372(2)
Dutton, William Hampden 341
Dwight, Harriet 278
Dyball, Helen Sarah Burrington (Mrs) 418
Dyball, Thomas Cooke (Lt) 418
Dyce, Agnes 376(2)
Dykes, Thomas (Rev) 254
Dymock, William 365
Eagar, Edward 89, 219, 252, 263, 305, 343, 374, 575, 370(2), 430(2), 508(2), 599(2)
Eagar, Edward 374, 555(C)
Eagar, Ellen 344

Eagar, Frances (Mrs) 343
Eagar, Geoffrey 344
Eagar, Jemima (Mrs) 344
Eagar, Richard 343
Eagers, Julia 174
Eagle, Elizabeth Charlotte 125
Eagle Hawk (Aborigine) 103
Eagle, Mary 425
Eagle, Solomon 125
Eales, Elizabeth (Mrs) 344
Eales, Jane Eleanor (Mrs) 345
Eales, John 344, 345
Eales, John (Jun) 345
Eardley-Wilmot, 436
Eardley-Wilmot, Augustus
    Hillier 346
Eardley-Wilmot, Charles
    Octavius 346
Eardley-Wilmot, Elizabeth
    Emma (Mrs) 345
Eardley-Wilmot, Elizabeth
    (Mrs) 345
Eardley-Wilmot, Frances (Mrs)
    345
Eardley-Wilmot, John 219
Eardley-Wilmot, John Eardley
    (Sir) 329, 345
Eardley-Wilmot, John (Gov)
    48(2), 50(2), 91(2)
Eardley-Wilmot, John (Lt. Gov)
    30 48, 339, 356, 361, 2(2),
    35(2), 40(2), 100(2), 118(2),
    163(2), 207(2), 247(2), 273(2),
    286(2), 296(2), 336(2), 351(2),
    372(2), 490(2), 501(2), 555(2)
Eardley-Wilmot, Robert
    Charles Chester 346
Earl, George Windsor 148
Earl St Vincent 258
Earl St Vincent (John Jervis)
    567
Earle, Augustus 348, 169(2),
    212(2), 366(2), 538(2)
Earle, Caroline (Mrs) 348
Earle, James 348
Earle, John 42
Earle, Ralph 348
Easton, Elizabeth 558, 559
Easty, John 349
Eatwell, Julia (Mrs) 253
Eatwell, William 253
Ebden, Antoinetta Adriana
    (Mrs) 349
Ebden, C.H. 252(2)
Ebden, Charles Hotson 349
Ebden, John Bardwell 349
Ebden, John Watts 349
Ebden, Tamar (Mrs) 350
Eckersberg, C.W. 27(2)
Eddington, Eliza 257
Eddington, Jessie M. 82
Eddington, Margaret 239
Edelsten, Alan 465
Edge, Fane 351
Edge, Sarah (Mrs) 351
Edinburgh, (Duke of) 317,
    50(2), 298(2), 455(2)
Ediss, Mary 143
Edmeades, Susannah Wilson
    539
Edmonston, Cecilia (Mrs) 219
Edmonston, William 219

Edwards, Agnes Ann 276(2)
Edwards, Ann 314, 600(2)
Edwards, Bridget 264(2)
Edwards, Edward 174, 151(2)
Edwards, G. (Lt) 124(2)
Edwards, Richard 175(2)
Edwards, Susannah 249
Edye, Lydia 202(2)
Egerton-Warburton, Augusta
    (Mrs) 466(2)
Egerton-Warburton, George
    Edward 466(2)
Eglinton, (Earl of) 362(2)
Egremont, (Earl of) 532
Egremont, (Lord) 283(2)
Ehrensvard, (Count) 302
Eipper, 509
Eipper, Albert James (Rev) 352
Eipper, C. (Rev) 422(2), 448(2)
Eipper, Christopher 351
Eipper, Harriet (Mrs) 351
Eipper, J.W. Christopher 352
Elau (New Hebridean native)
    85
Elder, Alexander Lang 341
Elder, J. 365
Elder, James 352, 76(2)
Elder, James (Rev) 632(2)
Elder, Mary (Mrs) 352
Eldred, Frances Maria 181
Elgar, Henry 275, 25(2)
Elgin, (Lord) 389
Eliott, (General) 11, 157(2)
Ellice, Edward 178, 348(2)
Elliot, Nathaniel 327
Elliott, Ann (Mrs) 355
Elliott, Anne 83(2)
Elliott, Eliza 545
Elliott, Elizabeth (Mrs) 354
Elliott, (General) 11, 157(2)
Elliott, Gilbert 406(2)
Elliott, Hugh 353
Elliott, Jane (Mrs) 354
Elliott, Margaret (Mrs) 353
Elliott, Thomas Frederick 353
Elliott, (William) Edward 354
Ellis, Alice 46
Ellis, Amie 308
Ellis, James 126, 312(2)
Ellis, John 7, 456(2)
Ellis, John (Capt) 541
Ellis, Susan (Mrs) 541
Ellis, William 46, 528(2), 599(2)
Ellison, Albinia Jane Martyn
    595(2)
Elliston, Edmund 355
Elliston, Margaret (Mrs) 355
Elliston, R.W. 595(2)
Elliston, Robert William 355
Elliston, W.G. 95, 163(2),
    164(2), 397(2)
Elliston, William Gore 355,
    595(2)
Elwall, Clara Ann 35(2)
Elwell, Julia 96
Elwes, Charles 381
Elwes, Eleanora Caroline 381
Emmett, Grace West (Mrs) 356
Emmett, Henry 356
Emmett, Henry James 356
Emmett, H.J. 396(2)
Emmett, Mary Thompson

(Mrs) 356
Empson, (Commodore) 527
Enderby, Charles 357
Enderby, Elizabeth 357
Enderby family 53(2)
Enderby, Mary (Mrs) 357
Enderby, Samuel 357, 44(2),
    58(2), 61(2)
Enderby, Samuel (Jun) 357
England, (Bishop) 165(2)
England, (Captain) 235
Eppes, Elizabeth 491(2)
Eppes, Elizabeth (Mrs) 491(2)
Eppes, William 491(2)
Eredia, Manuel Godinho de
    357
Erskine, (Colonel) 8, 11
Erskine, (Dr) 4(2)
Erskine, (Lord) 359(2)
Erskine, (Lt. Gov) 373
Erskine, G. (Rev) 567(2)
Erskine, J.F. (Col) 11
Erskine, James 323, 324, 358
Erskine, James (Lt. Col) 274(2)
Erskine, James (Sir) 271(2)
Erskine, Louisa (Lady) 271(2)
Erskine, Sarah (Mrs) 358
Espie, G. 21
Espie, Robert 264(2)
Essex, Mary 509
Evans, 9(2), 504(2), 575(2)
Evans, Ann (Mrs) 359
Evans, Ann Southern 421
Evans, G.W. 36, 242, 259, 273,
    421, 219(2), 429(2), 436(2)
Evans, George 369, 306(2)
Evans, George William 359
Evans, George William
    (Surveyor) 16(2)
Evans, Harriet 77
Evans, Jennett (Mrs) 359
Evans, Lucy Parris (Mrs) 360
Evans, Mabel Gwynne Ethel
    93(2)
Evans, Maria Amelia 385(2)
Evans, Mary 224(2), 225(2)
Evans, Thomas 93(2)
Evans, William 359
Evelyn, Philippa 115(2)
Evelyn, John 115(2)
Everett, (Lt. Col) 319(2)
Everett, James 294
Everett, Maria 319(2)
Everingham, Elizabeth (Mrs)
    361
Everingham, Matthew James
    360
Everleigh, Betty 549
Ewing, Louisa (Mrs) 361
Ewing, Thomas James 361
Exmouth, (Viscount) 348
Eyre, Adelaide Fanny (Mrs) 364
Eyre, Alfred John 365
Eyre, Anthony William 362
Eyre, Edward John 362, 470,
    497(2)
Eyre, E.J. 334, 478, 629(2)
Eyre, Elizabeth (Mrs) 365
Eyre, J. (Rev) 522
Eyre, John 253, 352, 365, 202(2)
Eyre, John (Mrs) 353
Eyre, Sarah (Mrs) 362

Eyre, Thomas 365
Fahie, J.J. 295
Fairfax, John 466, 41(2), 204(2), 491(2), 591(2)
Faithful family 215
Faithful, Alice 367
Faithful, George 311, 367
Faithful, Helen Eliza 367
Faithful, Margaret (Mrs) 367
Faithful, Maria (Mrs) 367
Faithful, Susannah (Mrs) 367
Faithful, William 126, 367
Faithful, William Pitt 367
Falfield, (Lord of) 566(2)
Fane, William 521(2)
Fantacchiotti, 527(2)
Faraday, 520
Farelly, Patrick S. 345(2)
Farmer, Catherine 94(2)
Farmer, Thomas 201(2)
Farnell, James Squire 468(2)
Farnell, Mary Ann (Mrs) 468(2)
Farnell, Thomas Charles 468(2)
Farquhar, (General) 283
Farquhar, Martha 290
Farquhar, Robert Townsend 399(2)
Farquhar, Walter (Sir) 290, 155(2)
Farquhar, William (Sir) 290
Farquharson, Harriet 264(2)
Farrell, J. (Rev) 335
Farrell, James (Rev) 378, 557
Farrow, Thomas (Rev) 440(2)
Faucett, Peter 535
Faunce, Alured Dodsworth 367
Faunce, Alured Dodsworth (Rev) 368
Faunce, Alured Tasker 367
Faunce, Anna Maria (Mrs) 367
Faunce, Elizabeth (Mrs) 368
Faunce, Thomas 367
Fawkner, 14, 9(2)
Fawkner, Eliza (Mrs) 369
Fawkner, Elizabeth 368
Fawkner, Hannah (Mrs) 368
Fawkner, John 368
Fawkner, John Pascoe 368, 520, 532, 457(2), 603(2)
Fawkner, J.P. 4
Fawkner, J.P. 69
Fawkner, J.P. 216, 316, 7(2), 50(2), 572(2), 576(2)
Feast, (Captain) 324
Fellows, Lydia 204(2)
Felton, Emma 26(2)
Felton, Maurice (Dr) 213(2)
Fenn Kemp, Anthony 71, 120
Fenn, Susannah 39(2)
Fennell, Robert 70
Fenton, (Mrs) 371
Fenton, Ann 622(2)
Fenton, Catherine 182
Fenton, Elizabeth (Mrs) 371
Fenton, Margaret (Mrs) 622(2)
Fenton, Michael 182, 371
Fenton, Richard 622(2)
Fenwick, N.A. 27, 43
Ferdinand, (King of Spain) 116(2)
Ferdinand, (Prince) 11
Fereday, Dudley 77, 371

Fereday, Samuel 371
Ferguson, Charles 372
Ferguson, Dora (Mrs) 372
Ferguson, Elizabeth 372
Ferguson, Isabella 372
Ferguson, Isabella (Mrs) 372
Ferguson, John 372
Ferriter, Elizabeth (Mrs) 24(2)
Ferriter, J.S. 24(2)
Festing, (Lieut) 123(2)
ffrench, Jemima 288(2)
Field, 525
Field, (Lieut) 64(2), 262(2)
Field, Barron 93, 152, 201, 263, 266, 305, 323, 373, 393, 463, 494, 558, 45(2), 552(2), 627(2)
Field, Barron (Judge) 393, 157(2), 370(2)
Field, Esther (Mrs) 373
Field, Henry 373
Field, Jane (Mrs) 373
Field, Martha (Ann) 255(2)
Field, William 394(2)
Fielding, Copley 212(2), 376(2)
Fields, J.T. 559(2)
Fiellerup, Louisa Augusta 415(2)
Finch, Eliza 298(2)
Fingall, (Earl of) 302(2)
Finn, Catherine (Mrs) 376
Finn, E. 521(2)
Finn, Edmund 82, 216, 376, 447(2)
Finn, Edmund (Jun) 376
Finn, William 376
Finnegan, John 123(2), 313(2)
Finnis, Elizabeth (Mrs) 376
Finnis, Gilbert 376
Finnis, J. (Capt) 341
Finnis, John 197, 376
Finnis, John Mercer 377
Finnis, Luduvina Rosa da Silva (Mrs) 377
Finnis, Mary Ann (Mrs) 377
Finnis, Samuel 377
Finniss, Anne Frances (Mrs) 377
Finniss, Boyle Travers 377
Finniss, Fanny Lipson 378
Finniss, John (Capt) 377
Finniss, Maria (Mrs) 377
Finniss, Sophia Florence Maud (Mrs) 379
Finniss, Susanna (Mrs) 377
Firth, Walter (Sir) 154
Fish, Elizabeth 347(2), 444(2)
Fisher, David 223(2)
Fisher, Eliza Romney 221(2)
Fisher, Elizabeth 262(2)
Fisher, Elizabeth (Mrs) 379
Fisher, Henrietta Harriet (Mrs) 379
Fisher, James 379
Fisher, James Hurtle (Sir) 379
Fisher, J.H. 166, 431, 539, 117(2), 262(2), 472(2), 482(2)
Fisher, Joseph 221(2)
Fisher, Robert 236(2)
Fisher, Thomas John 572(2)
Fitch, John 66(2)
Fitz, (Deputy Commissary) 459
Fitz, Ann (Mrs) 380

Fitz, Eunice (Mrs) 381
Fitz, Henry Bates 381
Fitz, Robert 157, 380
Fitz, William John 380, 381
Fitzgerald, 550
Fitzgerald, Catherine 27(2)
Fitzgerald, Charles 381, 5(2)
Fitzgerald, Eleanora Caroline (Mrs) 381
Fitzgerald, Elizabeth Henrietta (Mrs) 384, 402(2)
Fitzgerald, Ellen 274(2)
Fitzgerald, Lucy (Mrs) 381
Fitzgerald, Mary (Mrs) 383
Fitzgerald, R.D. 287
Fitzgerald, Richard 383, 59(2), 402(2)
Fitzgerald, Robert 381, 384, 402(2)
Fitzherbert, Thomas 524
Fitzpatrick, 565
FitzRoy, Augustus Charles Lennox (Capt) 387, 388
FitzRoy, C.A. (Gov) 98, 161, 4(2), 63(2), 80(2), 135(2), 241(2), 268(2), 295(2), 325(2), 415(2), 418(2), 463(2), 514(2), 524(2), 527(2), 588(2)
FitzRoy, Charles (Lord) 384
FitzRoy, Charles (Sir) 141, 452, 481
FitzRoy, Charles Augustus (Sir) 384, 483, 484
FitzRoy, Charles Lennox (Sir) 387
FitzRoy, Frances Anne (Mrs) 384
FitzRoy, Frances (Mrs) 384
FitzRoy, George 384, 387
FitzRoy, Margaret Gordon (Mrs) 388
FitzRoy, Mary (Lady) 384
FitzRoy, Robert 384
Fitzroy, Robert (Capt) 62(2), 212(2)
Fitzwilliam, (Earl) 133
Fitzwilliam, (Lord) 52, 419(2), 579(2), 583(2)
Flackwood, F.P. 29(2)
Flaxman, Charles 16, 33(2)
Fleetwood, Barbara 248(2)
Fleming, Fanny Maria (Mrs) 434(2)
Fleming, Valentine (Sir) 339, 434(2)
Fleming, William 480(2)
Flesher, Frances 451(2)
Fletcher, 427
Fletcher, Anne 252(2)
Fletcher, Martha 425
Fletcher, Sarah 425
Fletcher, William 425
Flinders, 283(2)
Flinders, Ann 391
Flinders, Ann (Mrs) 389
Flinders, Matthew 64, 72, 73, 119, 166, 170, 172, 177, 265, 266, 389, 391, 412, 468, 498, 528, 571, 27(2), 47(2), 61(2), 138(2), 272(2), 324(2), 390(2), 400(2), 443(2), 537(2), 574(2), 577(2), 592(2)

Flinders, Susannah (Mrs) 389
Flood, 162(2)
Flood, Bridget 269(2)
Flood, Edward 388
Florance, Elizabeth (Mrs) 392
Florance, Thomas 391
Flourens, Pierre 69(2)
Flower, Anne (Mrs) 575
Flower, Gilly 575
Flower, Horace 411(2)
Flower, John 575
Flower, Philip William 415(2)
Flynn (O'Flynn), Jeremiah
    Francis 299(2)
Fogg, Charlotte (Mrs) 333
Foley, Elizabeth 333(2)
Forbes, Amelia Sophia (Mrs)
    392
Forbes, Charles (Sir) 393,
    265(2)
Forbes, Francis (Chief Justice)
    55, 184, 200, 427, 464, 149(2),
    158(2), 169(2), 178(2), 211(2),
    319(2), 389(2), 477(2), 512(2),
    571(2), 578(2), 585(2)
Forbes, Francis 138, 153, 284,
    317, 319, 333, 374, 495, 554,
    52(2), 629(2)
Forbes, Francis (Dr) 392
Forbes, Francis (Sir) 305, 334,
    392, 394, 398, 501, 62(2)
Forbes, Francis E. 343, 575,
    547(2)
Forbes, George (Dr) 392
Forbes, Helen Johanna (Mrs)
    400
Forbes, James 399
Forbes, James (Rev) 82, 232,
    400, 522(2)
Forbes, Margaret (Mrs) 399
Forbes, Mary (Mrs) 392
Forbes, Peter 399
Ford, John 418
Ford, Mary 383
Ford, Mary Ann 418
Fordyce, Eliza 300(2)
Forlong, Agnes 401
Forlong, Andrew 400
Forlong, Christina 401
Forlong, Eliza (Mrs) 400
Forlong, James (Rev) 400
Forlong, Janet 400
Forlong, John 400
Forlong, Marion 401
Forlong, William 400
Forlonge, Andrew 401
Forlonge, Comtes de 400
Forlonge family 504(2)
Forlonge (Forlong), William
    400
Forlonge, Marion (Mrs) 401
Forlonge, William 401
Forrest, (Captain) 491
Forrest, Alexander 391(2)
Forrest, Austin (Capt) 16(2)
Forrest, George 402
Forrest, Jane (Mrs) 402
Forrest, Jemima (Mrs) 16(2)
Forrest, John 19, 391(2)
Forrest, John (Dr) 276(2)
Forrest, John (Sir) 391(2)
Forrest, Robert 150, 401

Forster, 36
Forster, Anne (Mrs) 407
Forster, Francis 411(2)
Forster, Johan Georg(e) Adam
    402
Forster, Johan Georg(e)
    Reinhold 402
Forster, Johann Georg Adam
    403
Forster, Johann Reinhold 402
Forster, Johann Reinhold 403
Forster, John 323(2)
Forster, John Randall (Lt. Col)
    404
Forster, M. 412
Forster, Martha 411(2)
Forster, Mary 546(2)
Forster, Matthew 41, 180, 346,
    404, 413, 414
Forster, Matthew (Capt) 500(2)
Forster, St Helena (Mrs) 404
Forster, Therese (Mrs) 403
Forster, William 210, 339(2)
Forth, Frederick 605(2)
Fosbrook, (Deputy
    Commissary) 435
Fosbrook, L. 517
Fosbrook, Leonard 126, 405,
    549
Foscari, Esther 27, 556
Foss, Ambrose 23(2)
Foss, Edward 558(2)
Foss, Edward Smith 558(2)
Fossey, Eliza (Mrs) 407
Fossey, John 457
Fossey, Joseph 406, 529
Fossey, Mary (Mrs) 406
Fossey, Thomas 406
Foster, Charlotte 50(C)
Foster, Henry 407
Foster, Jane (Mrs) 407
Foster, J.F.L. 126(2), 349(2)
Foster, John 194, 407
Foster, W. 389(2)
Foster, William 407
Fotheringham, Alexander 275
Fountain, (Dr) 214(2)
Foveaux, (Colonel) 422
Foveaux, (Major) 76, 491, 57(2)
Foveaux, Ann (Mrs) 409
Foveaux, F. 536
Foveaux, F. (Lt. Gov) 563
Foveaux, Francis 213(2)
Foveaux, J. (Col) 21(2)
Foveaux, Joseph 136, 157, 239,
    289, 308, 367, 407, 408, 409,
    47(2)
Foveaux, Joseph (Capt) 569
Foveaux, Joseph (Lt. Gov) 40,
    528, 575, 10(2), 98(2), 156(2),
    127(2), 131(2), 220(2), 272(2),
    283(2), 295(2), 318(2), 334(2),
    369(2), 403(2), 499(2), 520(2),
    530(2), 602(2), 608(2)
Foveaux, William 156
Foveaux, William (Gov) 351
Fowler, (Lieutenant) 390
Fowler, Robert (Lt) 592(2)
Fowler, John (Sir) 9
Fowles, Joseph 409, 242(2)
Fox, Charles James 87, 175
Fox, H.E. 175

Fox, William 479
Frances, Morgan 316(2)
Francis, James Goodall 300(2)
Francis, Mary Grant (Mrs)
    300(2)
Francis, Patrick 64
Francis, John (Rev) 159
Francis, Sarah 159
Frankland, (Surgeon Gen) 529
Frankland, Anne (Mrs) 410
Frankland, Augustus Charles
    411
Frankland, Catherine (Mrs) 410
Frankland, G. 143, 170(2),
    436(2)
Frankland, George 332, 410,
    114(2), 214(2), 429(2), 467(2),
    575(2)
Frankland, Georgina Anne 411
Frankland, Roger 410
Frankland, Sophia Catherine
    411
Frankland, Thomas (Admiral
    Sir) 410
Franklin family 494(2)
Franklin, Eleanor 413
Franklin, Eleanor Anne (Lady)
    437
Franklin, Eleanor Anne (Mrs)
    413
Franklin, Eleanor Isabella 437
Franklin, Eleanor (Mrs) 34(2)
Franklin, Hannah (Mrs) 412
Franklin, James (Major) 351(2)
Franklin, Jane (Lady) 97, 123,
    193, 355, 411, 413, 415, 418,
    437, 452, 457, 465, 492, 544,
    164(2), 247(2), 296(2), 349(2),
    421(2), 446(2), 464(2), 491(2),
    529(2), 542(2), 563(2)
Franklin, John 219
Franklin, John (Capt) 236
Franklin, John (Lt. Gov) 24, 38,
    411, 430, 440, 475, 476, 574,
    34(2), 37(2), 38(2), 40(2),
    114(2), 118(2), 185(2), 249(2),
    273(2), 315(2), 351(2), 397(2),
    413(2), 421(2), 454(2), 468(2),
    471(2), 490(2), 501(2), 595(2),
    605(2)
Franklin, John (Sir) 97, 105,
    143, 193, 253, 271, 278, 303,
    329, 355, 405, 412, 414, 416,
    417, 436, 437, 457, 465, 492,
    530, 544, 50(2), 94(2), 115(2),
    160(2), 164(2), 349(2), 446(2),
    472(2), 511(2), 542(2)
Franklin, Mary 351(2)
Franklin, Willingham 412
Franklyn, Nicholas 571
Franks, Charles 27
Franz, Friedrich Theodore
    Franz 421(2)
Fraser, 496(2)
Fraser, Charles 124(2)
Fraser, Donald 415
Fraser, Eliza Ann (Mrs) 468
Fraser, Henrietta Caroline 236
Fraser, James 82
Fraser, James (Capt) 468
Fraser, Jane 82
Fraser, Jane (Mrs) 415

Fraser, John (Dr) 530(2)
Fraser, Malcolm (Sir) 391(2)
Fraser, Mary (Mrs) 416
Fraser, Peter Gordon 415
Frazer, Charles 167, 267, 269, 485(2)
Frazer (Frazier or Fraser), Charles 416
Frederick, Augusta Maria 428(2)
Frederick, Charles (Col) 428(2)
Frederick the Great 353
Frederiksd, Agnes 555
Freeman, Thomas (Deputy Commissary) 97(2)
Freer, John 523(2)
Freer, Rebecca 523(2)
Fremantle, C.H. (Capt) 485(2)
Fremantle, S.G. (Capt) 63(2)
French, Rosetta 15, 18
Frere, H. Bartel 494(2)
Freycinet, 96(2), 556(2)
Freycinet, Louis de 324(2)
Freycinet, Louis Claude Desaulses de 71
Freycinet, Rose 72
Friday (Aborigine) 183(2)
Friell, Philip 407(2)
Friend, Charles 417
Friend, Daniel 417
Friend, George 417
Friend, Helen Sarah Burrington (Mrs) 418
Friend, John 417
Friend, Mary Ann (Mrs) 418
Friend, Mary (Mrs) 417
Friend, Matthew Curling 417
Friend, M.C. 457
Fristan, Elizabeth 208(2)
Fristan, Thomas 208(2)
Frith, Margaret Sayres Elizabeth 372(2)
Fritzsche, Dorette (Mrs) 33(2)
Fritzsche, Gotthard Daniel 33(2)
Frome, (Lieut) 497(2)
Frome, Edward Charles 418
Frome, Edward Charles (Lt) 432
Frome, Jane (Mrs) 419
Frome, J.T. (Rev) 418
Frost, Catherine 420
Frost, John 419, 601(2)
Frost, Mary (Mrs) 419
Frost, Sarah (Mrs) 419
Frost, Thomas 625(2)
Fry, Catherine (Mrs) 420
Fry, Elizabeth 45, 77, 411, 376(2), 563(2)
Fry, Elizabeth (Mrs) 209(2), 282(2)
Fry, Henry Phibbs 420
Fry, H.P. (Rev) 287(2)
Fry, Oliver 420
Fry, Oliver Armstrong 420
Fryer, Charlotte 136
Fryer, Thomas 136
Fryett, Ann Southern (Mrs) 421
Fryett, Daniel 421
Fryett, James Henry 421
Fryett, Richard William 421
Fuller, Charlotte Margaret

143(2)
Fullerton, Elizabeth 243(2)
Fulton, Ann (Mrs) 421
Fulton, Henry 260, 358, 421, 518
Fulton, Henry (Rev) 421, 59(2), 213(2), 279(2), 533(2)
Fulton, John Walker 514
Fulton, Thomas 84(2)
Furby, Mary 543
Furneaux, Tobias 243, 244
Furse, Charles Wellington (Archdeacon) 555(2)
Furse, Cory 555(2)
Furse, Elizabeth (Mrs) 555(2)
Furse, Elizabeth Theresa (Lily) 555(2)
Furse, Mary Theresa 555(2)
Furse, William Cory 555(2)
Furtado, David Ribeiro 250(2)
Fuseli, Henry 558(2)
Fyans, Elizabeth Alice (Mrs) 423
Fyans, Florence 423
Fyans, Foster 422, 424, 66(2)
Fyans, Gertrude 423
Fyans, John 422
Fyans, Letitia 423
Fyans, Margaret (Mrs) 422
Fyfe, Margaret 436(2)
Fyshe, Elizabeth (Mrs) 312(2)
Fyshe, Henry 312(2)
Gabber, Jimmy 183(2)
Gabbett, Lucy 294(2)
Gage, Henry William 504(2)
Gairdner, Edwin 425
Gairdner, Gordon 425
Gairdner, Jane Drummond (Mrs) 425
Gallie, Anne Maria 533
Gallie, Hugh 533
Galliott, Mary Anne 242(2)
Galt, John 630(2)
Galvin, 550
Gammon, George 276
Gammie, John 276
Gandy, Maria 117(2)
Gardiner, Anna Maria 425
Gardiner, Arthur 213
Gardiner, Charles 350
Gardiner, Charles John 348(2)
Gardiner, David 425
Gardiner, John 425, 524, 224(2), 572(2)
Gardiner, Letitia 213
Gardiner, Marguerite (Mrs) 348(2)
Gardiner, Martha (Mrs) 425
Gardiner, Mary (Mrs) 425
Gardiner, Sarah (Mrs) 425
Gardner, Alan (Sir) 550(2)
Gardner, William 425
Garibaldi 75(2)
Garling, Elizabeth 427
Garling, Elizabeth (Mrs) 426-8
Garling, F. 219, 16(2), 628(2)
Garling, Frederick 6, 89, 91, 426, 427, 428, 256(2)
Garling, Frederick Augustus 428
Garling, Jane 427
Garling, Nicholas 426, 427

Garling, Sarah Olivia (Mrs) 427
Garling, Sophia 427
Garner family 466(2)
Garnett, Richard 560(2)
Garnsey, C.F. (Rev) 484(2)
Garnsey, Mary Emma (Mrs) 484(2)
Garrard, 520
Garrard, C.J. 415(2)
Garratt, H.J. 489(2)
Garratt, Louisa French (Mrs) 489(2)
Garrett, James 428
Garrett, James (Rev) 21, 375(2), 421(2)
Garrett, Jane (Mrs) 428
Garrett, Robert 428
Garrett, Robert (Dr) 137
Garrow, William (Sir) 506
Garryowen, 602(2)
Garryowen, Edmund Finn 216, 376
Gascoigne, Olivia 139(2)
Gascoyne (Gascoigne or Gaskins), Olivia 139(2)
Gaskins, Olivia 139(2)
Gatehouse, Clement 429
Gatehouse, Edith (Mrs) 429
Gatehouse, George 428, 491
Gatehouse, Silas 429
Gatehouse, William 429
Gatenby, 372(2)
Gatenby family (Tas) 7
Gatenby, Andrew 429, 504(2)
Gatenby, Christopher 430
Gatenby, Hannah (Mrs) 429, 504(2)
Gatenby, Nancy 504(2)
Gates, William 430, 431
Gauden, (Bishop) 159
Gaudry, William 32(2)
Gavan, John (Rev) 169
Gavan, Julia Augusta 169
Gavan, William Henry 169
Gawler, (Colonel) 282
Gawler, George 244, 380, 431
Gawler, George (Gov) 478, 48(2), 64(2), 117(2), 201(2), 301(2), 379(2), 473(2), 482(2), 497(2), 535(2)
Gawler, Henry 435
Gawler, Julia (Mrs) 431
Gawler, Maria (Mrs) 431
Gawler, Samuel 431
Gaywal (Aborigine) 190
Gaze, William 632(2)
Geach, Mary 419
Gedye, Charles 281
Geibel, J. (Dr) 222(2)
Geils, (Commandant) 406
Geils, A. (Lt. Col) 295(2)
Geils, Andrew 435, 45(2)
Geils, Mary (Mrs) 435
Geils, Thomas (Lt. Gen) 435
Geiss, Mary 144(2)
Gell, Eleanor Isabella (Mrs) 437
Gell, J.P. 217, 420
Gell, John Philip 412, 436
Gell, Philip (Rev) 436
Gellibrand, 551, 9(2)
Gellibrand, Isabella 437

Gellibrand, John (Major Gen) 438
Gellibrand, Joseph Tice 437, 317(2)
Gellibrand, Joseph Tice (Rev) 438
Gellibrand, J.T. 27, 36, 68, 74, 339, 372, 566 214(2), 320(2), 409(2), 501(2), 516(2)
Gellibrand, Mary Selina 438
Gellibrand, Sophia Louisa (Mrs) 437
Gellibrand, Thomas Lloyd 438
Gellibrand, Walter Angus Bethune 437
Gellibrand, William 437
Gellibrand, William St Paul 438
Geoghegan, (Father) 512(2)
Geoghegan, Edward 161(2)
Geoghegan, P.B. (Rev) 522(2)
George, 108(2)
George, Ann 12
George, Henry 12, 414(2)
George II (King of England) 488
George III (King of England) 85, 191, 208(2), 245(2), 431(2), 456(2), 602(2)
George IV 279(2), 400(2)
George, Lucy 12
George, Mary Ann (Mrs) 95(2)
Gericke, Johann Wilhelm 422(2)
Gericke, J.W. 423(2)
Gerler, Carl Friedrich 422(2)
Gerrald, 218(2)
Gerrald, Joseph 438, 206(2), 266(2)
Geyl, P. 323(2)
Gibb, Matthew 297(2)
Gibbes, Augustus 439, 276(2)
Gibbes, Eliza Julia 331
Gibbes, Elizabeth (Mrs) 439
Gibbes, J.G.N. (Col) 275(2)
Gibbes, J.G.N. (Major) 331
Gibbes, John 439
Gibbes, John George Nathaniel 439
Gibbes, Mary 275(2)
Giblin, Robert 552
Giblin, R.W. 274(2)
Gibson, (Major) 214(2)
Gibson, Alice (Mrs) 367
Gibson, Andrew (Dr) 367
Gibson, Catherine (Mrs) 440
Gibson, David 439
Gibson, Elizabeth (Mrs) 439
Gibson, Frederick 626(2)
Gibson, James 271, 492
Gibson, James Alexander 440
Gibson, Mary Jane 316
Gibson, Rosetta (Mrs) 441
Gibson, William 440, 441
Gidley, (Attorney) 55(2)
Gilbart, Sarah 541(2)
Gilbert, (bushranger) 367
Gilbert, Grace 298
Gilbert, J. 470
Gilbert, John 325, 441, 466, 103(2), 349(2)
Gilbert, Margery 252
Gilbert, William 441

Gilbert, W.S. 276(2)
Gilchrist, Archibald (Rev. Dr) 82(2)
Gilchrist, Clara Elizabeth (Mrs) 442
Gilchrist, Helen Warden (Mrs) 442
Gilchrist, Isabella (Mrs) 442
Gilchrist, John 442
Gilchrist, William 442
Gilchrist, William Oswald 442
Giles, Clement 443
Giles, Emily Elizabeth (Mrs) 443
Giles, Mary (Mrs) 443
Giles, Mortimer 443
Giles, Sarah (Mrs) 443
Giles, Thomas 443
Giles, William 18, 443
Gill, Jane 15(2)
Gill, J.M. 324
Gill, S.T. 377
Gill, Samuel (Rev) 444
Gill, Samuel Thomas 444, 445
Gill, S.T. 18
Gill, Winifred Oke (Mrs) 444
Gillern, D. (Major) 133(2)
Gillern, Wilhelm von 301
Gillern, William de 301
Gilles, Hannah (Mrs) 445
Gilles, Lewis 445
Gilles, L.W. 24
Gilles, Osmond 175, 445, 446, 462, 290(2)
Gilman, (Captain) 3(2)
Gilroy, (bushranger) 312
Gipps, 378(2)
Gipps, (Lady) 221
Gipps, Elizabeth (Lady) 446
Gipps, George (Gov) 6, 103, 118, 192, 336, 345, 392, 399, 430, 546, 1(2), 63(2), 79(2), 90(2), 102(2), 120(2), 135(2), 185(2), 203(2), 236(2), 295(2), 303(2), 365(2), 399(2), 418(2), 424(2), 448(2), 454(2), 494(2), 495(2), 514(2), 524(2), 529(2), 540(2), 542(2), 543(2), 586(2), 588(2), 609(2), 616(2), 617(2)
Gipps, George (Rev) 446
Gipps, George (Sir) 202, 205, 221, 267, 271, 272, 300, 310, 315, 319, 384, 398, 423, 441, 446, 447, 448, 449, 451, 452, 532, 603(2)
Gipps, Reginald Ramsay 452
Gisborne, Elizabeth Fysche (Mrs) 453
Gisborne, Henry Fyshe (Fysche) 453
Gisborne, Thomas 453
Gisbourne, John 376(2)
Gisbourne, Maria (Mrs) 376(2)
Gladstone, 347, 285(2)
Gladstone, Helen 334
Gladstone, W.E. 347, 384, 446
Glanville, Richard 294
Glascott, Cradock (Rev) 528(2)
Glasgow, Isabella 71(2)
Glass, Hugh 70(2)
Glass, Janet 564(2)
Glasse, George Henry 149

Glasse, Harriet 149
Glasson, Annie (Mrs) 533(2)
Glasson, Gustavus 533(2)
Glasson, John 532(2)
Gleadow, Diana Harriet 454
Gleadow, John Ward 454, 532
Gleadow, J.W. 8(2), 371(2)
Gleadow, Robert 454
Gledstones, George (Col) 619(2)
Gledstones, Mary Amelia 619(2)
Glenelg, 378(2), 535(2)
Glenelg, (Baron) 380, 455, 488(2)
Glenelg, (Lord) 8, 446, 481, 541, 117(2), 482(2)
Glenelg, Charles (Baron) 52(2)
Glenelg, Charles (Lord) 401, 539
Glenelg, William 455
Glennie, Benjamin 448(2)
Gliddon, Mary 261(2)
Glindon, Suzannah 272
Glossop, Ann 158
Gloucester, (Bishop of) 613(2)
Gloucester, (Duke of) 223(2)
Glover, Ann (Mrs) 455
Glover, Henry 455
Glover, James 455
Glover, John 455, 456, 160(2)
Glover, John Richardson 456
Glover, Mary 456
Glover, Sarah (Mrs) 456
Glover, William 455, 407(2)
Gmelin, Johann Friedrich 89(2)
Goddard, Anna Maria 367
Godden, John 110
Goderich, (Viscount) 285, 456, 481, 179(2), 204(2), 247(2), 258(2), 470(2), 478(2)
Godman, Eva 363(2)
Godman, F. Du Cane 363(2)
Godwin, Mary 620(2)
Godwin, Mary Wollstonecraft 620(2)
Godwin, William 438, 376(2)
Goethe, Matthias (Rev) 423(2)
Goggs, Henry 433(2)
Goggs, Martha (Mrs) 433(2)
Goggs, Matthew 433(2)
Goggs, Phillis 433(2)
Goldie, 457
Goldie, Alexander 406, 457
Goldie, Louise Leman (Mrs) 457
Good, Peter 54
Goode, (Dr) 254
Goode, Benjamin 190
Goodwin, Sophia (Mrs) 458
Goodwin, William Lushington 457, 458
Goodwin, W.L. 417, 418
Goodwyn, Mary 357, 357(C)
Goold, (Bishop) 345(2)
Goold, J.A. 545(2)
Gooroobaroobooloo (Aborigine) 85
Gordon, 357
Gordon, (Colonel) 573(2)
Gordon, (Duke of) 384, 160(2)
Gordon, (General) 357

Gordon, (Major) 143(2), 393(2)
Gordon, (Mrs) 573(2)
Gordon, Adam Lindsay 160(2)
Gordon, Elizabeth Emily (Mrs) 458
Gordon, George William 364
Gordon, James 215, 458, 459, 72(2), 315(2)
Gordon, James (Sir) 75
Gordon, Jane 415
Gordon, John 458
Gordon, Peter Charles 160(2)
Gore, (Mrs) 200
Gore, (Provost Marshal) 159(2), 233(2), 628(2)
Gore, Harriet 111
Gore, Mary 460
Gore, Mary (Mrs) 52(2)
Gore, Thomas 52(2)
Gore, William 91, 200, 263, 422, 459, 460, 39(2), 213(2), 308(2)
Gorman, (Lieut) 310, 422(2)
Gorman, Ellen 344
Gorman, Owen 448(2)
Gorman, Owen (Lt) 509
Gorton, John 482(2)
Gorton, Margaret (Mrs) 482(2)
Gosling, Catherine (Mrs) 461
Gosling, Elizabeth Curtis (Mrs) 460
Gosling, John 460
Gosling, John William 460, 461
Gosling, William 461
Goss, Anne 301(2)
Goss, James 301(2)
Goss, Martha 528(2)
Gosse, Agnes Grant 525
Gossner, J.E. (Rev. Dr) 421(2)
Gostwick, Mary 247
Gostwick, William (Sir) 247
Gouger, Anne (Mrs) 461
Gouger, George 461
Gouger, Harriet (Mrs) 462
Gouger, Henry 461
Gouger, Robert 15, 46, 379, 461, 462, 463, 540, 7(2), 195(2), 559(2), 560(2)
Gouger, Sarah (Mrs) 463
Goulburn, (Major) 178(2), 430(2)
Goulburn, Frederick 153, 200, 463, 464, 503, 305(2), 510(2), 578(2)
Goulburn, Henry 67, 289, 463, 464, 365(2)
Goulburn, Munbee 463, 464
Goulburn, Susannah (Mrs) 463, 464
Gould, Ann (Mrs) 467
Gould, Charles 181, 465, 466
Gould, Eliza (Elizabeth) 465
Gould, Elizabeth (Mrs) 465
Gould, Franklin 465, 466
Gould, Henry 465, 466
Gould, J. 470
Gould, John 325, 414, 441, 442, 465, 466, 492, 89(2), 168(2), 349(2), 350(2)
Gould, W.B. 427(2)
Gould, William Buelow 467
Govett, John 467

Govett, Susanna Price (Mrs) 467
Govett, William Romaine 467, 468
Grafton (Duke of) 384
Grafton family 384
Grafton, Sarah 398(2)
Graham, Frances 65(2)
Graham, James (Sir) 180, 457
Graham, Jane 160(2)
Graham, J.B. 445
Graham, John 145, 294, 300, 468
Graham, Ralph 160(2)
Graham, Thomas 65(2)
Grant family 455
Grant, (Dr) 74(2)
Grant, Amelia Sophia 392
Grant, Charles 455
Grant, David (Dr) 392
Grant, Elizabeth 182
Grant, James 468, 111(2), 272(2)
Grant, James (Dr) 355(2)
Grant, James (Lt) 59(2), 318(2)
Grant, Jessie 499
Grant, John 108, 126, 469, 526, 111(2), 112(2)
Grant, Paddy (Capt) 486
Grant, Robert 468, 499
Grant, Robert (Prof) 544
Grantham, Baron 456
Grasse, de (Comte) 268(2)
Graves, John Woodcock 36(2)
Graves, Sharpland 458(2)
Gray, 287
Gray, Asa (Prof) 279
Gray, Helen 232
Gray, John Edward 470
Gray, Katherine Heath 58
Gray, Maria Emma (Mrs) 470
Gray, Mary 375(2)
Gray, Samuel Frederick 470
Gray, Sarah Kelleway 441(2)
Gray, Williamina Paton 167(2)
Greatheed, Samuel (Rev) 260
Greece (King of) 488(2)
Green, Ann 106
Green, Anne 205(2)
Green, H.M. 515, 533(2)
Greene, Charlotte 496(2)
Greenow, Sarah 155
Greenway, Ann (Mrs) 470
Greenway, Charles 472
Greenway, F. 109(2), 191(2), 554(2)
Greenway, Francis 259, 324, 325, 470, 471, 472, 139(2), 186(2), 291(2), 510(2)
Greenway, Mary (Mrs) 470, 472
Greenwood, 88(2)
Greenwood, Joseph 214(2)
Greeves, George (Dr) 43
Gregor, John 472, 473
Gregory, (Abbot) 165(2)
Gregory, (brothers) 253(2), 391(2)
Gregory, (Dr) 431
Gregory, A.C. 326
Gregory, Harriet Elizabeth (Mrs) 474

Gregory, Henry Gregory 473
Gregory, H.G. 339(2), 341(2)
Gregory, H.G. (Abbot) 293, 535, 199(2)
Gregory, John 405, 413, 474, 475
Gregory, Olinthus Gilbert 474
Gregory, William (Judge) 506
Gregory XVI (Pope) 270(2), 545(2)
Gregson, Jesse 306
Gregson, John 475
Gregson, John Compton 476
Gregson, T. 576(2)
Gregson, T.G. 38, 329, 371, 49(2), 225(2), 315(2), 385(2), 501(2), 593(2)
Gregson, Thomas 194, 164(2)
Gregson, Thomas George 475
Grenell, Martha 612(2)
Grenville, (Lord) 56(2)
Grenville, Richard (Sir) 550(2)
Greville, Charles 53, 61
Grey, (Earl) 61, 221, 222, 272, 347, 381, 385, 386, 456, 542, 262(2), 342(2), 412(2), 470(2), 524(2)
Grey, (Earl) 480
Grey, (Third Earl) 408(2)
Grey, Charles 480
Grey, Eliza Lucy (Mrs) 477, 466(2)
Grey, Elizabeth Anne (Mrs) 477
Grey, George 441
Grey, George (Capt) 434, 435, 391(2), 466(2), 489(2), 497(2)
Grey, George (Gov) 18, 29, 364, 418, 8(2), 301(2), 383(2), 408(2), 480(2), 611(2)
Grey, George (Lt) 253(2)
Grey, George (Lt. Col) 476, 477
Grey, George (Sir) 287, 476, 478, 479, 480, 576, 151(2), 450(2), 529(2)
Grey, Henry George 480, 482, 483, 484
Grey, H.G. (Gen) 506
Grey, Mary Elizabeth (Mrs) 480
Griffin, (Dr) 272
Griffin, Edmund 21(2)
Griffin, Jane 413
Griffin, John 411
Griffin, Joseph 70
Griffin, Mary 446(2)
Griffin, Mary (Mrs) 411
Griffiths, (Bishop) 341(2)
Griffiths, (Dr) 504
Griffiths, Ann 558(2)
Griffiths, Ann Grant (Mrs) 486
Griffiths, Annette Agnes (Mrs) 485
Griffiths, Elizabeth 36(2)
Griffiths, Elizabeth (Mrs) 485
Griffiths, Frederick 485
Griffiths, George Edward 558(2)
Griffiths, George Neville 485
Griffiths, George Richard 485
Griffiths, Herbert Tyrrel 485
Griffiths, John 197, 340, 485,

486, 487, 12(2), 231(2)
Griffiths, Jonathan 485, 486, 231(2)
Griffiths, Laetitia (Mrs) 485
Griffiths, Mary 12(2), 36(2)
Griffiths, Ralph 558(2)
Griffiths, Ralph (Dr) 558(2)
Griffiths, Sarah (Mrs) 485(C)
Griffiths, Thomas 485(C)
Griffiths, W. 402(2)
Griffiths, William Russell 485
Grigg, Anne 168
Grigor, James 472
Grigor, Jannet (Mrs) 472
Grimes, C. 306(2)
Grimes, Cassandra (Mrs) 488
Grimes, Charles 12, 351, 359, 487, 488, 219(2), 610(2)
Grimes, Charles (Surveyor) 566
Grimes, Esther (Mrs) 487
Grimes, George 488
Grimes, John 488
Grimes, Joseph 487
Grimes, Marianne 233(2)
Grimstone, Mary Leman Rede 3
Grisley, Jane Eleanor (Mrs) 345
Grono, (Captain) 519(2)
Grono, J. 220(2)
Grono, John 36(2)
Groom, Ann 115, 123(2C)
Groom, James 313(2)
Grose, Catherine (Mrs) 488
Grose, Elizabeth (Mrs) 489, 319(2)
Grose, Francis 12, 28, 49, 170, 237, 238, 383, 488, 489
Grose, Francis (Lt. Gov) 518, 563, 569, 570, 18(2), 22(2), 57(2), 97(2), 170(2), 206(2), 208(2), 281(2), 309(2), 312(2), 317(2), 319(2), 364(2), 373(2), 394(2), 468(2), 469(2), 531(2), 551(2)
Grose, Francis (Major) 568, 154(2), 329(2), 594(2)
Grose, Francis (Rev) 489
Grose, Irene 490(C)
Grose, J.H. 202(2)
Grose, Joseph Hickey 490, 137(2)
Grose, Mary Ann 490(C)
Grove, Daniel 490
Grove, James 490, 491
Grove, Susannah (Mrs) 490
Growse, Anne 99(2)
Grubb, Maria Susanna 372(2)
Guardi, Francesco 411(2)
Guest, George 104, 491
Guest, Jannett 402(2)
Guest, Mary (Mrs) 491
Guest, Sarah 104
Guest, Sarah 491
Guillan, John 245(2)
Guillemard, Mary 411
Gunn, Ann (Mrs) 492
Gunn, Eliza (Mrs) 492
Gunn, Frances Hannah (Mrs) 494
Gunn, James Arndell 494
Gunn, Margaret Legrand (Mrs) 493

Gunn, Margaret (Mrs) 492, 493
Gunn, R.C. 176, 440, 470, 530, 94(2), 230(2)
Gunn, Ronald Campbell 492, 493
Gunn, Ronald James William 492
Gunn, S. 491
Gunn, William 492, 493, 494
Gunn, William (Lt) 493
Gunning, George Weston 494
Gunning, Henry (Rev) 312(2)
Gurner, Henry Field 495
Gurner, John 494
Gurner, Mary 495
Gurner, Rebecca Ann (Mrs) 495
Gyles, Harriet 351
Gyles, John 252, 351, 495
Gyles, Maria (Mrs) 495
Hack, Bridget (Mrs) 497
Hack, J.B. 341, 498
Hack, John Barton 497
Hack, Maria (Mrs) 497
Hack, Stephen 497
Hack, Theodore 497
Hackett, (Captain) 250
Hackett, Marianne 250
Hacking, Henry 497
Hacking, Maria 549(2)
Hadden, Annie Maria 296
Hadden, Harriet 296
Hadden, James 296
Hadden, William 296
Haddington, (Earl of) 275, 415(2)
Haddon, F.W. 55(2)
Haeckel, 287
Hagen, 497
Hagen, Jacob 479, 498
Hagen, Mary (Mrs) 499
Hagen, van der, 13(2)
Hahn, Dirk 33(2)
Hahnemann, Samuel Christian Friedrich 448(2)
Haines, (politician) 350
Haines, William Clarke 606(2)
Haining, Jessie (Mrs) 499
Haining, John (Rev) 499
Haining, Robert 499
Haining, Wilhelmina (Mrs) 499
Haldon, John 398(2)
Haldon, Marina 398(2)
Hale, (Archdeacon) 620(2)
Hale, (Bishop) 122(2), 245(2)
Hale, Horatio 279
Hale, Mathew Blagden 509
Hale, Sabina (Mrs) 245(2)
Haley, Grace 126(2)
Haliburton, (Judge) 201
Hall, Angelina 246(2)
Hall, Anna 506(C)
Hall, Ben 313, 367
Hall, Charlotte (Mrs) 500
Hall, Edward (Jun) 500
Hall, Edward Smith 56, 285, 500, 537, 478(2)
Hall, Edward Swarbreck 502
Hall, Emily (Mrs) 501
Hall, E.S. 303, 318, 396, 69(2), 148(2), 179(2), 265(2), 359(2), 432(2), 511(2)

Hall, Frederick William 506
Hall, James 314, 503, 148(2)
Hall, Jane (Mrs) 500
Hall, Lydia Ann 506
Hall, Mary (Mrs) 502
Hall, Sarah (Mrs) 501
Hall, Smith 500
Hall, Thomas 240, 276
Hall, William 307, 503, 42(2)
Hallbeck, H.P. 89(2)
Hallen, Ambrose 58, 504, 112(2), 554(2)
Hallen, Edward 504
Hallen, Sarah (Mrs) 504
Hallen, Sophia (Mrs) 504, 505
Haller, Emma (Mrs) 506
Haller, John Friederick 505
Halloran, Elizabeth (Mrs) 507
Halloran, Henry 507, 515
Halloran, L.H. (Dr) 397
Halloran, Laurence Hynes 506
Halloran, Lydia Ann 506(C)
Halloran, Mary (Mrs) 506
Halls, Mary Ann 257, 257(C)
Hamelin, (Captain) 71
Hamersley, Anne Frances Elizabeth 155
Hamersley, Hugh 155
Hamilton, 277
Hamilton, Agnes 216(2)
Hamilton, Agnes Anna (Mrs) 65(2)
Hamilton, Archibald 65(2)
Hamilton, Charles (Sir) 392, 393
Hamilton, Edward 1(2)
Hamilton, Elennora 174(2)
Hamilton, Eliza Hamilton 337
Hamilton, E.W.T. 290
Hamilton, James 65(2)
Hamilton, Katherine 65(2)
Hamilton, Robert 65(2)
Hamilton, Sarah 565
Hamilton, Solomon 337
Hamilton, W. (Rev) 232
Hamilton, W.H. 500(2), 517(2)
Hamilton, William Henry 507
Hammett, James 132(2), 132 (2)
Hamond, Andrew Snape (Capt. Sir) 594(2)
Hampton, (Dr) 493
Hampton, (Major) 476
Hampton, Fanny (Mrs) 509
Hampton, G.E. 509
Hampton, George Essex 509
Hampton, Henry George 509
Hampton, John Stephen 508
Hampton, J.S. 347, 371, 393(2)
Hampton, Kennedy (Gov) 509
Hampton, Mary (Mrs) 509
Hampton, Stephen 576(2)
Hancox, Elizabeth 521, 522
Hand, John 548
Handt, J.C.S. (Rev) 352
Handt, Johann Christian Simon 509
Handt, Mary (Mrs) 509
Handyside, Margaret 500(2)
Hangan, 553
Hankinson, Catharine 316(2)
Hanks, Mary 257(2)
Hannaway, Ann 279(2)

Hanover (King of) 404(2)
Hansom, Charles 270(2)
Hansom, Joseph 270(2)
Hanson, (politician) 378
Hanson, R.D. 165
Hanway, Jonas 194(2)
Harbord, Martha 592(2)
Harbroe, Anne 253
Harbroe, Edward 253
Hardey, Ann (Mrs) 510
Hardey, John Wall 510
Hardey, Joseph 510
Hardey, Robert 510
Hardey, Sarah 511
Harding, Elizabeth 43
Harding, Sarah 605(2)
Harding, Sarah Elizabeth 619(2)
Harding, Tamar 350
Hardwicke, (Earl of) 456
Hardwicke, Charles Browne 511
Hardwicke, Elizabeth (Mrs) 511
Hardwicke, Frederick 511
Hardwicke, Sophia 380(2)
Hardy, Hannah 13
Hardy, Richard 150
Hardy, Thomas 206(2)
Hargraves, E.H. 494(2), 532(2)
Harington, Frances L. (Mrs) 512
Harington, John Herbert 511
Harington, Thomas Cudbert 511
Harley, Edward 431(2)
Harley, Elizabeth 110, 267
Harley, Jane Elizabeth (Mrs) 431(2)
Harley, Charlotte Mary (Lady) 46
Harmood, Jane Elizabeth 431(2)
Harmsworth, Alice (Mrs) 469(2)
Harmsworth, Thomas 469(2)
Harold, (King of England) 512
Harold, James 309, 512
Harold, James (Fr) 302(2), 340(2)
Harold, W.V. (Rev) 513
Harper, Anne 604(2)
Harper, George 513
Harper, Margaret Eleanor (Mrs) 513
Harper, Thomas 604(2)
Harpur, Charles 336, 337, 514, 515
Harpur, Charles Chidley 514
Harpur, Joseph 514
Harpur, Joseph Jehoshaphat 514, 515
Harpur, Mary (Mrs) 514
Harpur, Sarah (Mrs) 514
Harrington, (Earl of) 459
Harris, 359
Harris, 496(2)
Harris, (Captain) 308(2)
Harris, (Dr) 236
Harris, Alexander 515, 445(2)
Harris, Ann Jane (Mrs) 517
Harris, Ann (Mrs) 519

Harris, Eliza (Mrs) 519
Harris, Elizabeth 518, 87(2), 548(2)
Harris, Elizabeth (Mrs) 515
Harris, G.P. 227, 238, 240, 494
Harris, George Prideaux Robert 516
Harris, Grace 308(2)
Harris, Hannah 518, 87(2), 382(2)
Harris, John 252, 253, 260, 308, 517, 518, 519, 87(2), 548(2)
Harris, John (Const) 86(2)
Harris, John (Dr) 469, 129(2)
Harris, John (Rev) 259, 438(2)
Harris, John (Surgeon) 39, 12(2), 39(2), 61(2), 233(2), 281(2), 369(2), 382(2), 405(2)
Harris, Joseph (Dr) 372
Harris, Mary (Mrs) 518
Harris, Ursula (Mrs) 515
Harrison, Emma 480(2)
Harrison, James 520
Harrowby, (Lord) 288
Hart, 497
Hart, Ann 565(2)
Hart, Conway 330
Hart, Elizabeth 485
Hart, Thomas 565(2)
Hart, William Neville 485
Hartenstein, Ambrosius Theophilus William 421(2)
Hartogsz, Dirck 555, 556(2)
Harvey, John 91
Haslett, Mary 234(2)
Hassall family 337, 514
Hassall, Anne 567(2)
Hassall, Anne (Mrs) 523
Hassall, Eliza Cordelia 522, 566(2)
Hassall, Eliza Marsden 523
Hassall, Elizabeth (Mrs) 521, 522, 95(2)
Hassall, James 521
Hassall, James Samuel (Rev) 523
Hassall, John 532(2)
Hassall, Jonathan 402(2), 566(2)
Hassall, Lucy (Mrs) 227(2)
Hassall, Mary Cover 522, 95(2)
Hassall, Mary (Mrs) 402(2)
Hassall, Rowland 107, 205, 251, 260, 521, 522, 61(2), 95(2), 209(2), 402(2), 438(2), 566(2), 599(2)
Hassall, Samuel 522
Hassall, Samuel Otoo 521, 227(2)
Hassall, Susanna Marsden 522
Hassall, Thomas 150, 252, 521, 522, 551
Hassall, Thomas (Rev) 451(2)
Hassard, John (Col) 377
Hassard, Maria 377
Hastie, Thomas (Rev) 399
Hastings, (Marquis of) 288(2)
Hatherton, (Lord) 371
Haussman, Godfrey 422(2)
Haussman, John (Rev) 423(2)
Haussmann, Johann Gottfried 421(2)

Hawdon, Emma (Mrs) 524
Hawdon, Arthur Joseph 524(C)
Hawdon, John 523, 524
Hawdon, Joseph 350, 362, 425, 523, 524
Hawdon, Sarah Elizabeth (Mrs) 524
Hawke, (Admiral) 11, 85(2)
Hawes, Benjamin 482, 79(2)
Hawke, George 532(2)
Hawkes, J.H.M. 179
Hawkesworth, 314(2)
Hawkey, J.J. 388
Hawkey, Margaret Gordon 388
Hawkins, Caesar 85
Hawkins, Edward 93(2)
Hawkins, Elizabeth (Mrs) 524
Hawkins, George 524
Hawkins, Helen 525
Hawkins, Sarah (Mrs) 524
Hawkins, T.F. 362(2)
Hawkins, Thomas Fitzherbert 524
Hawkins, Thomas Jarman 525
Hawkins, Waterhouse 18
Hawkshaw, (General) 428
Hawksley, E.J. 141(2)
Hawley, Alfred 372(2)
Hawthorn, Beilby 392(2)
Hay, (Under Secretary) 324(2), 432(2)
Hay, Agnes Grant (Mrs) 525
Hay, Agnes (Mrs) 525
Hay, Alexander 525
Hay, James 479(2)
Hay, Peter 525
Hay, Robert (Archbishop) 526
Hay, Robert William 525, 377(2)
Hay, R.W. 217, 410, 554, 238(2), 258(2)
Hay, Susan (Mrs) 525
Hay, William Gosse 525
Haydock, Mary 373(2)
Haydon, R.B. 347
Hay-Drummond, Elizabeth Margaret (Mrs) 526
Hay-Drummond, George William Auriol (Rev) 526
Haydn, 89(2)
Hayes, (Father) 299(2)
Hayes, A.E. 285, 501
Hayes, Attiwell 526
Hayes, Bridget 295
Hayes, Catherine (Mrs) 527
Hayes, Fletcher 527
Hayes, Henry 137, 61(2)
Hayes, Henry Browne (Sir) 183, 469, 526, 388(2)
Hayes, John (Sir) 527
Hayes, Martha 137
Hayes, Michael 309, 527, 31(2), 299(2)
Hayes, Richard (Rev) 528
Hayes, Sophia 534
Hayter, Angelo Collen 222
Hayter, Charles 160(2)
Hayward, J. 600(2)
Hayward, James 353
Hayward, Mary (Mrs) 353
Hayward, Sophie 190
Hazard, Sarah (Mrs) 134(2)

Hazlitt, 558(2)
Heading, Ann 99(2)
Headlam, John 63
Heales-Brooke, (politician) 350
Heathorn, Elizabeth 158
Heathorn, Henrietta 577
Hebblewaite, William 261
Hellier, Mary 321
Hellyer, Betsy (Mrs) 528
Hellyer, Henry 406, 528
Hellyer, John 528
Helms, Mary Watson 618(2)
Helpman, Ann (Mrs) 529
Helpman, Benjamin Franklin 529
Hely, F.A. 575, 86(2), 554(2)
Hely, Forbes Francis (Col) 529
Hely, Frederick 265(2)
Hely, Frederick Augustus 529
Hely, Hovenden 530
Hems, Anne 109
Hems, Rachel 109
Henderson, E.Y.W. (Capt) 381
Henderson, E.Y.W. (Col) 509
Henderson, Jane 51
Henderson, Margaret 52
Henning, Amelia Tregenna 451(2)
Hennis, Peter (Dr) 14(2)
Henry, Ann (Mrs) 252
Henry, George 251
Henry, Martha Jane 55(2C)
Henry, Samuel 245
Henry, Samuel Pinder 252
Henry, Sarah 112, 252, 522
Henry, Sarah (Mrs) 251
Henry, William 112, 251, 521
Henshaw, (artist) 568(2)
Henslow, J.S. 287
Henslow, John (Sir) 530
Henslow, John Stevens 530
Henslowe, Anne (Mrs) 530
Henslowe, Cecilia Maria (Mrs) 530
Henslowe, Edward Prentis 530
Henslowe, Francis Boyle 531
Henslowe, Francis Hartwell 530
Henslowe, Frederic John Francis (Comm) 531
Henty brothers 239(2)
Henty family 297, 369, 231(2)
Henty, Anne Maria (Mrs) 533
Henty, Charles Shum 531
Henty, Charlotte (Mrs) 531
Henty, Edward 112, 340, 531, 411(2)
Henty, Eliza (Mrs) 533
Henty, Frances 531
Henty, Frances Elizabeth (Mrs) 531
Henty, Francis 531
Henty, George 531
Henty, Henry 531
Henty, James 440, 531, 94(2), 371(2), 372(2)
Henty, Jane 172, 531
Henty, Jane (Mrs) 529, 533
Henty, John 531, 9(2)
Henty, June (Mrs) 531
Henty, Mary Anne (Mrs) 533
Henty, Stephen 112, 531
Henty, Stephen George 529,

531, 533
Henty, Susan (Mrs) 532
Henty, Susannah Matilda (Mrs) 532
Henty, Thomas 335, 531
Henty, William 454, 531, 94(2), 617(2)
Hepburn, David 276
Hepburn, Graeme 276
Hepburn, John 425, 524
Herbert, Elizabeth (Mrs) 326(2)
Herbert, Henry 93(2)
Herbert, Louisa Katrina 268(2C)
Heritage, Charles 139(2)
Hesse, G.B.L. 27, 437(C)
Heustis, Daniel D. 430
Hewitt, James 340
Hewlitt, Mary 353
Hewson, Lucinda 568(2)
Heydon, Catherine 535
Heydon, C.G. 199(2)
Heydon, Charles Gilbert 536
Heydon, Ebenezer 534
Heydon, Emily 535
Heydon, George 535
Heydon, J.K. 343(2)
Heydon, Jabez King 534
Heydon, Louis Francis 536
Heydon, Miriam Josepha (Mrs) 199(2)
Heydon, Richard 534
Heydon, Sophia (Mrs) 534
Heydon, William 534
Heylin, Henry 577(2)
Heylman, Philip 503(2)
Heyne, Therese 403
Heywood, Peter (Capt) 403(2)
Heywood, Thomas 376
Hibbins, Ann (Mrs) 536
Hibbins, Constantia 536
Hibbins, Emmeline 536
Hibbins, T. 313
Hibbins, Thomas 536
Hicks, (Lieut) 243
Hicks, H.W. 224(2)
Hicks, Sarah 224(2)
Hicks, Sarah Westall 81
Hill, (Captain) 398(2)
Hill, (Lord) 431
Hill, Arthur 500
Hill, Eliza 538
Hill, James 538
Hill, John 5(2)
Hill, Joshua 288(2)
Hill, Louisa (Mrs) 538
Hill, Matthew Davenport (Q.C.) 186(2)
Hill, Phoebe Sapphira 537
Hill, Richard 523, 537
Hill, Rowland 365(2)
Hill, Rowland (Rev) 443
Hill, Samuel 605(2)
Hill, Samuel Prout 538
Hilson, Agnes 519(2)
Hindmarsh, (Captain) 116(2)
Hindmarsh, Jane 541
Hindmarsh, John 539, 541
Hindmarsh, John (Jun) 539, 541
Hindmarsh, John (Gov) 166, 431, 445, 462, 14(2), 117(2), 200(2), 262(2), 472(2), 473(2),

480(2), 482(2), 560(2), 624(2)
Hindmarsh, John (Sir) 378, 379, 538
Hindmarsh, Mary 541, 473(2)
Hindmarsh, Mary (Mrs) 538
Hindmarsh, Susan 541
Hindmarsh, Susannah Wilson (Lady) 539
Hindson, Matthew 1(2)
Hinson, Frances 435(2)
Hipkiss, Richard 541
Hitchcock, Benjamin 367(2)
Hitchcock, Eliza 367(2)
Hitchins, Frederic 26
Hoare, Catharine (Mrs) 316(2)
Hoare, Harriet Jane 14(2)
Hoare, Samuel 316(2)
Hobart, (Lord) 240, 348(2)
Hobart, Robert (4th Earl of Buckinghamshire) 542
Hobbs, (Mrs & Misses) 553
Hobbs, Ann Jane 517, 542
Hobbs, Charity 240
Hobbs, James 240, 542, 3(2)
Hobbs, James (Lt) 517
Hobbs, Judith Elizabeth 553
Hobbs, Mary Ann (Mrs) 543
Hobbs, Rebecca 3(2)
Hobbs, William 542
Hobbs, William (Lt) 553
Hobby, (Lieutenant) 83
Hobby, Thomas 39(2)
Hobler, Francis Helvetius 543(C)
Hobler, George 543
Hobler, Mary (Mrs) 543
Hobson, (Lt. Gov) 471(2)
Hobson, Edmund Charles 544
Hobson, Edward William 544
Hobson, Eliza (Mrs) 545
Hobson, Margaret (Mrs) 544
Hobson, Marie (Mrs) 545
Hobson, Martha (Mrs) 545
Hobson, Samuel 545
Hobson, William 187, 412, 545
Hobson, William (Capt) 544
Hodder, Edwin 18
Hoddle, 423
Hoddle, Agnes 548
Hoddle, Fanny Agnes (Mrs) 547
Hoddle, Mary (Mrs) 547
Hoddle, Robert 80, 376, 547, 125(2), 410(2), 472(2)
Hoddle-Wrigley, Constance 548
Hodges, Peter 251, 252
Hodgson, Arthur 406(2)
Hodgson, Pemberton 406(2)
Hogan, Frances 548
Hogan, Michael 548
Hogan, P. 5, 158
Hogan, P.G. 369
Hogan, Patrick Gould 548
Hogan, Sarah (Mrs) 549
Hogan, Sarah Maria 549
Hogan, Teresa Elizabeth 549
Hogan, William 548
Holcroft, Thomas 376(2)
Holden, Betty (Mrs) 549
Holden, George 427, 549
Holden, Henry Augustus 549

Holden, John Rose 549
Holden, Mary (Mrs) 549
Holden, Susan (Mrs) 550
Holden, William Rose (Rev) 549
Hole, Charles 483(2)
Hole, Grace (Mrs) 483(2)
Hole, Jane 483(2)
Holkar, 189(2)
Holl, Charlotte 500
Holl, Hugh Victor 500
Holland, (Lord) 404
Holland, Edward (Rev) 431(2)
Holland, J.J. 596(2)
Holland, Mary 504(2)
Hollands, David 254(2)
Hollands, Sarah Elizabeth 254(2)
Hollingdale, Robert 141(2)
Holmes, Sarah 501
Holmes, Susannah 31(2)
Holt, Hester (Mrs) 550
Holt, James 87(2)
Holt, John 550
Holt, Joseph 239, 258, 550, 38(2), 334(2)
Holt, Joshua 550
Holt, Thomas 616(2)
Hone, Elizabeth Augusta (Mrs) 551
Hone, Joseph 543, 551
Hone, Mary Ann 543
Honey, Honor 138
Hood, 558(2)
Hood, (Admiral) 83(2)
Hood, Thomas 402(2)
Hook, Charles 90, 551, 310(2)
Hook, Lionel (Capt) 551
Hook, Sarah (Mrs) 551
Hooker, 287
Hooker, Joseph (Sir) 493
Hooker, Joseph Dalton 492
Hooker, W.J. 230(2)
Hooker, W.J. (Prof) 492
Hooker, William 98, 167, 27(2)
Hooker, William (Sir) 269, 325, 566
Hooper, John 280
Hooper, Judith 280
Hope, (Captain) 431(2)
Hope, John (Gen. Sir) 492
Hope, Louis 334
Hope, Susan (Mrs) 334
Hopetoun, (Earl of) 334
Hopkins, Arthur 552
Hopkins, Frances Elizabeth 531
Hopkins, Henry 212, 552, 216(2), 229(2), 563(2), 572(2), 591(2)
Hopkins, John Rout 552
Hopkins, Martha 553
Hopkins, Mary (Mrs) 552
Hopkins, Sarah 553
Hopkins, Sarah Rout (Mrs) 552
Hopkinson, 496(2)
Hopley, Judith Elizabeth (Mrs) 553
Hopley, William 553
Hornby, Charlotte Margaret 470(2)
Hornby, Geoffrey (Rev) 470(2)
Horne family 375(2)

Horne, 'Orion' 160(2)
Horner, Hannah 254
Horrocks, J.A. 444
Horton, (Under Secretary) 461(2)
Hortle, Ann 292, 143(2)
Hortle, James 26, 143(2)
Horton, Anne Beatrix 554
Horton, Anne Beatrix (Mrs) 554
Horton, Eusebius 554
Horton, Robert Wilmot (Sir) 554
Horton, Samuel (Capt) 205(2)
Horton, William (Rev) 105(2), 216(2), 566(2)
Horton, Wilmot 67, 129, 270, 284, 343, 393, 395, 397, 462, 45(2), 560(2)
Hosking, Ann Elizabeth (Mrs) 554
Hosking, Eliza (Mrs) 555
Hosking, John 260, 554, 509(2)
Hosking, Martha Foxlowe (Mrs) 555
Hosking, Martha (Mrs) 555, 509(2)
Hosking, Peter Mann 555
Hotham, 492(2)
Hotham, Charles (Sir) 388, 349(2)
Houghton, (Colonel) 372
Houghton, (Major) 115(2)
Houghton, Philippa (Mrs) 115(2)
House, (Captain) 439(2)
Houston, George 82
Houston, William (Sir) 375
Houtman, Cornelis 555
Houtman, Frederik de 266, 555
Houtman, Vrouwtje Cornelisd (Mrs) 556
Hove, Anton Pantaleon 54
Hovell, Arndell John Palmer 557
Hovell, Elizabeth Emily 557
Hovell, Esther (Mrs) 556
Hovell, Sophia (Mrs) 557
Hovell, W.H. 27, 505(2)
Hovell, W.H. (Capt) 564
Hovell, William Hilton 68, 556
Howard, C.B. (Rev) 335, 446
Howard, Charles Beaumont 557
Howard, Grace Montgomery (Mrs) 557
Howard, William 557
Howe, 373, 427
Howe, (Admiral) 538, 567, 573(2)
Howe, (Lord) 50, 327(2)
Howe, Alfred Australia 559
Howe, Ann 167(2), 304(2)
Howe, Ann (Mrs) 558
Howe, Ann Wesley 559
Howe, Caroline (Mrs) 560
Howe, Catherine Broughton 321
Howe, Elizabeth (Mrs) 559, 560
Howe, Frances (Mrs) 560
Howe, George 260, 472, 557,

562, 60(2), 304(2), 605(2)
Howe, George Terry 559
Howe, G.T. 558, 163(2), 397(2)
Howe, Horatio 558
Howe, Jane 562
Howe, Jane (Mrs) 560
Howe, John 266, 321, 560, 220(2), 449(2)
Howe, Mary 560
Howe, Mary (Mrs) 561
Howe, Mary Ann Risdon 559
Howe, Mary McLeay 559
Howe, Michael 227, 328, 560, 566, 232(2), 278(2), 459(2), 469(2)
Howe, Robert 213, 557, 558, 167(2), 204(2), 304(2), 370(2), 533(2), 605(2)
Howe, Robert Mansfield 559
Howe, Sarah (Mrs) 558, 559, 605(2)
Howe, Thomas 557, 560
Howe, W. 578(2)
Howe, William 427, 561
Howell, Harriott 151
Howell, Sarah 490(C)
Howell, William Grose 490(C)
Howey, Henry 234(2)
Howey, Margaret Eleanor 513
Howey, Maria Matilda (Mrs) 234(2)
Howgill, Francis 46
Howick, 285
Howick, (Viscount) 480
Howick, Maria (Mrs) 480
Howitt, Richard 124, 249, 519(2)
Howley, (Archbishop) 160
Howley, (Bishop) 262, 401
Hoy, Helen 12
Huber, L.F. 403
Huber, Therese (Mrs) 403
Hudson, G.P. 261
Huerdd, Mary 290(2)
Hugessen, Dorothea 54
Hugessen, William Western 54
Hughes, Catherine 23(2)
Hughes, Esther (Mrs) 509(2)
Hughes, F.G. (Major Gen) 455(2)
Hughes, George 558, 562
Hughes, Henry (Dr) 375, 376
Hughes, J.T. 392(2)
Hughes, John Terry 555, 509(2)
Hughes, Matthew 521
Hughes, Thomas 364
Hull, Anna (Mrs) 562
Hull, Anna Munro 348(2)
Hull, George 429, 562, 348(2)
Hull, Mary Ann 226(2C)
Hull, Rose (Mrs) 562
Hull, Thomas 562
Hull, William 334(2)
Hulloch, John (Sir) 622(2)
Humboldt, Alexander von 403
Hume, (Major) 11
Hume, Abraham (Sir) 78
Hume, Andrew 361, 10(2)
Hume, Andrew Hamilton 563, 564
Hume, Elizabeth More (Mrs) 563

Hume, Elizabeth (Mrs) 564
Hume, Francis Rawdon 563, 565
Hume, H. 505(2)
Hume, Hamilton 67, 68, 556, 563, 564, 181(2), 495(2), 530(2)
Hume, Isabella 563
Hume, James 563
Hume, John 564
Hume, John Kennedy 563
Hume, Joseph 286, 501, 179(2), 616(2)
Humphrey, A.W. 560
Humphrey, A.W.H. 226, 532(2)
Humphrey, Adolarius William Henry 565
Humphrey, George 565
Humphrey, Harriet (Mrs) 566
Humphrey, Sarah (Mrs) 565
Humphreys, William 93(2)
Hungerford, Ann 139(2)
Hunt, John 552(2)
Hunt, Molly (Mrs) 259(2)
Hunt, Thomas 259(2)
Hunter, Alexander 572
Hunter, Alexander Maclean 572
Hunter, Andrew Francis 572
Hunter, Eliza Anne (Mrs) 572
Hunter, Helen (Mrs) 566
Hunter, Jacobina 181
Hunter, James Arthur Carr 572
Hunter, John 218, 238, 251, 298, 309, 313, 383, 572, 88(2)
Hunter, John (Admiral) 202(2)
Hunter, John (Gov) 28, 361, 421, 548, 563, 566, 572, 18(2), 46(2), 57(2), 58(2), 154(2), 170(2), 206(2), 208(2), 283(2), 313(2), 318(2), 364(2), 443(2), 444(2), 537(2), 573(2), 574(2), 602(2), 610(2)
Hunter, Louisa Harriett (Mrs) 573
Hunter, Mary 46(2)
Hunter, Matthew D. 306
Hunter, Robert 566
Hunter, William 566
Hunter, William Fergusson 572
Huntingdon, (Countess of) 251, 316
Huntly, (Marquis of) 160(2)
Huntly, George 160(2)
Huon de Kerilleau, Charles 573
Huon de Kerilleau, Elizabeth 573
Huon de Kerilleau (Kerillac), Gabriel Louis Marie 573
Huon de Kerilleau, Louise (Mrs) 573
Huon de Kerilleau, Paul 573
Hurd, Thomas (Capt) 61(2)
Hurst, Benjamin (Rev) 303(2), 540(2)
Huskisson, 523(2)
Huskisson, William 303
Hussey, Henry 17
Hutchins, (Archdeacon) 35, 311(2)
Hutchins, Joseph (Rev) 574
Hutchins, Rachel (Mrs) 574
Hutchins, William 573

Hutchins, William (Archdeacon) 420
Hutchinson, Jane (Mrs) 575
Hutchinson, John 130(2)
Hutchinson, John (Rev) 291(2)
Hutchinson, Margaret 325(2C)
Hutchinson, Mary 549
Hutchinson, Mary (Mrs) 291(2), 575
Hutchinson, William 549, 574, 363(2), 613(2)
Hutchinson, Y.B. 166
Hutchison, Janet Ranken 361(2)
Hutt, George (Sir) 577
Hutt, Gilly (Mrs) 575
Hutt, John 228, 326, 441, 487(2)
Hutt, John (Gov) 575, 122(2), 253(2)
Hutt, Richard 575
Hutt, William 575
Hutton-Browne, Mary 184(2)
Huxley, 287, 364
Huxley, Aldous 31
Huxley, George 577
Huxley, Henrietta (Mrs) 577
Huxley, Julian Sorell (Sir) 31
Huxley, Leonard 31
Huxley, Rachel (Mrs) 577
Huxley, T.H. 485, 44(2), 167(2), 471(2)
Huxley, Thomas Henry 577
Hynde, Sophia Louisa 437
Icely, Charlotte (Mrs) 2(2)
Icely, Louisa (Mrs) 2(2)
Icely, Thomas 105, 1(2), 80(2), 362(2)
Imlay, Alexander 2(2)
Imlay, Fanny 620(2)
Imlay, George 2(2)
Imlay, Jane (Mrs) 3(2)
Imlay, Peter 2(2)
Imlay, Sophia (Mrs) 3(2)
Inches, Caroline 84(2)
Inett, Ann 61(2)
Ingle, J. 159(2)
Ingle, John 76, 421, 560, 3(2), 366(2)
Ingle, Rebecca (Mrs) 3(2)
Ingle, Sophia Browell (Mrs) 3(2)
Inglis, Ann 224
Inglis, John 224
Ingram, Elizabeth 312(2)
Ingram, James 312(2)
Innes, Archibald Clunes 3(2), 180(2)
Innes, Barbara St Clair 182(2)
Innes, F.M. 458
Innes, George 4(2)
Innes, Gustavus Archibald Clunes Innes (Rev) 4(2)
Innes, J. Long (Capt) 228(2)
Innes, James (Maj) 3(2)
Innes, Joseph Long (Capt) 374(2)
Innes, Margaret (Mrs) 3(2), 180(2)
Irby family 614(2)
Iredale, Ann 549(2)
Iredale, Kezia (Mrs) 424(2)

Iredale, Lancelot 424(2), 549(2), 611(2)
Ireland, Anne 569(2)
Ireland, Eliza 492
Ireland, James 492
Ireland, Richard Davies 412(2)
Irinyi, Janos 624(2)
Irnham, (Lord of) 139(2)
Irvine, Charles James Irvine 182
Irving, David Williamson 562
Irving, Edward (Rev) 229(2)
Irving, Jane (Mrs) 562
Irving, John 4(2)
Irving, Washington 89(2)
Irwin, (Captain) 15
Irwin, Elizabeth (Mrs) 5(2)
Irwin, F.C. 228
Irwin, F.C. (Capt) 174(2), 253(2), 485(2), 487(2)
Irwin, F.C. (Col) 381
Irwin, Frederick Chidley 5(2)
Irwin, James (Rev) 5(2)
Jackey Jackey (Aborigine) 44(2)
Jackson, 224
Jackson, Burke 343
Jackson, Catherine (Mrs) 528(2)
Jackson, Edward Martin (Rev) 228
Jackson, Fanny Mary Jane 228, 253(2)
Jackson, Frances (Mrs) 228
Jackson, Harriet 462
Jackson, Henry 9(2)
Jackson, J. 415
Jackson, J.A. 225, 317, 452(2)
Jackson, Jane (Mrs) 9(2)
Jackson, John 528(2)
Jackson, John Alexander 7(2)
Jackson, John Serocold (Maj) 7(2)
Jackson, Maria Anne (Mrs) 7(2)
Jackson, Mary Ann (Mrs) 9(2)
Jackson, Samuel 9(2), 421(2)
Jackson, Susannah 518(2)
Jackson, William 9(2)
Jacky (Aborigine) 93(2)
Jacob, William 48, 64(2)
Jacquin, Baron Nikolaus von 73
James, Eliza 233
James, Maria 376(2)
James, T. Horton 480(2)
Jameson, Robert 119(2)
Jameson, Sarah 15
Jameson, Thomas 12(2)
Jamieson, Bobby 135(2)
Jamieson, Davie 493
Jamieson, Ellen (Mrs) 66(2)
Jamieson, John 10(2), 12(2), 308(2)
Jamieson, John (Dr) 144(2)
Jamieson, Margaret Legrand 493
Jamieson, Mary (Mrs) 10(2)
Jamieson, Polly 135(2)
Jamieson, S. (Mrs) 483(2)
Jamieson, William Thomas 10(2)
Jamison, (Surgeon) 369(2)
Jamison, John 153, 419(2)
Jamison, John (Sir) 118, 383, 10(2), 13(2), 36(2), 63(2),

148(2), 152(2), 169(2), 586(2)
Jamison, Mary (Lady) 12(2), 36(2)
Jamison, Rebecca (Mrs) 13(2)
Jamison, Robert Thomas 12(2)
Jamison, Thomas 115, 121, 156, 526, 528, 10(2), 12(2), 227(2)
Janssen (Janz), Willem 13(2), 556(2C)
Janssens, L. 358
Jaques, Jane 210
Jaques, William 210
Jaquin, Nicholas von (Baron) 73
Jardine, William (Sir) 97, 513
Jarrett, William (Rev) 420, 350(2)
Jarvis, Jane 21, 188(2)
Jarvis, Thomas 188(2)
Jay, John 630(2)
Jay, Margaret 630(2)
Jean, Harriet Elizabeth 474
Jean, Philip 474
Jebb, John 133
Jeffcott, Anne (Mrs) 14(2)
Jeffcott, Harriet Jane (Mrs) 14(2)
Jeffcott, John (Sir) 379, 541, 15(2), 50(2), 472(2)
Jeffcott, John William (Sir) 14(2)
Jeffcott, William 14(2)
Jeffcott, William (Sir) 15(2)
Jeffreys, (Captain) 127(2)
Jeffreys, (Lieut) 86, 142(2)
Jeffreys, (Lord) 127
Jeffreys, Arthur (Lt) 254(2)
Jeffreys, Charles 115, 327, 15(2), 216(2)
Jeffreys, Jane (Mrs) 15(2)
Jeffreys, Mary (Mrs) 15(2)
Jeffreys, Ninian 15(2)
Jeffries, (bushranger) 282
Jelf, Charlotte 613(2)
Jellicoe, Henry 475
Jenkins, Jemima (Mrs) 16(2)
Jenkins, John 572(2)
Jenkins, Mary 111, 442(2)
Jenkins, Robert 16(2), 130(2)
Jenkins, Robert Pitt 16(2)
Jenkins, William Warren 16(2)
Jenner, Edward 419(2)
Jennings, Henry 246(2)
Jennings, Maria 317(2)
Jennings, Sarah Tice 317(2)
Jennings, Sophia 409(2)
Jennings, Sophia Louisa 317(2)
Jerrold, Douglas 109(2)
Jervis, (Captain) 258, 567
Jervis, (Squire) 258
Jervis, John (Admiral Sir) 281(2)
Jervis, John (Earl St Vincent) 567
Jervis, John (Sir) 267(2), 397(2)
Jervis, Samuel Emanuel 258
Jim-the-Londoner 344
John, John William 111
John, Mary 111
Johnson, (Dr) 558
Johnson, Caroline Elizabeth 324(2)

Johnson, Elizabeth 379
Johnson, Ellen 614(2)
Johnson, Frances 247
Johnson, George French 227
Johnson, Georgiana Henrietta 50
Johnson, James 324(2)
Johnson, John 17(2), 27(2), 492(2)
Johnson, Mary Theresa (Mrs) 555(2)
Johnson, Mary Therese 555(2)
Johnson, Milbah 19(2)
Johnson, Richard 251, 298
Johnson, Richard (Rev) 49, 421, 570, 17(2), 31(2), 111(2), 208(2), 502(2)
Johnson, Samuel 201
Johnson, William Charles 555(2)
Johnston, (Colonel) 499(2)
Johnston, (Lt. Col) 422, 460, 520(2)
Johnston, (Major) 120, 383, 13(2), 39(2), 40(2), 47(2), 59(2), 96(2), 131(2)
Johnston, Anne Geogiana Henrietta 50(C)
Johnston, Blanche 21(2)
Johnston, David 19(2)
Johnston, Elizabeth 55(2)
Johnston, Esther (Mrs) 19(2), 22(2), 283(2)
Johnston, G. 487, 563
Johnston, George 2, 40, 51, 76, 78, 116, 117, 120, 144, 157, 204, 242, 308, 309, 526, 20(2), 22(2)
Johnston, George (Capt) 571, 572, 60(2)
Johnston, George (Col) 213(2), 219(2), 233(2), 609(2)
Johnston, George (Jun) 5
Johnston, George (Lt) 19(2)
Johnston, George (Lt. Col) 147(2), 190(2), 291(2), 602(2)
Johnston, George (Maj) 380, 408, 519, 563, 10(2), 97(2), 156(2), 232(2), 255(2), 283(2), 310(2), 318(2), 537(2), 538(2)
Johnston, Isabella 21(2)
Johnston, James Stewart 252(2)
Johnston, Janet 124(2)
Johnston, Julia 21(2)
Johnston, Louisa 228
Johnston, Maria 21(2)
Johnston, Robert 19(2)
Johnston, Rosanna 19(2)
Johnstone, Mary 435(2)
Joliffe, 344
Joliffe, (Captain) 406(2)
Jones, 214, 373
Jones, Algernon Burdett (Capt) 40(2)
Jones, Ann 197(2)
Jones, Anne 333
Jones, Caroline 221
Jones, Catherine (Mrs) 23(2)
Jones, David 23(2), 259(2), 600(2)
Jones, David Mander 24(2)
Jones, Edith 254

Jones, Edward Lloyd 24(2)
Jones, Eliza 24(2)
Jones, Elizabeth 24(2)
Jones, Elizabeth (Mrs) 25(2)
Jones, Elizabeth Ann (Mrs) 24(2)
Jones, Emily Ann 24(2)
Jones, Emily Ann (Mrs) 24(2)
Jones, Emma (Mrs) 26(2)
Jones, Fanny Edith (Mrs) 40(2), 144(2C)
Jones, Frances Sophia 25(2)
Jones, Frances Sophia (Mrs) 25(2)
Jones, George 24(2), 118(2)
Jones, Harriet (Mrs) 67(2)
Jones, Helen Ann 24(2)
Jones, Helen Ann (Mrs) 24(2)
Jones, Helena (Mrs) 245(2)
Jones, Herbert 164(2), 396(2)
Jones, Jane Hall (Mrs) 23(2)
Jones, John 25(2), 117(2), 372(2)
Jones, Joseph 197(2)
Jones, Lloyd 14
Jones, Louisa Alexandrine 25(2)
Jones, Margaret 353
Jones, Margaret (Mrs) 259(2)
Jones, Margaretta 48
Jones, Martha 545
Jones, Martha (Mrs) 25(2), 26(2)
Jones, Mary 259(2)
Jones, Mary Australia 25(2)
Jones, Mary Louisa (Mrs) 24(2)
Jones, Nancy 23(2)
Jones, Philip Sydney 24(2)
Jones, Richard 5, 105, 275, 290, 24(2), 25(2), 380(2), 381(2), 513(2), 520(2), 618(2)
Jones, Thomas 558, 23(2)
Jones, Thomas (Rev) 25(2)
Jones, Thomas Bowdler 24(2)
Jones, William 221, 419, 245(2), 601(2)
Joplin, T. 15
Jordan, Catherine 488
Jorgenson, Anna Lette (Mrs) 26(2)
Jorgenson, Jorgen 20, 21, 173, 566, 26(2)
Jorgenson, Norah (Mrs) 27(2)
Joseph, Joel 457(2)
Josephson, Jacob 109(2)
Josephson, Sarah Emma 109(2)
Joyce, Alexandra 29(2)
Joyce, Alfred 28(2)
Joyce, Alfreda 29(2)
Joyce, Caroline (Mrs) 28(2)
Joyce, Elizabeth (Mrs) 28(2)
Joyce, George 28(2)
Joyce, Helen (Mrs) 28(2)
Joyce, Thomas 28(2)
Judson, Jane Priscilla 4
Judson, William (Rev) 4
Jukes, Georgina Augusta (Mrs) 29(2)
Jukes, J.B. 111
Jukes, John 29(2)
Jukes, Joseph Beete 470, 29(2)
Jukes, Sophia (Mrs) 29(2)
Julian, Ann 457(2)

Julian, Esther 19(2), 22(2)
Julian, Moses 457(2)
Jussieu, (Professor) 323(2)
Juvenal, Pindar 516(2)
Kable, Eunice 381
Kable, Henry 120, 381, 31(2), 32(2), 129(2), 131(2), 227(2), 546(2)
Kable, James 32(2)
Kable, John 32(2)
Kable, Susanna(h) 227(2)
Kable, Susannah (Mrs) 31(2), 32(2)
Kane, (Mrs) 32(2)
Kane, Benjamin 32(2)
Kane, Caroline Jeanette (Mrs) 32(2)
Kane, Henry Neilly 32(2)
Kane, Henry Plow 32(2)
Kater, Henry 338
Kavanagh, (bushranger) 214, 247(2)
Kavel, August Ludwig Christian 33(2)
Kavel, Pastor 16
Kavenagh, (bushranger) 214, 247(2)
Kay, Clara Ann (Mrs) 35(2)
Kay, Clara Virginia Porden 35(2)
Kay, J.H. 446(2)
Kay, John 218(2)
Kay, Joseph Henry 34(2)
Kay, Maria (Mrs) 34(2)
Kay, Rosina Maria 34(2)
Kay, Sarah Henrietta (Mrs) 34(2)
Kay, William Porden 34(2)
Kay, W.P. 34(2), 555(2)
Kaye, (Mrs) 4
Kaye, Elizabeth 105(2)
Kaye, William (Rev) 105(2)
Kean, Charles 299(2)
Kearney, Anne (Mrs) 36(2), 134(2)
Kearney, Catherine (Mrs) 36(2)
Kearney, Margaret (Mrs) 36(2), 134(2)
Kearney, Susan (Mrs) 36(2)
Kearney, Thomas 36(2), 134(2)
Kearney, William 36(2), 134(2)
Keaston, Diana Harriet 454
Keates, William 632(2)
Kedah, (Sultan of) 116(2)
Keefe, Margaret 138(2)
Keeffe, Cornelius 294(2)
Keeling, (Miss) 281(2)
Keenan, Catherine 444(2)
Keightley, (Mr Solicitor) 284(2)
Keightley, Sarah 284(2)
Keith, Edward Joseph 256(2)
Kelley, Elizabeth 246
Kellor, (Counsellor) 216(2)
Kelly, Agnes 525
Kelly, Elizabeth (Mrs) 36(2)
Kelly, Isabella 567(2)
Kelly, James 104, 240, 273, 340, 392, 491, 36(2)
Kelly, Ned 313
Kelsall, (Captain) 24
Kelsall, Roger 37(2)
Kelso, Seth 253

Kemble, Francis 38(2)
Kemp, A.F. 30, 81, 194, 263, 428, 491, 379(2), 434(2), 442(2), 460(2), 461(2)
Kemp, A.F. (Capt) 97(2)
Kemp, Anthony Fader 39(2)
Kemp, Anthony Fenn 83, 39(2)
Kemp, Anthony Fenn (Capt) 462(2)
Kemp, Charles 40(2), 204(2)
Kemp, Edward 40(2)
Kemp, Elizabeth 30
Kemp, Elizabeth (Mrs) 39(2)
Kemp, Elizabeth Julia 40(2), 462(2)
Kemp, Ellen 40(2)
Kemp, Fanny Edith 40(2)
Kemp, George Anthony 40(2)
Kemp, Julia 462(2)
Kemp, Mary Ann (Mrs) 41(2)
Kemp, Simon 41(2)
Kemp, Sophia 40(2), 434(2)
Kemp, Stella (Mrs) 41(2)
Kemp, Susannah (Mrs) 39(2)
Kendall, Edward 42(2)
Kendall, Elizabeth 392
Kendall, Henry 515, 42(2), 160(2)
Kendall, Jane (Mrs) 42(2)
Kendall, John 210(2)
Kendall, Susanna (Mrs) 42(2)
Kendall, Thomas 307, 392, 42(2)
Kennedy, 389(2)
Kennedy, (Gov) 122(2)
Kennedy, Agnes 263(2)
Kennedy, David 244(2)
Kennedy, E.B.C. 7(2)
Kennedy, E.J. 471(2)
Kennedy, Edmund 578, 103(2)
Kennedy, Edmund Besley Court 43(2)
Kennedy, Elizabeth 564
Kennedy, Elizabeth Charlotte 158
Kennedy, Elizabeth More 563
Kennedy, Georgiana 244(2)
Kennedy, James 189
Kennedy, James R. 158
Kennedy, James Raworth 560
Kennedy, Jane 560
Kennedy, Mary (Mrs) 244(2)
Kennedy, Mary Ann (Mrs) 43(2)
Kennedy, Sarah 186, 189
Kennedy, Thomas (Col) 43(2)
Kennerley, Alfred 402(2)
Kennerley, Jane (Mrs) 402(2)
Kenny, (Dean) 241
Kenny, John 44(2)
Kensey, John 24, 25
Kensey, Martha 24, 25
Kent, (Captain) 359
Kent, (Duke of) 274(2)
Kent, (Lieut) 459(2), 573(2)
Kent, (Mrs) 572, 460(2)
Kent, Bartholomew (Lt) 46(2)
Kent, Eliza (Mrs) 47(2)
Kent, Henry 46(2)
Kent, John 47(2)
Kent, Mary (Mrs) 46(2)
Kent, Susannah Elizabeth

(Mrs) 48(2)
Kent, Thomas 44(2), 83(2)
Kent, William 46(2), 47(2), 283(2)
Kent, William (Capt) 572, 47(2)
Kent, William G.C. (Lt) 46(2)
Kent, William George Carlile 47(2)
Kentish, Nathaniel Lipscombe 48(2)
Kentish, N.L. 458, 505(2)
Kenton, Thomas 148
Kenvon, (Lord) 48
Kenworthy, J.R. (Dr) 57
Kerilleau, Huon de 150(2)
Kermode, Anne 14(2), 50(2)
Kermode, Anne (Mrs) 50(2)
Kermode, Anne Quayle (Mrs) 49(2)
Kermode, Elizabeth (Mrs) 49(2)
Kermode, Emily (Mrs) 50(2)
Kermode, Martha (Mrs) 50(2)
Kermode, R.Q. 26
Kermode, Robert Quayle 50(2)
Kermode, Thomas 49(2)
Kermode, W. 118(2)
Kermode, William 371, 14(2), 49(2), 50(2)
Kerr, Anne (Mrs) 50(2)
Kerr, Caroline Amelia (Mrs) 51(2)
Kerr, David 50(2)
Kerr, Isabella 297(2)
Kerr, John 106, 371, 566, 225(2)
Kerr, William 271, 50(2), 252(2)
Keyser, Pieter Dircksz 555
Kilgour, John Stewart 26
Killey, Elizabeth 49(2)
Kilpack, Elizabeth 232(2)
Kilray, (bushranger) 312
Kilroy, (bushranger) 312
Kimberley, Maria 470(2)
Kinchela, Anne (Mrs) 51(2)
Kinchela, Elizabeth (Mrs) 51(2)
Kinchela, J. 256(2)
Kinchela, James Butler 52(2)
Kinchela, John 185, 51(2), 266(2), 337(2)
Kinchela, Mary 52(2)
Kinchela, Rosina (Mrs) 51(2)
King, 151(2)
King, (Captain) 260(2)
King, (Ensign) 125(2)
King, (Mrs) 320, 521
King, Anna Josepha (Mrs) 52(2), 56(2), 61(2)
King, Anna Maria 61(2), 147(2)
King, Eliza Elflida (Mrs) 55(2)
King, Elizabeth 52(2), 61(2)
King, Elizabeth (Mrs) 55(2)
King, Harriet (Mrs) 61(2)
King, Henry 55(2)
King, James 54(2), 455(2)
King, John 536, 42(2), 57(2)
King, John Charles 55(2)
King, Louisa 121(2)
King, Maria 52(2), 53(2)
King, Martha Jane 55(2C)
King, Mary 53(2), 61(2).
King, Norfolk 52(2), 55(2), 61(2)

King, P.G. 116, 119, 156, 196, 203, 208, 218, 227, 238, 240, 241, 242, 259, 263, 264, 290, 309, 320, 468
King, P.G. (Lt) 326(2)
King, Philip 55(2)
King, Philip Gidley 383, 12(2), 63(2)
King, Philip Gidley (Gov) 357, 408, 421, 459, 469, 487, 519, 521, 526, 536, 568, 10(2), 20(2), 31(2), 36(2), 39(2), 44(2), 46(2), 52(2), 55(2), 61(2), 67(2), 120(2), 127(2), 147(2), 155(2), 171(2), 202(2), 206(2), 208(2), 217(2), 218(2), 222(2), 272(2), 279(2), 283(2), 295(2), 302(2), 305(2), 318(2), 332(2), 334(2), 369(2), 388(2), 401(2), 419(2), 499(2), 530(2), 536(2), 552(2), 575(2), 602(2), 622(2)
King, Philip Gidley (Lt. Gov) 351, 487, 518, 571, 281(2), 364(2), 469(2)
King, P.P. 98, 177, 266, 290, 545, 61(2), 111(2), 390(2), 400(2), 470(2), 494(2), 597(2)
King, P.P. (Capt) 53(2), 149(2)
King, Phillip Parker 464, 470, 52(2), 56(2), 61(2), 306(2)
King, Richard (Sir) 507
King, Robert Lethbridge (Rev) 63(2)
King, Sydney 52(2), 61(2)
King, Utricia 61(2)
Kingham, Harriet 20
Kinglsey, Charles 364
Kingscote, Henry 16
Kingsford, Georgiana Mary 99(2)
Kingsley, Henry 278, 556(2)
Kingston, 118(2)
Kingston, Emma Mary Ann Catherine (Mrs) 64(2)
Kingston, G.S. 197, 377, 378, 418, 433, 541, 116(2), 117(2), 262(2)
Kingston, George Strickland (Sir) 64(2)
Kingston, Harriet (Henrietta) Ann Stuart (Mrs) 64(2)
Kingston, Luduvina (Mrs) 197
Kingston, Luduvina Catherina da Silva (Mrs) 64(2)
Kinnaird, (Lord) 278
Kinnear, George 485
Kinnoull, (Earl of) 526
Kinross, John (Rev) 82(2)
Kirby, Elizabeth 566(2)
Kirchmann, Antoinetta Adriana 349
Kirk, Eliza 411(2)
Kirk, J.B. 4
Kirk, Mary 86
Kirk, Richard 411(2)
Kirkham, J.R. 411(2)
Kirkland, Ethel 65(2)
Kirkland, Isabella Christine 65(2)
Kirkland, John 65(2)
Kirkland, Katherine (Mrs)

65(2)
Kirkland, Kenneth William 65(2)
Kirkpatrick, Marion 574(2)
Kirton, Cornelia Ann 355(2)
Kirton, G.A. 355(2)
Kitching, Maria 78
Kite, Thomas 110
Knackston, Thomas 567
Knapp, Henrietta Harriet 379
Knapp, Henry 379
Knatchbull, Edward (Sir) 65(2)
Knatchbull, Frances (Mrs) 65(2)
Knatchbull, John 423, 424, 65(2), 135(2)
Knight, Isaac 223(2)
Knight, John 457
Knight, John (Mrs) 225
Knight, Mary Ann 209
Knight, Mary Anne 627(2)
Knight, Susannah Darke (Mrs) 225
Knight, William 626(2)
Knopwood, 373
Knopwood, Elizabeth (Mrs) 66(2)
Knopwood, Robert 476, 45(2), 66(2), 126(2)
Knopwood, Robert (Rev) 77, 490, 561, 231(2)
Knowles, Charles (Vice Admiral) 567
Knowles, Conrad Theodore 67(2)
Knowles, J.S. 161(2)
Knowles, John 67(2)
Knox, (Bishop) 421
Knox, (Dr) 39(2)
Knox, Catherine 440
Knox, Clara Elizabeth 442
Knox, Edward (Sir) 442
Knox, Elizabeth 371
Knox, James 505(2)
Knox, John Russell (Rev) 371
Knox, Sarah 424(2)
Knox, Thomas (Rev. Dr) 424(2)
Knox, Vicesimus 424(2)
Knox, Vicesimus (Rev. Dr) 424(2)
Knox, William (Bishop) 421
Kolp, Ann 252
Korff, John 202(2)
Kosciuszko, Tadeusz 494(2)
Krefft, G. 287
Krusenstern, I.F. 83
La Billardiere, Jacques Julien Houtou de 55, 167, 172, 69(2)
La Perouse, 171, 307, 69(2)
La Perouse, Barthez (Mrs) 85(2)
La Perouse, Dalmas (Mrs) 85(2)
La Perouse, Jean Francois de Galaup, Compte de 85(2)
La Perouse, Louise Eleanor (Comptesse) 85(2)
La Trobe, Benjamin 89(2)
La Trobe, C.J. 271, 272, 278, 347, 447, 532, 603(2)
La Trobe, C.J. (Supt) 234,

411(2)
La Trobe, Charles (Gov) 547, 125(2), 126(2)
La Trobe, Charles Joseph (Lt. Gov) 35(2), 50(2), 89(2), 160(2), 252(2), 349(2), 393(2), 455(2), 518(2), 543(2)
La Trobe, Christian 89(2)
La Trobe, Christian Ignatius 89(2)
La Trobe, Hannah (Mrs) 89(2)
La Trobe, Henri Bonneval 89(2)
La Trobe, Rose Isabelle (Mrs) 92(2)
La Trobe, Sophie 92(2)
La Trobe, Sophie (Mrs) 89(2)
Labouchere, 151(2)
Lackey, Maria 302(2)
Lackey, Michael 302(2)
Lacy, de (Sister) 339(2)
Ladds, William 228, 229
Laidley, Eliza Jane (Mrs) 69(2)
Laidley, James 69(2), 578(2)
Laidley, John 69(2)
Laidley, Maria 70(2)
Laidley, Sarah (Mrs) 69(2)
Laidley, Theresa 70(2)
Laing, Charles 331, 70(2), 410(2), 492(2)
Laing, Henry 71(2)
Laing, Isabella 128
Laing, Isabella (Mrs) 71(2)
Laing, James 71(2)
Laing, Robert 128
Lakeland, Emily Elizabeth 72(2)
Lakeland, James Gordon 72(2)
Lakeland, John 458, 71(2), 622(2)
Lakeland, John Thomas 72(2)
Lakeland, Louisa 72(2)
Lakeland, Mary Louisa (Mrs) 72(2)
Lamarck, 323(2)
Lamb, (Captain) 72(2)
Lamb, Alfred 73(2)
Lamb, Caroline (Lady) 279(2)
Lamb, Charles 374, 558(2)
Lamb, Edward William 73(2)
Lamb, Emma Trant (Mrs) 73(2)
Lamb, John 72(2), 415(2), 525(2)
Lamb, Walter 73(2)
Lambe, David 73(2), 527(2)
Lambe, Edward 207
Lambe, Harriet Catherine (Mrs) 73(2)
Lambe, Harriett Mary (Mrs) 73(2)
Lambe, Mary 56
Lambe, William 73(2)
Lambert, A.B. 120(2), 595(2)
Lambert, Aylmer Bourke 88(2)
Lambert, Johnston 500(2)
Lambert, Margaret 500(2)
Lambert, Margaret (Mrs) 500(2)
Lancaster, G.B. 143(2)
Lancey, John 369
Landale, Harriett (Mrs) 329, 74(2)

Landale, Thomas 74(2)
Landale, Thomas (Dr) 329
Landor, Edward Willson 74(2)
Landor, G.W. 74(2)
Landor, Henry 74(2)
Landor, Walter Savage 74(2)
Landrien, Antoine 371(2)
Landsborough, William 600(2)
Lane, (bookseller) 504(2)
Lane, Ann 532(2)
Lane, William 532(2)
Lanesborough, (Earl of) 334
Lang, 617(2)
Lang, (Dr) 505(2)
Lang, Andrew 75(2), 616(2)
Lang, Eliza Jane (Mrs) 210
Lang, Elizabeth (Mrs) 518,
  548(2)
Lang, Elizabeth Jane (Mrs)
  76(2)
Lang, G.S. 61, 426, 437(2)
Lang, George 80(2)
Lang, Gideon Scott 210, 75(2)
Lang, J.D. 4, 40, 93, 102, 153,
  154, 160, 184, 187, 210, 216,
  252, 260, 271, 304, 330, 334,
  352, 388, 447, 484, 550, 1(2),
  51(2), 114(2), 211(2), 338(2),
  347(2), 420(2), 448(2), 522(2),
  525(2), 529(2), 578(2), 611(2),
  616(2)
Lang, J.D. (Rev) 351, 399, 472,
  510, 108(2), 144(2), 166(2),
  172(2), 197(2), 220(2), 226(2),
  252(2), 289(2), 291(2), 304(2),
  343(2), 356(2), 361(2), 362(2),
  421(2), 431(2), 432(2), 454(2),
  510(2), 592(2), 599(2)
Lang, John Dunmore 76(2),
  325(2)
Lang, John George 518
Lang, Thomas 75(2)
Lang, Walter 518
Lang, William 75(2), 76(2)
Langdon, Anne 84(2)
Langdon, Anne (Mrs) 83(2),
  84(2)
Langdon, William 83(2)
Langdon, William (Rev) 83(2)
Langford, John 86(2)
Langford, Susannah (Mrs)
  86(2)
Langhorne, George 125(2)
Langlands, Caroline (Mrs)
  84(2)
Langlands, Christian (Mrs)
  84(2)
Langlands, George 85(2)
Langlands, Henry 84(2)
Langlands, Janet (Mrs) 84(2)
Langlands, Jessie (Mrs) 84(2)
Langlands, John 84(2)
Langlands, Robert 84(2)
Langle de, 85(2)
Langley, George 505
Langley, Sarah (Mrs) 505
Langlois, (Captain) 471(2)
Lansdowne, (Marquis of)
  107(2)
Lara, James 86(2)
Lardner, Frances 228
Lardner, Philip 228

Larnach, Emily (Mrs) 86(2)
Larnach, John 86(2), 265(2)
Larnach, Margaret (Mrs) 86(2)
Larnach, William 86(2)
Larnach, William James Mudie
  86(2)
Larra, James 518, 86(2)
Larra, Mary Ann (Mrs) 87(2)
Larra, Phoebe (Mrs) 87(2)
Larra, Susannah (Mrs) 86(2)
Lascelles, (Ensign) 327
Lascelles, Edwin 87(2)
Lascelles, Martha (Mrs) 87(2)
Lascelles, Mary Ann (Mrs)
  87(2)
Lascelles, Michael 87(2)
Lascelles, Thomas Allen 87(2),
  159(2), 214(2)
Latham, (Dr) 502
Latham, John 88(2)
Latham, Mary 502
Lathropp, Ann 273(2)
Lathropp, Ann (Mrs) 272(2)
Lathropp, Robert 272(2)
LaTrobe, (see La Trobe above)
Laud, William 215
Laurence, Samuel 262(2)
Lautour, Peter (Col) 576
Lavaud, (Commandant) 471(2)
Lavers, Jane Eleanor 345
Laverton, William (Leverton)
  613(2)
Law, Eliza Hamilton (Mrs) 337
Law, Georgina 337
Law, James Sylvius 337
Law, Mary Sophia Georgina
  337
Law, W. (Rev) 246(2)
Lawless, Burnett R. 93(2)
Lawless, Burnett William 93(2)
Lawless, Clement Francis 93(2)
Lawless, Ellen 93(2)
Lawless, Ellen (Mrs) 93(2)
Lawless, Emmeline Anne 93(2)
Lawless, Henrietta Babington
  (Mrs) 93(2)
Lawless, Ivan 93(2)
Lawless, John 93(2)
Lawless, John Paul 93(2)
Lawless, Mabel Gwynne Ethel
  (Mrs) 93(2)
Lawless, Mary (Mrs) 93(2)
Lawless, Noel 93(2)
Lawless, Paul 93(2)
Lawless, Warren (Sir) 93(2)
Lawrence, Catherine (Mrs)
  94(2)
Lawrence, Edward Billopp
  94(2)
Lawrence, Effingham (Capt)
  93(2)
Lawrence, Eliza 230(2)
Lawrence, John (Sir) 250
Lawrence, Mary Ann (Mrs)
  95(2)
Lawrence, Mary Anne 533
Lawrence, Robert William 492,
  95(2)
Lawrence, W.E. 25, 148, 492,
  533, 7(2)
Lawrence, William Effingham
  93(2), 230(2)

Lawrie, John 486
Lawry, Mary Cover (Mrs) 522,
  95(2)
Lawry, Walter 522, 95(2),
  566(2)
Lawry, Walter (Rev) 439(2)
Lawson, George (Dr) 327
Lawson, Nelson 96(2)
Lawson, Sarah 504
Lawson, Sarah (Mrs) 96(2)
Lawson, Sophia 504
Lawson, William 111, 116, 263,
  266, 314, 504, 96(2), 97(2),
  102(2), 134(2), 152(2), 260(2),
  571(2), 583(2)
Lawson, William (Lt) 526
Laycock, Elizabeth 97(2)
Laycock, Hannah (Mrs) 97(2)
Laycock, Isabella (Mrs) 98(2)
Laycock, Margaret (Mrs) 98(2)
Laycock, Mary (Mrs) 97(2)
Laycock, Sarah 76, 97(2)
Laycock, Thomas 126, 263,
  97(2), 170(2)
Laycock, Thomas William Eber
  Bunker 97(2)
Laycock, William 97(2)
Layman, George 190
Lazar, Abraham 98(2), 99(2)
Lazar, John 98(2)
Lazar, Julia (Mrs) 99(2)
Lazar, Rachel (Mrs) 98(2)
Lazar, Samuel 99(2)
Lazarev, Andrei 99(2)
Lazarev, Mikhail Petrovich
  99(2)
Lazarev, M.P. 83
Lazarus, John 98(2)
Lazarus, Rachel 98(2)
Le Maistre, Margaret 112
Le Massony, Margaret 112
Le Sage, Louise 573
Le Souef, Albert A.C. 250
Le Souef, Albert Sherbourne
  250
Le Souef, Caroline (Mrs) 250
Le Souef, Dudley 278
Le Souef, Ernest A. 250
Le Sueur, (artist) 323(2)
Leach, C. 8
Leadbeater, Sarah 96(2)
Leake, Ann Elizabeth 99(2)
Leake, Ann (Mrs) 99(2)
Leake, Anne (Mrs) 99(2)
Leake, Arthur 100(2)
Leake, Charles Henry 100(2)
Leake, Elizabeth (Mrs) 100(2)
Leake, George 99(2), 253(2),
  417(2)
Leake, Georgiana Mary (Mrs)
  99(2)
Leake, John 100(2), 605(2)
Leake, Luke 99(2)
Leake, Robert 100(2)
Leake, Sarah (Mrs) 100(2)
Leake, William 100(2)
Leaman, Elizabeth 344
Learmonth family 297, 438(2)
Learmonth, Alexander 101(2)
Learmonth, Andrew James
  100(2)
Learmonth, Anna (Mrs) 101(2)

Learmonth, Christian Donald (Mrs) 100(2)
Learmonth, John 100(2), 101(2)
Learmonth, John (Dr) 223(2)
Learmonth, John Franklin 101(2)
Learmonth, Louisa (Mrs) 101(2)
Learmonth, Margaret (Mrs) 101(2)
Learmonth, N.F. 231(2)
Learmonth, Somerville 100(2), 101(2)
Learmonth, Thomas 100(2), 223(2)
Lee, (Colonel) 121(2)
Lee, Charlotte 23
Lee, George 102(2)
Lee, John 102(2)
Lee, Maria 101(2)
Lee, Mary 121(2)
Lee, Mary (Mrs) 102(2)
Lee, Narcissa Sarah 590(2)
Lee, Samuel (Prof) 42(2)
Lee, Thomas 102(2)
Lee, William 110, 101(2), 505(2)
Lee, William (Jun) 102(2)
Lees, John 105(2)
Lefevre, C.S. 228(2)
Lefevre, John George Shaw 354
Lefroy, Gerald de Courcy 155
Lefroy, Henry Bruce (Sir) 619(2)
Lefroy, Rose Agnes (Mrs) 619(2)
Legge, Frances Blanche 332
Lehmann, Johann Georg Christian 349(2)
Leicester, Catherine 470(2)
Leicester, Oswald (Rev) 470(2)
Leichhardt, Charlotte Sophie (Mrs) 102(2)
Leichhardt, Christian Hieronymus Matthias 102(2)
Leichhardt, Friedrich Wilhelm Ludwig 102(2)
Leichhardt, Ludwig 22, 103, 176, 201, 441, 452, 530, 285(2), 387(2), 389(2), 407(2), 422(2)
Leichhardt, Ludwig van 43(2), 75(2)
Leigh, Catherine (Mrs) 105(2)
Leigh, Elizabeth (Mrs) 105(2)
Leigh, Samuel 135, 105(2)
Leigh, Samuel (Rev) 322, 95(2), 566(2), 599(2)
Leigh, William 270(2)
Leinster, (Duke of) 381, 384
Leith, James (Sir) 62
Lempriere, Charles D'A. 303(2)
Lempriere, Charlotte (Mrs) 106(2)
Lempriere, Harriet (Mrs) 105(2)
Lempriere, Lucy Parris 360
Lempriere, Maria (Mrs) 303(2)
Lempriere, Thomas 360
Lempriere, Thomas James 125, 105(2), 423(2)
Lennard, John 124
Lennox, David 106(2)

Lennox, Jane 107(2)
Lennox, Mary 107(2)
Lennox, Mary (Lady) 384
Leonhard, Carl Caesar von 222(2)
Leslie, C.R. 348
Leslie, Catherine (Mrs) 108(2)
Leslie, Christina 235
Leslie, George 276, 277
Leslie, Jane (Mrs) 108(2)
Leslie, Jannet 472
Leslie, Margaret 409(2)
Leslie, P. 149(2)
Leslie, Patrick 201, 276, 290, 107(2), 597(2)
Leslie, Walter 108(2)
Leslie, William 107(2)
Leslie, William Norman 108(2)
Lesseps, (French officer) 85(2)
Lesson, R.P. 266
Lethbridge, Harriet 61(2)
Lethbridge, Mary (Mrs) 53(2), 61(2)
Lethbridge, Robert 53(2), 61(2)
Levett, Clementina 392(2C)
Levey, Ann (Mrs) 110(2)
Levey, Barnett 67(2), 108(2), 298(2), 304(2), 445(2), 626(2)
Levey, Sarah Emma (Mrs) 109(2)
Levey, Solomon 245, 246, 109(2), 110(2), 321(2)
Levey-Roberts, John 110(2)
Levi, Frances 417(2)
Levy, 397
Lewin, 469
Lewin, Anna Maria (Mrs) 112(2)
Lewin, Henry (Rev) 262
Lewin, J.W. 470, 517, 558, 112(2)
Lewin, John 91
Lewin, John William 111(2)
Lewin, Thomas 111(2)
Lewin, William 111(2)
Lewin, William Arden 112(2)
Lewis, Anna Maria (Mrs) 258
Lewis, B. (Professor) 24
Lewis, Caroline (Mrs) 112(2)
Lewis, David 113(2)
Lewis, David (Rev) 113(2)
Lewis, Elizabeth (Mrs) 112(2)
Lewis, Elizabeth Isabel 179
Lewis, Frederick (Rev) 532(2)
Lewis, Isabella (Mrs) 113(2)
Lewis, John 236
Lewis, Margaret Louise 113(2)
Lewis, Mary (Mrs) 113(2)
Lewis, Mortimer 505
Lewis, Mortimer William 112(2)
Lewis, Neil 258, 113(2)
Lewis, Neil Elliot (Sir) 258
Lewis, Phillip 409(2)
Lewis, Richard 124, 179, 235, 257, 40(2), 113(2)
Lewis, Thomas 173
Lewis, Thomas Arundel 112(2)
Lewis, William 409(2)
Leycaster, 479(2)
Lhotsky, John 114(2), 242(2), 350(2), 494(2)

Liardet, Carolina Frederica (Mrs) 115(2)
Liardet, Francis (Capt) 115(2)
Liardet, Frank 115(2)
Liardet, Frederick 115(2)
Liardet, Hector 115(2)
Liardet, John Evelyn 115(2)
Liardet, John William Tell 115(2)
Liardet, Philippa (Mrs) 115(2)
Liardet, St Clere 115(2)
Liardet, Wilbraham Frederick Evelyn 115(2)
Liddon, Ann Warden 465(2)
Liebig, Justus von (Baron) 54(2)
Light, Alexander Whalley 419
Light, E. (Mrs) 116(2)
Light, Francis (Capt) 116(2)
Light, Jane 419
Light, Mary (Mrs) 116(2)
Light, W. 540
Light, William 539, 116(2)
Light, William (Col) 378, 379, 380, 432, 539, 64(2), 200(2), 480(2), 482(2), 535(2), 624(2)
Light, William Negus 116(2)
Lightfoot, James 486
Lillie, David 118(2)
Lillie, J. (Rev) 574
Lillie, John 118(2)
Lillie, John (Rev) 192, 220, 50(2), 467(2), 564(2)
Lillie, Mary Gascoigne (Mrs) 118(2)
Lilly, Elizabeth 524
Lincoln, (Earl of) 541
Lindesay, John (Lt. Col) 119(2)
Lindesay, Patrick (Sir) 333, 119(2)
Lindley, (Dr) 325, 244(2)
Lindsay, (Dr) 149(2)
Lindsay, (headmaster) 150(2)
Lindsay, Grace 23
Lindsay, John 15
Lindsay, W.S. 222
Lindsey, John 559(2)
Linnaeus, 53, 404, 456(2)
Linnaeus, Elizabeth Christina 456(2)
Linne, Carl von 456(2)
Linnell, John 558(2)
Lipscombe, John 451(2)
Lipson, (Captain) 64(2)
Lisle, William 150
Lissour, Caro 247
Lister, J.H.A. 532(2)
Liston, Robert 514(2)
Lithgow, William 119(2), 524(2), 578(2)
Little, John 25
Littlefield, Thomas 120(2)
Littlejohn, Robert 120(2)
Liverpool, (Earl of) 284
Liverpool, (Lord) 213(2)
Livingstone, Margaret 100(2)
Livingstone Learmonth, Thomas 101(2)
Lloyd, Anna Louisa 452(2)
Lloyd, G.A. 23(2)
Lloyd, Mary 113(2)
Loane, Mary (Mrs) 121(2)
Loane, Ro(w)land Walpole

120(2)
Loane, R.W. 494
Loch, J.D. 420
Lochee, Alfred 122(2)
Lochee, Charlotte Elizabeth Vigors 122(2)
Lochee, Constance 122(2)
Lochee, Emma (Mrs) 122(2)
Lochee, Francis 121(2)
Lochee, Mary Ellen Landor 122(2)
Lock, (artist) 225
Lockee, John 121(2)
Lockee, Louisa (Mrs) 121(2)
Lockie, Alison Hislop 493(2)
Lockwood, John 250
Lockwood, Matilda 250
Lockyer, Ann (Mrs) 123(2C)
Lockyer, Edmund 108, 123, 310, 534, 123(2)
Lockyer, Elizabeth (Mrs) 123(2)
Lockyer, Nicholas 124(2)
Lockyer, Thomas 123(2C)
Loder, George 632(2)
Loder, Jane 632(2)
Logan, Abraham 124(2)
Logan, Janet 361(2)
Logan, Janet (Mrs) 124(2)
Logan, John 442(2)
Logan, Letitia Anne (Mrs) 124(2)
Logan, Patrick 108, 233, 285, 294, 416, 124(2)
Logan, Robert Abraham 124(2)
Loine, Sarah Rebecca 288
Lomas, Joseph 70
Lomond, Ben 68
London, (Captain) 45(2)
Londonderry, (Marquis of) 384
Long, Alexandra (Mrs) 29(2)
Long, Basil 456
Long, George Merrick (Bishop) 29(2)
Long, Hester 550
Longbottom, William (Rev) 510
Longmore, Alexander 534
Longstaff, Hannah 544(2)
Lonsdale, 545, 547
Lonsdale, Martha (Mrs) 124(2)
Lonsdale, W. 522(2)
Lonsdale, W. (Capt) 472(2)
Lonsdale, William 69, 132, 91(2), 124(2)
Lonsdale, William (Capt) 447(2)
Lord Lyon of Scotland 237(2)
Lord, (landed proprietor) 457
Lord, Ann (Mrs) 128(2)
Lord, Cecilia 316
Lord, Corbetta (Mrs) 127(2)
Lord, David 126(2)
Lord, Edward 76, 158, 227, 240, 309, 439, 3(2), 127(2), 131(2), 225(2), 402(2), 502(2), 532(2), 578(2)
Lord, Edward (Lt) 517
Lord, Emma (Mrs) 456
Lord, Francis 131(2)
Lord, George William 131(2)
Lord, Grace (Mrs) 126(2)
Lord, Hannah (Mrs) 127(2)

Lord, James 257, 126(2), 127(2), 308(2)
Lord, John 127(2), 176(2), 308(2)
Lord, Joseph 127(2)
Lord, Maria 369
Lord, Maria (Mrs) 127(2)
Lord, Sarah Ann 361(2)
Lord, Simeon 13, 88, 116, 117, 120, 127, 170, 197, 353, 500, 506, 556, 16(2), 31(2), 45(2), 46(2), 128(2), 191(2), 257(2), 361(2), 388(2), 403(2), 520(2), 546(2), 548(2), 580(2), 598(2), 609(2)
Lord, Simeon (Jun) 131(2)
Lord, Susan (Mrs) 132(2)
Lord, T.D. (Maj) 316(2)
Lord, Thomas Daunt 131(2)
Lord, Wellington 132(2)
Lorraine, Claude 410(2)
Louis Philippe 315
Louis XVI (King of France) 171, 85(2), 266(2)
Louis XVIII (King) 455
Lovat, C. 544(2)
Love, (Mrs) 67(2)
Love, Andrew (Rev) 232, 423
Loveless, Elizabeth (Mrs) 133(2)
Loveless, George 132(2)
Loveless, Henry 132(2)
Loveless, James 132(2)
Lovell, Anne 36(2), 134(2)
Lovell, Anne (Mrs) 133(2)
Lovell, Esh 36(2), 133(2), 397(2)
Lovell, Margaret 36(2), 134(2)
Lovell, Samuel 133(2)
Lovell, Sophia Rebecca (Mrs) 133(2)
Lovell, William Esh 133(2)
Lovitt, (Captain) 433(2)
Low, Margaret 235(2)
Low, Mary 504(2)
Lowe, 617(2)
Lowe, Barbara (Mrs) 134(2)
Lowe, Caroline (Mrs) 136(2)
Lowe, Deborah 45
Lowe, Ellen (Mrs) 134(2)
Lowe, Georgiana (Mrs) 134(2)
Lowe, Henrietta (Mrs) 137(2)
Lowe, Hudson (Sir) 631(2)
Lowe, James 552(2)
Lowe, Margaret (Mrs) 137(2)
Lowe, May (Mrs) 137(2)
Lowe, Nathaniel 231
Lowe, Robert 61, 113, 114, 161, 162, 385, 388, 447, 449, 450, 481, 534, 66(2), 79(2), 113(2), 134(2), 141(2), 162(2), 182(2), 338(2), 514(2), 521(2), 587(2), 588(2), 616(2)
Lowe, Robert (Rev) 134(2)
Lowe, Robert (Viscount Sherbrooke) 134(2)
Lowe, Sarah (Mrs) 134(2)
Lowe, Sophia 552(2)
Lowe, T.Y. 302, 73(2)
Lowe, William 490, 137(2), 449(2)
Lowes, Anna Maria Theresa

(Mrs) 137(2)
Lowes, Mary Ann 137(2)
Lowes, Thomas Yardley 137(2)
Lowis, (Mr) 372
Lowth, (Dr) 558
Lowther, Mary Ann 9(2)
Lubbock, 287
Lucas, 283(2)
Lucas, James 138(2)
Lucas, James Hunt 138(2)
Lucas, Margaret (Mrs) 138(2)
Lucas, Nathaniel 471, 139(2)
Lucas, Olivia (Mrs) 139(2)
Lukin, Isabella (Mrs) 372
Lukin, L. 372
Lushington, (Lieut) 477
Lushington, Stephen 286
Luttrell, Ann (Mrs) 139(2)
Luttrell, Edward 139(2)
Luttrell, Martha (Mrs) 139(2)
Luttrell, Southcott Hungerford (Maj) 139(2)
Ly, Dorothea Agatha de 123(2C)
Lycett, Joseph 140(2), 468(2), 568(2)
Lynch, John 141(2)
Lynch, Margaret 324
Lynch, (Rev) 515
Lynch, Sophia Florence Maud 379
Lyon, Caleb 431
Lyon, Charles Hugh 14
Lyon, Robert 632(2)
Lyons, (Admiral Lord) 542(2)
Lyons, (Lord) 494(2)
Lyons, Abraham 142(2)
Lyons, Charlotte Margaret (Mrs) 143(2)
Lyons, George 142(2)
Lyons, George Herbert 143(2)
Lyons, Hannah 142(2)
Lyons, Israel 52
Lyons, Lydia 143(2)
Lyons, Mary (Mrs) 142(2)
Lyons, Samuel 109(2), 141(2), 142(2), 143(2), 143(2), 554(2)
Lyons, Saul 142(2)
Lyttleton family 329, 143(2)
Lyttleton, Ann (Mrs) 292, 143(2)
Lyttleton, Maria 291
Lyttleton, Thomas Hamilton 143(2)
Lyttleton, Westcote 143(2)
Lyttleton, W.T. 26, 173
Lyttleton, William Thomas 291, 143(2)
Lytton, (Lord) 559(2)
M'Donnell, Thomas 187
M'Konochie, Alexander 184(2)
Maben, Sarah 251
Macalister, Lachlan (Capt) 183(2)
Macalister, Matthew 183(2)
Macalister, Tom 183(2)
Macansh family 614(2)
Macarthur family 99, 393, 394, 1(2), 108(2), 236(2), 577(2)
Macarthur, Alexander 153(2)
Macarthur, Anna Maria (Mrs) 61(2), 147(2)

Macarthur, Anne (Mrs) 572(2)
Macarthur, Archibald 118(2), 144(2)
Macarthur, Archibald (Rev) 76(2), 300(2)
Macarthur, Catherine 108(2)
Macarthur, Charles 42, 464, 148(2)
Macarthur, E. (Mrs) 318(2)
Macarthur, Edward 144(2), 149(2), 154(2), 157(2)
Macarthur, Edward (Sir) 181(2)
Macarthur, Elizabeth 138, 53(2), 145(2), 186(2), 306(2), 584(2), 623(2)
Macarthur, Elizabeth (Mrs) 144(2), 147(2), 154(2), 157(2)
Macarthur, Emily (Mrs) 151(2)
Macarthur, Emmeline 145(2)
Macarthur, George Fairfowl 402, 149(2), 572(2)
Macarthur, Hannibal 42, 55, 277, 314, 375, 394, 53(2), 61(2), 62(2), 63(2), 145(2), 151(2), 499(2), 514(2), 554(2), 571(2), 572(2), 597(2)
Macarthur, Hannibal (Jun) 149(2)
Macarthur, Hannibal Hawkins 108(2), 147(2), 155(2)
Macarthur, J. 190(2)
Macarthur, James 230, 299, 387, 534, 573, 62(2), 145(2), 147(2), 149(2), 151(2), 154(2), 157(2), 162(2), 181(2), 182(2), 284(2), 513(2), 514(2), 525(2), 586(2)
Macarthur, John 39, 49, 51, 55, 74, 76, 79, 115, 117, 120, 137, 139, 144, 196, 201, 203, 206, 207, 208, 258, 259, 263, 290, 299, 306, 383, 384, 393, 396, 408, 435, 459, 463, 469, 487, 506, 514, 518, 519, 554, 561, 564, 569, 573, 10(2), 11(2), 13(2), 18(2), 20(2), 39(2), 60(2), 62(2), 63(2), 86(2), 96(2), 97(2), 98(2), 131(2), 144(2), 144(2), 145(2), 147(2), 150(2), 153(2), 158(2), 171(2), 193(2), 196(2), 208(2), 210(2), 213(2), 221(2), 233(2), 255(2), 281(2), 291(2), 307(2), 310(2), 318(2), 334(2), 337(2), 359(2), 369(2), 381(2), 432(2), 520(2), 538(2), 554(2), 573(2), 574(2), 578(2), 580(2), 584(2), 588(2)
Macarthur, John (Capt) 441, 471(2)
Macarthur, John   438(2)
Macarthur, John (Jun) 299, 393, 178(2), 478(2)
Macarthur, John (Lt) 488
Macarthur, John (Sen) 477(2)
Macarthur, Louisa Jean (Mrs) 144(2)
Macarthur, Maria (Mrs) 53(2)
Macarthur, Martha (Mrs) 144(2)
Macarthur, Mary 145(2)
Macarthur, Mary (Mrs) 144(2)
Macarthur, William 138, 230,

389, 573, 145(2), 150(2), 151(2), 157(2), 554(2)
Macaulay, (Dr) 519
Macauley, Zachary 298
MacCarthy, Mary 47
MacCarthy, M.S.J. 47
MacDermott, Caroline 341
Macdermott, Catherine Sarah (Mrs) 162(2)
Macdermott, Henry 141(2), 161(2)
MacDermott, Marshall 341
Macdonald, 397
Macdonald, (Captain) 292(2)
Macdonald, Isabella 292(2)
Macdonald, Malcolm Melville (Capt) 81(2)
Macdonald, Peter Fitzalan 606(2)
MacDonnell, (Gov) 244
MacDonnell, Ewen 197
MacDonnell, Mary 197
MacDonnell, Richard (Sir) 378
MacDonnell, Richard Graves 381
Macdougal, Mary 335
MacDougald, Christina 184(2)
Macdougall, Anna Maria 151
Macdougall, Archibald 356(2)
Macdougall, J.C. 559, 164(2), 221(2), 273(2)
Macdougall, John 163(2)
Macdougall, John Campbell 163(2)
Macdougall, Mary Ann 163(2)
Macdougall, Sarah Oakes (Mrs) 163(2)
Macdowell, Edward 214, 164(2), 247(2), 396(2)
Macdowell, Jane (Mrs) 164(2)
Macdowell, John 164(2)
Macdowell, Laura Jeanette (Mrs) 164(2)
Macdowell, Susan (Mrs) 164(2)
Macdowell, Thomas 163(2), 164(2)
MacFarlane, Duncan 341, 377
Macfarlane, Margaret 178
Macgill, Stevenson (Dr) 76(2)
MacGillivray, J. 471(2)
MacGillivray, John 111, 167(2)
MacGillivray, Paul Howard (Dr) 168(2)
MacGillivray, William 167(2)
MacGillivray, Williamina Paton 167(2)
Macintyre, Peter 280
Mack, Betty 67(2)
Mack, J.G. (Mrs) 43
Mackaness, John 348, 169(2), 478(2), 570(2)
Mackay, William 394(2)
Mackellar, Dorothea 167(2)
MacKellar, Duncan (Lt) 171(2)
Mackellar, Frederick (Dr) 167(2)
MacKellar, Isabella 113(2)
Mackellar, Isabella (Mrs) 167(2)
MacKellar, Neil (Capt) 327, 113(2), 170(2), 233(2), 283(2)
MacKellar, Patrick (Col) 170(2)

Mackenzie, A.K. 525
MacKenzie, Alastair 172(2C), 349(2)
Mackenzie, Alexander (Sir) 65(2)
Mackenzie, Augusta (Lady) 270(2)
Mackenzie, David 172(2)
Mackenzie, Elizabeth 368, 172(2C)
Mackenzie, Faith Compton 555(2)
Mackenzie, George (Sir) 25(2)
Mackenzie, Helen (Mrs) 525
Mackenzie, J.K. 368
Mackenzie, John Piper 525
Mackenzie, Louisa Alexandrine (Mrs) 25(2)
Mackenzie, Mary 172(2C)
Mackenzie, Robert Ramsay 247, 25(2)
Mackenzie, Sybilla (Mrs) 65(2)
Mackenzie, William Henry 525
Mackersey, Catherine (Mrs) 174(2)
Mackersey, James (Jun) 173(2)
Mackersey, James (Rev. Dr) 173(2)
Mackersey, John 173(2)
Mackersey, John (Rev) 329, 144(2)
Mackie, Elennora (Mrs) 174(2)
Mackie, John 306
Mackie, John Coningham 175(2)
Mackie, W.H. 253(2), 486(2)
Mackie, Wilhelmina 77(2)
Mackie, William Frederick 174(2)
Mackie, William Henry 5(2), 174(2)
Mackintosh, Maxwell 325
Mackintosh, Sarah 325
Macklin, R.B. 174(2)
Maclaine, (of Lochbuy) 186(2)
Maclaine, Farquhar 187(2)
Maclaine, John 192(2)
Maclaine, Margaret 187(2)
Maclaine, Murdoch 187(2)
Maclean, Allan (Col) 187(2)
Maclean, Sarah 623(2)
Macleay, Augusta (Mrs) 182(2)
Macleay, Bara St Clair (Mrs) 182(2)
Macleay, George 182(2), 496(2), 498(2)
Macleay, George (Sir) 180(2)
Macleay, Susan (Mrs) 526(2)
Macleay, William 177(2)
Macleay, William John 181(2), 182(2), 526(2)
Macleay, William Sharp 181(2), 182(2)
Macleay, W.S. 577, 578
Macmichael, W.T. 138(2)
Maconochie, (Captain) 448, 249(2), 413(2)
Maconochie, A. 165(2)
Maconochie, Alexander 45, 220, 405, 184(2), 466(2), 563(2)
Maconochie, Alexander (Capt)

413, 447
Maconochie, Allan 184(2)
Maconochie, Mary (Mrs)
  184(2)
Macquarie, (Mrs) 383, 500, 523
Macquarie, Charles 187(2),
  188(2), 192(2)
Macquarie, Donald 187(2)
Macquarie, Elizabeth (Mrs)
  435, 175(2), 189(2)
Macquarie, Elizabeth Henrietta
  186(2)
Macquarie, Hector 187(2),
  192(2)
Macquarie, Isabella Hamilton
  Dundas (Mrs) 187(2)
Macquarie, Jane Jarvis 186(2)
Macquarie, Margaret (Mrs)
  187(2)
Macquarie, Lachlan (Gov) 2, 5,
  6, 8, 21, 42, 87, 99, 103, 112,
  116, 121, 177, 178, 181, 199,
  200, 204, 208, 209, 211, 212,
  213, 219, 223, 227, 234, 235,
  239, 240, 241, 247, 252, 254,
  255, 259, 263, 264, 265, 273,
  288, 289, 301, 306, 308, 314,
  322, 324, 325, 327, 328, 343,
  353, 359, 365, 368, 373, 374,
  375, 380, 381, 383, 384, 391,
  392, 406, 409, 416, 421, 422,
  426, 428, 436, 463, 471, 485,
  491, 494, 506, 514, 537, 564,
  566, 573, 11(2), 15(2), 21(2),
  36(2), 40(2), 42(2), 45(2),
  61(2), 67(2), 105(2), 112(2),
  128(2), 131(2), 134(2), 139(2),
  140(2), 157(2), 159(2), 186(2),
  187(2), 192(2), 208(2), 215(2),
  219(2), 227(2), 234(2), 243(2),
  256(2), 259(2), 260(2), 264(2),
  278(2), 283(2), 291(2), 292(2),
  295(2), 299(2), 306(2), 307(2),
  308(2), 310(2), 318(2), 335(2),
  336(2), 361(2), 368(2), 370(2),
  371(2), 374(2), 376(2), 380(2),
  381(2), 382(2), 388(2), 393(2),
  394(2), 401(2), 427(2), 429(2),
  444(2), 459(2), 502(2), 507(2),
  508(2), 510(2), 520(2), 530(2),
  537(2), 538(2), 547(2), 548(2),
  550(2), 552(2), 566(2), 568(2),
  570(2), 575(2), 580(2), 583(2),
  598(2), 599(2), 608(2), 613(2),
  617(2), 620(2), 627(2)
Macqueen, Anne (Mrs) 196(2)
Macqueen, Malcolm 195(2)
Macqueen, Mariana (Mrs)
  195(2)
Macqueen, Thomas Potter 280,
  461, 168(2), 195(2)
Macready, William Charles
  68(2)
Macvitie, Ann (Mrs) 197(2)
Macvitie, Thomas 196(2)
Macwhirter, Anna 101(2)
Macwhirter, John (Dr) 101(2),
  223(2)
McAdam, John 276
McArthur, Donald Gordon
  589(2)
McArthur, Elizabeth 589(2)

McArthur, Margaret Campbell
  51
McArthur, Peter 51
McBrien, 494(2)
McCammon, Mary 199
McCandlish, Caroline Amelia
  51(2)
McCarthy (McCarty), Denis
  159(2)
McCarty, Denis 87(2)
McCarty, Mary Ann 87(2)
McCarty (McCarthy), Denis
  159(2)
McClintock, Leopold 412
McCluer, John 527
McComb, H.S. 547
McCombie, 602(2)
McCormack, James 309
McCoy, Frederick (Prof) 29(2)
McCrae, (Dr) 349(2)
McCrae, Andrew Murison
  160(2)
McCrae, Farquhar (Dr) 160(2),
  514(2)
McCrae, Farquhar Peregrine
  160(2)
McCrae, Hugh 161(2)
McCrae, George Gordon
  160(2), 161(2)
McCrae, Georgiana 142,
  424(2), 521(2)
McCrae, Georgiana Huntly
  160(2)
McCrae, Thomas Anne 233
McCrae, William Gordon 233
McCrone, Francis Nesbitt
  68(2), 161(2)
McCulloch, 234
McCulloch, James 82
McCulloch, J.R. 523(2)
McDermott, Henry 336
McDonald, Agnes (Mrs) 548
McDonald, Eleanor 485
McDonald, Grant 548
McDonald, Hugh 162(2)
McDonald, John 198
McDonald, Mary Ann (Mrs)
  162(2)
McDonnell, Thomas 187
McDonough, Felix (Capt) 64(2)
McDonough, Harriet
  (Henrietta) Ann Stuart 64(2)
McDougall, Andrew 320
McDougall, Bruce 320
McDougall, Elizabeth Maria
  320
McDougall, James 135
McDowell, Jane 428
McDuel, Jemima 344
McDuel, John 344
McDuff, Jacobina 74
McEachern, James 141(2)
McEncroe, (Archdeacon)
  270(2)
McEncroe, J. (Fr) 511(2),
  513(2), 544(2)
McEncroe, John 165(2), 341(2)
McEncroe, John (Archdeacon)
  534
McEncroe, John (Rev) 473,
  337(2), 338(2), 340(2)
McEncroe, Mary (Mrs) 165(2)

McEncroe, William 165(2)
McEntyre, (game keeper) 234
McEvoy, Edward 505
McFarland, 175(2)
McGammon, Anne 50(2)
McGarvie, 504(2)
McGarvie, Isabella (Mrs)
  167(2)
McGarvie, John 166(2), 176(2)
McGarvie, John (Rev) 76(2)
McGarvie, William 166(2),
  479(2)
McGeorge, Emily Elizabeth 443
McGibbon, John (Rev) 535
McGill, 102
McGill, John 102
McGillivray, 429
McGown, Agnes Mathie 430(2)
McGrath, James 560
McGuire, Elizabeth 605(2)
McGuire, Jane 3(2)
McIlwraith, Thomas (Sir)
  264(2)
McIntosh, A.M. 1
McIntosh, Ada 340
McIntosh, Edwin 340
McIntosh, Hugh 302
McIntosh, Sarah Thompson 96
McIntosh, Sophia 303
McIntyre, Ann 168(2)
McIntyre, Daniel (Donald)
  168(2)
McIntyre, Donald 195(2)
McIntyre, Donald (Daniel)
  168(2)
McIntyre, James 262
McIntyre, John 168(2), 195(2)
McIntyre, Louisa (Mrs) 262
McIntyre, Mary 168(2)
McIntyre, Peter 168(2)
McIver, Mary 232
McKaeg, John (Rev) 418(2)
McKay, Alexander 193, 529,
  170(2)
McKay, W.P. 528(2)
McKellar, Elizabeth 327
McKellar, Isabella 327
McKellar, Lilias 327
McKellar, Neil (see MacKellar)
  327
McKenny, John 171(2)
McKenzie, Alexander Kenneth
  172(2), 289(2)
McKenzie, Alistair 91(2)
McKenzie, Jane 289(2)
McKenzie, John Piper 172(2)
McKenzie, Mary Ann (Mrs)
  172(2)
McKinney, John 70
McKinnon, Margaret 420(2)
McKonochie, Alexander 184(2)
McLachlan, Charles 175(2),
  365(2)
McLachlan, Isabella (Mrs)
  176(2)
McLaren, Alexander 177(2)
McLaren, David 16, 443, 2(2),
  176(2), 480(2), 481(2)
McLaren, J.C. 290(2)
McLaren, Mary (Mrs) 176(2)
McLeay family 151(2)
McLeay, Alexander 97, 130,

133, 202, 283, 317, 334, 512, 558, 559, 3(2), 111(2), 177(2), 180(2), 182(2), 403(2), 523(2), 554(2), 587(2), 615(2)
McLeay, Barbara Isabella 202, 180(2)
McLeay, Christiana Susan 334, 180(2)
McLeay, Elizabeth (Mrs) 178(2)
McLeay, Frances L. 512
McLeay, George 180(2)
McLeay, James Robert 180(2)
McLeay, Margaret 3(2), 180(2)
McLeay, Rosa Roberta 180(2)
McLeay, William Sharp 180(2)
McLeod, (Dr) 571(2)
McManus, T.B. 294(2)
McManus, Terence 217(2), 234(2)
McMeckan, Anthony 247(2)
McMillan, 494(2)
McMillan, Angus 452, 453, 183(2), 184(2)
McMillan, Christina (Mrs) 184(2)
McMillan, Ewan 183(2), 184(2)
McNally, Catherine Christiana 363(2), 557(2)
McNaught, Janet 14
McNees, 269
McNicol, Helen 28(2)
McPherson, 103(2)
McRae, Margaret Forbes 514(2)
McRedmond, Edward 371(2)
Madden, Edward 508(2)
Madden, Rosetta (Rosata), (Mrs) 508(2)
Magarey, Elizabeth (Mrs) 197(2)
Magarey, James 197(2)
Magarey, Silvanus James 197(2)
Magarey, Thomas 197(2)
Magill (Aborigine) 103
Magill, Margaret 230
Mahon, Cecilia 149
Mahony, Ellen 93(2)
Maiden, J.H. 243
Maidment, Hannah 599(2)
Main, Edward 251, 252
Maine, Betsy 528
Mair, William 412(2)
Maitland, Peregrine (Sir) 603(2)
Major, Henry 358
Major, Susanna 377
Makdougall, Henry Hay (Sir) 151
Makinson, Henry Massey 199(2)
Makinson, Joseph 198(2)
Makinson, Mary (Mrs) 198(2)
Makinson, Miriam Josepha 199(2)
Makinson, Sarah Ann (Mrs) 198(2)
Makinson, T.C. 255
Makinson, T.C. (Rev) 162, 523, 406(2), 425(2), 569(2)
Makinson, Thomas Cooper 198(2)

Makkare (Aborigine) 236
Maloney, Margaret 344
Malpas, Ann 201(2)
Manchester, (Duke of) 248(2)
Mander, Jane Hall 23(2)
Mander, John Hall 23(2)
Mangles family 484(2)
Mangles, (Captain) 325
Mangles, Ellen 484(2)
Mangles, James (Capt) 244(2)
Manifold, Edward 200(2)
Manifold, Hannah 60
Manifold, James Chester 200(2)
Manifold, Jane Elizabeth (Mrs) 200(2)
Manifold, John 199(2)
Manifold, Marion (Mrs) 200(2)
Manifold, Mary (Mrs) 199(2)
Manifold, Peter 199(2)
Manifold, Thomas 59, 124, 199(2)
Manifold, William 199(2)
Manifold, William Thomson 200(2)
Mann, Ann Elizabeth 554
Mann, Ann (Mrs) 201(2)
Mann, Anne 569(2)
Mann, Bessie (Mrs) 201(2)
Mann, Charles 166, 244, 540, 200(2), 201(2), 472(2), 482(2)
Mann, David Dickenson 201(2)
Mann, D.D. 120, 365, 59(2)
Mann, Elizabeth (Mrs) 201(2)
Mann, Gother Kerr 230
Mann, Isabella Noble (Mrs) 201(2)
Mann, Maria Josepha (Mrs) 201(2)
Mann, Mary (Mrs) 201(2)
Mann, Sarah (Mrs) 200(2)
Manners-Sutton, Charles 348(2)
Manners-Sutton, Ellen (Mrs) 348(2)
Manning, 526(2)
Manning, Edye 137(2), 202(2), 203(2)
Manning, Fanny Elizabeth (Mrs) 202(2)
Manning, James (Rev) 202(2)
Manning, J.E. 389(2)
Manning, John Edye 202(2), 554(2)
Manning, Lydia (Mrs) 202(2)
Manning, Matilda Jordan (Mrs) 202(2)
Manning, William Montagu 203(2)
Mansfield, (Earl of) 504(2)
Mansfield, Ann (Mrs) 204(2)
Mansfield, Lucy (Mrs) 205(2)
Mansfield, Lydia (Mrs) 204(2)
Mansfield, Ralph 204(2)
Mansfield, Ralph (Rev) 213, 558, 479(2)
Manton, Anne (Mrs) 205(2)
Manton, J.A. (Rev) 205(2), 423(2)
Manton, Jane 205(2)
Manton, John Allen 205(2)
Manton, Thomas 205(2)
Mapleton, Sarah 362

Marceau, Joseph 353(2)
Margarot, 61(2), 218(2), 266(2), 449(2)
Margarot, Maurice 438, 526, 550, 206(2), 312(2), 388(2)
Markew (Aborigine) 236
Marks, Elizabeth Preston (Mrs) 242(2)
Marks, James 242(2)
Marks, John 242(2)
Marks, Sarah Jane (Mrs) 242(2)
Marlay, Fanny Jane 489(2)
Marnon, Elizabeth 307(2)
Marriott, Anne Frances (Mrs) 207(2)
Marriott, F.A. (Archdeacon) 256, 292, 493, 285(2), 311(2), 392(2)
Marriott, Fitzherbert Adams 207(2)
Marriott, George Wharton 207(2)
Marriott, Lydia (Mrs) 273(2)
Marriott, Selina Anne (Mrs) 207(2)
Marsden, Anne 523
Marsden, Charles 212(2)
Marsden, Elizabeth (Mrs) 208(2)
Marsden, Samuel 28, 54, 90, 105, 135, 144, 153, 159, 185, 199, 200, 205, 211, 219, 251, 252, 254, 255, 260, 262, 307, 314, 324, 352, 365, 432(2), 451(2), 483(2), 573(2), 576(2), 577(2), 580(2), 628(2)
Marsden, Samuel (Rev) 39, 374, 375, 394, 396, 402, 417, 421, 427, 495, 503, 509, 514, 518, 521, 522, 537, 550, 554, 561, 570, 17(2), 18(2), 19(2), 42(2), 105(2), 148(2), 157(2), 191(2), 207(2), 282(2), 359(2), 419(2), 438(2), 499(2), 508(2), 520(2), 529(2), 552(2), 567(2), 599(2), 632(2)
Marsden, Thomas 207(2)
Marsh, Esther 509(2)
Marsh, Henry 508(2)
Marsh, Maria 353(2)
Marsh, Robert 430
Marsh, Rosetta (Rosata) (Mrs) 508(2)
Marsh, Stephen 353(2)
Marsh, W. 522(2)
Marshall, (Lieut) 39, 469, 171(2)
Marshall, (shipwright) 490
Marshall, Alicia 273(2)
Marshall, Benjamin (Rev) 304(2)
Marshall, Elizabeth Margaret 526
Marshall, George 124
Marshall, James 137(2)
Marshall, James (Lt) 318(2)
Marshall, John 236, 294
Marshall, Joseph 355
Marshall, Mary 444(2)
Marshall, Sarah 304(2)
Marsham, Thomas 111(2)
Martens, Conrad 287, 349,

212(2), 409(2)
Martens, Elizabeth 212(2)
Martens, Henry 212(2)
Martens, J.C.H. 212(2)
Martens, Jane Brackenbury 212(2)
Martens, Rebecca 212(2)
Martin, Catherine 217
Martin, H.M. 515
Martin, James 210, 534, 228(2), 339(2), 505(2)
Martin, John 234(2), 235(2), 300(2)
Martin, Lily 306
Martin, Susannah 306
Martin, William 64, 336(2)
Martyn, John 52
Marwood, Henry (Capt) 26(2)
Maskelyne, Nevil (Rev. Dr) 297, 298
Mason, Anne 410
Mason, Catherine 376
Mason, Elizabeth 468(2)
Mason, Francis 215(2)
Mason, Horatio William 270
Mason, Martin 213(2), 499(2)
Mason, Michael 79
Mason, Thomas 88(2), 214(2)
Massey, Thomas 215(2)
Massie, J. (Rev) 246(2)
Massie, R. 14
Massie, R.G. 26(2)
Masson, Francis 54
Matcham family 291
Matcham, Catherine (Mrs) 291
Matcham, Elizabeth 291
Matcham, George 291
Matcham, Horatio Nelson 291
Matcham, Mary 16(2)
Matcham, Mary (Mrs) 367, 609(2)
Matcham, Susannah 367
Mather, Agnes (Mrs) 216(2)
Mather, Andrew 216(2)
Mather, Ann 216(2)
Mather, Elizabeth 184
Mather, Esther (Mrs) 216(2)
Mather, Joseph Benson 249
Mather, Robert 212, 552, 216(2)
Mather, Sarah 216(2)
Mather, Sarah Benson 562(2)
Mathew, Felton (Mrs) 80, 562
Matilda, (Queen of Denmark) 236
Matson, Henry Manifold 200(2)
Mattinson, Sophia 24
Maturin, Charlotte 48
Maturin, William 48
Maugham (Maum), William James 216(2)
Maughan, Anne 328, 329
Maughan, James 217(2)
Maum, Ann (Mrs) 217(2)
Maum (Maugham), William James 216(2)
Maum, Sophia (Mrs) 217(2)
Maum, W. 61(2)
Maw, Hannah 429
Maxwell, (Lieut) 573(2)
Maxwell, George 326

Maxwell, Isabella 372
Maxwell, James 372
May Day (Aborigine) 576(2)
May, Lawrence 246
May, Sarah 246
Mayne, William Colburn (Capt) 463(2)
Mayo, Herbert 85
Meach, James Thompson 503
Meadowbank, (Lord) 184(2)
Meagher, 235(2)
Meagher, Catherine (Mrs) 502, 217(2), 218(2)
Meagher, Henry Emmet Fitzgerald 217(2)
Meagher, T.F. 502, 234(2), 294(2)
Meagher, Thomas Francis 217(2)
Mealmaker, Alison (Mrs) 218(2)
Mealmaker, George 218(2), 312(2)
Mealmaker, John 218(2)
Mealmaker, Marjory (Mrs) 218(2)
Meares, Eleanor (Mrs) 218(2)
Meares, Richard Goldsmith 218(2)
Mears, Molly (Mrs) 259(2)
Mears, Thomas 259(2)
Medhurst, Frances Sarah 502(2)
Meehan, Hugh 129(2)
Meehan, J. (Surveyor Gen) 530(2), 598(2)
Meehan, James 359, 564, 59(2), 219(2), 570(2)
Meehan, Thomas 220(2)
Mein, James 220(2)
Mein, Susannah (Mrs) 220(2)
Melbourne, (Lord) 279(2), 407(2), 581(2)
Melbourne, (Viscount) 24
Melville, (Viscount) 337, 526
Melville, Eliza Romney (Mrs) 221(2)
Melville, Henry 37, 87, 163(2), 221(2), 397(2)
Melville, Jennett 359
Melville, Thomas 359
Mendana, Alvaro de 357(2)
Mendonca, Cristovao da 358
Menge, Anna Margaret (Mrs) 222(2)
Menge, Johann 222(2)
Menge, Johannes 33(2)
Menge, Nicholas 222(2)
Menke, Carl Theodor 350(2)
Menzies, (Lieut) 227(2)
Menzies, Archibald 54
Menzies, Charles (Lt) 530(2)
Menzies, Charles (Sir) 222(2)
Menzies, Maria Wilhelmina (Mrs) 223(2)
Menzies, Sarah (Mrs) 222(2)
Mercer, Anne Elliot 224(2)
Mercer, Anne Elliot (Mrs) 224(2)
Mercer, Elizabeth (Mrs) 223(2)
Mercer, Frances Charlotte (Mrs) 223(2)
Mercer, G.D. 224(2), 501(2)

Mercer, George 68, 223(2)
Mercer, George Duncan 223(2)
Mercer, J.H. 224(2)
Mercer, John Henry 223(2)
Mercer, Thomas 376
Mercer, W.D. 224(2)
Mercer, William 223(2)
Mercy, William Drummond 223(2)
Meredith, Charles 249, 225(2)
Meredith, Clara 329
Meredith, Edwin 225(2)
Meredith, George 9, 12, 24, 37, 81, 329, 475, 34(2), 224(2), 385(2), 502(2)
Meredith, Georgina Augusta 29(2)
Meredith, James 238, 349
Meredith, John 224(2), 225(2)
Meredith, Louisa 81, 354(2)
Meredith, Maria 34(2)
Meredith, Mary (Mrs) 225(2)
Meredith, Sally (Mrs) 224(2)
Meredith, Sarah (Mrs) 224(2)
Merewether, Augusta Maria (Mrs) 237(2)
Merewether, Edward Christopher 237(2)
Merewether, F.L.S. 315
Merewether, Francis 293, 181(2)
Meridith, Clara 225(2)
Mertho, (Captain) 491
Messent, Elizabeth 179
Messent, Mary Anne 179
Messent, Samuel 179
Mestre, Prosper de 131(2)
Meuron, Rose Isabelle de 92(2)
Meyndrix, Claesgie 503(2)
Mibaise, (explorer) 13(2)
Michelmore, G. 468
Michie, Archibald 216
Micklethwait, Benjamin 269
Micklethwait, Elizabeth 269
Micklethwait, Mary (Mrs) 269
Middleton, Charles 226(2)
Middleton, Charles (Sir) 573(2)
Middleton, George Augustus 226(2)
Middleton, Jane 617(2)
Middleton, Mary Ann (Mrs) 226(2C)
Middleton, Sarah (Mrs) 226(2)
Midgigoroo (Aborigine) 632(2)
Mileham, Elizabeth (Mrs) 227(2)
Mileham, James 12(2), 227(2)
Mileham, James (Dr) 522, 223(2)
Mileham, Lucy 227(2)
Mileham, Susanna(h) (Mrs) 227(2)
Miles, William Augustus 228(2)
Milford, (Justice) 196
Milford, Eliza 196
Mill, Hugh (Dr) 84
Mill, J.S. 364
Millar, John 266(2)
Milledge, Dinah 252
Miller, (shipwright) 262(2)
Miller, Andrew 229(2), 309(2)
Miller, Elizabeth 229(2)

Miller, Elizabeth (Mrs) 229(2)
Miller, Frederick (Rev) 553,
    229(2), 350(2)
Miller, George 230(2)
Miller, Harriet Beauvais 230
Miller, Henrietta Charlotte 107
Miller, Henry 108, 229(2),
    492(2)
Miller, Henry (Lt) 124(2)
Miller, Linus W. 431
Milligan, (Dr) 59, 492
Milligan, Alexander (Lt) 388
Milligan, Eliza (Mrs) 230(2)
Milligan, Joseph 230(2)
Millikin, William 271(2)
Millner, Eliza Elflida 55(2)
Mills, Charles Frederick 231(2)
Mills, G.G. 495
Mills, Jennifer Ann (Mrs)
    232(2)
Mills, John Brabyn 231(2)
Mills, Olive 231(2)
Mills, Peter 144, 359, 231(2),
    264(2)
Mills, Peter Bernard French
    (Lt) 232(2)
Mills, Richard 110
Milne, Robert Lyon 128
Milner family 208(2)
Milner, (Bishop) 340(2)
Milner, Sibella 476(2)
Milnes, Martha 424(2)
Milnes, Roger 424(2)
Milson family 233(2)
Milson, Ann (Mrs) 233(2)
Milson, David 337
Milson, Elizabeth (Mrs) 232(2)
Milson, James 207, 337, 232(2)
Milson, Marianne (Mrs) 233(2)
Milson, Rachel (Mrs) 337
Minchin, Ann 178
Minchin, Ann (Mrs) 233(2)
Minchin, George 233(2C),
    234(2)
Minchin, Maria Matilda 234(2)
Minchin, William 178, 263,
    233(2), 582(2)
Minshull, Mary 296
Minto, (Earl of) 353
Minto, (Lord) 170, 157(2)
Mitchel, Jane (Mrs) 234(2)
Mitchel, John 217(2), 234(2),
    294(2)
Mitchel, John (Rev) 234(2)
Mitchel, Mary (Mrs) 234(2)
Mitchell, (Captain) 571(2),
    578(2)
Mitchell, Alexander 101(2)
Mitchell, Augusta Maria 237(2)
Mitchell, Christina (Mrs) 401
Mitchell, David 235(2)
Mitchell, David Scott 237(2)
Mitchell, James 185, 353, 235(2)
Mitchell, James (Dr) 138,
    429(2)
Mitchell, Janet 84(2)
Mitchell, Janet (Mrs) 238(2)
Mitchell, John 238(2)
Mitchell, Livingstone 241(2)
Mitchell, Margaret (Mrs)
    235(2)
Mitchell, Mary (Mrs) 238(2)

Mitchell, T. 362
Mitchell, T. (Maj) 338, 532
Mitchell, T.L. 132, 269, 284,
    310, 311, 321, 350, 467, 504,
    547, 112(2), 119(2), 160(2),
    306(2), 324(2), 350(2), 409(2),
    471(2), 495(2)
Mitchell, T.L. (Maj) 526,
    243(2), 377(2)
Mitchell, T.L. (Surveyor Gen)
    106(2), 316(2)
Mitchell, Thomas 241, 287,
    313, 360(2)
Mitchell, Thomas (Sir) 61, 164,
    388, 448, 452, 43(2), 493(2),
    525(2), 543(2), 634(2)
Mitchell, Thomas Livingstone
    (Sir) 238(2)
Mitchell, William 573, 122(2)
Mitchell, William Fancourt 401
Mivart, 416(2)
Moase, G. (Rev) 528(2)
Mocatta, George 250(2)
Mocatta, Rebecca 250(2)
Moffitt, Elizabeth Preston
    242(2)
Moffitt, Henry 242(2)
Moffitt, Mary Anne 242(2)
Moffitt, Mary Anne (Mrs)
    242(2)
Moffitt, Sarah Jane 242(2)
Moffitt, Sophia Jane 242(2)
Moffitt, William 242(2), 504(2)
Moira, (Earl) 541(2)
Molesworth, (Viscount) 305(2)
Molesworth, William (Sir) 413,
    481, 525(2), 561(2)
Molle, (Colonel) 163(2)
Molle, G.J. (Col) 583(2)
Molle, George J. (Lt. Col) 358,
    581(2)
Molle, George James (Lt. Gov)
    15(2), 192(2), 243(2)
Molle (Mow), William 243(2)
Molle, William Macquarie
    243(2)
Mollison, Alexander Fullerton
    243(2)
Mollison, Crawford 243(2),
    244(2)
Mollison, Elizabeth (Mrs)
    243(2)
Mollison, W.F. 350
Mollison, William Thomas
    243(2)
Molloy, (Mrs) 372
Molloy, A.J.P. (Capt) 245(2)
Molloy, Amelia 245(2)
Molloy, Georgiana 244(2),
    245(2)
Molloy, John 245(2)
Molloy, John (Capt) 244(2)
Molloy, Mary 245(2)
Molloy, Sabina 245(2)
Mona, Menehem (Cantor)
    279(2)
Monds, Albert 246(2)
Monds, Angelina (Mrs) 246(2)
Monds, Benjamin 245(2)
Monds, Fanny (Mrs) 246(2)
Monds, Helena 245(2)
Monds, Helena (Mrs) 245(2)

Monds, Thomas 245(2)
Monds, Thomas Wilkes 258,
    245(2)
Monro, Anna 562
Montagu, 36
Montagu, Alfred Otter 247(2)
Montagu, Algernon 173, 420(2)
Montagu, Algernon Sidney
    246(2), 320(2)
Montagu, Barbara (Mrs) 248(2)
Montagu, Basil 246(2)
Montagu, Edward 248(2)
Montagu, Jessy (Mrs) 248(2)
Montagu, John 52, 77, 143, 182,
    191, 219, 253, 355, 405, 412,
    413, 414, 474, 530, 101(2),
    164(2), 246(2), 248(2), 397(2),
    507(2), 541(2), 542(2)
Montagu, John (Capt) 500(2)
Montagu, Laura (Mrs) 246(2)
Montagu, Maria Ann (Mrs)
    247(2)
Montefiore, Eliezer 250(2)
Montefiore, Eliezer Levi 251(2)
Montefiore, Jacob 251(2)
Montefiore, Joseph Barrow 376,
    250(2)
Montefiore, Judith (Mrs) 250(2)
Montefiore, Moses (Sir) 166
Montefiore, Rebecca (Mrs)
    250(2)
Montgomery, James 160(2)
Montmollin, Frederic Auguste
    de 89(2)
Montmollin, Sophie 89(2)
Moodie, 578(2)
Moodie, Affleck 316(2)
Moody, Elizabeth Sadlier
    293(2)
Moor, Elizabeth (Mrs) 251(2)
Moor, Henry 251(2)
Moor, Henry 50(2)
Moor, Henry Isaacs 251(2)
Moor, Marion (Mrs) 252(2)
Moor, Mary (Mrs) 252(2)
Moore, (newspaper proprietor)
    214
Moore, Andrew 98(2)
Moore, Ann 247, 257(2)
Moore, Ann Augusta (Mrs)
    254(2)
Moore, Anne (Mrs) 50(2),
    252(2)
Moore, Anne Quayle 49(2)
Moore, Annie Fletcher 619(2)
Moore, Charles 98
Moore, Charles Dodwell 256(2)
Moore, Elizabeth Jane 627(2)
Moore, Fanny Mary Jane (Mrs)
    228, 253(2)
Moore, Frederick Thomas
    254(2)
Moore, G.F. 165, 228, 381,
    175(2)
Moore, G.H. 118(2)
Moore, George Fletcher 252(2)
Moore, George Henry 50(2)
Moore, H. 303
Moore, J. Sheridan 345(2)
Moore, James 348(2C)
Moore, John 254(2), 255(2),
    627(2)

Moore, John (Rev) 49(2)
Moore, John (Sir) 49, 196, 270(2), 459(2)
Moore, Joseph 252(2)
Moore, Joshua John 254(2), 627(2)
Moore, Margaret (Mrs) 49(2)
Moore, Martha (Ann) (Mrs) 255(2)
Moore, Mary 307
Moore, Mary (Mrs) 257(2), 627(2)
Moore, Patrick 307, 308
Moore, Rachel (Mrs) 98(2), 254(2)
Moore, Sarah Elizabeth (Mrs) 254(2)
Moore, Thomas 21, 263, 41(2), 129(2), 254(2), 520(2), 595(2)
Moore, Thomas Matthews 256(2)
Moore, W.H. 6, 56, 89, 231, 247, 373, 426, 52(2), 550(2)
Moore, William Henry 255(2)
Moppy (Aborigine) 201
Moran, Alicia Mary 18
Moran, Anne 381(2)
Mordaunt, John (General Sir) 11
Morehead, Boyd Dunlop 258(2)
Morehead, Helen Buchanan (Mrs) 258(2)
Morehead, Margaret (Mrs) 257(2)
Morehead, Robert 257(2)
Morehead, Robert Archibald Alison 257(2)
Moreland, W.H. 323(2)
Moresby, Fairfax (Admiral) 288(2), 289(2)
Morgan, (convict) 95(2)
Morgan, Charles (Sir) 223(2)
Morgan, David 316(2)
Morgan, John 174, 258(2), 320(2)
Morgan, Molly 259(2)
Morgan, Rebecca 258(2)
Morgan, Rebecca (Mrs) 258(2)
Morgan, William 259(2)
Moriarty, 260(2)
Moriarty, Ellen 260(2)
Moriarty, Merion Marshall (Capt) 260(2)
Moriarty, Sylverius 260(2)
Moriarty, Sylverius (Vice Admiral) 259(2)
Moriarty, William 259(2), 260(2)
Morison, Grace 23
Morison, Jane 335
Morison, Margaret 232
Morison, Mary (Mrs) 232
Morison, M.W. (Capt) 232
Morisset, (Colonel) 13
Morisset, (Commandant) 226(2)
Morisset, (Major) 449(2)
Morisset, Edric Norfolk Vaux 261(2)
Morisset, Emily (Mrs) 261(2)
Morisset, James Thomas 260(2)

Morisset, J.T. 280
Morisset, J.T. (Capt) 569(2)
Morley, (Mrs) 189(2)
Morley, Hannah 127(2)
Morley, James 188(2)
Morphett, Elizabeth (Mrs) 262(2)
Morphett, George 261(2)
Morphett, H.C. 262(2)
Morphett, John 64(2), 384(2), 624(2)
Morphett, John (Sir) 261(2)
Morphett, Mary (Mrs) 261(2)
Morphett, Nathaniel 261(2)
Morrill, Eliza Ann (Mrs) 263(2)
Morrill (Murrills), James 262(2)
Morris, (Bishop) 511(2)
Morris, Augustus 4
Morris, Hannah 533(2)
Morris, George (Rev) 20
Morris, Sophia (Mrs) 241
Morris, William 341(2)
Morris, W.P. 544(2)
Morrison, Askin 407
Morrison, Catharine(2)
Morrison, Jean 206
Morriss, Sarah 123(2C)
Morse, Samuel 348
Mort, Henry 70(2)
Mort, Maria (Mrs) 70(2)
Mort, T.S. 197, 70(2), 569(2), 570(2)
Mort, Theresa (Mrs) 70(2)
Mortimer, Elizabeth 192
Moses, Abraham 84(C)
Moses, Elias 84
Moses, Julia 84(C)
Mosman, Agnes (Mrs) 263(2)
Mosman, Archibald 442, 263(2)
Mosman, George 263(2)
Mosman, Harriet (Mrs) 264(2)
Mosman, Hugh 263(2), 264(2)
Mundy, Louisa Katrina Herbert 268(2C)
Mountgarrett, Bridget (Mrs) 264(2)
Mountgarrett, Jacob 264(2)
Mountgarrett, John (Rev) 25, 264(2)
Mow, John 243(2)
Mow, Margaret (Mrs) 243(2)
Mowatt, Francis 275(2)
Mowle, Stewart 275(2), 276(2)
Moxon, Sarah 200(2)
Muddle, (Captain) 100(2)
Mudie, Emily 86(2)
Mudie, James 131, 52(2), 86(2), 264(2), 338(2), 449(2), 464(2), 479(2), 513(2), 615(2)
Mudie, James (Maj) 304(2)
Mudie, John 264(2)
Mudie, Margaret (Mrs) 264(2)
Mueller, (botanist) 491(2)
Muggleston, (Trooper) 312
Muir, Thomas 438, 266(2), 312(2), 449(2)
Muirhead, Mary 375(2)
Mulgrave, Peter Archer 94(2), 267(2), 622(2)
Muller, Flora Elizabeth 287(2)
Mulready, William 467
Multugerrah (Aborigine) 201

Mundy, Alfred Miller 541
Mundy, (Captain) 524
Mundy, (Colonel) 1(2), 4(2)
Mundy, Edward Miller 384
Mundy, Frances 384
Mundy, G.C. (Lt. Col) 385
Mundy, Godfrey Basil (Major Gen) 268(2)
Mundy, Godfrey Charles 268(2)
Mundy, Henry 339, 534(2)
Mundy, Jane (Mrs) 541
Mundy, Sarah Brydges (Mrs) 268(2)
Munro, Barbara 95
Munro, Hugh 562
Murchison, Roderick (Sir) 114(2)
Murdoch, Barclay (Mrs) 269(2)
Murdoch, Frances (Mrs) 269(2C)
Murdoch, George 269(2)
Murdoch, Grace (Mrs) 268(2)
Murdoch, James 268(2), 269(2), 269(2C)
Murdoch, John 268(2)
Murdoch, John Hugh Germain 269(2)
Murdoch, John Wallace 269(2)
Murdoch, Mary (Mrs) 268(2)
Murdoch, Peter 269(2), 296(2)
Murdoch, Robert Wallace 269(2)
Murdoch, Thomas William Clinton 354
Murphy, (Bishop) 193
Murphy, (convict) 108(2)
Murphy, (Dr) 509(2)
Murphy, Arthur 315, 269(2)
Murphy, Bridget (Mrs) 269(2)
Murphy, Francis 269(2)
Murphy, Francis (Bishop) 343(2), 545(2)
Murphy, Hester 315
Murphy, J.R. 545
Murphy, Margaret 43(2)
Murphy, Margaret (Mrs) 315
Murphy, Mary 142(2)
Murragingy (Aborigine) 234
Murray family 541(2)
Murray, 374, 396, 458
Murray, (Archbishop) 341(2)
Murray, (Dr) 276(2)
Murray, (Messrs) 493(2)
Murray, Agnes 271(2)
Murray, Alicia (Mrs) 273(2)
Murray, Andrew 271(2)
Murray, Anna Maria 274(2), 276(2)
Murray, Anne 271(2)
Murray, Anne (Mrs) 271(2)
Murray, Catherine (Mrs) 273(2)
Murray, D'Arcy Wentworth 458
Murray, David 271(2)
Murray, Edward Kent Strathearn 273(2)
Murray, Eleanor (Mrs) 273(2)
Murray, Elizabeth 328, 271(2)
Murray, Ellen (Mrs) 274(2)
Murray, George (Sir) 74, 284,

334, 404, 238(2), 246(2), 270(2), 321(2), 324(2), 485(2), 496(2), 578(2)
Murray, George Gilbert Aime 276(2)
Murray, Hubert (Sir) 276(2)
Murray, Hugh 271(2), 492(2)
Murray, James Aubrey Gibbes 276(2)
Murray, James Fitzgerald 274(2)
Murray, Jane 271(2)
Murray, Jean (Mrs) 271(2)
Murray, John 349, 272(2), 552(2)
Murray, John (Capt) 45(2), 46(2), 127(2)
Murray, John (Lt) 59(2)
Murray, John Hubert Plunkett 276(2)
Murray, Lilias 492(2)
Murray, Lillias 271(2)
Murray, Margaret 271(2)
Murray, Mary (Mrs) 275(2)
Murray, R.L. 86, 214, 437, 49(2), 163(2), 221(2), 300(2), 397(2)
Murray, Robert (Admiral) 288(2)
Murray, Robert William Felton Lathrop 272(2)
Murray, Robert 272(2)
Murray, T.A. 439
Murray, T.B. (Rev) 289(2)
Murray, Terence 274(2)
Murray, Terence Aubrey (Sir) 274(2)
Murray, William (Sir) 270(2), 272(2)
Murrell, (Aborigine) 185, 617(2)
Murrell, Margaret 207
Murtagh, J.G. 513(2)
Muskerry, (Lord) 291
Muzio, Charles 301(C)
Nagel, Charles 446(2)
Nairn, (Major) 81
Nairn, William 278 (2)
Nanningsz, Cornelis 556
Nanningsz, Guerte (Mrs) 556
Nanningsz, Vrouwtje Cornelisd 556
Nansen, Fridtjof 23
Napier, 495(2)
Napier, Cecilia 176
Napier, Charles (Sir) 116(2)
Napier, Charles James (Col) 539
Napier, George (Sir) 176
Napoleon, 55, 622(2)
Napoleon III (Emperor) 54(2)
Napper, Marie 545
Napper, Marie Anne Martha Sceline Helina 545(C)
Nash, 494
Nash, (Mrs) 278(2)
Nash, Ann (Mrs) 279(2)
Nash, Elizabeth 376
Nash, Ellen 93(2)
Nash, Ellen (Mrs) 93(2)
Nash, John 409(2)
Nash, Richard 278(2)

Nash, Richard West 122(2), 278(2)
Nash, Robert 494, 36(2), 278(2)
Nash, Susan 36(2)
Nash, William 93(2)
Nassau, (Grand Duke of) 54(2)
Nassau, Maria 313
Nathan, Charles 280(2)
Nathan, Henrietta (Mrs) 279(2)
Nathan, Isaac 336, 337, 279(2)
Nathan, Rosetta (Mrs) 279(2)
Naylor, Ellen Susannah 597(2C)
Neale, (Archbishop) 299(2)
Neales, Elizabeth (Mrs) 280(2)
Neales, John Bentham 280(2)
Neales, Margaret (Mrs) 280(2)
Neate, Christina 218
Neate, William 218
Negelin, (painter) 415
Nehrlich, Dorette 33(2)
Neill, P.C. (Mrs) 423
Neilley, Caroline Jeanette 32(2)
Neilly, William (Capt) 32(2)
Nelson, (Lord) 291, 367, 539, 97(2), 609(2)
Nelson, Catherine 291
Nelson, David 54
Nelson, Horatio 465(2)
Nelson, Isaac 599(2)
Nelson, Isabella 599(2)
Nelson, Jane 377(2)
Nepean, (Captain) 154(2)
Nepean, Evan 4(2), 281(2), 397(2)
Nepean, Johanna Francina Carolina (Mrs) 281(2)
Nepean, Nicholas 281(2)
Nettlefold, Frances 76
Neveaux, Marguerite Aurelie 353(2)
Nevill, John 110
Neville, Grace Montgomery 557
Newburgh, countess of 137
Newcastle, (Duke of) 387, 244(2), 408(2), 490(2)
Newcomb, (Miss) 71(2)
Newcomb, C.E. (Miss) 69
Newcomb, Caroline 330
Newcomb, Caroline Elizabeth 330
Newcomb, Samuel 331
Newenham, Charles Burton 244
Newenham, Emily Grace 244
Newland, (pastoralist) 525
Newland, (Captain) 509
Newland, Ridgway William 281(2)
Newman, 199(2)
Newman, Richard 457(2)
Newman, Sarah 64
Newton, E.T. 70
Newton, John 17(2)
Nias, (Captain) 546
Nicholas, John Liddiard 282(2)
Nicholls, R.N. 23(2)
Nichols, Charles 441
Nichols, Charles Hamilton 283(2)
Nichols, Elizabeth 439
Nichols, George Robert 283(2)

Nichols, Isaac 76, 313, 575, 19(2), 46(2), 170(2), 283(2)
Nichols, Isaac David 283(2)
Nichols, Jonathan 283(2)
Nichols, Mary (Mrs) 283(2)
Nichols, Rosanna (Mrs) 19(2), 283(2)
Nichols, Sarah (Mrs) 283(2)
Nicholson, 350, 51(2)
Nicholson, Charles 230, 293, 315, 182(2), 283(2)
Nicholson, Charles (Sir) 181(2), 241(2), 283(2), 293(2), 525(2)
Nicholson, Charles Archibald 285(2)
Nicholson, Jane 248
Nicholson, John 102(2)
Nicholson, Sarah (Mrs) 284(2)
Nicholson, Sydney 285(2)
Nicholson, William 51(2C), 55(2), 102(2), 244(2)
Nicolay, William (Major Gen) 324(2)
Nightingale, Florence 416(2)
Nightingall, Miles (Major Gen) 189(2)
Nique, Johann Peter 421(2)
Niquet, Peter 423(2)
Nisbet, John (Rev) 553
Nixon, (Bishop) 78, 192, 493, 205(2), 207(2), 311(2), 355(2), 392(2), 469(2)
Nixon, (Captain) 9(2)
Nixon, Anna Maria (Mrs) 287(2)
Nixon, F.R. (Bishop) 168, 256, 292, 346, 420, 576(2)
Nixon, Flora Elizabeth (Mrs) 287(2)
Nixon, Frances Maria 287(2)
Nixon, Frances Maria (Mrs) 287(2)
Nixon, Francis Russell 285(2)
Nixon, Harriet 287(2)
Nixon, Robert 287(2)
Nixon, Robert (Rev. Dr) 285(2)
Nobbs, George Hunn 288(2)
Nobbs, Sarah (Mrs) 288(2)
Noble, Mary 435
Nodder, Frederick Polydore 437(2)
Nodin, Francis 492(2)
Norfolk, (Duke of) 269, 532, 557
Norman, 151(2)
Norman, James 148
Norman, Leslie 351(2)
Normanby, (Lord) 446
Normanby, (Marquis of) 479
Norris, Sophia Isabella 320
North, James (Rev) 352(2)
Northumberland, (Duke of) 458, 20(2), 201(2)
Norton, Emma 307(2)
Norton, James 515, 289(2), 572(2)
Norton, Jane (Mrs) 289(2)
Norton, John 289(2)
Norton, Marian (Mrs) 289(2)
Norton, Mary (Mrs) 289(2)
Norton, Robert Wilmot (Sir) 554

Nott, Charles 614(2)
Nott, Henry 253
Nugent, George (Sir) 151
Nutt, R.W. 191
Nyland, Sarah 96
O'Beirne, Letitia Anne 124(2)
O'Brien, Catherine (Mrs) 292(2)
O'Brien, Charlotte (Mrs) 293(2)
O'Brien, Cornelius 565, 292(2)
O'Brien, Edward (Sir) 293(2)
O'Brien, Elizabeth Sadlier (Mrs) 293(2)
O'Brien, Harry 292(2)
O'Brien, Henry 201, 565, 292(2)
O'Brien, Henry (Jun) 293(2)
O'Brien, Lucy (Mrs) 294(2)
O'Brien, Rebecca (Mrs) 292(2)
O'Brien, Thomas 292(2)
O'Brien, William Smith 217(2), 234(2), 293(2)
O'Burne, James 227
O'Connell, (Captain) 246
O'Connell, Charles Philip 294(2)
O'Connell, Daniel 323, 234(2), 274(2), 294(2), 512(2), 608(2)
O'Connell, Daniel (General Count) 294(2)
O'Connell, Mary (Mrs) 295(2)
O'Connell, Mary Australia (Mrs) 25(2)
O'Connell, Maurice 122, 286
O'Connell, Maurice (Sir) 25(2), 284(2), 631(2)
O'Connell, Maurice Charles 295(2)
O'Connell, Maurice Charles Philip (Sir) 294(2)
O'Connell, William Bligh 25(2)
O'Connor, Feargus 296(2)
O'Connor, Francis 296(2)
O'Connor, Louisa Anna (Mrs) 296(2)
O'Connor, Roderic 56, 109, 182, 219, 372, 566, 269(2), 296(2), 429(2)
O'Connor, Roger 296(2)
O'Dogherty, 235(2)
O'Dogherty, K.I. 502
O'Donohoe, 217(2), 294(2)
O'Donohoe, Patrick 234(2)
O'Driscoll, Terence 323
O'Farrell, Henry 347(2)
O'Ferrall, R. 36
O'Ferrall, Rolla 517(2), 596(2)
O'Flaherty, Eliza (Mrs) 298(2)
O'Flaherty, Henry Charles 298(2)
O'Flynn, Jeremiah 509(2)
O'Flynn, Jeremiah (Rev) 528
O'Flynn (Flynn), Jeremiah Francis 299(2), 340(2)
O'Halloran, (Dr) 232(2)
O'Halloran, (Major) 434
O'Halloran, Anne (Mrs) 301(2)
O'Halloran, Elizabeth Minton (Mrs) 301(2)
O'Halloran, Frances (Lady) 300(2)

O'Halloran, Jane (Mrs) 301(2)
O'Halloran, Joseph (Major Gen) 300(2)
O'Halloran, Joseph Sylvester 301(2)
O'Halloran, Thomas Shuldham 300(2), 301(2)
O'Halloran, William Littlejohn 301(2)
O'Kelly, Eileen 337(2C)
O'Murrough (chief of) 315
O'Neil clan 302(2)
O'Neil, Peter 309, 302(2)
O'Neil, Peter (Fr) 340(2)
O'Reilley, Margaret 502(2)
O'Reilly, T. (Rev) 262
O'Shanassy, 350, 370, 84(2)
O'Shanassy, John 376
O'Shaughnessy, Edward 77(2), 304(2), 479(2)
Oakden, Georgina (Mrs) 290(2)
Oakden, Mary (Mrs) 290(2)
Oakden, Percy 290(2)
Oakden, Philip 445, 290(2)
Oakes, Francis 107, 251, 290(2), 467(2)
Oakes, Francis Rowland 291(2)
Oakes, George 291(2)
Oakes, George Spencer (Archdeacon) 291(2)
Oakes, Mary 291(2)
Oakes, Rebecca (Mrs) 291(2)
Oakes, Selina 407(2)
Oakes, Susannah Hassall 467(2)
Oakes, William Henry 107
Oatley, Frederick 292(2)
Oatley, James 291(2)
Oatley, Mary (Mrs) 291(2)
Odell, Aphrasia 461
Odell, John 538
Odell, Louisa (Mrs) 538
Officer, Isabella (Mrs) 297(2)
Officer, Jemima (Mrs) 297(2)
Officer, Robert 297(2)
Officer, Robert (Sir) 297(2)
Ogden, (bushranger) 308(2)
Ogilvie, 616(2)
Ogilvie, Eliza 527(2)
Ogilvie, Eliza Ann 300(2)
Ogilvie, Eliza (Mrs) 300(2)
Ogilvie, James 300(2)
Ogilvie, Mary Grant 300(2)
Ogilvie, Robert 120(2)
Ogilvie, Thomas 300(2)
Ogilvie, William 268
Oldham, James 388(2)
Oliver, Eliza Elliott 419(2)
Oliver, William Elliott 419(2)
Olley, Martha 26(2)
Olliver, June 531
Ommaney, J.M. 448(2)
Onslow, Arthur Pooley 180(2)
Onslow, Rosa Roberta (Mrs) 180(2)
Opie, 189(2)
Ord, Mary (Mrs) 431(2)
Ord, William 431(2), 432(2)
Ormonde, (Marquess of) 51(2)
Orr, Alexander 303(2)
Orr, Harriet (Mrs) 303(2)
Orr, Maria (Mrs) 302(2)

Orr, William Morgan 302(2)
Orred, George 134(2)
Orred, Georgiana 134(2)
Orsmond, John Muggridge 599(2)
Orton, Eleanor (Mrs) 303(2)
Orton, Elizabeth 614(2)
Orton, John 303(2)
Orton, Joseph Rennard 303(2)
Orton, Joseph (Rev) 532(2), 540(2), 567(2)
Osbech, 403
Osborne, Archie 303(2)
Osborne, Henry 303(2)
Osborne, James 304(2)
Osborne, Patrick Hill 304(2)
Osborne, Sarah (Mrs) 304(2)
Osmond, (Captain) 364
Osmond, Adelaide Fanny 364
Ossory, Upper (Earl of) 407
Oswald, John (Sir) 631(2)
Otter, (Lieut) 468
Ousten, Anne 133(2)
Outhwaite, Emma 524
Ovens, Georgina (Mrs) 305(2)
Ovens, J. (Maj) 598(2)
Ovens, John 305(2)
Ovens, John (Lt) 305(2)
Ovens, John (Maj) 464
Owen, (estate owner) 457
Owen, Corbetta 127(2)
Owen, Harriet 311(2)
Owen, Jeremiah (Rev) 574, 311(2)
Owen, John 127(2)
Owen, John (Lt. Gen) 127(2)
Owen, Rachel 574
Owen, Richard 85
Owen, Richard (Sir) 544, 181(2)
Owen, Robert 461, 132(2)
Owen, Susanna Price 467
Owen, William (Sir) 127(2)
Oxford, (Earl of) 46
Oxford, (5th Earl of) 431(2)
Oxley, Emma (Mrs) 307(2)
Oxley, Henry 307(2)
Oxley, Isabella 305(2)
Oxley, J. 359, 564
Oxley, John 111, 153, 188, 247, 259, 265, 266, 280, 299, 309, 325, 359, 416, 496, 504, 511, 520, 547, 564, 62(2), 111(2), 123(2), 219(2), 238(2), 305(2), 307(2), 313(2), 316(2), 319(2), 377(2), 400(2), 495(2)
Oxley, John Joseph William Molesworth 305(2)
Pace, Ann 529
Pace, Jane 529, 533
Pace, Walter (Capt) 529, 533
Pagan, John 312
Paganini, 567(2)
Page, Alfred 308(2)
Page, Charles Service 308(2)
Page, George 308(2)
Page, Grace (Mrs) 308(2)
Page, John 308(2)
Page, Louisa 308(2)
Page, Samuel 258, 308(2)
Page, Sarah (Mrs) 308(2)
Paine, Edward 190, 191

Paine, Sarah 191
Paine, Thomas 266(2)
Pakington, John (Sir) 387, 483, 408(2)
Palliser, Hugh 243
Palliser, Mary (Mrs) 316
Palliser, Richard 316
Palmer, Arthur (Sir) 264(2)
Palmer, Arthur Hunter 281
Palmer, Catherine Irene 198
Palmer, Catherine Irene (Mrs) 308(2)
Palmer, Christopher 309(2)
Palmer, Edwin Campbell 311(2)
Palmer, Elizabeth 453
Palmer, Fyshe 449(2)
Palmer, George 520(2)
Palmer, George Thomas 198, 308(2), 311(2)
Palmer, Harriet (Mrs) 311(2)
Palmer, Henry 467
Palmer, Jane 164(2)
Palmer, John 115, 157, 204, 215, 231, 409, 422, 10(2), 308(2), 309(2), 311(2), 395(2), 573(2), 608(2)
Palmer, John (Commissary) 380, 563, 233(2), 533(2)
Palmer, Jonathan 311(2)
Palmer, Philip 311(2)
Palmer, Philip (Rev) 77
Palmer, Phillip (Mrs) 574
Palmer, Sarah 551, 309(2)
Palmer, Sophia 198, 199, 206, 309(2)
Palmer, Sophia Susannah 231, 311(2)
Palmer, Susan 231
Palmer, Susan (Mrs) 308(2), 309(2)
Palmer, Thomas Fyshe 126, 178, 438, 206(2), 218(2), 266(2), 312(2)
Palmer, Ursula (Mrs) 311(2)
Palmerston, (Lord) 463(2)
Palmerston, (Viscount) 356, 377, 460
Pamby-Pamby (Aborigine) 294
Pamphlett, Thomas 313(2)
Panton, Alice 411(2)
Panton, George 365(2)
Panton, William 101(2)
Pantoney, Maria 101(2)
Pantoney, Sarah (Mrs) 101(2)
Pantoney, William 101(2)
Papineau, Louis 352(2)
Parbury, Frederick 72(2)
Park, Henrietta 236(C)
Park, Mungo 54, 166
Parker, 526(2)
Parker, (Captain) 56(2)
Parker, (overseer) 170(2)
Parker, (parliamentarian) 526(2)
Parker, Ann Mary (Mrs) 262
Parker, H.H. (Mrs) 262
Parker, H.W. 181(2)
Parker, Henry Harding 262
Parker, Letitia 136
Parker, Mary 115, 117
Parker, R.J. 454
Parker, Susannah 135

Parker, William (Sir) 136
Parkes, (Lady) 474(2)
Parkes, Henry 1, 211, 336, 515, 11(2), 26(2), 80(2), 136(2), 143(2), 181(2), 276(2), 505(2), 527(2)
Parkes, Henry (Sir) 388, 479, 501, 515, 534, 41(2), 339(2), 633(2)
Parkinson, Joel 314(2)
Parkinson, Stanfield 314(2)
Parkinson, Sydney 53, 314(2)
Parmeter, (Surgeon) 499(2)
Parr, Samuel (Dr) 438
Parr, William 560, 448(2)
Parramore, George 314(2)
Parramore, Patience (Mrs) 314(2)
Parramore, Thirza (Mrs) 315(2)
Parramore, W.T. 459
Parramore, William 315(2)
Parramore, William Thomas 314(2)
Parry, Caleb Hillier (Dr) 315(2)
Parry, Catharine (Mrs) 316(2)
Parry, Edward (Sir) 138, 280, 415, 350(2)
Parry, Elizabeth Emma 345
Parry, Isabella (Mrs) 315(2)
Parry, Sarah (Mrs) 315(2)
Parry, William Edward (Sir) 315(2)
Parsons, Cecil 316(2)
Parsons, Cecil Joseph 317(2)
Parsons, Charles Octavius 316(2)
Parsons, Frances (Mrs) 316(2)
Parsons, Guy 316(2)
Parsons, John Weddell (Rev) 316(2)
Parsons, Maria (Mrs) 317(2)
Parsons, Richard 313(2)
Partridge, Ann Maria 50, 50(C)
Partridge, Charlotte 516(2)
Partridge, Henry 516(2)
Partridge, Louisa French 489(2)
Partridge, Sarah 50, 50(C)
Pascoe, Hannah 368
Pasley, Charles 412(2)
Pasmore, Mary Anne 472(2), 478(2)
Passmore, Christiana 157
Paterson, (Captain) 569, 332(2)
Paterson, (Colonel) 334(2)
Paterson, (Mrs) 563
Paterson, Agnes 203
Paterson, Elizabeth (Mrs) 319(2)
Paterson, Elizabeth (Mrs) 489
Paterson, P.G. (Col) 487
Paterson, William 54, 76, 79, 83, 108, 139, 144, 157, 171, 238, 239, 240, 290, 328, 489, 571, 317(2), 537(2)
Paterson, William (Capt) 568, 154(2), 155(2)
Paterson, William (Col) 61, 517, 60(2), 111(2), 112(2), 215(2), 223(2), 499(2)
Paterson, William (Gov) 46(2), 380(2)
Paterson, William (Lt. Col) 408,

469, 519, 213(2), 310(2)
Paterson, William (Lt. Gov) 28, 39, 359, 380, 383, 409, 563, 573, 10(2), 20(2), 39(2), 45(2), 47(2), 53(2), 57(2), 87(2), 97(2), 130(2), 131(2), 140(2), 171(2), 190(2), 221(2), 233(2), 264(2), 306(2), 364(2), 394(2), 468(2), 520(2), 530(2), 537(2)
Patrick, Mary 48
Patterson family 297(2)
Patterson, Jane 297(2)
Patterson, Jemima 297(2)
Patterson, John 297(2)
Patterson, John Hugh 297(2)
Patterson, Myles 297(2)
Pattle, Eliza Ann Frances 559(2)
Patton, Alexander (Dr) 579(2)
Patton, Robert 192
Paulista, Jose Bonifacio Andrada 94(2)
Paxton, Joseph 244(2)
Payne, Catherine 527
Payne, J.H. 161(2)
Payne, William 455, 456
Paynter, Jane 9(2)
Peale, Portia Henrietta 61
Pearson, (Ms) 361(2)
Peate, William 139(2)
Pedder, John 319(2)
Pedder, John L. (Chief Justice) 302, 437, 249(2), 462(2)
Pedder, John Lewes (Sir) 318, 347, 372, 404, 413, 574, 247(2), 319(2)
Pedder, Maria (Mrs) 319(2)
Peddie, Robert 230(2)
Pedro, Dom 94(2)
Pedro, Don 47
Peel, Dorothy 321(2), 322(2)
Peel, Dorothy (Mrs) 320(2)
Peel, Frederick 322(2)
Peel, Julia 321(2)
Peel, Mary Charlotte Dorking (Mrs) 321(2)
Peel, Robert 137, 314, 500, 321(2)
Peel, Robert (Sir) 180, 394, 111(2), 401(2)
Peel, Thomas 236, 245, 110(2), 195(2), 219(2), 320(2), 322(2), 487(2), 560(2)
Peers, Agnes 224
Pelsaert, Francisco 322(2)
Pelzer, Eberhard 322(2)
Pemberton, Catherine Irene 308(2)
Pembroke, (Lord) 326(2)
Pemullaway (Aborigine) 234
Pendleton, (Captain) 127
Pendleton, Isaac 129(2)
Penfold, May 137(2)
Pennefather, William (Rev) 373(2)
Pennington, W.G. 515
Penrose, Mary 29
Penzance, (Lord) 627(2)
Peppin, George 75(2)
Perceval, Dudley 133
Percy, (Lord) 20(2)
Perigal, (Miss) 339

Perkins, Temperance 201
Perois, E. 116(2)
Peron, Francois 71, 391, 86(2), 323(2)
Perry, (Bishop) 322, 252(2), 406(2), 414(2), 522(2)
Perry, Caroline Elizabeth (Mrs) 324(2)
Perry, Elizabeth 405(2)
Perry, James 354
Perry, Jane 354
Perry, Samuel Augustus 139, 490, 324(2)
Perry, Susannah 385(2)
Perry, Thomas Augustus 324(2)
Pestalozzi, (writer) 211
Petchey, John 46(2)
Petchy, Elizabeth (Mrs) 325(2)
Petchy, John 325(2)
Petchy, Sarah Ann Russell 325(2)
Peters, Ann Augusta 254(2)
Peters, Elizabeth 27
Peters, John James (Lt) 254(2)
Peters, Thomas 27
Peterson, Frederick 554(2)
Peterson, Mary Louisa 24(2)
Petrie, 285(2)
Petrie, Andrew 98, 145, 201, 295, 325(2), 406(2), 448(2)
Petrie, Ann (Mrs) 391
Petrie, John 326(2)
Petrie, Margaret (Mrs) 325(2C)
Petrie, Mary (Mrs) 326(2C)
Petrie, Thomas 326(2)
Petrie, Walter 325(2C)
Petrie, William Flinders (Sir) 391
Petty, Martha (Mrs) 334
Petty, Thomas 334
Phelps, Elizabeth 150
Philip I (King of Portugal) 358
Philip III (King of Spain) 536(2)
Philips, Elizabeth Ann 24(2)
Phillip, Arthur 12, 22, 84, 122, 150, 183, 218, 234, 237, 237, 288, 297, 298, 308, 311, 374, 397
Phillip, Arthur (Capt) 56(2)
Phillip, Arthur (Gov) 351, 355, 403, 488, 562, 567, 20(2), 31(2), 53(2), 145(2), 154(2), 229(2), 309(2), 326(2), 347(2), 394(2), 397(2), 404(2), 420(2), 442(2), 463(2), 506(2), 551(2), 573(2), 594(2)
Phillip, Elizabeth (Mrs) 326(2)
Phillip, Isabella (Mrs) 333(2)
Phillip, Jacob 326(2)
Phillip, Margaret (Mrs) 326(2)
Phillips, Thomas 415, 316(2), 558(2)
Philo Free (nom de plume) 211(2)
Pickard, Eleanor Martha 77
Pickering, Charles 279
Pickering, Hannah 63
Pickering, Jane 63
Pickering, John 63
Pickett, Eleanor Martha 77
Pidgeon, Eliza (Mrs) 333(2)

Pidgeon, Nathaniel 333(2)
Pidgeon, Richard 333(2)
Piggott, Arthur Leary (Sir) 168
Pike, Emma 506
Pike, Mary 526
Pike, William 20
Pilmor, Eliza 623(2)
Pinnock, Charlotte 407(2)
Pinnock, J.D. 354
Pinnock, James Denham 333(2), 334(2)
Pinnock, Maria (Mrs) 333(2)
Pinnock, Philip 407(2)
Pinnock, Robert Denham (Dr) 334(2)
Pinnock, Sibyl Herlock (Mrs) 334(2)
Pinnock, Timothy Denham 333(2)
Piper, (Captain) 528, 145(2), 243(2)
Piper, (Ensign) 264(2)
Piper, Hugh 334(2), 335(2)
Piper, John 200, 245, 526, 172(2), 334(2), 510(2)
Piper, John (Capt) 469, 110(2), 129(2), 362(2), 388(2)
Piper, Mary Ann 172(2)
Piper, Mary Ann (Mrs) 335(2)
Piper, Sarah 335(2)
Pirce, Ann (Mrs) 350(2)
Piron, 172(C)
Pitcairn, Dorothea Jessie 336(2)
Pitcairn, John (Rev) 563(2)
Pitcairn, Robert 336(2)
Pitkethley, (Captain) 262(2)
Pitt family 215, 291
Pitt, Ann (Mrs) 336(2)
Pitt, Esther 609(2)
Pitt, Francis 336(2)
Pitt, Jane (Mrs) 336(2)
Pitt, Jemima 16(2)
Pitt, John 336(2)
Pitt, Mary 97(2)
Pitt, Mary (Mrs) 16(2)
Pitt, Richard 336(2)
Pitt, Robert 16(2), 609(2)
Pitt, Salome 336(2)
Pitt, Susannah (Mrs) 367
Pitt, Thomas Matcham 97(2)
Pitt, William 196, 180(2)
Pius VII (Pope) 509(2)
Pius IX (Pope) 21, 199(2), 345(2)
Place, Francis 462, 206(2)
Platt, George 599(2)
Platt, John Laurio 337(2)
Platt, Louisa Slade 337(2)
Platt, Roseanne (Mrs) 337(2)
Platt, William Thompson 337(2)
Plessos, Katerina Georgia 264
Plummer, T.W. 190(2)
Plunkett, Eileen 337(2C)
Plunkett, John Hubert 185, 52(2), 86(2), 165(2), 265(2), 276(2), 337(2), 341(2), 418(2), 505(2), 511(2), 513(2), 526(2), 544(2)
Plunkett, George 337(2C)
Pocock, I. 161(2)
Polack, A. 611(2)

Polding, J.B. (Archbishop) 48, 147, 534, 82(2), 165(2), 198(2), 338(2), 341(2), 425(2), 513(2)
Polding, J.B. (Bishop) 146, 161, 210, 336, 337, 473, 474, 535, 44(2), 270(2), 416(2), 511(2), 544(2)
Polding, John Bede 131, 242, 340(2)
Pollard, E.H. 219(2)
Polo, Marco 358
Pomare II (King of Tahiti) 108, 208, 233, 252, 343
Ponsonby, Mary Elizabeth 480
Ponsonby, William Brabazon 480
Poole, James 498(2)
Poore, Edward (Sir) 441
Popham, Letitia 630(2)
Porden, Eleanor 34(2)
Porden, Eleanor Anne 413, 437
Porden, Sarah Henrietta 34(2)
Porden, William 34(2)
Portarlington, (Lady) 516(2)
Porteous, (Bishop) 17(2)
Porteus, (Captain) 47(2)
Portland, (Duchesss of) 456(2)
Portland, (Duke of) 548, 569, 570, 57(2), 111(2), 312(2), 401(2), 537(2)
Portman, (Viscountess) 101(2)
Potter, Mariana 195(2)
Potter, H.E. (Rev) 15
Potter, Thomas 195(2)
Pounds, Phyllis 547(2)
Pourtales, Albert de (Count) 89(2)
Powditch, William 127
Powell, Edward 347(2), 444(2)
Powell, Elizabeth (Mrs) 347(2)
Powell, Jane 444(2)
Powell, Margaret 259(2)
Powell, Martha 507(2)
Powell, Mary Ann 547(2)
Powell, Philippa Bull 134
Powell, Thomas 134
Powell, Walter 322
Power, Anna Munro (Mrs) 348(2)
Power, Charles John 348(2)
Power, Daniel (Fr) 511(2)
Power, Edmond 348(2)
Power, Ellen 348(2)
Power, Ellen (Mrs) 348(2)
Power, Margaret Ellen 348(2)
Power, Marguerite 348(2)
Power, Mary Ann 348(2)
Power, Robert 251, 538, 48(2), 348(2), 467(2)
Powis family 211
Powlett, Charles (Rev) 349(2C)
Powlett, Frederick Armand 349(2)
Powlett, Margaret (Mrs) 349(2)
Poynter, (Bishop) 528, 340(2), 509(2)
Poynter, (Dr) 299(2)
Pracey, Rosetta (Rosata) 508(2)
Prado, Don Diego de 536(2)
Praed, W.M. 584(2)
Pratt, John Jeffreys 196

Pratt, Joseph (Rev) 209(2)
Preiss, Johan August Ludwig 349(2)
Preiss, Ludwig 325
Pressley, Sarah 433(2)
Preston, (Lieut) 236
Preston, Richard 244
Preston, W. (engraver) 569(2)
Preston, Walter 365
Price, Anna Clara 352(2)
Price, Anna Maria 149
Price, Catherine (Mrs) 350(2)
Price, Charles 350(2)
Price, Charles (Rev) 418
Price, Charles Seckerson Yahrah 351(2)
Price, Edward 455
Price, Elizabeth 227(2)
Price, Emily Mary 352(2)
Price, Frederick (Sir) 352(2)
Price, James Franklin 352(2)
Price, Jane de Winton 352(2)
Price, John 62, 168, 220, 350(2), 393(2), 474(2), 610(2)
Price, John Giles 351(2)
Price, Johyn Frederick 352(2)
Price, Mary 172(2C)
Price, Mary (Mrs) 351(2)
Price, Rose (Sir) 351(2)
Price, Thomas Caradoc 352(2)
Price, Tom, (Col) 352(2)
Price Warung (nom de plume for William Astley) 352(2)
Priddle, Charles Frederick Durham 572(2)
Priddle, Margaret Anne 572(2)
Priest, 605(2)
Priest, William 19
Priestley, 403
Priestley, (Dr) 558
Priestley, Joseph 126
Priestley, Joseph (Dr) 267(2), 312(2)
Prieur, Antoine 352(2)
Prieur, Archange (Mrs) 352(2)
Prieur, F.X. 430
Prieur, Francois Xavier 352(2)
Prieur, Marguerite Aurelie (Mrs) 353(2)
Prince, E.C. 466
Prince of Wales 474(2)
Prince Maurits (Dutch stadtholder) 555
Prince Regent (later George IV of England) 235, 349(2)
Pringle, Betty 429(2)
Pringle, John (Sir) 53
Prinsep, H.C. 190
Prior, Catherine 31
Proctor, Charles (Capt) 236
Proctor, Mary 236
Prothero, Thomas 419
Proud, Eliza 333(2)
Prout, Cornelius 353(2)
Prout, Frederick 354(2)
Prout, John Skinner 26, 41, 416, 456, 353(2)
Prout, Maria (Mrs) 353(2)
Prout, Matilda 354(2)
Prout, Samuel 353(2)
Prout, Skinner 538
Prout, Victor Albert 354(2)

Ptolemy, 358
Puckey, James 251, 252
Puckey, Margery (Mrs) 252
Puckey, William 251, 252
Puckey, William Gilbert 252
Puget, (Lieut) 551(2)
Pugh, (Mrs) 321
Pugh, Cornelia Ann (Mrs) 355(2)
Pugh, R.B. 476(2)
Pugh, William Bowdler 355(2C)
Pugh, William Russ 74(2), 355(2)
Pulteney, James (Lt. Gen) 459(2)
Punnett, Elizabeth 172(2C)
Purbrick, Hannah Read 316
Purbrick, Susannah Darke 225
Purkis, Emma 122(2)
Purkis, James 122(2)
Purves, W. 293
Purvis, Elizabeth 573(2)
Purvis, Liddell 573(2)
Putland, (Captain) 120
Putland, John (Lt) 119, 295(2)
Putland, Mary (Mrs) 119, 295(2)
Pybus, Elizabeth Margaret 194
Pybus, Mary 379(2)
Pybus, Richard 194
Pyche, Rajah 188(2)
Pye, Sarah 395(2)
Pyndar, Ellen 134(2)
Pyne, J.B. 387(2)
Pyne, Mary 93(2)
Pyne, Rose 387(2)
Quadra, Don Juan 551(2)
Quaife, Amelia (Mrs) 356(2)
Quaife, Barzillai (Rev) 165, 356(2)
Quaife, Eliza (Mrs) 357(2)
Quaife, Frederick Harrison 357(2)
Quaife, Maria (Mrs) 357(2)
Quaife, Thomas 356(2)
Quaife, William Francis 357(2)
Quast, 503(2)
Quayle, Margaret 49(2)
Quick, A.W. (Rev) 261
Quick, Charlotte Elizabeth Margaret 261
Quickfall, Jane 42(2)
Quilter, F.W. (Rev) 32(2)
Quincy, de 558(2)
Quinn, Patrick 321
Quintal, Edward 289(2)
Quiros, Dona Ana (Mrs) 358(2)
Quiros (Queiros), Pedro Fernandez de 358, 357(2), 536(2)
Raby, Margaret 379(2)
Race, Hannah 7
Radford, Frances Maria (Mrs) 464(2)
Radford, Henry Wyatt (Dr) 464(2)
Rae, John 354(2)
Raff, George 600(2)
Raff, Harriet (Mrs) 600(2)
Raffles, Stamford (Sir) 29
Raine, Elizabeth 359(2)
Raine, Fanny Eleanor (Mrs)

360(2)
Raine, John 269, 270, 396, 468, 359(2)
Raine, Mary (Mrs) 359(2)
Raine, Richard 359(2)
Raine, Thomas 359(2)
Raine, Thomas (Capt) 359(2), 361(2)
Ralph, Amelia 539(2)
Ramsay, David 197(2, 360(2), 361(2)
Ramsay, Edward Pearson 361(2)
Ramsay, Elizabeth 446
Ramsay, George (Major Gen) 446
Ramsay, John 361(2)
Ramsay, Sarah Ann (Mrs) 361(2)
Rand, Edward 433(2)
Randolph, Elizabeth 491(2)
Ranken, Arthur 362(2)
Ranken, George 361(2), 362(2)
Ranken, Janet (Mrs) 361(2)
Ranken, Janet Ranken (Mrs) 361(2)
Ranken, Thomas 362(2)
Ranken, W.B. (Mrs) 362(2)
Ranken, William Hugh Logan 362(2)
Rankin, John 48(2)
Rankin, Susannah Elizabeth 48(2)
Ransom, Anne 557(2)
Ransom, Thomas 362(2)
Raper, Catherine 363(2)
Raper, George 363(2)
Raper, Henry 363(2)
Rashleigh, Frances Mary 468(2)
Rashleigh, Thomas 468(2)
Rattigan, Arthur 296(2)
Rattigan, William 296(2)
Raven, Lucinda (Mrs) 364(2)
Raven, William 364(2)
Raven, William Thomas 364(2)
Ray, Joseph 445(2)
Raymond, Anna 124
Raymond, Aphrasia (Mrs) 461, 365(2)
Raymond, Catherine 461
Raymond, James 300, 461, 365(2)
Raymond, Margaret 300
Raymond, Robert Peel 365(2)
Raymond, William 365(2)
Raynor, Rebecca Eliza 480(2)
Read, Eliza (Mrs)(2)
Read, Elizabeth (Mrs) 366(2)
Read, G.F. (Jun) 366(2)
Read, George 429
Read, George Frederick 95, 365(2)
Read, Hannah 316
Read, Henry 366(2)
Read, Lydia 366(2)
Read, Margaret (Mrs) 366(2)
Read (Reid), Richard (Jun) 367(2)
Read, Richard 366(2), 367(2C)
Read, Sarah (Mrs) 366(2)
Receveur, Pere 85(2)
Reddall, Isabella 368(2)

Reddall, John 368(2)
Reddall, Luke 368(2)
Reddall, Martha (Mrs) 368(2)
Reddall, Thomas 198, 368(2)
Reddall, Thomas (Rev) 267(2)
Reddington, John 139
Rede, Leman Thomas 457
Rede, Louisa Leman 457
Redesdale, (Lord) 302(2)
Redfern, James Foveaux 370(2)
Redfern, Sarah (Mrs) 558, 370(2), 605(2)
Redfern, William 21, 99, 137, 260, 324, 575, 368(2)
Redfern, William (Dr) 112, 358, 393, 558, 172(2), 193(2), 570(2), 599(2), 605(2)
Redfern, William (Jun) 370(2)
Redfern, William Lachlan Macquarie 370(2)
Redhead, (Captain) 326(2)
Redmond, Edward 371(2), 594(2)
Redmond, John 371(2)
Redmond, Mary 371(2)
Redmond, Sarah 371(2)
Redmond, Winifred (Mrs) 371(2)
Reed, Benjamin 262
Reed, H.D. 373(2)
Reed, Henry 261, 486, 9(2), 260(2), 371(2)
Reed, Margaret Sayres Elizabeth (Mrs) 372(2)
Reed, Maria Susanna (Mrs) 372(2)
Reed, Mary (Mrs) 371(2)
Reed, Samuel 371(2)
Regent, Prince George of England 343
Regnier, de 323(2)
Reibey, Celia 374(2)
Reibey, Eliza 374(2)
Reibey, Elizabeth Ann 374(2)
Reibey, James Haydock 374(2)
Reibey, Mary 216
Reibey, Mary (Mrs) 528, 558, 373(2)
Reibey, Thomas 32, 306, 373(2), 374(2), 605(2)
Reid, Agnes (Mrs) 376(2)
Reid, Alexander 375(2)
Reid, Ann 429(2)
Reid, David 375(2)
Reid, Elizabeth 375(2)
Reid, Frances Charlotte 223(2)
Reid, James 541(2)
Reid, James 93(2)
Reid, Jane 375(2)
Reid, John (Dr) 223(2)
Reid, Lestock 101(2)
Reid, Mary (Mrs) 375(2)
Reid, (Read), Richard (Jun) 367(2)
Reid, Thomas 376(2)
Reid, William 127, 312(2), 420(2)
Reilly, Ann (Mrs) 512(2)
Remmington, Elizabeth 251(2)
Rendell, Maria Wood 453(2)
Rennie, (engineer) 306
Rennie, Elizabeth 5

Rennie, John 23, 376(2)
Repton, Edward (Rev) 424(2)
Repton, Elizabeth Catherine 424(2)
Reveley, Amelia 376(2)
Reveley, Henry Willey 165, 376(2)
Reveley, Maria (Mrs) 376(2)
Reveley, Willey 376(2)
Reynolds, 616(2)
Reynolds, (politician) 525
Reynolds, Ann 467
Reynolds, Joshua (Sir) 366(2), 555(2)
Reynolds, Letitia 547(2)
Reze, Mary Patricia 125
Rhind, Birnie 118(2)
Rhodey, Elizabeth 430(2)
Rhodey, Thomas 430(2)
Rhodius (Rodius), Charles 389(2)
Rice, Thomas Spring 132
Richards, John 280
Richards, Thomas 163(2), 221(2)
Richardson, Catharine (Mrs) 377(2)
Richardson, Elizabeth Melville 377(2)
Richardson, Jane (Mrs) 377(2)
Richardson, John (Sir) 577
Richardson, John Matthew 377(2)
Richardson, Samuel 431
Richardson, William 338
Richmond, (Duchess of) 218(2)
Richmond, (Duke of) 384, 385
Richmond, (3rd Duke of) 116(2)
Richmond, (5th Duke of) 384
Richmond, Charles, (Duke of) 384, 400(2)
Richmond, Thomas 53
Riddell, Campbell Drummond 130, 133, 202, 25(2), 265(2), 377(2), 513(2), 524(2)
Riddell, Caroline Stuart (Mrs) 377(2)
Riddell, James (Sir) 377(2)
Riddell, Margaretta (Mrs) 377(2)
Riddell, Rodney Stuart 378(2)
Riddell, Thomas Milles 377(2)
Riddell, Thomas Milles Stratford 378(2)
Riddiford, Anne 407
Riddle, (Captain) 36(2)
Riddle, T.C. 520
Ridgeway, Joseph 126
Ridgeway, Thomas 126
Ridley, Elizabeth 562(2)
Ridley, John 175, 443, 197(2), 301(2), 379(2)
Ridley, Mary (Mrs) 379(2)
Ridley, W. (Rev) 422(2)
Rigby, Sarah 315(2)
Righton, Charles 521(2)
Righton, Mary Ann 521(2)
Riley, Alexander 89, 115, 158, 170, 290, 562, 24(2), 39(2), 45(2), 379(2), 381(2), 520(2), 581(2)

Riley, Anne (Mrs) 381(2)
Riley, Annie Sophia 206
Riley, Edward 206, 263, 341, 562, 24(2), 310(2), 380(2), 381(2), 382(2)
Riley, Elizabeth 39(2), 434(2)
Riley, George 379(2)
Riley, Margaret (Mrs) 379(2)
Riley, Sophia (Mrs) 380(2)
Riley, William Edward 157, 230, 292(2)
Ring, James 211(2)
Ripon, (Bishop of) 207(2)
Ripon, (Earl of) 456
Risby, Elizabeth 437
Risby (Kerby) Isabella 437
Risdale, Thomas 264
Risely, Maria 127(2)
Ritchie, Hannah (Mrs) 382(2)
Ritchie, Harriet (Mrs) 319
Ritchie, John (Capt) 382(2)
Ritchie, Thomas 382(2)
Ritchie, W. 454
Riveau, Francois de 371(2)
Roadside, Helena 245(2)
Robb, Jean 139
Robe, F.H. (Gov) 301(2), 498(2)
Robe, F.H. (Lt. Gov) 335
Robe, Frederick Holt 499, 383(2)
Robe, Sarah (Mrs) 383(2)
Robe, William (Sir) 383(2)
Roberts, (miner) 543
Roberts, Adelaide 21
Roberts, Ann 110(2)
Roberts, Anne (Lady) 84(2)
Roberts, Caroline 304
Roberts, Eliza Elflida (Mrs) 55(2)
Roberts, James 53
Roberts, Jane 575
Roberts, John 9
Roberts, John Levey 322(2)
Roberts, Mary 577(2)
Roberts, Mary (Mrs) 458(2)
Roberts, Peter 21
Roberts, Thomas Howland (Sir) 84(2)
Roberts, William 55(2), 110(2), 458(2)
Robertson, Ann 510
Robertson, Charles 625(2)
Robertson, Elizabeth 28(2)
Robertson, Fanny 246(2)
Robertson, Gilbert 37, 459, 551, 164(2), 384(2), 397(2)
Robertson, John 102, 210, 514, 515, 26(2), 76(2), 82(2)
Robertson, John (Sir) 609(2)
Robertson, Mary 268(2)
Robertson, Robert 625(2)
Robertson, William 423
Robinson, 518(2)
Robinson, Cecelia 387(2)
Robinson, Elizabeth (Mrs) 388(2)
Robinson, Emma Trant 73(2)
Robinson, Frederick John 456
Robinson, George Augustus 20, 35, 75, 82, 165, 339, 400, 418, 451, 27(2), 71(2), 170(2),

385(2), 518(2), 577(2)
Robinson, John 73(2)
Robinson, Joseph Phelps 141, 387(2), 521(2)
Robinson, M.M. 42, 313, 559, 131(2), 192(2)
Robinson, Maria Amelia (Mrs) 385(2)
Robinson, Maria Josepha 165
Robinson, Michael 374, 61(2), 366(2)
Robinson, Michael Massey 387(2)
Robinson, Robert 165
Robinson, Rose (Mrs) 387(2)
Robinson, Susannah (Mrs) 385(2)
Robinson, Thomas (Baron Grantham) 456
Robinson, William 385(2)
Robison, (Captain) 478(2)
Robison, Robert (Capt) 286, 396
Robison, Sibella (Mrs) 478(2)
Robson, Robert 69
Rochford, Bernard 309, 163(2)
Rochford, Bernard 309
Rochford, Mary Ann (Mrs) 163(2)
Rockingham, marquis 579(2)
Rockliff, Mary 371(2)
Rodd, B.C. 1(2)
Rode, Joseph August 421(2)
Roderick, Colin 540(2)
Rodius, 104(2)
Rodius (Rhodius), Charles 7(2), 389(2)
Rodius, Charles Prossper 389(2)
Rodius, Harriet 389(2)
Rodius, Maria (Mrs) 389(2)
Rodney, (Admiral) 288, 567, 442(2)
Rodney, (Baron) 268(2)
Rodney, Caroline Stuart 377(2)
Rodney, Sarah Brydges 268(2)
Roe, J.S. (Lt) 486(2)
Roe, J.S. (Surveyor General) 253(2)
Roe, James (Rev) 390(2)
Roe, John Septimus 236, 326, 61(2), 122(2), 390(2)
Roe, Joseph 625(2)
Roe, Matilda (Mrs) 391(2)
Roe, Sophia (Mrs) 390(2)
Roemer, Charles William 392(2)
Rogers, Frederic (Sir) 509
Rogers, Frederick 354
Rogers, John William Foster 393(2)
Rogers, Phoebe 96
Rogers, Thomas (Rev) 168
Rogers, Sarah (Mrs) 392(2)
Rogers, Thomas George 392(2)
Rogers, Thomas (Rev) 220, 351(2), 352(2)
Rogers, Woodes (Capt) 277
Rogerson, Anne Frances 377
Rogerson, Mary 564(2)
Romaine, William (Rev) 518
Romer, (chemist) 624(2)

Romer, Wilhelm Maximilian von 392(2C)
Romilly, Samuel (Sir) 273(2)
Roossengin, Jan 13(2)
Roper, Abel 236
Roper, Sarah 443
Rosa. Salvator 410(2)
Roscommon, (4th Earl of) 579(2)
Rose family 180(2)
Rose, David 393(2)
Rose, Elizabethf (Mrs) 394(2)
Rose, George 180(2)
Rose, George (Sir) 327(2), 330(2)
Rose, Jane (Mrs) 394(2)
Rose, Robert 226(2)
Rose, Sarah 226(2), 394(2)
Rose, Sarah (Mrs) 395(2)
Rose, Thomas 347(2), 394(2), 548(2)
Ross, (Captain) 492
Ross, Alexander 396(2)
Ross, Anna Maria (Mrs) 396(2)
Ross, Catharine (Mrs) 396(2)
Ross, Daniel (Capt) 371
Ross, Eliza (Mrs) 24(2)
Ross, Eliza Ann 263(2)
Ross, Emma 181
Ross, George 559
Ross, Hugh Cokeley 395(2)
Ross, James 123, 177, 181, 316, 492, 396(2), 429(2)
Ross, James (Dr) 355
Ross, James Clark 415
Ross, James Clark (Capt) 415, 34(2)
Ross, Johan (Mrs) 398(2)
Ross, John 398(2)
Ross, John (Capt) 315(2)
Ross, Marina (Mrs) 398(2)
Ross, Robert 31, 54, 150, 226, 237, 288, 24(2), 397(2), 398(2)
Ross, Robert (Lt. Gov) 56(2)
Ross, Robert (Maj) 488, 568, 20(2), 328(2), 332(2), 506(2)
Ross, Robert (Rev. Dr) 24(2), 356(2)
Ross, Sarah (Mrs) 396(2), 398(2)
Ross, Susannah (Mrs) 396(2)
Rossi, (Captain) 261(2)
Rossi, Alexander Philip 399(2)
Rossi, Antoinette Genevieve (Mrs) 399(2)
Rossi, F.N. (Capt) 609(2), 615(2)
Rossi, Francis Nicholas 399(2)
Rossi, Francis Robert Louis 399(2)
Rossi, Philippe Francois Antoine, Comte de 399(2)
Rossiter, Thomas 288(2)
Rothery, Charlotte 2(2)
Rothery, Frederick 2(2)
Rothery, Nicholas Phillips 2(2)
Rothery, William Montagu 2(2)
Rothschild family 251(2)
Rouchouze, (Bishop) 341(2)
Rourke, Felix 512
Rous, Charlotte Whitaker (Mrs) 400(2)

Rous, Henry John 400(2)
Rous, John 400(2)
Rous, Sophia (Mrs) 401(2)
Rouse family 215, 509(2)
Rouse, Edwin 401(2)
Rouse, Eleanor 402(2)
Rouse, Elizabeth 402(2)
Rouse, Elizabeth (Mrs) 401(2)
Rouse, Elizabeth Henrietta 384, 402(2)
Rouse, George 401(2), 402(2)
Rouse, Jane 402(2)
Rouse, Mary 402(2)
Rouse, Richard 401(2)
Rowan, Ellis (Mrs) 250
Rowcroft, Charles 128(2), 402(2), 593(2)
Rowcroft, Horace 402(2), 593(2)
Rowcroft, Jane (Mrs) 402(2)
Rowcroft, Jannett (Mrs) 402(2)
Rowcroft, Thomas 402(2)
Rowe, Elizabeth Augusta 551
Rowe, W.H. 551
Rowlands, Isabella Noble 201(2)
Rowlands, Thomas Wood 74(2)
Rowlands, W.H. 201(2)
Rowlands, W.T. 385(2)
Rowley, Elizabeth 388(2)
Rowley, Thomas 403(2)
Rowley, Thomas (Capt) 128(2)
Rowling, Charles William 107(2)
Rowling, Jane (Mrs) 107(2)
Roxborough, Mary 538
Rozells, Martinha 116(2)
Rucker, W 370
Rudd, Ann Mary 615(2)
Ruffy, W.J. 20
Rumball, John 158
Rumball, Phoebe Ann 158
Rumball, Susannah 158
Rumker, Carl 338
Rumker, Charles Stargard 404(2)
Rumker, Charles Luis 404(2)
Rumker, Christian Carl Ludwig 154, 403(2)
Rumker, George F. (Prof) 404(2)
Rumker, J.F. 403(2)
Rumker, Mary Ann (Mrs) 404(2)
Rumker, P. Karl 404(2)
Rumsby, Ann 314, 374, 503, 211(2)
Runciman, Charles 61(2)
Runciman, Elizabeth (Mrs) 61(2)
Rusden, G. (Rev) 613(2)
Rusden, Sarah Anne 428(2)
Ruse, Elizabeth (Mrs) 405(2)
Ruse, James 519, 332(2), 404(2), 405(2), 420(2)
Rush, (farmer) 245(2)
Rush, Alfred 14
Rush, Laura 246(2)
Rush, William Beaumaris (Sir) 246(2)
Ruskin, (author) 364
Russell family 118(2)

Russell, Alexander 224, 409(2)
Russell, Anne (Mrs) 408(2)
Russell, Charlotte (Mrs) 407(2)
Russell, Euphemia 409(2)
Russell, Francis Thomas
  Cusack (Rev) 163, 405(2)
Russell, George 82, 330, 375(2),
  408(2), 523(2)
Russell, Georgiana Elizabeth
  (Mrs) 407(2)
Russell, H.D.G. 95
Russell, Helen Cunard 410(2)
Russell, Henry Stuart 406(2)
Russell, Isabella 408(2)
Russell, Isabella (Mrs) 408(2)
Russell, Janet 409(2)
Russell, John 409(2)
Russell, John (Lord) 36, 140,
  183, 353, 385, 419, 446, 481,
  541, 133(2), 136(2), 228(2),
  247(2), 407(2), 463(2), 495(2),
  523(2), 525(2)
Russell, John R. Stuart 407(2)
Russell, Julia 431
Russell, Margaret (Mrs) 409(2)
Russell, Mary Ann 377
Russell, Mary Ann Collis (Mrs)
  410(2)
Russell, Peter Nicol 224, 520
Russell, Philip 317(2), 408(2),
  409(2), 438(2)
Russell, Robert 376, 547,
  125(2), 213(2), 409(2)
Russell, Robert (Rev) 192
Russell, Sarah Ann 325(2)
Russell, Selina (Mrs) 407(2)
Russell, Sophia (Mrs) 409(2)
Russell, Sophia Louisa (Mrs)
  317(2)
Russell, Sydenham 406(2),
  407(2)
Russell, Thomas 409(2)
Russell, Thomas (Rev) 405(2)
Russell, W.G. Stuart 407(2)
Russell, William 409(2)
Rutledge family 297
Rutledge, Eliza (Mrs) 411(2)
Rutledge, James 411(2)
Rutledge, John 411(2)
Rutledge, Lloyd 411(2), 412(2)
Rutledge, Martha (Mrs) 411(2)
Rutledge, Richard 411(2)
Rutledge, Thomas 411(2)
Rutledge, William 112, 411(2)
Rutter, (Miss) 298
Ryan, Ann 128
Ryan, Charles 250
Ryan, Charles (Sir) 250
Ryan, Edmund 128
Ryan, Jeremiah 96
Ryan, Maria 149
Ryan, Marian (Mrs) 250
Ryan, Thomas 412(2)
Ryder, Dudley 288
Ryland, Archer 317
Rymes, Elizabeth 361
Ryrie, William 455(2)
Sadleir, Ann (Mrs) 414(2)
Sadleir, James 414(2)
Sadleir, Richard 414(2), 432(2)
Saggars, Mary 340
St Barbe, John 357

St Bernard of Clairvaux 544(2)
St Clair, (General) 275
St Leonards, (Lord) 392
St Vincent, (Earl of) 567
St Vincent, (Lord) 47(2)
Sainthill, Frances 345
Salaneta 422(2)
Saldanhade, Aires 358
Salisbury, Richard 167
Salmon, Charles Frederick
  415(2)
Salmon, Elizabeth (Mrs) 415(2)
Salmon, James 414(2)
Salmon, Joseph 415(2)
Salmon, Thomas 414(2), 415(2)
Salting, George 415(2)
Salting, Louise Augusta (Mrs)
  415(2)
Salting, Severin Kanute 392(2),
  415(2)
Salting, William 415(2)
Salvado, Dom Rosendo 147
Salvado, Peter 416(2)
Salvado, Rosendo 416(2)
Salvado, Rrancisca Rotea
  416(2)
Salvin, Osbert 363(2)
Sams, Augusta 182(2)
Sams, W.G.G. 4
Samson, Frances (Mrs) 417(2)
Samson, Lionel 417(2)
Samson, Michael 417(2)
Samson, William 417(2)
Samuel, Lydia (Mrs) 143(2)
Samuel, Sampson 143(2)
Samuel, Saul (Sir) 143(2)
Sandham, Augusta Catherine
  Anne (Mrs) 595(2)
Sandham, Henry 595(2)
Sandilands, James (Sir) 541(2)
Sandon, (Lord) 455
Sandwich, (Earl of) 52, 404,
  246(2)
Santos, (convict) 368
Sapieha, (Prince of Poland)
  494(2)
Sargent, Anna Maria 506(2)
Sargent, Robert 506(2)
Sargood, F.J. 84(2)
Satge, Oscar de 233(2)
Satterthwaite, Mary 124
Saumarez, (naval commander)
  538
Saunders, Elizabeth (Mrs)
  418(2)
Saunders, John 418(2)
Savage, Arthur 418(2)
Savage, John (Surgeon) 12(2),
  419(2)
Savage, Rebecca 43
Savery, Catherine 249
Savery, Eliza (Mrs) 420(2)
Savery, Eliza Elliott (Mrs)
  419(2)
Savery, Henry 459, 67(2),
  176(2), 221(2), 246(2), 247(2),
  419(2), 518(2), 576(2)
Savery, Henry Oliver 419(2)
Savery, John 419(2)
Savery, William (Rev) 249
Saward, (sugar refiner) 419(2)
Saxony, (King of) 474(2)

Sayce, 285(2)
Scamble, John 520
Schaeffer (Schaffer), Philip
  420(2)
Schaffer, Elizabeth 420(2)
Schaffer, Margaret (Mrs)
  420(2)
Schaffer, Philip 4(2), 420(2)
Schaffer (Schaeffer), Philip
  420(2)
Schanck, John (Capt) 468
Schaw, (Major) 436(2)
Schaw, Anne Frances 207(2)
Schaw, Anne Frances (Mrs)
  207(2)
Schaw, Charles 421(2)
Schaw, Charles (Major) 207(2),
  436(2)
Schaw, Frances Sarah 436(2)
Schaw, Sarah 421(2)
Schenley, E.W.H. 195(2)
Schmalfuss, 104(2)
Schmidt, 509
Schmidt, Karl Wilhelm Edward
  (Rev) 351, 421(2)
Schmittin, Anna Margaret
  222(2)
Schneider, Moritz 421(2)
Schoales, (Miss) 278(2)
Schoales, John 278(2)
Schofield, Ellen (Mrs) 424(2)
Schofield, Kezia (Mrs) 424(2)
Schofield, Martha (Mrs) 424(2)
Schofield, William 205(2),
  423(2)
Schofield, William (Rev) 138(2)
Schreiner, Gottlieb 351
Schreiner, Olive 351
Sconce, Edward 425(2)
Sconce, Elizabeth 425(2)
Sconce, Elizabeth Catherine
  (Mrs) 424(2)
Sconce, Madeline 425(2)
Sconce, R.K. 255, 198(2)
Sconce, R.K. (Rev) 162, 163,
  406(2), 484(2), 569(2)
Sconce, Robert Clement 424(2)
Sconce, Robert Knox 424(2)
Sconce, Sarah (Mrs) 424(2)
Sconce, Sarah Susanna 424(2)
Scott, 575(2)
Scott, (Admiral) 507
Scott, (Archdeacon) 35, 154,
  209, 169(2), 226(2), 368(2),
  414(2), 478(2), 510(2), 567(2),
  613(2)
Scott, Agnes Mathie (Mrs)
  430(2)
Scott, Ann (Mrs) 429(2)
Scott, Augusta Maria 429(2)
Scott, Augusta Maria (Mrs)
  237(2), 428(2)
Scott, Augusta Maria Frederick
  (Mrs) 237(2)
Scott, Betty (Mrs) 429(2)
Scott, Charlotte 431(2)
Scott, Daniel 425(2)
Scott, Daniel Henry 426(2)
Scott, David Charles Frederick
  428(2)
Scott, E.B. 363
Scott, Elizabeth 427(2)

Scott, Elizabeth (Mrs) 430(2)
Scott, Ellis Martin 426(2)
Scott, F. 449
Scott, Frances Harriet 426(2)
Scott, Francis 139
Scott, George 317(2), 429(2)
Scott, Georgina Caroline 543(2)
Scott, Helenus 428(2)
Scott, Helenus (Dr) 237(2), 428(2), 429(2)
Scott, James 140(2), 427(2), 427(2), 429(2), 431(2)
Scott, James (Admiral) 430(2)
Scott, James (Dr) 289, 467, 544
Scott, James (Serj) 105(2)
Scott, James Reid 430(2)
Scott, Jane Elizabeth 431(2)
Scott, Jane Elizabeth (Mrs) 431(2)
Scott, Jane (Mrs) 427(2)
Scott, Janet (Mrs) 426(2)
Scott, Johan 398(2)
Scott, John 487
Scott, Lucy Margaretta (Mrs) 289
Scott, Maria Jane (Mrs) 428(2)
Scott, Mary 431(2)
Scott, Mary (Mrs) 426(2)
Scott, Mary Anne (Mrs) 431(2)
Scott, Patrick 428(2)
Scott, Robert 428(2)
Scott, Rose 428(2)
Scott, Sarah Anne (Mrs) 428(2)
Scott, T.H. 169, 212, 315, 375, 393, 501, 537, 211(2)
Scott, T.H. (Archdeacon) 507
Scott, Thomas 57, 180, 360, 543, 36(2), 427(2), 429(2), 430(2)
Scott, Thomas A. 600(2)
Scott, Thomas Alison 430(2)
Scott, Thomas Hobbes 159, 431(2), 618(2)
Scott, W. (clerk) 263(2)
Scott, Walter (Sir) 333, 513, 161(2), 429(2)
Scott, William 352, 353, 543(2)
Scott, William Boxell 427(2)
Sea, Margaret 275
Seabright, Thomas (Sir) 19
Seal, Charles 433(2)
Seal, Phillis 433(2), 434(2)
Seal, Richard 433(2)
Seal, Sarah (Mrs) 433(2)
Seccombe, Elizabeth (Mrs) 434(2)
Seccombe, Ella Georgina 434(2)
Seccombe, Fanny Maria 434(2)
Seccombe, Sophia (Mrs) 40(2), 434(2)
Seccombe, William 40(2), 434(2)
Seckerson, Ann 350(2)
Sedgwick, (Prof) 29(2)
Sedgwick, Ann 592(2)
Sedgwick, Richard (Rev) 592(2)
Sellar, Robert 82
Selwyn, Elizabeth 403(2)
Selwyn, G.A. (Bishop) 163, 289(2), 570(2)
Sempill, H.C. 168(2), 195(2), 554(2)

Sephardi family 250(2)
Septima, Charlotte 534(2)
Serisier, Jean Emile 332
Serle, Esther Sarah 536(2)
Serra, (Bishop) 416(2), 417(2)
Serra, Dom Joseph 147
Serres, M.D. 160(2)
Servante, Emily Susan 335
Servante, F. (Comm) 335
Service, Jean 338
Sesa, (Duke of) 357(2)
Sewell, Martha 326
Seymour, Eleanor 218(2)
Seymour-Symers, Clementine (Mrs) 435(2)
Seymour-Symers, Thomas 435(2)
Seymour-Symers, Thomas Lyell 435(2)
Shadforth, Frances 435(2)
Shadforth, Frances (Mrs) 435(2)
Shadforth, Henry 435(2)
Shadforth, Henry John Tudor 435(2)
Shadforth, Mary Anne (Mrs) 435(2)
Shadforth, Robert William 435(2)
Shadforth, Thomas 435(2)
Shairp, J.C. 29
Shannon, John Campbell 311
Sharkey, Frances 553(2)
Sharland, Anne Jane 59, 436(2)
Sharland, Ella Georgina (Mrs) 434(2)
Sharland, F.B. (Rev) 434(2)
Sharland, Frances Sarah (Mrs) 436(2)
Sharland, Jane (Mrs) 436(2)
Sharland, John 59, 436(2)
Sharland, John Frederick 436(2)
Sharland, Margaret (Mrs) 436(2)
Sharland, Mary (Mrs) 436(2)
Sharland, Mary Jane (Mrs) 436(2)
Sharland, Sarah (Mrs) 421(2)
Sharland, W.S. 282, 215(2)
Sharland, William 421(2), 436(2)
Sharland, William Stanley 59, 436(2)
Sharling, Mary 449(2)
Sharling, Thomas 449(2)
Sharp, (Miss) 322
Sharp, William 178(2)
Sharpe, R.B. (Dr) 466
Shaw, (map maker) 520
Shaw, (pastoralist) 479(2)
Shaw, Ann (Mrs) 438(2)
Shaw, George 437(2)
Shaw, Harriet 442(2)
Shaw, James (Sir) 500
Shaw, Jonathan 438(2)
Shaw, Mary 326
Shaw, Thomas 4, 75(2), 101(2), 437(2)
Shaw, Thomas (Jun) 438(2)
Shaw, Timothy (Rev) 437(2)
Shea, (Captain) 226, 237
Shea, Annie 295

Shea, John 294
Shears, James 369(2)
Shears, Mary Ann 335(2)
Shee, Martin (Sir) 629(2)
Sheehy, Ellen 348(2)
Sheen, Maria 319
Shelley, Elizabeth 321
Shelley, Elizabeth (Mrs) 438(2)
Shelley, George 439(2)
Shelley, Lucy 205(2)
Shelley, P.B. 376(2), 620(2)
Shelley, Susanna Marsden (Mrs) 522
Shelley (Shelly), William 438(2)
Shelley, William 253, 321, 518, 522, 95(2), 205(2), 439(2)
Shelly (Shelley), William 438(2)
Shenton, Ann Catherina (Mrs) 440(2)
Shenton, Anna Marie (Mrs) 439(2)
Shenton, Charlotte Elizabeth Vigors (Mrs) 122(2)
Shenton, Edward 122(2), 440(2)
Shenton, Ernest 440(2)
Shenton, George 439(2), 440(2)
Shenton, George (Jun) 439(2)
Shenton, William 439(2)
Shenton, William Kernot 439(2)
Shepheard, Eliza Jane 69(2)
Shepherd, Ann 252
Shepherd, Isaac 252, 495
Shepherd, James 252
Shepherdson, George 440(2)
Shepherdson, John Banks 440(2)
Shepherdson, Marianne (Mrs) 440(2)
Shepherdson, Sarah Kelleway 441(2)
Sheppard, Bessie 201(2)
Sheppard, John 200(2)
Sheppard, Sherbourne 590(2)
Sherbrooke (Viscount) (Lowe, Robert) 134(2)
Sherer, John 444
Sheridan, R.B. 161(2)
Sherson, Georgina 500(2)
Sherwell, Elizabeth 547(2)
Sherwin, Amy 442(2)
Sherwin, Ann 409
Sherwin, Catherine (Mrs) 441(2)
Sherwin, Elizabeth (Mrs) 441(2)
Sherwin, George Green 441(2)
Sherwin, Isaac 441(2)
Sherwin, James 441(2)
Sherwin, John 441(2)
Sherwin, John Sargent 441(2)
Sherwin, William 112
Shipley, A.E. 556(2)
Shipman, Francis 406
Sholl, W.H. 6(2)
Shoobridge, Ebenezer 442(2)
Shoobridge, Harriet (Mrs) 442(2)
Shoobridge, Mary (Mrs) 442(2)
Shoobridge, Richard 442(2)
Shoobridge, Susannah 442(2)
Shoobridge, William 442(2)
Shore, John (Sir) 436(2)

Short, (Bishop) 7, 384(2), 465(2)
Short, (Captain) 408
Short, Joanna 598(2)
Short, Joseph 598(2)
Shortland, John 469, 442(2), 443(2)
Shortland, John (Lt) 571
Shortland, Thomas George 442(2)
Shortt, Francis 92, 93, 130(2)
Shuldham, (Lord) 281(2)
Shuldham, Mary 57
Shurtleff, Hannah 178(C)
Sibley, Anne 461
Sibly, Ann (Mrs) 281, 310
Sibly, Grace 280
Sibly, John 281, 310
Sibly, Margaret 310
Sibthorpe, Humphrey 52
Sibthorpe, John 73
Sidaway, Elizabeth 444(2C)
Sidaway, John 444(2C)
Sidaway, Robert 444(2)
Siddins, Jane (Mrs) 444(2)
Siddins, Joseph Richard 444(2)
Siddins, Richard (Capt) 36(2), 348(2), 444(2)
Sidney, John 445(2)
Sidney, Samuel 141, 444(2)
Sijgersd, Guerte 556
Silliman, Benjamin 279
Silliman, Harriet 279
Sills, Robert 597(2)
Silvester, Eliza Rebecca 505(2)
Simeon, Charles (Rev) 522
Simmonds, Ann 215(2)
Simmons, Charles (Dr) 236
Simmons, Joseph 68(2), 109(2), 161(2), 445(2), 626(2)
Simonov, Ivan Mikhailovich 83
Simpkinson de Wesselow, 306, 538
Simpkinson de Wesselow, Francis Guillemard 446(2)
Simpkinson, Emily (Mrs) 447(2)
Simpkinson, John Augustus Francis 446(2)
Simpkinson, Mary (Lady) 446(2)
Simpson, Caroline 164
Simpson, James 68, 164, 447(2)
Simpson, John 428, 251(2)
Simpson, Percy 111
Simpson, Roger 107, 158
Simpson, Sophia Ann 448(2C)
Simpson, Stephen (Dr) 145, 295, 344, 352, 448(2)
Simpson, T. Beckford (Capt) 7(2)
Sims, Hannah 89(2)
Simson, C. (Rev) 174(2)
Simson, Colin 409(2)
Simson, James 409(2)
Simson, John 409(2)
Simson, Robert 409(2)
Sinclair, J. 340
Singleton, Benjamin 560, 448(2), 618(2)
Singleton, Hannah (Mrs) 448(2)

Singleton, James 448(2)
Singleton, Joseph 448(2), 449(2)
Singleton, Mary (Mrs) 449(2)
Singleton, William 95(2), 448(2)
Skelmersdale, (Lord) 470(2)
Skelton, (Captain) 275
Skene, A.J. 520
Skene, Philip Wharton (Col) 531(2)
Skinner family 215
Skirving, 438, 218(2), 266(2)
Skirving, Rachel (Mrs) 449(2)
Skirving, William 126, 206(2), 312(2), 449(2)
Slade, Anna Eliza (Lady) 450(2)
Slade, Ernest Augustus 131, 450(2)
Slade, John (General Sir) 450(2)
Slaeger, Philip 365
Slater, Edward Bede (Bishop) 340(2), 341(2), 509(2)
Slater, Elizabeth 490(C)
Slatyer, W. (Rev) 23(2)
Sleeman, (Lieut) 57
Sloane, Anne 557(2)
Sloman, Amelia Tregenna (Mrs) 451(2)
Sloman, Samuel George 450(2)
Sloman, Thomas Martin 450(2)
Slyth, Maria 495
Small, Catherine Sarah 162(2)
Small, Francis (Lt) 162(2)
Small, John 291(2)
Small, Mary (Mrs) 291(2)
Small, Rebecca 291(2)
Smart, David (Capt) 548
Smeathman, Eliza 114
Smillie, William 433
Smirke, (artist) 253
Smirke, Robert (Sir) 409(2)
Smit, Detmer 173
Smith, (bushranger) 312
Smith, (Captain) 596(2)
Smith, Adam 184(2)
Smith, Ann 355
Smith, Ann Grant (Mrs) 486
Smith, Anna Louisa (Mrs) 452(2)
Smith, Anne Eliza 633(2)
Smith, Anne Margaret (Mrs) 452(2)
Smith, Arthur 452(2)
Smith, Charles 451(2)
Smith, Charlotte 106(2), 293(2)
Smith, Detmer 173
Smith, Dinah (Mrs) 252
Smith, E. 354(2)
Smith, Edward 150
Smith, Eleanor (Mrs) 452(2)
Smith, Eustace 452(2)
Smith, Eustace Alfred 452(2)
Smith, Frances (Mrs) 451(2)
Smith, Francis (Sir) 564(2), 593(2)
Smith, Gilbert Flesher 452(2)
Smith, Henry Gilbert 451(2), 453(2)
Smith, Henry Stinton 452(2)
Smith, Isobel 492(2)
Smith, James 312, 471
Smith, Jane 331
Smith, Jane Jeffreys (Mrs)

452(2)
Smith, Jemima Caroline 216
Smith, Jeremiah (Rev. Dr) 198(2)
Smith, John 57, 486, 532(2)
Smith, John 'Warwick' 455
Smith, John Frederick Sigismund (Sir) 33
Smith, John Galt 322
Smith, John William 253
Smith, Leny 184
Smith, Lewis 452(2)
Smith, M.L. (Capt) 32
Smith, Malcolm Laing 595(2)
Smith, Margaret 184, 308, 86(2)
Smith, Maria 357(2)
Smith, Mary 253, 352, 602(2)
Smith, Mary (Mrs) 532(2)
Smith, Mary Ann 262, 43(2)
Smith, Mary Ann Collis 410(2)
Smith, Maurice 221(2)
Smith, Penelope (Mrs) 453(2)
Smith, Philip Thomas 452(2)
Smith, Robert Hamilton 602(2)
Smith, Rosalie 301
Smith, Sarah 101(2)
Smith, Sarah Maria (Mrs) 453(2)
Smith, Susannah 396(2)
Smith, Sydney 193(2), 475(2)
Smith, Sydney (Sir) 47(2)
Smith, Thomas 16, 43(2), 451(2), 453(2)
Smith, Thomas Whistler 451(2), 452(2), 453(2)
Smith, Walter 201
Smith, William 216, 251, 252, 262, 101(2)
Smith, William (Sir) 406(2)
Smither, May Ann 95(2)
Smithies, John (Rev) 510
Smith-Rewse, Eustace Alfred 452(2)
Smith-Rewse, Gilbert Flesher 452(2)
Smith-Rewse, Henry Stinton 452(2)
Smyth, (Captain) 57
Smyth, (Major Gen) 142
Smyth, Arthur Bowes 453(2)
Smyth, Elizabeth Minton 301(2)
Smyth, P.J. 235(2)
Smyth, R. Brough 518(2)
Smyth, Sarah 392(2)
Smyth, Thomas 150, 263, 453(2)
Smythe, Benjamin 124(2)
Smythe, Martha 124(2)
Smythe, William H. 348
Sneyd, Caroline 136(2)
Sneyd, Thomas 136(2)
Snodgrass, Charlotte (Mrs) 250
Snodgrass, Charlotte Agnes 455(2)
Snodgrass, Janet (Mrs) 455(2)
Snodgrass, Janet Marion 455(2)
Snodgrass, John 455(2)
Snodgrass, Kenneth 265, 454(2)
Snodgrass, Kenneth (Lt. Col) 455(2)
Snodgrass, Peter 250, 455(2)

Snow, Samuel 431
Soanes, John Thomas 611(2)
Solander, Carl (Rev) 456(2)
Solander, Daniel 53, 403, 404, 456(2)
Solander, Magdalena (Mrs) 456(2)
Solomon, Abraham 444(2)
Solomon, Ann 458(2)
Solomon, Ann (Mrs) 457(2)
Solomon, Eliza (Mrs) 458(2)
Solomon, Emanuel 98(2)
Solomon, Frances 458(2)
Solomon, Frances (Mrs) 458(2)
Solomon, Isaac (Ikey) 457(2)
Solomon, John 457(2)
Solomon, Joseph 458(2)
Solomon, Judah 433(2), 458(2)
Solomon, Julia 99(2)
Solomon, Lion Henry 458(2)
Solomon, Mary 458(2)
Solomon, Moses 457(2)
Solomon, Samuel 444(2)
Solomon, Sarah 458(2)
Solomon, Vaiben 98(2)
Somerset, Charles (Lord) 129, 201(2)
Soper, Rebecca 296
Sorell, Elizabeth Julia (Mrs) 40(2), 462(2)
Sorell, Jane (Mrs) 459(2)
Sorell, Julia 30
Sorell, Louisa Matilda (Mrs) 459(2)
Sorell, W. (Gov) 94(2)
Sorell, William 30, 223, 240, 241, 242, 264, 270, 273, 274, 289, 328, 40(2), 459(2), 461(2)
Sorell, William (Jun) 462(2)
Sorell, William Alexander (Major Gen) 459(2)
Sorell, William (Lt. Gov) 24, 25, 76, 356, 360, 392, 421, 429, 492, 493, 542, 562, 566, 15(2), 40(2), 45(2), 49(2), 71(2), 121(2), 128(2), 133(2), 140(2), 159(2), 192(2), 215(2), 264(2), 267(2), 278(2), 300(2), 316(2), 319(2), 336(2), 366(2), 376(2), 396(2), 427(2), 462(2), 502(2), 564(2), 576(2), 577(2), 604(2)
Sorflitt, Susanna 42(2)
Sornay, Antoinette Genevieve 399(2)
Sorrell, (see Sorell)
Soulby, Sarah Ann 198(2)
Soult, (Marshal) 620(2)
South, James (Sir) 404(2)
Southam, Ann 359
Southcott, Joanna 625(2)
Southesk, (Earl of) 435(2)
Southwell, Daniel 462(2)
Southwell, Jane (Mrs) 462(2)
Spain, David 463(2)
Spain, Edward 149, 150
Spain, George 463(2)
Spain, Mary Elizabeth (Mrs) 463(2)
Spain, William 463(2)
Spark, Alexander Brodie 463(2), 554(2)
Spark, Frances Maria (Mrs)

464(2)
Sparrman, Andreas 404
Sparrow, John 444(2)
Speak, Julia 253
Speak, Samuel 253
Spence, (Surgeon) 273
Spencer, (Earl) 66(2)
Spencer, Ann Warden (Mrs) 465(2)
Spencer, Augusta 466(2)
Spencer, Eliza Lucy 477, 466(2)
Spencer, Herbert 364
Spencer, Mary Ann 124
Spencer, Richard 465(2)
Spencer, Richard (Sir) 477, 465(2)
Spengler, (Mr curator) 521(2)
Spicer, Charlotte 190
Spode, Josiah 466(2)
Sporing, H.D. 53
Spratt, Elizabeth 427
Sprent, Charles Percy 467(2)
Sprent, James 194, 251, 348(2), 466(2)
Sprent, Susannah (Mrs) 467(2)
Springer, Jan Meyndert 503(2)
Springer, Joanna (Mrs) 503(2)
Spurdon, Elizabeth 115
Spurdon, John 115
Spyers, C. 227
Squire, James 364(2), 467(2), 468(2)
Squire, James (Jun) 468(2)
Squire, Martha (Mrs) 468(2)
Squire, Mary Ann 468(2)
Stackhouse, Alfred (Rev) 26, 256, 468(2)
Stackhouse, Alfred Rashleigh (Rev) 469(2)
Stackhouse, Cecil Arthur 469(2)
Stackhouse, Ellen (Mrs) 469(2)
Stackhouse, Ernest Valentine 469(2)
Stackhouse, Frances Mary 469(2)
Stackhouse, Frances Mary (Mrs) 468(2)
Stackhouse, John 468(2)
Stackhouse, Melville Archer 469(2)
Standfield, Thomas 132(2)
Stanely, Owen (Capt) 577
Stanfield, (artist) 217
Stanfield, (Mrs) 67(2)
Stanfield, Alice (Mrs) 469(2)
Stanfield, Daniel 469(2)
Stanfield, Maria Kimberley (Mrs) 470(2)
Stanhope (Lord) 516(2), 518(2)
Stanislaus II (King of Poland) 279(2)
Stanley, (Dean) 285(2)
Stanley, (Lord) 345, 384, 385, 398, 405, 412, 446, 532, 286(2), 353(2), 470(2), 473(2)
Stanley, A.P. 436
Stanley, Catherine (Mrs) 470(2)
Stanley, Charlott Margaret (Mrs) 470(2)
Stanley, E.C. (Capt) 29
Stanley, Edward 470(2)
Stanley, Edward George

Geoffrey Smith 470(2)
Stanley, Edward Smith 470(2)
Stanley, Emma Caroline (Lady) 470(2)
Stanley, Isabella 315(2)
Stanley, John (Sir) 315(2)
Stanley of Bickerstaffe, (Lord) 470(2)
Stanley, Owen (Capt) 441, 546, 62(2), 167(2), 470(2), 543(2)
Stanton, Patrick 422
Stapylton, Catherine (Mrs) 471(2)
Stapylton, Granville Anson Chetwynd (Major Gen) 471(2)
Stapylton, Granville William Chetwynd 471(2)
Stapylton, Henry 471(2)
Stapylton, Martha 471(2)
Stapylton, Martha (Mrs) 471(2)
Staton, Mary 547
Staunton, George (Sir) 463(2)
Stawell, William Foster 91(2)
Stean, Janet 13
Stearn, W.T. 167
Steel, Margaret 137(2)
Stenhouse, N.D. 515
Stent, Anne 474(2)
Stephen, Alfred 36, 320, 411, 437, 164(2), 185(2), 247(2), 249(2), 320(2), 338(2), 395(2), 472(2), 478(2), 513(2)
Stephen, Alfred (Sir) 78, 87, 318, 616(2)
Stephen, Anne (Mrs) 474(2)
Stephen, Frances (Mrs) 436(2)
Stephen, Francis 436(2), 472(2), 478(2)
Stephen, G.M. 7, 244, 432, 540, 541, 482(2)
Stephen, George Milner 472(2)
Stephen, Harold 474(2)
Stephen, James 33, 34, 36, 47, 91, 130, 221, 317, 319, 347, 353, 354, 375, 385, 386, 393, 394, 395, 398, 434, 446, 452, 455, 478, 482, 526, 539, 541, 554, 151(2), 246(2), 247(2), 249(2), 334(2), 470(2), 474(2), 476(2), 483(2)
Stephen, James (Jun) 55, 393, 476(2), 628(2)
Stephen, James (Sir) 474(2)
Stephen, Jane Catherine (Mrs) 476(2)
Stephen, John 164, 312, 317, 393, 396, 472(2), 476(2), 478(2)
Stephen, John (Judge) 169(2), 204(2), 435(2), 436(2)
Stephen, John (Jun) 286
Stephen, Leslie 476(2)
Stephen, Mary Anne 435(2)
Stephen, Mary Anne (Mrs) 472(2), 478(2)
Stephen, Mary (Mrs) 541, 473(2)
Stephen, Samuel 378
Stephen, Sibella 478(2)
Stephen, Sibella (Mrs) 476(2)
Stephens, Alfred Ward 479(2)

Stephens, Charlotte Hudson (Mrs) 481(2)
Stephens, Edward 64(2), 480(2), 481(2)
Stephens, Eliza (Mrs) 479(2)
Stephens, Elizabeth 226
Stephens, Emma (MNrs) 480(2)
Stephens, John 480(2)
Stephens, John (Rev) 480(2), 481(2)
Stephens, John Raynor 480(2)
Stephens, Rebecca Eliza (mrs) 480(2)
Stephens, Samuel 16, 177(2), 481(2)
Stephens, Ward 102, 167(2), 305(2)
Stephenson, (Mrs) 13
Stevens, Mary 541(2)
Stevens, Rachel 193
Stevenson, George 540, 473(2), 481(2)
Stevenson, George John William 482(2)
Stevenson, Margaret (Mrs) 482(2)
Stewart, (Major) 25, 393(2)
Stewart, Ann 233(2)
Stewart, Donald 482(2)
Stewart, George 504(2)
Stewart, James 223
Stewart, James (Lord) 595(2)
Stewart, James Horne 483(2)
Stewart, Keith 387
Stewart, Keith (Mrs) 387
Stewart, Margaret 504(2)
Stewart, Margaret (Mrs) 504(2)
Stewart, Robert 498, 164(2), 397(2)
Stewart, Robert Pringle 220
Stewart, Susannah (Mrs) 397(2)
Stewart, Sylvia Anne (Mrs) 483(2)
Stewart, Thomas 626(2)
Stewart, William (Col) 55, 119(2), 482(2)
Stieglitz, Anne von (Mrs) 557(2)
Stieglitz, Catherine Christiana von 557(2)
Stieglitz, Catherine Christiana von (Mrs) 363(2)
Stieglitz, Charles Augustus von 557(2)
Stieglitz, Charlotte von (Mrs) 557(2)
Stieglitz, Christian Ludwig von 557(2)
Stieglitz, Emma von (Mrs) 557(2)
Stieglitz, Francis Walter von 557(2)
Stieglitz, Frederick Lewis von 556(2), 557(2)
Stieglitz, Frederick von 363(2)
Stieglitz, Heinrich Ludwig von (Baron) 556(2)
Stieglitz, Henry Lewis von 557(2)
Stieglitz, Hester Anna von (Mrs) 557(2)
Stieglitz, John Lewis von 557(2)

Stieglitz, Robert William von 557(2)
Stiles, Carter 483(2)
Stiles, Henry Tarlton 483(2)
Stiles, Jane (Mrs) 483(2)
Stiles, Mary Emma 484(2)
Stiles, Sophia (Mrs) 483(2)
Stilwell, Susan 308(2), 309(2)
Stirling, (Captain) 284, 325
Stirling, (Lady) 244(2)
Stirling, (Mrs) 236
Stirling, Andrew 484(2), 488(2)
Stirling, Anne 484(2)
Stirling, Anne (Mrs) 484(2)
Stirling, Charles (Rear Admiral) 484(2)
Stirling, Ellen (Mrs) 484(2)
Stirling, Frederick 488(2)
Stirling, James (Capt) 148, 164, 416, 123(2), 321(2)
Stirling, James (Gov) 230, 576, 426(2), 439(2)
Stirling, James (Lt. Gov) 174(2), 376(2)
Stirling, James (Sir) 176, 228, 236, 465(2), 484(2)
Stirling, Sarah 8
Stirling, Walter 488(2)
Stirling, Walter (Admiral Sir) 484(2)
Stoepel, Helen 568(2)
Stokes, Fanny Jane (Mrs) 489(2)
Stokes, Frederick 102, 167(2), 479(2)
Stokes, Henry 488(2)
Stokes, John Lort (Capt) 266, 470, 62(2), 488(2), 543(2)
Stokes, Louisa French (Mrs) 489(2)
Stokes, Mary 443
Stokes, R.M. 41(2)
Stone, Alfred Hawes 509, 489(2)
Stone, Charlotte Maria (Mrs) 489(2)
Stone, Edward 489(2), 555(2)
Stone, Elizabeth Theresa (Mrs) 555(2)
Stone, Emily 151(2)
Stone, Fanny 509
Stone, George Frederick 489(2)
Stone, Walter 266(2)
Stone, William 150
Stonhouse, Anne 38
Stonor, Alban Charles 489(2)
Stonor, Charles 489(2)
Stonor, Eliza Ann (Mrs) 490(2)
Stonor, Mary (Mrs) 489(2)
Storie, J. (Rev. Dr) 174(2), 542(2)
Story, Anna Maria (Mrs) 491(2)
Story, George 490(2)
Story, George Fordyce 249, 490(2)
Stow, Augustine 492(2)
Stow, Elizabeth (Mrs) 491(2)
Stow, Jefferson Pickman 492(2)
Stow, Randolph Isham 492(2)
Stow, Thomas Quinton (Rev) 443, 525, 201(2), 282(2), 491(2)

Stow, Wycliffe 492(2)
Stracey, J.C. 96
Stracey, John Charles (Capt) 96
Stracey, Charlotte Elizabeth 96
Strachan, Hugh (Jun) 492(2)
Strachan, Isobel (Mrs) 492(2)
Strachan, James Ford 492(2)
Strachan, John 492(2)
Strachan, Lilias (Mrs) 492(2)
Strachan, Louisa Anna 296(2)
Stradbroke, (Earl of) 400(2)
Strafford, (Earl of) 579(2)
Strahlow, Charlotte Sophie 102(2)
Strange, Frederick 470, 493(2)
Strathallan, (Viscount) 526)
Strathmore, (Earl of) 604(2)
Strathmore, (Lady) 317(2)
Streatfield, Frances Maria 287(2)
Street, James 230
Street, John 453(2)
Street, Maria Wood (Mrs) 453(2)
Street, Sarah Maria 453(2)
Street, Thomas George 25
Strickland, Harriet 21
Strickland, J.E. 21
Strode, Jemima Sarah 111
Strode, Thomas 26, 26(2)
Struth, (Admiral) 493(2)
Struth, Alison Hislop (Mrs) 493(2)
Struth, John 493(2)
Struth, Nathaniel (Sir) 493(2)
Strzelecki, Paul Edmund de (Sir) 414, 452, 453, 29(2), 49(2), 183(2), 355(2), 410(2), 494(2)
Stuart, Alexander 80(2)
Stuart, John McDouall 19, 498(2)
Stuart, Maria 236
Stubbs, George 314(2)
Stukeley, Simon 420(2)
Sturt, Charles 167, 284, 334, 362, 432, 466, 477, 565, 181(2), 292(2), 301(2), 306(2), 329(2), 365(2), 495(2), 497(2)
Sturt, Charles (Capt) 136, 376, 378, 419, 462, 117(2), 119(2), 473(2)
Sturt, Charlotte (Mrs) 496(2)
Sturt, Eliza 334
Sturt, E.P.S. 349(2)
Sturt, Napier George 497(2)
Sturt, Thomas Napier 495(2)
Stutchbury, Samuel 387, 29(2)
Sudds, Joseph (Private) 285, 394, 396, 235(2), 483(2), 571(2), 585(2)
Sugden, Edward 392
Sullivan, (bushranger) 308(2)
Sullivan, Benjamin 613(2)
Sullivan, Charlotte Albinia 613(2)
Sullivan, John 238
Sultan of Sulu 275
Summers, Charles 336(2)
Sumner, (Bishop) 159
Sumner, George Holme 552(2)
Surrey, (Lord) 532

Sutherland, (Duchess of) 448(2)
Sutherland, Alexander 161(2)
Sutton, Harriet 566
Suttor, (Mrs) 498(2)
Suttor, Francis Bathurst (Sir) 525, 500(2)
Suttor, George 54, 409, 213(2), 498(2)
Suttor, Sarah Maria (Mrs) 498(2)
Suttor, William Henry 500(2)
Swaine, Harriet 254
Swan, Elizabeth 223(2)
Swanbrooke, Thomas 110
Swanston, 9(2), 101(2), 250(2)
Swanston, Caroline 501(2)
Swanston, Catherine Elizabeth (Mrs) 291
Swanston, Charles 3, 68, 109, 291, 355, 164(2), 249(2), 500(2), 512(2)
Swanston, Charles (Capt) 361, 101(2), 223(2)
Swanston, Charles Lambert 501(2)
Swanston, Georgina (Mrs) 500(2)
Swanston, Kinnear 501(2)
Swanston, Laura Jeanette 164(2)
Swanston, Nowell 501(2)
Swanston, Oliver 501(2)
Swanston, Rebecca (Mrs) 500(2)
Swanston, Robert 500(2), 501(2)
Sydney, (Lord) 327(2)
Sylke, Ann 174(2)
Symers, Mary (Mrs) 435(2)
Symers, Thomas Lyell 435(2)
Symonds, Ann (Mrs) 458(2)
Symonds, Edward 458(2)
Symonds, Frances 458(2)
Symons (Captain R.N.) 156
Symons, (Lieut) 47(2)
Symons, J.C. 322
Synnet, Jane Elizabeth 200(2)
Synnet, Walter (Capt) 200(2)
Taber, Deborah 502(2)
Taber, Frances Sarah 502(2)
Taber, Frances Sarah (Mrs) 502(2)
Taber, George 502(2)
Taber, James 502(2)
Taber, Thomas 502(2)
Taber, Thomas (Jun) 502(2)
Talbot (Baroness) 502(2)
Talbot (Colonel) 172
Talbot, Julia 108
Talbot, Margaret (Mrs) 502(2)
Talbot, Richard 502(2)
Talbot, Richard Gilbert 503(2)
Talbot, Samuel Robdard John Neil 502(2)
Talbot, William 108, 225(2), 502(2)
Talfourd, Serjeant (Mr Justice) 437
Talfourd, T.N. 559(2)
Talleyrand, (French foreign minister) 267(2)
Tandy, Emily 501

Tanner, Jane 336(2)
Tanner, William 122(2)
Tasman, Abel Janszoon 503(2)
Tasman, Claesgie (Mrs) 503(2)
Tasman, Joanna (Mrs) 503(2)
Tate, Mary 12
Taylor family 401
Taylor, (actress) (Mrs) 611(2)
Taylor, (General) 33
Taylor, (Mrs) 611(2)
Taylor, Anne 299
Taylor, Catherine 441(2)
Taylor, David 504(2)
Taylor, Elizabeth 401(2)
Taylor, George 401, 504(2)
Taylor, Grace West 356
Taylor, Helen 166
Taylor, Henry 271(2), 470(2), 475(2)
Taylor, Henry (Sir) 353
Taylor, Herbert (Sir) 46, 404
Taylor, James 407(2)
Taylor, John 504(2)
Taylor, Margaret (Mrs) 504(2)
Taylor, Mary (Mrs) 504(2)
Taylor, Nancy (Mrs) 504(2)
Taylor, Robert 504(2)
Tayspill, Eliza 316
Teasdale, Margaret Mary 618(2)
Teast, Sidenham 107
Tegg, Caroline (Mrs) 505(2)
Tegg, Eliza Rebecca (Mrs) 505(2)
Tegg, James 337(2), 504(2)
Tegg, Mary (Mrs) 504(2)
Tegg, Samuel Augustus 504(2), 505(2)
Tegg, Thomas 504(2)
Teignmouth, Baron 436(2)
Telford, 106(2)
Telford, Thomas 504, 178(2)
Templeton, Andrew 400
Templeton, Janet 401
Templeton, Janet (Mrs) 400
Tench, Anna Maria (Mrs) 506(2)
Tench, Fisher 506(2)
Tench, John 506(2)
Tench, Margaret (Margaritta) 506(2)
Tench, Watkin 50, 150, 297, 312, 361, 403, 18(2), 506(2)
Tenerani, 589(2)
Tenney, Clarissa 607(2)
Tennyson, 415
Tennyson, Alfred 364, 221(2)
Tennyson, Frederick 221(2)
Tenterden, (Baron) 169(2)
Terry, Edward 126, 509(2)
Terry, Eleanor (Mrs) 402(2)
Terry, John 366(2), 402(2), 507(2), 509(2)
Terry, Leonard 70(2)
Terry, Margaret 366(2)
Terry, Martha 509(2)
Terry, Martha (Mrs) 507(2)
Terry, Martha Foxlowe 555
Terry, Mary Ann 126
Terry, Ralph 507(2)
Terry, Rosetta (Rosata), (Mrs) 508(2)

Terry, Samuel 41, 555, 575, 87(2), 402(2), 508(2), 548(2), 613(2), 618(2)
Tessier, Samuel 353
Theobold, Elizabeth 542(2)
Therry, Ann (Mrs) 512(2)
Therry, Eliza (Mrs) 509(2)
Therry, John Joseph (Rev) 75, 210, 241, 293, 504, 528, 165(2), 258(2), 270(2), 340(2), 341(2), 342(2), 343(2), 345(2), 432(2), 509(2), 513(2), 544(2), 553(2), 608(2)
Therry, John 509(2)
Therry, Roger 133, 231, 262, 394, 398, 25(2), 152(2), 265(2), 304(2), 337(2), 341(2), 378(2), 511(2)
Therry, Roger (Sir) 512(2), 544(2)
Thierry, Baron de 230
Thomas, (Miss) 498(2)
Thomas, Adele Zelee (Mrs) 521(2)
Thomas, Ann (Mrs) 514(2)
Thomas, Anna Jocelyn (Mrs) 516(2)
Thomas, Anne Margaret 452(2)
Thomas, B.B. (Capt) 170(2), 419(2)
Thomas, Bartholomew (Rev) 516(2)
Thomas, Bartholomew Boyle 516(2)
Thomas, Bartholomew William 516(2)
Thomas, Charles 515(2)
Thomas, Charlotte 518(2)
Thomas, Charlotte (Mrs) 516(2)
Thomas, David John 273, 514(2)
Thomas, E. 206
Thomas, Evan Henry 515(2)
Thomas, J. Davies 515(2)
Thomas, James Montgomery 516(2)
Thomas, Jocelyn 36
Thomas, Jocelyn Henry Connor 516(2)
Thomas, John (Rev. Sir) 477
Thomas, Louisa (Mrs) 516(2)
Thomas, Margaret Forbes (Mrs) 514(2)
Thomas, Marianne Burrell 516(2)
Thomas, Mary 218(2)
Thomas, Mary Ann 552(2)
Thomas, Mesac (Bishop) 198
Thomas, Robert 482(2)
Thomas, Sarah (Mrs) 516(2)
Thomas, Susannah (Mrs) 518(2)
Thomas, William 278, 514(2), 518(2)
Thompson family (of horsforth) 208(2)
Thompson, (Captain) 304(2)
Thompson, (Lieut) 568(2)
Thompson, (Private) 394, 396, 483(2), 585(2)
Thompson, Adam (Rev) 82(2)

Thompson, Agnes (Mrs) 519(2)
Thompson, Andrew 21, 87, 120, 383, 560, 59(2), 191(2), 194(2), 519(2), 580(2)
Thompson, Charles 395(2)
Thompson, Deas 446, 179(2)
Thompson, Eliza 68
Thompson, Henry (Capt) 178, 178(C)
Thompson, Isabella 178(C)
Thompson, Jane 612(2)
Thompson, John 313(2), 519(2)
Thompson, John Vaughan 235(2)
Thompson, Margaret 178, 367
Thompson, Margrett 178(C)
Thompson, Martha 608(2)
Thompson, Mary Ann (Mrs) 521(2)
Thompson, Patrick 285, 286
Thompson, Perronet (Col) 615(2)
Thompson, Richard 521(2)
Thompson, Sarah 216(2)
Thompson, William Fane 521(2)
Thoms, Christian 84(2)
Thoms, John 218(2)
Thoms, Marjory 218(2)
Thomsen, J.C. 349(2)
Thomsen, Margaret 349(2)
Thomsen, William (Dr) 349(2)
Thomson, 373, 35(2)
Thomson, (Dr) 331
Thomson, Adam Compton 521(2)
Thomson, Alexander 70, 272, 522(2)
Thomson, Alexander (Dr) 232, 330, 424
Thomson, Alice 527(2)
Thomson, Anne Maria (Mrs) 523(2)
Thomson, Barbara (Mrs) 522(2)
Thomson, Catherine (Mrs) 528(2)
Thomson, Deas 97, 385, 387, 378(2), 463(2)
Thomson, Edward Deas 133, 184, 385, 1(2), 181(2), 554(2), 589(2)
Thomson, Edward Deas (Sir) 523(2)
Thomson, Eliza (Mrs) 300(2), 527(2)
Thomson, Fanny 527(2)
Thomson, James 7, 109, 574, 118(2), 530(2)
Thomson, James Alexander 217, 300(2), 527(2)
Thomson, John Deas (Sir) 523(2)
Thomson, Joseph 527(2)
Thomson, Marion 200(2)
Thomson, Rebecca (Mrs) 523(2)
Thomson, Susan 526(2)
Thomson, William 527(2)
Thorne, Mary Anne (Mrs) 242(2)
Thorne, Robert 242(2)

Thornton, Edward 44(2)
Thornton, Elizabeth 51(2)
Thornton, Henry 17(2)
Thornton, Samuel 39
Thorpe, Charlotte 307(2)
Threlkeld, 226(2), 600(2)
Threlkeld, Lancelot Edward (Rev) 103, 260, 279, 226(2), 528(2), 599(2)
Threlkeld, Martha (Mrs) 528(2)
Threlkeld, Mary (Mrs) 528(2)
Threlkeld, Samuel Joseph 528(2)
Threlkeld, Sarah (Mrs) 529(2)
Throsby, Betsey (Mrs) 531(2C)
Throsby, Charles 263, 564, 147(2), 220(2), 530(2), 597(2), 633(2)
Throsby, Charles (Jun) 531(2)
Throsby, Jane 633(2)
Throsby, Jane (Mrs) 531(2)
Throsby, John 530(2)
Tibbs, Anne 105
Tickfold, Mary 5
Tiercx, Joanna 503(2)
Tierney, D.J. 534
Tilley, Thomas 124
Tilney, Anna Maria 248
Tims, Martin 77, 71(2), 531(2)
Tinnock, Jannette 596(2)
Tippahee (Maori chief) 170
Tippoo, Sahib 527
Tippoo Sultan 188(2)
Tittle, Margaret 169
Tod, Isabel 92
Todd, William (or Andrew) 68
Tom, Ann 532(2)
Tom, Annie 533(2)
Tom, Henry 532(2)
Tom, John 532(2)
Tom, Mary 532(2)
Tom, Nicholas 532(2)
Tom, Selina 533(2)
Tom, Wesley 532(2)
Tom, William 532(2)
Tomline, (Bishop) 158
Tompson, Charles 514, 559, 533(2)
Tompson, Charles (Jun) 422
Tompson, Elizabeth (Mrs) 533(2)
Tompson, Hannah (Mrs) 533(2)
Tondeur, Francis Oscar 138(2)
Toosey, Charlotte (Mrs) 534(2)
Toosey, Elizabeth (Mrs) 533(2)
Toosey, James Bramall 533(2)
Toosey, James Denton 533(2)
Toosey, James Denton (Jun) 534(2)
Toosey, Philip (Rev) 533(2)
Tooth, Robert 108(2)
Topp, Jane 394(2)
Torless, H.B. 530
Torrens, 380
Torrens, (Colonel) 482(2)
Torrens, Charity (Mrs) 536(2)
Torrens, Elizabeth (Mrs) 534(2)
Torrens, Esther Sarah (Mrs) 536(2)
Torrens, Robert 15, 166, 354,

434, 534(2), 560(2)
Torrens, Robert (Col) 379, 431, 445, 481
Torrens, Robert Richard 179, 435(2), 482(2), 536(2)
Torres, Luis Vaez de 276, 536(2)
Torrington, (4th Viscount) 407(2)
Torrington, Georgiana Elizabeth 407(2)
Towns, Robert 201, 221
Townsend, Mary Thompson 356
Townson, 403(2C)
Townson, (Lieut) 518
Townson, John 536(2), 537(2)
Townson, Robert 120, 536(2), 537(2)
Townson, Robert (Dr) 348
Traill family 614(2)
Tregurtha, Edward Primrose 538(2)
Tregurtha, Elizabeth (Mrs) 539(2)
Tregurtha, Mary (Mrs) 538(2)
Tress, 451(2)
Trevan, Betsy Alicia 226
Trevan, Elizabeth (Mrs) 226
Trevan, Matthew 226
Trevelyan, G.M. 31
Trigg, Amelia (Mrs) 539(2)
Trigg, Henry 539(2)
Trokes, Agnes Anna 65(2)
Troy, (Archbishop) 512
Truganini (Aboriginie) 14
Truro, (Lord) 627(2)
Truro, A.R. 490(2)
Truro, Eliza Ann 490(2)
Tuck, William 472(2)
Tucker, Fanny 540(2)
Tucker, James 539(2)
Tucker, James Rosenberg 539(2)
Tucker, James Stanyford 539(2)
Tucker, John 223(2)
Tucker, Louisa (Mrs) 540(2)
Tucker, Mary 392
Tucker, Thomas William 26(2)
Tucker, Valentine Kelso 540(2)
Tuckey, (Lieut) 238, 240, 517
Tuckfield, 522(2)
Tuckfield, (Rev) 303(2)
Tuckfield, Francis 540(2)
Tuckfield, Mary (Mrs) 541(2)
Tuckfield, Sarah (Mrs) 541(2)
Tull, John 67
Turnbull, Adam 530, 249(2), 541(2)
Turnbull, Adam (Dr) 220, 504(2)
Turnbull, Adam (Rev) 174(2)
Turnbull, Catherine 82
Turnbull, Elizabeth 507
Turnbull, Francis Moira 541(2)
Turnbull, George 82
Turnbull, Margaret (Mrs) 541(2)
Turnbull, Mary 19
Turnbull, Susan(na) (Mrs) 541(2)
Turner, (Captain) 41

Turner, Ann 438(2)
Turner, Ellen 559(2)
Turner, George 625(2)
Turner, J.M.W. 411(2)
Turner, Rachel 254(2), 595(2)
Turner, Sally 224(2)
Turner, Sarah 228
Turno, Aleksandryna (Adyna) 494(2)
Tuscany, (Grand Duke of) 69(2)
Twentyman, Mary 561
Twiss, Horace 485(2), 622(2)
Tyerman, Daniel (Rev) 275, 529(2)
Tyers, Charles James 112, 43(2), 542(2)
Tyers, Elizabeth (Mrs) 542(2)
Tyers, Georgina Caroline (Mrs) 543(2)
Tyers, John 542(2)
Tylor, Charles 46
Tyndall, (inventor) 520
Tyrrell, William (Bishop) 231, 262, 613(2)
Tyson, James 544, 532(2)
Ullathorn, William 544(2)
Ullathorne, 199(2)
Ullathorne, (Bishop) 199(2)
Ullathorne, Hannah (Mrs) 544(2)
Ullathorne, W.B. (Dr) 270(2), 608(2)
Ullathorne, William (Fr) 511(2)
Ullathorne, William Bernard 146, 185, 292, 341(2), 544(2)
Underwood, 131(2)
Underwood, (bushranger) 312
Underwood, Charlotte 547(2)
Underwood, Charlotte (Mrs) 548(2)
Underwood, Edward 547(2)
Underwood, Elizabeth (Mrs) 518, 547(2), 548(2)
Underwood, Frederick 548(2)
Underwood, James 61, 31(2), 32(2), 129(2), 348(2), 546(2), 546(2C), 547(2), 548(2)
Underwood, Joseph 120, 373, 485, 518, 1(2), 87(2), 547(2)
Underwood, Mary 547(2)
Underwood, Mary (Mrs) 546(2)
Underwood, Mary Ann (Mrs) 547(2)
Underwood, Richard 547(2), 548(2)
Underwood, Sarah 547(2)
Underwood, Thomas 546(2), 547(2), 548(2)
Unwin, Frederick Wright 613(2)
Upjohn, Rebecca 258
Upper Ossory, (Earl of) 407
Urquhart, George 107(2)
Urquhart, Mary (Mrs) 107(2)
Usher, Eliza Orde 33
Uthair, Maria del Rosaria Anna 74
Uther, Ann (Mrs) 549(2)
Uther, Eliza 555
Uther, John S. 611(2)

Uther, Maria (Mrs) 549(2)
Uther, Reuben 555, 130(2), 395(2), 548(2)
Uther, William 548(2)
Utterson, Louisa Harriett 573
Uxbridge, (Earl of) 76, 300(2)
Vaez de Torres, Luis 358(2)
Vale, Benjamin (Rev) 90, 256(2), 395(2), 550(2)
Valentijn, 13(2)
Valentine, William (Dr) 110
Valiant, Louisa 101(2)
Valiant, Thomas (Major Gen. Sir) 101(2)
Van Diemen, George 49(2)
Vancouver, Bridget (Mrs) 550(2)
Vancouver, George (Capt) 54, 56(2), 437(2), 550(2)
Vancouver, John 551(2)
Vancouver, John Jasper 550(2)
Vandermeulen, (Lieut) 126
Varley, John 160(2)
Varthema, Ludovico di 358
Vasiliev, Mikhail Nikolaevich 83
Vaughan, (Archbishop) 165(2)
Vaughan, Roger Bede (Archbishop) 44(2), 199(2), 347(2)
Vaughan, R.W.B. 337
Vaux, Daniel de 355
Vaux, Eleanor (Mrs) 553(2)
Vaux, Emily 261(2)
Vaux, Frances (Mrs) 553(2)
Vaux, Hardy 552(2)
Vaux, James Hardy 374, 60(2), 552(2)
Vaux, John 261(2)
Vaux, Louisa (Mrs) 261(2)
Vaux, Margaret de 355
Vaux, Mary Ann (Mrs) 552(2)
Vaux, Sophia (Mrs) 552(2)
Veale, Elizabeth 144(2), 154(2)
Veale, Grace 144(2C)
Veale, Richard 144(2C)
Venables, Ann 190
Venn, Jane Catherine 476(2)
Venn, John (Rev) 476(2)
Verco, Elizabeth 197(2)
Verco, James Crabb 197(2)
Verdon, George (Sir) 9(2)
Verge, Catherine (Mrs) 553(2)
Verge, John 96, 138, 142(2), 553(2)
Verge, Mary (Mrs) 553(2)
Verge, Nicholas 553(2)
Verge, Philip George 553(2)
Verner, Jane 234(2)
Victor, Anne Dashwood (Mrs) 555(2)
Victor, James Conway (Maj) 35(2), 38(2), 555(2)
Victor, Sophia 555(2)
Victoria, (Princess) 592(2)
Victoria, (Queen) 525, 279(2), 288(2)
Vidal, Francis (Rev) 555(2)
Vidal, Mary Theresa (Mrs) 555(2)
Vignoles, Elizabeth Anne 477
Vigors, (Mr) 122(2)

Villiers, 263
Villiers, Edward Ernest 354
Vincent, Francis (Sir) 195(2)
Vincent, Henry 601(2)
Vincent, John (Rev) 473, 523
Vines, F. 190
Viveash, C. Baskerville 271(2)
Viveash, Dora 372
Viveash, Samuel Waterman (Dr) 372, 122(2)
Vlamingh, Willem De 72, 556(2)
von (see also under main surname)
von Gillern, Wilhelm 301
von Humboldt, Alexander 403
von Jacquin, Baron Nikolaus 73
von Stieglitz (see Stieglitz)
Waddell, Isabella 212
Waddell, J.S. 3, 590(2)
Waghorn, Sarah 524
Wagner, Anna Catharine (Mrs) 422(2)
Wagner, Emily 447(2)
Wagner, George Henry Malcolm 447(2)
Wagner, Godfrey 422(2)
Wagner, Johann Gottfried 421(2)
Wainewright, Ann (Mrs) 558(2)
Wainewright, Eliza Frances (Mrs) 558(2)
Wainewright, Thomas 558(2)
Wainewright, Thomas Griffiths 558(2)
Wait, Benjamin 430
Wait, John 597(2)
Wakefield, (Captain) 123(2)
Wakefield, Arthur 559(2), 561(2)
Wakefield, Daniel 559(2), 560(2)
Wakefield, Edward 559(2)
Wakefield, Edward Gibbon 15, 128, 431, 433, 559(2)
Wakefield, Edward Jerningham 559(2)
Wakefield, E.G. 166, 461, 481, 539, 554, 576, 200(2), 261(2), 475(2), 514(2), 535(2)
Wakefield, Eliza Ann Frances (Mrs) 559(2)
Wakefield, Ellen (Mrs) 559(2)
Wakefield, Felix 559(2), 561(2)
Wakefield, Susan Priscilla (Nina) 559(2)
Wakefield, Susanna (Mrs) 559(2)
Wakefield, William 559(2)
Walbey (Warby), John 570(2)
Walch, James 505(2)
Waldron, (silversmith) 62
Waldron, John 87(2)
Waldron, Phoebe (Mrs) 87(2)
Walford, Benjamin 458(2)
Walford, Sarah (Mrs) 458(2)
Walker, (merchant) 485
Walker, Ann 421
Walker, Ann (Mrs) 565(2)
Walker, Anne (Mrs) 565(2)
Walker, Anna Elizabeth (Mrs) 564(2)

Walker, Archibald 566(2)
Walker, Eadith Campbell 565(2)
Walker, Edward 48
Walker, Eliza Cordelia (Mrs) 522, 566(2)
Walker, Elizabeth (Mrs) 562(2), 566(2)
Walker, G.W. 103, 192, 225, 249, 185(2), 216(2), 229(2), 441(2), 442(2), 529(2)
Walker, George Washington 45, 429, 441(2), 562(2)
Walker, Isabel 566(2)
Walker, James 566(2)
Walker, James (Rev) 421
Walker, James Thomas 565(2)
Walker, Janet (Mrs) 564(2)
Walker, John 224, 243, 246(2), 374(2), 501(2), 562(2), 563(2), 564(2)
Walker, John (Rev) 251
Walker, Julia 22, 566(2)
Walker, Julia Speke (Mrs) 564(2)
Walker, Maria Anne 7(2)
Walker, Mary Elizabeth 48
Walker, Mary (Mrs) 564(2)
Walker, Robert Thomas 563(2)
Walker, Sarah 222(2)
Walker, Sarah (Mrs) 216(2)
Walker, Sarah Benson (Mrs) 562(2)
Walker, Thomas 328, 275(2), 564(2), 565(2), 566(2)
Walker, W.G. 7(2)
Walker, William 24(2), 566(2)
Walker, William (Rev) 85, 522, 95(2)
Wall, Ann 510
Wall, Thomas 294(2)
Wallace, Alfred Russel 611(2)
Wallace, Catherine 174(2)
Wallace, Elisabeth 567(2), 568(2)
Wallace, Frances 269(2C)
Wallace, Helen (Mrs) 568(2)
Wallace, Isabella (Mrs) 567(2), 568(2)
Wallace, Wellington 567(2)
Wallace, William Vincent 124, 567(2), 568(2)
Waller, Hannah Maria (Mrs) 316
Waller, Kilner 316
Wallis, (Captain) 260(2)
Wallis, Anne (Mrs) 569(2)
Wallis, James 140(2), 568(2)
Wallis, Lucinda (Mrs) 568(2)
Wallis, Mary Ann (Mrs) 569(2)
Wallis, Richard 516(2)
Wallis, Sarah (Mrs) 516(2)
Walmsley, (bushranger) 312
Walond, Robert 21
Walpole, Bernard 125
Walpole, Robert (Sir) 447
Walsh, Anne (Mrs) 569(2)
Walsh, Isaac Richard 569(2)
Walsh, John 294(2)
Walsh, Mary 165(2)
Walsh, Sarah (Mrs) 569(2)
Walsh, Teresa 165(2)

Walsh, William Horatio (Rev) 425(2), 569(2)
Walters, Martha 139(2)
Wandi (David Bracewell) 326(2)
Warby, Sarah (Mrs) 570(2)
Warby (Walbey), John 570(2)
Ward, (Lieut) 428
Ward, Catherine (Mrs) 292(2)
Ward, Eliza Frances 558(2)
Ward, Elizabeth 428
Ward, Frances 560
Ward, Humphry (Mrs) 31
Ward, Janet Penrose 31
Ward, John 292(2)
Ward, R. Gerard 185(2), 186(2)
Ward, Susannah 389
Wardell, R. 148(2), 179(2), 256(2)
Wardell, R. (Dr) 319(2), 616(2)
Wardell, Robert 285, 318, 334, 395, 427, 570(2)
Wardell, Robert (Dr) 56, 74, 393, 478(2), 511(2), 585(2)
Wardlaw, Ralph 176(2)
Waring, Charlotte 42
Waring, James 301(2)
Waring, Jane 301(2)
Warland, W.H. 247
Warner, Sophia 618(2)
Warren, (Admiral) 443(2)
Warren, (Miss) 16(2)
Warren, A. 426(2)
Warren, Mary 283(2)
Warwick, (Earl of) 359
Washington, (President) 266(2)
Waterfield, Elizabeth (Mrs) 573(2)
Waterfield, William 572(2)
Waterhouse, (Captain) 46(2), 147(2), 309(2), 403(2), 420(2)
Waterhouse, (Miss) 574(2)
Waterhouse, Elizabeth 65
Waterhouse, Henry 64, 65, 283(2), 573(2)
Waterhouse, Susanna (Mrs) 573(2)
Waterhouse, William 573(2)
Watkins, John (Rev) 6
Watlin, Ham 574(2)
Watling, Thomas 238, 88(2), 574(2), 594(2)
Watson, Bridget 497
Watson, F.B. 161(2)
Watson, George 522(2)
Watson, Henry 497
Watson, James 13, 572(C)
Watson, John 224, 303, 572
Watson, Lucy 13
Watson, Robert 575(2)
Watson, Sydney Jamieson 451(2)
Watson, William 279
Watson, William (Rev) 509
Watt, (Scottish engineer) 306
Watt, J.B. 442
Watt, Sarah 383(2)
Watt, Thomas (Capt) 383(2)
Watt, William 216, 265(2), 304(2), 479(2)
Watts, J. 448(2)
Waugh, D.L. 58

Webb family 321
Webb, Ann 470
Webb, Charles 70(2)
Webb, Edmund 533(2)
Webb, P.B. 69(2)
Webb, Robert 4(2), 420(2)
Webb, Selina (Mrs) 533(2)
Webber, (bushranger) 312
Webster, A.G. 218
Wedge, 175
Wedge, Charles 575(2)
Wedge, Edward 575(2)
Wedge, Elizabeth 282
Wedge, John Helder 68, 174, 194, 282, 411, 73(2), 133(2), 539(2), 575(2)
Wedge, Maria Medland (Mrs) 576(2)
Wedgwood, Emma 287
Wedgwood, Josiah 286
Wedgwood, Susannah 286
Wedikind, (Major) 281(2)
Wedikind, Johanna Francina Carolina 281(2)
Weekes, Hannah 412
Weire, William 70
Weiss, Anna Catharine 422(2)
Welch, D.L. 505(2)
Weld, (Cardinal) 544(2)
Weld, (Gov) 509, 75(2), 391(2)
Weld, Frederick Aloysius 479
Wellesley, Arthur 151
Wellesley, Arthur (Sir) 190(2)
Wellington, 285, 116(2)
Wellington, (Duchess of) 159
Wellington, (Duke of) 46, 116, 159, 178, 285, 562, 124(2), 190(2), 194(2), 245(2), 271(2), 309(2), 475(2)
Wells, Charlotte (Mrs) 576(2)
Wells, Samuel Pullen 576(2)
Wells, Thomas 561, 576(2)
Welman, Abigail 215(2)
Welman, Harvey (Maj) 215(2), 434(2)
Welsh, (Captain) 170(2)
Welsh, (Major) 116(2)
Welsh, Harriett Mary 73(2)
Welsh, J. (Capt) 596(2)
Welsh, James 577(2)
Welsh, John 577(2)
Welsh, John (Capt) 73(2)
Welsh, Mary (Mrs) 577(2)
Welsh, P.W. 70
Wemyss, W. 153, 323, 352, 23(2)
Wemyss, W. (Deputy Com. Gen) 76(2), 230(2)
Wemyss, William 324, 513, 69(2), 577(2)
Wentworth, D'Arcy 52, 89, 91, 112, 115, 116, 120, 137, 207, 218, 242, 263, 358, 458, 460, 558, 11(2), 13(2), 58(2), 96(2), 97(2), 140(2), 191(2), 227(2), 234(2), 243(2), 273(2), 291(2), 369(2), 370(2), 399(2), 477(2), 508(2), 579(2), 582(2), 598(2), 628(2)
Wentworth, D'Arcy (Jun) 582(2)
Wentworth, John 581(2), 582(2)

Wentworth, Martha 368(2)
Wentworth, Martha (Mrs) 579(2)
Wentworth, Sarah (Mrs) 589(2)
Wentworth, W.C. 4, 5, 56, 74, 113, 116, 130, 153, 216, 248, 260, 285, 286, 293, 305, 315, 318, 336, 343, 344, 387, 389, 396, 447, 449, 463, 514, 526, 542, 543, 549, 11(2), 22(2), 41(2), 77(2), 96(2), 135(2), 142(2), 148(2), 150(2), 151(2), 152(2), 153(C), 160(2), 162(2), 172(2), 179(2), 181(2), 204(2), 216(2), 228(2), 233(2), 243(2), 256(2), 257(2), 275(2), 284(2), 335(2), 368(2), 511(2), 524(2), 525(2), 570(2), 571(2), 572(2), 581(2), 609(2), 614(2), 630(2)
Wentworth, William 579(2)
Wentworth, William Charles 3, 393, 427, 582(2), 605(2)
Wentworth Dillon 579(2)
Wentworth Woodhouse, Robert of 579(2)
Were, Arthur Bonville 590(2)
Were, Elizabeth (Mrs) 589(2)
Were, Frances (Mrs) 589(2)
Were, Francis Wellington 590(2)
Were, George 590(2)
Were, Jonathan binns 252(2), 589(2), 603(2)
Were, Jonathan Henry 590(2)
Were, Louisa 361
Were, Nicholas 589(2), 590(2C)
Were, Sophia Mullet (Mrs) 589(2)
Wesley, Charles 262
Wesley, John 261, 534, 333(2)
West, (Dr) 112
West, (Major) 312
West, Absalom 365
West, Ann (Mrs) 590(2)
West, John 48, 125, 239, 316, 351(2), 517(2), 590(2)
West, John (Rev) 3, 169, 81(2), 298(2), 350(2), 593(2)
West, John Beatty 185
West, Narcissa Sarah (Mrs) 590(2)
West, William (Rev) 590(2)
Westall, Ann (Mrs) 592(2)
Westall, Benjamin 592(2)
Westall, Martha (Mrs) 592(2)
Westall, Richard 592(2)
Westall, Robert 592(2)
Westall, W. (Rev) 592(2)
Westall, William 592(2)
Westgarth, William 350
Westlake, Mary 126
Weston, Ann Elphinstone (Mrs) 593(2)
Weston, Edward 593(2)
Weston, John 593(2)
Weston, Maurice 594(2)
Weston, William Pritchard 133(2), 593(2)
Wettenhall family 539(2)
Whateley, (Archbishop) 97
Whately, Richard 477

Wheatstone, 295
Wheeler, (Dr) (Surgeon) 295
Wheeler, Elizabeth 201(2)
Whistler, Eleanor 452(2)
Whistler, Penelope 453(2)
Whitaker, M.J. 159(2)
White, (apprentice boy) 262(2)
White, Andrew Douglass 595(2)
White, Augusta Catherine Anne 595(2)
White, Clara Christians 595(2)
White, G.B. 280, 332
White, Henry (Sir) 463(2)
White, John 27, 51, 157, 242, 403, 437(2), 506(2), 574(2), 594(2), 621(2)
White, John (Surgeon Gen) 88(2), 312(2)
White, Mary Elizabeth 463(2)
White, Mary Louisa (Mrs) 72(2)
White, Rachel 67
White, Richard Hamond 595(2)
White, Thomas H. 72(2)
White, William (Rev) 274(2)
Whitefoord, Albinia Jane Martyn (Mrs) 595(2)
Whitefoord, Caleb 595(2)
Whitefoord, John 595(2)
Whitehead, Isabella 333(2)
Whitfield, Charlotte Maria 489(2)
Whitfield, Eliza 533
Whitfield, Francis (Capt) 533, 489(2)
Whiting, Anne (Mrs) 436(2)
Whiting, Edwin (Capt) 60, 436(2), 539(2)
Whitten, Sarah 463
Whyte, James 330, 476, 163(2)
Whyte, Jane 95, 597(2)
Whyte, Jannette (Mrs) 596(2)
Whyte, Sarah Oakes 163(2)
Whyte, Thomas (Capt) 95, 596(2)
Whytehead, Thomas 198(2)
Wickham, Ellen (Mrs) 597(2)
Wickham, Ellen Susannah 597(2C)
Wickham, J.C. 62(2), 448(2)
Wickham, J.C. (Capt) 267, 473
Wickham, John Clements 489(2), 597(2)
Wickham, Samuel 597(2)
Widowson, Henry 517(2)
Wiere, William 177
Wilberforce, William 33, 67, 200, 205, 298, 375, 394, 500, 521, 522, 17(2), 89(2), 191(2), 208(2), 210(2), 282(2), 474(2)
Wilbraham, Edward Bootle 470(2)
Wilbraham, Emma Caroline 470(2)
Wilcox, James Fowler 167(2), 168(2)
Wild, Elizabeth (Mrs) 598(2)
Wild, Joseph 531(2)
Wilde, John Plaisted 627(2)
Wild(e), Joseph 597(2)
Wilde, Thomas 627(2)
Wilkes, Charles 279

Wilkes, John 206(2)
Wilkinson family 303(2)
Wilkinson, Anne 381(2)
Wilkinson, F. (Rev) 198
Wilkinson, George 293
Wilkinson, James 74, 253
Wilkinson, Sarah Olivia 427
Wilkinson, Sophia 557
Wilkinson, Susannah 86(2)
Wilkinson, Thomas White 427
Wilks, Matthew (Rev) 599(2)
Wilks, William 275
Willard, Barbara 134(2)
William III (King of England) 89(2), 579(2)
William IV (King of England) 413, 228(2), 279(2), 433(2), 631(2)
Williams, Ann 272(2)
Williams, Ann (Mrs) 600(2)
Williams, Anne 335
Williams, Emily Agnes 321
Williams, Francis 200, 130(2), 598(2)
Williams, George 232(2), 613(2)
Williams, Hannah (Mrs) 599(2)
Williams, Isabella (Mrs) 599(2)
Williams, Jane 292
Williams, Joanna (Mrs) 598(2)
Williams, Johan 602(2)
Williams, Johan (Mrs) 601(2)
Williams, John 522, 529(2), 577(2), 599(2), 600(2), 601(2)
Williams, John (Rev) 522, 430(2)
Williams, John Chauner 600(2)
Williams, Llewellyn 601(2), 602(2)
Williams, Margaret 280(2)
Williams, Margaret (Mrs) 280(2)
Williams, Mary (Mrs) 599(2), 601(2)
Williams, Rhoda 601(2), 602(2)
Williams, Richard 335
Williams, William 280(2), 600(2)
Williams, Zephaniah 419, 601(2)
Williamson, (servant) 280
Williamson, (Acting Comm) 572
Williamson, James 380, 602(2)
Willis, (Judge) 26, 216, 512, 15(2)
Willis, Ann Susanna Kent (Mrs) 604(2)
Willis, Anne (Mrs) 604(2)
Willis, Annette Agnes 485
Willis, Caroline 501(2)
Willis, Caroline Johnston 169
Willis, Edward 501(2)
Willis, Francis (Dr) 602(2)
Willis, John Walpole 602(2)
Willis, Joseph 604(2)
Willis, Joseph Scaife 485
Willis, J.W. 103, 271, 319, 125(2), 342(2)
Willis, Mary (Mrs) 602(2), 604(2)
Willis, Mary Isabella (Mrs) 604(2)

Willis, Richard 169, 604(2)
Willis, Richard (Jun) 605(2)
Willis, Robert Bruce 604(2)
Willis, William (Capt) 602(2)
Willoughby, William 70
Wills, Cedric 606(2)
Wills, Edward 558, 373(2), 374(2)
Wills, Edward Spencer 605(2)
Wills, Eliza 21, 558
Wills, Elizabeth 605(2)
Wills, Elizabeth (Mrs) 605(2), 606(2)
Wills, Horatio 514, 605(2)
Wills, Horatio Spencer 558(C)
Wills, Horatio Spencer Howe 605(2)
Wills, Maria Medland 576(2)
Wills, Mary (Mrs) 495
Wills, Sarah 558, 370(2)
Wills, Sarah (Mrs) 605(2)
Wills, Thomas 605(2)
Wills, Thomas Wentworth 606(2)
Wills, William Charles 495
Willson, (Bishop) 221, 258(2), 270(2), 343(2), 511(2)
Willson, Clarissa (Mrs) 607(2)
Willson, Edward 607(2)
Willson, R.W. 293, 324
Willson, Robert (Bishop) 351(2)
Willson, Robert (Dr) 504
Willson, Robert William 607(2)
Willson, William James 607(2)
Wilmot, (Lieut. Gov) 8, 192, 552
Wilmot, John Eardley (Sir) 505
Wilmot, Juliana Elizabeth (Mrs) 554
Wilmot, Robert (Sir) 554
Wilshire family 291
Wilshire, Austin Forrest 609(2)
Wilshire, Elizabeth 365
Wilshire, Esther (Mrs) 609(2)
Wilshire, Helen Eliza 367
Wilshire, James 25, 353, 365, 162(2), 608(2)
Wilshire, James Robert 80(2), 609(2)
Wilshire, Martha (Mrs 608(2)
Wilshire, Thomas Matcham Pitt 367
Wilshire, William 608(2)
Wilshire, William Pitt 609(2)
Wilson, (Bishop) 30, 40, 521(2)
Wilson, (Captain) 252
Wilson, Barbara 82
Wilson, C. & F. 611(2)
Wilson, Charles 353
Wilson, Charles Algernon 612(2)
Wilson, Edward 50(2), 252(2)
Wilson, George (Admiral) 364(2)
Wilson, Henry Croasdaile 609(2)
Wilson, Isabella 442
Wilson, J.Y. (Rev) 112, 521(2)
Wilson, James 8, 612(2)
Wilson, Jane (Mrs) 612(2)
Wilson, Janet 238(2)
Wilson, Jessie 84(2)

Wilson, John 498, 610(2)
Wilson, John Thomas 610(2)
Wilson, Katharine (Mrs) 612(2)
Wilson, Lucinda 364(2)
Wilson, Margaret 188, 492, 493, 257(2)
Wilson, Martha (Mrs) 612(2)
Wilson, Mary 612(2)
Wilson, Ralph (Capt) 379(2)
Wilson, Robert, (Sir) 116(2)
Wilson, Samuel 101(2)
Wilson, Sarah 8
Wilson, Sarah Emma 109(2)
Wilson, Sarah (Mrs) 516(2)
Wilson, Susan Mary 364(2)
Wilson, Theodore Percival (Rev) 612(2)
Wilson, Thomas 59, 594(2), 611(2)
Wilson, Thomas Braidwood 612(2)
Wilson, W. 242(2)
Wilson, Wilhelmina 499
Wilson, William 16(2), 227(2), 516(2)
Wilton, Charles Pleydell Neale 613(2)
Wilton, Charlotte Albinia (Mrs) 613(2)
Wilton, Charlotte (Mrs) 613(2)
Wilton, Elizabeth (Mrs) 613(2)
Wilton, William (Rev) 613(2)
Winder, Ellen (Mrs) 614(2)
Winder, Thomas White Melville 548(2), 599(2), 613(2)
Windeyer, Ann Mary 615(2)
Windeyer, Ann Mary (Mrs) 615(2)
Windeyer, Archibald 614(2)
Windeyer, Charles 449, 614(2), 615(2)
Windeyer, Elizabeth (Mrs) 614(2)
Windeyer, John 614(2), 615(2)
Windeyer, John Cadell 614(2)
Windeyer, Maria (Mrs) 54(2), 615(2)
Windeyer, Richard 135(2), 615(2)
Windeyer, Thomas Mark 614(2)
Windeyer, Walter 614(2), 615(2)
Windeyer, William Charles 616(2)
Windham, William 128
Windsor, Eliza Ann (Mrs) 300(2)
Windsor, William Henry 300(2)
Wingate, Eleanor (Mrs) 402(2)
Wingate, Mary 176(2)
Wingate, Thomas (Maj) 402(2)
Winstanley, Ann 298(2)
Winstanley, Eliza 298(2)
Winstanley, Eliza (Mrs) 298(2), 299(2)
Winstanley, William 298(2)
Winter, Samuel Pratt 406(2)
Wintle, Henry Saxelby Melville 221(2)
Winwright (Wainwright), Mary

Ann 87(2)
Wise, Henrietta Babington 93(2)
Wise, Thomas 93(2)
Wiseman, 199(2)
Wiseman, Jane (Mrs) 617(2), 618(2)
Wiseman, Solomon 41, 617(2)
Wiseman, Sophia (Mrs) 618(2)
Wishart, James (Capt) 231(2)
Witchell, Sarah 145, 145(C)
Withering, William (Dr) 194
Withers, (Captain) 139(2)
Withers, Sarah 485(C)
Witmarsh, Mary (Mrs) 321
Wittenoom, Annie Fletcher (Mrs) 619(2)
Wittenoom, Charles 618(2), 619(2)
Wittenoom, Edward 618(2)
Wittenoom, Edward Horne 619(2)
Wittenoom, Florence Mary Teasdale 619(2)
Wittenoom, Francis Frederick Burdett 619(2)
Wittenoom, Frederick Dirck 618(2), 619(2)
Wittenoom, Henry 618(2)
Wittenoom, James Cornelius 619(2)
Wittenoom, John 619(2)
Wittenoom, John Burdett 433(2), 618(2), 619(2)
Wittenoom, Margaret Mary 618(2)
Wittenoom, Mary Watson 618(2)
Wittenoom, Rose Agnes 619(2)
Wittenoom, Sarah Elizabeth (Mrs) 619(2)
Wittenoon, Thomas 618(2)
Witts, John (Capt) 537(2), 538(2)
Wixstead, (Corporal) 213(2)
Wolfe, (General) 367, 431
Wolfe, Sylvia Anne 483(2)
Wolfskehl, William Ernest 237(2)
Wollaston, Edward 619(2)
Wollaston, J.R. 74(2)
Wollaston, John Ramsden 619(2)
Wollaston, Mary Amelia (Mrs) 619(2)
Wollstonecraft, Edward 92, 305, 360(2), 538(2), 620(2)
Wollstonecraft, Elizabeth 92, 620(2), 621(2)
Wollstonecraft, Mary 376(2)
Wood family 215
Wood, Anna Maria 396(2)
Wood, Charles Alexander 354
Wood, Eliza 407
Wood, George Napoleon 150
Wood, Isaac 209, 495(2)
Wood, James Boteler 396(2)
Wood, Mark (Sir) 562(C)
Wood, Patrick (Capt) 297(2), 408(2), 409(2)
Wood, Thomas (Sir) 562
Woodbury, Richard 31(2)

Woodcock, Anna Maria 287(2)
Woodcock, Charles 287(2)
Woodcock, Samuel 257
Woodford, Alexander (Sir) 375
Woodford, J.A. 215
Woodriff, Allen 621(2)
Woodriff, Asia (Mrs) 622(2)
Woodriff, Daniel 621(2)
Woodriff, Daniel James 622(2)
Woodriff, George 621(2)
Woodriff, John 621(2), 622(2)
Woodriff, Robert 622(2)
Woodriff, Sarah (Mrs) 622(2)
Woods, Ann (Mrs) 622(2)
Woods, James Dominick 622(2)
Woods, Julian E. Tenison 622(2)
Woods, Roger Henry 622(2)
Woodward, Charles (Rev) 262
Woodward, F.J. 420
Woodward, Harriet (Mrs) 296
Woolf, Virginia 476(2)
Woolley, Eliza (Mrs) 623(2)
Woolley, Mary Honoria (Mrs) 623(2)
Woolley, Michael 623(2)
Woolley, Thomas 451(2), 623(2)
Woolly, Edward 393(2)
Woolner, Thomas 285(2)
Woore, John 306
Woore, Thomas 306
Wooreddy (Aborigine) 339
Wordsworth, Dorothy (Mrs) 246(2)
Wordsworth, William 374, 246(2), 464(2)
Worgan, George Bouchier 623(2)
Worgan, John 623(2)
Worgan, Sarah (Mrs) 623(2)
Worsley, (General) 360(2)
Worsley, Fanny Eleanor 360(2)
Worsley, Vaughan (Major Gen) 248(2)
Worsley, Jessy 248(2)
Worsley, St Helena 404
Worthington, Ann 204(2)
Worthington, Rosetta 279(2)
Wortman(n), Adolphus 623(2)
Wortman(n), Ignatz 623(2)
Wray, (Chief Justice) 603(2)
Wright, (Captain) 556
Wright, (Dr) 261(2)
Wright, Arthur Bridges 122(2)
Wright, C. 230
Wright, Charles 625(2)
Wright, Edward 624(2)
Wright, George 48(2)
Wright, Jane 360(2)
Wright, Janet 455(2)
Wright, Mary Ellen Landor (Mrs) 122(2)
Wright, Stephen 430, 431
Wright, W.H. 410(2)
Wroe, John 625(2)
Wroe, Mary (Mrs) 625(2)
Wullati (Aborigine) 337
Wyatt, Joseph 446(2), 625(2)
Wyatt, Richard 626(2)
Wyatt, William 626(2)
Wyld, James 240(2)

Wylde, Elizabeth Jane (Mrs) 627(2)
Wylde, John 91, 153, 323, 373, 374, 375, 426, 427, 176(2)
Wylde, John (Deputy Judge Adv) 561, 254(2)
Wylde, John (Judge Advocate) 358, 128(2), 157(2), 243(2), 581(2)
Wylde, John (Sir) 158, 184, 393 463, 500, 627(2)
Wylde, Mary Anne (Mrs) 627(2)
Wylde, Thomas 105(2), 256(2), 627(2)
Wylie (Aborigine) 363, 629(2)
Wyndham, (Mrs) 56
Wyndham, George 630(2)
Wyndham, Letitia (Mrs) 630(2)
Wyndham, Margaret (Mrs) 630(2), 631(2)
Wyndham, William 630(2)
Wynes, Temperance 288
Wynne Williams family 506(2)
Wynton, Marion 252(2)
Wynyard, Edward Buckley (Major Gen) 295(2), 631(2)
Wynyard, William (Lt. Gen) 631(2)
Wyon, W. (engraver) 123
Wyse, William 350
Ximenes, Ann (Mrs) 298(2)
Yagan (Aborigine) 632(2)
Yarnton, George S. 256(2)
Yates, Frances 189
Yates (Yeats), Mary 337
Yeates, Ann 239
Yeates, George 239
Yeo, T.R. 242(2)
Yeranibe (Aborigine) 234
York, (Duke of) 282, 573, 163(2), 189(2), 245(2), 316(2), 500(2), 604(2)
Yorke, Mary Jemima (Lady) 456
Yorke, Philip (Earl of Hardwicke) 456
Youl, Jane (Mrs) 632(2)
Youl, John 168, 260, 352, 353, 67(2), 527(2), 632(2)
Youl, John (Rev) 521
Young, (Gov) 339(2), 527(2)
Young, (Lt. Gov) 378
Young, Adolphus 633(2)
Young, Alexander 555(2)
Young, Anna Marie 439(2)
Young, Anne 271(2)
Young, Anne Dashwood 555(2)
Young, Anne Eliza (Mrs) 633(2)
Young, Dorothea Agatha 123(2C)
Young, Ellen (Mrs) 40(2)
Young, Fox 183
Young, Fox (Lt. Gov) 421(2)
Young, George 541(2)
Young, George (Sir) 235
Young, Henry (Lt. Gov) 508
Young, Henry Fox (Sir) 384(2)
Young, James 553(2)
Young, James Henry 40(2)
Young, Jane (Mrs) 633(2)

Young, John (Baron Lisgar) 428(2)
Young, John Adolphus 633(2)
Young, Margaret 541(2)
Young, Mary (Mrs) 634(2)
Young, Norwood 273(2)
Young, Thomas 247(2)
Yule, (landowner) 372
Yule, Benjamin 140
Yule, Charles (Lt) 111
Yule, Janet 140
Yuranigh (Aborigine) 634(2)
Zach, Franz Xavier de (Baron) 403(2)
Zastel, De (Spanish merchant) 620(2)
Zillman, Leopold (Rev. Dr) 423(2)
Zillmann, Johann Leopold 421(2)
Zouch, (Lieut) 269

Addenda — Names

Atholl, (Duchess of) 49(2)
Barry, James 42(2)
Boyes. (auditor) 416
Castlereagh, (Earl) 422
Coen, 13(2)
Collins, David 3(2)
Colnett, (Captain) 60(2)
Colville, Earl of 410
Cowper, Charles 26(2)
Dawes, (merchant) 24(2)
Derby, W. 415
Dighton, Robert 54(2)
Eckersberg, C.W. 27(2)
Edinburgh, (Duke of) 50(2)
Emma, Queen of Sandwich Is. 412
Enderbys (whalers) 53(2)
Fitzroy, (Gov) 7(2)
Forster, (politician) 26(2)
Foveaux, (Major) 57(2)
Fraser, (Dr) 416
Fyans, Letitia 423
Gawler, (Gov) 7(2)
George IV 11(2)
Goodwin, (editor) 417
Hahn, (Captain) 33(2)
Hoare, Harriet Jane 14(2)
Holt, Joseph 39(2)
Hongi (maori chief) 42(2)
Hume, (Supt) 10(2)
Huxley, T.H. 44(2)
Jeffcott, Harriet Jane 14(2)
Jones, (Captain) 15(2)
Lord, Simeon 45(2)
MacCormac, A. 65(2)
Nelson, (Lord) 16(2)
Nichols, Isaac 19(2)
Nichols, Rosanna 19(2)
Northumberland (Duke of) 22(2)
Parkes, Henry 26(2)
Paterson, (Mrs) 53(2)
Percy family 22(2)
Smith, (editor) 50(2)
Smith, (politician) 50(2)
Soames, (painter) 65(2)
Van Dieman, George 49(2)
Waikato (maori chief) 42(2)
Weston, (politician) 50(2)

Occupations

abbot: see Benedictine abbot
aboriginal guide 634(2)
absconder 294
accountant 445, 497, 100(2),
    176(2), 230(2), 257(2), 523(2),
    576(2), 598(2)
actor 355, 67(2), 98(2), 161(2),
    445(2), 498(2), 595(2)
actress 87(2), 298(2)
actuary 137(2)
adjutant 236
adjutant general (deputy)
    188(2)
administrator 297, 407, 5(2),
    124(2), 276(2), 383(2), 454(2)
administrator of charitable
    allowances 215(2)
administrator: see also public
    servant, civil servant, public
    official
admiral 83, 171, 258, 566, 99(2),
    326(2), 400(2)
admiral: see also rear admiral;
    vice admiral; port admiral
adventurer 306, 26(2)
adventurer: see also explorer
advocate-general 540, 174(2),
    200(2), 253(2), 278(2), 472(2),
    489(2)
agent 175, 252, 341, 356, 534,
    542, 110(2), 129(2), 131(2),
    283(2)
agent-general for emigration
    353
agent-general for QLD 23
agitator 469
agricultural superintendent 226
agriculturist 14, 63, 457, 541,
    7(2), 384(2), 531(2), 615(2)
aide-de-camp 11, 21, 33, 202,
    250, 303, 385, 464, 542, 3(2),
    116(2), 171(2), 223(2)
alderman 220, 261, 534, 547,
    51(2), 99(2), 268(2), 290(2),
    402(2), 557(2)
amanuensis 356
ambassador 11, 114(2)
anthropologist 577, 76(2)
antiquarian 488, 530(2)
apothecary 29, 64, 126, 134,
    314, 373, 74(2), 624(2)
apprentice boy 262(2)
apprentice (iron founder) 219
arbitrator 462(2), 510(2)
archbishop (Catholic) 340(2)
archbishop of Canterbury
    286(2)
archdeacon 254, 292, 472, 573,
    165(2), 211(2), 215(2), 619(2)
architect 23, 41, 96, 109, 217,
    224, 250, 304, 379, 426, 470,
    471, 504, 528, 9(2), 34(2),
    38(2), 64(2), 70(2), 73(2),
    112(2), 191(2), 213(2), 285(2),

290(2), 300(2), 325(2), 376(2),
    409(2), 414(2), 492(2), 527(2),
    553(2), 581(2), 607(2)
Arminian schoolteacher 260
army captain 371, 422, 431
army officer 296, 278(2), 536(2)
army officer, captain: see also
    soldier, officer
artillery officer 2, 233(2)
artilleryman 252
artisan 251, 252, 259
artist 18, 181, 123, 217, 339,
    348, 360, 365, 409, 419, 467,
    476, 538, 542, 88(2), 105(2),
    111(2), 123(2), 140(2), 160(2),
    212(2), 223(2), 353(2), 363(2),
    366(2), 367(2), 387(2), 389(2),
    409(2), 428(2), 446(2), 493(2),
    557(2), 558(2), 574(2), 609(2),
    612(2)
artist (female) 612(2)
artist: see also landscape painter
artist: see also miniature painter
artist: see also natural history
    artist
artist: see also painter
artist: see also portrait painter
art teacher 409
assessor 45(2)
assistant: see under main
    catagory
astronomer 52, 83, 298, 337,
    338, 403(2), 551(2)
astronomer royal 145
attache 182(2)
attorney 149, 218, 262, 360,
    373, 55(2), 75(2), 388(2),
    463(2), 516(2), 552(2), 572(2),
    633(2)
attorney's clerk 361
attorney's servant 361
attorney: see also barrister,
    lawyer
attorney general 55, 74, 168,
    231, 392, 393, 426, 476, 536,
    566, 51(2), 73(2), 91(2),
    143(2), 164(2), 201(2), 214(2),
    246(2), 247(2), 256(2), 314(2),
    337(2), 418(2), 482(2), 489(2),
    512(2), 516(2)
auctioneer 235, 246, 257, 301,
    355, 421, 490, 534, 542, 547,
    560, 16(2), 32(2), 55(2), 87(2),
    109(2), 113(2), 137(2), 142(2),
    280(2), 291(2), 401(2), 417(2),
    445(2), 451(2), 516(2), 611(2)
auditor general 350, 378, 5(2),
    119(2), 120(2)
Austrian consul 212(2)
author 26, 42, 97, 175, 181, 221,
    244, 267, 277, 376, 403, 444,
    15(2), 48(2), 74(2), 89(2),
    105(2), 111(2), 172(2), 201(2),
    221(2), 264(2), 268(2), 282(2),

352(2), 419(2), 426(2), 444(2),
    506(2), 552(2), 555(2C),
    559(2), 582(2), 590(2), 611(2)
author (colonial) 416
author of comic operas 228(2)
author (supposed) 539(2)
bailiff 276(2)
baker 352, 368-9, 84(2), 291(2),
    394(2), 444(2)
band sergeant 567(2)
bank manager 316, 451(2),
    480(2)
banker 3, 15, 290, 323, 338,
    349, 355, 485, 497, 500, 507,
    531, 105(2), 121(2), 122(2),
    151(2), 172(2), 196(2), 290(2),
    333(2), 365(2), 387(2), 411(2),
    419(2), 450(2), 453(2), 468(2),
    500(2), 510(2), 565(2)
Baptist minister: see minister
    (Baptist)
barrack master 7(2), 258(2),
    609(2)
barrister 55, 74, 128, 133, 196,
    198, 246, 393, 454, 476, 536,
    538, 541, 545, 74(2), 121(2),
    143(2), 164(2), 169(2), 224(2),
    283(2), 395(2), 446(2), 472(2),
    489(2), 570(2), 582(2), 615(2),
    622(2)
barrister-at-law 543, 564(2)
barrister: see also lawyer,
    attorney, conveyancing
    barrister
beachmaster 513
Benedictine abbot 473
Benedictine monk 416(2)
benefactor 565(2)
biographer 267
biologist 577, 167(2)
bishop (C. of E.) 158, 17(2),
    285(2), 470(2), 633(2)
bishop (Catholic) 146, 193, 292,
    504, 269(2), 340(2), 351(2),
    417(2), 607(2)
blacksmith 67, 294, 368, 207(2),
    216(2), 589(2)
bleacher 126, 51(2)
block-maker 365
boat builder 254(2), 362(2)
boatman 118(2)
boatswain 240, 62(2)
boatswain (dockyard) 575(2)
bookbinder 242(2)
book keeper 149(2), 257(2),
    602(2)
book merchant 504(2)
bookseller 317, 360, 474, 499,
    166(2), 204(2), 242(2), 379(2),
    504(2), 557(2)
botanical artist 73
botanical collector 377(2)
botanist 52, 98, 166, 176, 183,
    194, 215, 265, 267, 268, 269,

325, 416, 492, 530, 69(2),
  95(2), 223(2), 231(2), 239(2),
  244(2), 407(2), 485(2), 595(2)
botanist-explorer 119(2)
brassfounder 259(2)
brazier 252
brewer 59, 365, 428, 429, 24(2),
  314(2), 442(2), 467(2), 563(2)
brewer and distiller 269(2)
brewer: see also master brewer
brickmaker 313(2)
bricklayer 174, 264
bridgebuilder 106(2)
broker 149(2), 590(2)
brushmaker 528(2)
buccaneer 277
builder 49, 122, 249, 258, 304,
  352, 369, 9(2), 139(2), 300(2),
  325(2), 385(2), 539(2), 553(2),
  607(2)
builder: see also master builder
building contractor 527(2)
building superintendent 150
bushman 575(2), 597(2)
bushranger 147, 214, 293, 312,
  560
bushranger: see also General
  Index
businessman 3, 349, 31(2),
  40(2), 141(2), 147(2), 175(2),
  257(2), 283(2), 419(2), 453(2),
  519(2), 625(2)
businessman: see also merchant,
  company director, manager,
  trader
businesswoman 373(2)
butcher 179, 228, 70(2)
butler 552(2)
cadet 248
candlemaker 179, 398(2)
canon 256, 410, 472
captain: see army captain
captain: see post captain
captain's agent 129(2)
captain's clerk 289(2)
carpenter 12, 31, 74, 138, 149,
  251, 321, 521, 42(2), 139(2),
  187(2), 259(2), 271(2)
carpenter: see also house
  carpenter, master carpenter
carpenter's mate 621(2)
cartographer 358
cartographic surveyor 71
cartwright 224
cashier 76, 500, 533, 131(2),
  137(2), 172(2), 598(2)
castaway 123(2), 313(2)
catechist 220(2), 414(2)
Catholic bishop: see bishop
  (Catholic)
Catholic prelate: see prelate
  (Catholic)
Catholic priest: see priest
  (Catholic)
cattle breeder 124, 524
cattle dealer 178
cattle doctor 178
cedar getter 515
cellist 618(2)
censor 199
census collector 248
chairman: of directors 149(2)

— of quarter sessions 133
— of town trust 122(2)
— (deputy), Lloyds of London
  73(2)
— (deputy) of quarter sessions
  143(2)
chancellor 284(2), 470(2),
  526(2)
chancellor of the diocese 198
chancellor of the Exchequer
  456, 465, 136(2)
chaplain 49, 228, 252, 256, 260,
  347, 401, 469, 506, 518, 523,
  557, 42(2), 95(2), 165(2),
  207(2), 285(2), 349(2), 511(2),
  618(2)
chaplain (assistant) 262
chaplain (C of E) 351(2), 613(2)
chaplain (Catholic) 241
chaplain military (assistant) 77
chaplain to William III 291
chatelaine at Government
  House 387
cheesemaker 362(2)
chemist 134, 54(2), 439(2),
  490(2)
chemist: see also dispensing
  chemist
chief: assayer 296
— clerk 323
— clerk to Bench of
  magistrates 615(2)
— commissary of police 377
— commissioner of crown
  lands 349(2)
— constable 63, 106, 110, 241,
  511, 560, 248(2), 290(2),
  336(2), 458(2), 519(2), 520(2)
— district constable 12, 430
— engineer 376(2)
— justice 10, 99, 184, 244, 379,
  381, 392, 413, 14(2), 52(2),
  248(2), 489(2)
— officer 138(2)
— overseer of convict gangs
  283(2)
— police magistrate 219, 404-5,
  413, 580(2)
— justice of common please
  345
— secretary 262(2)
— secretary for Ireland 464
— surveyor of the navy 530
children's doctor 268(2)
churchman 82, 199, 261
city councillor 248
city treasurer 131(2)
civic leader 82
civil engineer 109, 188, 269,
  324, 64(2), 124(2), 376(2)
civil servant 155, 186, 530, 551,
  281(2)
civilian internee 116(2)
class leader (Methodist) 212
clergyman: 316, 506, 144(2)
— (C. of E.) 10, 48, 77, 150,
  156, 168, 211, 256, 261, 291,
  300, 311, 361, 401, 420, 436,
  520, 522, 537, 17(2), 198(2),
  207(2), 226(2), 311(2), 368(2),
  405(2), 424(2), 431(2), 468(2),
  483(2), 521(2), 550(2), 569(2),

602(2), 632(2)
— (Church of Ireland) 421
— (Independent)40
— (Moravian) 89(2)
— (Presbyterian) 327, 399, 472,
  499, 76(2)
— (protestant) 415
clergyman: see also bishop,
  chaplain, cleric, dean,
  minister, priest, rector
cleric 66(2)
clerk 14, 25, 42, 126, 149, 202,
  206, 216, 217, 218, 247, 254,
  265, 268, 300, 303, 313, 315,
  316, 323, 356, 376, 425, 494,
  547, 575, 23(2), 34(2), 51(2),
  71(2), 140(2), 178(2), 201(2),
  230(2), 333(2), 419(2), 576(2),
  599(2), 608(2)
— and constable of the Sydney
  Bench 273(2)
— of petty sessions 431(2)
— of the bench 381, 440(2)
— of the council 248(2), 276(2),
  523(2)
— of the court of requests 112
— of the crown 248(2)
— of the peace 356, 427, 495,
  396(2),490(2), 627(2)
— of the public market 291(2)
— of works 37(2), 410(2)
— to the judge advocate 254(2)
clerk: see also chief clerk,
  commissariat clerk, copying
  clerk
coach and chaise painter 574(2)
coachbuilder 467
coachmaker 15
coachman 217
coachmaster 457(2)
coach proprietor 257, 308(2)
coalmaster 188
coal miner 600(2)
collector of: customs 32, 38,
  197, 288, 372, 439, 475, 508,
  91(2), 192(2), 261(2), 399(2),
  415(2), 517(2)
— internal revenue 416, 508,
  563, 378(2)
— land fees and dog taxes
  219(2)
— quitrents 517, 219(2)
— taxes 204
colonial administrator 32
colonial agent 7(2)
colonial promoter 46, 320(2),
  559(2)
colonial secretary 97, 153, 168,
  228, 283, 378, 381, 385, 405,
  412, 413, 416, 463, 501, 559,
  3(2), 8(2), 91(2), 120(2),
  126(2), 156(2), 164(2), 178(2),
  248(2), 249(2), 250(2), 253(2),
  310(2), 473(2), 497(2), 523(2)
colonial secretary (asst) 512
colonial treasurer 23, 203, 206,
  350, 412, 413, 415, 416, 445,
  463, 474, 91(2), 113(2),
  120(2), 126(2), 131(2), 153(2),
  169(2), 225(2), 248(2), 265(2),
  349(2), 377(2), 498(2), 513(2),
  517(2)

colonization commissioner
534(2)
colonizer 195(2)
colporteur 252, 522
comedian 98(2)
comic performer 445(2)
commandant 49, 191, 197, 220,
223, 264, 127(2), 222(2),
260(2), 496(2), 506(2)
commandant of convicts 75,
125, 233, 273, 131(2)
commandant of native police
261(2)
commandant (Tasmanian
forces) 258
commander 47(2), 99(2), 213(2)
commander of Iron Gang 264
commander-in-chief (Black Sea
fleet) 99(2)
commercial agent 176(2)
commissariat clerk 126, 328,
125(2), 423(2), 472(2)
commissariat officer 25
commissariat store-keeper 524,
316(2)
commissary: 157, 292, 331,
229(2), 233(2), 308(2), 309(2),
564(2)
— (acting) 380
— (assistant) 322
— (deputy) 218, 365, 380, 405,
536, 52(2), 97(2), 232(2),
380(2)
— (deputy asst.) 247
— clerk 253
— general 578(2)
— general (assistant) 143, 562,
106(2)
— general (deputy) 5, 153,
69(2), 577(2)
— general (deputy assistant) 33,
247, 69(2)
— judge 182(2)
commissary: see also chief
commissary of police;
ecclesiastical commissary
commission agent 485, 55(2),
137(2), 516(2)
commissioner 67, 379, 356(C),
51(2), 74(2), 253(2), 598(2)
— (assistant) 228(2)
— for compensating West
Indian slave owners 372
— for reporting upon claims to
grants of land 196
— for taking affidavits 112,
376(2)
— for the Poor Law 133
— in bankruptcy 595(2)
— of affidavits 112, 376(2)
— of court of requests 168
— of crown lands 9, 112, 145,
448, 453, 331, 423, 492, 525,
160(2), 409(2), 447(2), 467(2),
471(2), 543(2)
— of crown lands and
immigration 280(2)
— of insolvent estates 168,
224(2), 462(2)
— of lands: see also chief
commissioner of crown lands
— of lands (assistant) 497(2)

— of land tax 455
— of police 288, 378, 228(2),
300(2), 301(2)
— of public works 525
— of public charities 228(2)
— of supreme court 495
— of survey and valuation
296(2)
— of works, roads and bridges
253(2)
commodore 233(2)
company agent 298, 440
company director 7, 504, 25(2),
38(2), 49(2), 73(2), 131(2),
435(2)
company manager 165, 269,
443, 61(2), 176(2), 481(2)
company official 511
company secretary 485
composer 233, 530, 566, 29(2),
416(2)
composer of church music
285(2)
compositor 515, 520, 534, 25(2)
comptroller 399(2)
comptroller general of convicts
220, 371, 493, 508
comptroller of steam machinery
316(2)
conchologist 168(2)
confidence man 127
Congregational lay leader
539(2)
Congregational minister: see
minister
congressman (USA) 548
connoisseur 283(2)
constable 214, 217, 264, 361,
383, 423, 430, 66(2), 27(2),
31(2), 71(2), 125(2), 159(2),
336(2), 348(2), 469(2), 570(2),
597(2)
constable: see also chief
constable
constitutional reformer 10(2)
consul 307, 212(2), 402(2)
controller general 405, 476
controller of medical services
427(2)
controller of railway accts. 497
convener 263(2)
conversationalist 181
conveyancer 184, 251(2),
395(2), 516(2)
conveyancing barrister 244
convict 31, 42, 48, 62, 67, 74,
78, 109, 123, 126, 144, 147,
170, 173, 178, 214, 215, 217,
218, 234, 240, 245, 246, 262,
264, 293, 294, 309, 312, 320,
328, 354, 360, 365, 368, 383,
430, 439, 468, 490, 491, 526,
527, 559, 560, 4(2), 19(2),
31(2), 36(2), 65(2), 86(2),
87(2), 95(2), 108(2), 110(2),
128(2), 132(2), 135(2), 139(2),
140(2), 141(2), 143(2), 159(2),
170(2), 206(2), 259(2), 266(2),
272(2), 299(2), 352(2), 373(2),
387(2), 404(2), 419(2), 444(2),
457(2), 502(2), 508(2), 539(2),
546(2), 547(2), 552(2), 570(2),

574(2)
convict: see also emancipist
cook 91, 215, 36(2)
cooper 245(2), 271(2)
copperplate engraver 230
copperplate printer 242(2)
copying clerk 436(2), 552(2)
corn merchant 190, 533(2)
coroner 19, 25, 149, 253, 365,
458, 500, 507, 551, 560, 566,
106(2), 111(2), 169(2), 214(2),
248(2), 256(2), 260(2), 267(2),
315(2), 365(2), 431(2), 434(2),
466(2), 482(2), 557(2), 595(2),
626(2)
cotton merchant 198(2)
councillor 370
county deputy lieut 38(2)
court registrar 202(2)
court councillor 403(2)
coxswain 192, 498
cricketer 533, 606(2)
critic 514
crown prosecutor 196, 427,
474(2), 490(2)
crown solicitor 149, 495,
165(2), 201(2), 256(2), 395(2),
472(2), 490(2), 627(2)
curate 10, 199
curate (assistant) 256
curator 279, 626(2)
curator of intestate estates
203(2)
customs officer 427, 125(2)
customs searcher 430(2)
customs waiter 430(2)
dancing master 506(2)
deacon 256, 260, 473
dealer 527, 371(2), 457(2)
dealer in machinery 528(2)
dealer in spirits 570
dean (episcopal) 257(2)
dean (rural) 256, 292
debt collector 356
diarist 143, 145, 225, 296, 349,
66(2), 106(2), 115(2), 160(2),
252(2), 354(2), 390(2), 427(2),
462(2)
die sinker 490
diplomat 595(2)
director of probation 414
director of public works 219,
35(2)
director of waterworks 220
dispencer 503
dispensing chemist 295
distiller 246, 137(2), 141(2),
546(2)
district constable see constable
doctor 189, 302, 69(2), 75(2),
284(2), 334(2)
doctor of medicine 314
doctor of music 623(2)
doctor: see also medical
practitioner, surgeon,
physician
domestic servant 263(2)
draper 42(2), 52(2), 153(2)
draughtsman 444, 538, 7(2),
527(2)
dressmaker 26(2), 259(2)
droget maker 283(2)

druggist 134, 44(2), 439(2)
dyer 519(2)
ecclesiastical commissary 533(2)
editor 3, 26, 216, 256, 355-6,
  369, 437, 462, 466, 474, 551,
  557, 48(2), 74(2), 88(2),
  121(2), 136(2), 163(2), 273(2),
  304(2), 384(2), 396(2), 402(2),
  419(2), 479(2), 481(2), 490(2),
  515(2), 521(2)
editor: see also newspaper
  editor
educational theorist 210
educationist 29, 191, 76(2),
  368(2), 599(2)
egyptologist 391, 285(2)
emancipist 517, 86(2), 109(2),
  110(2), 141(2)
emancipist: see also convict
emigration agent 165, 288, 540,
  48(2), 177(2), 418(2)
engineer 2, 11, 23, 27, 41, 57,
  60, 61, 81, 220, 224, 231, 250,
  297, 302, 306, 391, 419, 547,
  575, 34(2), 37(2), 48(2), 59(2),
  64(2), 71(2), 233(2), 305(2),
  412(2), 439(2), 527(2), 555(2)
engineer (assistant) 471
engineer: see also chief engineer
engineer: see also military
  engineer
engraver 123, 230, 339, 490,
  242(2)
ensign 101(2)
entomologist 111(2), 177(2),
  178(2)
entrepreneur 140, 206, 128(2),
  153(2)
estate agent 235, 490, 109(2),
  528(2)
estate manager 533(2)
evangelist 625(2)
examiner for the New South
  Wales Bar 198
examiner of the Census 215(2)
excise officer 208
experimenter 410(2)
explorer-botanist 119(2)
explorer 14, 61, 83, 108, 110,
  122, 194, 236, 240, 265, 268,
  277, 282, 309, 362, 412, 441,
  476, 497, 527, 528, 533, 542,
  556, 564, 577, 43(2), 65(2),
  96(2), 97(2), 99(2), 102(2),
  117(2), 119(2), 170(2), 180(2),
  183(2), 219(2), 272(2), 305(2),
  315(2), 317(2), 323(2), 390(2),
  406(2), 471(2), 488(2), 494(2),
  495(2), 506(2), 530(2), 570(2),
  575(2), 582(2), 610(2)
explorer: see also adventurer
factor 527
factory owner 302, 75(2)
faith healer 472(2)
farm labourer 42, 215
farm overseer 271(2)
farm agent 314(2)
farmer 27, 63, 68, 106, 110, 175,
  178, 197, 212, 263, 340, 354,
  399, 407, 428, 429, 443, 497,
  510, 519, 531, 548, 550, 562,
  563, 10(2), 20(2), 22(2), 28(2),

42(2), 50(2), 54(2), 55(2),
  73(2), 75(2), 102(2), 122(2),
  124(2), 144(2C), 159(2),
  170(2), 207(2), 232(2), 254(2),
  268(2), 283(2), 347(2), 361(2),
  393(2), 394(2), 420(2), 467(2),
  504(2), 519(2), 532(2), 533(2),
  613(2), 625(2), 630(2)
farmer: see also gentleman
  farmer
farm hand 311
farrier 194, 216(2)
federalist 224
fellmonger 608(2)
ferry proprietor 42
financier 110(2), 149(2), 250(2).
  424(2)
first lord of the admiralty 526,
  401(2)
fisherman 212, 115(2), 347(2),
  540(2)
flagmaker 426(2)
flour miller 258, 36(2), 366(2)
foreign secretary 67
foreman of the jury 227
forger 419(2)
furrier 548(2)
fustian maker 126(2)
gaol-bird 76(2)
gaoler 220, 632(2)
gaol governor 106
gardener 45, 176, 183, 227, 258,
  416, 465, 120(2), 244(2),
  353(2), 377(2)
general merchant 133(2)
general storekeeper 235
gentleman farmer 481(2)
geographer 122, 184(2)
geological surveyor 29(2)
geologist 11, 111, 181, 278, 387,
  465, 29(2), 222(2), 472(2)
geophysicist 34(2)
glazier 179
glovemaker 264
gold buyer 207, 590(2)
gold commissioner 365, 4(2),
  244(2), 349(2)
gold commissioner (asst) 514,
  4(2)
governess 465, 502, 35(2),
  576(2)
government medical officer 262
government messenger 493(2)
government printer 58, 213,
  472, 60(2)
government resident 219(2)
government resident in NT 378
government stores supervisor
  248
governor 118, 128, 151, 199,
  228, 250, 282, 353, 362, 375,
  377, 380, 381, 384, 390, 431,
  446, 476, 508, 538, 542, 545,
  566, 575, 55(2), 119(2),
  187(2), 281(2), 326(2), 484(2)
governor (acting) 202, 119(2)
governor (Newgate Gaol)
  558(2)
governor: see also lieutenant
  governor
governor's secretary 229(2)
governor general 384, 483

grain assessor 519(2)
grazier 57, 68, 139, 281, 306,
  310, 344, 500, 543, 544, 2(2),
  28(2), 107(2), 134(2), 254(2),
  271(2), 587(2)
grocer 349, 352, 23(2), 42(2),
  493(2)
guardian of minors 112, 278(2)
guardian of immigrant minors
  510, 99(2), 278(2)
guide 7(2)
gunner 538
gunner: see also master gunner
haberdasher 625(2)
handloom weaver 218(2)
harbourmaster 197, 240, 273,
  529, 36(2), 64(2), 138(2),
  231(2), 232(2), 264(2), 337(2),
  426(2), 575(2)
harpist 354(2), 602(2)
hatmaker 214
headmaster 361, 397, 401, 5(2),
  32(2), 149(2), 424(2)
headmaster: see also
  schoolmaster
health officer 296
hebrew scholar 437
helmsman 403(2)
high commissioner 479
high constable 383
high sheriff 99, 133, 371,
  316(2), 484(2)
historian 425, 44(2), 76(2),
  323(2), 406(2), 530(2)
home secretary 337, 465, 136(2)
homeopath 448(2)
hop grower 436(2), 442(2)
horse dealer 194
horsewoman 215
horticulturist 10, 63, 292,
  482(2)
hosier 216(2)
hotel proprietor 301
hotel keeper 272, 370, 115(2),
  374(2)
house carpenter 539(2)
housemaster 159
house painter 493(2)
house steward 552(2)
humanitarian 562(2)
huntsman 349(2)
hydrographer 275, 389, 61(2),
  62(2), 315(2), 488(2), 550(2)
illustrator 18, 26
immigrant (free) 142(2)
immigration agent 112, 291,
  372, 110(2), 334(2)
immigration organiser 76(2)
importer 56, 165, 251(2)
industrialist 235(2)
innkeeper 240, 270, 517, 347(2),
  347(2), 508(2), 515(2), 579(2)
insolvency commissioner 201(2)
inspecting field officer 288
inspector: 3(2), 160(2)
— general of hospitals 235(2)
— general of fortifications
  112(2)
— general of police 463(2)
— of cattle 241
— of distilleries 356, 577(2)
— of livestock 439, 393(2)

— of machinery 224
— of peat (Royal) 102(2)
— of penal settlements 261(2), 352(2)
— of police 300(C)
— of public works 240, 488, 494, 569, 64(2), 71(2), 127(2), 154(2), 278(2)
— of roads & bridges 296(2)
— of schools 29, 251, 292, 32(2), 311(2), 432(2), 564(2), 608(2), 626(2)
— of slaughtering houses 291(2)
instructor in surveying 48(2)
insurance agents 176(2)
insurance broker 257(2), 430(2)
interpreter 125(2), 263(2), 540(2)
inventor 245, 520, 379(2), 410(2)
Irish nationalist 217(2), 234(2), 293(2)
Irish rebel 550
Irish secretary 455
iron founder 504, 84(2), 282(2)
iron founder's apprentice 219
ironmonger 28(2), 55(2), 388(2), 445(2), 451(2), 549(2), 599(2), 611(2)
island trader 208
jeweller 488, 98(2), 109(2), 457(2)
joiner 251, 139(2)
joint secretary, Board of Control 136(2)
journalist 216, 335, 376, 457, 506, 515, 520, 25(2), 40(2), 50(2), 76(2), 114(2), 166(2), 221(2), 258(2), 272(2), 304(2), 444(2), 521(2), 615(2), 622(2)
judge 87, 99, 184, 195, 224, 244, 317, 349, 372, 373, 530, 536, 541, 548, 14(2), 51(2), 246(2), 319(2), 476(2), 495(2), 512(2), 513(2), 602(2)
judge: see also chief justice
judge advocate 373, 487, 500, 536, 39(2), 130(2)
judge advocate (deputy) 2, 38, 66, 87, 236, 237, 313, 404, 426, 519, 536, 190(2), 627(2)
judge advocate general 223(2)
justice of the peace 3, 22, 38, 77, 172, 173, 190, 197, 213, 219, 235, 237, 236, 247, 252-4, 261, 264, 273, 296, 302, 304, 317, 325, 329, 356, 394, 407, 419, 421, 457, 458, 459, 461, 485, 492, 512, 534, 536, 543, 545, 568, 11(2), 18(2), 40(2), 42(2), 45(2), 50(2), 72(2), 88(2), 94(2), 100(2), 113(2), 122(2), 124(2), 132(2), 138(2), 143(2), 148(2), 174(2), 176(2), 214(2), 219(2), 227(2), 245(2), 248(2), 258(2), 260(2), 265(2), 266(2), 282(2), 293(2), 355(2), 378(2), 383(2), 402(2), 411(2), 413(2), 414(2), 421(2), 430(2), 434(2), 441(2), 448(2), 450(2), 452(2), 464(2), 480(2), 497(2),

534(2), 557(2), 564(2), 580(2), 590(2), 593(2), 595(2), 626(2), 633(2)
King's advocate 392
labourer 147, 243, 132(2), 232(2), 259(2), 325(2)
labourer: see also farm labourer, farm hand
laceman 487
laird 202
land agent 218, 388
land commissioner 246, 49(2), 120(2), 126(2), 269(2), 429(2), 470(2), 532(2)
land surveyor 9, 406
land titles commissioner 334(2)
land waiter 118(C)
landed proprietor 371, 55(2), 252(2), 435(2)
landing waiter 427, 575
landholder 27, 51, 101, 519, 521, 259(2), 308(2), 403(2), 602(2)
landowner 7, 15, 24, 25, 42, 56, 117, 135, 178, 228, 256, 290, 329, 331, 332, 343, 421, 498, 549, 574, 1(2), 2(2), 10(2), 76(2), 83(2), 93(2), 116(2), 122(2), 123(2), 126(2), 149(2), 168(2), 172(2), 261(2), 264(2), 272(2), 274(2), 283(2), 296(2), 302(2), 320(2), 334(2), 371(2), 375(2), 382(2), 387(2), 414(2), 415(2), 429(2), 452(2), 466(2), 508(2), 516(2), 563(2), 582(2), 614(2), 620(2), 626(2)
landscape artist 592(2)
landscape painter 416, 455, 574(2)
language master 279(2)
language teacher 326(2)
lawyer 21, 55, 66, 74, 87, 101, 149, 168, 184, 190, 196, 218, 224, 227, 263, 343, 379, 437, 454, 551, 571, 51(2), 121(2), 252(2), 266(2), 337(2), 395(2), 452(2), 515(2)
lawyer: see also attorney, barrister
lecturer 40, 538, 114(2), 172(2)
lecturer in midwifery 268(2)
legal writer 246(2)
legislative councillor 3, 73(2), 131(2)
librarian 167, 192, 265, 403, 502, 538, 542, 229(2), 456(2)
librarian: see also musical librarian
library manager 301
lieutenant governor 33, 236, 288, 345, 358, 381, 384, 412, 419, 488, 89(2), 91(2), 243(2), 295(2), 317(2), 397(2), 459(2), 482(2)
lighterman (journeyman) 617(2)
lighthouse keeper 444(2)
linen draper 252, 84(2), 552(2), 562(2)
linen merchant 542(2)
linguist 160(2), 222(2), 398(2), 428(2)
lithographer 230, 410(2)

liveryman 109
livery taylor 191
lord advocate of Scotland 337
lord chancellor 67, 392, 627(2)
lord lieutenant and keeper of the rolls, Kilkenny, Irl 51(2)
lord lieutenant of Ireland 196
lord mayor 43(2)
lord of the admiralty 67, 337
lord of the treasury 67
lord president of the council 196
lord provost 566
lyric writer 337
magistrate 2, 12, 22, 27, 51, 56, 78, 99, 102, 115, 149, 155, 180, 190, 202-3, 210-1, 231, 233, 237, 253, 257, 259, 264, 275, 281, 321, 331, 363, 372, 380, 426, 427, 440, 442, 458, 477, 493, 513, 517, 519, 523, 525, 532-3, 538, 549, 551-2, 561, 563, 565-6, 570, 3(2), 4(2), 13(2), 18(2), 25(2), 40(2), 41(2), 43(2), 46(2), 67(2), 73(2), 96(2), 99(2), 119(2), 127(2), 131(2), 134(2), 147(2), 148(2), 149(2), 171(2), 172(2), 175(2), 178(2), 181(2), 191(2), 193(2), 196(2), 209(2), 213(2), 214(2), 225(2), 227(2), 228(2), 244(2), 247(2), 252(2), 255(2), 258(2), 260(2), 265(2), 267(2), 307(2), 308(2), 309(2), 316(2), 335(2), 351(2), 365(2), 366(2), 368(2), 370(2), 376(2), 380(2), 382(2), 393(2), 403(2), 411(2), 419(2), 421(2), 426(2), 427(2), 428(2), 440(2), 447(2), 449(2), 471(2), 479(2), 486(2), 489(2), 520(2), 530(2), 531(2), 538(2), 552(2), 564(2), 578(2), 595(2), 597(2), 598(2), 602(2), 605(2), 608(2), 612(2), 614(2), 620(2), 630(2)
magistrate (senior) 174(2)
magistrate: see also stipendiary magistrate, senior magistrate
mailman 524
maltster 406, 429
manager 3, 67(2), 122(2), 164(2), 445(2)
manager (bank) 500, 508
managing director 401
manufacturer 57, 179, 306, 54(2), 129(2), 257(2), 519(2), 548(2), 608(2)
manufacturer of earthenware 204(2)
manufacturers: see also industrialists, businessmen, merchants, traders etc.
map printer 528(2)
marine 236, 327, 349, 139(2), 469(2)
marine and army officer 281(2)
marine artist 427
marine engineer 493(2)
marine surveyor 489(2)
mariner 156, 197, 208, 13(2), 359(2), 503(2), 610(2)

mariner: see also sailor, seaman, master mariner, sea-captain, naval officer
market gardener 498(2)
master attendant 527, 567
master boat builder 254(2)
master brewer 375(2)
master bricklayer 122
master builder 403(2)
master carpenter 252, 264, 139(2), 279(2)
master (court records) 248(2)
master gunner 621(2)
master in chancery 345, 474(2)
master in equity 52(2)
master (lodge) 549(2)
master mariner 7, 14, 49, 56, 275, 376, 308(2), 364(2), 444(2), 463(2), 577(2), 596(2)
master mariner: see also sea captain, naval officer, mariner, seaman, sailor, master
master mason 106(2)
master (ship) 240, 243, 566, 72(2), 596(2)
master (supreme court) 495, 462(2)
master's mate 243, 468
match manufacturers & exporters 623(2)
mate (ship) 575(2)
mathematics master 298
matron 133(2), 613(2)
mayor 43, 317, 380, 419, 423, 549, 534, 554-5, 41(2), 43(2), 51(2), 98(2), 99(2), 113(2), 131(2), 162(2), 217(2), 251(2), 326(2), 414(2), 442(2), 463(2), 493(2), 522(2), 549(2), 609(2), 615(2)
mayor (acting) 125(2)
mayor (deputy) 233(2)
meat contractor 228, 394(2)
mechanic 12
mechanical engineer 493(2)
medical officer 51, 297(2)
medical officer: see also government medical officer
medical practitioner 1, 85, 112, 134, 248, 253, 272, 295, 335, 502, 40(2), 74(2), 355(2), 361(2), 398(2), 490(2), 514(2), 522(2), 541(2), 579(2), 612(2)
medical practitioner: see also doctor, surgeon, physician
member of parliament 210, 214, 384, 407, 515, 542, 552(2)
member of parliament: see also speaker, legislative councillor, politician, parliamentarian
mercantile agent 442
mercer 153(2)
merchant 6, 14, 15, 66, 80, 82, 84, 92, 95, 101, 104, 115, 117, 127, 156, 195, 198, 199, 202, 206, 209, 213, 229, 231, 233, 245, 257, 261, 270, 272, 275, 290, 304, 305, 338, 339, 343, 349, 373, 400, 407, 421, 442, 445, 460, 485, 490, 497, 505, 525, 527, 533, 545, 548, 551, 552, 554-5, 1(2), 3(2), 14(2),

16(2), 23(2), 24(2), 39(2), 44(2), 45(2), 48(2), 49(2), 51(2), 54(2), 65(2), 72(2), 73(2), 86(2), 93(2), 98(2), 99(2), 100(2), 105(2), 108(2), 110(2), 113(2), 118(2), 120(2), 127(2), 137(2), 161(2), 163(2), 196(2), 202(2), 203(2), 212(2), 217(2), 223(2), 250(2), 263(2), 266(2), 269(2), 271(2), 283(2), 290(2), 302(2), 303(2), 325(2), 352(2), 359(2), 361(2), 364(2), 365(2), 371(2), 379(2), 381(2), 392(2), 411(2), 414(2), 415(2), 417(2), 426(2), 430(2), 433(2), 439(2), 441(2), 458(2), 463(2), 465(2), 492(2), 500(2), 508(2), 547(2), 548(2), 563(2), 565(2), 566(2), 598(2), 600(2), 613(2), 617(2), 620(2), 623(2), 633(2)
merchant banker 129(2)
merchant, East India 402(2)
merchant, Tailor 419
merchant: see also businessman, manager, company director, industrialist, manufacturer, trader, linen merchant, general merchant.
metal refiner 368
Methodist leader 532(2)
Methodist schoolmaster 135
Methodist minister: see minister (Methodist)
Methodist missionary: see missionary (Methodist)
midshipman 233, 239, 468, 538, 138(2)
midwife 215, 268
military engineer 358
military officer 81, 144, 250, 258, 282, 324, 435, 439, 463, 170(2), 233(2), 334(2), 348(2)
military officer: see also soldier, army officer
military secretary 33, 282, 303, 188(2)
militia officer 562
miller 429, 494, 187(2), 197(2), 245(2), 246(2), 278(2), 361(2), 379(2), 441(2), 448(2), 563(2)
miller: see also flour miller
milliner 19(2), 133(2)
mill owner 468
millwright 57, 74, 306, 28(2), 246(2), 278(2)
mine manager 314(2)
mine owner 47, 601(2)
miner 188, 543, 540(2)
mineralogist 226, 278, 565-6
miniature painter 230, 140(2), 367(2), 574(2)
minister: (of religion) 74
— Baptist 316, 444, 418(2)
— Congregational 251, 525, 229(2), 281(2), 350(2), 356(2), 398(2), 491(2), 528(2), 572(2), 590(2)
— non-conformist 78, 515
— Methodist 212, 321, 67(2), 171(2), 205(2), 480(2), 490(2), 566(2)
— Presbyterian 232, 327, 351,

399, 428, 472, 563, 118(2), 166(2), 173(2), 234(2), 356(2), 435(2), 454(2), 541(2)
— protestant 415, 509
— Unitarian 312(2)
minister: see also clergyman
minister (government): see also secretary of state; under secretary of state.
minister for education 23
minister for lands & works 194
minister of justice & public instruction 6
minister of public instruction 526(2)
mission agriculturist 495
missionary: 192, 213, 251, 252, 259, 262, 275, 321, 351, 352, 365, 428, 429, 509, 518, 521, 42(2), 125(2), 204(2), 207(2), 222(2), 303(2), 402(2), 416(2), 421(2), 438(2), 528(2), 599(2)
— city 333(2)
— Independent 632(2)
— Methodist 95(2), 105(2), 423(2)
— Quaker 45
missioner 516, 133(2)
moderator 399
moneylender 263, 371, 142(2), 162(2)
monk: see Benedictine monk
mountaineer 89(2)
musical librarian 279(2)
musician 301, 29(2), 33(2), 122(2), 160(2), 279(2), 285(2), 298(2), 567(2)
muster master 214(2)
natural history artist 465
natural history collector 513
natural history draughtsman 314(2)
naturalist 18, 29, 45, 52, 71, 85, 194, 249, 325, 403, 441, 470, 480, 544, 571, 577, 69(2), 102(2), 111(2), 114(2), 120(2), 167(2), 182(2), 323(2), 349(2), 437(2), 456(2), 471(2), 491(2), 574(2), 594(2), 597(2), 611(2), 627(2)
naval agent 442(2)
naval captain 247, 65(2)
naval dockyard foreman 534
naval draughtsman 101
naval lieutenant 511, 542
naval officer 50, 52, 111, 118, 145, 148, 203-4, 207, 218, 240, 287, 290, 327, 458, 468, 519, 524, 527, 545, 563, 12(2), 15(2), 34(2), 46(2), 47(2), 55(2), 61(2), 72(2), 83(2), 127(2), 132(2), 143(2), 184(2), 283(2), 306(2), 315(2), 335(2), 382(2), 390(2), 414(2), 442(2), 443(2), 446(2), 462(2), 465(2), 470(2), 550(2), 573(2), 597(2), 621(2)
naval purser 248, 524, 86(2)
naval surgeon 29, 155, 169, 267, 310, 503, 2(2), 48(2), 139(2), 148(2), 375(2), 376(2), 418(2), 594(2)

navigator 122, 171, 243, 389, 85(2), 357(2), 536(2)
needleworker 133(2)
newspaper agent 87(2)
newspaper editor 395, 500, 558, 164(2), 204(2), 480(2), 570(2), 590(2)
newspaper editor: see also editor
newspaper proprietor 86, 227, 370
nightwatchman 31(2)
non-conformist minister: see minister (Noncomformist)
notary public 9, 227, 487, 359(2), 489(2), 516(2)
novelist 139, 143(2), 279(2), 402(2), 630(2)
nurse 215
obstetrician 268(2), 284(2), 369(2), 614(2)
officer 136, 306
officer: see also soldier, army officer, military officer, second officer
officer, Dutch East India Co 322(2)
officer of marines 225, 297, 127(2), 222(2), 264(2), 397(2), 506(2), 534(2)
official 115(2)
official assignee 143(2)
organist 301, 566, 416(2)
organizer and public servant 461
orientalist 511
ornithologist 88(2), 167(2), 361(2)
outlaw 610(2) see also bushranger
overlander 376, 524, 243(2)
overseer 214, 215, 217, 264, 430, 492, 31(2), 50(2), 66(2), 71(2), 86(2), 195(2), 214(2), 517(2), 527(2)
overseer: see also chief overseer
overseer of blacksmiths 419
overseer of government stock 575
overseer of lumber yard 217
overseer of town gang (deputy) 552(2)
page 573(2)
painter 18, 179, 339, 444, 542, 568(2)
painter (watercolour) 591(2)
painter: see also house painter; landscape painter; miniature painter; artist; illustrator
pamphleteer 554, 414(2), 468(2)
parish clerk 260, 365, 514, 502(2)
parliamentarian 523(2)
parliamentarian: see also member of parliament, politician, legislative councillor
parliamentary draftsman 393, 474(2)
parliamentary librarian 213(2)
parliamentary reporter 317, 41(2)

parliamentary undersecretart 482, 554
pastor 252, 260, 288(2)
pastor (Congregationalist) 259
pastor (Lutheran) 33(2)
pastoralist 7, 19, 22, 27, 38, 47, 95, 137, 155, 171, 172, 198, 201, 202, 206, 214, 225, 228, 247, 249, 257, 280, 298, 320, 326, 328, 341, 344, 349, 376, 400, 407, 425, 439, 465, 525, 541, 572, 3(2), 9(2), 24(2), 93(2), 75(2), 96(2), 100(2), 118(2), 127(2), 129(2), 131(2), 147(2), 153(2), 166(2), 180(2), 183(2), 197(2), 243(2), 263(2), 292(2), 303(2), 308(2), 316(2), 361(2), 379(2), 381(2), 406(2), 408(2), 433(2), 450(2), 455(2), 479(2), 502(2), 522(2), 533(2), 556(2), 605(2), 614(2), 630(2), 633(2)
pastoralist: see also squatter, farmer, pioneer, settler
pastry manufacturer 515(2)
patron of science 52
paymaster 142, 258, 377, 488, 39(2), 274(2), 500(2)
paymaster-captain 530
paymaster-general 456, 136(2)
paymaster general, deputy, (Bombay) 188(2)
penal administrator 351(2)
penal reformer 184(2)
pensioner 36(2)
philanthropist 7, 15, 57, 202, 221, 316, 552, 246(2), 254(2), 371(2), 444(2), 509(2)
philologist 279
philosopher 577
photographer 493(2)
physician 5, 63, 218, 235, 372, 544, 10(2), 24(2), 155(2), 235(2), 268(2), 283(2), 284(2)602(2)
physician: see also doctor, medical practitioner, surgeon
physician to the Prince of Wales 290
physiologist 69(2)
pianist 416(2)
pickpocket 62
pilot 277, 498, 36(2), 138(2), 231(2), 272(2), 374(2), 426(2), 444(2), 575(2)
pioneer 4, 67, 215, 276, 296, 368, 425, 445, 524, 531, 573, 74(2), 107(2), 231(2), 245(2), 281(2), 300(2), 404(2), 417(2), 507(2)
plant collector 325, 492, 349(2)
plantation manager 176(2)
planter (West Indies) 439
plasterer 600(2), 601(2)
ploughman 132(2), 271(2)
ploughwright 224
poet 267, 268, 469, 514, 538, 557, 42(2), 167(2), 304(2), 387(2), 533(2)
poet laureate 192(2), 366(2)
police commissioner 288
police constable 215(2), 415(2)

police magistrate 9, 19, 111, 112, 136, 180, 202, 213, 265, 292, 300, 365, 367, 378, 404, 407, 417, 423, 453, 458, 473, 492-3, 502, 508, 530, 551, 4(2), 52(2), 74(2), 88(2), 91(2), 100(2), 123(2), 124(2), 125(2), 132(2), 143(2), 149(2), 160(2), 201(2), 226(2), 228(2), 260(2), 261(2), 269(2), 271(2), 315(2), 349(2), 399(2), 407(2), 412(2), 421(2), 447(2), 450(2), 466(2), 595(2), 609(2), 613(2), 633(2)
police magistrate (assistant) 264, 251, 492, 323, 351(2), 622(2)
police magistrate: see also chief police magistrate.
police officer 278, 457(2)
police spy 206(2)
police superintendent 86(2), 191(2), 486(2)
policeman 217
political agitator 141(2)
political economist 534(2)
political prisoner 216(2)
political reformer 438, 266(2), 312(2), 449(2)
political transportee 218(2)
political writer 228(2)
politician 3, 7, 67, 106, 112, 191, 196, 198, 199, 202, 224, 254, 258, 261, 329, 341, 349, 371, 400, 454, 455, 456, 464, 475, 476, 480, 492, 498, 525, 542, 554, 25(2), 40(2), 55(2), 64(2), 72(2), 76(2), 84(2), 134(2), 147(2), 149(2), 161(2), 195(2), 261(2), 270(2), 274(2), 280(2), 297(2), 337(2), 455(2), 470(2), 492(2), 605(2)
politician: see also parliamentarian, member of parliament
politician: see also speaker, legislative councillor
polynesian scholar 599(2)
porcelain painter 467
port captain 548
port officer 417, 457, 260(2), 577(2)
port admiral 281(2)
portrait painter 348, 140(2), 367(2), 473(2), 493(2)
post boy 524
post captain 244, 47(2), 57(2)
postal agent 430
postmaster 66, 234, 281, 381, 514, 563, 139(2), 283(2), 365(2), 371(2), 431(2), 440(2)
postmaster (deputy) 241, 353
postmaster general 76, 300, 461, 365(2), 417(2)
poundkeeper 12, 179, 235, 241, 430, 348(2), 431(2), 632(2)
preacher 212, 251, 260, 261, 521, 132(2), 379(2), 424(2)
prebendary 134(2)
precentor 570(2)
precis writer 353
prelate (catholic) 544(2)

premier 378, 476, 479
premier of NSW 468(2)
premier of Queensland 258(2)
premier of Tasmania 402(2)
premier of Victoria 300(2)
Presbyterian clergyman &
   minister: see clergyman,
   minister
press associate 317
priest (Catholic) 269, 309, 503,
   512, 44(2), 165(2), 299(2),
   302(2), 509(2), 622(2)
prime minister 456, 470(2)
principal of night watch 86(2)
principal medical officer 434(2)
principal superintendent of
   convicts 227, 458, 529, 575,
   283(2), 466(2), 622(2)
principal superintendent of
   police 234(2)
printer 86, 95, 316, 355, 534,
   557, 559, 562, 26(2), 163(2),
   479(2)
printer: see also government
   printer
prison reformer 376(2)
prison warden (deputy) 552(2)
private secretary 32, 201, 303,
   443, 453, 530, 571, 87(2),
   119(2)
privateer 208, 277
privy councillor 455
produce merchant 600(2)
professor of: botany 287
— classics 403
— geography 185(2)
— Greek 128
— law 266(2)
— mathamatics 241(2)
— modern history 29, 476(2)
— moral philosophy and
   political economy 291
— obstetrics 614(2)
— Scots Law 219
— topographical drawing
   324(2)
propagandist 275
proprietor 87(2)
protagonist 505
protector of Aborigines 363,
   478, 385(2)
protector of Aborigines
   (assistant) 518(2)
prothonotary 495, 254(2)
provost 284(2)
provost of Wick 177(2)
provost-marshal 149, 200, 263,
   351, 459, 22(2), 39(2), 71(2),
   169(2), 308(2), 531(2), 583(2)
public auctioneer 129(2)
public official 105(2)
public prosecutor 627(2)
public servant 2, 8, 32, 38, 63,
   76, 106, 126, 135, 143, 157,
   164, 201, 218, 287, 314, 322,
   323, 324, 327, 328, 332, 335,
   353, 356, 377, 380, 383, 404,
   405, 425, 439, 453, 461, 492,
   507, 511, 513, 519, 525, 538,
   548, 554, 565, 574, 575, 7(2),
   34(2), 71(2), 87(2), 169(2),
   177(2), 218(2), 248(2), 258(2),

267(2), 269(2), 283(2), 296(2),
   314(2), 333(2), 334(2), 349(2),
   377(2), 387(2), 399(2), 401(2),
   447(2), 448(2), 466(2), 472(2),
   474(2), 495(2), 516(2), 523(2),
   531(2), 533(2), 541(2), 542(2),
   579(2), 602(2), 608(2), 622(2),
   626(2)
public servant: see also
   administrator, civil servant,
   official, public official
public vaccinator 273
publican 95, 192, 550, 308(2),
   362(2), 371(2), 394(2), 444(2)
publicist 227, 258(2), 534(2)
publisher 86, 316, 377, 534, 557,
   559, 163(2), 221(2), 466(2),
   504(2), 615(2)
pugilist 32(2)
puisne judge 184, 551, 52(2),
   246(2), 477(2)
purser 252, 524, 507, 523, 47(2),
   281(2), 309(2), 424(2), 614(2)
purveyor Army medical service
   242, 507, 523, 281(2), 424(2)
Quaker missionary 45
quartermaster 193, 497, 97(2),
   162(2)
quartermaster-general 33, 226,
   270(2), 500(2)
railway commissioner 41(2)
racehorse owner 349(2)
racing enthusiast 511
railway commissioner 41(2)
ratcatcher 259(2)
rear admiral 50, 146, 184, 412,
   541, 63(2), 400(2)
rear admiral: see also admiral
recorder 184, 15(2), 595(2)
rector 159, 256, 379, 134(2),
   278(2)
rector (C of E) 428
rector of Killarney, Irl 405(2)
rector: see also clergyman,
   minister
reformer 541
refugee 65(2)
regent in Brazil 94(2)
regimental paymaster 154(2)
registrar: 39, 379, 40(2), 50(2),
   65(2), 219(2), 254(2), 334(2),
   462(2), 523(2), 600(2)
— births, deaths and marriages
   492, 462(2), 489(2)
— brands 391(2)
— court of appeals 463
— court of chancery 248(2)
— deeds 442, 443, 248(2),
   462(2)
— general 378, 5(2), 497(2)
— probate 612(2)
— records 88(2), 524(2)
— supreme court 495
religious instructor 192, 392(2)
resident commissioner 379, 380,
   63(2), 117(2)
resident magistrate 180, 245(2)
retailer 129(2), 216(2)
returning officer 215(2)
revolutionary 402, 430
roadmaker 258
road trust commissioner 181(2)

Roman Catholic priest (etc): see
   priest (Catholic)
royal commissioner 99
sailmaker 123(2C), 610(2)
sailor 64, 101, 170, 529, 544,
   556, 231(2), 254(2), 262(2),
   337(2)
sailor: see also mariner, seaman,
   master mariner, sea-captain
sawyer 369, 621(2)
scalemaker 109
scholar 182(2), 283(2), 537(2),
   599(2)
schoolmaster 9, 135, 192, 209,
   210, 216, 251, 252, 259, 355-6,
   365, 401, 420, 506, 514, 515,
   518, 554, 577, 32(2), 42(2),
   201(2), 217(2), 289(2), 414(2),
   440(2), 502(2)
schoolmaster: see also
   Methodist schoolmaster,
   headmaster, teacher
schoolmistress 225, 315(2)
schoolteacher 252, 336, 509,
   288(2), 424(2), 599(2)
schoolteacher: see also teacher
scientist 297, 389, 34(2), 85(2),
   212(2), 494(2), 537(2)
sea captain 104, 105, 178, 340,
   372, 421, 538(2), 613(2)
sea captain: see also mariner,
   master mariner, seaman, naval
   officer, sailor, master, ship
   commander
seal engraver 230
sealer 36(2), 129(2), 170(2)
sealing master 547(2)
seaman 264, 277, 306, 497,
   272(2), 347(2), 363(2)
seamstress 389(2)
sea trader 435(2)
second officer 138(2)
secretary: see also private
   secretary; joint secretary;
   military secretary
secretary 63, 76, 126, 359,
   248(2), 456(2)
— at war 480
— for Ireland 470(2)
— for lands, Queensland 73(2)
— of state for the colonies 385,
   404, 455, 456, 496(2)
— of state for war & the
   colonies 196, 337, 542, 475(2)
— of state: see also under-
   secretary of state
— of the treasury 180(2)
— to the governor 218
senator 227
serjeant-at-arms 95, 302, 88(2),
   123(2), 348(2), 435(2)
serjeant-at-arms in parliament
   194
servant 102, 172, 215, 311, 424,
   120(2), 128(2), 232(2)
servant (female) 271(2)
servant: see also domestic
   servant
serving girl 116(2)
settler 12, 21, 42, 43, 76, 78, 92,
   95, 115, 126, 138, 144, 156,
   157, 180, 181, 189, 209, 224,

231, 235, 240, 248, 264, 301,
311, 324, 360, 367, 380, 383,
491, 494, 513, 524, 549, 556,
560, 561, 36(2), 49(2), 86(2),
87(2), 101(2), 120(2), 131(2),
143(2), 215(2), 218(2), 219(2),
220(2), 224(2), 231(2), 233(2),
269(2), 291(2), 336(2), 337(2),
365(2), 401(2), 411(2), 428(2),
448(2), 465(2), 469(2), 498(2),
516(2), 530(2), 536(2), 537(2),
553(2), 564(2), 600(2), 604(2)
settler (free) 252, 137(2)
settler: see also pastoralist,
squatter, pioneer, farmer
sheepbreeder 4
shepherd 133(2)
sheriff 77, 149, 183, 244, 275,
371, 415, 459, 500, 526,
169(2), 407(2), 447(2), 489(2),
517(2), 570(2), 618(2), 633(2)
sheriff (deputy) 112, 423, 160(2)
sheriff's officer 381
sheriff: see also high sheriff,
under sheriff
ship chandler 303(2), 605(2)
ship commander 384
ship's joiner 76(2)
ship's master: see master
ship's mate: see mate
shipbroker 110(2)
shipbuilder 302, 485, 486,
110(2), 137(2), 546(2)
shipowner 14, 104, 208, 240,
376, 485, 486, 533, 548, 1(2),
3(2), 110(2), 202(2), 254(2),
283(2), 360(2), 371(2), 433(2),
463(2), 522(2), 605(2)
shipping agent 176(2), 251(2),
539(2)
shipwright 13, 252, 254(2),
288(2), 621(2)
shoemaker 253, 42(2), 290(2),
353(2), 604(2)
shopkeeper 294, 291(2), 562(2)
silk mercer 66
silk weaver 411, 521, 350(2)
silversmith 98(2)
sinecurist 66
small landowner 24(2)
smallholder 354, 404(2)
smith 252, 271(2)
social worker 290(2)
soldier 2, 8, 11, 13, 21, 32, 46,
47, 49, 57, 60, 76, 78, 108,
171, 175, 191, 196, 220, 223,
264, 278, 301, 303, 358, 367,
377, 404, 407, 418, 431, 446,
488, 494, 542, 549, 573, 3(2),
5(2), 20(2), 37(2), 39(2),
97(2), 116(2), 119(2), 123(2),
124(2), 143(2), 153(2), 162(2),
218(2), 243(2), 248(2), 258(2),
259(2), 268(2), 270(2), 272(2),
294(2), 305(2), 317(2), 324(2),
383(2), 399(2), 403(2), 412(2),
421(2), 435(2), 454(2), 459(2),
482(2), 495(2), 516(2), 531(2),
555(2), 568(2), 574(2)
soldier: see also officer, army
officer, military officer
solicitor 5, 9, 184, 195, 220,

247, 262, 263, 379, 426, 435,
454, 494, 532, 536, 562, 70(2),
74(2), 214(2), 251(2), 255(2),
261(2), 269(2), 283(2), 289(2),
334(2), 336(2), 355(2), 395(2),
397(2), 418(2), 452(2), 489(2),
558(2), 611(2), 613(2), 620(2)
solicitor: see also crown
solicitor
solicitor general 349, 393, 407,
426, 86(2), 164(2), 165(2),
256(2), 337(2), 395(2), 477(2),
490(2), 511(2)
Speaker 330, 371, 64(2), 152(2),
180(2), 228(2), 262(2), 276(2),
284(2), 298(2)
speculator 2(2), 44(2), 359(2)
spy 390, 461
squatter 201, 247, 330, 101(2),
500(2), 587(2)
squatter (female) 330
squatter: see also settler,
pioneer, pastoralist
squire 475
stage manager 68(2)
statesman 283(2), 407(2), 582(2)
stationer 360, 520, 242(2)
stationmaster 51(2)
statistician 109, 362, 219(2)
staymaker 77, 312(2)
steamship owner 490
steward 571, 47(2), 73(2)
steward (racecourse) 295(2)
stipendiary magistrate 180, 288,
356, 378, 201(2), 441(2),
543(2)
stipendiary magistrate: see also
magistrate
stipendiary solicitor 256(2)
stockbreeder 155, 1(2), 2(2),
470(2)
stockbroker 98(2), 589(2)
stock keeper 133(2)
stonemason 352, 470, 141(2),
508(2)
stonemason: see also master
mason
storekeeper 218, 226, 227, 272,
328, 359, 490, 513, 536, 563,
106(2), 110(2), 223(2), 258(2),
279(2), 289(2), 380(2), 490(2),
540(2), 608(2)
storekeeper: see also
government storekeeper,
general storekeeper
student of the Aborigines 337
sub-agent for immigration
355(2)
sub-treasurer 125(2)
sugar grower 430(2)
summoning officer 302
supercargo 107, 49(2), 366(2),
548(2), 598(2)
superintendent (of): 3, 134, 136,
226, 264, 89(2), 279(2), 554(2)
— agriculture 262, 355, 383
— artificers 252
— boat builders 363(2)
— botanical gardens 195
— bridges 106(2), 107(2)
— carpenters 429, 139(2)
— coal mines 419, 601(2)

— convict barracks 450(2)
— convict chaplains 207(2),
286(2)
— convicts 126, 149, 183, 262,
264, 308, 383, 492, 563, 575,
10(2), 71(2), 223(2), 362(2),
420(2), 580(2)
— convicts: see also principal
superintendant of convicts
— emigration 576
— female factory 291(2)
— government affairs 209(2)
— government blacksmiths 252
— government boats 192,
577(2)
— government lumberyard
139(2)
— instruction 418
— labour 530(2)
— livestock 563, 22(2)
— police 22, 218, 529, 562, 566,
3(2), 123(2), 143(2), 261(2),
267(2), 399(2), 580(2)
— police (assistant) 615(2)
— probation station 302
— public works 487, 215(2),
283(2), 401(2), 539(2)
— road building (assistant) 220
— road gang 597(2)
— roads, bridges & streets
219(2)
— stock 380, 521, 10(2), 159(2),
215(2), 232(2), 308(2), 429(2),
447(2)
— stores 383
— Sunday School 192, 510
— telegraphs 267(2)
— timberyard 442(2)
— Sydney Botanic Gardens 269
— vaccinations 502
supervisor of swamp draining
220
surgeon: see also medical
practitioner, physician,
doctor, surgeon
surgeon 27, 51, 64, 104, 126,
134, 137, 191, 206, 213, 219,
235, 242, 252, 253, 273, 291,
295(C), 367, 372, 373, 389,
412, 467, 485, 508, 519, 537,
544, 553, 555, 556, 2(2), 4(2),
6(2), 12(2), 88(2), 139(2),
140(2), 174(2), 213(2), 227(2),
230(2), 264(2), 274(2), 280(2),
368(2), 369(2), 370(2), 419(2),
427(2), 434(2), 453(2), 490(2),
506(2), 530(2), 541(2), 580(2),
593(2), 612(2), 623(2), 624(2),
626(2)
surgeon general (NSW) 12(2)
surgeon's mate 4(2), 12(2)
surgeon superintendent (convict
transport) 268, 331, 503, 2(2),
369(2), 375(2), 376(2), 418(2),
427(2), 522(2)
surveyor: 11, 81, 96, 109, 183,
188, 193, 211, 220, 250, 265,
273, 280, 282, 297, 309, 332,
359, 377, 391, 410, 418, 448,
457, 467, 487, 504, 516, 528,
543, 547, 34(2), 43(2), 48(2),
64(2), 70(2), 71(2), 73(2),

112(2), 116(2), 125(2), 126(2),
    168(2), 213(2), 219(2), 231(2),
    232(2), 240(2), 264(2), 315(2),
    324(2), 390(2), 409(2), 429(2),
    436(2), 466(2), 471(2), 542(2),
    575(2)
— assistant 406
— customs 365(2)
— deputy 240, 359
— district 107(2)
— roads & bridges 487, 123(2)
— land 9, 406
— landing 427
— marine 64(2)
surveyor general 142, 241, 247,
    251, 388, 432, 464, 494, 538-9,
    112(2), 114(2), 116(2), 125(2),
    238(2), 305(2), 306(2), 348(2),
    391(2), 497(2), 507(2)
surveyor general (acting) 359
surveyor general (deputy) 64(2),
    348(2), 502(2)
surveyor: see also land
    surveyor; cartographical
    surveyor
tailor 252, 28(2), 51(2), 141(2)
tanner 29
taxidermist 465, 466
tea broker 250(2)
teacher 13, 514, 560, 42(2),
    212(2), 396(2), 502(2)
teacher of mathematics 403(2)
teacher: see also schoolteacher,
    schoolmaster; mistress
temperance worker 491(2)
tenant farmer 267, 133(2),
    408(2)
theatre critic 181
theatre director 108(2)
theatre lessee & owner 625(2)
theatre manager 355
theologian 424(2), 491(2)
ticket of leave convict 265(2)
timbergetter 601(2)
timber merchant 22, 372,
    129(2), 245(2)
tin plate worker 259
tinsmith 201
tobacconist 15
topographical artist 427
town clerk 184, 202, 206, 330,
    55(2), 251(2), 257(2)
town commissioner 433(2)
town surveyor 220
trader 56, 107, 115, 127, 209,
    263, 277, 533, 116(2), 373(2),
    438(2), 600(2), 605(2)
trader: see also merchant;
    island trader; sea trader;
    businessman; company
    director
trade unionist 132(2)
translator 40(2), 222(2)
traveller 348, 402, 282(2)
treasurer 204, 378, 463, 26(2)
treasurer of police fund 458
treasurer: see also sub-treasurer
treasurer: see also colonial
    treasurer
treasurer: see also city treasurer
trustee 598(2)
tutor 48, 63, 192, 210, 254, 376,

426, 428, 474, 558, 573, 50(2),
    118(2), 119(2)
under secretary: for colonies
    464, 480, 79(2), 470(2), 475(2)
— Dublin 464
— for law 509
— home office 464, 57(2),
    281(2)
— war office 268(2)
under sheriff 244, 255(2),
    353(2), 623(2)
Unitarian minister: see minister
    (Unitarian)
usher of the black rod 356,
    123(2), 348(2)
valuer 528(2)
vendue master 87(2), 142(2)
veterinary officer 246
vicar 199, 256, 362, 522, 573,
    49(2), 431(2), 440(2)
vicar apostolic 504
vicar general 146, 292, 472-3,
    207(2), 299(2)
vice admiral 99(2)
vice chancellor 11, 340(2),
    526(2)
vice consul 341
vice president 136(2)
vice regal secretary 199
vigneron 54(2), 371(2)
vigneron: see also winegrower
vine dresser 362(2), 616(2)
violinist 530
viticulturalist 186, 423(2)
warden 256
warehouse keeper 220
warehouse porter 448(2)
watchcase maker 444(2)
watch finisher 502(2)
watchmaker 419, 109(2),
    291(2), 463(2)
watchmaker (Royal) 26(2)
watchman 517
water conservator 394(2)
water colourist 115(2)
water police magistrate 149
weaver 13, 338, 365, 218(2),
    519(2)
Wesleyan layman 510
Wesleyan minister: see minister
    (Methodist)
Wesleyan missionary: see
    missionary (Methodist)
whaler 272, 533, 117(2), 231(2)
wharfinger 543, 575
wheat grower 294(2), 614(2)
wheelwright 222(2), 259(2)
wild white man 258, 468, 610(2)
wine & general merchant
    206(2)
wine & spirit merchant 162(2),
    271(2), 417(2)
wine cooper 616(2)
wine grower 614(2), 630(2)
wine merchant 178(2), 300(2),
    431(2), 553(2)
wool expert 437(2)
woolbroker 492(2)
woolbuyer 110(2), 437(2)
woolcomber 365
woolgrower 400, 498, 523
woollen draper 419, 314(2)

woolsorter 437(2)
writer 202, 206, 275, 402, 74(2),
    160(2), 166(2), 246(2), 424(2),
    555(2), 558(2), 576(2)
writer to the signet 227, 572,
    75(2), 160(2), 243(2), 271(2),
    336(2), 396(2)
yachtsman 232(2)
yeoman farmer 206(2), 254(2),
    333(2)
zoologist 111, 250, 279, 465-6,
    114(2), 181(2)

Placenames

This section is in the following order:—

Miscellaneous Places . . . . page 76

Countries or areas by modern name
from Antarctica to West Indies . . . . page 77

Australia: territories
Australian Capital Territory . . . . page 80
Norfolk Island . . . . page 80
Northern Territory . . . . page 81

Australia: states (formerly colonies)
New South Wales . . . . page 81
Queensland . . . . page 87
South Australia . . . . page 87
Tasmania . . . . page 88
Victoria . . . . page 92
Western Australia . . . . page 94

British Isles:
Island groups . . . . page 94
England . . . . page 95
Ireland . . . . page 99
Scotland . . . . page 100
Wales . . . . page 101

NOTE: Houses, buildings, properties, farms etc. are listed in the General Index under Houses etc.

Miscellaneous Places: Small
  Islands, Island Groups,
  Rivers, Bays, etc.
Actaeon Reef 260(2)
Adelaide Island 105
Admiralty Gulf 266
Admiralty Islands 172
Adriatic 400(2)
Alps 69(2)
Antipodes Island 130(2)
Arafura Sea 471(2)
Auckland Island 357
Baltic 290, 99(2)
Bass Islands 65
Bering Sea 85(2)
Bering Strait 315(2)
Bermuda 248, 392, 392, 503,
  234(2), 235(2)
Bermuda, St. George 392
Bintang Island 65
Biscoe Island 105
Bismarck Archipelago 172
Black Sea 181(2)
Bonaparte Archipeligo 390(2)
Booby Island 266
Borabora 306, 307
Bourbon (Reunion) Island
  492
Brunswick Bay 266
Buccaneer Archipelago 266
Bustard Bay 243
Calamos 264
Cape Barren 31(2)
Cape Horn 243, 277, 85(2),
  318(2)
Cape Leveque 71, 266
Cape Townshend 243
Cape Verde Islands 260(2)
Cape Voltaire 266
Cape Wessel 62(2)
Carnac Island 632(2)
Caroline Islands 348
Chatham Island 551(2)
Clarence Strait 266
Cloates Land 13(2)
Cocos Islands 527
Colbourg Peninsula 266
Columbia River 279
Cossack 266
Cumberland Isles 272(2)
De Witt's Land 503(2)
Dockhead 306
Dorey Harbour 527
Durley Island 31
Enderby Land 105, 357
Ercildoun 438(2)
Eromanga 600(2)
Exmouth Gulf 266, 390(2)
Falkland Islands 72, 157, 526,
  247(2)
Fitzroy Island 266
Foveaux Straits 130(2)
Friendly Islands 95(2)
Furneaux Islands 389, 272(2)
Galapagos Islands 357
Gilberts Islands 107
Goulburn Island 266
Graham Land 105
Guadalcanal, Solomon Islands
  142
Guam 348, 518, 312(2)
Guam Bay 127

Gulf of Riga 83
Gulf of Tartary 85(2)
Hawaiian Islands: see
  Sandwich Islands, USA:
  Hawaii
Henderson Island 360(2)
Hobson's Bay 115(2)
Ile Bourbon 171
Ile de France 171
Inaccessible Island 435(2)
Isle of Bourbon 146
Isle of Pines 275
Isles of Gold 358
Kent Group (islands) 272(2)
Kerquelen Island 492
King River 266
Koro Island 127
Leeward Islands 364, 384,
  529(2)
Lord Howe Is., Ball's
  Pyramid 50
Lord Howe Island 363(2),
  453(2)
Lorient 72(2)
Louisiade Archipelago 527,
  578, 167(2)
Louisiade Islands 471(2)
Loyalty Islands 141
Madeira 99, 370(2)
Malabar Coast 317(2)
Malta 129, 348, 474, 526,
  308(2), 403(2), 424(2),
  631(2)
Malta, Valetta harbour 465(2)
Mangareva 288(2)
Marquesas 178, 208, 259, 260,
  357(2)
Marquesas Islands 494(2)
Marshall Islands 107
Mediterranean 268, 279, 324,
  47(2), 61(2), 116(2), 224(2)
Mediterranean Station 72(2)
Menai Straits 106(2)
Moorea 208, 529(2), 599(2)
Mosquito Coast, Nicaragua
  33
Mozambique 548
Navigator Islands 85(2)
New Caledonia 172, 178, 480,
  527, 25(2), 46(2), 536(2)
New Hebrides 85, 141, 245,
  307, 480, 85(2), 168(2),
  358(2), 536(2), 600(2)
New Hebrides, New
  Jerusalem 358(2)
New Hebrides, Espiritu Santo
  536(2)
Norfolk Island: see Australia
North Sea 61(2)
North-West Passage 315(2)
Nukuhiva 208
Oesel 83
Ono Island 83
Pacific Islands 208, 307,
  209(2)
Pacific Ocean 205
Palm Island 266
Pass of Maya 264
Penantipodes Island 130(2)
Peter I. Island 83
Peter I. Land 83
Pitcairn Island 288(2), 360(2),

  361(2)
Plains of Promise 489(2)
Point Venus 111(2)
Polynesia 199
Port Walcott 266
Poyais settlement 385(2)
Preservation Island 64
Prince Edward Island 384
Prince of Wales Island 142(2)
Pyrenees 196, 264
Raiatea 430(2), 600(2)
Rarotonga 583(2)
Rarotonga 208
Reunion Island 146, 492
Rhio, Bintang Island 65
Rossel Island 527
St Allounan Island 172
St Eustacius 482(2)
St Helena 376, 417
St Jago 260(2)
St Marcouf Island 264(2)
Samoa 422(2), 600(2)
Samoa, Apia 422(2)
Samoa, Tutuila 85(2)
Sandwich Islands 65, 83, 235,
  244, 85(2)
Santa Cruz 85(2), 299(2),
  357(2)
Santa Cruz Islands 178
Sarawak 15(2)
Seychelles 298
Society Islands 245, 275, 306,
  365, 495, 444(2), 529(2)
Solomon Islands 142, 172,
  307
South-east Asia 277
South Georgia Islands 83
South Pacific 209
South Sandwich Island 105
South Seas 251, 258, 259, 260,
  275, 277
Stanley, Falkland Is. 248(2)
Straits of Magellan 470(2)
Straits of Malacca 32(2)
Sunda Strait 171
Surabaya 111
Suvorov Islands 99(2)
Swan Point 266
Tate Island 31
Tenerife 235
Termination Island 551(2)
Terre Napoleon 71
Tikopia, Solomon Islands 307
Tiku 14(2)
Timor Sea 489(2)
Tonga 253, 307, 321, 291(2),
  424(2), 438(2), 95(2)
Tonga Islands 503(2)
Tongatapu 127, 178, 518
Torres Strait 32, 276, 62(2),
  365(2), 390(2)
Tristan da Cunha 348, 469
Tuamotus 208, 439(2)
Tucopia 307
Upolu, Falealili 3(2), 422(2)
Valetta harbour 465(2)
Van Diemen's Gulf 266
Van Diemen's Land: see
  Tasmania
Vanikoro 307, 85(2)

Miscellaneous Countries:
    Where cities have been
    mentioned they are listed
    under the country in which
    they are situated.
Africa: see also entries under
    individual countries. 235
    Gambia 381, 14(2), 566(2)
    Gold Coast 248(2), 426(2)
    Liberia 509
    Nigeria, Lagos 248(2)
    Rhodesia 335
    Sierra Leone 298, 371, 495,
        509, 14(2), 248(2)
Antarctica: 83, 105, 34(2)
Antigua: 298, 364, 492, 430(2)
Argentina: 157
    Buenos Aires 128, 157, 439,
        573
    Cape Horn 243, 277, 85(2),
        318(2)
    Patagonia 62(2), 212(2)
    Tierra del Fuego 53, 212(2)
Austria: 71
    Feldberg 73
    Hietzing, Vienna 73
    Schonbrunn Palace 71
    Vienna 73, 99(2), 114(2),
        545(2)
Bahamas: 475
    Nassau 545
Barbados:
    Barbados 5, 62, 439, 492,
        69(2), 250(2)
    Bridgetown 69(2)
Belgium: (see also Flanders) 27,
    307, 218(2)
    Antwerp 512, 322(2)
    Brussels 27, 235(2), 294(2),
        630(2)
    Liege, 199(2)
    Louvain 309
    Ostend 446
    Quatre Bras 264
    Waterloo 264, 301
Bermuda:
    Bermuda 248, 392, 483, 503,
        234(2), 235(2)
    St George 392
Bolivia: 296(2)
Brazil: 235, 269, 348, 79(2),
    85(2), 114(2), 402(2)
    Botofogo 349
    Pernambuco 217(2)
    Port St Pedro (Rio Grande)
        233(2)
    Rio de Janeiro 18, 41, 53, 226,
        265, 310, 348, 349, 12(2),
        64(2), 94(2), 156(2), 212(2),
        229(2), 402(2), 427(2),
        457(2), 528(2), 599(2)
British Guiana:
    Berbice 183
    Demerara 384(2), 523(2),
        603(2)
    George Town 92
Burma:
    Burma 250, 371, 461, 527,
        546, 391(2), 471(2)
    Rangamati 231
Cambodia: 503(2)
Canada: 21, 142, 220, 322, 333,

    413, 430, 446, 488, 508, 5(2),
        69(2), 133(2), 258(2),
        268(2), 281(2), 368(2),
        407(2), 414(2), 475(2),
        481(2), 533(2), 586(2),
        603(2), 630(2)
    Baffin Bay 315(2)
    British Columbia 65(2),
        551(2)
    Capetown, Ontario 516
    Chateaugay 353(2)
    Halifax NS 236, 243, 20(2),
        234(2), 442(2)
    Hudson Bay 85(2)
    Ile aux Noix 353(2)
    King William's Land 412
    Labrador 52, 243
    Lake Champlain 220
    Lake Erie 268
    Lancaster Sound 315(2)
    London ONT 133(2)
    Lower Canada 353
    Montreal 2, 352(2)
    New Brunswick 142, 431,
        34(2), 234(2), 348(2)
    Newfoundland 52, 243, 290,
        392, 567, 29(2), 442(2)
    Nootka Sound 267(2), 550(2)
    Nova Scotia 201, 243, 187(2)
    Ottawa 333
    Prescott 430
    Quebec 243, 367, 431, 567,
        353(2), 383(2), 443(2),
        531(2)
    St Lawrence River 243
    St Polycarpe 352(2)
    St Timothee 352(2)
    Soulanges QUE 352(2)
    Upper Canada 37, 391, 430
Central America: 277
Ceylon: 101, 272, 375, 474, 554,
    5(2), 15(2), 123(2), 143(2),
    171(2), 295(2), 377(2),
    382(2), 399(2)
    Colombo 142(2), 188(2),
        377(2)
    Galle 123(2C), 188(2)
    Kandy 295(2)
    Trincomalee 310
Channel Islands: see British
    Isles
Chile: 208, 235, 348, 24(2),
    62(2), 85(2), 137(2), 503(2)
    Patagonia 62(2), 212(2)
    Tierra del Fuego 53, 212(2)
    Valparaiso 92, 548, 42(2),
        137(2), 212(2), 360(2),
        567(2)
China: 12, 208, 235, 275, 276,
    290, 305, 306, 59(2), 202(2),
    366(2), 446(2), 453(2),
    592(2)
    Canton 7, 107, 275, 290, 527,
        156(2), 307(2), 380(2),
        381(2), 501(2)
    Formosa 107, 235
    Hong Kong 106(2)
    Macao 65, 107, 127, 277,
        85(2), 156(2), 188(2)
Cuba: 183(2)
    Havana 182(2), 267(2), 326(2)
Cyprus: 69(2)

Czechoslovakia: 624(2)
    Galicia 114(2)
    Lemberg (Lwow) 114(2)
    Prague 114(2)
Denmark: 457(2), 590(2)
    Copenhagen 7, 264, 26(2),
        415(2)
    Jutland 285(2)
Dominica: 298, 317, 268(2),
    294(2), 324(2), 364(2),
    568(2)
    Roseau 294(2)
Dominican Republic: see San
    Domingo
Dutch East Indies: see
    Indonesia
East Indies: see Indonesia
Ecuador: 137(2)
Egypt: 13, 32, 324, 116(2),
    243(2), 270(2), 284(2),
    443(2)
    Aboukir 188(2)
    Aboukir Bay 465(2)
    Alexandria 8, 268, 539, 72(2),
        116(2), 188(2), 224(2),
        261(2)
    Cairo 47, 354, 188(2)
England: see British Isles below
Falkland Islands: 72, 157, 526,
    247(2)
Fiji: 199, 208, 306, 307, 518,
    573, 36(2), 129(2), 438(2),
    444(2)
Flanders: see also Belgium
    Flanders 151, 223, 247, 270(2)
France: 49, 71, 122, 196, 222,
    264, 269, 307, 315, 535,
    116(2), 149(2), 189(2),
    206(2), 406(2)
    Aix 171
    Albi 85(2)
    Alcantara 324(2)
    Alencon 69(2)
    Allier 323(2)
    Amelie-les-Bains 147
    Amiens 305
    Ancenis 539
    Bay of Biscay 322, 61(2)
    Belle-Isle 85(2)
    Biarritz 597(2)
    Bordeaux 431(2)
    Boulogne 417, 222(2), 450(2)
    Brest 171, 85(2), 281(2)
    Brittany 506(2)
    Brittany, St-Pol-de-Leon 573
    Caen 196(2), 315(2), 523(2)
    Calais 105(2)
    Cannes 455, 447(2)
    Cerilly 323(2)
    Chantilly 267(2)
    Cherbourg 417
    Corsica 399(2)
    Fontainebleau 193(2)
    Hautes-Pyrenees 568(2)
    Hyeres 193(2)
    Languedoc 400
    Le Havre 146, 315
    Lille 443(2)
    Mentone 182(2)
    Meuse 217
    Montelimar, Drome 71
    Nantes 85(2)

Nice 453(2)
Nivelle 49
Normandy 315(2), 523(2)
Paris 264, 308, 315, 455, 503, 69(2), 110(2), 235(2), 266(2), 294(2), 296(2), 387(2), 562(2), 584(2)
Pau 296
Quimper 506(2)
Rocheforte 83(2)
Rouen 122, 499(2)
St Dominique 122
St Malo 469
St-Pierre-de-Re 71
St Servan 469
Tagus 324(2)
Toulon 184, 539, 47(2), 193(2)
Verdun 116(2), 184(2)
Vieuzos 568(2)
Gambia: 381, 14(2), 566(2)
Germany: 42, 222, 77(2), 334(2), 441(2), 568(2), 611(2)
Aken-on-the-Elb, Saxony 509
Auggen, Baden 509
Bavaria 557(2)
Beeskow 104(2)
Berlin 33(2), 114(2), 403(2)
Brandenburg 33(2)
Carlsruhe 349
Cologne 389(2)
Cottbus 102(2)
Cuxhaven 341, 337(2)
Danzig 402, 403, 99(2)
Darmstadt 237(2)
Dirschau 403
Esslington 351
Frankfurt 326(2)
Gironde 403
Gottingen 403
Halberstadt 350(2)
Hamburg 338, 400, 445, 541, 33(2), 100(2), 105(2), 212(2), 290(2), 403(2), 404(2)
Hanau 222(2)
Heligoland 5, 419, 541, 119(2), 337(2), 473(2)
Herzberg am Harz 349(2)
Hesse 11, 222(2), 420(2)
Kaiserslautern 323(2)
Koblenz 476(2)
Leipzig 400, 392(2), 392(2C)
Liebenwerda, Saxony 33(2)
Lubeck 222(2)
Magdeburg 505, 323(2)
Mainz 403
Moselle 217
Munich 222(2)
Nassenhuben 402, 403
Pilsen, Bavaria 557(2)
Prussia 341, 504, 103(2)
Prussia, Stettin 137(2)
Rhine 217
Saxony 42, 281, 341, 24(2)
Silesia 341
Stargard, Mecklenburg-Strelitz 403(2)
Steinau 222(2)
Stettin 362(2), 566(2)
Stettin, Prussia 137(2)

Trebatsch 102(2)
Tschew, Prussia 403
Wurttemberg 351
Zaue 102(2)
Zullichau 33(2)
Gibraltar: 8, 11, 46, 125, 228, 375, 418, 419, 474, 483, 489, 538, 243(2), 281(2), 383(2), 399(2), 442(2), 536(2)
Gold Coast (Africa): 248(2), 426(2)
Granada: 61, 91, 168, 294(2), 482(2)
Greece:
Corfu 503
Ionian Islands 264, 631(2)
Guadeloupe: 62, 75, 443(2)
Guiana: see British Guiana
Holland: see Netherlands
Honduras: 15, 33, 131(2), 421(2)
Hungary: 537(2)
Nitra (Nyitra) 623(2)
Pest 624(2)
Iceland: 27(2), 222(2), 456(2)
India: 112, 203, 208, 211, 216, 224, 228, 233, 245, 250, 251, 253, 276, 290, 300, 303, 305, 306, 337, 371, 422, 465, 488, 542, 46(2), 49(2), 56(2), 64(2), 101(2), 116(2), 121(2), 123(2), 129(2), 222(2), 243(2), 248(2), 278(2), 301(2), 317(2), 366(2), 380(2), 400(2), 415(2), 436(2), 495(2), 569(2)
Agra 250, 322(2)
Belgaum 243(2)
Bengal 80, 253, 307, 455, 45(2), 292(2), 364(2), 419(2), 495(2), 598(2)
Berhampore 300(2)
Bhurtpore 268(2)
Bombay 7, 21, 37, 65, 83, 232, 316, 332, 507, 24(2), 188(2), 189(2), 281(2), 428(2), 468(2)
Calcutta 40, 117, 197, 203, 204, 208, 240, 250, 291, 307, 422, 527, 551, 46(2), 101(2), 116(2), 121(2), 130(2), 156(2), 223(2), 292(2), 301(2), 307(2), 364(2), 365(2), 373(2), 380(2), 381(2), 444(2), 464(2), 521(2), 547(2), 548(2), 566(2), 574(2), 613(2)
Calicut 188(2)
Cawnpore 488(2)
Chinsurah 197
Chittoor 575
Cochin 174(2), 188(2)
Coringa 435(2)
Fort St George 500(2)
Ghazipur 143
Goa 358
Gujarat 332
Kedgeree, Bengal 253
Kidderpore 455
Madras 82, 125, 185, 197, 208, 218, 221, 275, 276, 348,

359, 377, 542, 575, 243(2), 435(2), 500(2), 521(2)
Masulipatam 322(2)
Mysore 431
Negapatam 521(2)
Nellore 575
North Arcot 575
Peshawar 250
Poona 410
Royal Square, Calcutta 422
Sedasere 188(2)
Seringapatam 21
Sittana 250
Surat 322(2)
Tanjore 250, 521(2)
Ternate 527
Tinnevelly 500(2)
Travancore 500(2)
Vepery 521(2)
Indonesia: 29, 32, 527, 577(2)
Amboina 107, 172, 555, 155(2), 465(2)
Balambangan, Borneo 276
Banda 32
Bantam 555
Batavia 29, 32, 53, 243, 14(2), 235(2), 281(2), 314(2), 364(2), 365(2), 443(2), 503(2), 548(2), 596(2)
Bencoolen 29
Borneo 276
Ceram 503(2)
East Indies 235, 268, 272, 275, 290, 416, 46(2), 56(2)
Fort Henricus 13(2)
Jacatra 13(2)
Java 218, 527, 13(2), 69(2), 323(2)
Koepang (Kupang), Timor 174. 230(2)
Malacca 357, 15(2)
Malacca Straits 364(2)
Moluccas 171, 555
Padang 29
Solor 13(2)
Sumatra 29, 116(2), 323(2)
Timor 32, 72, 174, 266, 277, 62(2), 612(2)
Iran: see Persia
Iraq:
Baghdad 355, 189(2)
Basra 189(2)
Ireland: see British Isles below.
Israel: see Palestine
Italy: 222, 324, 116(2), 181(2), 376(2), 400(2), 406(2), 630(2)
Arno River 376(2)
Calabria 32
Como 75(2)
Elba 55
Florence 69(2)
Gaeta 538, 538(C)
Naples 538, 285(2), 416(2)
Norcia 416(2)
North Italy 149(2)
Rome 21, 293, 387(2), 417(2), 544(2)
Sicily 32, 57, 348, 454(2), 631(2)
Turin 530, 559(2)
Tuscany 69(2)

Vignolo, Lake Maggiore 287(2)
Jamaica: 33, 151, 183, 290, 322, 364, 372, 495, 538, 187(2), 243(2), 303(2), 412(2), 421(2), 440(2), 484(2), 550(2), 592(2), 621(2)
Falmouth 439
Kingston 10, 392
Port Maria 537
Port Royal 622(2)
Japan: 503(2)
Akkeshi 433(2)
Hokkaido 433(2)
Japan 202(2), 433(2)
Nagasaki 433(2)
Korea: 85(2)
Latin America: see individual countries.
Latin America: see South America
Lebanon: 69(2)
Beirut 624(2)
Liberia: 509
Liechtenstein: 73
Madagascar: 11, 283, 548, 340(2)
Malaya: 116(2)
Kuala Kedah 116(2)
Junkceylon 116(2)
Penang 116(2)
Malta: 129, 348, 474, 526, 308(2), 403(2), 424(2), 631(2)
Valetta harbour 465(2)
Marshall Islands: 107
Martinique: 10, 305, 306, 299(2)
Mauritius: 45, 47, 50, 71, 101, 127-8, 245, 266, 272, 283, 305, 306, 329, 332, 333, 377, 390, 407, 419, 474, 477, 539, 12(2), 62(2), 69(2), 70(2), 119(2), 121(2), 133(2), 196(2), 340(2), 372(2), 384(2), 390(2), 399(2), 400(2), 433(2), 500(2), 544(2), 548(2)
Port Louis, Mauritius 47, 283
Mexico:
235, 508, 357(2), 446(2)
Acapulco 358(2)
Mexico City 267(2)
Vera Cruz 267(2), 358(2)
Netherlands:
128, 174, 180, 460, 235(2)
Alkmaar 555-6
Amsterdam 13(2), 556(2)
Bergen op Zoom 631(2)
Egmont-op-zee, Holland 196
Gouda 555
Groningen 503(2)
Holland 8, 196, 399(2), 568(2)
Lutjegast 503(2)
North Holland 459(2)
Vlieland 556(2)
New Caledonia: 178, 480, 527, 25(2), 46(2), 536(2)
New Guinea: 172, 243, 276, 277, 167(2), 471(2), 503(2), 536(2), 592(2)
Fly River 111
Henry Reed Bay 373(2)

New Britain 277, 373(2)
Owen Stanley Ranges 471(2)
Papua 276(2)
New Hebrides: 85, 141, 245, 307, 480, 85(2), 168(2), 358(2), 422(2), 536(2), 600(2)
Espiritu Santo 536(2)
New Jerusalem 358(2)
New Zealand: 18, 49, 53, 57, 158, 178, 207, 214, 218, 229, 243, 244, 245, 252, 266, 267, 269, 275, 276, 281, 297, 306, 307, 357, 447, 479, 486, 556, 559, 42(2), 45(2), 50(2), 57(2), 63(2), 86(2), 95(2), 99(2), 115(2), 209(2), 212(2), 225(2), 263(2), 281(2), 303(2), 451(2), 463(2), 464(2), 471(2), 475(2), 494(2), 503(2), 520(2), 527(2), 559(2), 587(2), 598(2), 609(2), 631(2)
Akaroa 471(2) 182, 275, 392, 480
Auckland 541, 546
Banks Penisula 546, 471(2)
Bay of Islands 98, 170, 186, 269, 307, 349, 377, 479, 546, 42(2), 59(2), 105(2), 210(2), 535(2)
Canterbury 524, 524(C)
Canterbury North 50(2), 118(2)
Christchurch 118(2)
Cloudy Bay 48(2)
Cokeley 396(2)
Dusky Bay 364(2)
Foveaux Strait 178
Hawdon River 524
Hokianga 186, 187, 245, 360(2)
Kawau 479
Kororareka 546, 356(2)
Mahurangi 275
Mangonui 275
Mercury Bay 275
Napier 541
Nelson 29, 197(2)
New Plymouth 49, 2(2), 115(2)
North Canterbury 50(2), 118(2)
North Island 546
Official Bay 281
Omaka 49
Otago 297, 37(2)
Port Nicholson 546
Rangitikei River 396(2)
Rotorua 98
Russell 356(2)
Taupo 98
Tongariro 98
Vogeltown 115(2)
Waikato 108(2)
Waitangi 187-8, 546, 554(2)
Waitemata 546
Waiwera 297
Waiwera River 297
Wanganui 3(2)
Wellington 479, 546, 115(2),

396(2), 561(2)
Weraroa 479
Whangaroa 269, 25(2), 105(2)
Nicaragua: 385(2)
Mosquito Coast 33
Nigeria: Lagos 248(2)
Norfolk Island: see Australia
North America 233, 236, 244, 268, 276
Norway: 22, 46, 566
Larvik, Norway 22
Palestine: 435
Gaza 383(2)
Holy Land 124(2)
Panama: 446(2)
Papua: see New Guinea
Persia: 411, 285(2)
Persian Gulf 260(2)
Peru: 208, 548, 62(2), 137(2)
Callao 307, 348, 288(2), 357(2), 536(2)
Lima 92, 348, 402(2)
Phillipines: 252, 276, 277, 366(2)
Manila 127, 208, 348, 85(2), 313(2), 357(2), 536(2)
Poland:
Danzig 402, 403, 99(2)(see also Germany)
Gluszyna 494(2)
Pomerania 421(2)
Poznan 494(2)
Stargard 421(2)
Western Poland 494(2)
Portugal: 47, 197, 264, 94(2), 206(2), 270(2), 455(2), 463(2), 482(2), 601(2)
Evora 357(2)
Lisbon 184, 431, 474, 476, 562, 218(2), 404(2)
Oporto 47
Rarotonga: 208, 583(2)
Rhodesia: 335
Russia: 83, 402, 285(2), 494(2)
Astrakhan 398(2)
Kamchatka 107, 235, 85(2)
Kronstadt 83, 84
Neva 84
Orenburg 398(2)
Russian Tartary 398(2)
St Petersburg 189(2), 456(2)
Sakhalin 85(2)
Saratov 403
Sebastopol 388, 435(2)
Siberia 244, 222(2)
St Kitts: 228, 438, 557, 604(2)
Basse Terre 557, 476(2)
St Lucia: 92, 228, 482(2)
St Vincent 195, 298, 364, 172(2C), 482(2)
Samoa: 422(2), 600(2)
Apia 422(2)
Tutuila 85(2)
San Domingo: 300(2)
Saudi Arabia: Aden 106(2)
Scotland: see British Isles below.
Siam: 116(2)
Sierra Leone: 298, 371, 495, 509, 14(2), 248(2)
Freetown 248(2)
Singapore: 7, 348, 15(2), 348(2),

396(2), 471(2)
Solomon Islands: 172, 307
 Guadalcanal, Solomon Islands
  142
 Tikopia, Solomon Islands 307
South Africa: 18, 351, 404, 479,
  568, 89(2), 171(2), 317(2),
  380(2), 562(2)
 Cape Colony 101, 129, 202,
  455, 474, 547, 130(2), 196(2)
 Cape of Good Hope 145, 199,
  239, 242, 252, 262, 265, 308,
  318, 349, 359, 377, 384, 389,
  410, 506, 548, 229(2),
  235(2), 243(2), 250(2),
  329(2), 340(2), 363(2),
  420(2), 428(2), 459(2),
  573(2), 578(2), 629(2)
 Cape Town 129, 184, 376,
  404, 420, 477, 479, 492, 548,
  17(2), 77(2), 128(2), 250(2),
  285(2), 376(2), 398(2),
  574(2)
 Natal 256, 479
 Table Bay 359
South America: 208, 268, 287,
  307, 114(2), 574(2), 595(2),
  598(2), 631(2)
 Cape Horn 243, 277, 85(2),
  318(2)
Soviet Union: see Russia
Spain: 81, 208, 247, 264, 268,
  269, 282, 283, 331, 116(2),
  235(2), 243(2), 258(2)
 Albuera 8, 81, 196, 223, 264,
  260(2)
 Busaco 196
 Cadiz 92, 184, 538, 267(2),
  620(2)
 Compostela 416(2)
 Corunna 128, 282, 116(2)
 Douro 196
 Ferrol 224(2)
 Fuentes De Onoro 412(2)
 Galicia 128
 Madrid 431, 358(2)
 Minorca 324, 442(2)
 Nivelle 81
 Orthes 305(2)
 Orthos 81
 Pampeluna 305(2)
 Salamanca 81, 309
 San Sebastian 272
 Seville 267(2)
 Talavera 196
 Tuy 416(2)
 Vittoria 196, 305(2)
Sri Lanka: see Ceylon
Surinam: 294(2)
Sweden 454(2), 590(2)
 Norrland 456(2)
 Pitea 456(2)
Switzerland: 341, 89(2), 92(2),
  149(2)
 Berne 341, 89(2)
 Hofwyl 341
 Neuchatel 89(2)
Syria: 220, 434, 69(2), 181(2),
  624(2)
Tahiti: 53, 65, 107, 118, 119,
  178, 208, 233, 243, 244, 245,
  251, 252, 260, 307, 321, 343,

351, 353, 365, 495, 509, 518,
  521, 59(2), 110(2), 111(2),
  209(2), 212(2), 288(2),
  290(2), 314(2), 430(2),
  438(2), 494(2), 520(2),
  548(2), 599(2), 632(2)
 Tahiti, Matavai Bay, Tahiti
  65, 253, 522
 Tahitian Islands 551(2)
Thailand: see Siam
Timor: see Indonesia
Tobago: 168, 214(2)
Tonga: 253, 307, 321, 291(2),
  303(2), 424(2), 438(2), 95(2)
 Tonga Islands 503(2)
 Tongatapu 127, 178, 518
Trinidad: 92, 99, 228, 384(2)
Turkey: 181(2), 189(2)
United States of America: 220,
  235, 252, 253, 273, 288, 324,
  430, 39(2), 258(2), 266(2),
  294(2), 298(2), 457(2),
  568(2), 589(2)
 see also North America
 Alameda, California 544
 Alaska 85(2)
 Alaskan Peninsular 551(2)
 Baltimore 165(2), 299(2)
 Boston 611(2)
 Bunker's Hill 236, 397(2)
 California 235, 377, 543,
  85(2), 161(2), 411(2)
 California (Spanish) 267(2)
 Charleston 236, 348, 425,
  187(2)
 Chesapeake Bay 297, 309(2)
 Cincinnati 186(2), 402(2)
 Craney Island 220
 Crown Point 531(2)
 Fort Erie 233
 Franklin County 548
 Georgia 426, 502, 621(2)
 Hawaii (Sandwich Islands)
  65, 83, 107, 235, 244, 275,
  412, 85(2), 446(2), 494(2),
  551(2)
 — Honolulu 233
 — Karakakooa Bay 244
 — Kealakekua Bay 244
 Kent Island 220
 Lake Champlain 531(2)
 Louisiana 430(2)
 Massachusetts 78(2)
 Mississipi River 484(2)
 Missouri 218(2)
 Montana 218(2)
 Monterey 85(2), 267(2)
 New England 430
 New Orleans 184, 184(2)
 New York 21, 41, 252, 420,
  548, 20(2), 94(2), 187(2),
  217(2), 235(2), 243(2),
  294(2), 298(2C), 353(2),
  402(2), 423(2), 531(2),
  568(2)
 New York State 422(2),
  531(2)
 Norfolk VA 279
 Philadelphia 279, 305, 348,
  438, 513, 516, 221(2),
  298(2C), 300(2)
 Plymouth MA 178(C)

San Blas 267(2)
 San Francisco 235(2), 551(2)
 San Leander 544(C)
 Sandwich Islands: see Hawaii
 Skeneborough 531(2)
 South Carolina 78(2), 523(2),
  621(2)
 Susquehanna County 300(2)
 Ticonderoga 531(2)
 Utica 278, 279
 Virginia 235(2), 491(2)
 Washington 233, 279, 184(2)
Uruguay:
 Montevideo 128, 349, 439,
  465, 212(2), 484(2)
USSR: see Russia
Wales: see British Isles below.
West Indies: see also entries
  under individual countries.
  195, 223, 226, 228, 233, 240,
  248, 275, 282, 288, 290, 305,
  314, 316, 545, 51(2), 67(2),
  69(2), 89(2), 162(2), 175(2),
  224(2), 263(2), 426(2),
  442(2), 459(2), 482(2)
 Bahamas, Nassau 545
 Dominica, Roseau 294(2)
 Leeward Islands 364, 384,
  529(2)
 Martinique 10, 305, 306,
  299(2)
 St Kitts 228, 438, 557, 604(2)
 St Lucia 92, 228, 482(2)
 St Vincent 195, 298, 482(2)
 San Domingo 300(2)
 Tobago 168, 214(2)
 Trinidad 92, 99, 228, 384(2)

AUSTRALIA: Territories
  followed by States

Australian Capital Territory:
  see also under NSW
 Canberra 198, 199, 212,
  254(2), 400(2), 497(2),
  531(2)
 Civic Centre 254(2)
 Woden 274(2)
 Yarralumla 439, 275(2)
Norfolk Island:
  2, 13, 40, 49, 50, 64, 78, 92,
  145, 152, 181, 184, 195, 214,
  218, 220, 226, 233, 237, 239,
  242, 258, 264, 267, 313, 318,
  327, 328, 351, 353, 389, 405,
  408, 421, 423, 447, 448, 485,
  491, 513, 518, 527, 536, 563,
  566, 575, 4(2), 10(2), 12(2),
  13(2), 19(2), 36(2), 39(2),
  47(2), 52(2), 56(2), 57(2),
  59(2), 60(2), 61(2), 63(2),
  66(2), 85(2), 86(2), 96(2),
  97(2), 101(2), 131(2),
  138(2), 139(2), 165(2),
  170(2), 206(2), 208(2),
  217(2), 227(2), 261(2),
  265(2), 272(2), 279(2),
  281(2), 283(2), 287(2),
  288(2), 302(2), 309(2),
  317(2), 329(2), 331(2),
  334(2), 351(2), 354(2),

363(2), 364(2), 369(2),
388(2), 392(2), 398(2),
403(2), 419(2), 443(2),
463(2), 469(2), 483(2),
490(2), 496(2), 531(2),
536(2), 544(2), 573(2),
575(2), 580(2), 607(2)
Arthur Vale 518
Ball's Bay 50
Cascade Bay 568
Charlotte Field 226
Grenville Valley 518
Little Cascade 469(2)
Phillipsburgh 218
Queenborough 226
Sydney Bay 226
Sydney Vale 518
Northern Territory:
Arnhem Land 266
Bathurst Island 266
Fort Dundas 148
Fort Wellington 57, 148
Melville Island 148, 266,
230(2), 377(2), 391(2)
Point Pearce 489(2)
Port Curtis 61, 266
Port Darwin 62(2), 489(2)
Port Essington 148, 201, 363,
441, 452, 578, 103(2),
167(2), 240(2), 471(2),
542(2), 623(2)
Raffles Bay 57
Raine Island 167(2)
Rockingham Bay 578
Simpson Desert 498(2)
Victoria River 489(2)
West Alligator River 266
New South Wales:
42(2), 47(2), 48(2), 66(2),
124(2)
Abbotsbury 292(2)
Abbotsford 513
Abercrombie Ranges 523
Abercrombie River 359,
471(2)
Aberdeen 280, 352, 195(2),
168(2)
Acton 254(2)
Adelong (ACT) 150
Airds 252, 528, 573, 112(2),
368(2), 370(2), 395(2),
568(2)
Albury 212, 311, 341, 350,
173(2), 512(2)
Alexandria 109(2), 110(2)
Annandale 19(2), 371(2)
Anvil Creek 259(2)
Appin 158, 359, 563-4, 292(2),
307(2), 368(2), 548(2),
568(2)
Argyle County 205, 280, 306,
110(2), 433(2), 598(2)
Argyle Cut 505
Arkstone Forest 212
Armidale 199, 311, 44(2),
346(2)
Artarmon 460
Ashfield 12, 113, 523, 48(2),
63(2), 87(2)
Australian Alps 494(2)
Ball's Head 50
Balmain 40, 321, 333, 509,

205(2), 512(2)
Balranald 543
Bankstown 55, 19(2), 22(2),
87(2), 191(2), 220(2),
403(2), 405(2), 443(2)
Bargo 178, 305, 575, 570(2)
Bargo River 498
Bargo South 205
Barrington River 299
Barwon River 232, 239(2)
Bateman's Bay 524
Bathurst 110, 204, 205, 247,
259, 266, 267, 269, 287, 310,
312, 321, 331, 332, 359, 453,
460, 520, 522-4, 525(C),
1(2), 4(2), 11(2), 29(2),
52(2), 66(2), 75(2), 95(2),
96(2), 101(2), 102(2),
134(2), 142(2), 172(2),
191(2), 220(2), 238(2),
261(2), 292(2), 306(2),
310(2), 335(2), 346(2),
360(2), 370(2), 371(2),
376(2), 401(2), 451(2),
471(2), 483(2), 494(2),
495(2), 499(2), 500(2),
508(2), 530(2), 532(2),
544(2), 597(2)
Bathurst plains 292(2)
Baulkham Hills 260, 320, 352,
395(2), 499(2)
Baw Baw 254(2)
Beacon Hill 231
Beeboo 201
Bega 2(2)
Bell 80
Bell's Line of Road 80, 547
Belmont 529(2)
Belubula River 241, 359
Bendenine 292(2)
Bennelong Point 126
Bentley's Bridge 107(2)
Berrima 9, 111, 150, 510, 523,
523, 547, 564, 106(2),
107(2), 238(2)
Bethel Rock 533(2)
Bexley 537(2)
Binalong 150
Bingham 371(2)
Black Bob's Bridge 107(2)
Blackman's Swamp 111
Blacktown 432(2), 566(2)
Blakehurst 538(2)
Blandford 247
Blaxland 109(2)
Blue Mountains 116, 195, 259,
265, 279, 287, 310, 348, 385,
467, 498, 504, 547, 95(2),
96(2), 106(2), 109(2),
111(2), 187(2), 212(2),
233(2), 238(2), 292(2),
303(2), 401(2), 583(2)
Boatfalls 449(2)
Bodalla 570(2)
Bogan River 269, 310, 102(2),
239(2), 495(2)
Bokhara River 321
Bondi Junction 109(2)
Bong Bong 42, 111, 138, 523,
564, 575, 212(2), 512(2),
598(2)
Booligal 360, 532(2)

Boorowa 150, 205
Borambil 532(2)
Boree 240(2), 634(2)
Botany 130(2), 371(2), 538(2)
Botany Bay 53, 64, 389, 567,
58(2), 85(2), 131(2), 327(2),
335(2), 395(2), 457(2)
Bowral 307(2)
Boyd Town 141
Bradley's Head 145
Braidwood 196, 352, 368, 564,
241(2), 612(2)
Branxton 189, 226(2), 630(2)
Breadalbane Plains 2(2),
530(2)
Brewarrina 321
Brickfield Hill 609(2)
Brickfields 18(2), 111(2)
Brighton 452(2)
Brindabella 275(2)
Bringelly 58, 87, 200, 306,
312, 367, 500, 522, 575,
98(2), 134(2), 308(2)
Brisbane Grove 567(2)
Brisbane Water 294, 209, 338,
367, 203(2), 254(2), 431(2)
Broken Bay 212(2), 519(2)
Bronte 113(2)
Broulee 392(2)
Brownlow Hill 178(2)
Brush Farm 317(2)
Bulanaming 178, 308, 254(2)
Bulga Road 448(2)
Bulli 292(2)
Bundanoon Creek 530(2)
Bungonia 84, 564, 573 375(2)
Burragorang 523, 236(2)
Burragorang valley 62, 310,
556, 562, 570(2)
Burrowa 212
Burrundulla Swamps 111
Burwood 205(2), 236(2),
237(2), 381(2)
Butterwick 226(2)
Byalla 178(2)
Byrne's Gap 62
Cabramatta 76, 178, 373, 383,
495, 523, 10(2), 22(2), 98(2),
254(2), 439(2), 530(2),
602(2), 629(2)
Caley's Repulse 195
Camden 196, 208, 306, 315,
402, 511, 521, 523, 108(2),
149(2), 180(2), 183(2),
196(2), 203(2), 306(2),
317(2)
Camden County 280, 523,
257(2)
Campbell Fields 370(2)
Campbell River 96(2)
Campbell's Wharf, Sydney
198, 206
Campbelltown 9, 312, 402,
466, 562, 573, 134(2),
342(2), 365(2), 395(2),
511(2), 570(2)
Camperdown 119, 295(2)
Canowindra 241
Canterbury 205, 18(2), 38(2)
Cape Byron 400(2)
Cape Jervis 392
Capertree 11(2)

Carcoar 385, 2(2), 203(2)
Carcoar (Carcuan, Corcoran) 1(2)
Carlyle's Gully 247
Carrington 299
Carwoola 411(2)
Cassilis 229, 290, 310, 383
Castle Forbes 86(2)
Castle Hill 112, 192, 260, 521, 526, 20(2), 227(2), 232(2), 371(2), 499(2), 530(2), 613(2), 622(2)
Castlereagh 241, 260, 422, 105(2), 191(2), 220(2), 533(2)
Castlereagh River 505, 102(2), 238(2), 306(2), 401(2), 496(2), 566(2)
Cataract River 195
Cattai Creek 529(2)
Cawdor 464
Charleyong 352
Chippendale 559
Church Hill 387(2), 578(2)
Circular Quay 386, 72(2), 136(2)
Clarence district 311
Clarence River 139, 311, 490, 108(2), 202(2), 325(2), 400(2)
Clarence River valley 310
Clarence Town 490, 392(2), 449(2)
Clark Island 226
Clear Creek 499(2)
Clontarf 347(2)
Clydesdale 483(2)
Coal River (Newcastle) 215, 219, 263, 266, 289, 460, 213(2)
Coalcliff 64
Cobargo 2(2)
Cobbitty 523, 45(2)
Cockle Bay 157, 306, 439(2), 617(2)
Coolangatta 621(2)
Collaroi 108(2)
Collector 150, 212, 275(2)
Collector Valley 274(2)
Old Collector 274(2)
Collier's Point 223(2)
Concord (Longbottom) 260, 353, 150, 19(2), 96(2), 283(2), 305(2), 403(2), 564(2), 565(2)
Condamine 304
Condamine's River 304, 24(2)
Cook's River 205, 131(2), 254(2), 464(2), 572(2)
Cookbundoon 10(2)
Cookbundoon Range 150(2), 531(2), 598(2)
Cooke 381, 147(2), 134(2)
Coolangatta 93
Cooleman 275(2)
Cooma 292(2)
Cooyal 111
Cordeaux River 195
Cory's Camp Creek 247
Cowl-Cowl 532(2)
Cowpastures 21, 58, 64, 195, 196, 290, 297, 463, 498, 521,

523, 524, 21(2), 31(2), 111(2), 155(2), 157(2), 530(2), 531(2), 570(2)
Cowra 359
Cowra 370(2)
Cox's River 241, 267
Crook Haven 93
Crook Haven River 621(2)
Crossing Place 311
Crow's Nest 621(2)
Crudene River 110
Cudgegong River 110, 266, 96(2), 401(2)
Cullen Bullen 331
Cumberland County 306, 312, 523, 110(2), 134(2)
Cunningham's Gap (NSW-Qld) 267
Dabee 383
Dandaloo 269
Dangarfield 282
Dangarsleigh 282
Dapto 66, 562, 304(2), 353(2)
Darling Downs 24(2), 75(2)
Darling Harbour 157, 306, 73(2), 493(2), 609(2)
Darling Point 58, 452(2), 453(2)
Darling Point, Adelaide Place 113(2)
Darling River 269, 525, 543, 565, 75(2), 239(2), 360(2), 496(2)
Darlinghurst 57, 461, 537, 26(2), 73(2), 196(2), 276(2), 295(2), 347(2), 365(2), 616(2)
Darlinghurst (Potts Point) 442
Darlinghurst, Forbes St 527(2)
Dartbrook 102, 280, 168(2)
Dawes Battery 228(2)
Dawes Point 74, 199, 203, 297, 369(2), 566(2)
Delegate 205
Dividing Range 267, 112(2)
Dog Trap Road 115
Domain 113(2), 309(2)
Double Bay 416
Doughboy Hollow 294, 300
Douro 292(2)
Doyle's Creek 514, 560
Dr George Mountain, Bega 3(2)
Drummond 421
Dubbo 331, 332, 401, 451(2)
Duck Creek Bridge 107(2)
Dumaresq River (NSW-Qld) 267
Dundas 28, 258, 521, 522, 87(2), 227(2), 291(2)
Dundas, Larra Place 87(2)
Dungog 294, 553(2)
Dunn's Plains 139
Durham (County of) 319
Dusky Bay 65
East Maitland 472, 300, 472, 44(2)
Eastern Creek 499(2)
Eastern Farms 76, 364(2)
Eastwood 116, 411(2)

Ebenezer 13, 28, 560, 220(2), 529(2), 632(2)
Eden 387(2)
Eden Forest 148(2)
Edgecliff 11, 398(2)
Eglinton 362(2)
Eliza Point 335(2)
Elizabeth Bay 178(2), 192(2)
Emu Island 21(2), 538(2)
Emu Plains 189, 383, 397, 503, 11(2), 102(2), 191(2), 269(2)
Ermington 123(2)
Erskine Park 274(2)
Euroa 401
Euston 545
Evan 116, 144, 241, 295(2)
Evan district 140(2)
Fairlight 452(2)
Fal Brook 280
Farm Cove 308, 312, 416, 438, 527, 330(2)
Field of Mars 49, 51, 361, 86(2), 130(2), 220(2), 232(2), 411(2), 420(2), 444(2), 613(2)
Figtree 292(2)
Fish River 181(2), 361(2)
Five Dock 142(2)
Five Dock, Lyons Rd 142(2)
Five Islands (Illawarra) 108, 235, 292(2), 313(2), 598(2)
Fort Denison 60
Fort Phillip 59(2)
Foy Brook 280
Frogmore 295(2)
Garden Island 573(2)
Garden Island Cove 309(2)
George's Hall 19(2)
George's Head 2, 177, 192(2)
George's River 64, 195, 389, 13(2), 107(2), 254(2)
Gidley, Co. Cumberland 282(2)
Ginninderra (ACT) 368, 497(2)
Gladesville 199(2)
Glebe 11, 162, 199, 505, 51(2), 425(2), 554(2)
Glebe Point 533(2)
Glen Innes 334, 4(2), 264(2)
Glenderuel 523
Gloucester 300
Gloucester district 299
Goodradigbee 341, 123(2)
Gore Cave 460
Gore Hill 460
Gosford 294, 431(2)
Gostwyck 407
Goulburn 9, 84, 198, 199, 212, 232, 310, 311, 367, 368, 401, 523, 543, 547, 556, 564, 181(2), 203(2), 237(2), 238(2), 254(2), 261(2), 274(2), 275(2), 346(2), 382(2), 399(2), 400(2), 424(2), 530(2), 540(2), 610(2)
Goulburn Plains 58, 310, 564, 169(2), 220(2)
Goulburn River 266, 280, 524, 455(2)

Government Domain 202(2)
Govett's Leap 467
Grafton 199, 168(2)
Graham's Town 616(2)
Granville 115
Great Dividing Range 280
Great North Road 247, 281
Great Sirius Cove 263(2)
Green Hills (Windsor) 211, 518, 213(2), 519(2)
Gresford 211
Grose River 317(2)
Grose Valley 195, 310
Guildford 87(2)
Guilford, Larra Street 87(2)
Gulgong 401(2)
Gundagai 150, 151, 173(2), 496(2)
Gundaroo 368
Gunning 556, 556(C), 563, 564
Gunningbland 532(2)
Guntawang 401(2)
Gwydir River 201, 238(2), 239(2)
Haberfield 361(2)
Harris Farm 87(2)
Hartley 84, 111, 241
Hartley district 241
Hartley Vale 96(2)
Hastings River 299, 4(2), 62(2), 306(2)
Hawkesbury District 211, 252, 256, 259, 263, 309, 380, 383, 421, 472, 139(2), 170(2), 171(2), 373(2), 380(2), 405(2), 597(2)
Hawkesbury River 215, 246, 314, 320, 467, 284(2), 309(2), 330(2), 371(2), 374(2), 394(2), 508(2), 598(2)
Hay 75(2)
Haymarket 321
Hexham 293, 345, 613(2)
Hinton 226(2)
Homebush 549, 394(2), 582(2), 586(2)
Howe's Mountain 560
Howe's Park 560
Howe's Swamp 560
Howe's Valley 560
Hume Highway 107(2)
Huntawong 532(2)
Hunter River 195, 197, 201, 202, 231, 266, 268, 285, 312, 320, 348, 368, 469, 472, 514, 560, 10(2), 24(2), 86(2), 93(2), 103(2), 111(2), 113(2), 265(2), 272(2), 284(2), 464(2), 544(2)
Hunter River district 211, 247, 248, 280, 344, 537, 236(2)
Hunter River valley 214, 267, 279, 281, 294, 318, 543, 269(2), 414(2)
Upper Hunter district 310
Upper Hunter valley 397
Hunter's Hill 171, 498(C), 534, 12(2), 232(2), 283(2)
Hurstville 291(2), 537(2)

Hyde Park 236(2), 450(2), 583(2)
Illawarra 5, 9, 108, 157, 266, 267, 279, 289, 309, 312, 348, 359, 466, 523, 16(2), 187(2), 191(2), 212(2), 227(2), 292(2), 304(2), 313(2), 508(2), 530(2), 544(2), 581(2)
Ingleburn 220(2)
Inscription Point 374
Inverell 630(2)
Invermein 51
Irish Town 353(2)
Iron Cove 130(2)
Jamberoo 242(2)
Jenolan Caves 62
Jerry's Plains 514, 451(2)
Jervis Bay 195, 359, 564, 272(2), 306(2), 530(2), 597(2)
Jordan Hill 367
Jugiong 292(2)
Jugroy 195
Kanagra Plateau 62
Kelso 523, 524, 102(2), 500(2), 537(2)
Kempsey 296, 553(2)
Kensington 613(2)
Kiama 325(2), 431(2)
Kilnoorat 232
King's Cross 504
King's Grove 97(2)
King's Town 280, 223(2)
Kingdon Ponds 280
Kirribilli 136
Kissing Point 135, 251, 252, 253, 260, 353, 521, 542, 47(2), 364(2), 411(2), 468(2), 632(2)
Kittah Kittah 201
Knapsack Gully 106(2)
Krui River 290, 108(2)
Kurnell 55, 374, 457(2)
Kurrajong 448(2), 483(2)
Kyogle 630(2)
La Perouse 112(2)
Lachlan River 241, 259, 265, 310, 359, 102(2), 239(2), 306(2), 507(2)
Laidley's Plains 69(2)
Lake Alexandrina 524, 496(2)
Lake Bathurst 212, 247, 266, 490, 500, 564, 46(2), 220(2), 274(2), 530(2)
Lake George 21, 157, 266, 556, 275(2), 471(2), 598(2)
Lake Illawarra 64, 389, 22(2)
Lake Innes 3(2)
Lake Macquarie 103, 279, 226(2), 529(2)
Lamorran Brook 280
Lane Cove 102(2), 608(2)
Lang's Crossing Place 75(2)
Lansdowne Bridge 107(2)
Lapstone Hill 106(2)
Larras Lake 102(2)
Leichhardt 594(2)
Lennox Bridge 106(2)
Lennox Head 400(2)
Lett River 241
Leura 143(2)

Liberty Plains 353, 367, 97(2), 347(2), 394(2), 443(2), 573(2), 608(2)
Lidcombe 512(2)
Limestone Plains 198, 205, 362, 368, 254(2), 274(2), 311(2)
Linden 195
Lithgow 241, 212(2)
Little Redhead 300
Liverpool 21, 157, 178, 186, 211, 212, 213, 216, 247, 260, 368, 375, 461, 471, 521, 523, 549, 10(2), 52(2), 66(2), 105(2), 107(2), 110(2), 134(2), 139(2), 169(2), 191(2), 220(2), 226(2), 255(2), 304(2), 371(2), 380(2), 401(2), 414(2), 507(2), 508(2), 597(2), 599(2)
Liverpool Road 131(2), 257(2)
Liverpool Plains 266, 280, 299, 300, 325, 344, 362, 96(2), 168(2), 306(2), 316(2), 449(2)
Liverpool Range 266, 280, 281, 466
Lochinvar 614(2)
Lockhart 304(2)
Logan River 362(2)
Long Cove 130(2)
Longbottom 146, 353(2)
Longbottom (Concord) 305(2)
Lower Minto 405(2)
Lower Portland 320
Lower Portland Head 448(2)
Lower Tabratong 269
Luddenham 284(2)
Lue 566(2)
Lyndhurst 344(2)
Macdonald River 337
McDonald River 44(2)
Macintyre River 201, 168(2)
Macleay River district 296
Macpherson Range 267, 284
Macquarie Fields 555, 368(2), 405(2)
Macquarie Place 393, 373(2)
Macquarie River 310, 359, 360, 306(2), 335(2), 362(2), 495(2), 532(2)
Maitland 9, 202, 231, 265, 275, 280, 292, 294, 300, 318, 320, 321, 336, 345, 426, 469, 473, 543, 560, 26(2), 63(2), 168(2), 226(2), 237(2), 257(2), 259(2), 261(2), 265(2), 304(2), 337(2), 342(2), 344(2), 346(2), 540(2), 569(2), 613(2), 614(2)
Maitland: see also East Maitland
Mandagery Creek 359
Maneroo 183(2)
Manly 22, 84, 234, 452(2), 573(2)
Manly Cove 331(2)
Manning 300
Manning River 280, 299, 4(2)

Manning River district 211
Marshall Mount 304(2)
Marulan 84, 563, 123(2), 375(2)
Mayne River 201
Menangle 502(2)
Menangle Creek 548(2)
Menindee 239(2)
Merimbula 66
Merton 197
Merton District 7(2)
Miller's Point 442, 73(2)
Milson's Point 108(2), 333(2)
Minchinbury 234(2)
Minmi 345
Minto 252, 561, 112(2), 307(2), 368(2), 520(2), 530(2), 538(2), 605(2)
Mitchell's Pass 106(2)
Mittagong 575, 497(2)
Molong 385, 532(2), 634(2)
Molonglo 22, 368, 531(2), 605(2)
Molonglo Plains 362, 400(2), 451(2)
Molonglo River 205, 310, 555, 411(2)
Monaro 141, 245, 341, 368, 555, 572, 2(2), 114(2), 183(2), 305(2), 387(2)
Monaro Plains 598(2)
Moonbi Ranges 247
Moonbis 248
Moore Park 500
Moorebank 21, 255(2)
Moorundie 363
Morisset's Lagoon 260(2)
Morpeth 231, 265, 280, 344, 490, 560, 226(2)
Moscheto Island 613(2)
Mosman Bay 263(2), 407(2)
Moss Vale 575, 530(2)
Mount Banks 195
Mount Barney 119(2)
Mount Bell 80
Mount Cooper 205
Mount Cordeaux 247
Mount Dangar 282
Mount Dispersion 239(2)
Mount Harris 495(2)
Mount Keira 304(2)
Mount King George 310
Mount Ovens 305(2)
Mount Pleasant 483(2)
Mount Sibly 281
Mount Sion 109(2)
Mount Tomah 80, 136
Mount Towrang 610(2)
Mount Victoria 310, 238(2)
Mount Windeyer 615(2)
Mount York 80, 116, 241, 259, 66(2), 260(2)
Mudgee 110, 111, 259, 266, 96(2), 102(2), 134(2), 392(2), 401(2), 532(2), 566(2)
Mulgoa 198(2), 289(2), 435(2)
Mulgoa Forest 523
Mulgoa valley 259
Mulgrave Place 110, 127, 138, 171, 314, 518, 522, 560, 139(2), 448(2)

Mullengendry 341
Mulwaree Plains 401
Mulwaree Ponds 274(2), 533(2)
Mulwaree River 564
Mungadal 75(2)
Murray County 308(2)
Murray River 284, 311, 363, 350, 524, 119(2), 173(2), 181(2), 304(2), 481(2), 541(2)
Murrumbidgee 151, 543, 63(2), 75(2), 181(2), 292(2), 305(2), 496(2)
Murrumbidgee River 284, 310, 556, 123(2), 178(2), 181(2), 239(2), 243(2), 304(2), 531(2)
Murrurundi 139, 294
Muswellbrook 9, 138, 197, 280, 300, 334, 352, 7(2), 428(2), 613(2)
Myall Creek 300, 337, 338(2), 428(2), 617(2)
Myall Lakes 569(2)
Namoi River 11(2), 173(2), 238(2), 239(2)
Nandewar Range 119(2)
Narara, Brisbane Water 530
Narellan 402, 523, 556, 564, 573, 47(2), 181(2)
Narrabeen 195, 420(2)
Narrabri 321, 239(2)
Narrigo 315
Nattai 195, 523
Nattai River 62, 111(2), 570(2)
Nellingen 241(2)
Nelson, Upper 383, 227(2)
Nepean 241
Nepean District 555(2)
Nepean River 116, 234, 297, 498, 281(2), 289(2), 330(2), 506(2), 508(2), 548(2)
Nepean Upper 87(2)
Neutral Bay 141, 110(2), 232(2), 335(2)
Neutral Harbour (Bay) 232(2)
New England 248, 310, 311, 168(2), 195(2), 233(2), 387(2)
New England Highway 294
New Strathruddie 450(2)
Newcastle 9, 102, 204, 215, 219, 231, 264, 279, 280, 281, 284, 285, 292, 300, 365, 368, 369, 469, 526, 560, 571, 4(2), 29(2), 41(2), 59(2), 63(2), 86(2), 96(2), 103(2), 105(2), 140(2), 142(2), 158(2), 191(2), 206(2), 223(2), 226(2), 227(2), 237(2), 257(2), 259(2), 260(2), 306(2), 377(2), 428(2), 444(2), 493(2), 529(2), 530(2), 548(2), 568(2), 599(2), 601(2), 613(2)
Newtown 216, 223, 308, 398, 255(2), 374(2), 615(2)
Nobby Island 568(2)
Nobbys Head 231
North boundary 521

North Richmond 401(2)
North Shore, Sydney Harbour 120(2), 212(2), 232(2)
North Sydney 63(2), 261(2)
North Sydney, Mount St 44(2)
Northern Boundary 260
O'Connell 293(2)
O'Connell Plains 523, 102(2), 567(2)
Oaks, The 523, 570(2)
Oatley 291(2)
Oberon 62
Old Collector 274(2)
Old South Head Road 547(2)
Ophir 532(2)
Orange 111, 131(2), 239(2), 532(2)
Orton Park 532(2)
Ourimbah 530
Paddington 5, 246, 495, 356(2), 357(2)
Paddington, Glenmore Road 209, 495
Pages River 247
Palmers Hill 348
Pandora's Pass 266-7
Paroo River 525
Parramatta 12, 74, 119, 139, 183, 213, 260, 265, 304, 309, 312, 314, 321, 324, 338, 352, 355, 359, 361, 383, 401, 417, 509, 519, 521, 522, 524, 549, 564, 10(2), 36(2), 40(2), 53(2), 63(2), 86(2), 87(2), 95(2), 105(2), 106(2), 107(2), 108(2), 111(2), 112(2), 123(2), 137(2), 139(2), 140(2), 145(2), 147(2), 148(2), 149(2), 154(2), 157(2), 171(2), 172(2), 190(2), 192(2), 201(2), 205(2), 208(2), 213(2), 217(2), 218(2), 226(2), 227(2), 256(2), 259(2), 265(2), 281(2), 282(2), 291(2), 295(2), 303(2), 308(2), 310(2), 311(2), 316(2), 318(2), 330(2), 332(2), 334(2), 342(2), 348(2), 356(2), 359(2), 365(2), 394(2), 401(2), 402(2), 403(2), 404(2), 411(2), 419(2), 420(2), 424(2), 433(2), 438(2), 439(2), 467(2), 502(2), 508(2), 538(2), 544(2), 545(2), 548(2), 554(2), 564(2), 570(2), 573(2), 579(2), 581(2), 582(2), 595(2), 599(2), 605(2), 610(2), 613(2), 632(2)
Parramatta Streets:
— Buller St 95(2)
— Campbell St 107(2)
— Church St 107(2)
— George St. 192, 490
— Ross St 95(2)
Parramatta River 353(2)
Parramatta Road 66(2),

107(2), 289(2)
Parsley Bay 97(2)
Parson's Creek 537
Paterson 211, 247, 352, 226(2)
Paterson district 202
Paterson's Plains 226(2)
Paterson's River 322
Patrick's Plains 80, 280, 294,
   515, 560, 86(2), 226(2),
   377(2), 426(2), 428(2),
   449(2)
Peel River 247, 267, 306(2)
Pennant Hills 232(2), 577(2)
Penrith 146, 293, 331, 337,
   422, 555, 11(2), 24(2), 44(2),
   55(2), 108(2), 198(2),
   314(2), 401(2), 533(2),
   538(2), 555(2), 622(2)
Petersham 12, 122, 149, 337,
   367, 22(2), 130(2), 254(2),
   283(2), 319(2), 335(2),
   362(2), 403(2), 450(2),
   572(2)
Petersham Hill 31(2)
Pevensey 75(2)
Phoenix Park 226(2)
Picton 21, 22, 513, 403(2)
Pilcher's Mountain 294
Pinchgut Island 60
Pitt Town 260, 191(2), 220(2)
Pittwater 512(2)
Point Clare 431(2)
Point Hicks 243, 244
Point Maskelyne 297
Point Piper 243(2), 335(2)
Point Solander 457(2)
Ponds district 355
Porphyry Point, Seaham 211
Port Hacking 64, 498
Port Jackson 567, 46(2),
   61(2), 62(2), 88(2), 99(2),
   119(2), 139(2), 182(2),
   254(2), 327(2), 330(2),
   347(2)
Port Kembla 5
Port Macquarie 8, 102, 253,
   262, 265, 266, 296, 300, 314,
   348, 360, 496, 503, 523, 3(2),
   66(2), 124(2), 167(2),
   191(2), 211(2), 226(2),
   230(2), 306(2), 430(2),
   431(2), 521(2), 618(2)
Port Stephens 280, 299, 300,
   334, 348, 360, 487, 41(2),
   63(2), 158(2), 315(2),
   350(2), 443(2), 610(2),
   618(2)
Portland Head 13, 28, 260,
   361, 521, 166(2), 220(2)
Potts Point 281, 442, 284(2),
   554(2), 629(2)
Prince's Bridge 107(2)
Prospect 108, 144, 195, 241,
   505, 522, 563, 96(2), 97(2),
   394(2), 570(2), 599(2)
Prospect Creek 107(2)
Prospect Hill 570(2), 623(2)
Punchbowl 291(2)
Pyrmont 115
Quaker's Hill 312
Queanbeyan 84, 150, 198,
   212, 310, 332, 362, 368,

44(2), 392(2), 411(2), 531(2)
Queen's Wharf 106(2)
Quirindi 294
Raby 341
Randwick 315, 110(2), 264(2),
   280(2)
Ravensworth 178
Rawdon Island 496
Raymond Terrace 1, 54(2),
   392(2), 455(2), 613(2),
   614(2)
Razorback 506(2)
Red Point 5
Redbank 420(2)
Redfern 110(2), 317(2),
   370(2), 435(2)
Reid's Mistake 103, 205,
   529(2)
Reservoir Hill 403(2)
Retreat station 321
Richmond 78, 139, 213, 215,
   260, 266, 367, 422, 485, 486,
   564, 16(2), 191(2), 220(2),
   317(2), 395(2), 400(2),
   401(2), 483(2)
Richmond Hill 361
Richmond River 284, 311,
   11(2), 178(20, 630(2)
Riverina 199, 401, 75(2),
   614(2)
Riverstone 405(2)
Robertson 530(2)
Rocks, The 105(2), 212(2),
   255(2), 575(2)
Rooty Hill 200, 62(2)
Rose Bay 245, 334, 335(2)
Rose Hill 312, 154(2), 330(2)
Rossiville 399(2)
Rothbury 236(2)
Rouse Hill 119, 20(2), 401(2)
Roxburgh 96(2)
Rufus River 182(2)
Runnymede 317(2)
Rushcutter's Bay 495, 504,
   51(2), 107(2), 203(2), 547(2)
Ryde 150, 251, 252, 495, 534,
   542, 18(2), 123(2), 220(2),
   232(2), 468(2), 542(2)
Sackville Reach 320, 424(2)
St Leonards 44(2), 131(2),
   212(2)
St Leonards East 233(2)
St Omer 275(2)
St Vincent Co. 392, 72(2)
Salisbury Plains 247
Salisbury Waters 247
Scone 51, 102, 280, 281, 282,
   294, 300, 334, 352, 212(2),
   392(2)
Scotland Island 519(2)
Seaham 211, 226(2)
Segenhoe 226(2)
Seven Hills 355, 490
Shellharbour 221
Shoalhaven 81(2), 534(2),
   621(2)
Shoalhaven River 65, 93, 305,
   315, 573, 42(2), 219(2),
   530(2), 620(2)
Sidmouth Valley 134(2)
Singleton 80, 138, 189, 281,
   514, 560, 259(2), 377(2),

406(2), 428(2), 449(2)
Sirius Cove, Sydney Harbour
   263(2)
Snowy River 114(2)
South Bargo 205
South Creek 234, 306, 560,
   13(2), 53(2), 62(2), 131(2),
   519(2)
South Head 260, 324, 418(2),
   463(2), 575(2)
South Head Lighthouse 471
South Head Road 321
South Head Signal Station
   594(2)
Southern Tablelands 466,
   610(2)
Springfield 367, 532(2)
Springwood 96(2)
Stanmore 199, 172(2)
Stingray Bay 243
Stockton 236(2)
Stonequarry 523
Stonequarry Creek 22, 513,
   403(2)
Strathfield 394(2), 608(2)
Stroud 300
Subiaco 293, 344(2)
Surry Hills 157, 500, 549(2)
Surry Hills, Dowling St
   367(2)
Sutton Forest 575, 575(C),
   149(2), 530(2), 597(2)
Sydney 45(2), 62(2), 87(2),
   97(2), 102(2), 105(2),
   106(2), 108(2), 115(2),
   119(2), 139(2), 171(2),
   227(2), 254(2), 256(2),
   257(2), 263(2), 266(2),
   289(2), 304(2), 306(2),
   333(2), 350(2), 400(2),
   401(2), 415(2), 424(2),
   494(2), 508(2), 614(2)
Sydney: see also suburbs
Sydney Streets:
— Argyle Place 505
— Barrack Lane 23(2)
— Bathurst Street 58, 421,
   418(2)
— Bell Row 444(2)
— Bent Street 550
— Bligh Street 207, 196(2),
   613(2), 618(2)
— Brickfield Hill 371(2)
— Bridge Street 142(2),
   254(2), 567(2)
— Campbell Street 389(2)
— Castlereagh Street 209,
   111(2), 227(2), 368(2),
   374(2), 395(2), 626(2)
— Chapel Row 111(2), 395(2)
— Charlotte Place 461,
   142(2), 392(2)
— Charlotte Street 304(2)
— Circular Quay 113(2)
— Cleveland Street 228(2)
— College Street 209, 397,
   257(2)
— Cumberland Place 235(2),
   235(2)
— Cumberland Street 310,
   212(2), 428(2)
— Elizabeth Street 6, 395(2),

499(2)
— Essen (Essex) Lane 371(2)
— Fort Street 206, 142(2),
  293(2)
— George Street 6, 84, 115,
  217, 245, 246, 305, 470,
  23(2), 39(2), 110(2), 111(2),
  112(2), 142(2), 257(2),
  263(2), 283(2), 291(2),
  335(2), 367(2), 374(2),
  426(2), 464(2), 504(2),
  505(2), 548(2), 549(2)
  611(2) 623(2) see also
  Lower George St.
— 61 George St 445(2)
— 72 George St 109(2)
— 75 George St 142(2)
— George St North 505, 528,
  605(2)
— Goulburn Street 292(2)
— Grosvenor Place 461
— Hunter Street 6, 157, 207,
  415(2), 533(2), 548(2),
  567(2)
— Hyde Park 142(2)
— Imperial Arcade 549(2)
— Kent St 505, 534, 166(2),
  533(2)
— King and York Sts 446(2)
— King Street 209, 471,
  39(2), 257(2), 395(2), 493(2)
— 8 King St 242(2)
— Liverpool Road 426(2)
— Liverpool Street 305, 23(2),
  142(2), 333(2)
— Lower Fort Street 206
— 41 Lower Fort St 554(2)
— Lower George Street 442,
  142(2), 167(2), 255(2)
— Macquarie Place 500,
  129(2), 131(2), 374(2),
  453(2), 520(2)
— Macquarie Street 6, 368,
  550, 41(2), 105(2), 106(2),
  415(2)
— Market Street 356(2),
  395(2)
— Martin Place 509(2)
— O'Connell Street 442,
  251(2)
— Oxford Street 397
— Parramatta Road 207,
  426(2)
— Pembroke Terrace 505
— Phillip Street 260, 354(2)
— 95 Phillip Street 493(2)
— Pitt's Row 528
— Pitt Street 157, 505, 555,
  142(2), 212(2), 292(2),
  381(2), 508(2), 533(2),
  548(2) see also Upper Pitt
— 16 Pitt St 625(2)
— 23 Pitt St 242(2)
— 37 Pitt St 367(2)
— 59 Pitt St 367(2)
— 70 Pitt St 553(2)
— Prince St 371(2)
— Princes St 105(2), 305(2)
— Queen Street 203(2)
— Queen's Square 471,
  113(2)
— Roslyn Street 504

— South Head Road 51(2),
  54(2)
— Spring Street 376
— Sussex Street 58, 312, 505,
  555, 333(2), 493(2), 600(2)
— Tank Stream 365, 46(2),
  129(2), 254(2), 450(2),
  553(2)
— Upper Pitt Street 293(2)
— Wentworth Place 196
— Wynyard Square 631(2)
— York Street 163(2), 367(2),
  439(2)
Sydney Harbour 213(2)
Sydney-Windsor road 312
Talbragar River 139, 96(2)
Tamworth 248, 294, 238(2)
Taralga 150(2), 151(2)
Tarana 532(2)
Tarcutta 150, 350
Tempe 223, 465(2), 554(2)
Tenterfield 473
Terera 305
Terrible Vale 247
The Oaks see Oaks
The Rocks see Rocks
Three Legs o' Man Bridge
  106(2)
Tilba Tilba 66
Tobago 66
Tom's Lake 532(2)
Tomago 616(2)
Tomala 352
Tonalli Valley 62
Tongy 383, 384
Toongabbie 63, 170, 251, 252,
  260, 310, 320, 353, 383, 487,
  518, 521, 563, 10(2), 45(2),
  213(2), 330(2), 519(2),
  632(2)
Toronto 529(2)
Tottenham 266(2)
Towrang 84
Tressingfield 226(2)
Tuggerah 530
Tumut 150, 212, 422(2),
  439(2)
Tumut River 451(2)
Turon River 110
Tweed River 400(2)
Twofold Bay 65, 132, 141,
  266, 486, 2(2), 77(2), 305(2),
  360(2), 566(2)
Ulladulla 42(2), 178(2)
Undercliff 38(2)
Upper Hunter district 310
Upper Hunter valley 397
Upper Nelson 383, 227(2)
Upper Nepean 87(2)
Upper Paterson 345
Upper Williams River see
  Williams
Vaccary Forest 195
Vale of Clwydd 111, 241, 300
Varroville 466, 497(2), 605(2)
Vaucluse 526, 335(2), 586(2),
  589(2)
Vermont 523
Victoria Pass 241
Vinegar Hill 20(2), 401(2)
Vineyard 420(2)
Waddon 311(2)

Wagga Wagga 304(2)
Walcha 212(2), 306(2)
Wallaroi 532(2)
Wallerawang 22, 110, 566(2)
Wallis Plain 216, 280, 259(2),
  569(2)
Wallumbie (Wollombi) 232(2)
Walter Lawry Methodist
  Memorial Park 96(2)
Wanganella North 75(2)
Warragamba River 359, 11(2),
  12(2)
Warrah 352
Warren 401(2)
Waterloo 110(2)
Watson's Bay 444(2), 575(2)
Wattamolla 64
Waverley 424(2), 463(2)
Waverley Crescent 109(2)
Waverley Terrace 321
Wellington 9, 111, 348, 363,
  401, 453, 251(2), 362(2),
  401(2), 451(2), 494(2)
Wellington Co. 102(2)
Wellington Valley 266, 279,
  331, 509, 495(2)
Wentworth Falls 202(2)
Weston (Westow) 307(2)
White Bay 594(2)
White Hills 197
Whittingham 449(2)
Wilberforce 260, 191(2),
  220(2), 394(2), 618(2)
Wilbertree 134(2)
Wilga 532(2)
Williams River 74, 157, 211,
  472, 490, 54(2), 137(2),
  226(2), 426(2), 444(2),
  614(2), 615(2)
Williams River (Upper)
  614(2), 615(2)
Willoughby 61
Winburndale 499(2)
Winburndale Brook 261(2)
Winderradeen (ACT) 275(2),
  276(2)
Windsor 144, 211, 212, 213,
  221, 252, 259, 260, 262, 311,
  321, 343, 380, 381, 383, 471,
  514, 518, 548, 560, 31(2),
  101(2), 102(2), 105(2),
  191(2), 213(2), 220(2),
  342(2), 371(2), 374(2),
  395(2), 401(2), 402(2),
  405(2), 424(2), 484(2),
  512(2), 519(2), 533(2),
  544(2), 564(2), 608(2),
  632(2)
Windsor, Mileham St 227(2)
Wingecarribee River 107(2),
  610(2)
Wiseman's Ferry 618(2)
Wittingham 560
Wollar 383
Wollombi 210, 312, 321, 337
Wollombi Brook 127
Wollombi (Wallumbie) 232(2)
Wollondilly 598(2)
Wollondilly River 310, 147(2)
Wollongong 203(2), 257(2),
  292(2), 342(2), 452(2)
Wollstonecraft 621(2)

Woollahra 245, 442, 335(2), 592(2)
Woolloomooloo 189, 319, 123(2), 292(2), 382(2), 464(2), 565(2)
Woolloomooloo, Bourke St 292(2)
Woolloomooloo Cove 69(2)
Worgan River 623(2)
Wybong 280
Wyong 209
Yarralumla (Yarrowlumla) (ACT) 275(2)
Yass 9, 58, 150, 151, 201, 205, 212, 311, 312, 341, 524, 173(2), 181(2), 293(2), 381(2), 382(2), 392(2), 508(2), 511(2)
Yass Plains 564-5, 292(2)
Yawanba 205
Yea 455(2)
Yessabah 296
Queensland:
  Admiralty Gulf 62(2)
  Albany Passage 43(2)
  Albert River 93(2), 124(2), 489(2)
  Barcoo River 452, 43(2), 240(2)
  Barrier Reef: see Great Barrier Reef
  Beenleigh 422(2)
  Belyando River 240(2)
  Black River 262(2)
  Bowen 62(2), 263(2)
  Bowen Downs 257(2)
  Boyne River 407(2)
  Bribie Island 177
  Brisbane 295, 336, 416, 472, 547, 93(2), 108(2), 123(2), 212(2), 326(2), 406(2), 448(2), 452(2), 472(2), 601(2), 606(2)
  — George Street 295
  — Russell St 601(2)
  — Wickham Terrace 51
  — William St 108, 124(2)
  Brisbane River 266, 267, 393, 123(2), 124(2), 306(2), 313(2)
  Brunswick Sound 62(2)
  Bulimba 124(2), 601(2)
  Bunya Montains 422(2)
  Burdekin Delta 263(2)
  Burdekin River 262(2)
  Burnett 93(2), 422(2), 606(2)
  Burnett River 22
  Burpengary 422(2)
  Caboolture 422(2), 423(2)
  Canning Downs 108(2)
  Cape Bowling Green 262(2)
  Cape Cleveland 262(2)
  Cape York 243, 15(2), 168(2), 471(2)
  Cape York Peninsula 7(2), 43(2)
  Capricorn Islands 111
  Cardwell 263(2)
  Central Queensland 606(2), 634(2)
  Charters Towers 263(2), 264(2)

  Cleveland 201
  Cleveland Bay 266
  Condamine River 103(2)
  Cooktown 314(2)
  Cooper's Creek 43(2), 103(2)
  Cooyar 22
  Culgoa River 43(2)
  Cullinlaringo 606(2)
  Darling Downs 22, 175, 201, 267, 276-7, 284, 381, 441, 577, 103(2), 108(2), 212(2), 387(2), 406(2), 422(2), 438(2), 448(2), 606(2)
  Dawson 422(2)
  Dawson River 614(2)
  Dawson Track 606(2)
  Deception Bay 51
  Diamantina River 233(2)
  Duaringa 93(2)
  Dunwich 51, 400(2)
  Eagle Farm 145, 352, 448(2)
  Edinglassie 393
  Emerald 606(2)
  Emu Creek 22
  Endeavour River 53, 243, 266, 314(2)
  Escape River 7(2), 44(2)
  Fairfield 601(2)
  Farris 23
  Fitzroy Downs 22
  Fitzroy River 22, 606(2)
  Flinders River 257(2), 489(2)
  Fortitude Valley 201, 601(2)
  Gigoomgan 344
  Gladstone 378(2)
  Glass House Bay 389
  Glass House Mountains 326(2)
  Goodna 145, 313(2)
  Great Barrier Reef 111, 243, 578, 29(2), 167(2), 262(2), 359(2), 390(2)
  Gregory River 233(2)
  Gulf country 257(2), 407(2)
  Gulf of Carpentaria 390, 441, 13(2), 43(2), 390(2), 489(2)
  Gympie 423(2)
  Hervey Bay 471(2)
  Ipswich 473, 123(2), 124(2), 149(2), 422(2), 448(2), 597(2), 601(2)
  Isisford 240(2)
  Jimbour 103(2)
  Kangaroo Point 201, 295, 601(2)
  Keppel Bay 23
  Logan district 201
  Logan River 267, 124(2)
  Mackay 423(2)
  Maranoa River 240(2)
  Mary River 352, 93(2), 326(2), 406(2)
  Maryborough 23, 98, 344, 406(2), 422(2)
  Moggill 601(2)
  Molle Island 15(2), 243(2)
  Moreton Bay 51, 101, 108, 152, 201, 207, 233, 250, 266, 267, 294, 295, 310, 336, 351, 363, 393, 416, 423, 468, 473, 484, 509, 547, 25(2), 79(2), 123(2), 124(2), 306(2),

  326(2), 392(2), 407(2), 422(2), 448(2), 472(2), 540(2), 597(2)
  Moreton Bay District 22, 80(2), 93(2), 103(2)
  Moreton Island 313(2)
  Mount Barney 124(2)
  Mount Beerwah 326(2)
  Mount Beppo 124(2)
  Mount Elliot 262(2)
  Mount Jeffreys 15(2)
  Mount Martin 93(2)
  Mulgrave Island 352(2)
  New Farm 25(2), 124(2)
  Nundah 352, 473, 422(2)
  Owanyilla 344
  Oxley Creek 601(2)
  Peak Downs 606(2)
  Peak Downs district 23
  Percy Islands 266
  Port Curtis 306(2), 325(2), 471(2)
  Possession Island 243
  Princess Charlotte Bay 15(2)
  Rainbow Reach 400(2)
  Raine Island 111, 359(2)
  Raine Passage 359(2)
  Redbank 201, 448(2), 601(2)
  Redcliffe Point 108
  Repulse Bay 266
  Richmond River 124(2)
  Rockhampton 23, 284(2), 423(2), 606(2)
  Rockingham Bay 266, 43(2)
  Rous Channel 400(2)
  Sandy Cape 487
  Stanley River 123(2)
  Stradbroke Island 400(2)
  Swain Reefs 468
  Thomson River 43(2), 257(2)
  Thursday Island 352
  Tiaro 344
  Tinana 98
  Toolburra 108(2)
  Toorbul 422(2)
  Torres Strait 111, 390, 167(2), 352(2)
  Townsville 263(2)
  Victoria River (Barcoo) 452, 43(2), 103(2), 240(2)
  Warrego River 43(2), 240(2)
  Warwick 108(2)
  Westbrook 201
  Weymouth Bay 7(2), 44(2)
  Whitsunday Island 111
  Wide Bay 98, 145, 295, 344, 352, 468, 406(2), 422(2)
  Zion Hill 422(2)
South Australia:
  Adam Bay 378
  Adelaide 17, 179, 362, 376, 378, 432, 443, 444, 446, 478, 497, 524, 525, 540, 557, 99(2), 197(2), 251(2), 257(2), 262(2), 270(2), 356(2), 423(2), 435(2), 452(2), 472(2), 480(2), 481(2), 491(2), 498(2), 532(2), 627(2)
  Adelaide:
  — Angus Street 328
  — Flinders St 491(2)

— Franklin St 377, 624(2)
— Freeman St 491(2)
— Gawler Place 444
— Gilbert St 201(2)
— Gouger Street 328
— Grenfell Street 499
— Grote St 65(2), 197(2)
— Hindley St 179, 499, 98(2)
— King William Street 378
— Light Square 64(2)
— North Terrace 328, 262(2), 480(2), 491(2)
— Pemberton Terrace 497
— Rundle Street 525
— Stephen's Place 378
— Victoria Square 384(2)
— Wakefield Street 499
— Whitmore Square 244
— North Adelaide, Finniss St 482(2)
Adelaide River 378
Alberton 296
Angaston 16, 17, 19
Barossa Valley 16, 33(2), 222(2)
Beaumont 443, 525
Bethany 33(2)
Blinman 248
Brighton 481(2)
Buckland Park 7
Burnside 378
Burra 7, 179, 341, 497, 64(2), 280(2), 480(2)
Burra Burra 445
Camden Park 64(2)
Cape Jervis 57
College Park 175
Cooper's Creek 498(2)
Cygnet River 378
Dashwood Gully 335
Dry Creek 625(2)
Echunga 287, 557, 440(2)
Encounter Bay 57, 71, 378, 390, 497, 498, 540, 557, 117(2), 281(2), 282(2), 481(2)
Enfield 197(2)
Eucla 363
Eyre Peninsula 282, 197(2)
First Creek 378
Flinders Range 363, 445
Fowler Bay 390
Gawler 378, 557
Gawler Range 282, 363
Gawler River 7, 16, 473(2)
Glen Osmond 175, 446, 280(2)
Glenelg 248, 500, 557, 301(2)
Glenelg River 477
Guichen Bay 384(2)
Gulf St Vincent 46, 57, 377, 390, 462, 117(2)
Gumeracha 497, 525
Hahndorf 33(2)
Hanover Bay 477
Hawdon Vale 440(2)
Hindmarsh 557, 197(2), 379(2)
Holdfast Bay 248, 379, 446, 540, 557, 200(2), 480(2), 482(2), 624(2)
Howlong 524

Kadina 441(2)
Kangaroo Island 16, 18, 340, 378, 390, 443, 466, 486, 539, 117(2), 177(2), 222(2), 262(2), 372(2), 481(2), 482(2) 577(2), 624(2)
Kapunda 47, 179, 341
Kensington 463, 612(2)
Kensington Park 378
Kingscote 16, 378, 443, 177(2), 481(2)
Klemzig 16, 33(2)
Lake Cawndilla 497(2)
Lake Dutton 444
Lake Eyre 363
Lake Gill (Lake Dutton) 444
Lake Hindmarsh 362
Lake Torrens 362-3
Lake Wangary 282
Langmeil (Tanunda) 33(2)
Light River 47
Lindesay River 119(2)
Lobethal 33(2), 34(2)
Lofty Ranges 117(2)
Lyndoch Valley 378, 557
Macclesfield 248
Marble Ranges 282
Melville Island 485(2)
Mitcham 175, 328, 557
Montacute 341, 280(2)
Montefiore Hill 118(2)
Moorooroo 48
Moorundie 478, 497(2)
Morphett Vale 301(2)
Morphettville 262(2)
Mount Arden 362-3
Mount Barker 175, 341, 377, 378, 477, 497, 557, 440(2), 466(2)
Mount Dispersion 341
Mount Gambier 573, 423(2)
Mount Hopeless 363
Mount Lofty 57, 445, 539
Mount Lofty Ranges 433, 2(2)
Mount Lyell 477
Mount Remarkable 341
Murray River 525, 15(2)
Murray Scrub 466
Nairne 440(2)
Newland Bridge 282(2)
Newland's Head 282(2)
Noarlunga 301(2)
North Adelaide 378, 540, 557, 482(2)
Nuccaleena 248
Nuyts Island 172
O'Halloran Hill 301(2)
Palmerston 378
Port Adelaide 16, 288, 335, 377, 432, 442, 497, 499, 557, 117(2)
Port Adelaide River 117(2)
Port Augusta 248
Port Bowen 266
Port Clinton 266
Port Lincoln 18, 282, 362, 446, 539, 117(2), 280(2), 482(2), 626(2)
Port Vincent 46(2)
Preservation Creek 497(2)
Rapid Bay 175, 378, 117(2)

Rhine River 16
River Light 362
Robe 248, 384(2)
Rosetta Cove 540
Rowland Hill 64(2)
Semaphore 497
Sleaford Bay 197(2)
Spencer Gulf 363, 390, 564, 372(2)
Stephen Range 477
Streaky Bay 362-3
Sturt River 57, 557
Tanunda (Langmeil) 33(2)
Torrens River 419, 64(2), 262(2), 491(2)
Traversbrook 379
Victor Harbour 525, 282(2)
Waddikee Rock 282
Walkerville 540, 557
Wallaroo 441(2)
Wayville 379(2)
Wedge Hill 282
West Terrace 376, 557, 65(2)
Wheal Gawler 280(2)
Willunga 282(2)
Wimmera 362
Wudinna Hill 282
Yankalilla 378
Yankalilla Bay 57
Yelki 281(2)
Yorke Peninsula 441(2)
Tasmania:
Adventure Bay 172, 543, 244, 527, 543, 45(2), 429(2)
Allenvale 32(2)
Alma Pass 181
Anglewood 315(2)
Antill Ponds 138(2)
Apsley 409(2), 557(2)
Arthur Range 193
Arthur's Seat 4
Augusta Road, New Town 24
Avoca 197, 258, 36(2), 294(2)
Back River 356
Bagdad 27, 95, 191, 3(2), 308(2), 596(2)
Ballahoo 602(2)
Banks Strait 71
Bass Strait 486, 556, 111(2), 373(2), 386(2), 489(2)
Battery Point 8, 219, 339, 411, 563, 37(2), 67(2), 249(2), 397(2), 442(2)
Bellerive 502, 113(2), 273(2)
Ben Lomond 257, 456, 215(2)
Ben Lomond Rivulet 406, 133(2)
Betsy Island 81, 240, 492, 517
Bicheno 407, 231(2)
Big (Ouse) River 300(2)
Big River 386(2)
Birch's Bay 104
Birch's Inlet 104
Bishopsbourne 436, 286(2)
Black Brush 9
Bothwell 21, 106, 182, 251, 420, 428, 502, 144(2), 235(2), 297(2), 298(2), 300(2), 317(2), 336(2), 375(2), 395(2), 402(2), 409(2), 421(2), 427(2), 429(2), 436(2), 441(2),

593(2), 595(2)
Breadalbane 171, 468(2)
Break O'Day River 454
Bridgewater 24, 230, 430, 45(2), 296(2), 469(2)
Bridgewater Bridge 109
Brighton 421, 502, 436(2)
Brighton Plains 267(2)
Broadmarsh 269(2)
Brown's River 193, 419, 74(2)
Brumby's Plains 171
Bruny Island 172, 194, 244, 339, 517, 37(2), 385(2)
Buckland 256, 429
Burnie 440
Cambridge 78, 104, 181, 113(2), 268(2)
Campania 227
Campbell Town 8, 41, 63, 78, 109, 168, 192, 229, 257, 329, 356, 400, 74(2), 100(2), 173(2), 205(2), 215(2), 217(2), 229(C), 271(2), 290(2), 447(2), 452(2), 458(2), 504(2), 541(2), 542(2), 595(2), 604(2)
Canadian Point 392
Cape Grim 181, 271, 406, 457, 386(2)
Cape Leeuwin 71, 390, 551(2)
Cape Pillar 538
Cape Portland 407, 430(2)
Cape Sorell 138(2)
Carrick 172, 235, 258, 246(2)
Cascade Grove 137(2)
Cascades 254, 302, 71(2), 73(2), 132(2), 133(2)
Cascades Agricultural Settlement 214
Castray's Esplanade 303
Cataract Gorge 60
Cataract Hill 563(2)
Cheltenham 32(2)
Chudleigh 383(2)
Circular Head 3, 24, 270, 271, 406, 440, 457, 493, 528-9, 138(2), 595(2)
Clarence Plains 391, 420, 113(2), 126(2), 217(2)
Clarence Plains (Rokeby) 67(2)
Clarence Point 172
Clearlands (Cleveland) 317(2)
Cleveland 59, 174(2), 215(2)
Cleveland (Clearlands) 317(2)
Clyde River 106, 309, 507, 564, 566, 83(2), 98(2), 128(2), 297(2), 375(2), 402(2), 460(2), 467(2)
Coal River 137, 273, 359, 406, 36(2)
Colonial Hill 441(2)
Compton Ferry 43
Constitution Hill 81
Cormiston 200(2)
Cornelian Basin 527
Cornelian Bay 238
Cottage Green 36
Cradle Mountain 529
Cranbrook 12
Crayfish Point 356
Cressy 517(2), 534(2)

Cripps Range 529
Cross Marsh 270
Cygnet Bay 266
D'Entrecasteaux Channel 20, 71, 172, 138(2), 260(2), 412(2), 577(2), 539(2)
Dairy Lands 138(2)
Danbury Park 316
Darlington station 294(2)
Dasher River 528
Dawes Point 59(2)
Deloraine 8, 330, 407, 493, 48(2), 260(2), 429(2)
Denison 602(2)
Derwent 203, 227, 238, 239, 273, 353, 406, 410, 37(2), 47(2), 127(2), 138(2), 359(2), 365(2), 366(2)
Derwent River 166, 230, 240, 291, 507, 517, 59(2), 98(2), 120(2), 121(2), 219(2), 268(2), 336(2), 363(2)
Derwent valley 282, 302, 566
Derwent Water 84(2)
Devonport 214, 430(2)
Dingley East 32(2)
Don 245(2)
Don River 573(2)
Drummond district 442(2)
Dunrobin 528(2)
Eaglehawk Neck 34, 71(2)
Earlston 429(2)
East Devonport 602(2)
East Risdon 475
East Tamar 32(2)
Eastern Marshes 121(2), 126(2), 467(2)
Egleston 63
Elizabeth River 109, 251
Elizabeth Town 507(2)
Ellerslie 215(2)
Emu Bay 441, 48(2), 429(2)
Entally 32
Epping 174(2)
Epping Forest 308(2)
Esk Vale 192
Evandale 56, 192, 340, 439, 440, 454, 32(2), 458(2), 516(2), 522(2)
Fairfield 316
Fat Doe River 402(2)
Fingal 194, 502(2), 557(2)
Flinders Island 35, 45, 244, 451, 492, 230(2), 386(2)
Forester's River 430(2)
Forestier Peninsula 2(2), 37(2)
Formby 487
Formosa 94(2)
Forth 246(2)
Forth River 493, 573(2), 576(2)
Fosbrook's Point 406
Franklin River 181
Frederick Henry Bay 517, 350(2)
Freshwater Point 486
Frogmore 457
Furneaux group 287(2)
Geilston 436
Geographe Bay 71
George Town 4, 38, 60(C), 68, 126, 168, 197, 223, 224,

241, 257, 369, 417, 418, 458, 533, 38(2), 94(2), 215(2), 231(2), 297(2), 429(2), 596(2), 633(2)
George's Bay 557(2)
Gibson's River 439
Gipsy Village (Sandringham) 32(2)
Glamorgan municipality 249
Glen Ayr 133(2)
Glen Dhu 429(2)
Glen Leith 493
Glenorchy 214, 235, 406, 562, 120(2), 138(2), 415(2), 541(2)
Glenore 172
Gordon River 7, 193, 273, 392, 410, 159(2), 170(2)
Government House Point 553
Great Lake 170(2)
Great Lake road district 225
Great Swanport 34(2)
Green Lagoon 81, 470(2)
Green Point 486, 469(2)
Green Ponds 428, 430, 3(2), 40(2), 317(2), 336(2), 363(2), 532(2), 573(2), 595(2)
Grindstone Bay 429
Gun Carriage Island 35
Gunn's Plains 493
Guy Fawkes Rivulet 302
Hadspen 374(2)
Hagley 330, 143(2)
Halfmoon Bay 138(2)
Hamilton 156, 181, 251, 507, 302(2), 317(2), 436(2), 462(2), 466(2)
Hampshire Hills 429(2)
Handsome Sugarloaf 269(2)
Henty River 181
Herdsman's Cove 227, 217(2)
Highercombe 20
Hobart 2, 3, 5, 9, 29, 66, 78, 81, 86, 92, 134, 147, 155, 192, 220, 229, 339, 340, 353, 355, 356, 400, 404, 406, 407, 413, 421, 466, 491, 498, 552, 574, 34(2), 35(2), 36(2), 44(2), 49(2), 65(2), 67(2), 71(2), 73(2), 76(2), 83(2), 88(2), 97(2), 99(2), 100(2), 101(2), 105(2), 106(2), 113(2), 114(2), 118(2), 120(2), 121(2), 126(2), 126(2), 127(2), 128(2), 130(2), 132(2), 133(2), 137(2), 140(2), 142(2), 143(2), 144(2), 161(2), 163(2), 164(2), 170(2), 173(2), 199(2), 204(2), 205(2), 207(2), 214(2), 217(2), 220(2), 221(2), 225(2), 229(2), 232(2), 235(2), 245(2), 246(2), 248(2), 260(2), 267(2), 268(2), 269(2), 271(2), 278(2), 279(2), 285(2), 286(2), 288(2), 290(2), 291(2), 294(2), 296(2), 297(2), 298(2), 300(2), 302(2), 303(2), 308(2),

311(2), 314(2), 316(2),
319(2), 325(2), 336(2),
341(2), 344(2), 348(2),
349(2), 350(2), 351(2),
354(2), 355(2), 361(2),
363(2), 365(2), 385(2),
395(2), 402(2), 414(2),
433(2), 436(2), 445(2),
447(2), 457(2), 458(2),
459(2), 462(2), 466(2),
469(2), 472(2), 488(2),
490(2), 493(2), 504(2),
511(2), 522(2), 531(2),
562(2), 563(2), 598(2),
601(2), 607(2)
Hobart Streets:
— 13 Macquarie St 434(2)
— 20 Salamanca Place 433(2)
— Argyle Street 301, 36(2),
40(2), 113(2), 285(2),
458(2), 492(2)
— Barrack Street 224
— Bathurst St 339, 552,
144(2)
— Bridge St 140(2)
— Brisbane St 229(2)
— Campbell Street 24, 106,
123, 339, 492, 502, 37(2),
541(2)
— Collins Street 224, 225,
302, 491, 40(2), 113(2),
271(2)
— Colville St 271(2)
— Davey Street 507
— Elboden Street 528(2)
— Elizabeth Street 228, 264,
301, 339, 552, 144(2),
216(2), 229(2), 308(2),
505(2)
— Fitzroy Place 48
— Franklin Square 415
— Gore Street 420
— Goulburn 436
— Hampden Road 407, 420,
528(2), 555(2)
— Harrington Street 270,
491, 300(2)
— Liverpool Street 123, 230,
216(2), 267(2), 271(2),
300(2), 308(2), 436(2),
458(2), 466(2), 527(2)
— Macquarie Street 3, 58,
420, 436, 40(2), 72(2),
127(2), 434(2)
— Melville Street 261, 127(2),
133(2), 229(2)
— Murray Street 225, 230,
235, 74(2), 133(2), 363(2),
433(2)
— Paterson Street 261
— Salamanca Place 23, 224,
366(2)
— Trinity Hill 144(2)
— Upper Davey St 285(2)
— Warwick Street 324, 467(2)
Hobart Rivulet 36(2), 37(2)
Hobson's Bay 352(2)
Holbrook 330
Holdfast Bay 497, 301(2)
Hollow Tree 104, 300(2),
325(2)
Hope Island 126, 137

Horton 24
Humphrey's Rivulet 135,
120(2), 302(2), 415(2)
Humphrey's Rivulet
(Glenorchy) 406
Hunter River 167
Hunter's Island 240, 406,
269(2), 366(2)
Hunting Ground 100(2)
Huon 410, 351(2)
Huon River 137, 240, 412,
498, 566, 45(2)
Huon Valley 193, 282, 407
Impression Bay 48, 420,
601(2)
Inveresk 350(2)
Isis 225
Isis River 429
Jericho 20, 104, 106, 229, 301,
475, 506, 511
Jordan River 19, 421
Kangaroo Bottom 441(2)
Kangaroo Point 392, 45(2),
126(2), 133(2), 273(2),
325(2), 522(2)
Kelly Basin 37(2)
Kelly Island 37(2)
Kelly Point 37(2)
Kelly's Steps 37(2)
Kelso 59, 436(2)
Kelso, West Tamar 418
Kempton 301, 336(2), 557(2)
Kentish Plains 48(2)
Killymoon 363(2)
King Island 127, 219(2),
272(2), 287(2), 312(2)
King William's Land 415
King's River 181
Kingborough 500(2)
Kingston 576(2)
Kirklands 271(2)
Knocklofty 397(2), 602(2)
Lachlan River 87(2)
Lake Colac 271(2), 492(2)
Lake River 24, 251, 301, 302,
94(2), 97(2), 296(2), 517(2)
Lake Sorell 225, 217(2),
235(2)
Lake St Clair 96, 181, 193,
410, 414, 170(2), 354(2),
436(2)
Latrobe 407, 260(2)
Launceston 2, 3, 4, 38, 56, 59,
142, 147, 172, 191, 197, 209,
213, 214, 219, 220, 223, 224,
225, 234, 241, 251, 257, 278,
292, 296, 304, 316, 317, 328,
329, 330, 369, 400, 406, 417,
454, 457, 467, 486, 487, 493,
511, 518, 531, 543, 558, 563,
8(2), 9(2), 23(2), 32(2),
48(2), 65(2), 73(2), 74(2),
94(2), 95(2), 124(2), 143(2),
144(2), 161(2), 205(2),
215(2), 230(2), 231(2),
232(2), 245(2), 246(2),
260(2), 267(2), 290(2),
291(2), 298(2), 318(2),
350(2), 355(2), 371(2),
393(2), 413(2), 429(2),
430(2), 436(2), 441(2),
445(2), 458(2), 493(2),

504(2), 516(2), 539(2),
557(2), 563(2), 577(2),
590(2), 595(2), 633(2)
Launceston:
— Adelaide Street 317
— Barrack St 563(2)
— Brisbane Street 316, 9(2),
505(2)
— Cameron Street 304, 305,
9(2), 458(2), 633(2)
— Charles Street 9(2), 74(2),
245(2), 441(2), 493(2)
— Elizabeth Street 304
— Frankland Street 246(2)
— Margaret Street 304
— Paterson Street 59
— Prince's Square 317
— Rosemont High St 4
— St John Street 245(2)
— Wellington Street 373(2)
— York Street 305, 316, 317
Lawrence Vale Road 94(2)
Lawrenny 437
Leigh River 409(2)
Lemon Springs 308(2)
Lennox 137(2)
Leven River 573(2)
Lincoln 174(2)
Little Swanport 179, 543
Long Point, Maria Island 192
Longford 25, 32, 168, 171,
250, 251, 258, 291, 292, 302,
304, 333, 369, 491, 511, 9(2),
50(2), 133(2), 143(2),
383(2), 468(2), 469(2),
534(2), 593(2), 596(2)
Lovely Banks 104, 425, 577(2)
Low Head 257
Lower Clyde 433(2)
Lowes Park 138(2)
Loyola 21
Lymington 257, 32(2)
Macquarie 144(2)
Macquarie Harbour 34, 45,
104, 147, 191, 193, 273, 360,
412, 467, 491, 492, 543,
37(2), 62(2), 159(2), 230(2),
386(2), 423(2)
Macquarie Island 83, 485,
36(2), 45(2), 359(2), 360(2),
444(2), 548(2)
Macquarie Plains 81, 126,
507(2), 576(2)
Macquarie Point 406, 491
Macquarie River 7, 24, 251,
100(2), 173(2), 174(2),
429(2), 466(2), 504(2),
612(2)
Macquarie River district 425
Malvern 393(2)
Manor Owen 137(2)
Maria Island 34, 192, 194,
253, 38(2), 433(2)
Marlboro' 193
Mayfarm 356
Meander 143(2)
Medway Rivulet 106(2)
Melbille 359
Melrose 302
Melton Mowbray 416, 308(2),
434(2)
Meredith River 225(2)

Mersey 406
Mersey River 214, 270, 457, 487, 487, 528, 170(2), 602(2)
Middle Arm 304
Middlesex Plains 429(2)
Milford 516(2)
Mill's Plains 282, 456
Miller's Bay 120(2)
Minnow River 528
Mole Creek 290(2), 372(2), 373(2), 429(2)
Mona Vale 50(2)
Mooki River 424(2)
Moonah 254
Moriarty 260(2)
Morven 257, 454
Mount Bischoff 529
Mount Cameron 457
Mount Direction 230
Mount Dromedary 291
Mount Elephant 409(2)
Mount Emmett 357
Mount Farrell 529
Mount Mourice 430(2)
Mount Pleasant 466(2)
Mount Wellington 302, 303, 412, 502, 517, 566
Muddy Plains 216(2)
Mulgrave Battery, Hobart 303
Murchison River 529
New Norfolk 32, 43, 182, 213, 239, 291, 332, 333, 356, 371, 436, 440, 493, 502, 508, 527, 536, 560, 574, 73(2), 87(2), 88(2), 127(2), 159(2), 207(2), 214(2), 217(2), 221(2), 294(2), 297(2), 298(2), 366(2), 415(2), 427(2), 436(2), 442(2), 458(2), 466(2), 490(2), 507(2), 528(2), 576(2), 601(2), 607(2)
New Town 80, 81, 95, 125, 227, 254, 304, 356, 360, 429, 494, 511, 2(2), 113(2), 133(2), 214(2), 279(2), 285(2), 303(2), 336(2), 336(2), 366(2), 384(2), 415(2), 427(2), 458(2), 466(2), 500(2), 517(2), 576(2), 602(2)
New Town Bay 120(2)
New Town Creek 120(2)
New Town Rivulet 301
Nile 192, 557(2)
Nile River 56, 456
Nile Rivulet 371(2)
Nive River 291, 410
Norfolk Plains 32, 95, 257, 291, 486, 491, 7(2), 94(2), 143(2), 214(2), 231(2), 232(2), 264(2), 447(2), 596(2)
Norfolk Plains (Longford) 511
North Down 270
North Esk 486, 74(2)
North Esk River 171, 394(2)
North Hobart 291(2)
North-West Bay 549
North West Passage 415
Norwood 402(2)

O'Brien's Bridge 302(2)
Oatlands 4, 19, 20, 21, 81, 179, 257, 304, 430, 502, 561, 27(2), 121(2), 126(2), 215(2), 223(2), 269(2), 308(2), 415(2), 436(2), 595(2)
Old Wharf, Hobart 224, 303
Organ Pipes 302
Ouse 96, 317(2)
Ouse (Big) River 300(2)
Ouse district 32
Oyster Bay 225(2), 386(2)
Oyster Cove 230(2)
Panshanger 24
Pateena 258
Paterson's Plains 32(2)
Pembroke 323
Perry's Point 303
Perth 292, 316, 439, 468(2), 504(2), 593(2), 633(2)
Phillip Island 469
Piper's River 511, 430(2)
Pittwater 273, 436, 517, 560, 566, 16(2), 71(2), 87(2), 121(2), 268(2), 279(2), 300(2), 434(2), 577(2)
Plas y Dolan 113(2)
Pleasant Banks 440
Plenty 566, 365(2)
Plenty River 109, 566
Point Bougainville 132(2)
Point Effingham 94(2)
Point Lilias 492(2)
Point Louis 138(2)
Point Puer 125, 419, 71(2), 205(2)
Port Albert 407
Port Arthur 34, 45, 125, 192, 213, 214, 224, 253, 254, 303, 361, 419, 38(2), 71(2), 458(2), 576(2), 601(2), 607(2)
Port Dalrymple 2, 25, 49, 59, 71, 92, 112, 144, 166, 171, 197, 223, 226, 240, 252, 257, 273, 289, 290, 328, 359, 365, 368, 408, 439, 486, 487, 491, 511, 517, 553, 566, 15(2), 39(2), 46(2), 47(2), 59(2), 67(2), 97(2), 101(2), 143(2), 215(2), 232(2), 264(2), 267(2), 318(2), 336(2), 380(2), 382(2), 393(2), 394(2), 419(2), 459(2), 564(2), 596(2), 633(2)
Port Davey 104, 193, 37(2), 170(2), 386(2)
Port Esperance 126 Port Sorell 3, 270, 487, 528, 170(2), 430(2), 517(2)
Potter's Hill 216(2)
Preservation Island 170(2), 596(2)
Prince of Wales Bay 120(2)
Prosser Plains 128, 256, 429, 317(2)
Prosser River district 407
Providence Valley 442(2), 601(2)
Quamby district 258
Quamby's Plains 328

Queen's Bay Bluff 171
Race Course Marsh 179
Ralph's Bay 240, 273(2)
Recherche Bay 340, 368, 467, 492, 302(2), 325(2)
Redlands 365(2)
Richmond 8, 181, 253, 302, 359, 457, 458, 494, 36(2), 73(2), 133(2), 134(2), 258(2), 269(2), 315(2), 366(2), 384(2), 397(2), 421(2), 442(2), 577(2)
Richmond district 541(2)
Ringarooma River 430(2), 517(2)
Risdon 109, 134, 227, 230, 230, 238, 240, 268(2)
Risdon Cove 136, 137, 527
Rokeby 67(2)
Rosetta 7(2)
Ross 24, 41, 220, 235, 261, 339, 356, 407, 425, 502, 511, 49(2), 50(2), 205(2), 217(2), 314(2), 315(2), 429(2), 434(2), 452(2)
Ross Bridge 94(2), 447(2)
Rostella 32(2)
St Leonard's 271(2)
St Patrick's River 317, 430(2)
St Paul's River 36(2)
St Valentine's Peak 528
Safety Cove 125
Salmon Ponds 298(2)
Salt Pan Plains 36(2), 49(2), 176(2), 268(2)
Salt Water River 213, 71(2), 458(2)
Sandy Bay 7, 193, 517, 549, 40(2), 73(2), 74(2), 84(2), 126(2)
Sandy Cape 181
Sarah Island 104, 273, 549
Schouten Island 230
Scone 383(2)
Scottsdale 427(2)
Scottsdale district 430(2)
Shannon River 561, 297(2), 396(2)
Shooter's Hill 466(2)
Sidmouth 418
Sidmouth, West Tamar 428
Slopen Island 95
Smithton 357
Snake Banks 539(2)
Sorell 147, 273, 429, 437, 458, 502, 3(2), 16(2), 36(2), 45(2), 73(2), 126(2), 279(2), 366(2), 421(2)
Sorell district 323, 407, 493
Sorrento 238
South Arm 437
South Arm peninsula 325(2)
South Brighton 32(2)
South Cape 543, 429(2)
South Esk 67(2), 564(2)
South Esk River 2, 56, 59, 172, 339, 392, 439, 566, 215(2), 264(2), 383(2), 516(2), 633(2)
South Esk valley 36(2)
Southern Macquarie road district 225

Southport 176(2)
Spring Bay municipality 249
Spring Hill 81, 106
Stainsforth's Cove 120(2), 336(2)
Stanley 24, 428, 440
Stewarton 504(2)
Storm Bay 137, 172, 239, 302(2)
Storm Bay Passage 517
Styx River 72(2)
Sullivan Bay 238
Sullivan Cove 238, 406, 577(2)
Sullivan's Cove 24, 36, 368, 325(2), 366(2)
Supply River 566
Surrey Hills 270, 406, 230(2), 429(2)
Sussex District 87(2)
Swan Island 170(2), 386(2)
Swan River 12
Swanport 329, 437, 317(2)
Swansea 220, 329, 132(2), 225(2), 491(2)
Tamar River 258, 304, 356, 417, 566, 59(2), 94(2), 174(2), 199(2), 232(2), 372(2), 537(2)
Tarleton 602(2)
Tasman Peninsula 34, 213, 224, 244, 419, 420, 437, 71(2), 114(2), 601(2)
Tasmans Island 538
Tea Tree 442(2)
Tin Pot Marsh 179
Tooms Lake 179
Trinity Hill, Hobart 144(2)
Tullochgorum 493
Tully River 181
Tunbridge 36(2), 245(2), 542(2)
Upper Arthur River 493
Upper Macquarie 192
Van Diemen's Gulf 62(2)
Van Diemen's Land 387, 410, 40(2), 48(2), 50(2), 124(2)
Wanstead 604(2)
Waratah 181
Waterloo Point 249, 132(2), 225(2), 490(2)
Wesley Dale 372(2), 373(2)
Westbury 328, 502, 143(2), 260(2)
Western District 316
Western River 273
Western River district 3
Westernport 68, 372(2)
Westmorland County 500(2)
West Point 511
White Hills 106
Whitefoord Hills 596(2)
Windermere 304, 393(2), 522(2)
Windmill Hill 417, 590(2)
Winton 541(2)
Wood's Lake 97(2)
Woodbridge 104
Woodlands 436(2)
Woolnorth 271, 406
Wyld's Craig 282
Wynyard 631(2)

York Town 318(2)
Zeehan 214
Victoria:
Abbotsford 271
Alberton 160(2), 412(2)
Anderson's Creek 349(2)
Anderson's Inlet 14
Arthur's Creek 38
Arthur's Seat 544
Austin's Ford 43
Australia Felix 532, 239(2), 243(2), 471(2)
Avenel 14
Avoca River 28(2)
Avon River 28(2), 183(2)
Bacchus Marsh 543, 349(2), 521(2)
Bakery Hill, Ballarat 26
Balham Hill 249
Ballan 557(2)
Ballanee 14
Ballarat 229, 278, 80(2), 91(2), 101(2), 199(2), 334(2), 349(2), 393(2), 423(2), 492(2), 534(2)
Balmoral 406(2)
Barunah Plains 409(2)
Barwon River 330, 303(2), 540(2)
Bass Strait 59(2)
Batesford 409(2)
Batman's Hill 69
Beechworth 311, 474(2)
Belfast (Port Fairy) 399
Bellarine Peninsula 68, 330, 71(2)
Bendigo 91(2), 168(2), 222(2), 423(2)
Birregurra 540(2)
Blacknose Point 340
Boorabool Hills 282
Box Hill 402(2)
Branxholme 406(2)
Bream Creek 174
Brighton 234, 350, 32(2), 71(2), 590(2)
Broken River 367
Brunswick 331, 474(2), 519(2)
Buninyong 399, 75(2)
Campbellfield 399
Cape Patterson 14
Caledonia Australia 183(2)
Corner Inlet 411(2)
Carngham 409(2), 438
Casterton 9(2), 406(2)
Castlemaine 349(2)
Champion Bay 326
Chancery 67(2)
Clunes 520
Colac 385(2)
Cole's Wharf 233
Coleraine 406(2)
Coliban River 243(2)
Collingwood, Brunswick St 110
Collingwood, Smith St. 371
Corinella 14
Corio Bay 556, 564, 492(2)
Cranbourne 572
Creswick 160(2)
Crooked River 184(2)
Dandenong 524

Darebin Creek 545, 65(2)
Dargo 184(2)
Delatite River 249
Diamond Creek 38
Digby 406(2)
Dight's Falls 488
Dingley 32(2)
Dowling Forest 229
Dromana 160(2)
Drysdale 71(2), 330
Dunolly 95
Durdidwarrah 557(2)
Eagle Point 543(2)
East Melbourne 216, 506(C), 334(2), 340(2), 367(2C), 410(2), 447(2)
Echuca 231(2)
Elderslie 409(2)
Eltham 455(2)
Eureka 85(2)
Fitzroy 410(2), 625(2)
Fitzroy, Brunswick St. 70(2)
Forest Creek 222(2)
Fowler's Bay 20
Frederick Henry Bay 134
Freeman Street 443
Freshwater River 369
Fulham, Gippsland 198
Fyansford, Geelong 70
Fyansford 423
Gabo Island 543(2)
Gardiner's Creek, Melbourne 425
Geelong 27, 43, 68, 70, 81, 82, 229, 232, 330, 331, 399, 423, 510, 520, 565, 44(2), 48(2), 65(2), 70(2), 88(2), 101(2), 161(2), 176(2), 224(2), 297(2), 372(2), 385(2), 409(2), 423(2), 492(2), 501(2), 522(2), 539(2), 540(2), 557(2), 593(2), 606(2)
Gellibrand Point 125(2)
Germantown 510, 423(2)
Gippsland 124, 407, 452, 572, 573, 160(2), 183(2), 184(2), 410(2), 494(2), 518(2), 532(2), 543(2)
Gisborne 349(2)
Gisborne-Sunbury district 4
Glenelg 125(2)
Glenelg River 543(2)
Golf Hill 224(2), 409(2)
Goulburn River 14, 556, 541(2)
Goulburn River valley 249
Grampians 606(2)
Great Swan Port 502(2)
Griffith's Island 487
Griffith's Point 14
Grovedale 423(2)
Hamilton 533
Hamilton (the Grange) 406(2)
Harrow 112, 406(2), 501(2)
Heathcote 271
Heatherlea 75(2)
Heidelburg 124, 524
Henty 407(2)
Hepburn 160(2)
Heywood 406(2)
Hobson's Bay 369, 545,

534(2)
Hopkins River 124, 197
Horsham 85(2)
Hunter's River 59(2)
Iguana Creek 184(2)
Indented Head 68, 369,
  224(2)
Ingleby country 27
Jackson's Creek 9(2)
Jolimont 84(2)
Kardinia 522(2)
Kew 244(2)
Kilmore 160(2), 411(2)
Koolomurt 501(2)
Koroit 411(2)
Kyneton 222, 244(2), 349(2)
Lake Alexandrina 75(2)
Lake Colac 423
Lake Corangamite 423, 200(2)
Lake Gnarpurt 200(2)
Lake Hindmarsh 557(2)
Lake Murdeduke 552
Lake Purrumbete 199(2)
Landsborough 349(2)
Langi Kal Kal 409(2)
Latrobe 602(2)
Lexington 606(2)
Light's Pass 423(2)
Loddon River 28(2), 239(2)
MacAlister River 183(2)
Malmsbury 296
Malvern 224(2), 352(2)
Mangalore 14
Maryborough, Nightingale St.
  28(2)
Matlock 184(2)
Melbourne 14, 70, 109, 399,
  423, 430, 453, 460, 495, 533,
  544, 547, 28(2), 65(2), 89(2),
  92(2), 115(2), 125(2),
  160(2), 164(2), 176(2),
  203(2), 251(2), 257(2),
  270(2), 290(2), 303(2),
  320(2), 334(2), 344(2),
  372(2), 392(2), 406(2),
  409(2), 411(2), 424(2),
  442(2), 447(2), 455(2),
  458(2), 464(2), 474(2),
  492(2), 512(2), 521(2),
  522(2), 543(2), 572(2),
  589(2), 593(2), 603(2),
  607(2)
Melbourne Streets:
— Acland Street 9(2)
— Bank Place 70(2)
— Bourke Street 547, 28(2),
  68(2), 160(2), 410(2),
  565(2), 603(2)
— Collins Street 350, 444,
  55(2), 229(2), 455(2), 572(2)
— Elizabeth Street 425, 55(2),
  70(2)
— Flinders Lane 272, 70(2)
— Flinders Street 9(2)
— King St 410(2), 603(2)
— Little Bourke Street 232
— Little Collins St 425, 9(2)
— Little Flinders St 447(2)
— Little Lonsdale St 70(2)
— Lonsdale Street 272, 322,
  407, 126(2)
— Market Street 272, 492(2),

572(2)
— Prince's Bridge 107(2)
— Queen Street 55(2)
— Russell Street 572(2)
— Spencer Street 233, 547,
  455(2)
— Swanston Street 232, 70(2)
— Toorak Road 112
— William Street 272, 572(2)
Melbourne North, Victoria St
  70(2)
Merai 197
Merino 406(2)
Merri River 200(2)
Mitta Mitta River 556
Mitchell River 183(2)
Moorabool River 423, 199(2),
  409(2)
Mordialloc 82
Moroka River 184(2)
Mount Aitken 4
Mount Alexander 243(2)
Mount Ararat 606(2)
Mount Egerton 101(2)
Mount Elephant No. 2 (sheep
  run) 4
Mount Leura 199(2)
Mount Macedon 38, 350,
  28(2), 243(2), 349(2)
Mount Martha 126(2)
Mount Mcleod 183(2)
Mount Napier 572
Murray River 173(2), 181(2),
  541(2)
Narmbool 75(2)
Narrawang 112
Narre Warren 278, 518(2)
Nicholson River 183(2)
North Geelong 9(2)
North Melbourne 322, 82(2)
Old Port 543(2)
Old Settlement Point 14
Omeo 91(2), 183(2), 184(2)
Ovens River 311, 367, 556,
  305(2)
Pentland Hills 349(2)
Perry River 183(2)
Pirron Yallock 423
Plaistow 28(2)
Plenty River 14
Point Gellibrand 545
Point Henry 330, 423, 521,
  199(2), 372(2), 539(2),
  606(2)
Point Lonsdale 126(2)
Point Nepean 545, 281(2)
Port Albert 410(2), 543(2)
Port Essington 391(2)
Port Fairy 197, 296, 340, 399,
  486, 231(2), 411(2)
Port Melbourne 115(2)
Port Phillip 38, 66, 226, 362,
  365, 368, 399, 401, 487, 490,
  517, 524, 531, 543, 545, 547,
  556, 564, 38(2), 59(2), 65(2),
  67(2), 77(2), 84(2), 88(2),
  91(2), 101(2), 120(2),
  125(2), 126(2), 127(2),
  135(2), 219(2), 224(2),
  243(2), 252(2), 271(2),
  272(2), 303(2), 317(2),
  353(2), 366(2), 372(2),

387(2), 409(2), 411(2),
  452(2), 472(2), 492(2),
  501(2), 513(2), 514(2)
Port Phillip Bay 240, 369,
  544, 553, 621(2)
Port Phillip District 311, 385,
  447, 451, 453, 492, 48(2),
  89(2), 90(2), 107(2), 120(2),
  392(2), 518(2), 540(2),
  565(2), 606(2)
Portland 297, 423, 510, 75(2),
  239(2), 252(2), 504(2),
  543(2), 557(2)
Portland Bay 112, 197, 340,
  369, 399, 485, 486, 531,
  43(2), 231(2), 372(2),
  387(2), 412(2)
Portland Head 76(2)
Powlett Plains 14
Prahran 461
Pyalong 349(2)
Queenscliff 26, 232, 455(2)
Rabbit Island 487
Richmond 88(2), 410(2)
Richmond, 283 Burnley St
  410(2)
Rocky Point 520
Rosebrook 197
Rowville 232
Rowville, Wellington Road
  232
Rupertwood 9(2)
Rye 545
St Helier's 271
St Kilda 176, 322, 407, 543,
  573, 9(2), 86(2), 334(2),
  393(2)
Sale 457
Saltwater River 69, 75(2)
San Remo 14
Sandford 407(2)
Sandhurst 244(2)
Sandringham (Gipsy Village)
  32(2)
Schouten Islands 340
Seymour 521(2)
Sorrento 67(2)
South Port 413(2)
South Yan Yean 297
South Yarra 14, 82, 198, 401,
  544, 34(2), 455(2)
South Yarra, Caroline St. 198
Station Peak 229, 447(2)
Stieglitz 557(2)
Stoneleigh 409(2)
Stony Rises 200(2)
Stratford 184(2)
Studley Park 160(2)
Sunbury 51(2)
Swan Hill 545
Swan Reach 543(2)
Talbot 474(2)
Tambo River 183(2)
Taradale 410(2)
Tarwin River 14
Thomson River 183(2)
Traralgon 545
Trawalla 112, 65(2)
Tullaroop 28(2)
Turon 388
Wallup 175
Wangaratta 311, 75(2), 376(2)

Wannon River 532, 406(2)
Wannon valley 297
Warragul 573
Warrnambool 197, 529,
    200(2), 352(2), 406(2)
Werribee 401, 409(2), 522(2),
    557(2), 576(2)
Werribee River 27, 349(2),
    447(2)
Western District 412(2)
Western Port 15, 61, 65, 71,
    195, 285, 369, 452, 556, 564,
    59(2), 272(2), 305(2),
    349(2), 494(2)
Western Port Bay 14
Williamstown 547, 115(2),
    125(2), 352(2)
Wilson's Promontory 61, 65,
    71, 202(2), 410(2)
Wimmera 557(2)
Winchelsea 43, 552
Wodonga 573
Wonthaggi 14
Yarra River 233, 271, 369,
    487-8, 544, 90(2), 107(2),
    115(2), 125(2)
Yarram 184(2)
Yering 14
York 326
You Yangs 229
Western Australia:
  Admiralty Gulf 62(2)
  Albany 227, 236, 272, 325,
    326, 382, 477, 465(2),
    486(2), 487(2), 488(2),
    618(2), 620(2), 629(2)
  Albany River 325
  Albrohos 272 see also
    Houtamn
  Albrohos Islands 529
  Arrowsmith River 326
  Augusta 189, 325, 244(2),
    245(2)
  Australind 372, 576, 489(2),
    561(2), 619(2)
  Avon 219(2)
  Avon River 510, 253(2)
  Avon valley 180, 325, 122(2)
  Beeliar 632(2)
  Bernier Island 477
  Beverley 174(2)
  Blackwood River 189, 244(2)
  Broome 352, 440(2)
  Bunbury 176, 122(2), 488(2),
    489(2), 619(2)
  Busselton 175, 176, 189, 190,
    245(2)
  Camden Sound 266
  Canning River 230, 278(2)
  Cape Leeuwin 172, 189, 389,
    390(2)
  Cape Riche 325, 326
  Champion Bay 529, 253(2),
    489(2)
  Champion Bay district 180
  Champion Bay River 382
  Clarence 321(2)
  Cockburn Sound 110(2),
    321(2), 487(2)
  Collie 236
  Collie River 236
  Collier Bay 266

Darling Range 325, 486(2)
Dedelsland 555
Dirk Hartog Island 266,
    556(2)
Eendracht's Land 13(2)
Esperance 363, 391(2), 629(2)
Fair Lawn 244(2)
Flinder's Bay 244(2)
Fowler's Bay 629(2)
Fremantle 66, 165, 155, 227,
    272, 381, 382, 510, 576,
    74(2), 122(2), 174(2),
    245(2), 252(2), 278(2),
    321(2), 377(2), 391(2),
    417(2), 426(2), 433(2),
    439(2), 488(2), 612(2),
    618(2), 632(2)
Gage Roads 487(2)
Gantheaume Bay 477
Garden Island 165, 236,
    376(2)
Gascoyne River 477
Geographe Bay 245(2)
Geraldine 382
Geraldton 382, 122(2), 323(2),
    426(2), 439(2)
Gingin 155
Greenough River flats 439(2)
Guangan 325
Guildford 382, 74(2), 219(2),
    486(2), 488(2), 618(2)
Gwambygine 618(2)
Hay River 465(2)
Helena valley 325
Henley Park 5(2)
Herne Hill 155
Houtman Albrohos 266, 441,
    555, 253(2), 323(2) see also
    Albrohos
Kalgan River 230
Kelmscott 433(2), 488(2)
King George Sound 57, 71,
    219, 236, 266, 266, 285, 287,
    340, 477, 533, 61(2), 123(2),
    465(2), 485(2), 629(2)
King River 629(2)
King Sound 266, 277
King's Park 391(2)
Kojonup 227
Leschenault 372, 576
Lucky Bay 326
Mandurah 322(2), 440(2)
Maylands 510
Melville Island 123(2)
Middle Mount Barren 326
Montebello Islands 266
Moora 325
Moore River 326
Mount Caroline 326
Murchison River 326, 382,
    439(2)
Murray River 322(2)
New Norcia 416(2), 417(2)
North West Cape 477, 13(2),
    61(2)
Northam 155, 325, 253(2)
Northampton 439(2)
Nundah 509
Perth 147, 165, 477, 509, 510,
    6(2), 74(2), 175(2), 258(2),
    322(2), 391(2), 417(2),
    433(2), 487(2), 489(2),

    612(2), 618(2), 632(2)
— Causeway 253(2)
— Hay & Irwin Sts. 165
— Mount Street 372
— St George's Terrace 236,
    372, 377(2), 439(2)
— William Street 175(2)
Perth-Fremantle Road 372
Picton 619(2)
Pinjarra 175, 176, 322(2),
    439(2)
Point Moore 253(2)
Port Gregory 180
Port Grey 489(2)
Port Leschenault 477, 619(2)
Preston River 236
Ravensthorpe 326
Rockingham Beach 219(2)
Roebourne 391(2)
Roebuck Bay 266, 277, 440(2)
Rose Hill 489(2)
Rossiter Bay 629(2)
Rottnest 272
Rottnest Island 227, 236, 266,
    325, 509, 556(2)
Russell Range 391(2)
Salt River 325, 326
Shark Bay 71, 277, 382, 477,
    556(2)
Stirling Range 326
Surry River 340
Swan River 46, 57, 164, 230,
    236, 285, 325, 372, 416, 441,
    510, 531, 555, 5(2), 51(2),
    99(2), 110(2), 122(2),
    123(2), 195(2), 244(2),
    245(2), 258(2), 278(2),
    321(2), 349(2), 376(2),
    391(2), 433(2), 485(2),
    489(2), 556(2), 618(2)
The Rocks, Clarence 219(2)
Thistle Cove 363
Toodyay 326, 372, 489(2)
Toodyay valley 325
Upper Swan 180, 252(2)
Vasse River 189, 325, 244(2)
Victoria Plains 325, 416(2)
Wallemarra 326
Walyormouring 326
Wanneroo 439(2), 440(2)
Wedderburn 372
West Mount Barren 326
Wilson's Inlet 612(2)
Wongan Hills 325
Yandergine 122(2)
York 175, 510, 74(2), 122(2),
    174(2), 175(2), 219(2),
    252(2), 278(2), 440(2),
    488(2)
York district 180, 227, 253(2)

British Isles

Channel Islands:
    290, 116(2), 267(2), 268(2),
    285(2), 390(2)
  Jersey 33, 224, 334, 105(2),
    268(2)
  Guernsey 164, 197, 303, 324,
    419, 43(2), 234(2), 536(2)
Isle of Man: 49(2), 50(2), 391(2)

England:

Acton Burnell 340(2)
Addlestone SRY 327
Alcester WAR 558
Alderley CHS 315(2), 470(2)
Aldgate LND 39(2), 457(2)
Aldridge STS 9, 368(2)
Allhallows 326(2)
Alnwick NBL 188
Alphington 506, 506(C)
Alresford HAM 499
Alrewas 570(2)
Ambleside CUL 246(2)
Ampfield HAM 324(2)
Ansley WAR 573
Appleby 455
Arlingham GLS 16(2)
Ash 285(2)
Ashburton DEV 344
Askrigg 507(2)
Aswarby LIN 64
Aylesbury BKM 487, 608(2)
Baldock HRT 406
Balham Hill LND 249
Ball's Pond 418(2)
Baltonsborough SOM 42, 43
Banbury OXF 196(2)
Barfield, Ryde IOW 304
Barham Downs KEN 11
Barnard Castle 562(2)
Barnet HRT 158, 285(2),
    312(2)
Barnstaple DEV 218(2)
Barrow upon Humber LIN
    510
Bartley HEF 144(2)
Bashford 337(2)
Basingstoke HAM 125
Bath 21, 63, 216, 245, 292,
    335, 355, 574, 141(2),
    145(2), 309(2), 315(2),
    319(2), 387(2), 514(2)
Bath, 19 Bennett St 333(2)
Battersea Rise SRY 485
Bayswater LND 195, 442,
    144(2)
Beaminster DOR 549
Beccles SFK 29
Bedale 507(2)
Bedford BDF 247
Bempton 440(2)
Benham BRK 46
Berkshire 299, 515, 224(2)
Bermondsey 357
Bermondsey LND 308(2),
    546(2)
Bermondsey SRY 254(2)
Berwick upon Tweed 404,
    216(2), 481(2), 500(2),
    573(2)
Bethnal Green LND 212
Bexley 418
Bierton BKM 437(2)
Biggleswade BDF 205(2)
Bingham NTT 134(2)
Biningham DUR 63
Birmingham 1, 9, 123, 126,
    180, 419, 490, 541, 29(2),
    64(2), 79(2), 224(2), 444(2),
    546(2), 607(2), 610(2)
Bittern HAM 2(2)

Blackburn LAN 320(2)
Blackheath 418, 468(2)
Blackheath KEN 225
Blackwater HAM 461
Blandford DOR 394(2)
Bledlow BKM 298
Bletchley 583(2)
Blisland CON 532(2)
Blyth NTT 534(2)
Bodmin CON 118, 95(2)
Bolton LAN 126, 245, 252
Bolton Percy YKS 287(2)
Bolton YKS 126(2)
Boroughbridge YKS 224, 557
Boston LIN 64, 385(2)
Bothwell 83(2)
Bow LND 299
Bowling YKS 625(2)
Bracknell BKS 287
Braddan 49(2)
Bradford YKS 270(2)
Bradford YKS 211, 423(2)
Bridekirk CUL 527
Bridgerule CON 154(2)
Bridgewater SOM 297
Brighton 246, 286, 541,
    176(2), 189(2), 251(2),
    252(2), 320(2), 355(2),
    425(2), 593(2), 595(2)
Bristol 10, 74, 107, 257,
    257(C), 258, 264, 367, 431,
    441, 470, 508, 79(2), 203(2),
    288(2), 419(2), 483(2),
    539(2)
Brixton, Tulse Hill SRY
    547(2)
Bromborough CHS 199(2)
Brompton KEN 308(2)
Broxwood HEF 474
Budleigh Salterton 530
Buntingford HRT 491(2)
Burrswood KEN 532
Burslem STS 322, 441(2)
Burton on Trent 9, 26
Bury LAN 373(2)
Bury St Edmunds 384, 552(2)
Butcombe SOM 419(2)
Buxted SSX 437
Calne WIL 283(2)
Cambridge 10, 288, 417, 453,
    456, 464, 474, 480, 66(2),
    246(2), 627(2)
Cambridge Heath 229(2)
Canterbury 11, 159, 291, 446,
    279(2)
Carlesley WAR 214(2)
Carlisle CUL 137, 311, 244(2)
Carshalton SRY 562
Castletown 49(2), 50(2)
Catton DBY 554
Chaddesley Corbett WOR
    207(2)
Chapel-en-le-Frith 453
Charlton, Woolwich, London
    169
Charmouth DOR 465(2)
Chatham 11, 101, 157, 170,
    539, 27(2), 385(2), 434(2),
    534(2), 595(2)
Cheadle STS 599(2)
Cheapside LND 66, 23(2),
    392(2), 504(2)

Chelsea LND 134, 217,
    115(2), 156(2), 462(2),
    498(2)
Cheltenham 358, 473, 5(2),
    47(2), 50(2), 498(2), 564(2)
Cheriton 155
Chertsey KEN 415(2)
Cheshire 59, 65(2)
Cheshunt HRT 78
Chester 245, 557, 215(2),
    313(2), 353(2), 506(2),
    601(2), 633(2)
Chester-Le-Street DUR
    493(2)
Chichester SSX 256, 391, 497
Childesoakford, Carshalton
    SRY 562
Chipping Ongar ESS 313,
    133(2)
Chirbury SAL 24(2)
Chishall ESS 144(2)
Christchurch 553(2)
Chudleigh DEV 431
Clapham 39, 476(2)
Clapham Common LND 249
Clapham Park 73(2)
Clapham SRY 275
Clerkenwell MDX 134(2),
    404(2)
Clevedon SOM 418
Clifton 10
Clifton, Bristol 508
Clifton GLS 102(2), 569(2)
Clothall 406
Cockermouth CUL 283(2)
Colchester 316
Colchester, Stanwell Street
    316
Cold Bath, Islington 431
Coleshill WAR 590(2)
Collompton DEV 356(2)
Compton DEV 149
Cookham Dean BKM 256
Cornwall 212, 213, 252, 61(2),
    334(2)
Cotesbach LEI 207(2)
Covent Garden 552(2)
Coventry WAR 178, 365, 521,
    522, 214(2), 350(2), 546(2)
Cowes 146, 406, 419(2),
    463(2)
Cowes, Isle of Wight 15(2)
Cranfield BDF 175
Craven YKS 194
Crediton DEV 288
Cripplegate LND 368
Crondall SRY 47
Croydon SRY 489
Cummins DEV 261(2)
Darenth KEN 111(2)
Darlington DUR 45, 309
Dartford 88(2)
Dartmouth DEV 259
Daventry NTH 184
Dawlish DEV 15, 301(2)
Deal KEN 524
Denmark Hill, London 176
Dent YKS 592(2)
Deptford 552, 137(2)
Deptford KEN 621(2)
Deptford LND 196, 115(2)
Derby 572(2)

Derby, Friar Gate 431
Devizes WIL 256, 258
Devon 212, 213, 247, 296,
    529, 123(2), 224(2)
Devonport 538, 506(2)
Diddlebury SAL 259(2)
Dinton WIL 630(2)
Dobroyd YKS 128(2)
Doncaster 510, 371(2), 372(2)
Donington LIN 389
Dorchester DOR 132(2)
Dorset 299(2)
Dover 7, 219, 240, 302, 376,
    188(2)
Downe KEN 128(2)
Downside 292, 340(2), 544(2)
Dudley Hill 423(2)
Dulverton SOM 19
Dungeness 119
Dunstan NBL 188
Dunster SOM 139(2)
Durham 233, 612(2)
Ealing LDN 577 9(2)
East Clandon SRY 552(2)
East Coker SOM 277
East Heslerton YKS 440(2)
East Riding YKS 133(2)
East Smithfield LND 23(2)
Eastbourne SSX 578, 92(2)
Edenbridge KEN 278(2)
Edgbaston 31
Egg-Buckland DEV 226
Egremont CUL 12(2)
Ellington KEN 100(2)
Elm CAM 256
Eltham KEN 88(2)
Ely 312(2), 516(2)
Ely CAM 256
Ems 316(2)
Enfield MDX 105
Enfield MDX, Baker Street
    9(2)
Enfield racecourse 63
Englefield Green SRY 485
Essex 250, 299, 418, 262(2),
    604(2), 617(2)
Ewell SRY 419
Exeter 135, 506, 506(C),
    450(2)
Exeter DEV 98, 516, 14(2),
    202(2)
Falkingham LIN 500
Fareham HAM 321
Farnham SRY 47, 159
Farningham KEN 122
Farsley YKS 207(2)
Faversham KEN 452(2)
Feltwell Place NFK 534(2)
Fen Ditton CAM 256
Finchley MDX 96(2)
Finsbury, London 109
Fleet HAM 471(2)
Flushing 119
Foleshill WAR 290(2)
Forcett 507(2)
Forcett YKS 458
Fordwich KEN 115, 117
Fowey CON 119, 173
Framlingham SFK 215, 491(2)
Fulham 262, 160(2)
Fulham LND 530
Gateshead DUR 452(2)

Germoe CON 540(2)
Gestingthorpe ESS 48
Gillingham KEN 101
Glassenbury KEN 84(2)
Glastonbury 43
Glenfield LEI 530(2)
Gloucester 169, 316, 485, 491,
    106(2), 539(2)
Gloucestershire 414(2)
Gluvian CON 212
Gosport 316(2), 491(2),
    622(2)
Gosport HAM 105(2)
Grangemouth 101(2)
Grantham LIN 232(2)
Gravesend 17, 293, 38(2),
    371(2), 491(2)
Great Ayton 243
Great Bentley ESS 298
Great Billing NTH 381
Great Houghton NTT 451(2)
Great Marlow BKM 193, 333
Great Staughton HUN 443
Great Wakering ESS 590(2)
Great Yarmouth 439, 143(2)
Greenwich 338, 377, 36(2),
    39(2), 251(2), 316(2),
    583(2), 621(2), 622(2)
Greenwich KEN 563, 251(2)
Greenwich LND 268
Greenwich SRY 300
Gretna Green 559(2)
Grosvenor Hotel, London 101
Guildford SRY 476, 488(2)
Hackney LND 57(C), 58, 572,
    149(2C), 229(2)
Hadleigh SFK 491(2)
Halifax YKS 126(2), 392(2)
Halliford MDX 406(2)
Hammersmith LND 406,
    172(2), 276(2), 618(2)
Hampshire 275, 553(2)
Hampstead 418
Hanley 105(2)
Hanley STS 281(2), 438(2)
Harrogate YKS 372(2)
Harrow 245(2)
Hartley Wespall HAM 159
Hastings 223(2), 289(2)
Hatfield YKS 510
Hatherleigh DEV 52(2),
    528(2)
Hawkshurst KEN 256
Headingley 564(2)
Helperthorpe 133(2)
Hendon MDX 569(2)
Henley-on-Thames OXF 244
Hereford 230, 54(2)
Hertford 24, 25, 592(2)
Hertfordshire 543
Heston, London 54
Hexham NBL 15
High Wycombe BKM 4,
    218(2)
Highbury 40
Highercombe SOM 19
Highgate 250(2)
Highgate LND 223
Hints STS 82
Holborn, Great Turnstile
    552(2)
Holborn LND 109, 306,

139(2)
Holloway LND 73(2)
Holsworthy DEV 154(2),
    186(2), 189(2)
Homerton 184
Hoo SFK 215
Hopesay 259(2)
Horbling 389, 389(C)
Hornby Castle 507(2)
Horningsea 627(2)
Horningsea CAM 254(2)
Hornsea 362
Hornsey MDX 453(2)
Horsforth YKS 208(2)
Horton 424(2)
Horwich LAN 126
Houghton on the Hill 455
Hounslow 190
Hounslow, London 54
Hovingham 440(2)
Hoxton 540(2)
Hoxton LND 111(2)
Hull 254, 400, 100(2), 303(2),
    371(2)
Hull YKS 560, 576
Hull: see also Kingston-upon-
    Hull
Hunstanworth DUR 519
Huntingdonshire 207(2)
Hutton SOM 106, 416
Hyde Park, London 84
Hyning, LAN 124
Hythe KEN 172(2)
Ickwell BDF 312(2)
Ide DEV 261(2)
Ightham KEN 42
Ilford 15
Ilfracombe DEV 136
Ingersby 455
Iping-cum-Chithurst SSX 256
Ipswich 215, 289(2)
Ireby CUM 209
Ireton DBY 574
Isle of Thanet 417
Isle of Wight 125, 304, 261(2),
    364(2), 456(2), 463(2)
Isleworth, London 54
Islington 351, 543, 543(C),
    229(2), 385(2), 483(2)
Islington LND 504, 73(2)
Itchen Stoke HAM 431(2)
Kelmscott 431(2)
Kelsale SFK 115
Kelvedon ESS 248
Kendal WES 401, 402
Kenilworth WAR 463
Kennington Common LND
    409(2)
Kensal Green 568(2)
Kensington 343, 528(2)
Kensington LND 505, 253(2)
Kent 139(2)
Kentish Town LND 20, 21,
    354(2)
Kew Gardens LND 53, 73,
    194, 480
Kew LND 120(2)
Kew SRY 265-268, 120(2)
Kewstoke SOM 106
Kinfield SSX 532
King's Lynn NFK 533(2),
    550(2)

Kingsbridge 483(2)
Kingston Russell DOR 407(2)
Kingston SSX 531
Kingston SRY 364
Kingston-on-Thames SRY 50(C), 122
Kingston upon Hull YKS 454
Kirk DBY 574
Kirkham LAN 557
Kirkoswald CUL 604(2)
Kirmington LIN 42(2)
Knightsbridge LND 248(2)
Knowsley Park LAN 470(2)
Lake District 455
Laleham MDX 29
Lambeth SRY 122, 306, 15(2), 392(2C), 474(2)
Lampeter 522
Lancashire 134(2), 197(2), 470(2), 539(2), 545(2)
Lancaster 347(2)
Landrake CON 311(2)
Langdon Hills ESX 311(2)
Langley BKS 469
Langstone Harbour 508(2)
Larkhill WOR 550
Lauder NBL 216(2)
Launceston CON 55(2), 404(2)
Leamington Spa WAR 425
Leatherhead SRY 312(2)
Lee, Kent 531
Leeds 254, 54(2), 393(2), 480(2)
Leeds YKS 45
Leek 438(2)
Leicester 455
Lenham KEN 356(2)
Levels YKS 510
Lewes 437
Leytonstone ESS 539(2)
Lichfield 9, 123, 258, 455, 448(2), 570(2)
Limehouse, London 170
Lincoln 65, 4(2), 607(2)
Lincoln's Inn Field LND 407, 207(2)
Lindfield SSX 440(2)
Liskeard CON 221, 311(2), 623(2)
Litlington 92(2)
Little Chelsea LND 122(2)
Littlehampton SSX 531
Liverpool 96, 213, 223, 224, 269, 272, 311, 400, 502, 25(2), 65(2), 93(2), 94(2), 242(2), 254(2), 290(2), 340(2), 426(2), 430(2), 545(2), 552(2)
Loders DOR 281(2)
London: see also under suburban names.
London: Misc. Refs. 159, 275, 34(2), 40(2), 43(2), 79(2), 93(2), 94(2), 112(2), 121(2), 143(2), 446(2), 509(2)
London: Streets etc.
— Adelphi Terrace 262
— Baker St 324(2)
— Belgrave Square 271(2)
— Bell Lane 457(2)
— Blackfriars 58, 419(2)

— Bloomsbury 427, 73(2), 553(2)
— Bond Street 19
— Bread St 326(2)
— Camberwell, Cold Harbour Lane 418(2)
— Camberwell Grove 468(2)
— Chancery Lane 359(2)
— Chelsea, Milman's Row 498(2)
— Chelsea, Paradise Row 498(2)
— Crutched Friars 212(2)
— Drury Lane 355
— Eaton Place 176(2)
— Fitzroy Square 460
— Fleet St 452(2)
— Green Street 379
— Holborn, Brook Street 306
— Holborn, King Street 427
— Holborn, Red Lion St 139(2)
— Horseshoe Alley 444(2C)
— Houndsditch, Gravel Lane 457(2)
— Hyde Park 84
— Judd Street, Brunswick Square 134
— Judd St, New Rd, Hackney 572
— Leicester Square 354(2)
— Mason Court 419(2)
— Moorgate Street 127
— New Bond St 339
— New Burlington St 52
— New Gravel Lane, Shadwell 282(2)
— Old Kent Road 518(2)
— Oxford Street 23(2)
— Palace Gardens Terrace 384(2)
— Panorama, Strand 348
— Petticoat Lane 457(2)
— Piccadilly 246, 388, 542(2), 552(2)
— Portland Place 463
— Portland Square 448(2)
— Ratcliffe Highway 246
— Red Lion Square 426
— Regents Park 295
— Regent's Park, Park St 527(2)
— St Mary at Hill 165
— Smith Square 272(2)
— Soho Square 53, 167, 456(2)
— Southwark, Maid Lane 306
— Stepney, Gloucester Terrace 414(2)
— The Strand 295
— Tower of London 159
— Tower Street 295
— Walbrook 544
— Warwick Square, Newgate St. 627(2)
— Waterloo Place 415
— Watling Street 190, 225
— Westbourne Terrace 128(2)
— Wigmore Street 225
— Wood Street, Cheapside 23(2)

— Wych Street 76
Long Riston 362
Longton STS 550(2)
Loughborough 451(2)
Lower Edmonton 599(2)
Lowlynn NBL 475
Ludgate Hill LND 316
Ludlow SAL 259(2)
Lyme Regis DOR 465, 465(2)
Lymington 355, 17(2)
Lymington HAM 257
Lympton DEV 21
Lyndhurst HAM 326(2)
Lynn NFK 566, 621(2)
Macclesfield CHS 174
Maida Vale 480(2)
Maidstone 282
Malvern Wells 333
Manchester 41, 126, 147, 453, 70(2), 89(2), 177(2), 198(2), 290(2), 313(2), 466(2), 508(2)
Mangotsfield 470
Market Deeping LIN 511
Marshalsea prison 75
Martley WOR 355
Martock SOM 84(2)
Marton CHS 174
Marton-in-Cleveland YKS 243
Marylebone LND 461(2)
Maryport CUL 425
Matlock DBY 436
Mayfair LND 407(2)
Melton Constable NFK 196(2)
Middlesex 255(2)
Milton STS 105(2)
Milton next Gravesend 488
Minehead, SOM 444
Mitcham SRY 50(C), 562
Mitton 322
Montacute SOM 83(2)
Moorfields LON 504
Morden SRY 186(2), 395(2)
Mordington 500(2)
Morpeth NBL 15, 431(2)
Mottingham KEN 442(2)
Much Woolton 340(2)
Nacton SFK 215
Nailsworth GLS 63
Narrow Wall, Lambeth LND 306
Newark NTT 618(2)
Newbury BRK 46, 97, 224(2), 390(2)
Newby Head WES 311
Newcastle 15, 562(2)
Newcastle under Lyme 554
Newcastle upon Tyne 15, 18, 46(2), 218(2)
Newington KEN 117
Newlyn CON 538(2)
Newport MON 419
Newport Pagnell 260
Newport SAL 394(2)
Newton Abbot DEV 281(2)
Nine Elms, Vauxhall, London 127
Nore 369(2)
Norfolk 66(2)
North Cray KEN 285(2)

North Meols LAN 311
North Shields NBL 139, 480(2)
North Thoresby LIN 42(2)
Northallerton YKS 254
Northampton 467
Northampton NTH 221, 223
Northgate Barracks, Canterbury KEN 291
Norton 65(2)
Norwich 45, 66(2)
Norwood 149(2)
Norwood Green LND 522(2)
Norwood LND 278(2)
Notting Hill 437
Nottingham 461, 337(2), 493(2), 607(2)
Nottinghamshire 354, 607(2)
Odiham HAM 281(2)
Oldbury KEN 42
Oldmixon SOM 106
Orleigh DEV 3(2)
Ormskirk, LAN 52
Osmaston DBY 554
Oswestry SAL 113(2), 196(2)
Ottery St Mary DEV 295, 407(2)
Oxford 31, 155, 311. 420, 245(2), 431(2)
Oxfordshire 244, 401(2), 489(2)
Paddington, LND 17
Padiham 420
Paignton DEV 331
Parkstone DOR 377(2)
Parson's Green 248(2)
Patterdale 456
Peckham LND 250(2)
Peelfold LAN 320(2)
Penn 570(2)
Penrith 72(2)
Pentonville LND 376(2)
Penzance CON 322, 353(2), 473(2), 506(2)
Perriton, SOM 444
Petersfield HAM 258(2)
Petersham SRY 554, 551(2)
Pimlico LND 206
Plymouth 32, 38, 85, 118, 149, 194, 240, 243, 259, 322, 362, 404, 444, 508, 533, 534, 542, 47(2), 83(2), 133(2), 147(2), 153(2), 259(2), 280(2), 281(2), 353(2), 404(2), 434(2), 442(2), 534(2), 589(2), 626(2)
Plympton DEV 1(2)
Plymstock DEV 73(2)
Pocklington YKS 544(2)
Poling SSX 531
Pontefract YKS 560
Poole DOR 476(2)
Port Erin 49(2)
Portchester HAM 528
Portsea 352
Portsea HAM 189, 500
Portsmouth 297, 349, 368, 377, 383, 567, 572, 57(2), 105(2), 127(2), 258(2), 264(2), 362(2), 439(2), 463(2), 479(2)
Powys Castle 211

Prestbury GLS 569(2)
Preston 470(2)
Preston Bissett BKM 124
Provender KEN 54, 65(2)
Puckington SOM 228
Purfleet 614(2)
Putney LND 265
Pyrton 155
Quinton NTT 451(2)
Ramsgate KEN 417, 465, 100(2), 216(2)
Rawdon 254
Reading BRK 518, 27(2), 282(2), 377(2)
Redbourne LIN 560
Redmire YKS 507(2)
Revesby Abbel LIN 52
Richmond 558(2)
Richmond Park SRY 408(2)
Rickmansworth HEF 176
Ridgmont BDF 195(2)
Ringwold KEN 446
Ripley SRY 253
Ripon YKS 224, 456
Robin Hood's Bay YKS 7
Rochester KEN 424(2), 534(2), 574(2), 615(2)
Romford ESS 325(2)
Romney Marsh 155
Romsey HAM 88(2)
Rotherham 362
Rowton SAL 536
Roydon ESS 246(2)
Rutheren 95(2)
Ryde IOW 304, 575, 261(2)
St Alban's 569(2)
St Botolph's, Aldgate LND 228
St Catherine's MDX 179
St Giles LND 207(2)
St James 359
St John's Wood 592(2)
St Leonard's 447(2)
St Leonards-on-Sea SSX 225, 356(2), 623(2)
St Margarets, Queen's Square LND 48
St Martin's 71(2)
St Martin's parish LEI 180
St Marylebone 517
St Neot CON 280, 310
St Paul's Cray KEN 175
St Thomas's Square 229(2)
St Tudy CON 118
Salford LAN 147
Salisbury WIL 256
Saltash CON 291, 281(2)
Saltash DEV 542
Sandgate 285(2)
Sandhurst 193, 332, 271(2)
Sandhurst BKS 264
Saxmundham SFK 115
Scarborough YKS 429, 544(2)
Scotton LIN 171
Settle YKS 407
Sevenoaks KEN 396(2)
Severn River 106(2)
Shadwell LND 170, 243
Shaldon DEV 82
Sheerness 503, 595(2)
Sheffied YKS 269
Sherborne DOR 84(2)

Shifnal SAL 552(2)
Shoreditch LND 109, 351, 418(2), 444(2C), 593(2)
Shrewsbury SAL 286, 530, 340(2)
Shropshire 349(2), 536(2)
Shudy Camps CAM 575(2)
Slaugham SSX 291
Smithfield LND 228
Soho, LND 57
Somerset 228, 383, 495, 514, 83(2)
Somerset House LND 562
South Creake NFK 433(2)
South Kensington 319(2)
South Lambeth 298
Southam WAR 590(2)
Southampton HAM 321, 621(2)
Southgate MDX 497, 498
Southport LAN 311
Southsea 435, 605(2)
Southwark 200(2)
Southwark LND 306, 528(2), 548(2)
Southwell 134(2)
Spilsby LIN 412, 205(2)
Spithead 226, 369(2), 427(2)
Sprotbrough 480
Stafford 453, 291(2)
Staffordshire 371, 105(2), 136(2), 140(2), 466(2), 570(2), 614(2)
Staithes 243
Stamford LIN 188, 461
Stanmore 438
Stanwick 458
Stapleton 420
Stepney LND 414(2)
Steyning SSX 55
Stockbridge 470(2)
Stockwell 552(2)
Stoke Albury NTH 379
Stoke Damerel DEV 226, 153(2), 281(2), 517(2)
Stoke Newington LND 418(2)
Stoke SAL 470(2)
Stoke-on-Trent 466(2), 550(2)
Ston Easton SOM 316
Stone GLS 485(C)
Stourbridge WOR 143(2)
Stow GLS 613(2)
Stowmarket SFK 491(2)
Strand, Salisbury St LND 87(2)
Strand-on-the-Green 267
Streatham LND 402(2)
Stubbington HAM 143
Stydd, DBY, 290(2)
Suffolk 257
Sunbury MDX 379, 369(2)
Sunderland DUR 379(2)
Surrey 294, 468(2)
Sussex 116(2), 134(2), 243(2)
Sutton SFK 556(2C)
Sutton Coldfield WAR 123
Swilly, Stoke Damerel DEV 226
Sydenham 67
Syleham SFK 200(2)
Tallentire 527

Tavistock 364
Teddington MDX 252(2)
Tenterden KEN 209, 442(2)
Thames River LND 306
Theberton SFK 116(2)
Thetford NFK 590(2)
Threxton 66(2)
Ticknall DER 27
Tiverton DEV 288, 467,
    336(2)
Tolleshunt D'Arcy ESS
    453(2)
Tolpuddle DOR 132(2),
    133(2)
Tonbridge KEN 44(2)
Topsham DEV 156
Torbay 74
Torquay 339, 376, 421(2)
Torrington DEV 555(2)
Totnes DEV 344, 416
Tottenham High Cross LND
    599(2)
Towchester 451(2)
Toxteth Park LAN 204(2)
Tranmere CHS 134(2)
Trengwainton CON 351(2),
    352(2)
Tring 466(2)
Troutbeck WES 402
Trowbridge WIL 368(2)
Truro CON 31, 134, 555
Tuckingmill CON 213
Tunbridge Wells 256, 372(2)
Turnham Green 167
Tweedmouth 500(2)
Twickenham MDX 174(2)
Ullswater CUL 455
Upton, West Ham, LND 109
Vale Place 406
Walkerfield DUR 524
Wallingford 169(2)
Walsall STS 470
Waltham Abbey 105
Walthamstown ESS 175
Walton BKM 256
Walworth SRY 209
Wangford SFK 400(2)
Wantage 256
Warlingham SRY 136(2)
Warrington LAN 402, 403
Warwick 123, 490
Waterloo 65(2)
Waterloo Bridge 376(2)
Wednesbury STS 296
Wellington HEF 316(2)
Wellington SAL 211
Wellington SOM 589(2)
Wells SOM 135, 228, 410,
    472(2), 476(2), 600(2)
Welton YKS 17(2)
Wentworth Woodhouse YKS
    579(2)
West Boldon 379(2)
West Bromwich 9
West Felton SAL 272(2)
West Heslerton YKS 440(2)
West Hill 49(2)
West Tarring SSX 531
West Wickham CAM 619(2)
Westminster 52, 158, 359,
    525, 547, 565, 71(2), 255(2),
    470(2), 518(2), 555(2), 600(2)

Westmorland 246(2)
Weston-Super-Mare 416
Westow YKS 305(2)
Wetmore Hall DBY 314(2)
Weymouth 186(2)
Whenby 429
Whipsnade BDF 362
Whissonett NFK 433(2)
Whitby 243, 429
Whitby YKS 75
White Haven CUL 407
Whitechapel LND 28(2)
Whitfield 431(2), 433(2)
Whittington LAN 254
Whittlesey CAM 25
Wickham HAM 321
Wighill YKS 471(2)
Willington 247
Wimbledon SRY 265, 268,
    246(2)
Wimborne DOR 258, 589(2)
Winchester 143, 48(2), 333(2),
    439(2), 618(2)
Winchester HAM 529
Windsor BRK 196, 441, 515,
    208(2), 470(2)
Wirksworth DBY 574
Wisbech CAM 256
Wivenhoe 477
Woking 456(2)
Wolverhampton WAR 9, 60,
    29(2), 340(2)
Wolveton DOR 458(2)
Woodbridge SRY 484(2)
Woodchurch CHS 50(C)
Woodcote OXF 250
Woodford ESS 488
Woodlands DOR 418
Wooler 521(2)
Woolwich KEN 251, 308,
    418, 446, 474, 563, 578,
    17(2), 362(2)
Worcester WOR 192, 264
Worle SOM 106
Worthing SSX 531, 595(2)
Wye Valley 353(2)
Yardley WAR 541
Yarmouth 556, 288(2), 552(2)
    see also Great Yarmouth
Yeovil SOM 385(2)
York 46, 439, 560
Yorkshire 510, 283(2), 363(2),
    564(2), 579(2)
Yorkshire East Riding 133(2)

Ireland:
    272, 548, 116(2), 245(2),
    281(2), 288(2)
Antrim 337, 274(2), 515(2)
Ardsallagh 165(2)
Ardstraw LDY 278(2)
Armagh 337, 557(2), 579(2)
Athlone 264, 579(2)
Baladicken 333(2)
Ballinate ARM 200(2)
Ballinlough 502(2)
Ballinvonear 168
Balliston LIM 274(2)
Ballydaniel 550
Ballygawley TYR 261
Ballymacoda 302(2)
Ballymagirl 411(2)

Banbridge DOW 234(2)
Bandon COR 64(2), 414(2)
Bantry COR 248, 248(C)
Bawnboy CAV 411(2)
Belfast 48, 192, 266(2)
Bellevue WEX 333(2)
Belmont DON 228
Birr 264
Bishopscourt WAT 108
Bond's Glen 252(2)
Burrin Farm CAV 308
Cahir TIP 314
Caledon TYR 199
Camnish 234(2)
Carlow 456, 509(2)
Carrickfergus, ANT 10(2)
Cashel TIP 165(2)
Castle Town, SLI 182(C), 371
Castlebridge WEX 309
Castletown SLI 182
Cavan 146, 308, 379(2)
Charleville COR 216(2)
Clare 214, 242
Clonmel IRL 294(2)
Clontarf DUB 422
Cloydagh 516(2)
Cloyne COR 93(2), 302(2)
Coleraine 337, 171(2)
Colp MEA 425
Connaught 337(2)
Cookstown TYR 557(2)
Coona COR 302(2)
Cork 242, 258, 409, 526, 548,
    162(2), 414(2), 509(2),
    512(2), 568(2), 569(2)
Crossabeg WEX 309
Denaghee, Hogstown 192
Derry 421, 116(2), 174(2),
    274(2)
Devonport COR 296
Dingle KER 259(2)
Dirnaseer TYR 303(2)
Donemana TYR 252(2)
Down 55(2), 197(2), 557(2)
Drogheda 62, 512, 409(2)
Dromara 55(2)
Dromoland CLA 293(2)
Dromore DOW 304(2)
Drumbanagher ARM 264(2)
Drumsally, County Limerick
    128
Dublin 23, 39, 62, 128, 168,
    172, 195, 218, 241, 312, 314,
    320, 324, 377, 425, 464, 502,
    36(2), 51(2), 89(2), 231(2),
    278(2), 304(2), 392(2),
    502(2), 553(2), 567(2),
    596(2)
Dun Laoghaire 550
Dunboyne 269(2)
Dundalk 468
Dungannon TYR 376(2)
Dungiven DRY 234(2)
Dunloe 93(2)
Ennis 294(2)
Enniscorthy WEX 214
Enniskillen FER 5(2), 372(2)
Everton 516(2)
Fairview Clontarf 513
Fermanagh 412(2)
Ferns 309
Fethard TIP 180

Galway 163(2), 292(2)
Harveyhill LDY 534(2)
Hillsborough DOW 563
Hogstown 192
Holymount MAY 292(2)
Inishmagrath, LET 371
Kerry 300, 294(2), 299(2)
Kilbrin 291
Kilcullen 513
Kildare 371(2)
Kilkee, CLA 381
Kilkenny 149, 51(2)
Killaloe 421
Killarney KER 343, 299(2),
    405(2)
Killeavy ARM 264(2)
Killensule TIP 314
Kilmore 147
Kilrea LDY 440
King's County (Offaly) 236
Kinsale COR 514
Langford (Longford) 411(2)
Lifford LEI 371
Limerick 75, 128, 129, 272,
    376, 404, 294(2), 365(2)
Lismore DOW 602(2)
Lismore WAT 357
Listowel 291
Londonderry 116(2) see also
    Derry
Longford 411(2)
Loughlinn ROS 21
Louth 422
Malahide 502(2)
Mallow COR 168, 291, 93(2)
Marlborough COR 291
Marlton WIC 164(2)
Maryborough 358
Maynooth 62, 241
Mayo 36(2), 292(2)
Meath 306, 506, 579(2)
Moira 563
Monaghan 241
Moneymore LDY 519
Mount Plunkett 337(2)
Mount Vernon 526
Movida 274(2)
Mullingar MEM 377
Navan MEA 269(2)
Newry 493
Newry ARM 199
Newry DOW 234(2), 301(2)
Northern 77(2)
Nurney KIL 47
Palmerston 320
Portadown 579(2), 582(2)
Queen's County (Leix) 317,
    358, 516(2)
Raphoe DON 5(2)
Rathcoole 512
Riversdale KER 461
Roscommon 161(2)
Roundwood 550
Roxburgh KER 536(2)
Royal Canal, DUB 23
St Catherine FER 305(2)
St Peter's Parish DUB 557
Shrule MAY 168
Slieve Russel CAV 31
Sligo 251, 295, 420
Strathbane TYR 273
Tanderagee 579(2)

Thurles 567(2)
Tipperary 23, 376, 233(2)
Tralee KER 14(2), 260(2)
Tubberneering 309
Tyrone 182, 261(C), 529,
    529(C), 302(2)
Ulster 78(2), 79(2), 178(2)
Walls Town COR 169
Waterford 409, 421, 545,
    217(2), 294(2), 567(2),
    568(2)
Westmeath 502(2)
Wexford 108, 214, 216, 309,
    315, 328, 527, 159(2), 516(2)
Wicklow 320, 512, 550, 458(2)
Woodview, Cloyne COR 93(2)
Youghal COR 21, 291, 93(2)

Scotland:
    306, 415, 74(2), 77(2),
    116(2), 119(2), 317(2),
    397(2), 456(2)
Aberdeen 166, 336, 468, 492,
    506, 108(2), 167(2), 257(2),
    375(2), 395(2), 396(2),
    476(2), 490(2), 522(2)
Aberdeenshire 2(2)
Aberdour 235(2)
Airds 186(2)
Aldie 223(2)
Annandale 55(2)
Annandale DFS 561, 20(2)
Appin 186(2), 482(2)
Appin ARL 162(2)
Ardnamurchan ARL 377(2)
Argyllshire 551, 65(2), 153(2)
Ashfield 202, 206
Auchingill CAI 86(2)
Auchtermuchty FIF 372
Auchtyfardle LKS 263(2)
Ayr 106(2)
Ayrshire 361(2), 595(2)
Bal Freike PER 222(2)
Balado KRS 268(2)
Balhepburn PER 51
Balvaird 504(2)
Banff 300(2), 321(2)
Banffshire 427(2)
Beith 338
Ben Lomond 520
Berwickshire 493(2)
Blair-Athol PER 416
Blairs 336
Bluefield 335
Boganduie 468
Bonnymuir 13
Borthwick MLN 233
Breadalbane PER 201
Brechin 435(2)
Broadmeadows SEL 139
Brodie 250
Bromielaw 294
Caithness 492, 178(2), 482(2)
Caledonian Canal 188
Calton Hill 450(2)
Calton Hill, Edinburgh 313(2)
Cambock FIF 56
Camelon STI 13
Capelrig RFW 269(2)
Capledrae 235(2)
Chartershall 232
Chirnside BEW 243(2)

Clyde 375(2)
Coldingham BEW 124(2)
Coul 25(2)
Countesswells 182
Coupar-Angus PER 227
Craigend 238(2)
Craigow KRS 268(2)
Crail FIF 327
Crieff PER 74, 270(2)
Culloden; Battle of 178(2)
Culzean AYR 189
Cupar FIF 56
Dalswinton DFS 267
Damhead FIF 449(2)
Dornoch 95
Driminasalie, Kilmallie INV
    196
Drumpellier LKS 484(2)
Dumfries 196(2), 230(2),
    574(2)
Dunbarrow, Forfar 169
Dunbarton DNB 118(2)
Dunbartonshire 435, 529(C)
Dundee 372, 84(2), 218(2),
    297(2), 312(2)
Dunfermline 525
Dunlop AYR 338
Dunnideer 235
Dunse BEW 81
Dynnyrne 272(2)
Earlston BEW 429(2)
East Lothian 138, 375(2)
Edenshead FIF 566(2)
Edinburgh 5, 19, 29, 186, 213,
    233, 235, 275, 337, 352, 442,
    455, 499, 508, 513, 572,
    74(2), 79(2), 98(2), 101(2),
    119(2), 167(2), 184(2),
    187(2), 192(2), 223(2),
    230(2), 235(2), 257(2),
    268(2), 271(2), 272(2),
    313(2), 314(2), 325(2),
    336(2), 370(2), 384(2),
    398(2), 437(2), 449(2),
    450(2), 490(2), 501(2),
    523(2), 574(2), 579(2)
Edinburgh, Buccleuch Place
    541(2)
Edinburgh Castle 541(2)
Edinburgh, Nicholson Street
    144(2)
Ednam 563(2)
Elgin 463(2)
Elie FIF 328
Falkirk 442, 101(2)
Faskine 484(2)
Feuar 235(2)
Fife 92, 140, 44(2), 235(2),
    325(2), 408(2)
Folla 107(2)
Forfarshire (Angus) 264(2)
Forgie BAN 472
Forres, Elgin 208
Forres MOR 468
Fura 187(2)
Galashiels 220(2)
Galawater, Heriot-mill 12
Garioch 399
Glasgow 118, 253, 327, 335,
    339, 400, 425, 518, 520,
    65(2), 166(2), 176(2),
    257(2), 266(2), 370(2),

430(2), 466(2), 574(2)
Glenbrittle 183(2)
Golfhill 330
Grantham 362
Greenock 82, 202, 206, 48(2),
    65(2), 76(2), 422(2)
Haddington 189, 457, 527(2)
Hallyards FIF 531(2)
Hamilton 330
Harburn MLN 555(2)
Hawthornden MLN 325, 327
Helensburgh 528(2)
Herbertshire STI 257(2)
Horn and West Hall ABD
    276
Humbie 375(2)
Inch WIG 428
Inner Hebrides 187(2)
Insch ABD 235
Inverness INV 198, 455
Irvine 76(2)
Isle of Skye 183(2)
Jacksbank 297(2)
Kelso 563(2)
Keoldale SUT 13
Kilmarnock 428
Kilninian 187(2)
Kilravock 180(2)
Kincardineshire 290
Kinghorn FIF 224
Kircudbright 14
Kirkaldy 232
Kirkaldy FIF 224
Kirkcaldy 330, 449(2)
Kirkhill 415
Kirkpatrick 96(2)
Knockshinnock 361(2)
Lanark 461, 263(2)
Lanarkshire 47(2)
Largs AYR 151
Lauder 12
Leith 139, 219, 232, 253, 566,
    101(2), 137(2), 143(2),
    166(2), 176(2), 375(2),
    382(2), 385(2), 398(2),
    426(2), 565(2), 597(2)
Leith Fort 188
Leochel-Cushnie, ABD 399
Lesmahagow LKS 263(2)
Libberton LKS 449(2)
Loch Ryan 188
Lochbuy 186(2), 187(2),
    188(2)
Mains 243(2)
Makerstoun 151, 338
Maxton ROX 499
Maybole AYR 334(2)
Meikle Kinnaird 51
Melrose 12
Merton Hall WIG 140
Middlebie DFS 80
Midlothian 223(2)
Montrose 3, 11, 51, 492(2)
Monzievaird (by Crieff) PER
    74
Muirkirk AYR 428
Mull 187(2), 188(2), 193(2)
Musselburgh 119(2), 427(2)
New Braes 399
New Hailes MLN 275
Ochtertyre PER 270(2)
Old Wynd, Glasgow LKS 294

Paisley 454(2)
Perth 22, 439, 176(2), 186(2),
    189(2), 230(2), 361(2),
    565(2)
Perthshire 69(2)
Peterculter ABD 182
Pitteuchar FIF 330, 223(2)
Portobello 5, 119(2)
Portpatrick 337, 266(2)
Potterhill 223(2)
Prestonfield 449(2)
Priestwells 235
Princeland, Coupar-Angus
    PER 227
Pyle GLA 97
Rayne ABD 290
Renfrewshire 265, 268
Renton DNB 520
Rhynd PER 51, 382(2)
Rispond 13
Rockmoor 160(2)
Ross-shire 177(2)
Roxburgh 338
Roxburghshire 513
Rutherglen 400
Sedbergh 362
Selkirk 75(2)
Skye 420(2)
South Shetland Is. 105
Stirling 13, 232, 327, 137(2),
    632(2)
Stirling Castle 188
Stirlingshire 101(2), 257(2)
Stranraer 428
Sunipol 197(C)
Sunipole, Mull 197
Thrumster 3(2)
Todhillbank RFW 269(2)
Tolcross 541(2)
Tomcairn PER 168(2)
Towie ABD 335
Tulchan PER 223(2)
Tymaen GLA 97
Ulva 187(2)
Uphall WLN 612(2)
Warthill ABD 107(2)
West Calder 173(2)
West Morrison 429(2)
Westbrook MLN 233
Wheatfield MLN 140
Whitehill 361(2)
Wick 492
Wigtownshire 50(2)
Wilsontown LKS 219

Wales: 12, 76
Abernant CMN 113(2)
Anglesea 76
Bangor 294(2)
Blaina MON 419, 601(2)
Brecon 321
Cardiff 601(2)
Carmarthen 485, 574, 23(2),
    311(2)
Coalbrookvale 601(2)
Conwil CMN 113(2)
Eglwyswrw PEM 23(2)
Glamorgan 215(2)
Grwyne Fechan, BRE 429
Haverfordwest PEM 224(2),
    489(2)
Hayscastle PEM 12

Holyhead 119
Lampeter 150
Llandilo 23(2)
Llandissilio 113(2)
Llangadock CMN 514(2)
Llawhaddon 150
Merthyr Tydfil GLA 601(2)
Monmouthshire 601(2)
Newport 601(2)
Orielton 127(2)
Pembroke 127(2)
Plas Newydd, Anglesea 76
Pontypool 419
Presteigne 316(2)
Radnorshire 316(2), 611(2)
Swansea 98, 321, 332
Usk MON 292
Welshpool MGY 158
Wrexham 572(2)

Abbreviations

ABD	Aberdeen, SCT	ESS	Essex, ENG	MO	Missouri, USA
ACT	Australian Capital Territory, AUS	FER	Fermanagh, IRL	MOG	Monaghan, IRL
		FIF	Fife, SCT	MON	Monmouthshire, WLS
AGY	Anglesey, WLS	FL	Florida, USA	MOR	Moray, SCT
AK	Alaska, USA	FLN	Flintshire, WLS	MS	Mississippi, USA
AL	Alabama, USA	GA	Georgia, USA	MT	Montana, USA
ALB	Alberta, CAN	GAL	Galway, IRL	NAI	Nairn, SCT
ALD	Alderney, CHI	GLA	Glamorgan, WLS	NB	New Brunswick, CAN
ANS	Angus, SCT	GLS	Gloucestershire, ENG	NBL	Northumberland, ENG
ANT	Antrim, IRL	GSY	Guernsey, CHI	NC	North Carolina, USA
AR	Arkansas, USA	HAM	Hampshire, ENG	ND	North Dakota, USA
ARL	Argyll, SCT	HEF	Herefordshire, ENG	NE	Nebraska, USA
ARM	Armagh, IRL	HI	Hawaii, USA	NFD	Newfoundland, CAN
AUS	Australia	HRT	Hertfordshire, ENG	NFK	Norfolk, ENG
AYR	Ayr, SCT	HUN	Huntingdonshire, ENG	NH	New Hampshire, USA
AZ	Arizona, USA	IA	Iowa, USA	NJ	New Jersey, USA
BAN	Banff, SCT	ID	Idaho, USA	NM	New Mexico, USA
BC	British Columbia, CAN	IL	Illinois, USA	NRY	North Riding, YKS
BDF	Bedfordshire, ENG	IN	Indiana, USA	NS	Nova Scotia, CAN
BEW	Berwick, SCT	INV	Inverness, SCT	NSW	New South Wales, AUS
BKM	Buckinghamshire, ENG	IOM	Isle of Man	NT	Northern Territory, AUS
BRE	Brecknockshire, WLS	IOW	Isle of Wight, UK	NTH	Northamptonshire, ENG
BRK	Berkshire, ENG	IRL	Ireland	NTT	Nottinghamshire, ENG
BUT	Bute, SCT	IRL	Ireland	NV	Nevada, USA
CA	California, USA	JSY	Jersey, CHI	NWT	North West Territories, CAN
CAE	Caernarvon, WLS	KCD	Kincardine, SCT		
CAI	Caithness, SCT	KEN	Kent, ENG	NY	New York, USA
CAM	Cambridgeshire, ENG	KER	Kerry, IRL	NZ	New Zealand
CAN	Canada	KID	Kildare, IRL	OFF	Offaly (Kings), IRL
GAR	Carlow, IRL	KIK	Kilkenny, IRL	OH	Ohio, USA
CAV	Cavan, IRL	KKD	Kirkcudbright, SCT	OK	Oklahoma, USA
CGN	Cardiganshire, WLS	KRS	Kinross, SCT	OKI	Orkney, SCT
CHI	Channel Islands	KS	Kansas, USA	ONT	Ontario, CAN
CHS	Cheshire, ENG	KY	Kentucky, USA	OR	Oregon, USA
CLA	Clare, IRL	LA	Louisiana, USA	OXF	Oxfordshire, ENG
CLK	Clackmannan, SCT	LAN	Lancashire, ENG	PA	Pennsylvania, USA
CMN	Carmarthen, WLS	LDY	Londonderry, IRL	PEE	Peebles, SCT
CO	Colorado, USA	LEI	Leicestershire, ENG	PEI	Prince Edward Is., CAN
CON	Cornwall, ENG	LET	Leitrim, IRL	PEM	Pembroke, WLS
COR	Cork, IRL	LEX	Leix (Queens), IRL	PER	Perth, SCT
CT	Connecticut, USA	LIM	Limerick, IRL	QLD	Queensland, AUS
CUL	Cumberland, ENG	LIN	Lincolnshire, ENG	QUE	Quebec, CAN
DBY	Derbyshire, ENG	LKS	Lanark, SCT	RAD	Radnorshire, WLS
DC	Dist. of Columbia, USA	LOG	Longford, IRL	RFW	Renfrew, SCT
DE	Delaware, USA	LND	London, ENG	RI	Rhode Island, USA
DEN	Denbighshire, WLS	LOU	Louth, IRL	ROC	Ross & Cromarty, SCT
DEV	Devon, ENG	MA	Massachusetts, USA	ROS	Roscommon, IRL
DFS	Dumfries, SCT	MAN	Manitoba, CAN	ROX	Roxburgh, SCT
DNB	Dunbarton, SCT	MAY	Mayo, IRL	RSA	Republic South Africa
DON	Donegal, IRL	MD	Maryland, USA	RUT	Rutland, ENG
DOR	Dorset, ENG	MDX	Middlesex, ENG	SA	South Australia, AUS
DOW	Down, IRL	ME	Maine, USA	SAL	Shropshire, ENG
DRY	Derry, IRL	MEA	Meath, IRL	SAS	Saskatchewan, CAN
DUB	Dublin, IRL	MER	Merioneth, WLS	SC	South Carolina, USA
DUR	Durham, ENG	MGY	Montgomeryshire, WLS	SCT	Scotland
ELN	East Lothian, SCT	MI	Michigan, USA	SD	South Dakota, USA
ENG	England	MLN	Midlothian, SCT	SEL	Selkirk, SCT
ERY	East Riding, YKS	MN	Minnesota, USA	SFK	Suffolk, ENG
SHI	Shetland, SCT	TYR	Tyrone, IRL	WEX	Wexford, IRL
SLI	Sligo, IRL	UK	United Kingdom	WI	Wisconsin, USA
SOM	Somerset, ENG	USA	United States	WIC	Wicklow, IRL
SRK	Sark, UK	UT	Utah, USA	WIG	Wigtown, SCT
SRY	Surrey, ENG	VA	Virginia, USA	WIL	Wiltshire, ENG
STS	Staffordshire, ENG	VIC	Victoria, AUS	WLN	West Lothian, SCT
STI	Stirling, SCT	VT	Vermont, USA	WLS	Wales
SSX	Sussex, ENG	WA	Washington, USA	WOR	Worcestershire, ENG
SUT	Sutherland, SCT	WA	Western Australia, AUS	WRY	West Riding, WKS
TAS	Tasmania, AUS	WAR	Warwickshire, ENG	WV	West Virginia, USA
TIP	Tipperary, IRL	WAT	Waterford, IRL	WY	Wyoming, USA
TN	Tennessee, USA	WEM	Westmeath, IRL	YKS	Yorkshire, ENG
TX	Texas, USA	WES	Westmorland, ENG		

Courtesy: *Genealogical Research Directory*

General Index

The General subject index comprises a number of broader subject areas, some consisting of hundreds of sub-entries, listed in an alphabetical sequence which also includes more specific subject areas with a very small number of references. They range from references to specific entities such as a school or a newspaper to more general subjects such as education or exploration. They reflect the growth of a colonial society based on primary production, with the spread of settlement involving exploration and contact with the Aborigines. The development of both private and public institutions, as well as the importance of the churches and armed services are also highlighted. The names of houses, farms and estates mentioned in the biographies are indexed, as well as the names of ships in which persons sailed to and from the colonies.

The broader subject areas include the following:

Aborigines	industries, primary production
army, military etc.	law
banks	newspapers
books	organisations, miscellaneous
churches	organisations, government
companies, business	politics
convicts	religion
courts	religious organisations
education	schools
exploration	ships
hospitals	universities
houses, farms	

Many of these larger subject areas are further subdivided by geographical area. This reflects the division of Australia into six colonies and aims to assist local and regional historians and researchers using the index. Politics, for example, begins with a number of miscellaneous entries, followed by entries grouped under geographical area, listed alphabetically (Australia, England, Ireland, New South Wales, Queensland, Scotland, South Australia, Tasmania, Victoria, Western Australia).

Readers interested in the broader aspect of a particular subject are advised to carefully check references under the "miscellaneous" category, as well as under the various geographical subdivisions. For example, the issue of Chinese coolie labour, mentioned in a number of biographies, is listed under politics with references spread among sub-entries for various colonies.

Wherever possible more specific subjects have been listed under broader subject areas. Smallpox, for example, is listed under the heading Diseases, the Rum Rebellion (1808) and the Castle Hill Irish uprising (1804) are listed under Rebellions, and the American Civil War is listed under Army: Wars. The great variety of subjects and organisations listed under the broader subject categories has precluded the insertion of a cross reference for all of them in the main alphabetical sequence. As a result a certain amount of browsing is required to make the fullest use of these large groups of references.

Other subjects with a small number of entries not suitable for inclusion under a broader subject area are listed in the main alphabetical sequence; examples include astronomy, entomology, bushrangers and women.

Aborigines: miscellaneous
 references
  45, 84, 108, 177, 234, 287,
  294, 386, 391-2, 441, 452, 457,
  482, 564, 18(2), 324(2),
  562(2), 600(2), 612(2)
 customs 326
 language 279, 326
 native police corps 278, 261(2)
 place names 241(2)
 rock carvings 228(2)
Aborigines: New South Wales
  22, 84, 103, 145, 195, 205,
  212, 213, 231, 234, 252, 255,
  267, 269, 297, 298, 299, 337,
  349, 384, 468, 497, 516, 7(2),
  18(2), 60(2), 61(2), 62(2),
  75(2), 86(2), 102(2), 111(2),
  147(2), 170(2), 183(2), 192(2),
  226(2), 239(2), 243(2), 313(2),
  314(2), 331(2), 347(2), 362(2),
  389(2), 401(2), 414(2), 428(2),
  432(2), 439(2), 463(2), 468(2),
  471(2), 496(2), 506(2), 510(2),
  529(2), 566(2), 568(2), 570(2),
  597(2), 606(2), 610(2), 614(2),
  617(2), 618(2), 634(2), 634(2)
 Aboriginal Police Corps 103
 Awabakal tribe (Newcastle) 102
 Broken Bay 177
 contact with first settlers 22
 missions 567(2)
 Myall Creek Massacre 300, 451,
  516, 338(2), 617(2)
 Native Institution 79, 537,
  134(2), 192(2), 209(2), 234(2),
  368(2), 370(2), 439(2)
 Newcastle tribe 102
 portraits of 574(2)
 smallpox epidemic 22
Aborigines: Northern Territory
  489(2)
Aborigines: Queensland
  145, 344, 44(2), 93(2), 103(2),
  124(2), 262(2), 263(2), 313(2),
  326(2), 407(2), 421(2), 422(2),
  448(2), 472(2), 606(2)
 Carbaraks tribe 145
 language 295
 massacre of whites 233, 606(2)
 native police force 423(2)
Aborigines: South Australia
  282, 288, 363, 378, 433, 434,
  477, 478, 222(2), 281(2),
  282(2), 301(2), 482(2), 498(2),
  626(2), 626(2)
 Board of Aboriginal Protection
  557
 Murray tribe 301(2)
Aborigines: Tasmania
  14, 20, 68, 123, 194, 197, 258,
  339, 392, 404, 418, 451, 458,
  543, 561, 49(2), 114(2),
  170(2), 215(2), 230(2), 258(2),
  303(2), 375(2), 384(2), 385(2),
  386(2), 429(2), 432(2), 441(2),
  460(2), 504(2), 517(2), 563(2),
  577(2), 591(2)
 Black War 35
 kidnapping of aboriginal
  children 385(2)
 portraits of 123

 relations with 68
Aborigines: Victoria
  68, 125, 278, 367, 545, 65(2),
  75(2), 125(2), 183(2), 372(2),
  387(2), 518(2), 519(2), 522(2),
  541(2), 543(2), 576(2)
 Aboriginal missions 400
 Aboriginal welfare office 400
 Port Phillip Protectorate 451
 Watourong tribe 174
Aborigines: Western Australia
  326, 382, 477, 509, 577, 5(2),
  75(2), 123(2), 245(2), 253(2),
  322(2), 323(2), 408(2), 416(2),
  417(2), 439(2), 440(2), 487(2),
  556(2), 620(2), 629(2), 632(2)
 corroborees 632(2)
 Murara-Murara, Victoria Plains
  416(2)
 Pinjarra tribe 486(2)
Aborigines: individuals
 Abaroo 18(2)
 Arabanoo 22
 Askabout 177
 Bennelong 84, 18(2), 331(2),
  468(2), 566(2)
 Biraban 529(2)
 Boatman 177
 Boni 337
 Boorong 234
 Botany Bay Colebe 234
 Broomstick 177
 Brown, Harry 103
 Bun-bo-e 610(2)
 Bungaree 177
 Coalby 234
 Colebe 145, 234, 331(2)
 Creek Jimmy 234
 Dicky 634(2)
 Gaywal 190
 Gooseberry 177
 Jackey Jackey 7(2)
 Makkare 236
 Markew 236
 May Day 576(2)
 Midgigoroo 632(2)
 Milmendjeri 433
 Moppy 201
 Multugerrah 201
 Murragingy 234
 Murrell 185, 617(2)
 Onion 177
 Pamby-Pamby 294
 Pemullaway 234
 Pincher 177
 Truganini 14
 Wooreddy 339
 Wullati 337
 Wylie 363, 629(2)
 Yagan 632(2)
 Yeranibe 234
 Yuranigh 634(2)
Agriculture: see Industries:
  Wheat, grain etc.
Albino 134(2)
Anaesthesia 355(2), 514(2)
Anatomy: see Medicine
Archaeology 285(2)
Architecture: 304, 186(2)
 England 149
 Gothic 110, 554(2)
 Greek Revival 554(2)

 Hobart 23
 Melbourne 9(2)
 NSW 96, 471, 112(2), 191(2),
  553(2)
 Regency style 553(2)
 Sydney 191(2)
 Tas 41, 109, 35(2), 71(2)
 Victoria 71(2)
 WA 377(2)
Army: (armed services,
  miscellaneous military
  references)
  196, 219, 233, 247, 250, 258,
  264, 273, 303, 314, 322, 367
 see also Marines, occupations
  (soldier, officer, army officer)
 Chatham Infantry and Invalid
  Depot 488
 Dutch army 226
 Fort Phillip NSW 233(2)
 French army 294(2)
 Gunnery School NSW 176
 Hanoverian army 301
 Indian army 258, 426
 List 143(2)
 Madras army 348(2)
 Maidstone Recruiting Depot
  488
 Martial Law (Norfolk Island)
  398(2)
 Martial Law (TAS) 289, 328
 Medical Service 242
 military engineers 60
 prisoners of war (French &
  Irish 233(2)
 Royal Military College,
  Sandhurst: see schools,
  England
 Rum Rebellion see rebellion
 Sepoy batallion 250
 Spanish revolutionary army
  116(2)
 Treaty of Amiens 305, 359, 553
 United States Army 523(2)
 Victoria Barracks, Sydney 60
 Victorian Defence Forces
  334(2)
 War Office (England) 153, 356
 Waterloo Point Military
  Station, TAS 490(2)
Army: British army regiments and
  other military detachments:
 1st Battalion 422
 1st Foot 273(2)
 1st Regiment 428
 1st Royal Scots Regiment 561
 1st West India Regiment 294(2)
 1st West York Militia 419(2)
 2nd Life Guards 218(2)
 2nd Regiment 12
 2nd West India Regiment
  131(2)
 3rd Foot Guards 270(2)
 3rd Regiment 196, 233, 250,
  377, 3(2), 482(2)
 4th Dragoons 116(2)
 4th Garrison Battalion 439,
  516(2)
 4th Regiment 174, 269, 367,
  368, 423, 468, 109(2), 124(2),
  125(2), 294(2)
 5th Regiment 108, 294(2)

6th Regiment 223, 278, 435
6th Royal Veteran Battalion 51
7th Dragoon Guards 95(2)
7th Foot Regiment 273(2)
7th Regiment 33
8th Regiment 11
9th Light Dragoons 516(2)
9th Regiment 333
11th Dragoons 96, 291
11th Hanoverian Regiment 281(2)
13th Dragoons 463, 602(2)
13th Light Infantry 371
13th Regiment 488
14th Light Dragoons 448(2)
14th Regiment 223, 254(2)
15th Hussars 530
16th Lancers 224(2)
16th Regiment 558(2)
17th Lancers 46
17th Light Dragoons 516(2)
17th Regiment 549, 233, 292(2), 300(2)
17th Rifle Brigade 388
18th Regiment 314, 516(2), 536(2)
19th Light Dragoons 435
19th Regiment 123(2)
20th Regiment 423, 348(2), 631(2)
21st Fusiliers 125
21st Regiment 175, 202, 474, 421(2)
22nd Light Dragoons 250
22nd Regiment 358
23rd Dragoons 463
24th Regiment 13, 404, 410
25th Light Dragoons 62
25th Regiment 419
28th Regiment 264
29th Regiment 143, 567(2)
31st Regiment 459(2)
33rd Regiment 62
34th Regiment 2, 154, 270(2)
35th Regiment 269(2)
36th Regiment 377, 579(2)
38th Regiment 151, 301(2)
39th Regiment 57, 136, 367, 123(2), 162(2), 293(2), 495(2), 496(2)
40th Regiment 49, 108, 147, 191, 439, 248(2), 450(2)
41st Regiment 250
43rd Regiment 175
45th Regiment 282
46th Regiment 228, 300, 404, 416, 140(2), 162(2), 192(2), 243(2), 278(2), 459(2), 550(2), 568(2)
47th Regiment 215(2), 435(2)
48th Regiment 8, 81, 223, 224, 231, 273, 324, 358, 416, 460, 235(2), 243(2), 260(2), 274(2), 278(2), 299(2), 569(2)
50th Regiment 13, 14, 41, 296, 412(2), 413(2), 509(2)
51st Regiment 282
52nd Regiment 431, 488, 248(2)
53rd Regiment 125
54th Regiment 180, 450(2)
55th Regiment 202, 439
56th Regiment 377, 416

57th Regiment 285, 303, 304, 123(2), 124(2), 215(2), 235(2), 305(2), 435(2), 541(2)
58th Regiment 324, 631(2)
60th Regiment 408, 421(2)
61st Regiment 308(2)
62nd Regiment 300, 131(2)
63rd Regiment 75, 32(2), 336(2), 485(2)
64th Regiment 133, 248(2)
67th Regiment 422
68th Regiment 154(2)
69th Regiment 151, 115(2), 399(2)
71st Regiment 187(2), 222(2), 270(2)
72nd Regiment 492, 7(2)
73rd Regiment 21, 29, 79, 431, 435, 491, 494, 15(2), 46(2), 87(2), 143(2), 186(2), 189(2), 278(2), 295(2), 305(2), 317(2), 348(2), 393(2), 582(2)
74th Regiment 305(2)
77th Regiment 187(2)
78th Regiment 13, 119(2)
80th Regiment 260(2), 295(2)
81st Regiment 295(2)
82nd Regiment 50, 377
83rd Regiment 477
84th Regiment 187(2), 383(2)
85th Regiment 404, 488, 421(2)
86th Regiment 188(2)
87th Regiment 47, 383(2)
88th Regiment 377
89th Regiment 202
90th Regiment 62, 454(2)
91st Regiment 32, 348(2)
92nd Regiment 196, 435
93rd Regiment 492, 281(2)
94th Regiment 243(2)
95th Regiment 238(2), 245(2)
96th Regiment 488, 455(2)
97th Regiment 301(2)
98th Regiment 327, 98(2), 317(2)
99th Regiment 61, 300(2)
100th Regiment 516(2)
101st Regiment 62, 482(2)
102nd Regiment 144, 128(2), 138(2), 233(2), 449(2)
104th Regiment 463, 412(2)
121st Regiment 324
134th Regiment 324
Anglo-Corsican batallion 399(2)
Armagh Company (First) 579(2)
Army Medical Corps 235(2)
Bedfordshire yeomanry 195(2)
Bengal army 248(2)
Bengal Native Infantry 224(2)
Black Watch 188(2)
Bombay Artillery 83
Bombay Native Infantry 332
Bourbon Regiment 493
Breadalbane Fencibles 162(2)
Brunswick Oels Corps 301
Buckingham Volunteer Rifle Corps 138(2)
Buffs 119(2)
Castlemaine Rifles 349(2)
Channel Squadron 539

Cheshire Militia 174
Coldstream Guards 562, 301(2)
Dublin City Corps, Liberty Rangers 557
Duke of York's Cavalry 117
Durham Light Infantry 154(2)
East Adelaide Rifles 64(2)
Fifeshire Regiment of Fencibles 166
First Armagh Company 579(2)
German Rifle Corps 420(2)
Grenadier Guards 128, 631(2)
Guernsey Artillery 164
Hampshire Militia 275, 488
Hertford Southern Yeomanry 78
Highland regiment 276
Hobart Town Garrison 413(2)
Horse Guards 46, 282, 384, 404
Hull Volunteers 100(2)
Irish Brigade 294(2)
Irish Volunteers 579(2)
Isle of Man Corps 39
Kent Militia 573
King's Own Regiment 427
Leitrim Militia 348(2)
Liberty Rangers, Dublin City Corps 557
Light Brigade 459(2)
Light infantry regiment 409
Madras Artillery 435
Madras Native Infantry 258
Malta Regiment 439
Manchester Volunteers 11
Moira Regiment of Volunteers 563
New Jersey Volunteers 21
New South Wales Corps 2, 49, 51, 61, 74, 76, 78, 83, 117, 126, 144, 171, 237, 258, 288, 297, 327, 351, 351(C), 407, 408, 488, 519, 548, 569, 570, 571, 573, 13(2), 17(2), 20(2), 31(2), 39(2), 47(2), 53(2), 57(2), 59(2), 60(2), 96(2), 97(2), 129(2), 143(2), 144(2), 154(2), 156(2), 170(2), 189(2), 190(2), 223(2), 233(2), 281(2), 283(2), 310(2), 317(2), 329(2), 332(2), 334(2), 364(2), 379(2), 403(2), 469(2), 531(2), 536(2), 537(2), 573(2)
New South Wales Corps (Committee of Paymastership) 39(2)
New South Wales Veterans Company 79, 144, 96(2)
New York Volunteer Regiment 187(2)
Ogle's Loyal Blues 333(2)
Poona Auxiliary Horse 500(2)
Queen's Lancers 47
Queen's Own Regiment 37
Queen's Royal Regiment 8
Royal African Corps 234(2)
Royal Artillery 176
Royal Engineers 24, 60, 219, 296, 391, 418-9, 446, 492, 37(2), 170(2), 528(2), 555(2), 595(2)
Royal Engineers' Department 254

Royal Fusiliers 218(2)
Royal Highland Emigrants 187(2)
Royal Lancashire Regiment 134
Royal Manx Fencibles 272(2)
Royal Saxon Regiment 392(2C)
Royal South Lincoln Militia 254(2)
Royal Staff Corps 142, 303, 333, 324(2)
Royal Veterans 286
Royal Waggon Train 273(2)
Rum Corps 401(2)
Scots Brigade 243(2)
Scots Greys 187(2)
South Australian Volunteer Force 378
South Cork militia 526
Surrey Militia 488
Swiss chasseurs 11
Trinity House Volunteers 364(2)
Victorian Mounted Rifles 352(2)
Volunteeer Infantry, 1st Battalion 301(2)
Volunteer Force, NSW 1
West Indian Squadron 364(2)
West Middlesex Militia 76
Yeomanry and Volunteer Corps of Sussex 531
York Chasseurs 13, 33
Army Ranks: less common
adjutant 220, 282, 367, 233(2)
brevet captain 87(2)
brevet colonel 239, 119(2)
brevet lieut-colonel 223, 289, 413(2)
brevet major 220, 288, 301
brigade major 404
brigadier-general 258
cornet 250
paymaster 274(2)
quartermaster 97(2)
subaltern 223(2)
Army: Wars, battles, actions, military campaigns
see also Navy:
Albuera, Spain, battle of 196, 223, 264, 260(2), 435(2)
Alexandria, Egypt, blockade of 268
American Civil War 218(2), 235(2)
American colonies 542
American war 226, 233, 322, 324, 98(2), 124(2)
American War of Independence 21, 332, 391, 488, 567, 21(2), 85(2), 154(2), 234(2), 281(2), 309(2), 397(2), 484(2), 506(2), 531(2), 541(2)
American War of 1812. 105, 151, 258(2)
Amiens, Treaty of see: army (miscellaneous references)
Anglo-Danish 27(2)
Badajoz 358, 431, 446, 477, 238(2), 324(2)
Balaclava, battle of 47
Bunker's Hill, battle of 236
Burma 527

Busaco, Spain, campaign at 13, 196, 450(2)
Camperdown, battle of 119, 288
Canada, action at frontier 220
Carour (Karur), siege of 317(2)
Chesapeake Bay, action off 297
Chinese War of 1840. 148
Ciudad Rodrigo 238(2)
Copenhagen, Denmark, action at 264
Corunna, Spain, battle of 282
Craney Island, action at 220
Crimean War 47, 176, 356, 23(2), 32(2), 268(2), 402(2), 435(2), 494(2)
Culloden, battle of 178(2)
Douro, Spain, campaign at 196
Egmont-op-zee, Holland, battle of 196
Egypt, campaign in 324
Fort Erie 233
France, action in 264
France, campaign in southern 196
French war: see Napoleonic
Fuentes de Onoro, battle of 13, 450(2)
Gibraltar, seige of 11
Greek war of independence 264
Guadeloupe, capture of 13, 60, 137
India, North West Frontier, action at 250
Italy, campaign in 324
Kaffir wars 455, 479, 250(2)
Kandahar 419
Kent Island, action at 220
Louisberg, seige of 243, 397(2)
Maharajpore 413(2)
Maida, battle of 13
Malta, blockade of 81
Maori war 463(2), 511(2)
Maratha campaign 14
Martinique, capture of 62, 75, 137
Mediterranean, campaign in 324
Minorca, capture of 324
Napoleonic wars 8, 13, 49, 220, 226, 265, 354, 524, 561, 100(2), 184(2), 235(2), 265(2), 316(2), 382(2)
New Orleans, battle of 235(2)
Nive, battle of the 324(2), 454(2)
Nivelle 324(2)
Orthes, battle of 454(2)
Paris, occupation of 264
Pass of Maya, Pyrenees, action at 264
Peninsular War 13, 49, 57, 60, 81, 108, 128, 142, 143, 151, 191, 196, 219, 223, 231, 247, 314, 333, 358, 404, 422, 446, 463, 3(2), 5(2), 69(2), 116(2), 124(2), 238(2), 245(2), 260(2), 271(2), 273(2), 305(2), 324(2), 412(2), 421(2), 450(2), 454(2), 495(2), 555(2), 564(2), 577(2)
Peninsular War Medal 435
Portugal, action in 264
Punniar, India, battle of 14, 233

Pyrenees, campaign in 196
Quatre Bras, action at 264
Quebec, capture of 243, 397(2)
St Sebastian, siege of 421(2)
Salamanca 238(2)
San Domingo 358
San Sebastian, siege of 272, 454(2)
Seringapatnam, battle of 188(2)
Seven Years' war 171
Sobraon 413(2)
South African war 352(2)
Spain, action in 264
Sutlej campaign 413(2)
Syrian campaign 220
Syrian campaign of 1840-41 383(2)
Talavera, Spain, campaign at 13, 196
Torres Vedras (lines of) 13
Toulon, capture of 61
Trafalgar, battle of 622(2)
United States, war against 220
Vinegar Hill, battle of 358
Vittoria, Spain, campaign at 196, 454(2)
Walcheren expedition 32, 282, 439, 539, 412(2)
Waterloo, battle of 108, 178, 180, 247, 264, 301, 333, 384, 431, 463, 524, 32(2), 218(2), 245(2), 248(2), 254(2), 269(2), 308(2), 563(2), 564(2), 595(2)
Art 98, 217, 230, 348, 365, 409, 416, 11(2), 140(2), 212(2), 314(2), 353(2), 415(2) see also occupations — artist
Associations: see Organisations: miscellaneous
Astronomy 154, 243, 276, 297, 418, 213(2), 221(2), 463(2), 506(2), 551(2)
Asylums: see Hospitals and also Organisations
Australian Agricultural Co.: see Organisations: Business
Banks: Australia
Australian Joint Stock Bank 242(2)
Bank of Australasia 59, 95, 127, 138, 149, 461, 533, 541, 8(2), 94(2), 160(2), 196(2), 251(2), 290(2), 372(2), 410(2), 447(2), 501(2), 563(2)
Bank of Australia 202, 247, 303, 401, 442, 461, 547, 555, 1(2), 12(2), 25(2), 66(2), 120(2), 142(2), 148(2), 149(2), 158(2), 196(2), 236(2), 237(2), 261(2), 289(2), 307(2), 428(2), 435(2), 464(2), 547(2), 565(2), 611(2), 620(2)
British and Australian Bank 127
Commercial Bank of Australia 334(2)
Royal Bank 140
Royal Bank of Australia 140, 142, 387(2)
Union Bank of Australia 275, 415(2)
Banks: England
Bank of Australasia 485

Bank of England 109, 490, 547, 44(2), 229(2), 558(2)
English, Scottish and Australian Bank 9(2)
Hull Banking Co 480(2)
London and County Joint-stock Bank 38(2)
London Chartered Bank 28(2)
London Joint Stock Bank 549
Royal Bank 141
Stourbridge Bank 141(2)
Union Bank of Australia 421(2)
Banks: India
Bank of India 216
Banks: Ireland
Bank of Ireland 199
Banks: New South Wales
Bank of New South Wales 6, 21, 61, 76, 95, 105, 200, 204, 207, 245, 246, 305, 323, 325, 344, 350, 373, 384, 427, 460, 500, 520, 549, 551, 555, 558, 575, 11(2), 16(2), 25(2), 81(2), 110(2), 120(2), 131(2), 142(2), 148(2), 172(2), 196(2), 233(2), 234(2), 255(2), 289(2), 307(2), 335(2), 360(2), 370(2), 371(2), 380(2), 382(2), 389(2), 395(2), 426(2), 508(2), 509(2), 565(2), 566(2), 578(2), 580(2), 598(2), 620(2), 627(2)
Bathurst Bank 172(2), 451(2)
Commercial Banking Co. 490, 530, 26(2), 451(2), 453(2)
Commercial Banking Co. of Sydney 58, 461, 41(2), 73(2), 196(2), 256(2), 392(2), 411(2), 428(2), 464(2), 513(2)
Finance 5
Savings Bank 6, 58, 114, 374, 1(2), 41(2), 120(2), 192(2), 203(2), 255(2), 415(2), 435(2), 464(2)
Savings Bank (Campbell's Bank) 16(2)
Savings Bank of New South Wales 451(2)
Sloman's Bank 451(2)
Sydney Bank 392(2)
Sydney Banking Co. 538, 555, 109(2), 142(2), 230(2), 237(2)
Union Bank 450, 485, 451(2)
Union Bank of Australia 442
Banks: New Zealand
New Zealand Bank 242(2)
Banks: Scotland
Bank of Scotland 574(2)
Paisley Union Bank SCT 400
Scotch Bank 141
Banks: South Australia
Bank of Adelaide 197(2)
Bank of Australasia 341
Provincial National Bank 15
Savings Bank 380, 525, 251(2)
South Australian Banking Co. 15, 8(2), 480(2), 262(2)
Union Bank 16
Union Bank of Australia 15
Banks: Tasmania
Bank of Van Diemen's Land 20, 37, 77, 80, 95, 191, 155, 225, 235, 425, 429, 49(2), 106(2),

113(2), 128(2), 137(2), 176(2), 300(2), 366(2), 395(2), 427(2), 433(2), 441(2), 460(2), 458(2), 563(2)
Colonial Bank 230, 323
Commercial Bank 3, 191, 339, 100(2)
Commercial Bank of Tasmania 95, 176(2), 441(2)
Cornwall Bank 59, 257, 328, 454, 533, 74(2), 94(2), 268(2), 374(2), 576(2)
Derwent Bank 3, 20, 37, 339, 467, 508, 100(2), 164(2), 176(2), 249(2), 250(2), 268(2), 374(2), 500(2), 512(2), 564(2)
Derwent Savings Bank 500(2)
Hobart Savings Bank 324, 552, 271(2), 441(2), 542(2), 562(2), 563(2)
Hobart Town Savings Bank 506, 433(2)
Launceston Bank for Savings 3, 59, 63, 169, 261, 316, 246(2), 290(2), 441(2)
Tamar Bank 290(2)
Tasmanian Bank 339
Union Bank 290(2)
Union Bank of Australia 323
United Banking Co of Aust. & Van Diemen's Land 290(2)
Van Diemen's Land Bank 2, 123, 552, 40(2), 126(2), 402(2)
Wesleyan Sunday School Penny Bank, TAS 261
Banks: Victoria
Bank of NSW 80(2)
Bank of Victoria 112, 407, 334(2)
Colonial Bank 229
Commercial Bank of Melbourne 75(2)
Derwent Bank 501(2)
English, Scottish and Australian Bank 70(2)
Melbourne Banking Corporation 334(2)
Port Phillip Bank 350, 425, 224(2)
Savings Bank 412(2)
State Savings Bank 533
Union Bank 112, 370, 425, 501(2), 522(2)
Banks: Western Australia
Bank of Western Australia 577, 99(2)
Western Australian Bank 122(2), 489(2), 440(2)
Battles: see Army: wars, battles etc.
Bigge Report 99
Blue Mountains, NSW (see Places and Exploration)
Boers: South Africa 45
Books mentioned:
A.B.C. of Colonization 222
Abentheuer auf einer Reise nach Neu-Holland 403
Aboriginal Mission, New South Wales 530(2)
Aborigines of Australia 75(2), 303(2), 414(2)

Aborigines of NSW 520
Aborigines of Victoria 518(2)
Abridgement of Blackstone's Commentaries 345
Account of a Memorial ... by Captain Pedro Fernandez de Quir 337
Account of the Colony of Van Diemen's Land, principally designed for the use of emigrants 270
Account of the Discoveries made in The South Pacifick Ocean 276
Account of the English Colony in New South Wales 238, 574(2)
Account of the Manners & Customs of Aborigines 364
Account of the State of Agriculture & Grazing in New South Wales 42
Acts and Ordinances of the Governor & Council of New South Wales 196
Acts of Council 380
Acts of Parliament enacted for, and applied to, the Colony, with notes & index 196
Address to the Inhabitants of the Colonies, established in N.S.W. and Norfolk Island 18()
Adelaide Miscellany of Useful and Entertaining Knowledge 481(2)
AEgyptiaca, comprising a catalogue of Egyptian antiquities... Museum of Sydney 285(2)
Albenstock; or Sketches of Swiss Scenery and Manners 89(2)
Alleged Slavery in Qld. 23
Analysis of Blackstone's Commentaries 373
Analytical view of the Census of New South Wales for the year 1846. 205(2)
Annals of Natural History 266
Ansichten vom Niederrhein .. 403
Appeal from the unjust decision of the Very Rev. Vicar General 336
Aroldo and Clara, An Historical Poem. Translated from the Italian of Silvio Pellico 336
As Much As I Dare 555(2)
Aseroe rubra 104(2)
Astronomical Observations made at the Observatory at Parramatta in New South Wales 404(2)
Atrocious Case of infamously false & malicious libel 458
Attractive Piety, Being Memorials of William Banks Carvosso 213
Australasiatic Reminiscences of Twenty-three Years'

Wanderings 177
Australia 354(2)
Australia, a Popular Account 19
Australia's Colonial Culture 118(2)
Australian Diary and Almanack 242(2)
Australian Geography 240(2)
Australian Grammar... of the Language Spoken by Aborigines... of Hunter's River 530(2)
Australian Magistrate 337(2), 505(2)
Australian Manual of Horticulture 176
Australian Melodies 337
Australian Merino 75(2)
Australian Sheet Almanack 242(2)
Australian Sketch Book 444, 505(2)
Authentic Information regarding the British Colony of Tasmania 128
Autobiography of T.W. Monds 246(2)
Autobiography of Henry Taylor 271(2)
Baker's Australian County Atlas 426
Battle of Trafalgar, a Poem 507
Bengala: or, Some Time Ago 556(2)
Beowulf 31
Best means of Security against the Prevailing Epidemic 314
Biographical Index of Deceased British and Irish Botanists 245(2)
Birds 112(2)
Birds of Australia 466
Birds of Europe 465
Birds of Great Britain 111(2)
Birds of New Guinea and the adjacent Papuan Islands 466
Birds of New Holland with their Natural History 111(2)
Birds of New South Wales with their Natural History 558
Bitter Sweet — So is the World 299(2)
Bleak House 222
Bligh and the Bounty 119
Book of the Horse 445(2)
Botanical Miscellany 417
Botanists Repository for new, and rare plants 120(2)
Brandy and Salt; being an effectual cure ... 505(2)
Brief Jottings of my Life 534(2)
Brief Journal of the Proceedings of William Light 117(2)
Brief Statement... in Connection with an Overland Expidition 556
Bush in South Aust. 48(2)
Bushman, or Life in a New Country 74(2)
Bushranger of Van Diemen's Land 402(2)

Bushrangers, A Play in Five Acts and other Poems 515
Cabramatta Store 555(2)
Capt. Dampier's Vindication of his Voyage to the South Seas in the Ship St George 277
Cardinal 140
Castles and Abbeys of Monmouthshire, The 353(2)
Catalogue of 7385 Stars from Observations made at the Observatory at Parramatta 338
Catalogue of British Insects (1770) 403
Catalogue of Scientific Papers 404(2)
Catalogue of Stars 338
Catholic Mission in Australia 545(2)
Centenary History of the Midland Agricultural Association 49(2)
Century of Birds from the Himalayan Mountains 465
Characteristics of Volcanoes 279
Childe Harold 46
Chronicles of Early Melbourne 376
Clockmaker, or, the Sayings and Doings of Samuel Slick of Slick Vale 201
Close and Crisis of Waterloo 431
Colonial Observer 505(2)
Colonization of South Australia 535(2)
Colony of South Aust. 335
Comfort for the Poor! Meat Three Times a Day!! Voluntary Information from the People of New South Wales 222
Coming Event; or the United Provinces of Australia 80(2)
Commerce du Grand Ocean 123
Companion to the Botanical Magazine 266
Compendious Latin Grammar, for the use of the Australian College, Sydney 211
Complete Account of the Settlement at Port Jackson in New South Wales ... 507(2)
Concerning the Differences in the magnetic needle ... Transactions, 1805, pt 2 391
Condensed view of the proper design and uses of the Lord's supper 356(2)
Confessions of an Etonian 402(2)
Conquest of Siberia..... from the Earliest Period 308
Constitutional History of South Australia 378
Converted Atheist's Testimony ... being the autobiography of Ales. Harris, author etc. 516
Convict Ship; a Narrative of

the Results.....Discipline 169
Correspondence 352(2)
Correspondence, etc 351(2), 352(2)
Correspondence relating to the resignation of Mr Gordon as Police Magistrate of Richmond 459
Correspondence relating to the Dismissal of the Rev. T. Rogers, from his Chaplaincy at Norfolk Island 393(2)
Crime and Punishment, The Mark System 186(2)
Crown Ward 140
Cruise of the Beacon 287(2)
Cultivation of the Cotton Plant in New South Wales 426
Culture of the Grape-Vine, and the Orange, in Australia and New Zealand 499(2)
De Tetano 242
Defence of Transportation 34
Delameres of Delamere Court 140
Der Eggsberiences ov Hans Schwarts ... with humourous interleaves. 376
Des Capitain Jacob Cook's dritte Entdeckungs-Reise 403
Descent of Man 287
Description of the Barossa Range 18
Description of the Genus Pinus 73
Descriptiones Animalium qyae in itinere ad maris australis terras per annos 1772 etc.. 404
Descriptive Vocabulary of the Language in Common Use amongst the Aborigines of WA.. 253(2)
Descriptive Vocabulary of the Native Language of W. Australia 147
Desmoro 299(2)
Diary of our trip around the world 246(2)
Diary of Ten Years Eventful Life of an Early Settler in Western Australia 253(2)
Dicks' English Novels 299(2)
Dictionary of National Biography 268, 476(2)
Digitalium Monographia 73
directories 258(2)
Discoveries in Aust. 489(2)
Doctor's Disciples 420
Domestic and Other Pieces 246(2)
Dominion of Australia 362(2)
Drunkenness, the Enemy of Britain 213
Duchess: or Womans Love and woman's hate 140
Dunorlan Tracts 373(2)
Early Experiences of Colonial Life in South Australia 175
Early History of Warwick District and Pioneers of the Darling Downs 276
Early Settlement of Queensland

and Other Articles 201
Edward Wilson's Rambles at the Antipodes 444
Elementa Botanica 456(2)
Elementary Free-Hand Drawing Books 409
Emancipation of Jews 435
Emigrant Family, or The Story of an Australian Settler 516
Emigrant's Guide; or Ten Years' Practical Experience in Australia 173(2)
Emigrant's Notebook and Guide 258(2)
Emigration and Transportation relatively considered 222
Emigration for the Relief of Parishes practically considered 462
Encyclopaedia Britannica 182(2)
England and America. A Comparison of the social and political State of both Nations 560(2)
England's Exiles; or a View of a System of Instruction & Discipline 169
Enquiry into the Effect produced by the Deluge upon...Gold 426
Entomologia Britannica 111(2)
Entrances and Exits 299(2)
Essay on Prison Discipline 397(2)
Essay on the History and Theory of Music ... Human Voice 279(2)
Essays in Ecclesiastical Biography 476(2)
Essentials of Good Skirmishing 431
Ethnography and Philology 279
Evidences of an Inland Sea collected from the Natives of the Swan River Settlement 253(2)
Evidences of Christianity 431
Excursions in and about Newfoundland during the yuears 1839 and 1840 29(2)
Exile's Return 431
Experimental Guide to Chemistry 295
Exposition and Defence of Earl Bathurst's Administration 67
Extracts from the Letters ... of George Fletcher Moore, Esq.... Swan River Settlement 253(2)
Facts relating to the punishment of death in the metropolis 559(2)
Felonry of New South Wales 304(2), 464(2), 615(2)
Female Immigration, considered in a brief account of the Sydney Immigrants' Home 221
Female Volunteer; or, the Dawning of Peace; a Drama 507

Fiction for Family Reading 299(2)
First Fruits of Australian Poetry 374, 558
Flora Australiensis 167, 245(2)
Flora Gaeca 73
Flora Tasmaniae 287
For Her Natural Life: a tale of 299(2)
For the Term of His Natural Life 352(2), 393(2), 397(2)
Forty Reasons for Leaving the Church of Rome 420
Frankenstein 376(2), 620(2)
Freedom and Independence for the Golden Lands of Australia 80(2)
Garryowen Sketches 376
Gatherings of a Naturalist in Australasia 86
Geelong Almanac 520
General Biographical Dictionary 482(2)
General History of Birds 88(2)
General Synopsis of Birds 88(2)
General Zoology 437(2)
Genesis of Queensland 407(2)
Geoffry Hamlyn 278
Geographical and Descriptive Delineations of the Island of VDL 16(2)
Geographical Dictionary 538
Geographical, Historical and Topographical Description of Van Diemen's Land 360
Geographical Memoirs of New South Wales 94, 266, 374, 463
George Mayford: An Emigrant in Search of a Colony 402(2)
Georgiana's Journal 161(2)
Gold and Silver 494(2)
Gold Digger: A Visit to the Gold Fields of Australia in February 173(2)
Goldfinder of Australia 444
Grammar and Vocabulary of the Language of New Zealand 42(2)
Great Efficacy of Faith in the Atonement of Christ 213
Guide to Port Stephens in N.S.W., the Colony of the Australian Agricultural Company 516
Guide to the Laws of England Affecting Roman sCatholics 21
Handbook for Emigrants 505(2)
Hangman and the Judge 559(2)
Hansard of the Houses of Parliament of South Australia 377
Heads of the People 444
Hebrew Melodies 279(2)
Herball or generall historie of plantes 52
Hermit in Van Diemen's Land 420(2)
Hints for Australian Emigrants 268
Hints Relating to Emigrants

and Emigration 210
Historical and Critical Account of a Grand Series of National Medals 265(2)
Historical and Statistical Account of NSW 77(2), 211(2)
Historical Collection of...Discoveries in the South Pacific Ocean 276
Historical Journal of the Transactions at Port Jackson and Norfolk Island 146, 568, 58(2)
History of Margaret Catchpole 215
History of Tasmania 316, 591(2)
History of the Commencement and Progress of Catholicity in Australia, up to 1840 44(2)
History of the Island of Van Diemen's Land from the year 1824 to 1835 221(2)
History, Resources and Future Prospects of Queensland 23
Hobart Town Almanack 492
Hobart Town Almanack and Van Diemen's Land Annual 355
Homestead History 29(2)
Horrors of Convict Life 420
Horrors of Transportation 545(2)
Hortus Kewensis 265, 268
Humane Policy; or Justice to the Aborigines of New Settlements 56
Husbandman's Assistant 449(2)
Icones Planatarum Rariorum 73
Icones Planatarum Syriae rariorum discriptionibus et observationibus illustratae 69(2)
Iconographia Generum Planatarum 73
Illustrated Handbook of the Voyage to Australia 354(2)
Illustrationes Florae Novae Hollandiae 73
Illustrations of Australian Plants 456(2)
Illustrations of Australian Plants collected in 1770. 54
Illustrations of Ornithology 97
Illustrations of the Present State and Future Prospects of the Colony of N.S.W. 114(2), 242(2)
Impending Crisis 630(2)
Impressions of Australia Felix ... Australian Poems 249
Incidents in the life of the Rev. Henry Dowling 316
Index and Directory to Map of the County bordering upon the River Hunter 280
Index Ornithologicus, sive systema ornithologiae 88(2), 89(2)
Indian Archipelago 128
Information for the People

114(2)
Inquiry into the Nature of Benevolence 97
Inquiry into Poor Laws 97
Insolvent Law of New South Wales 185, 242(2)
Intellectual Sciences, 1-2, 356(2)
Ireland and its Oeconomy 97
Jahangir's India. The Remonstrantie of Francisco Pelsaert 323(2)
Jail Manual 168
Jews in Van Diemen's Land 458(2)
John Price's Bar of Steel 352(2)
Journal d'un Exile Politique aux Terres Australes 353(2)
Journal of a recent visit to the principal vineyards of Spain and France 186
Journal of a Tour of Discovery accross the Blue Mountains in NSW 116
Journal of a Tour through some of the Vineyards of Spain and France 186
Journal of a voyage from Plymouth to Sydney ... 353(2)
Journal of a Voyage in the Missionary Ship Duff 252
Journal of a Voyage in the Barque 'Parkfield' ... in the year 1843. 249
Journal of a Voyage to New South Wales 437(2), 594(2)
Journal of a Voyage to the South Seas 314(2)
Journal of an Expedition into the interior of Tropical Australia 240(2)
Journal of Mrs Fenton, a narrative of her life...1826-1830. 371
Journal of researches into the Geology and Natural History of the various countries visited by H.M.S. Beagle 287
Journal of Two Expeditions of Discovery in North-West & WA...1837-9. 477
Journals of Expeditions of Discovery into Central Australia...1840-1 364
Journals of Two Expeditions into the Interior of New South Wales 306(2)
Journey from Sydney to the Australian Alps 114(2)
Journey of Discovery to Port Phillip ... 114, 556, 505(2)
Judicial Establishments of New South Wales and of Vand Diemen's Land 100
Kafirs Illustrated 18
Key to the Structure of the Aboriginal Language
King's Bench Reports 1822-31. 317
Korao no New Zealand; or, the New Zealander's First Book 42(2)

Lachrymae Hibernicae; or, The Genius of Erin's Complaint, a Ballad 507
Language and Dialects spoken by the Aborigines of Tasmania 194
Language of the Aborigines 176
Language of Theology Interpreted 136
Latest Information with regard to Australia Felix 26
Law Reform 179
Lay of the Last Minstrel 429(2)
Lecture on National Education 336
Lectures, Historical, Doctrinal and Practical, ...Catechism of the Church of Eng. 285(2)
Lectures on Prophecy and the Kingdom of Christ 356(2)
Lectures on the History of France 476(2)
Legends of Australia 505(2)
Leila 68(2)
Letter from John Smith to John Jones 421
Letter from Sydney, the principal town of Australasia 559(2)
Letter to the Magistrates of England 345
Letter to the People of Great Britain and Ireland on transportation 420
Letters from an exile at Botany-Bay to his Aunt in Dumfries .. 574(2)
Letters from Charles Dickens to Angela Burdett-Coutts 186(2)
Letters from France 506(2)
Letters from Van Dieman's Land 430
Letters from Victorian Pioneers 29(2)
Letters to The Rt. Hon. Robert Peel 343
Letters written to France, ... 507(2)
Life and Adventures of William Buckley 174, 258(2)
Life and Labours of George Washington Walker 46
Life of Captain Andrew Barclay 57
Lost and Found; or Light in the Prison 490
love story 140
Magical Trip to the Gold Regions 354(2)
Magistrates' Cases 1822-27. 317
Mammals of Australia 466
Manual for the Cultivation of the Vine and Olive in Western Australia 122(2), 278(2)
Manual of Plain Directions for Planting and Cultivating Vineyards and for making Wine in New South Wales 186
Manuscript Book 250(2)
Map of the District of Geelong

520
Map of the Town and Suburbs of Geelong 520
Melbourne Almanac and Port Phillip Directory 216, 51(2)
Memoir of ... Joseph Monnier 337
Memoirs Historical and Scientific of the Right Honourable Sir Joseph Banks 500(2)
Memoirs of James Hardy Vaux 374, 60(2)
Memoirs of Rowland Taylor 491(2)
Memoirs of the First Thirty-Two Years of the Life of James Hardy Vaux ..... 552(2)
Memoirs of the Royal Astronomical Society 338
Memories of the Past by a Lady in Australia 297
Michael Howe, the Last and Worst of the Bushrangers 561
Mineral Kingdom of South Australia 222(2)
Mistress of Hawk's Crag 299(2)
Modern Parables, or the Voices of Revelation and Nature interpreted and harmonized 136
Molluscorum Novae Hollandiae specimen 350(2)
Monody on the Death of St George Gipps 538
Month in the Bush of Australia 565(2)
Moral and Political Catechism of Man 218(2)
Musurgia Vocalis 279(2)
My Jail Journal, or Five Years in British Prisons 235(2)
Narative of...the history of Van Diemens Land 415
Narrative and Recollections ... during a Three Years' Captivity 431
Narrative and Successful Result of a Voyage in the South Seas ... to Ascertain the Actual Fate of La Perouse's Expedition 307
Narrative of a journey to...the Polar Sea...1819-22 415
Narrative of a Nine Months' Residence in New Zealand in 1827. 349
Narrative of a Survey of the Intertropical and Western Coasts of Aust... 1818-1822. 266, 62(2)
Narrative of a visit .. to the New Missionary Settlement of the United Brethren ... 89(2)
Narrative of a Visit to the Australian Colonies 46
Narrative of a Visit to the Mauritius and South Africa 46
Narrative of a Voyage around the World 446(2)

Narrative of a Voyage of
  Discovery 469
Narrative of a Voyage round
  the World 612(2)
Narrative of a Voyage to
  N.S.W. & V.D.L. in the ship
  Skelton during the year 1820
  216(2)
Narrative of a Voyage to New
  Zealand ... 282(2)
Narrative of an Expedition into
  Central Australia 167
Narrative of Four Journeys into
  the Country of the Hottentots
  and Caffraria 317(2)
Narrative of proceedings of
  William Cox, Esq., of
  Clarendon ... in the years
  1814 & 1815 259
Narrative of the Adventures
  and Sufferings of Captain
  Daniel D.Heustis 430
Narrative of the Expedition to
  Botany Bay ... 507(2)
Narrative of the Overland
  Journey...from Hobart Tonw
  to Macquarie Harbour, 1842
  182
Narrative of the Settlement of
  The Scots Church, Sydney,
  New South Wales 76(2)
Narrative of the Surveying
  Voyage of H.M.S. Fly 29(2),
  167(2)
Narrative of the Surveying
  Voyages of His Majesty's
  Ships, Adventure and Beagle
  62(2)
Narrative of the Voyage of
  H.M.S. Rattlesnake 167(2)
National Importance of
  Emigration 47
Native Tribes of South
  Australia 627(2)
Naturalists' Miscellany 437(2)
Naval Chronicle (Vol 6, 1801)
  572
Neuholland und uie brittische
  Kolonie in Botany-Bay,
  November 1786 403
New British Province 200(2)
New British Province of South
  Australia 560(2)
New South Wales Calendar and
  General Post Office Directory
  242(2)
New South Wales General
  Standing Orders 558
New South Wales; Its Present
  State and Future Prospects
  151(2)
New South Wales Pocket
  Almanack 505(2)
New System of Stenography
  550(2)
New Voyage round the World
  277
New Zealanders Illustrated 18
Newgate 507
Nine Years on the North-West
  Frontier of India, from 1854
  to 1863 250

Notes d'un condamne Politique
  de 1838. 353(2)
Notes of an Exile in Van
  Dieman's Land 431
Nouveau Dictionnaire
  d'Histoire Naturelle 323(2)
Nova Hollandiae Plantarum
  Specimen 69(2)
Novae Hollandiae Plantae
  Specimen 167
Nung-Ngnun (poem) 337
Observations made during a
  Voyage Round the World, on
  Physical Geography etc. 404
Observations on the Coasts of
  Van Diemen's Land, on Bass's
  Straight and its Islands... part
  of NSW 389
Observations on the Flora of
  Geelong 493
Observations on the Philosophy
  of Criminal Jurisprudence 97
Observations upon Secondary
  Punishment 34
Odes, Poems and Translations
  507
On the Evidence of
  Accomplices 340(2)
On the expediency and
  necessity of encouraging
  distilling and brewing from
  grain in NSW 42
On the Government of British
  Colonies 604(2)
On the Land Policy of New
  South Wales 630(2)
On the Most Effectual Means
  of Encouraging Scientific
  Undertakings 404(2)
On the Motions of the Earth
  and Heavenly Bodies 268
On the Origin of Species by
  means of Natural Selection
  287
Ordinances of the Colony of
  Sierra Leone 248(2)
Our Antipodes 4(2), 268(2)
Outlines of the Method of
  Conducting a
  Trigonometrical Survey 418
Oyster Culture 194
Parliamentary Pocket
  Companion 615(2)
Passages in a Wandering Life
  31
Paul's Letters to his Kinsfolk
  333
Pedestrian: A Summer's Ramble
  in the Tyrol 89(2)
Peerage of England 236
Pen and Pencil Sketches, being
  the Journal of a tour in India
  ... 268(2)
Philosophical Transactions 338,
  404(2)
Philosophy of Mineralogy
  537(2)
Physical Description of New
  South Wales and Van
  Diemen's Land 494(2)
Pickwick Papers 242(2)
Picturesque Antiquities of

Bristol 354(2)
Picturesque Tour of the River
  Thames 592(2)
Pioneer Hymn Book 373(2)
Plan for extending the
  Commerce of this Kingdom
  and of the East-India-
  Company 276
Plantae Preissianae sive
  enumeratio ... L. Preiss 350(2)
Plays, and Fugitive Pieces in
  verse 182
Plea for the New South Wales
  Constitution 336
Poems on Various Occasions
  507
Poet's Home 515
Poetical Fragments 490(2)
Polynesia, a Popular
  Description 19
Pomara, a Tale of Real Life 19
Popular politics 559(2)
Posthumous Papers of the
  Pickwick Club 316
Practial View of Homeopathy,
  Being an Address to British
  Practitioners 448(2)
Practical Treatise on Sheep
  Breeding and Wool Growing
  438(2)
Practice of the Local Courts of
  South Australia 441(2)
Preliminary Catalogue of Fixed
  Stars ... Reduced from the
  Observations made ...at
  Parramatta 404(2)
Present Picture of New South
  Wales 365, 202(2)
Present State of Australia 299
Present state of Australia, with
  particular hints to emigrants
  221(2)
Present State of Moral
  Principle in the Supreme
  Government of the British
  Colonial Empire 45
Priest's Secret 376
Proceedings of the Royal
  Society of Tasmania 362
Prodromus Entomology 112(2)
Prodromus Florae Norfolkicae
  73
Propdromus Entomology,
  Natural History of
  Lepidopterous Insects of
  NSW 111(2)
Prophecy fulfilled, 1869, The
  Central Asian Question 250
Protestant 420
Psellus' Dialogue on the
  Operation of Daemons 505(2)
Psycologia Australica 493
Queensland: her History,
  Resources, and Future
  Prospects 23
Question of Questions 48(2)
Quintus Servinton 221(2),
  420(2)
Races of Man 279
Ralph Rashleigh 540(2)
Ramble in Malta and Sicily in
  the Autumn of 1841. 18

Rambler in Mexico 89(2)
Rambler in North America 89(2)
Rambles in New Zealand 98
Rankens of Bathurst 362(2)
Real Property Act... with Analytical and Critical Notes 380
Recollections of a Peninsula Veteran 13
Recollections of a Rambling Life 23
Recollections of Geoffrey Hamlyn 556(2)
Recollections of Life in Van Dieman's Land 430
Refutation of the Chevalier Dillon's Slanderous Attacks 307
Relation du Voyage a la recherche de La Perouse 69(2)
Remarks on a Passage to Botany Bay, 1787-1792. 427(2)
Remarks on Drill, with rough sketches of field days 250
Reminiscences 13
Reminiscences of the Life of a Bushman 623(2)
Reminiscences of Thirty Years' Residence in N.S.W. & Victoria 513(2)
Reminiscences of Twelve Years' Residence 41
Reply to Certain Calumnies and Misrepresentations ... 211
Report of the late trial for libel!!! Clarke versus MacFaul 227
Report on the State of Prison Discipline in Van Diemen's Land 185(2)
Resident Song Birds of Great Britain 249
Review of Dr. Hampton's First Report on Norfolk Island 351(2)
Rhetoric in Miniature 550(2)
Rhyme 515
Robinson Crusoe 389
Royal South Australian Almanack and General Directory 481(2)
Rules of the Final Judgment 356(2)
Sailing Directions.. Coasts of.. Patagonia.. Straits of Magellan.. Tierra del Fuego 62(2)
Savage Life and Scenes in Australia and New Zealand 18
Scenery in... Sydney 444
Scope of Piety 491(2)
Scriptural Evidence of the Apostolic Ministry and Tradition of the Church Catholic 420
Sea Wolves & Bandits 351(2)
Secrets of Alexander Harris, a frank autobiography .. 516
Serious Admonition to the Public on the Intended Thief-Colony at Botany Bay 276
Sermons Preached in Boroughbridge Chapel 557
Settlers and Convicts: or Recollections of sixteen years' labour... Aust. Backwoods 516
Seven Years of my Life 430
Shifting Scenes in Theatrical Life 299(2)
Sicilian Scenery 116(2)
Sidney's Australian Handbook 445(2)
Simple Rules for the Guidance of Persons in humble Life 505(2)
Six Months in South Australia 480(2)
Six Views of the Gold Field of Ophir 19
Sketch of a Proposal for Colonizing Australasia 462, 559(2)
Sketch of the Physical Structure of Australia ... 29(2)
Sketch of Three Colonial Acts, suggested for adoption in... South Australia 379
Sketches Illustrative of the Native Inhabitants and Islands of New Zealand 349
Sketches in the environs of Sydney 212(2)
Solace of Song 89(2)
Some Account of New Zealand .... Customs of the Natives, etc. 419(2)
Some Account of.... the Native Tribes of Tasmania 194
Song Birds of Great Britain 249
South Australia and its Mines 341
South Australia Illustrated 18, 19
South Australia in 1837: a series of letters, with a postscript as to 1838. 463
South Australian Almanack 248
South Australian Church Hymn Book 557
Southern Colonies: their municipal annexation ... 561(2)
Spanish Sketches 376
Speeches of George Canning 512(2)
Squatting Orders. Orders in Council. Locking up the lands 370
Stastistical, Historical and Political Description of the Colony of N.S.W.... 584(2)
State and Position of Western Australia, Commonly Called the Swan-River Settlement 5(2)
State of Agriculture and Trade in the Colony of New South Wales 100
State of Religion and Education in New South Wales 185
State of the Colony of New South Wales 100
Statement of the Origin, Condition, and Prospects of the German Mission to the Aborigines at Moreton Bay 352
Statement of the services of Mr Dawson, as chief agent of the Australian Agricultural Co. 29
Statistical Account of the British Settlements in Australasia 343
Statistical, Historical, and Political Description of The Colony of N.S.W. 582(2)
Stolen Moments 505(2)
Stray Suggestions on Colonization 278(2)
Summary View of the Statistics & ..Commerce... Principal Shores... Pacific Ocean.. 185(2)
Sunday Services adapted to the use of Country Congregations 169
Swing unmasked, or the cause of rural incendiarism 559(2)
Sydney Illustrated 354(2)
Sydney in 1848. 409
Sydney's First Four Years 507(2)
System of Penal Discipline 420
Systema Naturae 89(2)
Tales for the Bush 555(2)
Tales of the Colonies, or, the Adventures of an Emigrant 402(2)
Tales of the Colonies 593(2)
Tales of the Old Regime 352(2)
Tarquin the Proud, and other poems 538
Tasmania Illustrated 354(2)
Tasmania Journal of Natural Science 362
Tasmanian Industries 194
Tasmanian Letters 366(2)
Testimony to the Truth; or, The Autobiography of an Atheist 516
Theological Repository 312(2)
Thoughts: A Series of Sonnets 515
Three Colonies of Aust. 445(2)
Three Expeditions into the interior of Eastern Australia 240(2)
Three Years Residence in Van Diemen's Land 271
Tom Cringle's Log 545
Tower of the Dream 515
Tracts of Truth 316
Tradesman's and Housekeeper's Diary 316
Tranquillization of Syria and the East 435
Travels in Ireland, in the year 1822, exhibiting brief sketches... 376(2)
Travels with Leichhardt 177
Treatise on Navigation 357(2)
Treatise on the Culture of the Vine and the Art of Making

Wine 186
Tribute of Affection 316
Twenty Straws 299(2)
Twenty-three Years'
  Wanderings in the Australias
  and Tasmania, including
  Travels with Dr Leichhardt
  177
Two Voyages to New South
  Wales and Van Diemen's
  Land 376(2)
Two Years in New South Wales
  268
Van Diemen's Land Pocket
  Almanack 86
Van Diemen's Land Warriors
  182
Veritas 221(2)
Victims of Whiggery 133(2)
Victoria Gold Diggings and
  Diggers as They Are 444
Victoria Illustrated 444
View of the Art of
  Colonization 577, 561(2)
Views in Australia 348, 140(2)
Views in New South Wales, and
  Van Diemen's Land 349
Views of Melbourne and
  Geelong 354(2)
Views of Pompeii 116(2)
Views of the Gold Regions of
  Australia 19
Views through Hobart Town
  41
Vindication of the Practice of
  not allowing Counsel for
  Prisoners accused of Felony
  to Make Speeches for Them.
  375
Vindication of Van Diemen's
  Land 182
Vocabulary of the Dialects
  spoken by the Aboriginal
  Races of South-Western
  Australia 477
Vocabulary of the Dialects of
  Some of the Aboriginal Tribes
  of Tasmania 230(2)
Vocabulary of the Flash
  Language 552(2)
Voice from South Australia
  481(2)
Voice from Tasmania 40(2)
Voice from the Far Interior of
  Australia 445(2)
Voyage around the World in
  His Britannic Majesty's Sloop
  Resolution ..(1777) 402
Voyage de Decouvertes aux
  Terres Australes ... sure les
  Corvettes le Geographe,...
  324(2)
Voyage De La Perouse autour
  du Monde, 1-4. 85(2)
Voyage of discovery to the
  North Pacific Ocean 551(2)
Voyage of Governor Phillip to
  Botany Bay 146, 88(2), 594(2)
Voyage round the World in His
  Britannic Majesty's Sloop
  Resolution.. (1777) 404
Voyage to China (Osbech) 403

Voyage to Terra Australis 73,
  167, 391, 592(2)
Voyage to the south sea (by W.
  Bligh, 1792) 119
Walch's Almanack 493
Wanderings in NSW 85
Wanderings of the Clerical
  Eulysses 41
What is To Be will Be 299(2)
Who translated the Bible 503
Wild Notes, from the Lyre of a
  Native Minstrel 559, 533(2)
Woodlands, etc. of Tasmania
  194
Woodleigh Farm 556(2)
Work in the Bush ... Thought
  in the Bush ... Life in the Bush
  of Van Diemen's Land 48(2)
Wreck of the 'Admella' and
  other poems 19
Wroeites' faith 625(2)
Wyndabyne 362(2)
Zoology of New Holland
  437(2)
Botanical gardens: see
  Organisations: Misc.
Botanical organisations: see
  Organisations: Misc.
Botanists: see Occupations
Botany 52-55, 73, 167, 194, 195,
  266, 267, 268, 269, 325, 468,
  102(2), 318(2)
Bridges: 486
  Bridgewater Bridge 462(2),
  528(2)
  Ross Bridge 413(2)
  Tasmania 41
British army: see army
Building 122, 304, 191(2)
Bushrangers: (see also in
  Personal Names Index)
Misc: 12, 147, 214, 293, 312,
  429, 560
NSW: 214, 367, 397
— Collins, Patrick 570(2)
— Davis, Edward 293
— Jewboy gang 293-4
TAS 19, 34, 95, 147, 172, 282,
  407, 429, 430, 493, 560,
  159(2), 308(2), 375(2), 396(2),
  458(2), 459(2), 469(2), 470(2),
  504(2)
Tasmanian:
— Brady, Matthew 147, 493,
  566, 225(2), 504(2), 575(2),
  596(2)
— Cash, Martin 214, 164(2)
— Crawford, James 504(2)
— Howe, Michael 560, 232(2),
  278(2)
— Kavanagh, 247(2)
— Martin, William 336(2)
— Mills, Peter 231, 264(2)
— Ogden, 308(2)
— Sullivan, 308(2)
Victoria 455(2), 605(2)
Businesses: see Companies
Cape Colony: see South Africa
Capital punishment 369, 177(2),
  247(2), 261(2), 320(2)
Cartoons (political) 458
Castle Hill Irish convict rebellion

(1804): see Rebellions: NSW
Cattle (breeds):
  Durham 271, 534(2)
  Hereford 544, 93(2), 409(2),
  630(2)
  Shorthorn 124, 1(2), 96(2),
  200(2), 534(2)
Celtic Language 302(2)
Cemeteries: listed geographically
Cemeteries: Canada
  Montreal, La Cote des Neiges
  353(2)
Cemeteries: England
  Bathampton, St Nicholas 333(2)
  Blackheath KEN, Lee
  churchyard 225
  Broadwater, St Mary's 595(2)
  Brompton, 415(2)
  Hackney, Old Cemetery 572
  Highgate, London 9(2)
  Kensal Green 143(2), 494(2)
  Lower Tooting, St Nicholas
  61(2)
  St Giles in the Field, LND 52
  St John's, Westminster 574(2)
  Turnham Green, LND
Cemeteries: Ireland
  Old Richmond, Dublin 513
Cemeteries: Italy
  Stresa 287(2)
Cemeteries: New South Wales
  Botany 143(2), 371(2)
  Bungonia, Church of England
  376(2)
  Bunnerong 263
  Campbelltown, St Peter's
  395(2)
  Camperdown 123(2), 228(2),
  292(2)
  Camperdown, St Stephen's 58
  Cook's River, St Peter's 2(2),
  365(2)
  Devonshire Street. see Sydney
  East Maitland 472, 300(C)
  Gore Hill 44(2), 166(2)
  Haslem's Creek 217
  Kelso, churchyard 102(2),
  261(2)
  La Perouse 227(2), 389(2),
  575(2)
  Liverpool 158, 531(2)
  Maitland, Christ Church 337(2)
  Newcastle 102
  Newtown, St Stephen's 626(2)
  North Sydney, St Thomas's
  261(2), 305(2), 621(2)
  Parramatta, St John's 12, 231,
  355, 5(2), 107(2), 134(2),
  218(2)
  Parramatta, Wesleyan 95(2)
  Penrith, St Mary's (formerly
  South Creek) 53(2)
  Petersham 347(2)
  Point Frederick 431(2)
  Prospect, St Bartholomew's
  97(2)
  Richmond, St Peter's 367,
  402(2)
  Rookwood 217, 205(2)
  Ryde, St Charles's 199(2)
  St Jude's Anglican 49
  Sandhills (see Sydney,

Devonshire Street)
Singleton cemetery 449(2)
Singleton C. of E. 86(2)
South Head cemetery 113(2)
Sydney, Devonshire St. 192,
  255, 294, 308, 337, 427, 495,
  87(2), 109(2), 112(2), 142(2),
  170(2), 307(2), 340(2), 371(2),
  389(2), 575(2)
Waverley 207, 20(2), 299(2),
  549(2)
Wilberforce, St John's 361,
  394(2)
Wollombi 337
Yass 565
Cemeteries: South Australia
Adelaide, West Terrace 378,
  491(2)
Victor Harbor 282(2)
Cemeteries: Tasmania
Cornelian Bay, C. of E. 407
Evandale, C. of E. 57
Geelong, Eastern Cemetery
  38(2)
Glenorchy, St Paul's C. of E.
  138(2)
Hobart: Presbyterian 340,
  271(2)
— St David's 302, 574, 36(2),
  337(2), 427(2), 462(2)
— St George's 40(2), 138(2),
  260(2)
Launceston: C. of E. 264(2)
— Charles St. 441(2)
— Cyprus St. 516(2)
— Presbyterian 493
— St John's 143(2)
New Town, St John's 360, 405,
  653
Presbyterian 144(2)
Richmond 217(2)
Richmond, St Luke's 397(2)
West Hobart, Providence
  Valley 563(2)
Cemeteries: Victoria
Brighton 198
Geelong 523(2)
Geelong East 331
Heidelberg (Warringal) 349(2)
Melbourne general 297(2),
  367(2C), 410(2), 447(2)
St Kilda 401, 34(2)
Sale 184(2)
Warringal (Heidelberg) 349(2)
Cemeteries: Western Australia
East Perth 372
York 219(2)
Censorship 583(2), 585(2)
Census 8(2), 275(2), 489(2)
Central America: see Places:
  Latin America
Charities: see Organisations:
  Miscellaneous
Chemistry 295
Child sexual abuse 19
Chinese coolie labour see
  Immigration
Chloroform 372
Churches and Parishes: listed
  geographically
Churches: Canada
Halifax, St Paul 236

Churches: England
Barley. HEF, Congregational
  Chapel 144(2)
Bath Abbey 333(2)
Bristol, St James's 257(C)
Bury St Edmund's SFK 303(2)
Cambridge, St Benedict's 627(2)
Canterbury Cathedral 164, 452,
  285(2), 413(2)
Canterbury, St Mildred 159
Christchurch, Priory 553(2)
Clifton, Dowry Square chapel
  10
Derby, All Saints' 409
Devonport DEV, St Andrew
  153(2)
Durham Cathedral 433(2)
Guildford, Stoke Church
  484(2)
Halstead ESS, Old Independent
  Church 491(2)
Hambleton, St Mary's 557
Hull, St John's Church 254
Kidderminster Congregational
  Church WOR 398(2)
Liverpool, St Patrick's 270(2)
London, Covent Garden, St
  Paul's 552(2)
— Episcopal Jews' Chapel
  229(2)
— Hackney, St John's 229(2)
— Hammersmith, St Paul's
  324(2)
— Hatton Garden, Caledonian
  Church 229(2)
— Holborn, St Andrew's 623(2)
— Holywell Mount Chapel
  251, 365
— Knightsbridge, St Paul's
  207(2)
— Limehouse Wesleyan Chapel
  303(2)
— London Wall, Church of All
  Saints 499(2)
— Marylebone New Church
  196(2)
— St Antholin 19(2)
— St Dunstan's 178(2)
— St George in the East 178(C)
— St George's, Hanover
  Square 134, 482(2)
— St Giles in the Fields 52
— St James's, Hampstead Road
  391
— St James's, Picadilly 65
— St Luke's, Old Street 216(2),
  550(2)
— St Martin-in-the-Fields
  52(2), 56(2)
— St Leonard's, Shoredich
  444(2C)
— St Pancras New Church 291
— St Paul's Cathedral 480
— St Thomas's Square,
  Independent Chapel 229(2)
— Southwark Chapel 321
— Southwark, St George's
  528(2)
— Swedish Church 456(2)
— Westminster Abbey 415,
  285(2)
— Westminster Cathedral

424(2)
— Westminster, St Anne's
  357(2)
— Westminster, St James's
  521(2)
— Westminster, St Margaret's
  Chapel 550(2)
— Zion Chapel 259
Manchester, St Ann's 198(2)
Mitton, Leigh Memorial Chapel
  322
Nottingham, St Barnabas
  Cathedral 607(2), 608(2)
Petersham, St Peter's 551(2)
Plymouth, St Andrew's 123(2C)
Portsea, Congregational chapel
  632(2)
Portsea, St Mary's 427(2)
Ryde, New Church 261(2)
Southampton, Church of All
  Saints 376(2)
Surrey Chapel 599(2)
Tilney All Saints NFK 256
Tilney St Laurence NFK 256
Weigh House Chapel 165
West Orchard Congregational
  Church 521
Churches: Germany
Berlin, Bethleham Bohemian
  Church 421(2)
Churches: Gibraltar
Cathedral Church of St Mary
  the Crowned 375
Churches: Ireland
Belfast, Berry St. Church 192
Dublin, St Peter's Parish 557
Rosecrea, St Cronan's 421
Sligo, St John's 124(2)
Churches: Italy
Rome, St Isadore's 309
Churches: New South Wales
Alexandria, St Mark's 406(2)
Bathurst, All Saints' 451(2)
Bathurst, St John's Bathurst 522
Braidwood, St Bede's,
  Braidwood 196
Bungonia, Christ Church
  554(2)
Camden, St John the Evangelist
  113(2)
Campbelltown, St Peter's
  292(2), 368(2)
Canberra, St John the Baptist
  198, 199, 205, 439
Carcoar, St Paul's 2(2)
Chippendale, St Paul's 451(2)
Cobbitty, St Paul's 523, 554(2)
Cook's River, St Peter's 205,
  198(2), 464(2)
Ebenezer Chapel 13, 166(2)
Field of Mars 402
Goulburn, St Saviour's 199
Grafton Cathedral 472
Heber Chapel 523
Hunter River Valley 113(2)
Ingleburn, Denham Court, St
  Mary the Virgin 554(2)
Kelso, Holy Trinity 524, 525
Liverpool, St Luke's 158, 471,
  139(2), 255(2)
Morpeth, St James 231, 560
Mulgoa, St Thomas 523

Newcastle, Christ Church (Cathedral) 140(2), 226(2), 227(2), 568(2), 613(2)

Parramatta, Leigh Memorial Centenary Church 105(2)

Parramatta, Scots Church 96(2)

Parramatta, St John's 184, 205, 207, 312, 402, 417, 523, 16(2), 21(2), 59(2), 95(2), 209(2), 211(2), 217(2), 255(2), 564(2), 566(2)

Parramatta North, All Saints 402

Port Macquarie, St Thomas 262, 555(2)

Salem Chapel 523

Scone, St Luke's 334

Singleton, All Saints 281

South Creek, St Mary Magdalene 198(2), 425(2)

South Head, Congregational Church 529(2)

Sutton Forest, All Saints 523

Sydney:
— Baptist Chapel 554(2)
— Bridge Street Synagogue 84
— Christ Church St Laurence 305, 70(2), 392(2), 425(2), 484(2), 540(2), 569(2)
— Church Hill, St Patrick's 166(2)
— Darling Point, St Mark's 406(2), 453(2), 570(2)
— Holy Trinity 565(2C)
— Hunter's Hill, Marist Fathers' Church, Villa Maria 199(2)
— Independent Chapel 554(2)
— Macquarie Street, Wesleyan Chapel 356(2)
— Mariners' Church 529(2)
— Miller's Point, Holy Trinity 206, 41(2)
— North Sydney, St Mary's 44(2)
— Parramatta: see Parramatta
— Penrith, St Stephen's 425(2)
— Pitt Street, Congregational 96, 261, 353, 356(2), 398(2), 491(2), 600(2)
— Randwick, St Jude's 73(2), 276(2), 527(2)
— Ryde, St Anne's 251
— Scots Church, 205, 76(2), 78(2), ,79(2), 81(2), 82(2), 96(2), 172(2), 197(2), 307(2), 356(2), 360(2), 361(2), 431(2), 464(2), 566(2), 578(2)
— St Andrew's Cathedral 206, 210, 259, 461, 501, 41(2), 255(2), 425(2), 570(2)
— St Andrew's Church 269
— St Andrew's Scots Church 166(2)
— St James 10, 159, 212, 324, 331, 377, 442, 471, 501, 537, 41(2), 143(2), 180(2), 198(2), 237(2), 257(2), 275(2), 293(2), 296(2), 298(2), 307(2), 360(2), 389(2), 411(2), 418(2), 425(2), 432(2), 554(2), 569(2), 572(2)
— St Mary's Cathedral 293, 504, 166(2), 270(2), 279(2), 293(2), 342(2), 347(2), 346(2), 425(2), 510(2), 567(2)
— St Patrick's 545(2)
— St Philip's 159, 199, 205, 217, 226, 245, 247, 254, 255, 303, 305, 344, 537, 59(2), 98(2), 101(2), 232(2), 255(2), 293(2), 366(2), 367(2), 377(2), 450(2), 469(2), 550(2), 596(2)
— Watson's Bay, Presbyterian 269
— Woollahra, Ocean Street Congregational 356(2)
— York St, Synagogue 84, 294, 142(2)

Windsor, St Matthew's 211, 311, 259, 262, 383, 471, 227(2), 211(2), 483(2), 533(2)

Yass, St Clement's 151, 565, 293(2)

Churches: New Zealand
Nelson, Ebenezer Chapel 197(2)

Churches: Queensland
Brisbane, Nazareth Lutheran 423(2)
— St John's pro-Cathedral 277, 473
— Wharf Street Congregational 600(2)

Churches: Scotland
Kelso Free Church 564(2)
Kirk Yetholm 519(2)
Secession Chapel 144(2)
Tron Church 76(2)

Churches: South Australia
Adelaide:
— Congregational 491(2)
— Grote St., Church of Christ 179
— Holy Trinity 335, 440(2)
— Kermode St., Church of Christ 179
— Mitcham, St Michael 244
— North Terrace, Scots 328
— Pirie Street Church 321
— Port Adelaide, St Paul's 335
— St Francis Xavier's Cathedral 270(2)
— St John's C. of E. 499
— Stow Memorial Church 491(2)
— Trinity Church 378, 380, 419, 446, 499, 557, 64(2), 201(2), 473(2), 626(2)
Draper Memorial Church 322
Glen Osmond, St Saviour's 446
Newland Memorial Church 282(2)
O'Halloran Hill, Christ Church 301(2)
St Andrew's 499
Unley Church of Christ 179
Wallaroo, St Mary's 441(2)

Churches: Switzerland
Chapelle de l'Hermitage 92(2)

Churches: Tasmania
Bagdad, Congregational 110
Bothwell, Presbyterian 375(2)
Bothwell, St Luke's 24
Buckland, St John 429

Campbell Town, C. of E. 100(2)
Campbell Town, St Andrew's 542(2)
Cranbrook, Gala Kirk 12, 35(2)
Evandale, St Andrew's 257
Hagley, St Mary's 330
Hobart:
— All Saints 553
— Brisbane Street Chapel 553
— Collins Street church 553
— Davey Street Methodist 553
— Holy Trinity 110
— Melville St., Methodist 133(2)
— Memorial Congregational 191
— Penitentiary Chapel 35(2)
— Presbyterian 235
— St Andrew's 494, 118(2), 176(2), 271(2), 298(2), 564(2)
— St Andrew's Presbyterian 542(2)
— St David's 77, 225, 239, 253, 256, 264, 292, 301, 330, 356, 361, 429, 553, 73(2), 127(2), 207(2), 247(2), 285(2), 286(2), 297(2), 302(2), 316(2), 336(2), 366(2), 452(2)
— St George's 538
— St George's, Battery Point 24, 110, 219, 361, 574, 249(2)
— St John Baptist Church 256
— St John the Baptist, Goulburn St 436
— St John's 192, 298(2)
— St Joseph's 324, 504, 511(2), 528(2)
— St Mary's Cathedral 241
— St Virgil's chapel 241
— Synagogue 528(2)
— Trinity 311(2)
— Wesleyan Methodist 229(2)
Hobart South, St George's 420
Kempton, St Mary's 110
Kirklands Church 173(2)
Launceston:
— Central Baptist 317
— Chalmers Church 494
— Christ Church 246(2)
— Church of the Apostles 304
— Holy Trinity 110, 304, 533, 32(2), 288(2), 595(2)
— Margaret St. Chapel 441(2)
— Memorial Church 373(2)
— Paterson St. Methodist 372(2)
— St Andrew's 430
— St John's 168, 316, 486, 511, 73(2), 303(2), 458(2), 539(2), 597(2), 633(2)
— St John's Sq. Chapel 590(2)
— St Joseph's Margaret St. 304
— St Joseph's 528(2)
— Tamar St. Chapel 350(2)
— Vincent St. Chapel 350(2)
— Wesleyan 290(2)
Longford, Christ Church 25, 26, 304, 490(2), 593(2)
Lymington, St Peter's 257
New Norfolk, St Matthew's 73(2)

New Town Congregational 110
New Town, St John's 24, 109, 174, 357, 429, 35(2), 311(2)
Oatlands, St Peter's 20, 304
Prosser PLains, St John Baptist 256
Richmond, St Luke's 24, 315(2), 527(2)
Rokeby, St Matthew's 110
Ross, Methodist 290(2)
Stanley, St James 428
Swansea, All Saints 329
Westbury, St Andrew's 110
Windermere, St Matthias 304
Churches: Victoria
Eastern Hill, St Peter's 70(2), 521(2)
Geelong, St George's Presbyterian 492(2)
Maryborough, Congregational 29(2)
Melbourne:
— Albert St., Baptist 84(2)
— Camperdown, St Paul's 200(2)
— Coburg, St Paul's 9(2)
— Scots Church 9(2), 271(2), 455(2)
— St Francis' 9(2)
— St James's 521(2)
— St James's Old Cathedral 410(2)
— St Mary of the Angels 9(2)
— St Patrick's Hall 9(2)
— St Paul's 296
— St Peter's 334(2), 447(2)
— Wesley Church, Lonsdale St. 322
Portland, church 541(2)
Churches: Wales
Lampeter, St David's 150
Churches: Western Australia
Albany, St John's 465(2)
Middle Swan, St Mary's 372
Perth: — All Saints' C. of E. 175(2)
— St George's Cathedral 618(2)
— Wesley Church 440(2)
Upper Swan, All Saint's 254(2)
Churches: West Indies
Barbados, St Michael's 364(2)
Clubs: see Organisations:
Colleges: see schools
Colonial governments: see Organisations: Government
Companies: see also Organisations
Companies, business organisations, partnerships, private enterprise.
Adam Turnbull & Son TAS 542(2)
Adelaide Chamber of Commerce SA 251(2)
Adelaide Corn Exchange 175
Adelaide Life Association & Guarantee Co. 166
Adelaide Mining Co. SA 499
Adelaide Smelting Co. SA 296
Albion Mills NSW 354(2)
Albion Mills TAS 246(2)

Alexander Birnie & Co. 104, 129(2)
Alexander & Co. India 307(2)
Alexander & Co. NSW 548(2)
Allen Allen & Hemsley 6
Allen & Son 6
Alliance Assurance Co. NSW 461, 26(2)
Allport & Roberts 9
Allport, Roberts & Allport 9
G.F. Angas & Co. 16
Appleton & Co. NSW 23(2)
Appleton & Jones NSW 23(2)
Archers, Gilles & Co. 24, 25, 486
Argyle Store NSW 84
Aspinall, Brown(e) & Co. ENG & Sydney 461, 232(2)
Australasian Colonial & General Life Assurance Co. 633(2)
Australasian Sugar Co. NSW 38(2)
Australian Agricultural Co. 116, 138, 188, 247, 280, 284, 285, 290, 299, 300, 334, 341, 345, 393, 512, 554, 41(2), 62(2), 63(2), 150(2), 158(2), 196(2), 236(2), 237(2), 241(2), 289(2), 307(2), 308(2), 315(2), 335(2), 337(2), 350(2), 432(2), 485(2), 529(2), 614(2), 616(2)
Australian Auction Co. NSW 505, 25(2), 142(2), 264(2), 392(2)
Australian Brewery, NSW 245
Australian Co. Edinburgh SCT 176(2)
Australian Co. Leith SCT 176(2)
Australian Co. of Sydney & Leith NSW 426(2)
Australian, Colonial & General Life Assurance & Annuity Co. ENG 38(2)
Australian Fire & Life Assurance Co. 73(2), 202(2)
Australian Gaslight Co. 505, 26(2), 109(2), 202(2), 204(2), 230(2), 233(2), 237(2), 284(2), 435(2), 453(2), 464(2), 611(2), 623(2), 633(2)
Australian General Insurance Co. 453(2)
Australian Loan Co. 127, 464(2)
Australian Mining Co. 203(2)
Australian Mutual Provident Society 23(2), 237(2), 269(2), 441(2), 569(2)
Australian Navigation Co. 203(2)
Australian Stationery Warehouse NSW 167(2)
Australian Steam Conveyance Co. 204(2), 611(2)
Australian Steam Navigation Co. 344, 41(2), 233(2), 453(2), 565(2)
Australian Sugar Refining Co. NSW 38(2)
Australian Trust Co. 453(2)
Australian Union Benefit

Society 435(2), 611(2)
Australian Wheat & Flour Co. 542, 575, 435(2)
Australian Wood Co. 140
Bagot, Shakes & Lewis 48
Baring & Co. ENG 290
Barker & Co. 58
Bartlett & Beddone 611(2)
J. & W. Bateman 67
Beck's steam factory, Coventry 178
Bell & Wilkinson 24(2)
Bells & Buchanan 82
Benjamin & Moses 84
Berry & Wollstonecraft NSW 534(2), 620(2)
Bingle & Co. 102
Birmingham & Manchester Warehouse NSW 623(2)
Bitter Beer 487
James J. Blundell & Co. VIC 444
Blaxland's Salt Works 623(2)
Boston & Co. NSW 127, 312(2)
Brisbane Water Steam Co. NSW 203(2)
British & Tasmanian Charcoal Iron Co. TAS 430(2)
British Australian Gold Mining Co. VIC 474(2)
British Australian Steam Navigation Co. 120(2)
British Australian Telegraph Co. SA 378
British Colonial Bank & Loan Co. NSW 450
Britten & Boulger NSW 245(2)
Brown, Cobb & Co. 209
Brown & Gotobed ENG 379
J. & A. Brown NSW 236(2)
Henry Buckle & Co. ENG 372(2)
Buckles, Bagster & Buchanan ENG 72(2)
W.H. Burfod & Sons 179
Burra Mining Co. SA 296
Burwood & Newcastle Smelting Co. NSW 237(2)
Butler, Nutt & Butler, TAS 191
Button's Mill TAS 246(2)
Campbell, Clark & Co. 203
Campbell & Clarke, India 551
Campbell & Co. (NSW) 198, 199, 203, 204, 206, 207, 16(2)
Robert Campbell & Co. 437(2)
Campbells, Hook & Co. India 551
Canada Co. 554, 630(2)
Canada Land Co. Wales Branch 258(2)
Cannon foundry ENG 282(2)
Carr & Rogers NSW 633(2)
Cartwright & Allport 9
Cataract Mills TAS 246(2)
Chace, Chinnery & Co. 208
Chamber of Commerce 204, 207
Chamber of Commerce NSW 25(2), 426(2), 464(2), 525(2), 566(2), 620(2)
Chamber of Commerce TAS 182, 317, 552, 176(2), 269(2)

Chamber of Commerce Vic 590(2)
Cheap Wholesale & Retail Warehouse NSW 625(2)
Cheapside Stores 84
City & Port Railway Co. SA 280(2)
Clyde Co. TAS 317(2), 375(2)
Clyde Company VIC 409(2)
Colchester warehouse NSW 109(2)
Collins & Co. ENG 589(2)
Colonial Railway Co. SA 626(2)
Colonial Sugar Refining Co. NSW 485, 38(2), 233(2)
Colonization Assurance Corporation 122(2), 278(2), 322(2)
Commercial Society of Sydney 547(2)
Company of Apothecaries 248
Constantia Brewery TAS 427(2)
Constantia distillery TAS 301
Cook & Sherwin TAS 441(2)
Cooper & Levey NSW 245, 109(2), 110(2), 142(2), 321(2)
Cornwall Fire & Marine Insurance Co. 3, 290(2)
Cornwall Insurance Co. TAS 305, 590(2)
Coutts & Co. 222
Cressy Co. TAS 517(2)
Cressy Land Co. TAS 430(2)
Crookes & Hudson TAS 261
Currawang mine NSW 237(2)
Dalgety & Co. ENG 441
Dangar, Gedye & Malloch NSW 281
David Jones Ltd. NSW 23(2)
Davidson & Co. (Canton, China) 290
Davy & Co. ENG 295
Dawes & Son ENG 452(2)
Messrs J. & A. Dennistoun, Glasgow 82
Dennys Lascelles Ltd. VIC 88(2)
Derwent & Tamar Fire, Marine & Life Assurance Co. TAS 37(2)
Derwent & Tamar Insurance Co. TAS 230, 164(2)
Derwent brewery TAS 300(2)
Derwent Co. TAS 224(2)
Dickey, Shaw & Co. ENG 163(2)
Donaldson, Wilkinson & Co. ENG 380(2)
Douglas River Coal Co. TAS 407, 564(2)
Douglas River Coal Mining Co. TAS 230(2)
Dowling, Swain & Co. 317
Dutch East India Co. 555, 322(2), 364(2), 556(2)
Dynnyrne Distillery TAS 273(2)
East Coast Steam Navigation Co. TAS 249
East India Co. 7, 26, 56, 83, 112, 156, 158, 178, 203, 216, 221, 228, 232, 235, 250, 275, 276, 290, 305, 316, 332, 357, 428, 435, 527, 529, 551, 575, 14(2), 16(2), 58(2), 59(2), 72(2), 101(2), 116(2), 129(2), 131(2), 174(2) 188(2), 223(2), 257(2), 297(2), 364(2), 365(2), 373(2), 380(2), 403(2), 406(2), 408(2), 419(2), 428(2), 435(2), 451(2), 468(2), 484(2), 495(2), 500(2), 521(2), 538(2), 548(2), 571(2), 578(2), 579(2), 583(2)
Ellinthorp Vale Mill, TAS 225
Enderbys 105
English Railway Co. SA 262(2)
Equitable Building Society TAS 246(2)
Ewing & Reid, Glasgow SCT 176(2)
Fairbairn & Co. NSW 344
Fairlie, Ferguson & Co. ENG 566(2)
Fingal Gold Exploration Co. TAS 231(2)
James Finlay & Co. SCT 257(2)
Fire & Life Assurance Co. NSW 505, 203(2), 392(2), 415(2), 435(2)
Fletcher & Fearnell's Blackwall shipyard ENG 539
Floating Bridge Co. NSW 264(2)
Flower, Salting & Co. NSW 415(2)
Forbes & Co. (India) 24(2)
Fremantle Whaling Co. 66
Gas Co. TAS 317
Gaslight Co. 6, 61, 345, 25(2)
Geelong Melbourne Railway Co. VIC 522(2)
Geraldton Smelting & Mining Co. WA 426(2)
Gilchrist, Alexander & Co. NSW 442
Gilchrist, Watt & Co. NSW 442
Gilchrist, Watt & Sanderson Pty. Ltd. NSW 442
Glasgow & Co. VIC 520
Glasgow Water Works SCT 177(2)
Gleadow & Henty, solicitors 69
Goldsbrough, Mort & Co. 48, 214
Gosling, Browne & Co. NSW 461
Robert Gouger & Co. SA 462
Great Lake Co. VIC 176(2)
Great Northern Mining Co. SA 248
Griffiths & Connolly TAS & VIC 486
Griffiths, Fanning & Co. NSW 485
Griffiths, Gore & Co. NSW 485
Guillan & Symes TAS 246(2)
Haberdashers' Company 109
Hallen & McEvoy 505
Harris & Co. Egypt 261(2)
Harwood & Pincott, Geelong solicitors 70
Heath & Furze ENG 214(2)
Henry Buckle & Co. ENG 372(2)
James Henty & Co. TAS 533
Herries, Farquhar & Co. ENG 290
Hewitt, Gore & Co. VIC 340
Hindmarsh Flourmill SA 197(2)
Hobart Exchange TAS 176(2), 528(2)
Hobart Gas Co. TAS 552
Hobart Town & Launceston Marine Insurance Co. 81
Hobart Town Gas Co. TAS 407
Hobart Town, Launceston & Port Phillip Steam Co. 418
Horse Breeding Co. ENG 534(2)
Horse Breeding Co. TAS 517(2)
Howe & Ross TAS 396(2)
Howe's coach factory, London 15
Howrah distillery, India 551
Hudson Bay Co. CAN 551(2)
Hughes & Hosking NSW 555, 264(2), 509(2)
Hullett & Co. NSW 156(2)
Hunter River Navigation Co. NSW 479(2)
Hunter River Railway Co. NSW 41(2), 237(2)
Hunter River Steam Navigation Co. 344, 490, 236(2), 237(2), 601(2)
Hutchinson, Terry & Co. NSW 245, 110(2)
Illawarra Steam Co. NSW 435(2)
Illawarra Steam Navigation Co. 202(2)
Inglis, Forbes & Co. ENG 523(2)
Jardine, Matheson & Co. China 501(2)
Jones & Riley NSW 500, 24(2), 380(2)
Jones, Riley & Walker NSW 24(2)
Jones & Walker NSW 24(2)
Kable & Underwood NSW 31(2), 36(2), 405(2)
Keir, Buxton & Co NSW 147(2)
Kemp & Gatehouse TAS 429, 40(2)
Kemp & Co. TAS 40(2)
Kennedy & Sons TAS 224
Kerr & Bogle TAS 339
King's Wharf TAS 35(2)
Lachlan & Waterloo Co. NSW 110(2)
Lachlan & Waterloo Flour Mills NSW 613(2)
Lachlan Flour Mills NSW 613(2)
Lamb, Buchanan & Co. ENG 72(2)
Lamb & Co. NSW 72(2)
Launceston Chamber of Commerce 3
Launceston Gas Co. TAS 305, 441(2)
Launceston Marine Insurance

Co. TAS 407
Launceston Shipping Co. TAS
  290(2)
Launceston Steam Navigation
  Co. TAS 261
Leaf, Levers & Co. ENG 224
T. & S. Learmonth TAS 101(2)
Lempriere & Co. 127, 106(2)
R. Lewis & Sons TAS 113(2)
Liddell & Reid SCT 375(2)
Light, Finniss & Co. SA 378,
  117(2)
Lloyds of London 157, 234,
  73(2), 295(2)
London Agency 317
London Agency for Van
  Diemen's Land 24
London, Liverpool & Globe
  Insurance Co. 26(2), 285(2)
London Stock Exchange 417(2)
London Stores (Sydney) 84
Lord, Kable & Underwood
  16(2), 31(2), 129(2), 307(2)
Lord & Williams NSW 130(2),
  598(2)
Maitland Steam Navigation Co.
  NSW 320
Marine Assurance Co. NSW
  305, 25(2)
Marine Insurance Co. NSW
  575, 256(2)
Maude & Robinson, of the
  Cape 307(2)
Melbourne Fire & Marine
  Insurance Co. 425
Melbourne, Mount Alexander
  & Murray River Railway Co.
  VIC 350
Merino Import Co. 243(2),
  438(2)
Mersey & Deloraine Tramway
  Co. TAS 407, 552, 138(2)
Messrs Mosman NSW 263(2)
Metropolitan & Counties
  Permanent Investmt &
  Building Society NSW 23(2)
Milson's Point Ferry Co. NSW
  233(2)
G. Mitchelmore & Co. NSW
  468
J.B. Montefiore & Co. NSW
  251(2)
Mount Morgan Goldmining
  Co. 214
Mount Bischoff Tin Mining Co.
  3
Mutual Benefit Insurance
  Society
Mutual Fire Insurance
  Association NSW 575, 41(2)
Mutual Fire Insurance Co.
  NSW 305, 549, 23(2)
Mutual Fire Insurance Co. TAS
  430(2)
Mutual Insurance Society TAS
  246(2)
Mutual Protection Association
  NSW 162(2)
Napier & Postlethwaite NSW
  493(2)
Neales Bentham SA 280(2)
New Brunswick Land Co ENG

34(2)
New Norfolk Bridge Co. TAS
  35(2), 215(2)
New Town Pottery 441(2)
New Zealand Co. 188, 512, 546,
  463(2)
New Zealand Colonisaton Co.
  188
New Zealand Land Co. 561(2)
Newcastle Chamber of
  Commerce 102
Newcastle Coal & Copper Co.
  237(2)
North Shore Ferry Co. NSW
  233(2)
Old Mill, TAS 225
Paddington House (store)
  NSW 445(2)
Palmer & Co. 240
Thomas Peel & Co. ENG
  110(2)
W.C. Penfold & Co. NSW
  242(2)
Penfolds Wines Ltd. NSW
  630(2)
Peninsular & Orient Steamship
  Co. ENG 285(2)
Plummer, Barham & Co. ENG
  129(2)
T.W. & J. Plummer & Co.
  ENG 31(2)
Raine & Ramsay 207, 360(2),
  361(2)
Read & Bethune TAS 366(2)
Reed & Donald TAS 261
Reed & Duncan TAS 371(2)
Thomas Reibey & Co. NSW &
  TAS 374(2)
Reid, Irving & Co ENG 461
Risby Bros. TAS 224
Ritchie Parker (legal firm, SA)
  383(2)
Robert Gouger & Co. SA 462
Royal Exchange Co. NSW 505,
  204(2)
Royal Exchange NSW 442, 461,
  256(2), 453(2)
Royal South Australian Mining
  Co. 251(2)
Russian American Co. 99(2)
William Rutledge & Co. VIC
  411(2)
St George's Steam Packet Co.
  140
St Paul's Wharf LND 357
Scottish Australian Co. SCT
  257(2)
Shoalhaven Steam Navigation
  Co. NSW 202(2)
Siebe Brod, Holborn ENG 520
Sierra Leone Co. 298
J.T.Simes & Co. ENG 437(2)
Simmons & Marks TAS 445(2)
Sinnett, F. & Co. 216
Sloman & Ashe NSW 451(2)
Smart & Wilson SA 611(2)
Smith Bros. NSW 453(2)
Smith, Croft & Co. NSW
  453(2)
J. & J. Solomon TAS 458(2)
South Australian Co. 16, 17,
  128, 378, 442-3, 525, 2(2),

117(2), 177(2), 222(2), 379(2),
  464(2), 480(2), 481(2), 497(2)
South Australian Cattle Co
  440(2)
South Australian Land Co. 15,
  47, 456, 462, 535(2), 560(2)
South Australian Mining
  Association 7, 166, 64(2),
  280(2)
Spode's factory, Liverpool
  ENG 467
Staniforth & Gosling ENG 460
Steam Mill NSW 505
Steam Navigation Co. VIC
  447(2)
Steamboat Store TAS 415(2)
Stephens & Soakes 102, 242(2)
Stock Exchange of Melbourne
  VIC 590(2)
Stock Exchange of SA 251(2)
Strachan & Co. Ltd. VIC
  492(2)
Struth's Wharf NSW 493(2)
Supply Mills TAS 246(2)
Swanston & Willis VIC 501(2)
Sydney Alliance Assurance Co.
  275, 485, 73(2)
Sydney & Van Diemen's Land
  Packet Co. 49(2), 360(2)
Sydney Chamber of Commerce
  245, 461, 73(2)
Sydney Exchange 58
Sydney Exchange & Assurance
  Co. NSW 233(2)
Sydney Exchange Co. 38(C),
  73(C), 453(2), 453(2C)
Sydney Ferry Co. NSW 203(2),
  237(2), 264(2).
Sydney Fire Insurance Co.
  NSW 41(2)
Sydney Floating Bridge Co.
  204(2)
Sydney Gas Co. 345
Sydney Ice Co. NSW 520
Sydney Marine Insurance Co.
  NSW 26(2)
Sydney Railroad Co. NSW
  73(2)
Sydney Railway Co. 58, 388,
  41(2), 123(2), 452(2)
Tamar Brewery TAS 487
Tamar lime works TAS 304
Tamar Steam Navigation Co.
  TAS 328, 94(2)
Tasmanian Fire & Life
  Insurance Co. 81, 138(2)
Tasmanian Fire, Life & Marine
  Insurance Co. 164(2)
Tasmanian Insurance Co. 552
Tasmanian Permanent Building
  & Investment Association 356
Tasmanian Permanent Trustees
  & Executors 246(2)
Tasmanian Steam Navigation
  Co. 230, 74(2)
Tasmanian Store 458(2)
J. Tegg & Co. NSW 505(2)
Tegg & Co. (Cheapside ENG)
  520
Tennant & Trail RSA 548
Thomas Peel & Co. ENG
  110(2)

Thomas Reibey & Co. NSW &
  TAS 374(2)
Thomas & William Ward ENG
  307(2)
Thomas Wilson & Co. ENG
  415(2)
Thompson & Giles NSW 23(2)
Thomson & Cookney TAS
  528(2)
Tod's counting house ENG
  463(2)
Tomlins & Sloman NSW
  623(2)
Travis & Leake ENG 100(2)
Trustees Executors & Agency
  Co. Ltd. VIC 401
Tucker, Cracknell & Fells NSW
  26(2)
Union Assurance Co. NSW
  256(2)
United Fire & Life Insurance
  Co. of Sydney 41(2)
Van Dieman's Land Co. 440
Van Diemen's Land Assurance
  Association 137(2)
Van Diemen's Land Assurance
  Co. 176(2)
Van Diemen's Land Co. 3, 36,
  128, 241, 270, 287, 406, 457,
  492, 528, 531, 554, 3(2), 27(2),
  170(2), 230(2), 386(2), 429(2),
  467(2), 575(2)
Van Diemen's Land Insurance
  Co TAS 441(2)
Victoria Mills, NSW 490
Victorian Fire & Marine
  Insurance Co. 350, 252(2)
Victorian Life & General
  Assurance Society 334(2)
Waddington & Smith ENG 349
T.B.Walker, Shipping ENG
  372(2)
Walker Bros. & Co. ENG
  566(2)
William Walker & Co. NSW
  565(2), 566(2)
Thomas & William Ward, LND
  307(2)
Warren & Scott NSW 426(2)
Waterloo Co. NSW 245
Waterloo Mill TAS 225
Waterloo Warehouse NSW
  245, 110(2), 142(2)
Weavers' Company ENG
  216(2)
Were, J.B. & Son VIC 590(2)
West Australian Co. 477
West Australian Land Co. ENG
  619(2)
Western Australian Co. 576,
  488(2), 489(2), 561(2)
Western Port Coal Co. VIC
  252(2)
Wilcock & Clark, ENG 224
William Rutledge & Co. VIC
  411(2)
William Walker & Co. NSW
  565(2), 566(2)
Williamson & Thomas 317
Wilson & Curtis 611(2)
Thomas Wilson & Co. ENG
  415(2)

Convicts:
see: Convicts: Places of Trials
see: Penal settlements
see: Occupations Index: convict
see: Transportation
Convicts: Miscellaneous
  31, 42, 48, 62, 67, 74, 109,
  123, 126, 145, 147, 152, 170,
  173, 178, 215, 217, 285, 354,
  360, 365, 368, 383, 405, 430,
  439, 468, 491, 526, 527, 559,
  560, 574, 575, 4(2), 19(2),
  36(2), 65(2), 86(2), 87(2),
  95(2), 108(2), 134(2), 135(2),
  140(2), 266(2), 272(2), 299(2),
  327(2), 328(2), 387(2), 393(2),
  419(2), 444(2), 457(2), 502(2),
  508(2), 523(2), 539(2), 546(2),
  552(2), 570(2), 574(2), 622(2)
assignment 249(2)
Bigge Report 99-101
corporal punishment 165(2),
  191(2)
emancipists 426, 506, 87(2),
  331(2), 338(2), 404(2), 509(2),
  520(2), 571(2). 580(2)
emancipists, attitudes toward
  83, 89-91, 99, 206, 246, 263,
  369, 464, 11(2), 17(2), 25(2),
  179(2), 186(2), 191(2), 243(2),
  370(2), 585(2)
England 217(2)
female 173, 215, 226, 327,
  19(2), 259(2), 373(2)
French Canadian 352(2)
Indian convicts to Mauritius
  399(2)
Irish 550, 20(2), 509(2)
Stocks 175(2)
New South Wales 131, 214,
  217, 218, 234, 240, 245, 246,
  262, 293, 305, 309, 312, 320,
  327, 485, 503, 517, 558, 569,
  170(2), 191(2), 193(2), 215(2),
  259(2), 273(2), 302(2), 305(2),
  312(2), 329(2)
— Assignment Board 285
— Irish 146, 258, 571, 599(2),
  610(2)
— women 215, 226
Norfolk Island 264
penal reform 186(2)
Queensland 233, 250
Tasmania 42, 68, 78, 134, 264,
  273, 328, 560, 71(2), 170(2),
  217(2), 230(2), 294(2), 612(2)
Transportation 8, 107, 55(2),
  286(2), 327(2), 339(2), 503(2)
Transportation, abolition of
  106, 204, 206, 386, 336(2),
  375(2), 407(2), 418(2), 445(2)
Transportation, opposition to
  renewal 275(2)
treadmill 261(2)
Western Australia 382
Convicts: Places of Trials
Bradford 126(2)
Chester 597(2)
Clonmel TIP 217(2), 234(2),
  294(2)
Colchester Q. Sessions 493(2)
Cork Summer Assizes 343

Cornwall Assizes 404(2)
Coventry Assizes 365
Croydon Sessions 259(2)
Croydon SRY 354
Dorchester Assizes 132(2)
Dublin 234(2), 304(2), 388(2)
Edinburgh 266(2)
Edinburgh Court of Justiciary
  596(2)
Essex Assizes 539(2)
Glasgow 170(2)
Gloucester 485, 403(2)
Hereford 71(2)
Hertford 570(2)
Huntington 101(2)
Jedburgh 519(2)
Kent Assizes 458(2)
King's County 371(2)
Kingston SRY 467(2)
Lancashire Q. Sessions 126, 147
Lancaster Assizes 313(2)
Lincoln ENG 4(2)
London Gaol Delivery 576(2)
Maidstone 546(2)
Manchester Q. Sessions 128(2)
Middlesex ENG 362(2)
Middlesex Gaol Del. 217, 428
Monmouth 601(2)
Newgate 527(2)
New Sarum Assizes 547(2C)
Northampton Q. Sessions 467
Old Bailey, London 63, 78, 109,
  145, 170, 174, 240, 293, 517,
  574, 19(2), 86(2), 110(2),
  139(2), 201(2), 278(2), 388(2),
  444(2), 448(2), 457(2), 458(2),
  552(2), 579(2), 617(2)
Perth SCT 312(2)
Salford Q. Sessions LAN
  508(2)
Salop Assizes 140(2)
Shrewsbury 394(2)
Shrewsbury Assizes 259(2)
Southampton Assizes 291(2)
Stafford 373(2)
Staffordshire Assizes 582(2)
Suffolk Summer Assizes 215
Surrey Assizes 66(2)
Sussex Assizes 174, 377(2)
Thetford NFK 31(2)
Tipperary 421
Warminster Sessions 283(2)
Warwick Assizes 123, 178, 490,
  558, 533(2)
Warwickshire Q. Sessiosns 345
Waterford 294(2)
Westminster 383, 389(2)
Wexford 159(2)
Wigan LAN 610(2)
Winchester Assizes 146
York Assizes 560
Conchology 19
Court Cases: 77(2), 98(2)
Attorney General v. Brown
  616(2)
Bank of Australasia v. Breillat
  616(2)
Baughan, John v. New South
  Wales Corps 571
Bradley v. Arthur 131(2)
Bullock v. Dodds 374
Burn v. Howe 373, 427, 628(2)

Child (NSW) 38(2)
Court Martial 47(2), 580(2),
    628(2)
Eagar v. de Mestre 374
First civil suit 31(2)
Hall v. Douglass 148(2)
Hill, John 5(2)
Laidley v. Hall 69(2)
Lord v. Rowcroft 128(2)
Macarthur, John (NSW) 39(2)
Macdonald v. Levy 184, 396-7
Marsden v. Campbell 100, 17(2)
Nichols, Isaac (NSW) 46(2)
Philo Free libel case 324
R. v. Farrell & Dingle 478(2)
R. v. Paxton et al 244
Raine v. Macarthur 396
Sudds-Thompson 178(2),
    256(2)
Symmonds v. Morgan 247(2)
Wentworth v. Mansfield 478(2)
Courts: listed geographically
Courts: Bermuda
Vice-Admiralty Court 39
Courts: Canada
Supreme Court of
    Newfoundland 392
Courts: England
Chancery 426, 475(2)
Common Pleas 313, 196(2),
    251(2), 627(2)
Court of the Exchequer 627(2)
Criminal Jurisdiction 426
High Court 395
House of Lords 130(2)
King's Bench 374, 426, 196(2),
    370(2), 457(2), 463(2)
King's Bench Division 200(2)
Middlesex Gaol Delivery 217
Midland Circuit 180, 164(2)
Old Bailey 63, 240, 293, 517,
    574, 388(2)
Oxford Circuit 244
Privy Council 208, 371, 376,
    15(2), 81(2), 82(2), 479(2),
    604(2)
Quarter Sessions, ENG 184
Supreme Court 426
Vice-Chancellor's Court 343,
    273(2)
Westminster Hall 318
Courts: Gibraltar
Court of Civil Pleas 375
Courts: India
District Court, Nellore 575
Supreme Court 337
Supreme Court of Calcutta 511
Courts: Ireland
Equity Courts 51(2)
Prerogative Court 51(2)
Courts: Norfolk Island
Criminal Court 181, 536, 490(2)
Courts: New South Wales
Appeals Court 463, 628(2)
Bathurst court house 95(2)
Berrima court house 112(2)
Civil Court 88, 237, 263, 290,
    421, 328(2), 330(2)
Civil Jurisdiction 204, 16(2)
Consistorial Court 211(2)
Criminal Court 40, 88, 145,
    226, 237, 313, 393, 426, 460,

463, 568, 39(2), 46(2), 52(2),
    98(2), 283(2), 328(2), 330(2),
    397(2), 443(2)
Darlinghurst court house
    112(2)
District Court 536
Equity Court 93, 81(2)
Governor's Court 426, 500,
    561, 16(2), 45(2), 254(2),
    578(2), 580(2), 628(2)
Hartley court house 112(2)
Industrial Arbitration Court
    536
Judge Advocate's Court 219,
    263
Land Commissioners' Court
    204(2)
Lieut. Governor's Court 421
Magistrates' Court 22
Norfolk Island 107
Parramatta court house 112(2)
Petty Sessions 91, 149(2)
Quarter Sessions 55, 153, 196,
    393, 407, 427, 143(2), 259(2),
    265(2), 319(2), 359(2), 378(2),
    389(2), 477(2), 513(2), 571(2)
Quarter Sessions, Windsor
    221(2)
Requests 9, 111, 133, 300, 315,
    381, 407, 495, 261(2), 378(2),
    477(2), 511(2), 512(2)
Richmond court house 73(2)
Supreme Court 55, 75, 88, 91,
    94, 149, 151, 158, 184, 196,
    200, 208, 219, 242, 263, 275,
    284, 294, 312, 317, 318, 319,
    320, 367, 374, 393, 395, 396,
    427, 472, 494, 495, 38(2),
    52(2), 81(2), 82(2), 111(2),
    134(2), 169(2), 192(2), 202(2),
    203(2), 212(2), 232(2), 237(2),
    251(2), 256(2), 293(2), 319(2),
    400(2), 435(2), 455(2), 472(2),
    477(2), 478(2), 508(2), 513(2),
    567(2), 571(2), 585(2), 603(2),
    610(2), 629(2)
Supreme Court of Civil &
    Ecclesiastical Jurisdiction
    395(2)
Supreme Court of Civil
    Judicature 373, 393
Sydney court house 502(2)
Sydney Police Court 392(2)
Vice Admiralty 11, 88, 117, 392,
    396, 52(2), 229(2), 254(2),
    328(2), 627(2)
Courts: Queensland
Petty Sessions 448(2)
Supreme Court 513(2)
Courts: Scotland
Court of Session 81(2)
Supreme Court 227
Courts: South Africa
Supreme Court, Cape Colony
    184, 375
Vice Admiralty Court 548
Courts: South Australia
Appeals 611(2)
Insolvency 201(2)
Quarter Sessions 472(2)
Resident Magistrate's Court
    379

Supreme Court 380, 499, 14(2),
    201(2), 384(2), 624(2)
Courts: Tasmania
Criminal Court 168, 35(2)
Deputy Judge Advocate's Court
    270
Governor's Court 511
Hobart Court House 74(2)
Hobart Town General Sessions
    552
Insolvency Court 164(2)
Launceston Court House 418,
    350(2)
Licensing Court 214, 452(2)
Lieut. Governor's Court 2, 104,
    171, 240, 392, 458, 126(2),
    366(2), 395(2), 415(2)
Medical Examiners 297(2),
    434(2)
Quarter Sessions 32, 551,
    215(2), 267(2), 396(2), 421(2),
    434(2), 516(2), 595(2)
Requests 2, 32, 300(C), 302,
    356, 492, 551, 214(2), 258(2),
    267(2), 315(2), 595(2)
Supreme Court 2, 77, 156, 168,
    302, 373, 437, 454, 486, 551,
    35(2), 40(2), 100(2), 132(2),
    214(2), 247(2), 314(2), 319(2),
    336(2), 452(2), 462(2), 472(2),
    542(2)
Vice Admiralty Court 462(2)
Courts: Victoria
Petty Sessions 543(2)
Requests 112, 65(2)
Supreme Court 495, 15(2),
    334(2)
Courts: Western Australia
Civil Court 175(2), 253(2)
Petty Sessions 174(2)
Quarter Sessions 174(2), 253(2)
Requests 74(2), 175(2)
Small Debts Courts 175(2)
Courts: West Indies
Supreme Court, Jamaica 530
Vice Admiralty Court
    (Trinidad) 99
Cricket 32, 216, 533, 340(2),
    416(2)
Crime: see Convicts
Currency, NSW 577(2)
Customs Duty 246, 476, 483, 498,
    16(2), 176(2), 190(2), 196(2),
    335(2), 525(2), 580(2), 616(2)
Depressions:
1816-17. 54(2), 563(2)
1820's. 283, 541, 70(2), 148(2),
    176(2), 381(2)
1826-28. 371(2), 620(2)
1840's. 16, 24, 58, 97, 140, 175,
    185, 207, 216-7, 221, 224,
    228-9, 231, 250, 275, 311,
    345-6, 401, 414, 419, 426, 440,
    443, 450, 463, 476, 485, 490,
    497, 532, 533, 555, 577, 4(2),
    5(2), 23(2), 25(2), 36(2),
    37(2), 63(2), 70(2), 91(2),
    108(2), 135(2), 141(2), 142(2),
    149(2), 181(2), 257(2), 293(2),
    302(2), 325(2), 336(2), 348(2),
    354(2), 359(2), 379(2), 428(2),
    433(2), 441(2), 452(2), 455(2),

492(2), 501(2), 512(2), 566(2),
576(2), 612(2), 617(2), 626(2)
Diseases:
  aque 508
  apoplexy 124, 417, 537, 74(2)
  asthma 350, 408, 365(2)
  cataract 225
  catarrhal fever 522
  cholera 240, 359, 422, 508,
    434(2)
  consumption 277
  deafness 537(2)
  diabetes 34(2)
  diptheria 502, 453(2)
  dropsy 26, 89, 285
  dysentry 170, 351, 314(2)
  epilepsy 156, 517
  gout 53(2), 618(2)
  heart disease 273, 465(2)
  hepatitis 508
  hypochondria 183, 558(2)
  influenza 183, 215, 523
  jaundice 577(2)
  kidney disease 22
  melancholia 146(2)
  pneumonia 114, 278, 435
  pulmonary disease 257, 595(2)
  rheumatic fever 249
  rheumatism 194, 44(2), 622(2)
  sandy blight 326(2)
  scarlet fever 467(2)
  scurvy 10(2), 497(2), 551(2)
  smallpox 22, 502, 12(2), 60(2)
  syphilis (nasal) 70
  tetanus 576(2)
  tuberculosis 45, 438, 515
  typhoid 110, 321, 354
  typhus 51, 359(2)
  whooping cough 268
  yellow fever 226, 348
Drama 98(2), 340(2) see also
  Theatre, Opera
Druidism 550(2)
Duels 51, 83, 112, 144, 199, 234,
  355, 475, 503, 506, 563, 14(2),
  49(2), 59(2), 154(2), 164(2),
  171(2), 241(2), 310(2), 318(2),
  321(2), 334(2), 349(2), 396(2),
  398(2), 455(2), 503(2), 572(2),
  580(2)
Dynamometer 324(2)
Early settlement:
  Norfolk Island 56(2)
  NSW 283(2) 567, 569
  — first settlement 226, 236,
    237, 297
  — Newcastle 223(2)
  — Parramatta 12
  New Zealand 186
  Northern Territory 57, 61, 148
  South Australia 15, 16, 248,
    462, 540, 557, 116(2), 262(2),
    281(2)
  Tasmania 136, 171, 553, 566,
    3(2), 264(2)
  — first land grant to a woman
    181
  — first settlement 136, 227,
    239, 240
  Victoria 14, 68, 126, 134, 226,
    240, 439, 447, 531, 545, 547,
    566, 125(2), 223(2)

  — Melbourne, foundation of
    68
  WA 14, 155, 236, 245, 576, 5(2),
    195(2), 535(2)
East India Co.: see Companies
Economics:
  see Customs Duties
  see Depressions
  see Free Trade
  interest rates 251(2), 257(2)
  laissez faire 135(2)
  price control 58(2)
  stamp duty (newspapers) 501
Education: see also Schools:
  Miscellaneous references 209,
    210, 211, 225, 387(2), 432(2)
  Board of National Education in
    Ireland 470(2)
  British and Foreign Schools
    system 20
  England, Council of Education
    136(2)
  Fellenberg system 211
  Irish National System 30, 35,
    58, 160, 211, 305, 450, 451,
    179(2), 204(2), 244(2), 267(2),
    275(2), 338(2), 340(2), 343(2),
    361(2), 362(2), 470(2), 533(2),
    616(2)
  Lancastrian plan 260
  Madras system of instruction
    368(2)
  monitorial system of education
    252
  National system: see Irish
    National System
  Parochial schools 35
  reform 30
  Stanley's Irish School system
    544(2)
  teacher rotation 432(2)
Education: New South Wales
  6, 11, 13, 113, 131, 209, 210,
  397, 402, 422, 450, 514, 575,
  25(2), 44(2), 59(2), 76(2),
  135(2), 162(2), 183(2), 257(2),
  275(2), 342(2), 346(2), 368(2),
  513(2)
  Catholic 165(2), 342(2)
  denominational 275(2)
  Irish National education 179(2)
  Irish National School System
    131, 160, 247, 305, 450, 83(2),
    162(2), 309(2), 338(2), 340(2),
    362(2), 455(2), 533(2), 616(2)
  Irish system 451, 204(2)
  Madras system 209
  non-denominational 135(2)
  schools 13, 48, 131, 209, 210
  schools (C.of E.) 11
  secular education 247
  state aid 153, 160, 535, 6(2),
    83(2)
Education: South Australia
  384(2), 440(2), 616(2)
  state aid 201(2), 262(2), 384(2)
Education: Tasmania
  29, 30, 347, 414, 574, 44(2),
  94(2), 118(2), 287(2)
  Board of Education 32(2)
  denominational system 505
  schools 20, 29, 30

  state aid 20, 287(2)
Education: Victoria 399
  bush schools 399
  Irish National system of
    education 244(2)
  public education 399
  state aid 399
Education: WA 6(2), 278(2)
Electricity 246(2)
Embezzlement 599(2)
Engineering 57, 219, 224, 250
Engineers see Occupations
England:
  see: Cemeteries — England
  see: Churches — England
  see: Houses etc. — England
  see: Newspapers — England
  see: Organisations — England
  see: Places Index — England
  see: Politics — England
  see: Religion — England
  see: Schools — England
  see: Universities — England
Entomology 182(2)
Ethnology 19
Eucalyptus oil 297(2)
Excise (spirits) 335(2) see also
    Customs duty
Exhibitions, fairs, shows:
  Australian Floral and
    Horticultural Society 289(2)
  Associated Artists Exhibition
    592(2)
  Eng. Brighton Flower Show 234
  Eng. Exhibition 1862 231(2)
  Eng. Great Exhibition 342
  Eng. London Exhibition, 1851.
    196
  Eng. London Exhibition 1862
    153(2)
  France. Paris Exhibition 54(2),
    431(2)
  France. Paris International
    Exhibition 1867. 527(2),
    630(2)
  New South Wales:
  — Broughton exhibition 206
  — Exhibition of 1862. 41(2)
  — Exhibition of fine arts 1849.
    230
  — Floral and Horticultural
    Society shows 1840 & 1841.
    431(2)
  — Forrest exhibition 206
  — Grand Complimentary
    Benefit 446(2)
  — Horticultural Show 464(2)
  — Hunter River Show 321
  — International Exhibition
    75(2)
  — Paris Exhibition 276(2)
  — Regatta 400(2)
  — Salting Exhibition 415(2)
  Qld. Gayndah 93(2)
  Qld. Maryborough Show 93(2)
  Tas. Launceston Art Exhibition
    493(2)
  Victoria:
  — Ballarat Eisteddfod 515(2)
  — Intercolonial Exhibition
    1867. 474(2)
  — Melbourne Exhibition 520,

531(2), 590(2)
— Melbourne Exhibition of
Australian Gems 1865. 474(2)
— Melbourne show 125
— Villiers & Heytesbury
Agricultural Society Show
1854 412(2)
WA. York Fair 219(2)
Exploration: Miscellaneous
195, 266, 267, 269, 282, 243,
452, 315(2)
Antarctic 83, 105
Arctic 83, 315(2), 471(2)
French Pacific exploration 171
geophysical 34(2)
north west passage 412
Pacific 123, 243, 85(2), 357(2),
551(2), 552(2)
Exploration:
Australia 243, 389-391, 29(2),
497(2)
— Dieppe maps 358
— discovery of 277
— Geology 29(2)
New South Wales:
— Misc: 62, 64, 116, 195, 266,
284, 360, 466, 468, 547, 564,
96(2), 181(2), 183(2), 238(2),
239(2), 240(2), 306(2), 318(2),
377(2), 495(2), 496(2), 531(2),
597(2)
— Blue Mountains, NSW 62,
64, 116
Northern Territory 266
Papua New Guinea 111, 167(2)
Queensland:
— Misc: 22, 111, 266, 7(2),
43(2), 103(2), 108(2), 124(2),
167(2), 240(2)
— geographical surveys 62(2)
— Great Barrier Reef 578
— Zoological 168(2)
South Australia 57, 362, 389,
2(2), 117(2)
Tasmania:
— Misc: 64, 137, 410, 468, 517,
27(2), 37(2), 170(2), 430(2),
460(2), 551(2), 552(2)
— Bass Strait 272(2)
— French 71
— Geological 114(2)
USA year 1838. 279
Victoria:
— Misc: 556, 564, 183(2),
272(2)
— French 71
— Gippsland 572
Western Australia:
— Misc: 266, 277, 103(2),
253(2), 391(2), 486(2), 556(2)
— Dutch 555
— French 72
Faith healing 474(2)
Federation 408(2), 591(2)
Ferry Service TAS
First Fleet to Australia 11, 31, 74,
150, 157, 173, 218, 226, 237,
242, 264, 288, 297, 349, 353,
354, 360, 491, 517, 562, 567,
10(2), 12(2), 17(2), 20(2),
31(2), 139(2), 281(2), 309(2),
327(2), 363(2), 397(2), 404(2),

427(2), 442(2), 443(2), 444(2),
453(2), 462(2), 467(2), 469(2),
506(2), 573(2), 575(2), 582(2),
594(2), 610(2), 623(2) See
also: Second and Third Fleet.
Floods (NSW 1806) 220(2)
Forgery 574(2)
Fossils 362(2)
Free trade 386, 484, 29(2),
523(2), 526(2)
France:
see: Places Index — France
see: Organisations: France
Gaelic language 399
Gambling 405(2)
Gardening 186(2)
Gardens: see Organisations:
Miscellaneous
Gas companies: see Companies
Geology 29(2), 102(2), 114(2),
494(2), 521(2)
Germany:
see: Organisations — Germany
see: Places Index — Germany
see: Religion — Germany
see: Universities — Germany
Goldfields:
California 23, 142, 528(2)
NSW 387, 514-5, 275(2)
Vic 26, 278, 322, 370, 388, 440,
444, 497, 91(2), 126(2),
160(2), 222(2), 244(2), 349(2),
410(2), 423(2), 474(2), 606(2),
625(2)
— Dunolly 28(2)
— Gippsland 543(2)
— Maryborough 28(2)
— pioneer 184(2)
Warden of 160(2)
Governments, government
departments, boards,
committees
see: Organisations: Government
Graphic arts 410(2)
Great Britain: see England,
Wales, Scotland
Hansom cab 270(2)
Harvesting machine 379(2)
Health 1
Aboriginal 22
homeopathic 414(2)
infant mortality 1
mental 607(2)
smallpox epidemic 22
vaccination 12(2), 60(2), 419(2)
see also Diseases
see also Hospitals
see also Occupations Index:
doctors, medical practitioners,
surgeons
see also Public health
Highway robbery 502, 560,
584(2)
Historiography 591(2)
Homeopathic medicine 414(2)
Homosexuality 347, 457
Horse Breeding, racing 572,
36(2), 96(2)
Horses:
Akbar 428(2)
Archer 305
Captain 221

Clydesdales 271, 411(2)
Creamy (horse) 523(2)
Dover 428(2)
Gig 583(2)
Hadji Baba 257
Hector 207
Iris 400(2)
Peter 423
St Andrew 276
St George 276, 277
Shetland ponies 411(2)
Speedy 207
Suffolk Punch 271
Sultan 21(2)
Toss 428(2)
Trumpet 428(2)
Young Pompey 217(2)
Horticulture 179(2), 181(2),
218(2)
Hospitals: Miscellaneous
British military hospital,
Belgium 235(2)
Canberra Community Hospital,
ACT 254(2)
Fever Hospital & Infirmary IRL
314
Lisbon Hospital 463(2)
Sir John Watson's Hospital 499
Swansea Infirmary WLS 514(2)
Hospitals: England
Bethlem Hospital (Bedlam)
624(2)
Charing Cross Hospital 577
Chelsea & Brompton
Dispensary LND 134
Chelsea Hospital 250, 577
Dalston German Hospital,
LND 114(2C)
Greenwich Hospital 170, 34(2),
316(2), 622(2)
Guy's Hospital, London 295
Hanwell Asylum 134
Haslar Hospital 316(2)
Marine Infirmary, Woolwich,
ENG 156
Middlesex Hospital 85
Royal Lying-in Hospital,
Golden Square 514(2)
Royal Naval Hospital 47(2)
St Bartholomew's Hospital 1,
85, 295
St Bernard's Hospital 134
Hospitals: New South Wales
Colonial Hospital 27(2)
Dame Eadith Walker
Convalescent Hospital for
Men 565(2)
Dispensary 359(2)
Gladesville hospital 112(2)
Goulburn Hospital 274(2)
Homeopathic Dispensary
569(2)
Liverpool Asylum 540(2)
Liverpool Hospital 472, 389(2)
Lunatic Asylum 499(2)
Maitland Hospital 231, 232
Parramatta Hospital 27, 401(2)
Prince Alfred Hospital 197,
540(2)
Rum Hospital 471, 139(2),
380(2), 581(2)
St Vincent's Hospital 337,

339(2), 346(2), 512(2)
Sydney Dispensary 113, 304,
  427, 555, 166(2), 178(2),
  538(2), 623(2)
Sydney Hospital 260, 315,
  113(2), 235(2), 237(2), 581(2)
Sydney Infirmary 1, 549, 2(2),
  166(2), 280(2), 527(2)
Tarban Creek asylum 608(2)
Thomas Walker Convalescent
  Hospital 565(2)
Hospitals: Queensland
  Brisbane General Hospital 51,
  295, 448(2)
Hospitals: South Australia
  Adelaide Hospital 335
  Edinburgh New Town
    Dispensary 268(2)
Hospitals: Tasmania
  convict hospital 38(2)
  Cornwall Free Hospital 441(2)
  Cornwall Infirmary 134
  General Hospital TAS 317
  Hobart Colonial Hospital
    434(2)
  Hobart General Hospital 213,
    258(2)
  Hobart Hospital 502, 427(2),
    434(2)
  Hospital for the Insane 254
  Launceston Colonial Hospital
    434(2)
  Launceston General Hospital
    441(2)
  Launceston, St John's Hospital
    355(2)
  Longford Hospital 534(2)
  New Norfolk Hospital 297(2)
  public hospital 590(2)
  Queen's Asylum for destitute
    children 454
  St John's Hospital 454, 290(2)
  St Mary's Hospital 35(2),
    138(2), 559(2)
  St Mary's Hospital, Hobart 78
Hospitals: Victoria
  Austin Hospital, Melbourne 43
  Kew Asylum 515(2)
  Melbourne Benevolent Asylum
    70(2)
  Melbourne Hospital 350, 544,
    9(2), 95(2), 514(2), 515(2),
    521(2)
  Melbourne Lunatic Asylum 273
  Royal Melbourne Hospital
    93(2)
  Yarra Bend Lunatic Asylum 273
Hottentots 130
Houses of Parliament: see
  Organisations: Government
Houses of Assembly: see
  Organisations: Government
Houses, Properties, Farms,
  Estates, Stations — listed
  geographically
Houses etc: England
  Aigburth Hall 134(2)
  Ampthill Park BDF 407
  Angel Court 452(2)
  Appley House 575
  Ardencaple Castle 118(2)
  Armitstead Hall 407

Ashcombe Park 136(2)
Ashfold Lodge 291
Basing House 125
Becket 299
Bellevue House 269
Bentley Lodge 299
Benton House, NBL 99
Berry Pomeroy Castle 344
Buckingham Palace 409(2)
Buriton Manor 439(2)
Burswood KEN 616(2)
Bushel Hall SAL 333
Castle Hill 485
Castle Mona 49(2)
Chulmleigh Hall 431
Clapham House 92(2)
Clifton 367
Courthouse Farm 199(2)
Crosby Lodge 244(2)
Cumberland House 573(2)
Denston Hall 599(2)
Denton Court 38(2)
Dews Hall, Essex 250
Dinton House 630(2)
Dover Castle 188(2)
Dunorlan Villa 372(2)
Efford manor 226
Eldon 335
Ellinthorp Hall 224
Ettingshall Park STS 371, 372
Exeter Hall, London 295, 462
Frogmore House 461
Garter Court 169
Gategill KKD 293(2)
Glasshayes 326(2)
Glendon SRY 428(2)
Grange Villa 466(2)
Groombridge Place KEN
  616(2)
Grosvenor Hotel LND 101
Hadleigh ESS 285(2)
Hagley Hall 143(2)
Hare Hatch House BRK
  633(2), 634(2)
Henham Hall 400(2)
Highgate 402
Hopley House, Alresford HAM
  499
Howard Lodge 480(2)
Howick 484
Howick House NBL 480
Huish Cottage 218(2)
Hutton Court 106
Inwood Lodge 83(2)
Kensington Palace 631(2)
Kirkham Abbey 305(2)
Knowsley Hall LAN 442
Knowsley Park 470(2)
Lambeth Palace 160
Little Aston Hall STS 270(2)
Longcrofts Hall 26
Lumley Castle 233
Marwell Hall 275
Merly House 589(2)
Moorland Cottage 107
Moulsey 87
Newtown House 460
Norley House 32
Over Hall 48
Paddington House 547(2)
Pembroke Lodge 408(2)
Portman Market 611(2)

Prior Park 21
Rhodes Hall 564(2)
Ridge Hall 453
Seacombe 481(2)
Segenhoe manor, Ridgmont
  BDF 195(2)
Shenstone Park 258
Shipley Hall DBY 384
Silverlands 415(2)
Somerset House 460
Stoke Hall 354
Stoke Lodge 466(2)
Stratfieldsaye 159
Sudbrooke Park 554
The Hermitage 574(2)
The Mill 507(2)
Totteridge Grange 285(2)
Vernals Farm 326(2)
Walreddon Manor 364
West Felton Hall 273(2)
Weston Zoyland 228
Winchmore Hall MDX 293(2)
Windsor Castle 299(2)
Yarra House 9(2)
Houses etc: France
  Chateau de Haget 568(2)
Houses etc: India
  Staffa Lodge 188(2)
Houses etc: Ireland
  Castle Talbot 108
  Deer Park 182
  Dublin Castle 278
  Fyanstown Castle 579(2)
  Geraldine House, Kilkee 383
  Hollymount House 529
  Kilcroan 93(2)
  Killymoon Castle TYR 557(2)
  Knockbarragh Park DOW
    557(2)
  Lewis Hill 557(2)
  Malahide Castle 172, 502(2)
  Thornfield 128
Houses etc: Jamaica
  Harding Hall 530
Houses etc: New South Wales
  Aberglasslyn 543
  Agnes Bank 519(2)
  Ajamatong 274(2)
  Alloway Bank 335(2), 362(2).
    500(2)
  Annandale Farm 22(2)
  Annandale House 19(2)
  Apsley House 74
  Apsley Lodge 142(2)
  Arajoel 304(2)
  Ashfield Park 548(2)
  Askrigg 126
  Austral Edcen 553(2)
  Bahtahbah
  Barbigal 332
  Barham 527(2), 554(2)
  Barren Garry 304(2)
  Bayly Park 76
  Beardy Plains 4(2)
  Beckham station 247
  Belaringar 451(2)
  Belle Vue 121(2)
  Belmont 79, 290
  Ben Bullen 331
  Bendenine 293(2)
  Bengalla 428(2)
  Berkeley 16(2)

Berry Park 344
Biragambil 401(2)
Birling Gap 134(2)
Blackdown 524
Blairmore 168(2)
Bligh House 206
Boamboll 151
Bombira Hill 96(2)
Boonara 24(2)
Boree Station 239(2), 360(2)
Boulevarde, The 337
Box Hill 508(2)
Box Hill Farm 381
Brimbine 4(2)
Brisbane Meadow 573
Brooking 304(2)
Brougham Lodge 319
Brownlow Hill 181(2)
Brucedale 499(2)
Brush Farm 116, 258, 259, 550,
  130(2)
Buckingham 573
Bukkulla 630(2)
Bulgamatta 136
Bungarribee 1(2)
Burgalia 524
Burrin Farm 308
Burwood 236(2)
Burwood House 331
Byron Lodge 264(2), 280(2)
Byron Plains 168(2)
Camden Park 522, 145(2),
  149(2), 151(2), 157(2), 158(2),
  554(2)
Canning Downs 290
Canterbury Vale 18(2)
Carr Field House 225
Castle Forbes 265(2)
Castle Meehan 368(2)
Castlereagh House 422
Cavan 123(2), 381(2)
Cheshunt Park 362
Cheverells 461
Claremont 331, 102(2)
Clarendon 256, 259
Clarens, Darlinghurst 485
Clee Villa 387(2)
Cleveland 334
Cliefden 2(2)
Clifton 311
Clifton station 183(2)
Closebourne 231
Clunes 199
Clydesdale 533(2)
Coates Park 500
Cobborah 401(2)
Collaroi 290
Collaroi station 277
Collingwood 178
Collingwood Dale 178
Colonial Architect's House
  113(2)
Commissariat Store 124(2)
Cooma Cottage 565
Coombing Park 1(2)
Coomsby Hill 10(2)
Corinda 80
Cornwallis 548
Corrundaroo 573
Cory Vale 247
Cremorne 233(2)
Crossland 262

Crows Nest House 94
Currawang 183(2)
Curribie 392
Customs House 410(2)
Dalwood 630(2)
Deepwater 614(2)
Denbeigh 551
Denbigh 523
Denham Court 157, 554(2)
Dobroyd estate 130(2)
Dobroyd Farm 361(2)
Dochairn 172(2)
Doon Moor Cottage 533(2)
Dubbo Station 332
Duckenfield Park House 345
Dundallamal 451(2)
Dunheved 108(2)
Duntroon 198205, 206, 232
Durham House 205(2)
Duxford, Paddington 495
Eagleton 455(2)
Ecclesbourne 453(2)
Edinglassie 397
Elamong 233(2)
Elder House 352
Elderslie 511, 524
Elizabeth Bay House 181(2),
  182(2), 554(2)
Elizabeth Farm 145(2), 149(2),
  154(2), 554(2)
Elizabeth Farm House 2(2)
Ellengerah 332
Elswick 289(2)
Engehurst 554(2)
Entally House 373(2)
Ermington House 534
Eurolie 565
Eveleigh House 435(2)
Ewenmar 401(2)
Experiment Farm Cottage 519
Falconer 168(2)
Fernhill 256
Fleurs 24(2)
Fort Macquarie 324
Foveaux's Gift 22(2)
Foxlowe 555
Furracabad 334, 4(2)
Furracabad station 264(2)
Gilimatong 555
Gillendoon 401(2)
Ginninderra Station 198, 308(2)
Glasgow 519(2)
Glen Alpine 368(2)
Glen Logan 362(2)
Glendon 428(2)
Glenfield 530(2)
Glenlee 561
Glenrock 563, 564, 453(2)
Glenrose 226(2)
Goorangoola 300
Gordon Brook station 311
Gostwyck 247, 248
Government House 204, 218,
  234, 260, 263, 312, 21(2),
  233(2), 310(2)
Government House, Parramatta
  385, 401(2)
Government House, stables 471
Grabberback 556
Grantham 281
Greenknowe 442
Greystones 2(2)

Guyra 168(2)
Hambledon 310(2)
Hamond Hill Farm 594(2)
Hardwicke 292(2)
Harrington Park 208
Harrisford 360
Hartwell Farm 487
Henrietta Villa 335(2)
Herald 304(2)
Hereford 259
Hereford House 505, 51(2)
Hermitage Farm 12
Hermitage, Norfolk Island 351
Horningsea 254(2)
Humewood 565
Hyde Park Barracks 615(2)
Illulaung 231
Innes Creek 4(2)
Innestown 4(2)
Inverary Park 376(2)
Iron Bark Hill 337(2)
Irrawang 54(2), 455(2)
Jarvisfield 21, 22
Jerrabombera 311(2)
Juniper House 51(2)
Keelgyrah 630(2)
Kelburn 401
Kelloshiel 362(2)
Kentucky 4(2)
Kerarbury 181(2)
Kilgra 630(2)
Killarney 321
Killarney 321, 519(2)
Kill-me-cat 451(2)
King's Grove 131(2)
Kinross 614(2)
Kirkham 306(2, 307(2)
Kirkton 189
Lachlan Vale 158
Lake Innes Cottage 4(2)
Lampeter Farm 523
Larbert Lodge 73(2)
Leitrim Lodge 398
Leppington 247
Lisgar 428(2)
Lismore 479(2)
Llangollen (Llangothlin) 325(2)
Llangothlin (Llangollen) 325(2)
Lockyersleigh 123(2)
Lord's Folly 131(2)
Luskentyre 599(2)
Lyndhurst 11, 162, 425(2),
  554(2)
Lyndhurst Vale 553(2)
Lyons Terrace, Sydney 96,
  23(2), 142(2)
Macquarie Field 220(2)
Macquarie Grove 551
Marchmont 565
Marshall Mount 304(2)
Maryland 58
Meadows Station 451(2)
Mereworth 42
Midlorn 320
Milbrodale 537
Milgarra 80
Mill Farm 618(2)
Molle's Maines 243(2)
Moore Park 226(2)
Moredun 426
Morpeth House 231
Moulsey 87

Mount Foster 332
Mount Gilead 395(2), 548(2)
Mount Mitchell 426
Mount Philo 200
Mount Pleasant 555, 167(2), 508(2)
Mowbla 505
Moxham's Farms 519(2)
Mugabareena 350
Mulla Villa 337
Mullingundy 332
Mummel 58
Murrindindi 455(2)
Nanima station 251(2)
Naval Pavilion 335(2)
Neotsfield 281
Nest, The 263(2)
Newington House 205(2)
Nonorrah 58
Nurrabri 321
Oban 426
Octagon 452(2)
Oldbury 42
Ormonde House 51(2), 52(2)
Orwell, Woolloomooloo 485
Paika 543
Palmerston 463(2)
Pemberton Grange 308(2)
Pickering 80
Pitnacree 168(2)
Plattsburg 337(2)
Police Office, Sydney 472
Priory, The 61
Puen Buen 102, 479(2)
Queepolli 344
Raby 380(2), 382(2)
Rainbarn 360(2)
Ramornie station 310, 311
Ranghaoo estate 359(2)
Rathluba 9
Ravensfield 464(2)
Ravenswood 435(2)
Ravensworth 138
Raworth 560
Redbourneberry 560
Regentville 11(2), 13(2)
Retreat Farm 341, 549
Rhodes 564(2)
Richmond House 276(2)
Richmond Villa 113(2)
Riverston 295(2)
Rockvale 426
Rockwall 554(2)
Rose Hall 504
Rosemount 86(2)
Roseneath Cottage 401
Roslyn Hall 58, 504
Roxburgh Place 320
Runnymede 479(2)
St Andrew's 520(2)
St Aubins 334
St Heliers 334, 500
St Leonard's Lodge 120(2)
Saltram 1(2), 362(2)
Saumarez, Armidale 334, 426
Scone Hospital 334
Segenhoe 168(2), 195(2)
Seven Creeks 401
Skellater 397
Snugsburough 291(2)
Somerset Lodge 367(2)
South Head lighthouse 444(2)

Spencer Lodge 73(2)
Spicer's Creek 332
Springfield Station 367
Stargard 403(2)
Stoneleigh 26(2)
Strath 483(2)
Stratheden 479(2)
Stratheden station 310
Sugarloaf Station 233(2)
Sunning Hill Farm 130(2), 361(2)
Swilly Farm 16(2)
Sydney House 84
Tahlee House 334
Tarmons 284(2)
Teddington 533(2)
Telford Place 504
Tempe 464(2)
Tempe House 554(2)
Temple Court 139
Terara 305
Terry's Buildings 508(2)
Thanks 119, 60(2)
Throsby Park 531(2)
Tilbuster 334
Tilligra 615(2)
Tivoli 334
Toganmain 181(2)
Tomago 54(2), 617(2)
Townson's Retreat 131(2)
Toxteth Park 6, 554(2)
Turanville 281, 282
Tusculum 464(2), 554(2)
Ulinbawn 320
Ultimo 519
Ultimo House 382(2), 478(2)
Uriara 243(2)
Varro Ville farm 538(2)
Varroville 365(2)
Vaucluse House 526, 97(2), 335(2)
Vauxhall Gardens 452(2)
Vermont 203(2), 583(2)
Veteran Hall 505, 96(2), 97(2)
Villa Maria 534
Vineyard, The, Rydalmere 277, 53(2), 147(2), 554(2)
Walholla 344
Walmer 525
Wantabadgery 614(2)
Warby's Station 496(2)
Wardle Bank 519(2)
Warrah 290
Waterloo 4(2), 168(2)
Waverley House 109(2)
West Hill 519(2)
Westbourne 335(2)
Westgrove 359(2)
Wharf House 199
Willow Cottage 367(2)
Windellama 368
Windermere 614(2)
Winderradeen 275(2)
Windsor Court House 471
Woden 274(2)
Woodhay Farm 548
Woodlands 362
Woolloomooloo 309(2), 310(2)
Wooriwyrite Station 438(2)
Wooroowoolgen Station 485
Wyoming 530
Yaralla 565(2)

Yarralumla 439
Yarras 4(2)
Yarrowick 387(2)
Yarrowlumla (Yarralumla) 275(2)
Yarrows 4(2)
Yarrundi 466
York House 123(2)
York Lodge 144
Houses etc: New Zealand
Otama 501(2)
Treaty House 554(2)
Houses etc: Queensland
Bluff Plains 93(2)
Boonimba 93(2)
Booubyjan 93(2)
Bowen Downs 257(2)
Bunya Creek 93(2)
Burrandowan station 407(2)
Cecil Plains 406(2), 407(2)
Cogoon 103(2)
Coonambula 22
Durundur 22
Eidsvold 22
Eton Vale 406(2)
Goomally 93(2)
Goomburra 277, 108(2), 149(2)
Government House 263(2)
Gracemere 23
Imbil 93(2)
Mundoolun 93(2)
New Farm 25(2)
Newstead House 108(2), 597(2)
Nindooinbah 93(2)
Pikedale 381
Tamrookum 201
Victoria Downs 131(2)
Windera 93(2)
Yelvertoft 407(2)
Zion Hill 352
Houses etc: Scotland
Ardmore 435
Balvaird Farm 504(2)
Brisbane House 151
Carnousie 321(2)
Craignish Castle 187(2)
Dryden House 223(2)
Dumbuck 435, 436
Dunsinnan House 227
Geilston 435
Gordon Castle 160(2)
Gorthy PER 223(2), 224(2)
Huntingtower PER 224(2)
Inchdrewer Castle 427(2)
Inchmarlo estate 290
Jarvisfield 187(2), 189(2), 194(2)
Kilrie farm 330
Melrose 220(2)
Netherby 457
Old Ratho Bank 375(2)
Oskamull 187(2)
Parkhall 101(2)
Ratho 375(2)
Strathruddie 449(2)
Wantonwalls farm 235
Houses etc: South Australia
Anlaby 341, 377
Bowyer 175
Calagandoo 573
Craike Farm 440(2)
Cummins 262(2)

Echunga Springs 497, 498
Felixstow 491(2)
Government House 64(2)
Koonunga 47
Linden 525
Lindsay Park 17
Lytton Lodge 482(2)
Moorak 573
Mount Breckan 525
Mount Dispersion station 377
Naracoorte 197(2)
Noarlunga 197(2)
Nurney House 47
Prospect Hall 17
Prospect House 445
Ramornie station 202(2)
Theberton Cottage 378
Theberton (Thebarton) 117(2)
Traversbrook 378
Tulkea 197(2)
Vale Farm 445
Walkerville 445
Weymouth House 441(2)
Houses etc: Tasmania
Abernant 113(2)
Adelphi 329
Alice Place 441(2)
Allanvale 576(2)
Ancanthe 411
Annandale, Tas 81
Anstey Barton 19, 21, 308(2)
Anstey Park 19
Ashfield 74(2)
Ashgrove 21
Askrigg 507(2)
Athol Brae 317(2)
Barrington Lodge 35(2)
Barton 429
Beaufront 452(2)
Beauty Lodge 356
Belle Vue 81, 328
Belmont 181, 225(2), 564(2)
Benham 296(2)
Berriedale 317(2)
Bifrons Court, Launceston 169
Billopp 94(2), 95(2)
Birch Grove Farm 159(2)
Bishopsbourne 576(2)
Bishopstowe 285(2)
Bloomfield 317(2)
Blue Hills 126(2)
Bluff 113(2)
Boa Vista 285(2), 427(2)
Bona Vista 197
Bourbon 493
Bowhill 429(2)
Brickendon 25
Brighton Lodge 356
Bronte 291
Bronti 291
Buckinghamshire House 225
Cairns Mount 383(2)
Cambock 56
Cambria 329, 225(2)
Camperdown 56
Carr Field House 225
Carr Villa 225
Carrington 397(2)
Carrington House 134(2)
Cheshunt 25
Chigwell 355
Cilwen 113(2)

Clarendon 257, 564(2)
Cluny 593(2), 594(2)
Clyde Villa 182
Coburg 429
Colebrook Dale 36(2)
Corra Lynn 394(2)
Cottage Green Estate 407, 67(2)
Craigow 268(2)
Cressy House 534(2)
Danbury Park 94(2)
Dennistoun 408(2)
Derwent Park 437
Dunorlan 260(2)
Dunorlan Cottages 373(2)
Dunrobin 96
Dynnyrne House 273(2)
Eden 300(2)
Ellangowan 181
Ellenthorpe 308(2), 434(2)
Ellerslie 316, 420
Ellinthorp Hall estate 225
Elphin 328, 329, 74(2)
Entally 374(2)
Erskine Park 359
Esk Farm 7(2)
Evandale 408(2)
Everton 516(2)
Fairfield 25
Fawcett 459
Fenton Forest 371, 500(2)
Fernhill 257
Ferry House 230
Formosa 95(2)
Fosterville 407
Four Square Gallows 81
Frogmore 16(2), 87(2), 260(2)
Gaddesden 173(2)
Gala 12
Glen Ayr 302
Glen Dhu, Launceston 494
Government Cottage 633(2)
Government Cottage, Launceston 35(2)
Government House 239
Government House, Hobart 35(2)
Green Lawn 557(2)
Hagley House 329, 143(2)
Hall Green 298(2)
Halstead 128
Hangan's Farm 553
Hattondale 246(2)
Hawthorn 246(2)
Hermitage 396(2)
Highfield 270
Hobart Markets 35(2)
Humbie 375(2)
Humphreyville 566
Hunterston 297(2)
Hutton Park 106, 416
Hythe 9(2), 593(2)
Illawarra 333
Ingle Hall 3(2)
Ivadene 254
Ivanhoe 73(2), 366(2)
Janefield 612(2)
Jutland 24
Kelso House 199(2)
Kelvedon 249, 490(2)
Kelvin Grove 308(2)
Kenilworth 401, 504(2)

Kent Cottage 442(2)
Kerry Lodge 63
Kewstoke 106
Kilderry 440
Killafaddy 543
Killard 241, 242
Killymoon House 557(2)
Kimbolton 317(2)
Kinvarra 366(2)
Laburnum Park 457, 36(2), 134(2)
Lake House 430
Lambe's Gardens 74(2)
Lauderdale 216(2)
Lawrence's Paddock 94(2)
Lawrenny 457, 128(2)
Lee Mount 121(2)
Lewis Hill 557(2)
Leyburne 366(2)
Lizard Lodge 301(2)
Llanherne 113(2)
London House, Hobart 216(2)
Lovely Banks 106, 229, 223(2)
Lowestoft 138(2)
Malahide 502(2)
Marion Villa 257
Marylands 356
Mauriceton 594(2)
Medlands 576(2)
Melrose 528(2)
Melville Grove 421
Milford 113(2), 518(2)
Millbrook 87(2)
Mona Vale 14(2), 49(2)
Montford 156
Mount Morriston 429(2)
Mount Pleasant 261, 373(2)
Mount Vernon 308(2)
Mountain Villa 373(2)
Munmurra 229
Murray Hall 221(2)
Nabowla House, Launceston 305
Narryna 563(2)
Native Hut Corner 372(2)
Neck 113(2)
New Grange 317(2)
Newlands 320(2)
Newnham 417
Newstead estate 493
Newtown Park 500(2)
Nonesuch 429
Norley Cottage 32
North Down 517(2), 518(2)
Northbury 25
Northumbria 475, 308(2)
Oakhampton 132(2)
Orielton 457
Ornley 258
Palmerston 25
Panshanger 25, 143(2)
Paraclete 397(2)
Patterdale 456
Penquite 493, 94(2)
Perth 383(2)
Pinefield 143(2)
Pisa 430
Plaisance 59
Pleasant Banks 316, 439
Point Effingham 95(2)
Punchbowl 94(2)
Quamby 328, 329

Quorn Hall 229, 257
Ratho 375(2)
Ravensdale 543
Redbanks 225(2)
Rendlesham 257
Restdown 134, 475
Rhodes 564(2)
Richmond Hill 534(2)
Richmond Park 126(2)
Ring Farm 456
Riverview 549, 458(2)
Rock House 37(2)
Rosebank Farm 36(2)
Rosedale 100(2)
Roseneath 42
Roseway Lodge 427(2), 517(2)
Rosny 247(2)
Rossbank 34(2)
Rostella 32(2)
Rothiemay 427(2)
Roxburgh House 144(2)
Royal Hotel, Bagdad 95
Runnymede 285(2), 336(2)
St Johnstone 504(2)
St Kilda House 434(2)
Sandhill 106
Saundridge 25
Schawfield 421(2)
Secheron 411, 320(2)
Seton 366(2)
Shawfield 564(2)
Shene 191
Sherwood 441(2)
Skelton Castle 430
Somercotes 205(2)
Speedwell 174(2)
Springvale Tea Gardens 113(2)
Stethorn Farm 415(2)
Stoke 125
Stoke Cottage 466(2)
Stone Buildings 528(2)
Stonehenge 308(2)
Stowell 191, 249(2)
Strathbarton 409(2)
Strathmore 257
Streanshalh 7
Summerhome 552
Sunnyside 557(2)
Surrey House 58
Syndal 452(2)
The Grove 458
The Lawn 291
Thornhill(2)
Thorpe 106
Tolosa 562
Trafalgar 56
Trefusis 308(2)
Tremayne 434(2)
Tressick, Northcote 511
Trevallyn 59, 534(2)
Uplands 230
Valleyfield 504(2)
Vermont 94(2)
Vron 7(2)
Warwick Lodge 360
Wentworth 273(2)
Westella 552
Weston Lodge 494
Wetmore 314(2), 315(2)
Whisloka 257
Willingham 412
Wimborne 257

Windermere 355
Windfalls 229
Winton 504(2), 541(2)
Wivenhoe 407
Woodburn 430, 384(2)
Woodlands 308(2)
Woodsden 256
Woodside 25
Woolmers 25, 469(2)
Houses etc: Victoria
Alcove 297
Arthur's Seat 160(2)
Avalon freehold 43
Avoca 82
Balla Balla 572
Banyule 524
Barwon Park, Vic 43
Batesford 101(2)
Bell Bird Balyang 423
Bell Park 81
Belle Vue 606(2)
Black Forest station 43
Black Rock House 350
Boisdale 407
Bona Vista 544
Bonegilla 350
Bongmire station 297
Boninyong 101(2)
Bontharambo 311
Boronggoop 330
Borrumbeet 101(2)
Buntingdale 540(2)
Bushy Park 183(2)
Campbellfield 124
Carlsruhe 350
Castleburn 407
Clunie 112
Clutha 232
Como 27
Congbool 27
Corhanwarrabul 232
Coryule 330, 331, 71(2)
Cullinlaringo 606(2)
Cupumnimnip 320(2)
Dargo 407
Doogallook 249
Dryden 224(2)
Dundas 542(2)
Elcho 27
Ensay 183(2)
Ercildoun 101(2)
Erinvale 407
Eureka Hotel 349(2)
Fairlie 14
Farnham 411(2)
Field Place 533
Findon 533
Fulham 27
Fyansford House 224(2)
Gheringhap 224(2)
Glencoe 407
Glenfalloch 407
Gnawarre 501(2)
Golfhill 409(2)
Grasmere 124
Grassmere 200(2)
Greenmount 112
Hermitage 27, 43
Irrewarra 81
Kanawalla 224(2)
Kangerong 545
Kardinia 330

Kingston 68
Koorakooracup 9(2)
Lake Colac 81
Laurence Park 101(2)
Leighton 124
Lunan 492(2)
Maintoongoon 249
Mawallock 409(2)
Mayfield 160(2)
Merino Downs 533
Merri Ville Lodge 519(2)
Mervyn 28(2)
Minnieburn 573
Mooleric 492(2)
Moorabbin House 590(2)
Mooroolbark 425
Morongo 81
Mount Gellibrand station
    492(2)
Mount Koroite 542(2)
Mount Mercer 224(2)
Mount Sturgeon 27
Muntham 533
Murgheboluc 501(2)
Murndal 406(2)
Native Creek No.2. 409(2)
Native Creek No.3. 501(2)
Netherwood 14
Norwood 28(2)
Numbla Munjie 183(2)
Nuntin 183(2)
Oakhill 232
Ocean Grove 501(2)
Offington 533
Old Colonists' Homes,
    Melbourne 606(2)
Pascoe Vale 370
Paywit 501(2)
Pirron Yalloak 124
Plaistow 28(2)
Point Lonsdale 501(2)
Priory 43
Purrumbete 200(2)
Pyalong 243(2)
Rhyll 32(2)
Rodborough Vale 28(2)
Rosebrook 231(2)
Roseneath 229
Royal Terrace 70(2)
St Albans stud 330
St Ninian's 234
Sandford station 533, 9(2)
Seabank 543(2)
Sinclair's 297
Springburn 297
Station Peak 557(2)
Strathfieldsaye 124
Tabberabbera 184(2)
Tahara estate 406(2)
Tallarook 524
Tangel 407
Tarndwarncoort 539(2)
Tarringower 243(2)
Tarwin Meadows 545, 572
Terinallum 409(2)
The Heart at Sale 407
Tirhatuan 232
Tivoli (see Triviola)
Tootgarook 545
Tower House, Flinders Street,
    Melbourne 9(2)
Trivolia (Tivoli) 82

Tulchan 224(2)
Turkeith 27
Wangaratta Station 367
Warrambeen station 224(2)
Watch Hill 81
Wattle House 9(2)
Weatherboard Station 224(2)
Wild Cattle Run, Wonthaggi 14
Windermere 27
Winnimburn 542(2)
Wolfscrag 271
Woodside run 28(2)
Wooloomanata 27, 423
Wormbete 27, 552
Yambuck station 296
Houses etc: Wales
  Newton Hall MON 316(2)
  Talymaes Park 429
Houses: Western Australia
  Adelphi 189
  Bassendean 165
  Bower, Guildford 219(2)
  Bowes station 180
  Cattle Chosen 190
  Cheriton 155
  Deepdale 372
  Fair Lawn 245(2)
  Government House 376(2)
  Gwambygine 619(2)
  Hawthornden 325, 326
  Henley Park 174(2), 175(2)
  Merino Downs 533
  Millendon 252(2)
  Narrawong 340
  Old Court House 377(2)
  Peel estate 236
  Peninsula 510
  Richmond House 227
  Rose Hall 439(2)
  Round House 377(2)
  Seabrook 155
  Strawberry Hill 465(2)
  Tipperary 180
  Tranby House 510
  Whitehall 175(2)
  Woodbridge 486(2)
Hulks: see also Ships
    118, 308, 537, 17(2)
  Victoria 352(2)
  Bahama 27(2)
  Captivity 490
  Dunkirk 173, 404(2)
  Fortunee 508(2)
  Phoenix 66(2)
  Zetland 457(2)
Hydrography 111, 171, 551(2)
Immigration:
    221, 222, 270, 354, 382, 554,
    63(2), 77(2), 79(2), 136(2),
    377(2), 414(2), 559(2), 562(2)
  Assisted 484, 576
  American 370
  Bounty scheme 449, 454
  Chile 96(2)
  Chinese 14, 345, 370, 499, 6(2),
    606(2)
  Coolie labour issue 281, 499,
    564, 45(2), 123(2), 141(2),
    181(2), 293(2), 305(2), 587(2),
    623(2)
  German 281, 33(2)
  Indian 345, 123(2), 284(2),
    623(2)
  Irish 523(2)
  Jewish 110(2)
  Kanaka 484
  NSW 584(2)
  Paupers 462
  Scottish 77(2), 176(2)
  Scottish Highlanders 78(2)
  South Australia 16, 432
  Victoria, policy 14, 606(2)
  Wakefield system 222
  Welsh miners 564(2)
  Western Australia 382, 383(2)
Import Duty: see Customs Duty
Incest 536
India: see Places Index: India
India: Tamil language 522(2)
Indian coolie labour: see Politics
  & Immigration
Indonesia: see Places Index
  see: Organisations: Indonesia
Inns of Court: see Organisations:
  Miscellaneous — England
Industries, trades, manufacturing,
  primary production (misc
  refs)
  (see also under geographic
  areas below).
apples 470(2)
apricots 145(2)
almonds 145(2)
agricultural 139(2)
aniseed 268(2)
bakery 302
baking bread 246
Baltic trade 243
bananas 431(2)
banking 177(2), 196(2), 276(2),
  500(2)
beef salting 362(2), 521(2)
bee keeping 612(2)
beetroot 268(2)
bloodstock 248
boatbuilding 485, 129(2),
  488(2), 546(2)
boiling-down works 281, 344,
  91(2), 362(2)
book binding 397(2)
book selling 265(2), 466(2),
  480(2)
brewing 59, 246, 302, 306, 487,
  31(2), 58(2), 362(2), 488(2),
  508(2), 569(2)
brickmaking 394(2)
candle making 245(2), 609(2)
cattle 117, 198, 200, 201, 209,
  229, 249, 257, 271
cattle (shorthorn) 124
cedar see also timber 246, 368,
  45(2), 130(2), 137(2), 292(2),
  313(2), 360(2), 520(2), 613(2),
  617(2), 621(2)
cheese 1(2), 335(2)
clothmaking 132(2)
coach service 257
coal 201, 485, 2(2), 45(2), 71(2),
  236(2), 520(2), 529(2), 614(2),
  617(2)
coffee 577(2)
copper 419, 443, 237(2), 251(2),
  383(2), 465(2), 480(2), 536(2)
  see also mining.
corn chandling 268(2)
cotton, 502, 79(2), 195(2)
curing fish 272
curing meat 201
dairyfarming 497, 36(2), 65(2),
  360(2)
deer 257
distilling 246, 58(2), 71(2),
  137(2), 541(2), 547(2)
earthenware 441(2)
engineering 224
export of timber 240
fishery 486
flax 275, 563, 56(2), 195(2),
  598(2)
flax treating factory 307
flour milling 109, 246, 302, 306,
  486, 504, 109(2), 168(2),
  225(2), 359(2), 379(2), 383(2),
  439(2), 488(2), 507(2), 508(2),
  563(2)
foundry 1(2)
fur 233, 266(2)
glass 237(2), 130(2)
glue 608(2)
gold 91(2), see also under
  goldfields
grain 520(2) see also wheat etc.
gunpowder 246
hatmaking 130(2), 548(2)
haymaking 186(2)
hops 371, 168(2), 362(2), 468(2)
horse breeding 257, 36(2),
  629(2)
horseracing: see racing
horses 200, 271, 401(2)
insurance 464(2)
iron 123(2)
ironmongery 611(2)
kangaroo shooting 230(2)
lead 446, 480(2)
leather 31(2)
liquor 86(2), 126(2), 197(2),
  543(2)
maize 124(2)
manufacturing 520, 59(2),
  130(2), 493(2), 598(2)
marine surveying 541(2)
marine steam engine 224
masts 275
meat 249, 265(2), 403(2)
meat preserving works 281
meat salting 493(2)
medicinal herb growing 268(2)
medicines (selling of) 5
metal casting 493(2)
millinery 260
milling flour 246, 302, 306
mining (copper) 47, 296, 479,
  498
oil 129(2), 359(2)
oil refining 28(2)
opium 233, 268(2)
oranges 361(2)
paddle steamer 233
paling trade 246(2)
parchment 609(2)
pastoralism 197, 198, 201, 205,
  209, 225, 247, 249, 257, 259,
  499, 509, 70(2), 380(2), 460(2)
peach 318(2), 319(2)
pear 145(2)

pearl fishing 233
pearl shell trade 208, 382
perfumes 268(2)
pineapple 496, 510
porcelain 237(2)
pork 13(2)
pork (South Sea Islands)
    156(2), 438(2), 520(2)
pottery 54(2), 130(2), 282(2),
    438(2), 466(2)
printing 534, 397(2)
property development 225
rabbit-breeding 126, 54(2)
racing 345, 475, 511, 532, 549,
    562, 572, 11(2), 36(2), 115(2),
    192(2), 317(2), 335(2), 365(2),
    375(2), 383(2), 400(2), 412(2),
    428(2), 515(2), 630(2)
retail 230
rum trade 571
saddlery 562(2)
salt 268(2), 519(2)
salt pork trade 208
sandalwood 233, 245, 275, 558,
    6(2), 13(2), 31(2), 36(2),
    147(2), 156(2), 438(2), 583(2)
sandalwood trade 208
sawmilling 302, 440(2)
seal fishery 240
sealing 104, 105, 107, 127, 203,
    208, 245, 485-6, 24(2), 25(2),
    27(2), 31(2), 36(2), 129(2),
    231(2), 302(2), 309(2), 312(2),
    364(2), 366(2), 371(2), 374(2),
    520(2), 605(2)
seaweed fertilizer 234
sheep 4, 24, 141, 155, 196, 197,
    209, 229, 247, 248, 249, 257,
    259, 270, 271, 290, 514, 531,
    49(2), 100(2), 130(2), 145(2),
    155(2), 208(2), 315(2), 401(2),
    438(2), 502(2), 553(2), 566(2),
    574(2), 576(2), 604(2), 606(2),
    630(2)
sheep breeding 437(2)
sheep (Leicester breed) 229
shipbuilding 303, 485-6, 32(2),
    115(2)
shipping 199, 203, 204, 208,
    216, 233, 240, 245, 305, 344,
    28(2), 54(2), 94(2), 176(2),
    177(2), 566(2), 617(2)
silver 446, 480(2)
slaughtering 609(2)
slave trading 400(2)
smelting 237(2), 528(2)
soap & candle works 306
soap making 245(2), 608(2)
sorghum 606(2)
sperm whale fishery 240
spirits 489, 24(2), 28(2)
starch production 295
steam engine 224, 306, 359(2),
    379(2)
steam flourmill 281
stud farm 281
sugar 495, 572, 4(2), 38(2),
    65(2), 195(2), 372(2), 419(2)
sugar beet 234, 268(2)
Sugarcane 572, 600(2)
tallow 23(2)
tanning 45(2), 59(2), 130(2),

132(2), 225(2), 519(2), 608(2)
tea 578(2)
Teeswater sheep 458
timber 201, 1(2), 42(2), 137(2),
    148(2), 196(2), 254(2), 439(2),
    598(2), 621(2)
timber export 240
timber, Norfolk Island pines
    22(2)
timber (sandalwood) 208
timber: see also cedar,
    sandalwood
tinning works 281
tobaco 431(2), 600(2), 616(2),
    621(2)
trade 203, 245, 272, 524(2)
trade (Aust.-Malaya) 148
trade (NSW-India) 462, 130(2),
    365(2), 381(2)
trade (Sydney-Hunter) 490
vinegrowing 150(2)
viticulture, NSW 211
wattle bark 249, 231(2), 372(2)
weaving cloth 246, 130(2)
whaling 16, 66, 104, 141, 178,
    197, 233, 240, 245, 272, 275,
    305, 357, 442, 486, 497, 532,
    24(2), 27(2), 31(2), 49(2),
    54(2), 70(2), 155(2), 177(2),
    196(2), 231(2), 245(2), 263(2),
    302(2), 322(2), 330(2), 332(2),
    359(2), 360(2), 366(2), 371(2),
    372(2), 417(2), 426(2), 444(2),
    481(2), 566(2)
wheat 249, 13(2), 100(2),
    139(2), 197(2), 265(2), 360(2),
    489(2), 494(2), 606(2)
wheat (harvesting machine)
    301(2), 379(2), 616(2)
wine 186, 524, 24(2), 54(2),
    157(2), 499(2)
wool 104, 207, 229, 245, 440,
    543, 552, 23(2), 100(2),
    101(2), 128(2), 150(2), 196(2),
    208(2), 250(2), 257(2), 262(2),
    265(2), 359(2), 375(2), 380(2),
    392(2), 437(2), 488(2), 593(2)
wool processing 11(2), 54(2),
Industry: New South Wales
    beer brewing 468(2)
    boiling down works 293(2)
    cattle 205, 1(2), 22(2), 53(2),
        58(2)
    coal 58(2), 309(2)
    coal mining 345, 63(2), 236(2),
        257(2)
    cotton 58(2)
    crops 18(2)
    dairy 216, 1(2), 304(2)
    flax 58(2)
    flour milling 57, 74, 493(2)
    glass manufacturing 54(2)
    goldmining 525(2)
    grain 383, 18(2)
    hemp 58(2)
    horse racing 207, 345
    horsebreeding 108(2), 428(2)
    horses 205, 11(2)
    indigo 58(2)
    liquor distilling 58(2)
    manufacturing industry 57
    marine insurance 380(2)

match making 624(2)
merchants 57
mining 1(2)
pastoral 96(2), 4(2), 380(2)
pottery 353(2)
racing 582(2)
retail 207
rum trade 52, 581(2)
sandalwood 129(2)
sealing 58(2), 129(2), 380(2),
    547(2), 548(2)
sheep 141, 205, 1(2), 24(2),
    150(2), 293(2)
sheep grazing 344
shipbuilding 202(2), 312(2),
    519(2), 546(2)
smelting 236(2)
steam ferries 233(2)
sugar 4(2)
sugar cane 430(2)
sugar refining 38(2)
tallow 293(2)
tanning 609(2)
timber 58(2), 572(2)
tobacco 58(2), 430(2)
trade 203, 309(2)
trade (NSW-China) 290
tweed manufacturing 236(2)
vineyards 58(2)
Waterloo flour mill 575
whaling 376, 2(2), 58(2), 263(2),
    380(2)
wheat 344, 572(2)
wine 54(2)
wine growing 616(2)
wine making 630(2)
wool 146(2), 155(2), 156(2),
    208(2), 381(2)
Industry: Queensland
    burning shells & coral for lime
        201
    castor oil 201
    cattle 93(2)
    coal 601(2)
    cotton 201
    grazing 22
    salt 201
    sponge gathering 201
    sugar 201, 431(2)
Industry: South Australia
    building 525
    copper mining 7, 47, 296, 341,
        525, 64(2), 257(2)
    iron ore 280(2)
    lead 280(2)
    manufacturing 379(2)
    mining 280(2), 383(2)
    sheep 341
    Shipping 15
    silver 280(2)
    smelting 280(2)
    wheat (harvesting machine)
        616(2)
    wine 498, 616(2)
Industry: Tasmania
    banking 3
    brewing 59
    candle 230
    coal mining 602(2)
    fine wool 460(2)
    flour milling 12, 246(2), 279(2),
        507(2), 563(2)

grain 45(2)
hay 45(2)
hop growing 371, 442(2)
Insurance 3
pastoral 49(2), 100(2)
racing 511
rum 45(2)
salt 230
sealing 371(2)
sheep 96, 49(2)
ship building 302(2), 325(2)
shipping 374(2)
shoemaking 132(2)
soap 230
tanning 45(2)
whaling 37(2), 176(2), 225(2),
    302(2), 325(2), 371(2), 433(2),
    538(2)
woolgrowing 40(2), 45(2),
    502(2), 504(2)
Industry: Victoria
  beef cattle 124, 200(2)
  coalmining 14
  goldmining 542(2)
  horsebreeding 411(2)
  iron 84(2)
  sealing 231(2)
  sheep 401, 411(2)
  sheep breeding 4
  sheep farming 4
  shipping 411(2)
  whaling 340, 231(2)
  wool 28(2), 101(2)
Industry: Western Australia
  copper mining 435(2), 439(2)
  lead mining 439(2)
  timber 439(2)
  whaling 435(2)
Institutions: see Organisations:
    Miscellaneous
Insanity 105, 19(2)
Insurance companies: see
    Companies
Ireland, Irish Australians,
    connections with Ireland:
  see: Cemeteries — Ireland
  see: Churches — Ireland
  see: Houses etc. — Ireland
  see: Newspapers — Ireland
  see: Organisations — Ireland
  see: Places Index — Ireland
  see: Politics — Ireland
  see: Religion — Ireland
  see: Schools — Ireland
  see: Universities — Ireland
Irish language & literature 399,
    302(2)
Irish National System of
    education: see Education
Irish ordnance survey 409(2)
Irrigation 11(2), 222(2), 441(2)
Italy:
  see Places Index: Italy
  see also: Organisations
Journalism 26, 216, 227
Kangaroos 350(2)
Koalas 610(2)
Land companies: see
    Organisations and Companies
Land:
  (see also Squatting)
  Conveyancing 251(2)

Crown Land, alienation of
    408(2)
Crown Land, grants 409(2)
Crown Land, occupation of
    113, 152, 448
Crown Land, sale of 275(2)
Land Grant, first in NSW
    405(2)
Land Grants, NSW 331(2)
Minimum price, NSW 415(2)
NSW 481, 331(2), 332(2)
Occupation of NSW 132
Register of Deeds 628(2)
Register of Land Grants NSW
    331(2)
Regulations, NSW 205(2)
Robertson Land Bills 526(2)
South Australia 446, 525
Survey, title deeds 238(2)
Tasmania, quitrents 248(2)
Tasmania, titles 551
Tenure of Land 401, 338(2)
Title Deeds, NSW 332(2)
Torrens system 186, 536(2)
Victoria 401, 531, 547
Latin America: see Places Index
Law (see also Court Cases):
    195, 196, 218, 219, 227, 244,
    262, 263
  enforcement 175(2)
  independence of judiciary
    211(2)
  juries, emancipists on 245
  libel 37, 43, 48, 86, 286, 317,
    367, 427, 501, 503, 506, 559,
    38(2), 48(2), 69(2), 204(2),
    385(2), 473(2), 529(2), 571(2),
    585(2), 591(2), 592(2)
  trial by jury 130, 200, 205,
    96(2), 98(2), 581(2), 585(2),
    616(2)
Law firms: see Organisations and
    Companies
Laws:
  1 Wm. IV, (no.1) 253(2)
  10 Geo. IV, (No.9) 513(2)
  13 Anne. (c.15) 397
  32 Geo. III, c.42 as amended
    1809. 392
  4 Geo. IV, (c.96) 147(2)
  4 Geo. IV, (c.96) 393
  4 Geo. IV, (c.96) 395
  4 Geo. IV, (c.96, s.6) 319(2)
  4 Geo. IV, (c.96 s.29) 394
  4 Geo. IV. (c.96 s.27 & 29) 395
  5 & 6 Vic. (c.76) 398
  Vic 18 & 19, c.56 408(2)
  5 Geo. IV, (c.86) 158(2)
  6 Geo. IV, (no.16) 477(2)
  6 Wm. IV, (no.16) 398
  Wm IV, no 7 NSW 609(2)
  9 Geo. IV, (c.83) 395
  9 Geo. IV, (c.83) 395
  9 Geo. IV, (c.83) 396
  9 Geo. IV, c.83 397
  9 Geo. IV, (c.83) 398
  Act of 1842. 447
  Act of Indemnity 394
  Act of Indemnity (59 Geo. III,
    c.114) 373
  Algerine Laws 404
  Articles of War 12(2)

Australian Colonies
    Government Act of 1850. 17,
    386, 483, 9(2), 91(2), 320(2),
    408(2)
Australian Constitution bills
    136(2)
Australian Lands Act of 1842.
    448
Bastardy Act 1871 417(2)
Bourke's Church Act 1836.
    171(2)
Bullion Act 17, 480(2)
Bushranging Act 397
Charter of Justice 1814. 219,
    192(2)
Charter of Justice 263, 343, 374,
    393
Charter of Justice (TAS) 225(2)
Charter of Office 397
Church Act 1836 (7 Wm. IV,
    No.3) 399, 77(2), 338(2),
    341(2), 433(2), 511(2), 513(2),
    544(2)
Church Act 1837 TAS 174(2)
Church Building Act 1818. 41
Civil Court Ordinance and
    Rules 1836. 175(2)
Constitution 1842. 384
Constitution Act 463(2)
Constitution Bill 525(2)
Convicts Prevention Act 1852.
    14, 51(2)
Corn Laws 384(2), 630(2)
Corporation Act 125(2)
Country Towns Police Act
    1838. 202
Crown Lands Act 293(2)
Crown Lands Occupation Act
    132, 102(2)
Differential Duties Act TAS
    320(2)
District Courts Act 1858. 196
Districts Road Act 1871 155
Divorce Act 81(2)
Dog Act TAS 320(2)
East India Act 337
Edict of Nantes 400, 89(2)
Education Act 1885, Tas 30
Education Act 383(2)
Electoral Act 386, 26(2)
English Catholic Emancipation
    Act, 1829. 513(2)
Forbes Act 251(2)
Forbes Act of 1834 397
Foundation Act (4 & 5 Wm IV,
    c.95) 201(2)
General Education Act 251(2)
Government Order 21
    November 1821. 578(2)
Government Order 302(2)
Habeas Corpus 234(2)
Imperial Pension Act 194
Indemnity Act 396
Industrial Schools Act 1874
    417(2)
Insolvency Act 75, 302, 543
Insolvent Debtors' Relief Act
    202(2)
Intestate Act 257(2)
Intestate Act of 1834. 172(2)
Intestates' Estates Act (13 Vic.
    no.44) 203(2)

Jury Act 130
Jury Act 1833. 79
Libel Act 1843. 617(2)
Market Act TAS 35(2)
Market Commissioners' Act NSW 338(2)
Masters and Servants Act 141, 26(2), 162(2), 275(2)
Municipal Corporation Act of 1835. 419
Mutiny Act 419(2)
National Schools Bill 179(2)
Navigation Act 305, 177(2), 550(2)
Navigation Acts 1849. 177(2)
Navigation Acts 256(2)
New South Wales Act, 1823 (4 Geo. IV, c.96) 88, 100, 374, 370(2), 476(2), 585(2), 628(2)
New South Wales Bill 407(2)
New South Wales Constitution 481
New Zealand Constitution Act 1852. 561(2)
Newspaper Act 405
Newspaper Licensing Act TAS 248(2), 319(2)
Newspaper Licensing Act 319(2)
Newspaper Regulating Act 285, 394, 395, 501
Order in Council 381, 79(2)
Order in Council 1 May 1840 407(2)
Order in Council 1847. 401, 481, 543, 92(2), 240(2), 244(2)
Order in Council 1847 VIC 229
Order in Council of 9 March 1847. 385
Order in Council (transportation) 1840. 447
Oyster Fisheries Act 244(2)
Passengers Act 1852. 222
Peel's Act (7 & 8 Geo. IV, c.27) 395
Pleuro Pneumonia Act 244(2)
Police Act 1862. 463(2)
Poor Laws 97, 228(2)
Presbyterian Church Act 1837. 78(2)
Press Licensing Act 475, 427(2)
Press Licensing Act Tas. 127(2), 176(2), 302(2)
Prisoners' Counsel Act (6 & 7 Wm. IV, c.114) 375
Public Schools Act 1866. 346(2)
Public Schools Act 1868, Tas. 30
Railways Act 1854. 41(2)
Real Property Act 1847. 63
Real Property Act 1864. TAS 230
Reform Act 431, 518(2), 586(2)
Reform Act 1832. 15, 336, 384, 407(2)
Reform Act 1836. 136(2)
Robertson's Land Acts of 1861. 293(2), 565(2)
Scab Act 244(2)
Scab Act 1869. 63
South Australian Act 499, 539, 261(2), 535(2)

South Australian Act 1834. 15, 462, 64(2)
South Australian Act (4 & 5 Wm IV, c.95) 379
South Australian bill 408(2)
South Head Road bill 1832. 148(2)
Squatting Act 1839. 411(2)
Squatting Act 1846. 79(2)
Stamp Act 204
Supreme Court Act 1861. 489(2)
Sydney Police Act (4 Wm IV, no.7 NSW) 399(2)
Tasmanian Act 304, 386
Tram Road Act 237(2)
Transportation Act, 1824. 343
Treason Felony Act 234(2)
Treaty of Waitangi 463(2)
Waste Lands Act 140
Waste Lands Act, TAS 593(2)
Waste Lands Act, VIC 229
Waste Lands Occupation Act of 1846 (9 & 10 Vic.c.104) 385
Waste Lands Occupation Act 481
Water Acts 220
Water Police Amendment 228(2)
Legal firms and organisations: see Organisations and Companies
Legislative assemblies: see Organisations: Government
Legislative councils: see Organisations: Government
Legislatures: see Organisations: Government
Libel: see Law
Libraries: see Organisations: Miscellaneous
Lighthouses 335(2), 418(2), 5433(2), 556(2), 575(2)
Literature:
  Irish 302(2)
  see also Books, Opera, Pamphlets, Poems
  see also Author, writer etc.
Lithography 41, 353(2), 528(2)
Local Government: see Organisations: Government
Lottery 236(2)
Machinery, harvesting 301(2)
Mail service 66(2), 115(2), 308(2)
Manufacturing: see Industries
Manuscripts 284(2) see also Books
Marines (Royal Marines): 220, 226, 236, 288, 297, 20(2), 127(2), 222(2), 224(2), 506(2)
  69th Company 264(2)
  Bombay Marines 253
  Channel Squadron 236
  Chatham Division 236
  Marines (Royal Marines)
  Plymouth Division 221, 236, 506(2)
  Portsmouth Division 226
  Woolwich Division of Marines 288
  Royal Marine Artillery 223(2)
  Royal Marines 221, 115(2), 121(2), 258(2)

  Royal Marine Corps 288
  second lieutenant 281(2)
Martial Law (Norfolk Island) 398(2)
Mechanics' institutes: see Organisations: Miscellaneous
Medical journalism 1
Medicine:
  213, 214, 235, 242, 248, 253, 268, 272, 295, 369(2)
  anaesthesics 280(2), 514(2)
  anatomy 468, 578, 88(2)
  chloroform 515(2)
  Hunterian School of 85
  mental health 607(2)
  see also Disaeses
  see also Health
Military campaigns: see Army: wars, battles etc.
Military references: see Army
Military forces: see also Marines
Military ranks: see Army: Ranks
Mill, roller 246(2)
Mining companies: see Organisations and Companies
Morality 77(2)
Morphology 578
Municipal councils: see Organisations: Government
Museums: see Organisations: Miscellaneous
Music:
  301, 89(2), 251(2)
  A Song of Freedom 280(2)
  Australia the Wide and Free 279(2)
  Australian Melodies 280(2)
  Church music 570(2)
  Currency Lasses 279(2)
  Don John of Austria 280(2)
  Hail, Star of the South 279(2)
  Irish folk music 340(2)
  Koorinda Braia 280(2)
  Leichhardt's Grave 279(2)
  Long Live Victoria 279(2)
  The Greeting Home Again 279(2)
  The Southern Euphrosyne 280(2)
Musical Instruments:
  cello 629(2)
  flute 115(2), 629(2)
  guitar 115(2)
  harp 251(2)
  piano 251(2), 623(2), 629(2)
  violin 557, 340(2), 567(2)
  violoncello 301(C)
Names of Persons: see Personal Names Index
Nationalities:
  (English, Irish, Scottish, Welsh not included)
  American 21, 278, 305, 348, 516, 65(2), 218(2), 235(2), 308(2), 568(2), 598(2)
  Aragonese 357
  Austrian 73, 212(2), 624(2)
  Breton 149(2)
  Canadian 446, 65(2), 352(2)
  Czechoslovakian 114(2), 624(2)
  Danish 26(2), 27(2), 415(2)
  Dutch 555, 13(2), 340(2),

503(2), 556(2)
Flemish 361(2)
French 61, 71, 122, 171, 184,
  223, 305, 339, 407, 69(2),
  72(2), 85(2), 86(2), 89(2),
  121(2), 267(2), 371(2), 39(2)
German 11, 16, 326, 351, 402,
  508, 509, 29(2), 33(2), 212(2),
  222(2), 326(2), 349(2), 362(2),
  389(2), 392(2), 392(2C),
  403(2), 420(2), 557(2), 616(2),
  624(2)
Greek 409
Hungarian 623(2), 624(2)
Macassarese 357
Malay 57, 390(2)
Malay-Portuguese 357
Polish 403, 279(2), 421(2),
  494(2)
Portuguese 290, 357, 357(2),
  454(2)
Portuguese Eurasian 116(2)
Prussian 33(2), 114(2), 494(2),
  616(2)
Russian 83, 99(2)
South American 288(2)
Spanish 536(2)
Swedish 456(2)
Swiss 89(2), 115(2)
National School System: see
  Education: Irish National
  School System
Natural history 18, 19, 45, 544,
  12(2), 88(2), 106(2), 112(2),
  119(2), 230(2), 317(2), 349(2),
  361(2), 363(2), 456(2), 526(2),
  537(2), 594(2)
  see also Occupations: Botanist,
  Naturalist etc.
Navy, Royal Navy, other navies,
  naval institutions:
  50, 56, 118, 145, 169, 233,
  235, 240, 243, 268, 272, 275,
  290, 331, 566, 567, 72(2)
Anglo-Swedish Fleet 99(2)
Baltic Fleet 10(2)
Black Sea Fleet 99(2)
Bombay Marine 527
Chilean Navy 288(2)
Coastguard 381
Egyptian 539, 116(2)
French 71, 171
Mediterranean Fleet 538
Mutiny at the Nore 369(2)
Swedish 10(2)
Toulon Fleet 72(2)
United States 523(2)
Navy: England
  306, 310, 553, 99(2), 184(2)
Admiralty 526, 569, 576, 61(2),
  316(2)
Channel Fleet 56(2), 369(2),
  452(2), 506(2), 534(2)
Channel Squadron 233, 538
Chatham Yard 595(2)
Hampshire Sea Fencibles 333(2)
Mutiny of the Nore 119, 288,
  369(2)
Navy Board 53, 503
Navy Office 523(2)
Plymouth Dockyard 508
Royal Naval Academy 259(2)

Royal Naval College 446(2)
Royal Naval College,
  Dartmouth 287
Royal Yacht Squadron 140
sea cadets 403(2)
Sheerness Navy Yard 595(2)
Thames Flotilla 364(2)
Water Guard service 290
Naval ranks
  Able seaman 363(2)
  First class volunteer 417, 72(2),
    83(2)
  Helmsman 403(2)
  Master's Mate 468, 305(2)
  Mate 272(2)
  Midshipman 468, 56(2), 61(2),
    72(2), 184(2), 272(2), 305(2),
    363(2), 452(2), 462(2)
  Pilot 272(2)
  Purser 507, 523, 281(2), 424(2),
    614(2)
  Quartermaster 497
  Second Master 272(2)
Naval Battles & Engagements:
  Misc. 99(2)
  American War of Independence
    567, 56(2), 337(2)
  Brest, blockade of 315(2)
  Copenhagen, Battle of 7, 412,
    259(2)
  Genoa, blockade of 47(2)
  Glorious First of June 538
  Java, capture of 539
  Napoleonic War at sea 417
  Navarino, Battle of 99(2)
  Nile, Battle of the 538
  Rio de la Plata, Battle of 484(2)
  Seven Years' War 326(2)
  Spanish-Portuguese war 326(2)
  Trafalgar, Battle of 148, 412,
    539, 375(2)
New South Wales:
  see: Cemeteries — NSW
  see: Churches — NSW
  see: Houses etc. — NSW
  see: Newspapers — NSW
  see: Organisations — NSW
  see: Places Index — NSW
  see: Politics — NSW
  see: Religion — NSW
  see: Schools — NSW
  see: Universities — NSW
New South Wales Corps: see
  Army: Regiments
Newspapers freedom of the press
  (NSW) 571(2)
Newspapers, magazines, journals,
  periodicals: Miscellaneous
  see also under geographic areas
  below.
  Australian Magazine 213
  Berwick Journal 407
  Chamber's Miscellany 65(2)
  Church News 256
  Colonial Magazine 182, 185
  Colonies and India 19
  Congregational Magazine
    491(2)
  Eclectic Review 419(2)
  Empire 515, 81(2)
  Farmers' Journal 20
  Freeman's Journal 534

Gospel Magazine 253
Hood's Magazine and Comic
  Miscellany 402(2)
Household Words 222
Independent 32
Inquirer 325
Journal of Mental Science
  608(2)
Journal of the Agricultural and
  Horticultural Society of
  Western Australia 122(2)
Nautical Magazine 105, 63(2)
Naval and Military Gazette 97
Rural Magazine 177
Saturday Magazine 468
Solicitors' Journal 9
South-Asian Register 94
Tasmanian Journal of Natural
  Science 250, 118(2)
The Record, or Pastorals for
  Guildford 122(2)
Zoological Journal 63(2)
Zoologist 167(2)
Newspapers: Australia
  Australian: see NSW
    newspapers
  Australian Magazine 558
  Australian Medical Journal 1,
    114, 515(2), 523(2)
  Australian Quarterly Journal of
    Theology, Literature and
    Science 400(2), 613(2)
  Australian Quarterly Journal 42
  Australian Zoologist 19
  Freeman's Journal 345(2)
Newspapers: England
  Annals of Agriculture 54
  Archaeologia 54
  Blackwood's Magazine 304(2)
  Bow Bells 299(2)
  British Banner 79(2)
  Christian Advocate 480(2)
  Constitutional 164(2)
  Courier 402(2)
  Courier (London) 25
  Gentleman's Magazine 52
  Globe 482(2), 535(2)
  Globe and Traveller 262(2)
  Guardian 11
  Illustrated London News
    355(2), 445(2)
  John Bull 193(2)
  Journal of the Royal
    Geographical Society of
    London 267
  Lancet 114
  Law Chronicle and Estate
    Advertiser 615(2)
  Liverpool Chronicle 25(2)
  London Dispatch 133(2)
  London Gazette 273(2)
  London Journal of Botany 493
  London Magazine 552(2),
    558(2)
  London Naval and Military
    Gazette 347
  Mirror of Parliament 615(2)
  Morning Chronicle 3, 354, 481,
    559(2), 615(2)
  Penny Magazine 397(2)
  People's Journal 516
  Proceedings of the Geological

Society, London 267
Proceedings of the Zoological
  Society 19
Punch 21
Representative 615(2)
Sidney's Emigrant's Journal and
  Traveller's Magazine 445(2)
Spectator 46
Statesman 571(2)
Sun 615(2)
Times 198, 345, 557, 75(2),
  136(2), 615(2)
Tracts for the Times 10
Traveller 535(2)
Westminster Review 200(2),
  535(2)
Newspapers: Ireland
  Catholic Question, The 302(2)
  Clonmel Gazette 348(2)
  Dublin Penny Journal 337
  Nation 234(2)
  United Irishman 234(2)
Newspapers: New South Wales
  Freedom of the Press 583-5(2)
  Misc: 558
  Atlas 61, 140, 449, 60(2),
    135(2), 356(2), 505(2), 521(2)
  Australasian Chronicle 87, 336,
    534, 25(2), 342(2), 513(2),
    545(2)
  Australian 55, 285, 332, 333,
    334, 337, 393, 394, 395, 501,
    69(2), 102(2), 178(2), 194(2),
    259(2), 261(2), 319(2), 354(2),
    432(2), 511(2), 521(2), 571(2),
    585(2), 587(2), 615(2)
  Australian Almanac 417, 472
  Australian Magazine 204(2)
  Balmain Reporter 515
  Bell's Life in Sydney and
    Sporting Chronicle 409
  Bent's News and and New
    South Wales Advertiser 87
  Bulletin 474(2)
  Catholic Press 534
  Catholic Weekly 534
  Christian Pleader 356(2)
  Christian Standard 356(2)
  Colonial Observer 77(2)
  Colonist 210, 248, 50(2), 77(2),
    204(2), 236(2), 304(2), 529(2)
  Commercial Journal 149
  Currency Lad 514, 558, 605(2)
  Duncan's Weekly Register, of
    Politics, Facts and General
    Literature 336
  Empire 501, 535, 356(2), 592(2)
  Free Press 609(2)
  Freeman's Journal 165(2)
  Gleaner 507
  Government Gazette 82(2),
    204(2)
  Guardian 274(2)
  Heads of the People 446(2)
  Herald 305(2), 505(2)
  Hunter River Gazette 26(2)
  Illawarra Mercury 81(2), 356(2)
  Illustrated Sydney News 409
  Kiama Examiner 81(2)
  Kiama Pilot 515
  Literary News: A Review &
    Magazine 505(2)

Literary News 520
Maitland Mercury and Hunter
  River General Advertiser 337,
  352, 26(2)
Monitor 42, 56, 200, 210, 285,
  303, 333, 343, 394, 395, 396,
  500, 520, 537, 25(2), 41(2),
  179(2), 196(2), 265(2), 432(2),
  511(2), 582(2)
Morning Chronicle 462
New South Wales Literary,
  Political and Commercial
  Advertiser 114(2)
New South Wales Magazine
  114(2)
New South Wales Medical
  Gazette 1
New South Wales Pocket
  Almanack 559
New South Wales Sporting
  Magazine 428(2)
People's Advocate and New
  South Wales Vindicator 534
Press, The 77(2), 80(2)
Quarterly Review 375
Spectator 521(2)
Statesman 585(2)
Sydney Gazette 42, 85, 94, 199,
  216, 233, 263, 315, 327, 367,
  368, 381, 464, 524, 12(2),
  17(2), 46(2), 48(2), 50(2),
  60(2), 69(2), 77(2), 87(2),
  114(2), 166(2), 167(2), 172(2),
  194(2), 204(2), 210(2), 211(2),
  261(2), 263(2), 265(2), 273(2),
  283(2), 304(2), 366(2), 367(2),
  370(2) 382(2), 388(2), 394(2),
  401(2), 405(2), 444(2), 479(2),
  496(2), 510(2), 578(2), 583(2),
  600(2), 605(2)
Sydney Gazette and New South
  Wales Advertiser 558
Sydney Herald 102, 130, 150,
  196, 221, 466, 520, 41(2),
  48(2), 108(2), 142(2), 166(2),
  167(2), 265(2), 479(2)
Sydney Magazine 26
Sydney Magazine of Science
  and Art 1
Sydney Mail 287, 299(2)
Sydney Monitor: see Monitor
Sydney Morning Herald 6, 48,
  61, 94, 344, 409, 449, 535,
  26(2), 42(2), 75(2), 81(2),
  204(2), 275(2), 338(2), 418(2),
  479(2), 540(2), 591(2), 626(2)
Sydney Times 515, 48(2)
Tegg's Monthly Magazine
  504(2)
Trumpeter 163(2)
Voice of Jacob 84
Weekly Orthodox Journal
  341(2)
Weekly Register 514, 342(2)
Newspapers: New Zealand
  Bay of Islands Gazette 356(2)
  Bay of Islands Observer 356(2)
  Maori Messenger 182
  New Zealand Advertiser 356(2)
  New Zealand Herald 182
Newspapers: Queensland
  Brisbane Courier 201

Newspapers: Scotland
  Edinburgh Philosophical
    Journal 403(2)
  Edinburgh Review 220, 193(2),
    419(2), 476(2)
  Glasgow Herald 167(2)
Newspapers: South Australia
  Adelaide Examiner 295
  Adelaide Observer 175, 481(2)
  German 222(2)
  Government Gazette 482(2)
  Guardian 473(2)
  Observer 197(2)
  Port Lincoln Herald 280(2)
  Register 2(2), 197(2), 482(2)
  South Australia Illustrated 444
  South Australian 262(2), 356(2)
  South Australian Advertiser 377
  South Australian Colonist
    480(2)
  South Australian Gazette and
    Colonial Register 378, 379,
    444, 540, 473(2), 482(2)
  South Australian Gazette and
    Mining Register 482(2)
  South Australian Magazine 248,
    611(2)
  South Australian News 480(2)
  South Australian Oddfellows'
    Magazine 612(2)
  South Australian Register 445,
    525, 481(2), 482(2)
  Southern Australian 166,
    201(2), 473(2), 482(2), 624(2)
  Southern Star 478
Newspapers: Tasmania
  86, 558, 163(2), 164(2),
    230(2), 576(2)
  Advertiser 591(2)
  Australasian 194
  Austral Asiatic Review 49(2)
  Bent's News 359(2), 472(2)
  Bent's News and Tasmanian
    Threepenny Register 87
  Britannia 320(2), 385(2)
  Britannia and Trades' Advocate
    258(2)
  Church News 298(2)
  Colonial Advocate 3
  Colonial Advocate &
    Tasmanian Monthly Review
    87
  Colonial Times 37, 43, 48, 87,
    347, 411, 475, 46(2), 48(2),
    163(2), 215(2), 221(2), 273(2),
    354(2), 420(2)
  Colonial Times & Tasmanian
    Advertiser 86
  Colonist 356, 475, 384(2),
    576(2)
  Cornwall Chronicle 417, 457,
    458, 48(2)
  Derwent Star & Van Diemen's
    Land Intelligencer 86, 227,
    517
  Examiner 493(2), 590(2), 591(2)
  Hobart Mercury 48, 168, 194
  Hobart Town Advertiser 506,
    163(2), 258(2)
  Hobart Town Almanack 177,
    397(2), 429(2)
  Hobart Town Chronicle 397(2)

Hobart Town Courier 95, 302, 316, 339, 355, 538, 574, 72(2), 163(2), 164(2), 247(2), 300(2), 396(2), 452(2)
Hobart Town Gazette 289, 356, 559, 273(2), 279(2), 336(2), 396(2), 515(2), 516(2)
Hobart Town Gazette and Van Diemen's Land Advertiser 86
Hobart Town Gazette and Southern Reporter 86
Hobart Town Guardian 48, 303
Hobart Town Herald 420
Hobart Town Magazine 221(2)
Independent 457
Launceston Advertiser 316, 369, 418, 458, 7(2)
Launceston Courier 316
Launceston Examiner 3, 25, 258, 316, 458, 355(2)
Morning Advertiser 258(2)
Murray's Austral-Asiatic Review 273(2)
Observer: a Van Diemen's Land Journal of Politics, Agriculture, Commerce... 505
People's Advocate 214
Quarterly Review 561
Spectator 164(2), 490(2)
Tasmanian 459, 559, 163(2), 221(2), 258(2), 273(2), 396(2)
Tasmanian and Austral Asiatic Review 163(2), 221(2), 273(2)
Tasmanian and Port Dalrymple Advertiser 559
Tasmanian and Southern Literary and Political Journal 221(2)
Tasmanian Church Chronicle 95, 287(2)
Tasmanian Journal of Natural History 414
Tasmanian Journal of Natural Science 59, 493, 544, 106(2)
Tasmanian Messenger 205(2)
Tasmanian News 437, 438
Tasmanian Tribune 194
Tasmanian Weekly Dispatch 258(2)
Teetotal Advocate 316, 441(2)
True Colonist 37, 164(2)
True Colonist & V.D.L.Political Despatch..& Commerical Advertiser 385(2)
Trumpeter 221(2)
Van Diemen's Land Chronicle 355, 412, 164(2), 249(2)
Van Diemen's Land Gazette 368
Van Diemen's Land Gazette and General Advertiser 86
Van Diemen's Land Monthly Magazine 397(2)
Van Diemen's Land Temperance Herald 316
Newspapers: USA
American Journal of Science 279
Citizen 235(2)
Daily News 235(2)
Irish News 218(2)
New York Tribune 235(2)

Saturday Evening Post 516
Southern Citizen 235(2)
United States Catholic Miscellany 165(2)
Newspapers: Victoria
Misc: 26
Advertiser 520
Advocate 393(2)
Age 520, 474(2)
Argus 26, 176, 351, 50(2), 55(2), 80(2), 84(2), 90(2), 252(2), 474(2)
Australia Felix Monthly Magazine 520
Colonist 88(2)
Corio Chronicle 26
Daily News 252(2)
Geelong Advertiser 520
Geelong Register 520
Herald 216, 474(2), 603(2)
Intelligencer 520
Journal of Australasia 176
Melbourne Advertiser 370, 50(2), 125(2)
Melbourne Herald 48(2)
Melbourne Morning Herald 252(2), 438(2)
Melbourne Morning Herald and General Daily Advertiser 216
Port Phillip Christian Herald 399
Port Phillip Gazette 26, 216, 399, 125(2), 603(2)
Port Phillip Herald 26, 216, 376, 453, 50(2)
Port Phillip Patriot 216, 271, 520, 50(2), 125(2), 603(2), 604(2)
Port Phillip Patriot and Melbourne Advertiser 370
Victoria Colonist and Western District Advertiser 385(2)
Victorian Agricultural and Horticultural Gazette 176
Newspapers: Western Australia
Inquirer 6(2), 74(2), 278(2)
Inquirer: A Western Australian Journal of Politics and Literature 122(2)
Perth Gazette 74(2), 632(2)
Perth Inquirer and Commercial News 392(2)
Swan River Guardian 227
New Zealand:
see: Cemeteries — NZ
see: Churches — NZ
see: Houses etc. — NZ
see: Newspapers —NZ
see: Organisations — NZ
see: Places Index — NZ
see: Politics — NZ
see: Religion — NZ
see: Schools — NZ
see: Universities — NZ
New Zealand
Early settlement 170, 186, 187, 546
Land policy 479
Magna Carta 546
Maori culture 480
Maori land rights 356(2)

Maori language 42(2)
Maori War 49, 463(2), 511(2)
Maoris 479, 130(2), 209(2)
Politics 187
Treaty of Waitangi 546, 463(2)
Waitangi treaty 188
Nursing 369(2)
Occult 221(2)
Occupations: see Occupations Index
Oceanography 85(2)
Opera 98(2), 568(2)
Operetta: Sweethearts and Wives 279(2)
Organisations: Banks, Companies, Hospitals, Prisons etc. see under B, C, H, P etc.
Organisations Government: see below following Organisations Miscellaneous.
Organisations Religious: see Religious Organisations.
Organisations: including associations, institutions, movements, libraries, museums, societies, clubs, political, legal, scientific, botanical and sporting organisations, inns of court, charities, mechanics' institutes, orphanages, parks, gardens etc.
Listed geographically after:
Organisations: Miscellaneous:
Academy of Sciences, Russia 456(2)
Acclimatization Society 86
Alexander Turnbull Library, Wellington, NZ 363(2)
Alpine Club, Switzerland 89(2)
American Academy of Sciences, USA 279
Basel Missionary Society, Switzerland 351
Bombay Civil Service, India 101(2)
British Legation, Switzerland 89(2)
Council of the Indies 14(2)
Indian Medical Service 419(2)
Literary Institute, Brazil 79(2)
Military Institute, India 500(2)
Museum of Florence 69(2)
Naturhistorische Hofmuseum, Vienna 73
New York Philharmonic Society, USA 568(2)
New Zealand Association 561(2)
New Zealand Co. 115(2)
Pennsylvania Academy of Fine Arts, USA 348
Public Museum, Swansea WLS 98
Rijksmuseum NL 556(2)
Russian Antarctic Expedition 99(2)
Sans Souci Club (Bombay), India 188(2)
Societe d'Histoire Naturelle (Mauritius) 12(2)

South Sea Academy 599(2)
Stockholm museum, Sweden 521(2)
Turko-Persian Boundary Commission 18
Zoological Society 19
Organisations Miscellaneous: Australia
(see also under states etc.)
Aborigines Protection Society 617(2)
Agricultural and Horticultural Society 379(2)
Anti-Transportation League 63, 51(2)
Australasian League 82, 225, 317, 55(2), 336(2)
Australasian League for the Prevention of Transportation 591(2)
Australian Advisory Committee .62(2)
Australian Association for the Advancement of Science 59
Australian Club 387(2), 400(2), 411(2), 609(2)
Australian Immigration Association 300, 203(2), 237(2)
Australian League 80(2)
Australian Medical Association 1
Australian Medical Board 311
Australian Patriotic Association 113, 575, 11(2), 142(2), 148(2), 151(2), 586(2)
Australian Philosophical Society 94
Australian School Society 204(2), 398(2), 616(2)
Australian Society for the Promotion of... Colonial Produce and Manufactures 509(2)
Australian Society for Deposits and Loans 120(2)
Australian Subscription Library 304, 398(2), 435(2)
Colonial Reform Society 482
Committee of the Australian Colonists 244(2)
Federal Convention 480
Freemasonry 528(2)
Freemasonry: Aust Lodge of the Independent Order of Oddfellows 242(2)
General Association of the Australian Colonies 589(2)
Gould League of bird lovers 467
Loyal National Association 141(2)
National Library, Canberra 445, 354(2)
National School Society 387(2)
Philosophical Society of Aust. 374, 62(2)
Royal Agricultural and Horticultural Society 379(2)
Society for the Promotion of Fine Arts 409, 367(2), 389(2)
Organisations Miscellaneous:

Canada
Association des Chasseurs 352(2)
North American Colonial Association 561(2)
Reformatory 353(2)
Organisations Miscellaneous: England
see also under Organisations Government
Agricultural Hall Co. 445(2)
Agricultural Society 45(2)
Anti-Corn Law movement 615(2)
Antiquaries Society 345
Apothecary's Hall 295
Ashmolean Society of Oxford 613(2)
Association for Founding the Settlement of Canterbury 561(2)
Australasian League 9(2)
Bar 168, 14(2)
Birmingham Political Union 541
Board of Longitude, ENG 54
British and Foreign Sailors' Society 15
British & Foreign School Society 30, 35, 420
British Association 285(2)
British Association for the Advancement of Science 182(2)
British Committee 204(2)
British consular service 197
British Convention of the Friends of the People 206(2)
British Fisheries Society 178(2)
British Institution 339
British Museum 54, 167, 252, 470, 492, 102(2), 120(2), 137(2), 456(2), 462(2), 595(2)
British Museum of Natural History 168(2), 363(2), 314(2), 437(2), 574(2)
British Patriotic Fund 32(2)
British Relief Association 494(2)
Bureau of Political Economy 391
Cambridge Philosophical Society 613(2)
Canterbury Association 437, 577
Central Queensland Separation League 285(2)
Chancery barrister 319(2)
Chichester Mechanics' Institute 497
Church Missionary Society 252
Coin Committee, ENG 54
College of Physicians 242
Colonial Bishops' Committee 198
Colonial Office 193
Colonial Society Club, London 182
Committee of Trade, ENG 54
Company of Surgeons 64, 594(2)
Company of Surgeons, London

264(2)
Conservative Club 589(2)
Court of Medical Examiners 355(2)
Covent Garden Opera House 442(2)
Crystal Palace Exhibition 84
Cumberland House 573(2)
Dilettante Society 53
Dissenters' Academy, Warrington 403
Ecclesiastical Board for the Colonies 432(2)
Engineers' Society 53
English Bar 224, 337(2), 512(2)
English Society for the Improvement of Prison Discipline 185(2)
Ethnological Society 529(2)
Ethnological Society of London 228(2)
Exeter Hall 15
Family Colonization Loan Society 222
Friendly Society of Agricultural Workers 132(2)
Furnival's Inn 251(2)
General Association for the Australian Colonies 408(2), 412(2)
Gray's Inn 74, 551, 246(2), 314(2), 559(2), 602(2)
Horticultural Society 53, 244(2), 355(2)
Horticultural Society of London 566
Howard Association 509
Hydrographic Office 391(2)
Inner Temple 99, 184, 244, 14(2), 174(2)
Institut de France 53
Institute of British Architects 34(2)
International Statistical Congress 1860 153(2)
Jewish Ladies' Benevolent Society 222
Jockey Club 401(2)
Kensington Museum 480
Kew Gardens and Herbarium: see Royal Botanical Garden, Kew
Kew Botanical Gardens 325
Kew Herbarium 168(2), 244(2)
Lincoln's Inn 29, 55, 74, 128, 139, 265, 392, 456, 134(2), 203(2), 251(2), 428(2), 475(2), 490(2), 552(2)
Linnean Society 19, 29, 53, 65, 85, 97, 98, 167, 267, 325, 345, 493, 88(2), 111(2), 112(2), 114(2), 178(2), 181(2), 182(2), 183(2), 231(2), 391(2), 437(2), 457(2), 499(2), 526(2), 537(2)
Literary and Scientific Institution 626(2)
Literary Club 53
London Agency 225
London Agency Association 9(2)
London Agency for Van Diemen's Land 290(2)

London Botanical Society 407(2)
London Company of Surgeons 368(2)
London Corresponding Society 438, 206(2)
London Emigration Committee 333(2)
London Itinerant Society 260
London Mechanics' Institute 28(2)
London Society for the Encouragement of Arts, Manufactures and Commerce 11(2)
London Society of Arts and Manufacture 54(2)
Manchester Free Grammar School 194
Manchester School of Botanists 194
Medico-Botanical Society 417
Middle Temple 21, 89, 97, 139, 168, 169, 180, 210, 360, 457, 9(2), 169(2), 319(2), 473(2), 570(2), 583(2), 615(2)
National Colonization Society 195(2), 535(2)
National Maritime museum 316(2)
National Portrait Gallery LND 333(2)
Natural History Museum 319(2)
New Zealand Association 535(2)
Ordnance Survey 193
Patriotic Fund 72(2), 295(2)
Philharmonic Society 301
Phrenological Society 624(2)
Political Economy Club 535(2)
Reading Society 578(2)
Repeal Association 217(2)
Royal Academy 222, 339, 348, 455, 160(2), 558(2), 574(2), 592(2)
Royal Agricultural Society 445(2)
Royal Astronomical Society 338, 403(2), 404(2), 471(2)
Royal Botanical Garden, Kew 265, 268, 325
Royal Botanical Garden, Kew (Herbarium) 168(2), 244(2)
Royal College of Physicians 56
Royal College of Science 30(2)
Royal College of Surgeons 1, 85, 112, 295, 314, 502, 74(2), 102(2), 297(2), 368(2), 376(2), 418(2), 434(2), 514(2), 515(2), 626(2)
Royal Colonial Institute 285(2), 301(2)
Royal Commonwealth Society 592(2)
Royal Geographical Society 105, 363, 477, 565, 103(2), 185(2), 473(2), 494(2), 498(2), 576(2)
Royal Geological Society 473(2)
Royal Humane Society 426(2)

Royal Institution 53
Royal Jennerian Society 419(2)
Royal Military College, Sandhurst 193
Royal National Lifeboat Association 322
Royal Observatory 338
Royal Society 52, 98, 151, 167, 243, 244, 275, 338, 345, 391, 403, 413, 457, 470, 493, 531, 554, 578, 34(2), 62(2), 88(2), 114(2), 137(2), 178(2), 183(2), 315(2), 318(2), 319(2), 404(2), 437(2), 456(2), 471(2), 494(2), 535(2)
Royal Society Club 53
Royal Society of Arts 119, 285(2)
Royal Society of Literature 457
Royal Society of London 154, 578, 34(2)
Royal United Services Institution 316(2)
Royal Zoological Society 250
Scott Polar Research Institute, Cambridge 316(2)
Societies of the Friends of the People 449(2)
Society for Promoting Arts, Manufactures and Commerce 160(2)
Society for the Encouragement of Arts and Science 45(2)
Society for the Reform of Colonial Government 561(2)
Society of Antiquaries 53
Society of Apothecaries 1, 134, 502, 434(2), 514(2)
Society of Arts 53, 157(2)
Society of Arts & Commerce 123, 359(2)
Society of Arts, Commerce & Manufactures 325(2)
Society of British Artists 455
Society of Painters in Water Colours 455, 353(2)
Society of Painters in Oils and Water Colours 455
Society of Telegraph Engineers 295
South Australian Association 261(2)
South Australian Literary Association 262(2), 624(2)
South Australian School Society 440(2)
South Kensington Museum 354(2)
Statistical Society 539, 228(2)
Temperance Society 562(2)
Theological Institution 540(2)
Trinity House 567, 93(2), 364(2)
Union Society 480
Watercolour Society 455
Western Australian Association 5(2)
Western Literary & Scientific Institution 354(2)
Worshipful Company of Apothecaries 626(2)
Zoological Society 85, 182(2)

Zoological Society of London 441, 465, 363(2)
Organisations Miscellaneous: France
French Academy 69(2)
Geographical Society 103(2)
Geographical Society of Paris 413
Institut de France 69(2), 403(2)
Jardin des Plantes 102(2)
L'Academie Royale des Sciences 69(2)
Museum d'Histoire Naturelle 228(2)
Paris Museum 323(2)
Royal Academy of France 389(2)
Royal Statistical Society of France 417
Societe de Geographie 105
Organisations Miscellaneous: Germany
Bavarian Botanical Society 114(2)
Geological Society of Germany 474(2)
Heimat Museum 104(2)
Jacobin Club 403
National History Society of Dresden 474(2)
Organisations Miscellaneous: Ireland
Bar 51(2)
Belfast Mechanics' Institute 192
Board of National Education 470(2)
Cork Botanical Gardens 325
Fenian Movement 347(2)
Galbally Abbey 376
Irish Bar 195, 278(2), 337(2), 512(2)
Irish Distress Committee 129
King's and Queen's College of Physicians of Ireland 314
National Society for the Education of the Poor in Ireland 512(2)
Repeal Association 234(2), 294(2)
Royal Irish Academy 314
Royal Irish Constabulary 202
Seamen's Friend Society 192
Ulster Teachers' Association 192
United Irishmen 512, 550, 206(2), 296(2)
United Irishmen of Dublin 266(2)
Young Ireland Movement 217(2), 234(2), 294(2), 342(2)
Organisations Miscellaneous: New South Wales
Aborigines Protection Society 600(2)
Aborigines' (Natives) Institution 370(2)
Agricultural & Horticultural Society 6, 42, 417, 11(2), 25(2), 69(2), 148(2)
Agricultural Association 629(2)
Agricultural Society 144, 152, 157, 259, 305, 306, 314, 325,

490, 530, 562, 153(2), 158(2), 178(2), 196(2), 307(2), 362(2), 426(2), 464(2), 538(2), 566(2)
Agricultural Stock Club 562, 134(2)
Ancient Masonry 39(2)
Anti-Transportation Committee 26(2)
Art Gallery of NSW 445
Atlas Office and Book Repository 505(2)
Australasian Pioneers' Club 402(2)
Australian Clerks' Benevolent Fund Society 538
Australian Club 202, 411(2), 527(2)
Australian Jockey Club 549, 527(2)
Australian Landowners Association 113
Australian Library 26(2)
Australian Medical Association 114
Australian Medical Subscription Library 114
Australian Museum 19, 12(2), 178(2), 181(2), 182(2), 237(2), 284(2), 361(2), 497(2)
Australian Patriotic Association 210, 325, 481
Australian Racing & Jockey Club 11(2)
Australian Racing Club 114, 325, 427, 562, 69(2)
Australian School Society 260
Australian Steam Navigation Co. 199
Australian Subscription Library 201, 210, 237(2)
Australian Union Benefit Society 542
Bachelors' Ball 283(2), 367(2)
Bar 195
Benevolent Asylum 233(2), 420(2)
Benevolent Society 1, 6, 42, 113, 135, 157, 255, 260, 304, 314, 315, 344, 374, 427, 464, 500, 537, 554, 575, 12(2), 16(2), 131(2), 134(2), 178(2), 192(2), 196(2), 359(2), 370(2), 381(2), 464(2), 509(2), 527(2), 578(2), 617(2), 629(2)
Botanical Gardens 416, 12(2), 103(2), 181(2), 377(2)
British and Foreign Society 450
British Medical Association, NSW Branch 357(2)
Charities 6
Church & School Corporation 432(2)
Clergy & School Lands (Trustees of) 211(2)
Commercial Reading Rooms & Library 538
Committee to Establish a Free Port at Newcastle 26(2)
Constitutional Association 534, 542, 136(2)
Corporation of the Trustees of Church and School Lands

432(2)
Council of Education 6
Debating Society 617(2)
Denominational School Board 58
Domain (Government) 187(2)
Destitute Childrens' Asylum 58
Dixson Gallery, Sydney 333(2), 354(2)
Evan District Committee of Emancipated Colonists 241
Female and Male Orphans Institutions 427
Female Immigrants Home 221
Female Orphan Institution 234(2), 295(2), 307(2), 311(2), 319(2)
Floral & Horticultural Show 149
Floral & Horticultural Society 96, 542
Free Public Library of Sydney 337
Freemasonry 1, 206, 207, 384, 526, 191(2), 243(2)
Gaol Committee 519
Hawkesbury Benevolent Society 79, 144, 384, 227(2), 425(2)
Hawkesbury Racing Club 11(2)
Horticultural Committee 538(2)
Horticultural Improvement Society 168(2)
Horticultural Society of Sydney 54(2)
Hunter River Agricultural Association 320, 26(2)
Hunter River Steam Packet Association 137(2), 202(2)
Hunter River Vineyard Association 54(2)
Institution for the Civilisation, Care and Education of Aborigines 243(2)
James King or Irrawang Travelling Scholarship 55(2)
lending library 109(2)
Library (circulating) 167(2), 211(2)
Liverpool Asylum 217, 492
Lord Mayor's dinner 411(2)
Loyal Associations 59(2)
Loyal Parramatta Association of Volunteers 521, 87(2)
Loyal Sydney Volunteer Association 51, 255(2)
Macleay Museum 180(2), 181(2), 183(2)
Macquarie Memorial fund 259
Maitland Hospital Committee 320
Male and Female Orphan Institutions 537
Male Orphan Institution 234(2), 307(2)
Masonic Lodge 526, 509(2)
Masonic Lodge (No. 266, 260) 109(2)
Mechanics' Institute 113, 613(2)
Mechanics' School of Arts 538, 172(2)
Medical Board 418(2)

Mitchell Library, Sydney 445, 307(2), 333(2), 335(2), 354(2), 363(2)
Mrs King's Orphanage 53(2)
Mutual Protection Association 141(2)
National Colonization Society 462
National Herbarium, Sydney 167, 493
Native Institution 114, 359, 427, 537, 134(2), 192(2), 209(2), 234(2), 368(2), 439(2)
Newcastle Mechanics' Institute 237(2)
Nicholson Museum 285(2)
Normal Institution 210
Northern Districts Stock owners' Association 11(2)
Oberlin Friendly Aid Society 233(2)
Observatory (Parramatta) 63(2)
Orange Society 347(2)
Orphan Asylum, Parramatta 61
Orphan Committee 519, 201(2)
Orphan School Quarry 107(2)
Orphanage (male) 192(2)
Parramatta Catholic Orphanage Board 346(2)
Parramatta Loyal Association 290, 355, 10(2), 111(2), 419(2), 602(2)
Parramatta Observatory 338
Parramatta Volunteer Association 380
Parramatta-Castle Hill tramway 107(2)
Pastoral Association 141, 311, 449, 135(2), 587(2), 617(2)
Patriotic Association 343, 542
Philanthropic Society 105, 135, 551, 16(2), 17(2), 295(2)
Philosophical Society 1, 94, 314, 315, 562, 241(2), 307(2)
Philosophical Society of Aust. 463, 538(2)
Police Fund 435
Portland Head Society 632(2)
Public Library of NSW 304, 26(2), 178(2), 237(2), 257(2), 435(2)
Railway Association 120(2)
Riverine Association 75(2), 75(2C)
Royal Society, NSW 1, 86, 315, 374, 578, 357(2), 474(2)
Royal Sydney Yacht Squadron 233(2)
St Cecilia's Philarmonic Society 337
St George Coffee Lounge 547(2)
Separation Association 90(2)
Society for Affording Protection to the Natives of the South Sea... 210(2)
Society for Destitute Children 315, 527(2)
Society for the Abolition of Capital Punishment 276(2)
Society of Emigrant Mechanics 542

Southern Association 198
Southern Cattle Association 120(2), 203(2)
Standing Committee of the Emancipated Colonists of NSW 547(2)
Stock Club, NSW 42
Stock Fund Committee 538(2)
Stockholder's Committee 203(2)
Subscription Library 178(2), 293(2)
Sydney Benevolent Society Asylum 87
Sydney Bethel Union 58
Sydney Botanic Garden 269, 180(2)
Sydney College Committee 203(2)
Sydney Female Refuge Society 58
Sydney Institution 42, 374, 578(2)
Sydney Jewish Library 84
Sydney Loyal Association 122, 215(2), 403(2)
Sydney Philharmonic Society 265
Sydney Pilot Service 73(2)
Sydney racecourse 395(2)
Sydney Reading Room 395(2)
Sydney Sailors' Home 233(2)
Sydney Turf Club 11(2)
Temperance Hall 474(2)
Temperance Movement 270(2)
Temperance Society 6, 260, 617(2)
Total abstinence movement 418(2), 515
Turf Club 114, 315, 169(2), 172(2), 256(2)
Union Club 197, 207, 472, 41(2), 453(2)
United Masonic Fraternity 12(2)
Victoria Club 41(2)
Waterloo Fund 131(2), 221(2)
Windsor Benevolent Society 259
Windsor Charitable Institution 144, 381, 221(2), 227(2)
Zoological Society 86
Organisations Miscellaneous: Queensland
Ipswich Racecourse 124(2)
Moreton Bay & Northern Districts Separation Association 311
Temperance Movement 229(2)
Walter and Eliza Hall Trust 214
Organisations Miscellaneous: Scotland
Caledonian theatre, Edinburgh 182
Church of Scotland 79(2)
Clan Macquarie 187(2)
College of Justice 227
College of Surgeons 219
Edinburgh Astronomical Institution 154
Edinburgh Botanical Gardens

188
Edinburgh museum 119(2)
Edinburgh Royal Observatory 154
Edinburgh University Museum 94
Faculty of Advocates 337, 266(2)
Friends of Liberty 218(2)
Glasgow Associated Friends of the Constitution and of the People 266(2)
Glasgow Edinburgh Union Canal 219
Glasgow Mechanics' Institute 520, 520(C)
Highland Society, SCT 188
Hunterian Medical Society of Edinburgh 284(2)
Royal College of Physicians, Edinburgh 268(2)
Royal College of Surgeons, Edinburgh 230(2), 235(2), 427(2)
Royal Society of Edinburgh 154, 537(2)
Scottish Societies of the Friends of the People 266(2)
Society for the Promotion of Fine Arts 242(2)
Speculative Society 455
Turriff Hunt 321(2)
United Scotsmen 218(2)
Wernerian Natural History Society of Edinburgh 12(2)
Organisations Miscellaneous: South Australia
Acclimatization Society 626(2)
Adelaide Gardens 176
Adelaide Hunt Club 384(2)
Adelaide Marksmen 378
Adelaide Mechanic's Institute 296
Agricultural Society 262(2)
Bar 244, 380
Botanic Gardens 557, 626(2)
Building Committee, SA 377, 379
Caldeonian Society 525
Freemasonry 335
German Rifle Club 446
Immigrants' Welcome Committee 626(2)
Institution of Civil Engineers 342
Literary & Scientific Association, SA 462, 200(2)
Lobethal Lutheran Semaniry 222(2)
Lodge of Unity 335
Mechanics Institute 248, 497, 384(2), 612(2)
National Gallery of SA 19
Natural History Society 482(2)
North Adelaide Institute 612(2)
Old Colonists' Festival Dinner 380
Parliamentary Candidate Society 462
Pastoral Aid Fund 7
Royal Geographical Society (SA branch) 19

Royal Society 626(2)
St Patrick's Society 248
School Society 626(2)
Secondary Towns Association 262(2)
Society of Arts 626(2)
South Australian Association 165, 462, 535(2), 560(2)
South Australian Bar 244, 380
South Australian Club 378, 557, 626(2)
South Australian Colonization Commission 462
South Australian Farmers' Co-operative Union 444
South Australian Football League (Australian Rules) 197(2)
South Australian Institute 626(2)
South Australian Jockey Club 380
South Australian Lodge of Friendship 64(2)
South Australian Museum 19
South Australian School Society 16, 327, 440(2)
South Australian Society 541
South Australian Temperance Alliance 197(2)
Statistical Society 498, 64(2)
Total Abstinence League, SA 48
Wyatt Benevolent Institution 525(2), 627(2)
Zoological Gardens 525
Organisations Miscellaneous: Tasmania
Acclimatization Society 298(2)
Agricultural & Commercial Association 176(2)
Agricultural Society of Van Diemen's Land 402(2)
Anniversary Regatta 37(2)
Anti-State Aid Association 192
Anti-Transportation League 329, 484, 552, 393(2), 593(2), 594(2)
Bellerive Library 110
Benevolent Society 191, 317, 359, 502, 552, 290(2)
Botanical Gardens 490(2)
Bothwell Literary Society 428, 436(2)
Colonial Medical Service 541(2)
Cornwall Agricultural Society 532
Cornwall Turf Club 454, 511
Cross Marsh Agricultural Association 375(2)
Cross Marsh Market Committee 421, 375(2)
Deane's Library 229(2)
Derwent Circulating Library 505(2)
Derwent Whaling Club 37(2)
Female Factory, Hobart 71(2)
Freemasonry 230, 458, 221(2), 273(2)
Glamorgan Library 491(2)
Hobart Airport 113(2)
Hobart Anniversary Regatta 414

Hobart Art Exhibition 35(2)
Hobart Domain 453(2)
Hobart Infant School Society 564(2)
Hobart Mechanics' Institute 118(2), 258(2), 385(2), 528(2)
Hobart, St David's Park 347
Hobart Town Agricultural Society 225
Hobart Town Book Society 191
Horticultural Society 261, 317, 492
Immigrants' Home, Tas 174
Immigration Aid Society 317
Infant School Society 144(2)
Ladies' Patriotic Committee 261
Launceston & Deloraine Railway Association 330
Launceston Association 261
Launceston Auxiliary Temperance Society 143
Launceston Benevolent Society Asylum 258, 454, 441(2)
Launceston Horticultural Society 418, 292, 290(2), 441(2)
Launceston Mechanics' Institute 456
Launceston Public Library 4
Legislative Council, Tas 20
Licensed Victuallers' Society 258(2)
London Agency 261
London Agency Association 8(2)
London Agency for Van Diemen's Land 433(2)
Manchester Unity Independent Order of Oddfellows 138(2)
Mechanics' Institute 4, 98, 217, 261, 305, 339, 418, 176(2), 290(2), 351(2), 385(2), 466(2), 542(2), 590(2)
Medical Court of Examiners 213
Merchant Seamen's Institution 260(2)
Midland Agricultural Association 225, 430, 94(2), 452(2)
Museum of Natural History 411
New Norfolk Asylum 156
New Town Race Course 138(2)
Northern Tasmanian Railway League 330
Orange Lodge 258(2)
Philharmonic Society 356
Queen Victoria Museum, Launceston 330
Queen Victoria Museum & Art Gallery 373(2)
Regatta Association 433(2)
Royal Hobart Regatta 356
Royal Society 411, 32(2), 118(2), 315(2), 355(2)
Royal Society of Tasmania 10, 46, 493, 544, 34(2), 67(2), 106(2), 138(2), 230(2), 231(2), 298(2), 354(2), 427(2), 447(2), 490(2), 563(2), 576(2)

Royal Society of Van Diemen's Land 346, 230(2)
St Andrew's Club(2)
Southern Tasmanian Council of the Australasian League 506
Tasmanian Club 407, 531, 298(2)
Tasmanian Ladies' Society for the Reformation of Female Prisoners 411
Tasmanian Museum & Art Gallery 447(2)
Tasmanian Natural History Society 414
Tasmanian Public Library 10, 98
Tasmanian Racing Club 308(2)
Tasmanian Society 10, 436, 457, 492, 530, 544, 29(2), 118(2), 355(2), 613(2)
Tasmanian Society for the Prevention of Cruelty to Animals 438
Tasmanian Teetotal Society 441(2)
Tasmanian Turf Club 511, 36(2)
Temperance movement 504
Temperance Society 144(2), 563(2)
Union Club 235
United Irishmen 302(2)
Van Diemen's Land Agricultural Society 128(2)
Van Diemen's Land Auxiliary Temperance Society 551
Van Diemen's Land Folk Museum 563(2)
Waterloo Club 327
Wellington Bridge Stationery Shop and Library 505(2)
Organisations Miscellaneous: Victoria
Anti-Transportation Committee 252(2)
Anti-Transportation League 542(2)
Athenaeum Library 453
Austin Homes, Geelong 43
Ballarat Art Gallery 101(2)
Benevolent Asylum 350, 93(2)
Botanic Gardens 93(2)
Constitutional Association 350
Deaf and Dumb Institute 515(2)
Flagstaff Gardens 410(2)
Geelong Botanical Gardens 492(2)
Gippsland Caledonian Society 184(2)
Historical Society of Victoria 445
Horticultural Society 524, 334(2)
Irish & Scotch Destitution Relief Fund 82
Ladies' Benevolent Association 331
League of Solemn Engagement of the Australian Colonies 593(2)
Mechanics' Institute 220, 400,

453, 93(2), 125(2), 447(2)
Mechanics' Institute, Melbourne 26
Medical Board 544
Medical Society of Victoria 515(2)
Melbourne Botanical Gardens 176
Melbourne Chambers 410(2)
Melbourne Club 273, 350
Melbourne Cricket Club 216, 349(2)
Melbourne Debating Society 400
Melbourne Herbarium 326
Melbourne Hospital Committee 590(2)
Melbourne Ladies' Benevolent Society 400
Melbourne Public Library 444
Melbourne Race Club 38
Melbourne Total Abstinence Society 400
Melbourne Turf Club 572
Melbourne Union Benefit Society 26, 273
National Gallery of Victoria 445
National Herbarium (Vic) 167
Old Colonists' Association of Victoria 547
Orangemen 51(2)
Pastoral & Agricultural Society 453, 524, 447(2), 501(2)
Pastoralists' Association 387(2)
Port Phillip Association 4, 38, 68, 282, 423, 437, 101(2), 224(2), 447(2), 501(2), 576(2)
Port Phillip Immigration and Anti-Shipwreck Society 82
Port Phillip Medical Association 273, 515(2)
Port Phillip Separation Association 51(2)
Royal Australasian College of Surgeons 160(2)
Royal Geological Society of Victoria 473(2)
Royal Historical Society of Victoria 604(2)
Royal Philharmonic 93(2)
Separation Committee 79(2)
Separation League 271
Separation Society 216
Sheep & Cattle Mutual Assurance Co 48(2)
State Library of Victoria 544, 71(2)
Sunbury Boys' Home 523(2)
Temperance movement 29(2)
Villiers & Heytesbury Agricultural Society 412(2)
Organisations Miscellaneous: Western Australia
Agricultural & Horticultural Society 253(2)
Agricultural Society 99(2), 278(2), 489(2), 618(2), 630(2)
Book Society 175(2)
Botanical Gardens, Perth 175(2)
Children's Friend Society 99(2)

Colonization Commission 477
Freemasonry 122(2)
Fremantle Town Trust 66
Guildford Mechanics' Institute 155
Perth Museum 391(2)
St George Lodge 122(2)
St John Lodge 122(2)
Stirling Gardens 175(2)
Swan Agricultural Society 155
Swan River Mechanics' Institute 391(2), 440(2)
Total Abstinence Society 440(2)
Vineyard Society 122(2), 175(2), 440(2)
Western Australian Agricultural Society 219(2)
Western Australian Society 122(2)
York Agricultural Society, WA 180
York Race Club 219(2)
Organisations Government: including government departments, boards, commissions, committees, local government, legislatures and parliaments. Listed geographically.
Organisations Government: Canada
Canadian General Assembly 561(2)
Gosford Commission 353, 446
House of Assembly 603(2)
Legislative Council 234(2)
Organisations Government: England
Admiralty 243, 275, 276, 277, 287, 288, 289, 392, 404, 415, 446, 526, 569, 61(2), 281(2), 316(2), 573(2)
Admiralty Victualling Board 576
Audit Board 120(2)
Board of Control 136(2)
Board of Customs 439
Board of Longitude 297
Board of Ordnance 614(2)
Board of Trade 67, 455, 457, 136(2), 475(2)
Bow Street Police Office 399(2)
British Embassy Paris 182(2)
British Food Corporation 606(2)
British Ordnance Department 547, 32(2), 115(2)
British Parliament 294(2)
British Treasury 120(2), 258(2)
Central Board of Health, ENG 1
Charity Commissions 282(2)
Chatham Dockyard 75
Colonial Land and Emigration Commission 51, 354, 485, 535(2), 407(2)
Colonial Office 49, 117, 149, 200, 202, 205, 217, 219, 239, 251, 254, 257, 270, 271, 283, 284, 285, 286, 287, 288, 289, 291, 298, 299, 302, 306, 308, 314, 315, 317, 324, 323, 329, 372, 375, 379, 384, 385, 386, 387, 395, 396, 397, 398, 401, 404, 410, 415, 425, 431, 434, 436, 446, 449, 456, 478, 480, 512, 526, 8(2), 44(2), 45(2), 47(2), 52(2), 61(2), 62(2), 70(2), 77(2), 78(2), 80(2), 86(2), 90(2), 92(2), 110(2), 120(2), 121(2), 125(2), 133(2), 210(2), 333(2), 407(2), 475(2), 483(2), 560(2), 576(2), 605(2)
Colonization Commission 541, 117(2)
Colonization Commission for South Australia 228(2)
Commission on Eastern Colonies 474
Commissioners of sewers
Committee on transportation (see select committee)
Comptroller's Office 310(2)
Convict Department 207(2)
Corporation of London 257(2)
Council on Education 136(2)
Customs Office 118, 118(C), 216(2)
Department of Marine and Colonies 391
Emigration Commission 353
Engineers' Department 385(2)
Home Department 536, 281(2)
Home Office 314, 464, 569
House of Commons 21, 37, 53, 67, 113, 139, 187, 196, 286, 290, 337, 339, 345, 384, 446, 449, 451, 455, 464, 554, 19(2), 25(2), 64(2), 136(2), 193(2), 228(2), 236(2), 273(2), 400(2), 401(2), 424(2), 475(2), 550(2), 561(2), 587(2), 600(2), 633(2)
House of Lords 220, 222, 298, 456, 542, 546, 228(2), 286(2), 470(2), 490(2), 561(2), 584(2), 607(2)
House of Lords (select committee on transportation) 107, 122
Land & Emigration Commission 576, 334(2)
Marine Board 527
Medical Board, ENG 65
Metropolitan Police 28(2), 228(2), 609(2)
Molesworth Committee on Transportation 185(2), 249(2)
Navy Board 53, 503, 272(2)
Navy Office 523(2)
Ordnance Office, Portsmouth 297
Postmaster General's Dept. 474
Prisoners of War Office 178(2)
Privy Council 37, 53, 54, 263, 306, 309, 396, 463, 542, 548, 554, 228(2), 247(2), 287(2), 476(2)
Privy Council Committee for Trade and Plantations 482, 155(2)
Royal Constabulary Commission 228(2)
Royal Dockyard 115(2), 137(2)
Royal Engineers Department 614(2)
Select Committee on Colonial Lands 576
Select Committee on Transportation 107, 122, 185, 572, 19(2), 178(2), 191(2), 266(2), 310(2), 407(2)
South Australian Colonization Commission 576, 251(2), 356(2)
Stamp Office 172(2C)
Survey Department 230
Transport Board 235, 468, 548, 178(2), 306(2), 621(2)
Treasury 5, 36, 156, 158, 289, 434, 570, 52(2), 578(2)
Trinity House 567
Victualling Board 526
War Office 153, 215, 253, 273, 315, 356, 268(2)
Organisations Government: France
Directory 267(2)
National Assembly, France 171
Parlement of Provence 171
Organisations Government: India
Bengal Postal Department 253
Madras Civil Service 352(2)
Revenue & Topographical Survey Dept. 332
Supreme Council of Bengal 511
Organisations Government: New South Wales
Assignment Board 529
Audit Board 8(2)
Audit Commission 70(2)
Board of General Purposes 200, 178(2), 483(2)
Board of General Services 119(2)
Board of Magistrates 529
Board of National Education 210, 495
Carters' Barracks, Sydney 304
Caveat Board 242
Central Railway Station 112(2)
Church & School Corporation 6, 136, 159, 186, 284, 507, 211(2), 368(2)
Church and School Lands Corporation 537
Civil Medical Department 580(2)
Clergy & School Lands Corporation 209
Colonial Architect's Office 539(2)
Colonial Medical Department 235(2)
Colonial Secretary's Office 533(2)
Commissariat Dept. 5, 157, 227, 247, 322, 323, 383, 406, 511, 513, 562, 69(2), 98(2), 120(2), 190(2), 202(2), 221(2), 230(2), 309(2), 310(2), 435(2), 464(2), 577(2), 602(2), 608(2)
Commission of Survey & Valuation 269(2)
Committee for the Erection of Jails 201(2)

Convict Assignment Board
523(2)
Convict Department 622(2)
Crown Solicitor's Office 52(2)
Council of Education 337, 409,
257(2), 346(2)
Customs House 113(2)
Customs Office 336, 427
Denominational Board 6
Department of Public Works
219, 539(2)
Department of Roads &
Bridges 238(2)
Emu Plains Agricultural
Establishment 539(2)
Engineer's Department 242(2)
Executive Council 184, 202,
271, 283, 284, 286, 294, 300,
303, 320, 333, 387, 393, 395,
446, 482, 119(2), 120(2),
135(2), 178(2), 183(2), 228(2),
240(2), 284(2), 295(2), 307(2),
339(2), 378(2), 454(2), 523(2),
524(2), 525(2), 526(2), 529(2),
631(2)
Executive Society 204(2)
Female Factory 202, 304, 314,
333, 471, 524, 211(2), 218(2),
282(2), 291(2), 295(2), 308(2),
508(2), 545(2)
General Post Office 509(2)
Government House 111(2)
House of Assembly 348(2)
Hyde Park barracks 293,
113(2), 162(2)
Land Board 200, 207, 284, 333,
178(2), 483(2), 549(2)
Lands & Public Works Dept.
276(2)
Lands Department 565(2)
Legislative Assembly 6, 58, 80,
199, 206, 281, 325, 374, 401,
536, 575, 26(2), 41(2), 73(2),
75(2), 82(2), 83(2), 102(2),
108(2), 131(2), 153(2), 181(2),
276(2), 292(2), 304(2), 339(2),
431(2), 435(2), 453(2), 500(2),
526(2), 533(2), 589(2), 609(2)
Legislative Council 6, 55, 58,
61, 74, 79, 80, 94, 114, 118,
130, 139, 141, 153, 159, 185,
189, 198, 199, 200, 202, 204,
206, 207, 231, 246, 259, 271,
281, 283, 284, 285, 303, 305,
311, 315, 319, 320, 334, 336,
345, 346, 350, 367, 384, 386-8,
393, 394, 397, 398, 407, 439,
446, 447, 464, 483, 484, 485,
550, 525, 534, 536, 546, 561,
1(2), 11(2), 23(2), 25(2),
26(2), 41(2), 52(2), 62(2),
72(2), 73(2), 75(2), 77(2),
79(2), 80(2), 90(2), 97(2),
102(2), 113(2), 119(2), 120(2),
123(2), 135(2), 142(2), 147(2),
148(2), 152(2), 158(2), 162(2),
178(2), 179(2), 180(2), 181(2),
197(2), 203(2), 224(2), 228(2),
236(2), 237(2), 240(2), 243(2),
251(2), 252(2), 256(2), 276(2),
284(2), 289(2), 295(2), 304(2),
307(2), 309(2), 338(2), 339(2),

343(2), 378(2), 387(2), 399(2),
406(2), 407(2), 414(2), 431(2),
435(2), 452(2), 454(2), 455(2),
463(2), 477(2), 479(2), 483(2),
493(2), 497(2), 500(2), 512(2),
513(2), 514(2), 522(2), 523(2),
524(2), 525(2), 526(2), 531(2),
532(2), 533(2), 545(2), 565(2),
585-9(2), 616(2), 617(2),
630(2), 631(2)
Light, Pilot & Navigation
Board 73(2)
Medical Board 1, 237(2),
284(2), 357(2)
Metropolitan Water Board
97(2)
Mounted Police 86(2), 454(2),
483(2)
Municipal Council of Sydney 6,
292(2)
National & Denominational
Boards 346(2)
National Board of Education
337, 409, 514, 183(2)
National Schools Board 339(2),
340(2)
Ordnance Department 326(2),
454(2)
Parliament 40(2), 143(2)
Parliament House 113(2)
Parramatta Council 95(2),
107(2)
Police Force 519(2)
Police Fund 111(2), 190(2),
234(2), 580(2)
Police Office 273(2), 389(2)
Prospect Reservoir 97(2)
public administration 67
Public Works Dept. 60, 389(2)
Roads Dept. 106(2), 324(2)
Royal Commission 241(2)
Scone District Council 334
Survey Department 210, 216,
280, 238(2), 240(2), 409(2)
Surveyor General's Dept. 309,
7(2), 43(2)
Sydney City Council 1, 442,
461, 549, 555, 23(2), 162(2),
180(2), 242(2), 292(2), 446(2),
623(2)
Sydney District Council 210
Sydney Municipal Council
38(2), 257(2), 279(2)
Sydney Town Hall 112(2)
Treasury 202, 70(2)
Turnpike Board 191(2)
Water police 192, 335(2)
Wentworth Committee 339(2)
Yass District Council 293(2)
Organisations Government: New
Zealand
Auckland Provincial Council
188
Canterbury Provincial Council
561(2)
House of Representatives 479
Legislative Council 524
New Zealand General Assembly
561(2)
Organisations Government:
Queensland
Board of Public Education

600(2)
Customs Dept. 263(2)
Denominational Schools Board,
Qld 51
Legislative Assembly 23, 423(2)
Legislative Council 284(2),
448(2)
Public Estate Department 332
State Observatory 124(2)
State Stores 124(2)
Steam Navigation Board 336
Organisations Government:
Scotland
Board of Customs 184(2)
Organisations Government:
South Africa
Naval Store-Keeper's
Department 359
Survey Dept. 432, 478
Organisations Government:
South Australia
Adelaide City Council 478,
99(2)
Adelaide Municipal Council
64(2), 201(2)
Board for Superintendence of
the Relief of the Destitute
Poor 443
Board of Aboriginal Protection
557
Board of City Commissioners
280(2)
Board of Education 17, 335
Central Board of Main Roads
443
Colonization Commission 15,
16, 379
Council of Government 379,
462, 201(2), 472(2)
Destitute Board 499
District Council 197(2)
Emigration Department 432
Executive Council 244, 245,
378, 497(2)
Forest Board 378
Government Assay Office 296
Government House 433
Hospital Board 557
House of Assembly 179, 378,
525, 540, 64(2), 197(2),
201(2), 482(2)
Land Office 379
Land Titles Office 295, 435
Legislative Assembly 342
Legislative Council 17, 47, 287,
288, 341, 342, 378, 380, 478,
498, 499, 525, 64(2), 197(2),
262(2), 280(2), 301(2), 383(2),
384(2), 408(2), 480(2)
Medical Board 335, 626(2)
Municipal Corporation of
Adelaide 179, 262(2), 482(2),
611(2)
Royal Commission 378
South Australian Colonization
Commission 434, 177(2),
560(2)
South Australian Commission
407(2)
Survey Dept. 282, 432, 478,
64(2)
Organisations Government:

Spain
Archives of the Indies 267(2)
Organisations Government:
Tasmania
Assignment Board 217, 474, 492
Audit Board 7(2)
Audit Department 23
Avoca Road Trust 557(2)
Bridgewater Bridge
Commission 35(2), 138(2),
467(2)
Carrick Road Trust 246(2)
Caveat Board 182, 183, 410,
474, 530, 551, 542(2)
Colonial & Convict Medical
Dept. 297(2)
Colonial Engineer's
Department 71(2)
Colonial Secretary's Office
419(2)
Commissariat 549, 566, 106(2),
128(2), 143(2), 217(2), 316(2)
Convict Department 329, 371
Convicts, Board for
Distributing of 230(2)
Council of Government 419
Education, Council of 181,
298(2)
Education Department 113(2)
Education, Board of 4, 30, 181,
330, 357, 474 287(2), 452(2),
462(2)
Executive Council 181, 219,
270, 339, 347, 401, 404, 416,
474, 492, 566, 574, 38(2),
214(2), 247(2), 248(2), 285(2),
297(2), 311(2), 319(2), 320(2),
429(2), 436(2), 472(2), 517(2),
541(2), 542(2), 564(2), 622(2)
Female Factory 174, 132(2),
291(2), 563(2)
Government House 127(2),
555(2)
Hobart High School
Committee 298(2)
Hobart Municipal Council
528(2)
House of Assembly 3, 8, 21, 60,
95, 261, 230, 302, 317, 329,
330, 333, 339, 438, 454, 476,
492, 494, 530, 533, 538, 50(2),
269(2), 298(2), 430(2), 436(2),
593(2)
Immigration Department 297(2)
Infant School Board 454
Land Board 229, 417, 508, (2),
317(2)
Land Commission 530, 542(2)
Lands, Department of 35(2)
Launceston City Council 458,
430(2)
Launceston General Hospital
Board 60, 261, 430(2)
Launceston Municipal Council
261
Launceston & Western Railway
261, 317
Legislative Assembly 441
Legislative Council 2, 3, 8, 20,
21, 25, 30, 77, 96, 97, 106,
143, 181, 230, 249, 251, 257,
270, 324, 329, 330, 339, 356,

371, 404, 407, 413, 416, 437,
454, 458, 459, 475, 476, 492,
508, 530, 552, 566, 35(2),
38(2), 50(2), 51(2), 84(2),
95(2), 100(2), 114(2), 127(2),
138(2), 164(2), 176(2), 248(2),
260(2), 269(2), 296(2), 298(2),
303(2), 311(2), 319(2), 320(2),
372(2), 436(2), 447(2), 452(2),
466(2), 500(2), 541(2), 542(2),
544(2), 557(2), 564(2), 576(2),
591(2), 593(2)
Marine Board 317
Medical Board 490(2)
Medical Examiners, Board of
253
Medical Department 253
New Norfolk Lunatic Asylum
Commission 298(2)
Oatlands Municipal Council
179
Ordnance Department 37(2)
Parliament House 330
Paterson Barracks 73(2)
Paterson's Plains Road Trust
430(2)
Police Department 253, 404
Postal Department 235, 248(2)
Prisoners' Barracks 291(2)
Public Works, Board of 555(2)
Public Works Department 109,
303, 35(2)
Queen's Asylum for Orphans
254
Registrar-General's Dept.
462(2)
Road Trust 249
Roads & Bridges, Dept. of 109
Rokeby watchhouse 35(2)
Ross Municipal Council 225
Salmon Commission 298(2)
Survey Department 251, 282,
529, 538, 170(2), 429(2),
436(2), 467(2), 575(2), 576(2)
Tasmanian Lands & Surveys
Dept. 467(2)
Treasury 95, 416
Upper House 564(2)
Westbury Council 246(2)
Westbury Road Trust 290(2)
Organisations Government:
Victoria
Aborigines, Central Board for
the Protection of 519(2)
Civil List 91(2)
Commission on tenure of waste
lands 401
Education Department 492(2)
Executive Council 350, 34(2),
91(2), 126(2), 349(2)
Geelong Town Council 423
Goldfields Commission 492(2)
Hampden Road Board 200(2)
Hampden Shire Council 200(2)
Heytesbury Road Board 200(2)
House of Assembly 371
Immigration Board 590(2)
Land Board 605(2)
Legislative Assembly 82, 316,
350, 401, 520, 533, 29(2),
55(2), 81(2), 84(2), 184(2),
244(2), 352(2), 412(2), 455(2),

474(2), 523(2), 590(2), 606(2)
Legislative Council 14, 222,
229, 234, 326, 370, 376, 436,
533, 84(2), 88(2), 91(2), 92(2),
126(2), 224(2), 252(2), 334(2),
352(2), 412(2), 455(2), 474(2),
492(2), 501(2), 519(2), 523(2),
605(2), 606(2), 633(2)
Medical Board 273, 515(2)
Melbourne City Council 547,
55(2)
Melbourne Town Council
38(2), 90(2), 334(2)
Police Force 91(2)
Port Phillip customs house
113(2)
Sewers & Water Supply 51(2)
Toodyay Road Board 326
Trade & Customs Department
543
Treasury 88(2)
Victoria Plains Road Board 326
Victorian Legislative Council
401
Warrnambool Shire Council
and Roads Board 412(2)
Yan Yean reservoir 51(2)
Organisations Government:
Western Australia
Albany Town Trust 435(2)
Education, Board of 510, 6(2),
278(2), 618(2)
Education Committee 122(2),
489(2)
Executive Council 174(2),
253(2), 391(2), 486(2), 619(2)
Fremantle Town Council 67
Fremantle Town Trust 417(2),
426(2)
Government House 372
Lands & Surveys Department
488(2)
Legislative Council 66, 155,
165, 180, 190, 382, 576, 99(2),
174(2), 175(2), 253(2), 322(2),
391(2), 408(2), 417(2C),
440(2), 486(2), 487(2), 619(2)
Mounted Police 487(2), 619(2)
Perth City Council 440(2)
Perth Town Trust 165, 99(2),
440(2)
Roads Trust 180, 99(2), 322(2)
Swan Road Board 155
Town Trust 122(2)
Vaccination Board 372
Works, Board of 510, 99(2),
489(2)
Organisations Government: West
Indies
House of Assembly, Dominica
294(2)
Organisations Miscellaneous:
listed above Government
Orphanages: see Organisations:
Miscellaneous
Ornithology 362, 465, 541
Paddle steamer 490, 362(2),
601(2)
Palaentology 494(2)
Pamphlets:
Address to young persons who
are of age to be confirmed

469(2)

An Answer to certain calumnies in the late Governor Macquarie's pamphlet, & etc.. 208(2)

An Appeal to the British Nation 273(2)

Annulosa Javanica; or an Attempt to Illustrate ... Insects collected in Java ... 182(2)

Answers to the question, why do I submit to the Teaching of the Church 425(2)

Australia as she is and as she may be 196(2)

Australia May be an extensive Wine-growing Country 54(2)

Australian Essays on Subjects, Political, Moral and Religious 289(2)

Australian Merino 437(2)

Australian sketches, no 1 114(2)

Brief Statement of Facts... an Overland Expedition from Lake George to Port Phillip 565

Case of E.W. Landor, Esq., J.P., Police Magistrate, Western Australia 75(2)

Catalogue of Scientific Papers 114(2)

Christian Liberality 282(2)

Church of the Incarnation, our guide and refuge 207(2)

Condition of the Colony of New South Wales 289(2)

Congratulatory Address to the National Convention of France 206(2)

Convention the only means of saving us from ruin... to the people of England 438

Convicts' Bank; or a Plain Statement of the Case of Alleged Embezzlement 80(2)

Corrected Report of the Speeches of the Honourable Edward Deas Thomson 525(2)

Correspondence between Major Gen. Sir Richard Bourke ,,, and Alexander McLeay 179(2)

Darkness made Light 468(2)

Divine Right of private judgment in matters of Religion 469(2)

Eight Lectures on the Signs of the Times 469(2)

Essay on Capital Punishment 48(2)

Essays and Reflections in Australia 289(2)

Facts for the Protectionists 289(2)

Family Prayers 469(2)

Felonry of New South Wales 52(2), 266(2)

Fragmens du dernier voyage de la Perouse 85(2)

Free Trade and Protection 289(2)

General Observations on the

Smallpox 12(2)

George Milner Stephen and His Marvellous Cures 474(2)

Gorham Heresy and the Non-natural Explanation .. England 469(2)

Governor Hunter's Remarks on... Colonial Expense of the Establishment of N.S.W.... 571

History of the Rise and Progress of the new British Province of South Australia 480(2)

Horae Entomologicae; or, Essays on the annulose animals 182(2)

Hunger and revolution; On cases of death by starvation 114(2)

Illustrations of the Annulosa of South Africa 182(2)

Is a Penal Colony reconcileable with God's constitution of human society ... 207(2)

Land and Labour in Australia 75(2)

Land of Promise 480(2)

Letter Addressed to His Excellency ... against the Renewal of Transportation 207(2)

Letter from Sydney 462

Letter to Viscount Sidmouth 193(2)

Letter to Lord Sidmouth 584(2)

Letter to the Rev. W. B. Ullathorne 422

Letter to the Right Honourable His Majesty's ... 479(2)

Life in the Bush 65(2)

Mediums and their Dupes 474(2)

Message from God 468(2)

Michael Howe, the last and worst of the Bush Rangers of Van Diemen's Land 577(2)

Observations on the 'Hole and Corner Petition' 304(2)

On the Anatomy and Affinities of the Family of the Medusae 578

On the maritime geography of Australia 62(2)

Parochial System, The 207(2)

Party Politics Exposed 265(2), 304(2), 479(2)

Pastoral Letter to the Congregation 550(2)

Patronage and Justice of the British Treasury Exemplified in a Plain Narrative 230(2)

Political Economy of New South Wales 48(2)

Preliminary Notes on the Fossil Remains of a Chelonian Reptile, ... 578

Present State of New South Wales 48(2)

Proposal for a Grand National Jubilee 206(2)

Reasons for submitting to the

Catholic Church 425(2)

Reasons for the Purchase of Land in South Australia ... Capital 261(2)

Religious Objections to Teetotal Societies, Considered... with Christian Duty 469(2)

Reply to Judge Burton 545(2)

Report on the Statistics of Western Australia in 1840 ... 122(2)

Some Words for and to the Capitalists and Shareholders ... New South Wales 257(2)

Songs of Australia 515

State of the Country in 1832 195(2)

State of the Nation at the Close of 1830 195(2)

Statement 396

Statement of Facts relating to the Recent Altercation .. 49(2)

Statement of the Case of Jas Mitchell, Esq ... 236(2)

Statement of the Improvement and Progress of the Breed of Fine Wooled Sheep in N.S.W. 155(2)

Story of 'Old Sam' the Christian Jew 468(2)

Strictures upon a Letter lately written by Roger Therry, Esq. to Edward Blount Esq., 422

Thoughts on Revolution 206(2)

Two letters written in Van Diemen's Land showing.. oppression & tyranny of government 221(2)

Unpaid Magistrate 265(2)

Vindication of James Mudie & John Larnach... certain reflections... convict servants 86(2), 265(2)

Voluntary support of the Christian Ministry Alone Scriptural and Defensible 591(2)

Wretched Greenwood 88(2)

Parishes: see Churches

Parliaments: see Organisations: Government

Parliamentary seats: see Politics: Parliamentary seats

Partnerships: see Businesses

Penal reform 447, 186(2) see Laws

Penal Settlements: 424
see also Convicts
see also Transportation of Convicts
Misc: 8, 75, 233
Australia 45, 296
Coal Harbour, NSW 222(2)
Impression Bay convict station, Tas 434(2)
Macquarie Harbour penal station, Tas 75
Macquarie Harbour, Tas 37(2), 71(2), 106(2), 138(2), 204(2), 205(2), 230(2), 316(2), 460(2)
Maria Island, Tas 37(2), 71(2),

106(2), 132(2), 269(2), 294(2), 316(2)
Moreton Bay 45, 108, 233, 250, 386, 274(2), 313(2), 600(2)
New South Wales 8
Newcastle, NSW 552(2), 599(2)
Norfolk Island, 45, 220, 408, 447, 165(2), 185(2), 260(2), 261(2), 351(2), 393(2), 580(2)
Port Arthur, Tas 114(2), 205(2), 294(2), 420(2), 429(2)
Port Macquarie, NSW 8, 45, 540(2), 553(2)
Queensland 233, 406(2)
Rocky Hills probation station, Tas 302
Sarah Island, Tas 460(2)
Tasmania 34, 45, 75, 191, 192, 273, 71(2), 316(2)
Victoria 352(2)
Western Australia 484
Pensions 228(2)
Personal names: see Personal Names Index
Pharmaceutical research 355(2)
Philosophy 356(2)
Philosophy (natural) 376(2)
Photography 426, 445, 410(2), 493(2)
Places: see Place Names Index
Plays:
Bandit of the Rhine 516(2)
Black-eyed Susan 109(2)
Brutus 161(2)
Bushranger; or Norwood Vale 221(2)
Busybody and the Poor Soldier 562
Clari, or the Maid of Milan 298(2)
Coriolanus 161(2)
Giovanni in London 109(2)
Grahames' Vengence 540(2)
Hibernian Father 161(2)
Irishman in London 109(2)
Iron Chest 161(2)
Isabelle of Valois; or, the Tyrant of Navarre 298(2)
Jemmy Green in Australia 540(2)
Leigh Hunt's Reflector 374
Leila; or the Siege of Granada 68(2)
Miller and his Men 109(2)
Mountaineers 161(2)
Pizarro 161(2)
Ravenswood 161(2)
Recruiting Officer 562
Rob Roy MacGregor 161(2)
Salathiel 68(2)
William Tell 161(2)
Poems:
New Song made in NSW 388(2)
Ode to Spring 533(2)
Panegyric on an Eminent Artist 470
Poetry (NSW) 514
Police: 202, 217, 278, 300, 478, 518, 572, 580(2)
Politics:
(see also Politics: Parliamentary seats)
Misc: 66, 198, 199, 204, 206, 234, 246, 261
Chartism, Wales 601(2)
liberalism 30
New Zealand 187, 356(2)
radical reformers 29
political ecomomy 523(2), 536(2)
prison reform 45
protectionism 234
slavery, abolition of 470(2), 474(2)
slavery, anti 67, 91, 101, 298, 79(2), 84(2), 89(2), 180(2), 182(2), 235(2), 480(2), 494(2)
South Africa, responsible government 479
universal suffrage 438
Politics: Australia
anti-transportation league 51(2)
Australian Federation 527(2)
constitution 408(2)
Federal Convention 480
federation 480, 233(2), 408(2), 591(2)
franchise qualifications 483
republicanism 80(2)
responsible govt. 482, 484
separation movement 591(2)
transportation, abolition of 204, 206, 386, 83(2), 152(2), 275(2), 336(2), 375(2), 383(2), 407(2), 418(2), 479(2), 587(2)
transportation, agitation against 198
Politics: England
67, 126, 206(2), 266(2)
agrarian disturbances 132(2)
Anti-Corn Law Movement 615(2)
Chartist 419, 133(2), 480(2)
London Corresponding Society 438, 206(2)
Luddism 178
radical 461
Scottish Martyrs 126
Scottish Radicals 13
slavery issue 298, 381, 480 see misc.
Toryism 589(2)
trade unions 131(2)
Politics: Ireland
266(2), 294(2), 296(2), 302(2)
agrarian riots 245(2)
Fenian movement 347(2)
United Irishmen 512, 550, 206(2)
Young Ireland Movement 217(2), 234(2), 294(2), 342(2)
Politics: New South Wales
6, 55, 79, 94, 99-101, 113, 118, 130, 153, 160, 185, 186, 198, 199, 246, 248, 283, 319, 386, 387, 393, 447, 480, 514, 575, 11(2), 26(2), 150(2), 151(2), 153(2), 156(2), 162(2), 276(2), 495(2), 526(2), 581(2)
abolition of transportation 281
ballot voting 339(2), 514(2)
censorship 583-585(2)
constitution 114
Coolie labour Issue (Chinese & Indian) 281, 564, 45(2), 123(2), 141(2), 181(2), 293(2), 305(2), 623(2), 630(2)
customs duties 190(2)
Democrats 42(2)
education (Schools) 275(2)
free trade 257(2), 275(2)
freedom of the press 285, 599, 571(2), 583-585(2)
Irish home rule 79(2)
judical independence 211(2)
land policy 534, 165(2), 205(2), 339(2), 526(2)
local government 162(2)
liberals 42(2)
male suffrage 542, 136(2), 339(2), 514(2)
responsible government 113, 131, 284, 387, 501, 534, 542, 549, 135(2), 152(2), 181(2), 205(2), 407(2), 445(2), 475(2), 479(2), 524(2), 525(2), 585(2), 586(2)
squatting (see Squatting)
state aid 131, 160, 535, 83(2)
temperance movement 77(2)
trial by jury 374, 481, 501, 575, 16(2), 96(2), 98(2), 585(2)
Whiggism 588(2)
Politics: Queensland
Central Queensland separation movement 23
Politics: Scotland
218(2), 266(2)
republicanism 206(2)
Scottish Martyrs 126, 438, 206(2), 266(2), 312(2)
Scottish radicals 13
trade unionism 13
Politics: South Australia
47, 248, 431-434, 540, 541
ballot voting 262(2)
coolie labour issue 499, 383(2)
elections 17
free trade 616(2)
republican 64(2)
responsible government 478, 616(2)
sectarianism 17
self government 17
state aid 17, 47, 499, 201(2), 262(2), 384(2)
Politics: Tasmania
3, 8, 20, 21, 25, 30, 97, 106, 230, 317, 346, 475, 8(2), 40(2)
Champ ministry 21
Chartism 469(2)
constitution for 8
convict transportation 106, 169, 420, 476, 506, 552, 50(2)
dog tax 247(2)
freedom of the press 475, 273(2), 515(2)
import duties 176(2)
Patriotic Six 8, 97, 106, 324, 329, 346, 371, 476, 8(2), 50(2), 100(2), 273(2), 372(2), 501(2), 557(2)
protectionism 538
responsible government 476, 336(2)

separation from NSW 475, 138(2)
state aid 287(2)
taxation 372(2)
trial by jury 475
Politics: Victoria 82, 271, 51(2), 90(2)
Chinese immigration 14, 606(2)
convict transportation 350
land policy 38(2), 50(2), 92(2), 606(2)
male suffrage 370
penal reform 606(2)
responsible government 370, 126(2)
rights of married women 370
secret ballot 51(2)
separation from NSW 350, 385, 453, 482, 533, 38(2), 48(2), 51(2), 90(2), 108(2), 240(2), 243(2), 268(2), 504(2), 522(2)
state aid 443
temperance movement 85(2)
Politics: Western Australia 66, 382
responsible government 509
Politics: Parliamentary seats named
Adelaide 280(2)
Albot 370
Anglesey 455(2)
Bligh NSW 334
Bourke Ward NSW 251(2)
Brighton 564(2)
Brisbane 334
Buckingham 298(2)
Burnett 108(2)
Burra 64(2), 201(2), 280(2)
Campbell Town 50(2)
Canterbury 143(2), 292(2)
Capricornia 23
Central Cumberland 143(2)
Central Province 234, 370
Clare 64(2)
Collingwood 474(2)
Cumberland 139, 550, 96(2)
Cumberland, North Riding 453(2)
Devon 329
Durham 26(2)
Durham County 616(2)
East Adelaide 342
East Macquarie NSW 525
East Torrens 482(2)
Ennis 294(2)
Evelyn 55(2)
Geelong 252(2), 492(2), 523(2)
George Town 60(C), 430(2)
Georgiana NSW 275(2)
Gippsland 234
Glebe electorate 199
Glenorchy 298(2)
Gloucester 180(2)
Gloucester, County of 455(2)
Grant 224(2)
Great Yarmouth 633(2)
Gumeracha SA 497, 525
Gwydir 75(2)
Helston CON 633(2)
Heytesbury 401, 412(2)
Hobart 564(2)
Hunter NSW 334

Hunter, Brisbane & Bligh 281
Huon TAS 230, 458(2)
Kidderminster 136(2)
King NSW 275(2)
Kingborough TAS 230
Kyneton 244(2)
Light 342
Limerick 294(2)
Liverpool Plains 75(2)
Liverpool Plains NSW 41(2)
Lonsdale Ward 252(2)
Lower Hunter 414(2)
Macquarie 180(2)
Maranoa 108(2)
Moreton 108(2)
Morpeth NSW 231
Morven 576(2)
Murray NSW 275(2)
New Norfolk 371
Noarlunga 301(2)
North Adelaide 280(2)
North Esk TAS 576(2C)
Northumberland 281
Orange 401
Port Adelaide 442
Port Phillip 51(2), 79(2), 240(2), 284(2), 565(2)
Port Phillip District 350, 633(2)
Portland 252(2)
Queanbeyan 198
Richmond 476
Ringwood 593(2)
Roxburgh 102(2)
South Coast district 198
South Esk 452(2)
South Gippsland 455(2)
South Grant 606(2)
Southern Province VIC 229
Stanley 64(2), 180(2), 201(2), 280(2)
Stanley, County of 455(2)
Sydney Hamlets 199
Tamar TAS 3, 329
Upper Hunter 281
Villiers 401, 412(2)
West Camden 153(2)
West Sydney 73(2)
West Torrens 197(2)
Wide Bay 108(2)
Winchelsea ENG 480
Yass 293(2)
Yatala 442, 443
Portugal: see Places Index
Postal system 235, 365(2)
Primary Industry: see Industries & see also Organisations
Prisons:
Adelaide Jail 64(2)
Berrima Gaol NSW 523
Cascades female prison TAS 502
Cold Bath Fields prison ENG 419
Darlinghurst Gaol NSW 1, 616(2)
Debtor's Prison TAS 576(2)
Female Factory NSW see: Organisations Government: NSW
Female House of Correction, TAS 213, 133(2), 291(2), 458(2), 457(2)

Female Penitentiary, TAS 134
Fleet LND 27(2), 552(2)
Fremantle Gaol WA 382, 377(2), 416(2)
Hobart Gaol TAS 106, 183
Hyde Park Convict Barracks NSW 471, 236(2)
Ipswich Gaol ENG 215
King's Bench Prison ENG 46, 462
Longford Gaol 110
Male House of Correction TAS 492, 493
Maria Island Penitentiary 132(2)
Maria Island Probation Station, TAS 249
Newgate London 438, 461, 490, 19(2), 27(2), 457(2), 558(2), 559(2)
Parkhurst Prison SA 577, 280(2)
Pentonville Prison, London 192, 381, 411
Prisoners' Barracks, Hobart TAS 493
Richmond TAS 458(2)
Savoy Prison, London 233(2)
Private enterprise: see Companies
Prostitution 503
Pseudonyms:
Ariele 299(2)
Cornelius Van Vinkbooms 558(2)
Egomet Bonmot 558(2)
Humanitas 265(2), 304(2)
Janus Weathercock 558(2)
Majorca 400(2)
Oedipus 521
Otto von Rosenberg 540(2)
Peutetre 393(2)
Philo Free 211(2)
Rolf Boldrewood 573
Vox Populi 571(2)
Public health 1, 369(2)
Public Houses & Inns: England
Brighton, Castle Inn 189(2)
Queen's Hotel 196(2)
Royal Oak Inn, Newport 419
Victoria Hotel 623(2)
White Swan 246
Public Houses: New South Wales
Angel Inn 259(2)
Bob's Pub 332
Duke of York Inn 87(2)
Freemasons' Arms 86(2)
Halfway House 348(2)
Macquarie Inn 332
Petty's 334
Pilgrim Inn 109(2)
Rose and Crown Inn 395(2)
Royal Hotel 109(2), 540(2)
St Aubin Arms 294
Sportsman's Arms Hotel 292(2)
Steam Packet Hotel 192
Tavistock Hotel 446(2)
The Golden Fleece 241
Union Inn 318
Woolpack Inn 352
Public Houses: Queensland
Brazier's Hotel 201
Captain Piper Hotel 601(2)

Sovereign Hotel 277
Public Houses: South Australia
  Freemason's Tavern 380
  Thebarton Hotel 624(2)
Public Houses: Tasmania
  Albion Hotel 257, 516(2)
  British Hotel and Brandy (later
    Wine) Vaults 300(2)
  Cornwall Hotel 25, 257, 369
  Cornwall Hotel, Launceston
    305
  Derwent Hotel 407
  Devonshire Hotel 113(2)
  Glasgow Wine and Spirits
    Vaults 308(2)
  Help-Me-Through-The-World
    inn 302
  Highlander Inn 113(2)
  Hobart, Cat and Fiddle Hotel
    516(2)
  Joiners' Arms 363(2)
  Lake Dulverton Inn 308(2)
  Macquarie Hotel 257
  Nelson Head 7
  Oatlands Hotel 308(2)
  Parr's Hotel 373(2)
  Royal Oak Inn 363(2)
  Saracen's Head 27
  Seven Stars Inn 492
  The Retreat 113(2)
  Waggon and Horses Inn 302(2)
  York Hotel 257
  York Wine Vaults 271(2)
Public Houses: Victoria
  Albion Hotel 115(2)
  Angel Inn 407
  Brighton Pier Hotel 115(2)
  Chusan Hotel 115(2)
  Fyansford Inn 224(2)
  Gilleo's Hotel 184(2)
  Pier Hotel 115(2)
  Swan Hotel 224(2)
Public Houses: Wales
  Royal Oak Inn 601(2)
Queensland:
  see: Cemeteries — QLD
  see: Churches — QLD
  see: Houses etc. — QLD
  see: Newspapers —QLD
  see: Organisations — QLD
  see: Places Index — QLD
  see: Politics — QLD
  see: Religion — QLD
  see: Schools — QLD
  see: Universities — QLD
Rank (military): see Army: Ranks
Railways:
  Railway companies: see
    Businesses
  guages 483
  NSW 345, 388, 41(2), 275(2)
  SA 536(2)
  TAS Launceston-Deloraine
    railway 467(2)
  — Launceston and Western
    Railway 63
  — Great Western Railway 493
  VIC 533, 522(2)
Rebellions:
  Bounty mutiny 118
  Castle Hill, NSW (1804) 2, 144,
    258, 550, 20(2), 59(2), 97(2),

206(2), 209(2), 222(2), 479(2),
  622(2)
  Eureka Hotel riot, Vic 349(2)
  French Revolution 438, 573,
    206(2), 218(2), 227(2), 266(2),
    449(2)
  Indian mutiny 488(2)
  Ireland (1798). 421, 571
  Matabele rising 335
  Polish insurrection (1830)
    494(2)
  Rum Rebellion, NSW 2, 28, 40,
    76, 78, 79, 115, 116, 117, 120,
    156, 157, 308, 408, 422, 519,
    558, 563, 20(2), 47(2), 96(2),
    98(2), 139(2), 147(2), 156(2),
    190(2), 202(2), 210(2), 213(2),
    220(2), 233(2), 255(2), 283(2),
    291(2), 310(2), 318(2), 348(2),
    388(2), 401(2), 514(2), 537(2),
    538(2), 602(2)
  Scotland (1745) 544(2)
Refrigeration 520
Registration of Births, Deaths &
  Marriages 472(2)
Religions, churches: General
  199, 205, 211, 212, 213, 241,
  251, 252, 254, 255, 256, 259,
  260, 261, 262, 291, 292
  see also Churches & Cemeteries
  see also Religious
    Organisations
  see also by geographic area
    below.
  Anglican: see Church of
    England below
  Anglican-Methodists 67
  Anglican, NZ 197(2)
  Anglo-Catholics 425(2)
  Assyrian Christians (mission to)
    169
  Baptists 15, 97, 224, 316, 317,
    444, 177(2)
  Baptists (Scottish) 179
  Calvinism 103, 213
  Calvinist Evangelicals 33
  Catholic 21, 30, 34, 48, 195,
    216, 221, 231, 241, 255, 258,
    270, 288, 307, 308, 309, 324,
    370, 506(C), 118(2), 211(2)
    see further references under
    individual states.
  Catholic emancipation 511(2),
    512(2)
  Church of England 198, 199,
    205, 209, 211, 213, 234, 235,
    244, 252, 255, 281, 288, 300,
    305, 311, 315, 320, 328, 330,
    370, 118(2), 207(2), 226(2),
    534(2), 613(2)
  Church of Scotland 210, 232,
    328, 118(2)
  Churches of Christ 179
  Collegiate Church of
    Propaganda 147
  Congregational Church 3, 260,
    505(C), 600(2)
  Congregational, NZ 356(2)
  Dissenters 225, 252, 255, 260,
    563(2)
  Druidism 550(2)
  Free Church of Australia 399

  Free Church of Scotland 232
  Free Presbyterian Church of
    Australia Felix 82
  Huguenots 400, 89(2), 121(2),
    137(2)
  Independent Church 109, 443
  Independents 41, 179
  Jacobin 126
  Judaism 84, 217, 293, 435,
    19(2), 33(2), 458(2)
  Lutheran, Germany 104(2)
  Lutheran, USA 422(2)
  Methodism 6, 33, 34, 94, 135,
    252, 293, 344, 495, 497,
    216(2), 290(2)
  Methodism see also Wesleyan
  Methodist Society 321
  Moravian 421(2)
  Nonconformist 78
  Plymouth Brethren 190
  Presbyterianism 13, 41, 49, 94,
    96, 192, 197, 205, 220, 224,
    293, 327, 330, 472, 82(2)
  Protestant 216, 231, 247, 328,
    79(2)
  Protestant Irish 228
  Prussian church 421(2)
  Quakers 45, 192, 248, 249, 497,
    498
  Reformed Church, Netherlands
    503(2)
  Roman Catholic: see Catholic
  Salvation Army 35(2)
  Scottish National Church 205
  Secession Church of Scotland
    327, 328
  Society of Friends: see Quakers
  Unitarian Church 1
  United Presbyterian Church of
    Scotland 328
  Wesleyan 212, 213, 255, 260
  Wesleyan Conference 322
  Wesleyan Conference of 1814.
    212
  Wesleyan Methodist 261, 330
  Wesleyan Methodist
    Missionary Society 307
  Wesleyan Methodist Society
    330
  Wesleyan missionaries 307
  Wesleyan, NZ 197(2)
  Wesleyan Society 261
  Wesleyan Society, NSW 79
Religions: England
  Baptist 84(2), 418(2), 599(2)
  Calvinist 105(2)
  Calvinist Methodist 528(2),
    599(2)
  Catholic 503, 198(2), 285(2),
    424(2), 489(2), 509(2)
  Catholic Emancipation 84(2)
  Christian Israelitism 625(2)
  Christian philanthropists 475(2)
  Church of England 420, 17(2),
    43(2), 100(2), 198(2), 208(2),
    285(2)
  Clapham Sect 208(2), 475(2)
  Congregational 352, 105(2),
    229(2), 281(2), 290(2), 438(2),
    599(2)
  Dissenter 461
  Independent Church 105(2),

572(2)
Irish Catholics 542
Irish Church disestablishment
  136(2)
Jew 86(2), 250(2)
Jewish Episcopal Church 212
La Trappe reform 299(2)
Methodism 554, 105(2), 204(2),
  207(2), 303(2), 379(2), 423(2),
  540(2)
Methodist: see Wesleyan
Moravian 89(2)
Nonconformist 552, 353(2)
Presbyterian 399
Quaker 243, 387(2), 562(2),
  589(2)
Tabernacle Church 599(2)
Unitarianism 149(2), 312(2)
Wesleyan 510, 67(2), 132(2),
  133(2), 205(2), 481(2), 518(2),
  562(2)
Wesleyan Methodist 133(2),
  303(2), 440(2)
Wesleyan Society 290(2)
Religions: Ireland
  Anglican 274(2)
  Catholic 431, 542, 165(2),
    269(2), 274(2), 294(2), 337(2),
    512(2), 567(2)
  Franciscans 299(2)
  Irish Jesuits 217(2)
  Methodism 333(2)
  Presbyterian 55(2), 234(2)
  Protestant 293(2)
  Quaker 526
  Roman Catholic see Catholic
  Sisters of Charity 545(2)
  Unitarian Presbyterian 234(2)
  Wesleyan Methodist 171(2)
Religions: New South Wales
  302(2)
  Anglicans: see Church of
    England
  Baptist 82(2), 204(2)
  Benedictines (English) 165(2),
    340(2)
  Calvinism 82(2)
  Calvinistic Methodism 521, 522
  Catholic Association 535
  Catholic Church 77(2)
  Catholicism (see also Religions:
    miscellaneous) 185, 474, 513,
    515, 528, 25(2), 76(2), 77(2),
    141(2), 152(2), 165(2), 172(2),
    198(2), 235(2), 255(2), 275(2),
    293(2), 299(2), 337(2), 338(2),
    340(2), 342(2), 371(2), 378(2),
    389(2), 405(2), 425(2), 510(2),
    512(2), 513(2), 553(2), 569(2)
  Catholics, Marist Fathers 534
  Church of England (see also
    Religions: Miscellaneous) 10,
    159, 232, 374, 2(2), 41(2),
    53(2), 84(2), 95(2), 105(2),
    135(2), 146(2), 171(2), 198(2),
    204(2), 208(2), 255(2), 276(2),
    305(2), 311(2), 338(2), 341(2),
    401(2), 414(2), 433(2), 449(2),
    464(2), 599(2)
  Church of Scotland 81(2),
    82(2), 454(2)
  Church of Scotland: see also

  Presbyterian
  Congregational 353, 519, 23(2),
    78(2), 81(2), 82(2), 356(2),
    398(2), 439(2), 452(2)
  Diocesan Committee 461
  Dissenting 523, 599(2)
  Dissenting Chapel 521
  Dissenting Presbyterians 76(2)
  Erastianism 78(2)
  Free Churches 79(2), 82(2)
  Irish Catholics 550, 340(2)
  Judaism 84, 517, 87(2), 109(2),
    142(2), 321(2)
  Lutherans 509, 77(2)
  Methodism 322, 523, 537, 555,
    558, 18(2), 95(2), 171(2),
    179(2), 204(2), 291(2), 333(2),
    338(2), 424(2), 484(2), 509(2),
    532(2), 566(2), 599(2)
  Nonconformists 338(2)
  Particular Baptist Church
    428(2)
  Presbyterianism 28, 40, 352,
    353, 510, 521, 560, 562, 564,
    76(2), 77(2), 78(2), 81(2),
    96(2), 166(2), 196(2), 220(2),
    255(2), 292(2), 335(2), 338(2),
    356(2), 360(2), 361(2), 362(2),
    449(2), 454(2), 464(2), 493(2),
    510(2)
  Protestant 81(2), 142(2), 204(2),
    299(2)
  Quakers 179(2), 529(2)
  Scots Church, Sydney 105
  Unitarians 515, 275(2)
  Wesleyans: see Methodism
Religions: Queensland
  Anglican 423(2)
  Congregational 423(2)
  Methodist 423(2)
  Presbyterian 352, 423(2)
Religions: Scotland
  Calvinist 119(2)
  Church of Scotland 472, 567,
    76(2), 108(2), 118(2), 119(2),
    144(2), 398(2)
  Congregationalists 176(2)
  Presbyterian 76(2), 118(2),
    144(2), 166(2), 173(2), 563(2)
  Quaker 314(2)
  Scottish Baptists 176(2)
  Scottish Presbyterians 144(2)
  United Associate Presbytery
    428
Religions: South Australia
  Baptists 499, 177(2)
  Catholics 270(2), 384(2)
  Church of Christ 197(2)
  Church of England 335, 384(2),
    441(2)
  Congregational 47, 463, 525
  Dissenters 177(2)
  Dissenters (voluntaryist) 384(2)
  Independent Chapel 443
  Jewish 251(2)
  Lutheran 16, 33(2), 384(2)
  Methodism 303(2), 480(2)
  Plymouth Brethren 197(2)
  Presbyterian 499, 500, 525,
    482(2)
  Protestants 270(2)
  Representative Methodist

  Church 480(2)
  Scotch Baptist 197(2)
  United Evangelical Lutheran
    Church of Australia 33(2)
  Wesleyan 499, 480(2)
Religions: Tasmania
  192, 574
  Catholicism 241, 502, 504,
    142(2), 287(2), 296(2), 320(2),
    393(2), 544(2), 608(2)
  Church of England 574, 94(2),
    118(2), 127(2), 260(2), 287(2),
    311(2), 336(2), 436(2), 452(2),
    462(2), 576(2)
  Church of Scotland 144(2)
  Congregationalism 553, 229(2),
    317(2), 320(2), 350(2), 573(2),
    591(2), 593(2)
  Dissenters 311(2), 493(2)
  Independent 229(2)
  Methodist 127(2), 133(2),
    320(2), 442(2)
  Nonconformist churches 404
  Presbyterianism 139, 428, 440,
    505, 574, 118(2), 127(2),
    174(2), 176(2), 271(2), 298(2),
    300(2), 350(2), 427(2), 504(2),
    542(2)
  Protestant 36(2), 287(2)
  Quakers 45, 249, 216(2),
    441(2), 442(2), 491(2), 563(2)
  Wesleyan 339, 454, 138(2),
    205(2), 246(2), 350(2), 372(2),
    441(2)
Religions: Victoria
  Baptist Church 399
  Catholic 51(2)
  Church of England 50(2),
    200(2) 252(2), 412(2), 590(2)
  Congregationalism 553, 572(2)
  Evangelical Lutheran 423(2)
  Free Church 399
  Free Presbyterian 70(2)
  Independent Church 425
  Knox Church 399
  Lutheran 510
  Methodism 303(2)
  Nonconformists 84(2)
  Presbyterianism 232, 423,
    101(2), 184(2), 522(2)
  Protestant 51(2)
  Scots Church 399
  Scottish Free Church 399
  United Presbyterian Church
    Synod 510
  Wesleyan (see Methodism)
Religions: Western Australia
  Catholic 6(2), 278(2)
  Church of England 5(2), 6(2),
    99(2), 278(2), 426(2), 486(2),
    618(2), 619(2)
  Congregational 539(2)
  Methodist 440(2), 539(2)
Religious Organisations: (misc
  refs)
  Anglo-Catholicism 414(2)
  Australian Religious Tract
    Society 537
  Australian Wesleyan Methodist
    Conference 322
  Auxilary Bible Society 6(C)
  Benedictine Monastery 293

Benedictine Nuns 293, 472-4
Benedictine Order 534
Catholic emancipation 84(2)
Christian Brothers 473
Church Missionary Society 186
clergy — Church of England 254, 256
clergy — Congregational 251
clergy — NSW 10, 48, 49
clergy — Roman Catholic 241
Congregation for the Propagation of the Faith 376
Edict of Nantes 400
Evangelical Movement 10, 67, 168, 251-255, 431, 522
Irish Catholics in NSW 309
Irish Sisters of Charity 474
Jesuits (French) 171
Jesuits (Goa, India) 358
latitudinarianism 30, 437, 476(2)
League for the Preservation of Religious Freedom 166
Lectures on the Papal Claim of Jurisdiction 10
Lutheran Theological seminary 34(2)
Manchester Church Congress, 1888 256
Marist mission 308
marriage 48
NZ Church Missionary Society 282(2)
Nonconformist missionaries 15
papal knight 21
Puseyites 292, 420, 198(2), 426(2)
Sabbatarianism 22
sectarianism 30
Spanish Benedictines 147, 416(2)
Switzerland, Basle Mission Institute 509
Tractarianism 10, 161, 254-5, 420, 522(2)
Tridentine doctrine 163
Religious Organisations: AUS
Australian Wesleyan Conference 261
Bishop's Conference 255
Bishop's Council of Advice 256
Colonial Missionary Society 553
Congregational Union of Australasia 351(2)
New Guinea Mission 373(2)
Sisters of Charity 165(2)
Synod of Australia 81(2)
Religious Organisations: England
Baptist Missionary Society 418(2)
Benedictine Congregation 340(2)
Benedictine Order 292, 473, 340(2), 511(2), 544(2)
Bristol Clerical Education Society 483(2)
British & Foreign Bible Society 4, 6, 45, 255, 328, 500, 209(2), 222(2)
British & Foreign School Society 45, 440(2)

British Conference of Methodists 95(2)
China Inland Mission 373(2)
Church Building Society 41
Church Missionary Society 255, 298, 307, 351, 509, 559, 42(2), 209(2), 483(2)
Church of England Assurance Institution of London 461
Colonial Missionary Society 281(2), 356(2), 398(2), 491(2), 572(2), 590(2)
Congregation of St Catherine of Siena 546(2)
Convent of our Lady of Consolation of Cambray 340(2)
East London Christian Mission 373(2)
Eclectic Society 17(2)
Elland Society 207(2)
Evangelical 518, 208(2), 483(2)
London Missionary Society 4, 40, 107, 153, 205, 251, 259, 352, 365, 495, 518, 521, 522, 552, 553, 23(2), 209(2), 229(2), 398(2), 422(2), 430(2), 438(2), 491(2), 528(2), 599(2), 600(2), 632(2)
Lulworth Abbey 299(2)
Methodist Conference 105(2)
Methodist Society 205(2)
Missionary College 491(2)
Missionary Society 105, 251, 259
Oxford movement 10, 21, 534, 198(2), 286(2)
Quakers (London Yearly Meeting) 45
Religious Tract Society 45, 23(2)
Salvation Army 373(2)
Shaftesbury circuit 105(2)
Society for Promoting Christian Knowledge 289(2)
Society for Propagation of the Gospel in Foreign Parts 502(2)
Society for the Furtherance of the Gospel 89(2)
Society for the Propagation of the Faith 270(2)
Society for the Propagation of the Gospel 10, 49, 150, 160, 162, 17(2), 198(2), 288(2), 392(2), 406(2), 521(2), 569(2)
Society of Friends 562(2)
St Gregory's Monastery, Downside 292
St Wilfred's Theological College 534(2)
Sunday School Union 15
Temperance Society 45
Tractarianism 162
Trappist 299(2), 544(2)
Wesleyan Methodist Conference 423(2), 480(2)
Wesleyan Methodist Missionary Society ENG 307
Wesleyan Missionary Society 510
Wesleyan Overseas Committee

566(2)
Wesleyan Society 105(2)
West Orchard Chapel, Coventry 350(2)
Westminster Confession of Faith 78(2)
Religious Organisations: Germany
Evangelical Union for the Spread of Christianity among the Heathen 421(2)
German Mission to the Aborigines 422(2)
Missionary Society of Leipzig 422(2)
Religious Organisations: Ireland
St Patrick's seminary 269(2)
Cistercian monastery 299(2)
Maynooth seminary IRL 165(2)
Society for the Propagation of the Gospel 420
Ursuline Convent 567(2)
Religious Organisations: Italy
Congregation for the Propagation of the Faith (Propaganda) 340(2)
Religious Organisations: NSW
Archdeaconry of Sydney 289(2)
Australian Religious Tract Society 25(2)
Auxiliary Bible Society 304, 16(2), 131(2), 509(2)
Auxiliary Missionary Society 600(2)
Auxiliary Wesleyan Missionary Society 204(2)
Bathurst Bible Society 172(2)
Benedictine monastery 545(2)
Bethel Mission for Seamen 15
Bible & Religious Tract Societies 353, 23(2)
Bible Society 135, 157, 427, 464, 537, 134(2), 192(2), 234(2), 307(2), 398(2), 578(2)
Board of Missions 461
British & Foreign Bible Society auxiliary 255(2)
Catholic Association 338(2)
Chapter House, Sydney 255(2)
Christian Brothers 342(2), 344(2)
Church & School Corporation 77(2), 613(2), 510(2)
Church Corporation 259(2)
Church Missionary Society 537, 172(2)
Church of England Constitution Defence Association 414(2)
Church of England Lay Association 461
Church Society 11, 2(2)
Colonial Auxiliary Bible Society 105(2)
Convent of the Good Samaritan 554(2)
Diocesan Church Society 484(2)
Enfield, Leigh Theological College 105(2)
Evangelicals 38(2), 76(2), 33(2), 414(2)

General Assembly 82(2)
General Committee of Protestants 260
General Wesleyan Missionary Society 95(2)
German Mission to Aborigines 398(2)
Irish Sisters of Charity: see Sisters of Charity
Marist Order 534, 536, 44(2), 165(2)
Marsden House (Marsden Training School for Women Missionaries) 523
Methodist Society 6, 554
Moore Theological College 41(2), 63(2), 255(2)
New South Wales Society for promoting Christian Knowledge among the Aborigines 537
New South Wales Society 422(2)
New South Wales Sunday School Institution 522
Newcastle Church Society 613(2)
Parramatta Bible Association 365
Passionist Order 342(2)
Presbyterian Synod 422(2)
Presbytery of New South Wales 77(2), 78(2), 144(2)
Presbytery of Sydney 78(2), 82(2)
Provincial Synod 339(2)
Puseyite 162
Religious Tract Society 6, 255, 23(2), 172(2), 398(2)
Sacred Heart Presbytery, Darlinghurst 347(2)
St James's Theological College 406(2)
St Magdalene's Retreat 554(2)
St Mary's Seminary, Sydney 48, 198(2), 425(2)
schools, NSW 11
Scots Church Committee 335(2)
Sectarians 166(2)
Sisters of Charity 337, 535, 339(2), 344(2), 512(2)
Sisters of Mercy 165(2)
Sisters of St Joseph 44(2)
Society for Promoting Christian Knowledge 255, 358, 500, 554, 530(2)
Society for Promoting Christian Knowledge amongst the Aborigines 374, 537, 134(2)
Society for Promoting Christian Knowledge & Benevolence 105(2)
Society for the Propagation of the Gospel 255, 473, 381(2)
Society for the Propagation of Christian Knowledge (Portland Head) 205
Subiaco Convent 554(2)
Sunday School Institution 365
Sydney Bethel Union 6, 387(2),

529(2)
Sydney Diocesan Committee 41(2)
Synod of NSW 510, 78(2), 81(2), 356(2)
Tractarian 414(2), 406(2), 484(2), 569(2)
Wesleyan Auxiliary Missionary Society 381, 255(2)
Wesleyan Methodist Conference 205(2)
Wesleyan missionaries 464
Wesleyan Missionary Society 6
Wesleyan Society 105(2)
Windsor Bible Society 144, 221(2), 227(2)
York Street House 424(2)
Religious Organisations: Queensland
Bethesda Aboriginal Mission 423(2)
Society of the German Mission to the Aborigines 352
Religious Organisations: Scotland
Presbytery of Irvine 81(2)
Benedictines 44(2)
Edinburgh Gratis Sabbath School Society 352
Edinburgh Missionary Society 352, 398(2)
Evangelicals 76(2)
General Assembly of the Church of Scotland 78(2)
Scottish Disruption of 1843. 232
Scottish Missionary Society 144(2), 398(2)
United Associate Presbytery of Edinburgh 144(2)
Religious Organisattions: South Australia
Benedictine order 336
Church of Scotland Society of SA 499
Congregational Union of SA 491(2)
evangelical 177(2)
Evangelical Lutheran Synod of Australia 33(2)
League for the Preservation of religious Freedom 480(2)
sectarianism, SA 17
Society for Promoting Christian Knowledge 557
Society for Propagating the Gospel in foreign parts 262(2)
Society for the Preservation of Religious Freedom 443
Society for the Propagation of the Gospel 557
South Australia Dissent 443
South Australian Church Society 378, 557
South Australian League for the Maintenance of Religious Freedom 384(2)
Young Men's Christian Association 525
Religious Organisations: Tasmania
Auxiliary Bible Society 144(2),

385(2)
Bethel Union 229(2)
Bible Society 169, 261, 317, 359, 552, 351(2), 394(2)
British & Foreign Bible Society 311(2)
Church of England Synod 286(2)
Church Missionary Society TAS 455
City Mission 552, 351(2), 590(2)
Colonial Missionary Society 229(2)
Cornwall Auxiliary Bible Society 418, 454
Diocesan Registry 288(2)
Evangelical 599(2)
Evangelical Union 505
Hobart Presbytery 298(2)
Hobart Town Auxiliary Bible Society 225, 100(2), 315(2)
Kirk Session 144(2)
Methodist Mission 442(2)
Methodist Society 212, 204(2)
Missionary Society 454
Presbyterian Tract Society 564(2)
Puseyites 286(2), 426(2)
Quakers: Hobart Friends 249
Quakers: Launceston Meeting 249
Quakers: Tasmanian Yearly Meeting 249
Quakers: Van Diemen's Land Yearly Meeting 45
Quakers: York Retreat 45
Religious Tract Society 311(2)
St Andrew's Club 176(2)
St Mary's Seminary, Hobart 193
Salvation Army 35(2)
School Society 45
Seamen's Friend & Bethel Union Society 385(2)
Society for the Propagation of the Gospel 59, 292
Tasmanian Congregational Union 351(2)
Tasmanian Presbytery 542(2)
Town Mission 454
Tractarianism 420
Van Diemen's Land Missionary Society 144(2), 494
Wesleyan Methodist School's Committee for Hobart 442(2)
Cornwall Auxiliary Bible Society 454
Methodist Society 212
Religious Organisations: Victoria
Anglican Church Assembly 334(2)
Bible Society 590(2)
British & Foreign Bible Society 522(2)
Buntingdale mission 303(2), 522(2)
Church of England Assembly 349(2)
Diocesan Registry, Melbourne 252(2)
Diocese of Melbourne 252(2)

Downside Benedictines 344(2)
Erastian (anti) 399
Presbyterian Female Visiting
  Society 400
St James's Visiting Society
  521(2)
Wroeites 625(2)
Religious Organisations: WA
  Anglican sunday school 382
  Church of England Property
    Trust 254(2)
  Irish Sisters of Mercy 6(2)
  Subiaco Convent 293, 514(2)
  Western Australian Missionary
    Society 175(2)
Retail trade, businesses: see
  Companies
Revolution: see Rebellions
Roadbuilding 259, 170(2), 528(2)
Royal Marines: see Marines
Rum Corps: see Army: Regiments
Russia: see Places Index: Russia
Salt pans 223(2)
Sanitation 1, 369(2)
Schools (& Colleges): see also
  Education
Schools: Miscellaneous
  Builders' Academy, Germany
    403(2)
  Cerilly College, France 323(2)
  Collegium Carolinum (Kassel),
    Germany 403
  Dresden Gymnasium, Germany
    33(2)
  Elizabeth College, Guernsey
    43(2)
  Female School of Industry for
    the Daughters of European
    Soldiers, Madras, India 221
  Jewish, Germany 33(2)
  School for Maori children, NZ
    42(2)
Schools: England
  Ackworth School 248
  Appleby Free School 455
  Appleby Grammar School 311
  Atherstone Grammar School
    574
  Barnet Grammar School 158
  Bath Grammar School 37(2)
  Beaminster DOR 83(2)
  Benedictine College 292
  Birmingham Oratory School 31
  Blundell's School 467
  Bridgeworth High School 278
  Brighton College 415(2)
  Burney's (Rev Charles P.)
    school, Greenwich 251(2)
  Bury St Edmunds 66(2)
  Catholic College, Bath 21
  Central National School LND
    368(2)
  Central School LND 267(2)
  Charterhouse 73(2), 207(2),
    319(2), 351(2), 602(2), 619(2)
  Cheam SRY 248(2)
  Christ's Hospital 298, 469,
    506(C), 575, 390(2), 542(2)
  Christ's Hospital Mathematical
    School 390(2)
  Claybrook House 160(2)
  Colchester 399

College of St Edmund, Old
  Hall Green 504
Crediton Grammar School 249
Daventry Grammar School 184
Donington School 389
Dr Lindsay's Grove Hall
  School 299
Dr Seabrook's Academy 444
English Academy, Kensington
  151
Eton 10, 46, 52, 453, 485, 536,
  554, 37(2), 293(2), 312(2),
  402(2), 415(2), 421(2), 424(2),
  470(2), 516(2), 555(2)
Exeter Grammar School 236
Fairfield Boys' Boarding School
  89(2)
Free Grammar School,
  Colchester 316
Garcia's Academy 250(2)
Great Queen Street Charity
  School, London 135
Greenwich Academy 558(2)
Greenwich school for the sons
  of seamen 326(2)
Hale School, Perth 190
Harrow 52, 353, 384, 453, 456,
  245(2), 294(2), 321(2), 406(2),
  495(2), 523(2), 630(2)
Heath School, Halifax 407
Highbury College 229(2),
  350(2)
Honiton Grammar School
  472(2)
Hoxton Academy LND 356(2)
Hull Grammar School 208(2)
Hurwitz's school 250(2)
Kemplay's Academy, Leeds 407
Kimbolton Grammar School
  443
King Edward's Grammar
  School, Salisbury 256
King Edward's School,
  Birmingham WAR 29(2)
King's School 446
King's School, Canterbury 115,
  117, 158, 159
Kingston upon Hull 17(2)
Lampeter 401
Lampeter College 401, 522
Leeds Wesleyan Acadamy
  480(2)
Manchester Grammar School
  198(2)
Manchester School 502(2)
Merchant Taylors' School 209,
  256, 88(2), 214(2), 285(2)
Mill Hill School 165
Morden Academy 395(2)
New Road Boarding School
  LND 160(2)
Newark Grammar School
  618(2)
Newcastle Grammar School,
  ENG 99
Newport ESX 66(2)
Old College, Hoxton 281(2)
Old Hall College 340(2)
Oscott College 258, 546(2),
  607(2)
Oswestry Grammar School
  419(2)

Ottery St Mary's 451(2)
Portsmouth Naval Academy
  61(2)
Postwick NFK 362
Putney academy 268
Rev Charles P. Burney's school
  251(2)
Rochester Mathematical School
  452(2)
Rotherham College YKS 572(2)
Royal Academy School 592(2)
Royal Hospital School,
  Greenwich 240
Royal Hospital School 621(2)
Royal Military Academy 418,
  474, 446, 122(2)
Royal Military Academy,
  Woolwich 60
Royal Military College,
  Sandhurst 142, 193, 264, 303,
  377, 48(2)
Royal Military College 128,
  303, 332, 333, 404, 431, 477,
  271(2), 300(2), 324(2), 555(2)
Royal Naval Academy,
  Portsmouth 145, 259(2)
Royal Naval College 541,
  446(2), 470(2)
Royal Naval College,
  Dartmouth 136
Royal School of Mines 578
Rugby School 29, 436, 602(2),
  606(2)
St Bees 401
St Bees College CUL 401
St Gregory's Benedictine
  College 340(2)
St Ives and Lough Grammar
  School 412
St Paul's School, London 317,
  627(2)
Sedgeley Park school 269
Stonehouse 555(2)
Stonyhurst College LAN
  217(2), 539(2)
Tattingstone SFK 362
Tavistock Grammar School 18
Thompson's Academy 229(2)
Tonbridge School 424(2)
Ushaw College 269
Walsham School NFK 533(2)
Westminster School 99, 128,
  506, 542, 180(2), 182(2),
  226(2), 272(2), 359(2), 400(2),
  407(2), 559(2)
Winchester School 29, 189, 529,
  65(2) 134(2), 534(2), 618(2)
Woolwich Academy 428(2),
  583(2)
Wymondham 66(2)
Schools: Ireland
  Bandon Classical School 414(2)
  Belfast College 192
  Belfast Royal Institute 55(2)
  Charleville school 168
  Clongowes College KID
    217(2), 512(2)
  Dr Bell's grammar school 291
  Dr Henderson's school 234(2)
  Dr John Ellison's Kilkenny
    College 51(2)
  Flynn's Grammar School 165(2)

Foyle College LDY 252(2)
Kilworth 302(2)
Royal College Maynooth
  269(2)
Royal Grammar School 5(2)
St Finian's College, Navan
  269(2)
St Patrick's College 509(2)
Schools: New South Wales
  48, 131, 368(2)
Academy of Singing 279(2)
All Saints' College, Bathurst
  525, 525(C)
Ascham School 453(2)
Australian Academy 135
Australian College 58, 210,
  77(2), 158(2), 166(2), 172(2),
  356(2), 361(2), 422(2)
Bathurst, All Saints' College
  451(2)
Camden College 553, 23(2),
  356(2), 592(2)
Drawing School, Sydney 366(2)
Elfred House Private School
  209
Female Orphan School 135,
  147(2), 243(2), 368(2), 483(2),
  567(2), 613(2)
Female School of Industry 304,
  464(2)
Free Grammar School 76(2)
Georgian School 368(2)
Glebe Point Collegiate 410
Grammar School 354(2)
King's Orphan School 623(2)
King's School, The 160, 185,
  198, 205, 206, 255, 360, 401,
  402, 410, 76(2), 149(2),
  295(2), 402(2), 554(2), 572(2)
King's School, Sydney 160, 205
Ladies' school, Parramatta
  265(2)
Lyndhurst College 410
Lyndhurst, St Mary's College
  199(2)
Maitland School of Arts 26(2)
Male Orphan School,
  Cabramatta 135, 186, 212,
  368(2), 414(2)
Methodist Ladies' College,
  Burwood 424(2)
Moore Theological College
  255(2)
Music school 567(2)
Muswellbrook Presbyterian
  School 514
National Schools 25(2)
Native Institution 192(2)
New School 410
New South Wales Sunday
  School Institution 522
Newington College 205(2)
Normal Institution 354(2)
O'Halloran's (Dr) school
  232(2)
Orphan School 554, 563, 10(2),
  319(2), 510(2), 545(2), 547(2)
Orphan School (Girls) 59(2)
Public School Institution 307(2)
Roman Catholic Orphan
  School 535, 25(2)
Roman Catholic School 295(2)

St James' Parochial School
  395(2)
St James' Sunday School 304
St James's College, Sydney 11,
  162, 425(2)
St James's Grammar School,
  Sydney 11
St Mary's Benedictine College,
  Lyndhurst 344(2)
St Mary's College, Lyndhurst
  210, 293, 425(2)
St Philip's Infant School 502(2)
Schofield Hall 424(2)
School for Aboriginals 147(2)
School of Gunnery 176
School of Industry 359(2),
  432(2), 578(2)
Sunday School 402, 95(2),
  209(2)
Sunday School Institution,
  NSW 135
Sydney Academy 209
Sydney Church of England
  Girls' Grammar School
  527(2), 554(2)
Sydney College 6, 58, 113, 209,
  210, 397, 555, 575, 12(2),
  76(2), 110(2), 142(2), 158(2),
  509(2), 616(2)
Sydney Free Grammar School
  6, 374(2)
Sydney Free Public Grammar
  School 245, 507
Sydney Grammar School 58,
  209, 409, 504, 506, 12(2),
  110(2), 415(2), 472(2)
Sydney Mechanics' School of
  Arts 58, 210, 211, 542, 616(2)
Sydney Public Free Grammar
  School 209, 575, 395(2)
Sydney Public Grammar School
  110(2), 509(2)
Sydney Public School 209
Sydney School of Arts 60, 96,
  113, 538, 166(2), 425(2)
Schools: Queensland
  Largs Brisbane Academy 154
  School of Arts 336
Schools: Scotland
  Aberdeen, Marischal College
  166, 396(2)
  Blackford School 232
  Blue Coat School 253
  Cupar Grammar School 92
  Edinburgh High School 337,
  270(2), 523(2), 541(2), 559(2)
  Forres Grammar School 208
  Glasgow College 176(2)
  Glasgow Evening College 520
  Glasgow High School 335
  Haddington school 275, 449(2)
  Heriot's Hospital 398(2)
  King's College, Aberdeen 399,
  468, 472, 506
  Kircudbright Academy 14, 15
  Largs parish school 76(2)
  Leith's Academy 498(2)
  Marischal College 166, 396(2)
  Montrose Academy 166
  Royal High School 187(2)
  St Andrews 428(2)
Schools: South Australia

Adelaide, Collegiate School of
  St Peter 612(2)
Collegiate School of St Peter 7,
  166, 335, 380, 201(2), 262(2),
  301(2), 482(2), 626(2)
Pulteney Street Grammar
  School 7
Ridley Agricultural College
  379(2)
South Australian High School
  166
Sunday School 433
Schools: Tasmania
  192, 32(2)
Boys' Training School 254
Cambridge House Academy
  192
Carrington Boarding School
  397(2)
Catholic School 44(2)
Christ's College 256, 292, 333,
  412, 414, 436, 574, 207(2),
  249(2), 286(2), 490(2), 534(2),
  576(2)
Church of England Grammar
  School 304
Church Grammar School
  286(2)
Cornwall Collegiate Institution
  257, 94(2)
Ellinthorp Hall 339, 174(2)
Friend's School 285(2)
Hobart, Church of England
  school 312(2)
Hobart High School 29, 505,
  552, 118(2), 467(2), 590(2),
  591(2)
Hobart Orphan School 386(2)
Hobart School of Arts 258(2)
Hobart Town Academy 4, 193
Horton College 261
Hutchins School, Hobart 292,
  414, 436, 574, 118(2), 286(2)
Infant School 316, 260(2),
  290(2), 298(2)
Ireland's Collegiate School,
  Hobart 193
King's Orphan Schools, Tas 77
Kirklands 329
Launceston Church of England
  Grammar School 96, 169, 304,
  414, 436, 574, 32(2), 94(2)
Launceston, Paterson Street
  Methodist Sunday School
  9(2)
Launceston Sunday School 418
Longford Grammar School 355
Longford Hall Academy 21,
  355
New College 118(2)
New Town Academy 552
New Town, St John's 361
Normal School 8, 30
North Hobart, Friends' School
  563(2)
Officer College 298(2)
Orphan School 143, 156
Philip Smith Training College
  30, 453(2)
Presbyterian Sunday School
  220
Prospect Place Academy 133(2)

public school 466(2)
Queen's Orphan Schools 30,
  125, 361, 505, 40(2), 298(2)
Queen's School 420, 436
Ragged School 552
Roxburgh House 436(2)
St John's schoolhouse 304
St Mary's Seminary 193
Sunday School 454, 216(2)
Schools: Victoria
  Geelong Church of England
    Girls' Grammar School 27
  Geelong Grammar School
    501(2)
  Geelong National Grammar
    School 492(2)
  Grange School for boys 401
  John Knox School 399
  Malmsbury Common School
    296
  Matthew Flinders School
    492(2)
  Melbourne Academy 399
  Melbourne Hebrew School
    393(2)
  Merri Creek Aboriginal School
    399
  Scots College 399, 84(2)
  Scots School 399
  Wesley College, Melbourne 322
Schools: Western Australia
  Wesley College 511
Science 34(2), 318-319(2)
Science (natural) 525(2)
Scientific organisations: see
  Organisations
Scotland:
  see: Cemeteries — Scotland
  see: Churches — Scotland
  see: Houses etc. — Scotland
  see: Newspapers — Scotland
  see: Organisations — Scotland
  see: Places Index — Scotland
  see: Politics — Scotland
  see: Religion — Scotland
  see: Schools — Scotland
  see: Universities — Scotland
Secondary Industry: see
  Industries
  see also Organisations
  see also Businesses
Second Fleet to Australia 2, 237
  18(2), 86(2), 154(2), 259(2),
  279(2), 329(2), 347(2), 594(2)
Sedition 419, 421, 438
Sewage (Sydney) 1
Sheep:
  breeding 574(2)
  gadegast 100(2)
  Hampshire 553(2)
  Lincoln 411(2)
  merino 4, 19, 24, 155, 429, 531,
    543, 565, 101(2), 130(2),
    145(2), 208(2), 292(2), 438(2),
    460(2), 502(2), 566(2), 573(2),
    576(2), 604(2)
  saxon 4, 96, 290, 400, 443,
    24(2), 49(2), 100(2), 292(2),
    380(2), 502(2), 606(2)
  saxon merino 566(2)
  silesian 4
  southdown 630(2)

Spanish 573(2)
  steiger 100(2)
  teeswater 2(2)
Shipping companies: see
  Companies
Shipwrecks, Tas 20
Ships:
  Aberdeenshire 572(2)
  Acasta 539
  Achilles 353(2)
  Active 63, 204, 260, 307, 495,
    210(2), 282(2), 529(2)
  Adamant 232(2), 414(2)
  Adelaide 41, 572(2)
  Aden 256
  Admiral Barrington 283(2),
    546(2)
  Admiral Cockburn 20, 80, 92,
    225, 327, 348, 49(2), 172(2),
    374(2)
  Admiral Gambier 290, 13(2),
    156(2), 202(2)
  Admiral Juul 27(2)
  Adrian 32, 33, 73(2), 248(2),
    434(2), 593(2)
  Adventure 243, 62(2), 470(2)
  Advocate 74(2), 75(2)
  Africaine 166, 340, 462
  Agamemnon 503
  Agincourt 47(2), 268(2)
  Ajax 66(2)
  Alacrity 423(2)
  Aladdin 433(2)
  Albemarle 111, 278(2)
  Albion 52, 136, 178, 203, 206,
    232(2), 308(2), 364(2), 403(2),
    438(2), 517(2), 534(2)
  Aldborough 145
  Alert 421
  Alexander 51, 150, 156, 264,
    491, 27(2), 443(2), 444(2),
    506(2), 550(2), 610(2), 617(2)
  Alfred 178, 25(2), 169(2),
    370(2), 570(2)
  Alfred Hawley 372(2)
  Allies 247
  Alligator 148, 269, 541, 542(2)
  Almorah 155, 571(2), 578(2)
  Amelia 357, 365(2)
  Amelia Thompson 333(2)
  Amethyst 72(2)
  Amity 266, 123(2), 377(2),
    612(2)
  Amsterdam 555
  Andromache 503
  Andromeda 425, 454, 86(2),
    100(2)
  Angelina 134, 138(2)
  Ann 7, 84, 467, 143(2), 451(2)
  Ann & Amelia 312
  Ann Gale 38(2)
  Ann Jamieson 429(2)
  Anna 348
  Anna Josepha 253, 518, 438(2)
  Anna Robertson 372
  Anne 211, 260(2), 302(2)
  Anne Royden 296
  Anson 134
  Antipodes 466(2)
  Apollo 272(2)
  Appoline 544
  Arab 169

  Arabian 420
  Archduke Charles 548(2)
  Ardent 172, 65(2), 170(2),
    296(2), 397(2)
  Arethusa 240
  Argo 136, 156, 290, 155(2)
  Argyle 160(2), 424(2)
  Ariadne 50, 145, 56(2), 326(2)
  Ariel 142, 263(2), 382(2)
  Arkwright 195
  Arnon 372(2)
  Arrogant 443(2)
  Ascendant 17
  Asia 123, 221, 467, 66(2),
    304(2)
  Asiatic 180
  Astraea 552(2)
  Atalanta 16(2)
  Athenian 222
  Atlanta 414(2)
  Atlantic 31, 184, 332(2)
  Atlas 156, 162, 526, 561, 12(2),
    39(2), 371(2), 528(2)
  Augusta Jessie 296
  Augustus 18
  Augustus Caesar 109
  Auriga 3, 522(2)
  Aurora 546(2), 598(2)
  Australian 37(2)
  Avon 133(2)
  Azov 99(2)
  Bacchante 400(2)
  Badger 83(2)
  Bahama 27(2)
  Ballarat 222
  Barham 184
  Baring 72(2), 375(2), 596(2),
    597(2)
  Barwell 76, 138, 192, 203, 313,
    254(2), 388(2), 394(2), 546(2)
  Batavia 323(2)
  Bathurst 266, 62(2), 390(2)
  Beagle 267, 287, 349, 384, 477,
    529, 539, 62(2), 212(2),
    488(2), 489(2), 597(2)
  Bee 111(2)
  Belinda 308(2)
  Belle Poule 118
  Bellerophon 389, 412, 538, 539,
    375(2), 573(2), 622(2)
  Belliqueux 290
  Bellona 347(2), 394(2)
  Belvidera 381, 470(2)
  Benbow 66(2), 403(2)
  Bencoolen 63, 461
  Berwick 19, 225, 407, 429, 524,
    567
  Betsey (Whaler) 518
  Betsy 253, 438(2)
  Betty Ann 532(2)
  Birman 47
  Bitter Beer 487
  Blanch 93
  Blanche 465(2)
  Blazer 272(2)
  Blenden Hall 435(2)
  Blenheim 333(2)
  Blonde 542(2)
  Blossom 230, 235
  Blundell 222
  Boadicea 310
  Boddingtons 388(2)

Bolina 275
Bombay 527, 348(2), 372(2)
Borrowdale 443(2)
Bounty 118, 174
Boyd 92, 158, 170, 45(2),
  130(2), 210(2)
Bramble 111, 387(2)
Brazen 484(2)
Breeze 2(2)
Bridgewater 83
Brilliant 65(2), 465(2)
Britannia 51, 178, 218, 238, 357,
  359, 488, 508, 575, 60(2),
  61(2), 213(2), 254(2), 281(2),
  309(2), 364(2), 371(2), 373(2),
  446(2), 621(2)
British Sovereign 60
Britomart 148, 217, 441, 546,
  122(2), 300(2), 428(2), 471(2)
Brixton 466(2), 566(2)
Brothers 116, 117, 299, 398,
  503, 556, 576, 36(2), 62(2),
  129(2)
Broxbornebury 470, 11(2),
  550(2)
Bucephalus 417
Buckinghamshire 7
Buffalo 115, 252, 269, 275, 359,
  379, 430, 445, 487, 539, 542,
  557, 572, 19(2), 46(2), 47(2),
  61(2), 111(2), 138(2), 213(2),
  305(2), 352(2), 364(2), 465(2),
  482(2), 552(2)
Burrill 600(2)
Bussorah Merchant 124(2),
  392(2), 622(2)
Butterworth 260
Buzzard 381
Calcutta 155(C), 174, 218, 226,
  238, 240, 296, 368, 439, 490,
  542, 553, 126(2), 222(2),
  249(2), 447(2), 530(2), 555(2),
  621(2), 622(2)
Caledonia 77, 80, 219, 435(2),
  447(2), 522(2), 596(2)
Calista 230, 99(2), 417(2),
  426(2)
Cambrian 146
Camden 160, 293, 600(2)
Camel 484(2)
Camelion 465(2)
Camilla 137, 340
Campbell Macquarie 246, 36(2),
  121(2), 444(2), 547(2), 548(2),
  596(2)
Canada 110, 365, 620(2)
Canton 175, 430
Cape Packet 3, 270, 406, 528
Captain Cook 418(2)
Caroline 444, 531, 128(2),
  171(2), 174(2), 502(2), 538(2),
  579(2)
Caroline Chisholm 222
Carysfort 384, 567
Castle Forbes 49, 143, 268(2),
  297(2), 375(2), 427(2), 458(2)
Casuarina 72
Catherine Adamson 73(2)
Catherine Stewart Forbes 283,
  332
Celestial Queen 297
Centaur 567, 621(2)

Ceres 137(2), 202(2)
Challenger 485(2)
Champion 529, 83(2)
Chance 548
Chapman 199, 373, 581(2),
  628(2)
Charles Eaton 415(2)
Charlotte 31, 122, 173, 506(2),
  539(2), 582(2)
Chatham 355, 550(2), 551(2)
Cherokee 382(2)
Cherubin 402(2)
Chesapeake 220
Chesterfield 31
Cheviot 433(2)
Children 197
Chili 4
Chilli 9(2)
Christian VII. 50
Christiana 7
Christina 74(2)
Circassian 303
City of Edinburgh 92, 171(2),
  469(2), 541(2)
City of London 189(2)
City of Melbourne 233
Civilian 263(2)
Clansman 400
Clarence 197, 407
Clarkstone 553(2)
Claudine 269, 577(2)
Cleopatra 252(2)
Clifton 290(2)
Clonmel 202(2)
Clyde 367
Cochin 576(2)
Collector 548
Colonist 611(2)
Columbia 442
Combatant 382(2)
Comet 146, 137(2), 167(2)
Commerce 104, 129(2), 382(2),
  546(2)
Competitor 374
Concord 104, 513
Congo 170
Conqueror 184
Contest 546(2)
Coquille 123, 266
Cornubia 61, 141, 387(2)
Coromandel 248, 428, 469, 560,
  200(2), 220(2), 480(2), 530(2),
  533(2)
Coronet 168, 457(2)
Countess of Durham 426(C)
Countess of Harcourt 77
County Durham 426, 426(C)
Courageux 236, 382(2)
Courier 301, 604(2)
Crafty 465(2)
Criterion 129(2), 598(2)
Cruiser 381
Culdee 572
Cumberland 42, 170, 189, 390,
  426(C), 487, 66(2), 132(2),
  363(2), 402(2)
Curler 51(2)
Currency Lass 345, 614(2)
Cyclops 115, 208
Cygnet 277, 378, 64(2), 116(2),
  117(2), 262(2), 439(2), 624(2)
Cyprus 467, 302(2)

Czar 400
Daedalus 49, 50, 469(2), 551(2),
  594(2)
Dalhousie 294(2)
Daniel J. Draper 322
Daphne 208
Darling 275
Dart 207
David Owen 7(2)
David Shaw 299(2), 367(2)
Dawsons 7(2)
De Weser 148
Dedaigneuse 208
Delaware 279
Denmark Hill 112, 209, 442(2)
Dependance 621(2)
Deptford 208
Derwent 250, 249(2), 354(2),
  355(2), 375(2), 423(2), 516(2),
  539(2)
Deveron 228
Diadem 484(2)
Diana 275, 25(2), 31(2), 61(2),
  546(2)
Dick 61(2), 390(2)
Diligence 382(2)
Diligent 240
Director 119, 288, 398(2)
Discovery 550(2)
Dolphin 369, 443(2)
Don Juan 201
Donegal 156
Dordrecht 555
Doris 235
Doterel 66(2)
Dowson 428
Dragon 178
Dromedary 87, 143(2), 190(2),
  318(2)
Druid 470(2)
Dublin 221, 188(2)
Dubuc 104
Duchess of Bengal 527
Duchess of Kent 611(2)
Duckenfield 75, 246
Duff 251, 253, 259, 365, 518,
  521, 522, 290(2), 438(2),
  632(2)
Duke 272(2), 364(2)
Duke of Clarence 527
Duke of Gloucester 348
Duke of Roxburgh 207(2),
  285(2), 611(2)
Duke of Wellington 240, 391,
  299(2)
Duke of York 481(2), 596(2)
Dumfries 124
Dunbar 316
Duncan 265, 310
Dundee Merchant 433(2)
Dunvegan Castle 112(2)
Dusty Miller 246(2)
Duyfken 13(2)
Eagle 243, 551, 567, 465(2)
Eamont 433(2)
Earl Cornwallis 508(2)
Earl Grey 169, 315, 555(2)
Earl Spencer 6, 57, 78, 246, 306,
  556, 282(2), 366(2), 367(2),
  552(2)
Eclipse 102
Eden 280(2)

Edward 601(2)
Edward Coulson 540(2)
Edward Lambe 440
Edwin 309(2), 373(2)
Eendracht 556(2)
Egmont 326(2)
El Plumier 127, 518, 312(2)
Eldon 144(2)
Eleanor 509
Eliza 227, 3(2), 180(2), 566(2)
Elizabeth 115, 178, 275, 340,
    376, 486, 511, 51(C), 2(2),
    254(2), 274(2), 416(2), 436(2),
    438(2), 447(2), 613(2), 627(2)
Elizabeth & Mary 485, 444(2),
    548(2)
Elizabeth Henrietta 188,
    187(2), 596(2)
Elk 138(2)
Ellen 3, 362, 633(2)
Ellida 23
Elphinstone 37, 169, 383(2)
Emerald 12, 24, 475, 225(2)
Emerald Isle 221
Emigrant 51
Emilie 138(2)
Emily 555(2)
Emma 105
Emma Eugenia 108(2)
Emu 2, 143, 440, 114(2), 137(2),
    202(2), 590(2)
Endeavour 4, 53, 243, 275,
    32(2), 314(2), 444(2), 456(2),
    546(2)
Endymion 148
Enterprise 4, 178, 369, 9(2)
Era 233(2)
Erebus 415, 492, 34(2)
Esmeraldas 288(2)
Essex 178, 406, 360(2)
Essington 340, 231(2)
Estramina 232(2), 305(2),
    370(2)
Europe 56(2), 326(2)
Eurydice 465(2)
Eveline 487, 133(2)
Expedition 363(2)
Experiment 409, 139(2), 202(2),
    217(2), 259(2), 380(2), 449(2)
Fair American 127
Fair Tasmanian 303
Fairlie 150, 574, 25(2), 295(2),
    569(2)
Fairy 231(2)
Fame 486, 98(2)
Fanny 272
Favorite 208
Favourite 115, 13(2)
Ferrett 137, 419(2)
Fifeshire 197(2)
Fisgard 447(2)
Fishguard 578
Flirt 64
Florenita 106(2), 623(2)
Fly 83, 92, 111, 29(2), 34(2),
    167(2)
Forester 553
Formidable 85(2)
Forth 267, 407, 290(2), 566(2)
Fortitude 79(2)
Fortune 5, 409, 326(2)
Foudroyant 567, 397(2)

Fox 412
Fram 23
Francis 127, 170, 344, 389,
    223(2), 575(2)
Francis & Eliza 426, 427
Francis Freeling 214, 114(2)
Frederick 112, 178, 613(2)
Friends 500
Friendship 27, 74, 226, 247,
    309, 527, 31(2), 159(2),
    219(2), 443(2), 444(2), 467(2),
    564(2)
Fury 511
Gambia 288(2)
Ganges 67, 576, 227(2), 470(2),
    573(2), 597(2)
Gannet 235
Gem 69, 352(2)
General Graham 135
General Hewitt 470, 511, 519,
    140(2), 295(2), 369(2), 568(2),
    581(2)
General Wellesley 170, 129(2)
Geordy 32(2), 159(2)
George 309(2)
George Bass 528
George Hibbert 418(2)
George Horne 630(2)
George the Third 412(2)
Georgiana 75, 125, 503, 245(2)
Gibraltar 50, 220
Gilmore 48, 87, 219(2), 321(2)
Gipsy 94(2), 539(2)
Glatton 119, 136, 218, 575,
    264(2), 272(2), 419(2)
Glenbervie 247(2)
Globe 322
Glory 217, 486, 484(2)
Gneering 601(2)
Golden Grove 17(2)
Goliath 572
Gorgon 49, 64, 174, 183, 218,
    226, 237, 487, 10(2), 56(2),
    97(2), 215(2), 427(2), 506(2)
Governor Arthur 3, 224, 94(2)
Governor Bligh 25(2), 36(2),
    519(2)
Governor Hunter 283(2)
Governor King 546(2)
Governor Macquarie 115, 178,
    208, 252, 348, 374(2)
Governor Phillip 66(2), 185(2)
Governor Ready 612(2)
Grace 402(2)
Grampus 567, 364(2)
Grasshopper 184(2)
Greencock 504(2)
Greenlaw 505
Greenock 492, 2(2), 166(2)
Greenwich 357
Grenada 268
Grenville 243
Greyhound 208, 518, 382(2)
J.L.Griffiths 487
Guardian 308, 563, 329(2),
    331(2), 398(2), 420(2), 499(2)
Guerrera 375
Guildford 2, 25, 86, 144(C),
    170, 331, 365, 416, 242(2),
    313(2)
Guillaume Tell 465(2)
Gulnare 178

Halcyon 115, 438(2)
Haldane 566(2)
Hamlet 63(2)
Hampshire 406(2)
Harbinger 548, 26(2)
Harmony 261(2)
Harrier 446(2)
Harriet 219, 380(2), 411(2),
    529(2)
Harriett 25(2), 66(2), 126(2)
Harrington 178, 208, 438(2)
Hartley 443, 440(2), 491(2)
Hashemy 169, 206, 386, 72(2),
    136(2)
Hawk 469
Hawkesbury 519(2)
Hawkesbury Packet 617(2),
    618(2)
Hazard 231(2)
Heather Bell 303(2)
Hebe 463, 105(2)
Henrietta Packet 104, 37(2)
Henriette 523
Henry 340, 486, 371(2), 372(2),
    539(2)
Henry Reed 372(2), 373(2)
Henry Wellesley 246(2), 420(2)
Herald 142, 546, 167(2)
Hercules 12(2), 484(2)
Hero 629(2)
Heroine 225, 282, 339, 552,
    103(2), 216(2), 563(2), 575(2)
Hesper 112
Hibernia 41, 208, 252, 352, 537,
    319(2)
Highlander 433(2)
Hillsborough 262, 575, 201(2),
    508(2), 605(2)
Hind 48(2)
Hindoo 165, 505
Hindostan 29, 40, 204, 206,
    143(2), 190(2), 499(2)
Honduras 417
Honduras Packet 546(2)
Hooghly 286, 317
Hoogly 468
Hope 106, 115, 302, 339,
    216(2), 519(2), 598(2), 617(2)
Hopefull 105
Horatio 390(2)
Horssen 174
Howe 488(2)
Hudson 419(2)
Hugh Crawford 429, 24(2),
    83(2), 168(2), 195(2)
Hunter 203, 129(2), 155(2)
Hunter of Boston 235
Hyacinth 111, 212(2)
Hyderabad 294(2)
Hyperion 348
Imogene 187
Impetueux 572
Indefatigable 29, 560, 288(2),
    325(2)
Indemnity 28(2)
Indian 552(2)
Indispensable 570(2)
Indus 330, 488(2)
Inflexible 265(2)
Insolent 553
Integrity 137, 254(2)
Intrepid 567

Investigator 54, 73, 166, 167, 177, 265, 389, 390, 412, 498, 47(2), 139(2), 272(2), 443(2), 592(2)
Irresistible 594(2)
Isabella 41, 57, 109, 157, 352, 497, 35(2), 123(2), 147(2)
Island Queen 576
Isles of the South 35(2), 528(2)
James 373(2)
James Hay 208, 127(2)
James Lucas 138(2)
James Pattison 219, 614(2)
James Watt 272, 399, 490
Jane 26(2), 263(2)
Jane Frances 552
Janet 3, 316
Janet Izard 105
Janus 241, 509(2)
Jarvey 423(2)
Java 310
Jeddo 448(2)
Jenny 233(2)
Jenny Lind 303
Jessica 614(2)
Jessie 149, 280
Jessie Lawson 420(2)
J.L.Griffiths 487
John 159, 460, 461, 309(2), 418(2), 600(2), 601(2), 612(2)
John Barry 99, 137, 133(2), 235(2)
John Bull 108(2)
John Craig 595(2)
John Palmer 374(2)
John Pirie 177(2), 481(2)
John Renwick 97, 626(2)
John Wickliffe 29
Joseph Albino 377
Joseph Cripps 407
Julia 275
Juliana 147
Julie 348
Juliet 191
Juno 141, 63(2)
Junon 443(2)
Jupiter 250(2), 446(2), 532(2)
Kains 457
Kangaroo 86, 115, 327, 368, 407, 511, 522, 15(2), 127(2), 138(2), 142(2), 202(2), 363(2), 366(2), 575(2)
Katherine Stewart Forbes 244, 335
Kent 567, 410(2)
King George 36(2), 444(2), 546(2), 548(2)
King Henry 377
King William the Fourth 490
Kinnear 10
Kitty 242, 621(2)
Kreiser 99(2)
L'Astrolabe 85(2)
L'Esperance 171, 69(2)
L'Heroine 267
L'Orient 538
L'Uranie 72
La Boussole 85(2)
La Manche 506
La Recherche 171
La Recherche 69(2)
La Revolution 171

La Thetis 72(2)
La Ville de Bordeaux 435(2)
Lady Barlow 137, 203, 58(2), 374(2)
Lady Bird 529
Lady Castlereagh 81, 95(2)
Lady Emma 303
Lady Harewood 142
Lady Juliana 308, 491, 563, 347(2), 420(2)
Lady Loch 407
Lady Mary Pelham 340
Lady Melville 45(2)
Lady Nelson 8, 105, 136, 148, 170, 178, 240, 468, 469, 498, 27(2), 47(2), 111(2), 223(2), 272(2), 306(2), 568(2), 596(2)
Lady Nugent 310
Lady of the Lake 457(2)
Lady Penrhyn 12, 122, 242, 264, 312, 4(2), 19(2), 20(2), 444(2), 453(2)
Lady Shore 233(2), 234(2)
Lady Stirling 426(2)
Laing 339
Lancaster 136
Lang 23, 102, 291, 229(2), 451(2)
Larkins 144
Lass of Geraldton 440(2)
Latona 443(2)
Launceston 567
Laura 499(2)
Lavinia 224
Layton 145, 504
Le Geographe 390
Le Naturaliste 71, 39(2)
Le Seographe 71
Le Tigre 47(2)
Leda 184, 264(2)
Lenox 145
Leonidas 66(2)
Leslie 487
Letitia 260(2)
Liberty 392
Lilias 492(2)
Lindsays 371
Linton 487
Lion 9(2), 557(2)
Litherland 433(2)
Lively 105
Liverpool 56(2)
Lloyds 81
Lochnagar 372(2)
Lonach 452(2)
London 322, 28(2)
Lord Auckland 61
Lord Eldon 137, 157(2)
Lord Goderich 611(2)
Lord Hawkesbury 92
Lord Hobart 281(2)
Lord Liverpool 94(2), 614(2)
Lord Melville 373, 494, 202(2)
Lord Wellington 155
Los Tres Reyes Margos 536(2)
Lotus 41
Louisa 134, 473(2)
Louisa Campbell 177(2), 514(2)
Lucy 438(2), 598(2)
Lucy Anne 377(2)
Ludlow Castle 621(2)
Lusitania 45(2), 83(2), 361(2)

Lynher 477
Lynx 365(2), 444(2)
Madagascar 310
Madeira Packet 340
Madras 388
Magistrate 418(2)
Magnet 305, 24(2)
Maitland 4(2), 202(2)
Majestic 272
Mandarin 419, 601(2)
Mangles 435(2), 531(2C), 548(2), 566(2), 612(2)
Marchioness of Exeter 361(2)
Marcia 129(2)
Margaret 169
Margaret & Agnes 197
Maria 433, 289(2), 301(2)
Maria Ann 314
Maria Orr 302(2), 433(2)
Marian 547(2)
Marianne 96, 541
Mariner 257, 495(2)
Maritana 568(2)
Marlborough 440
Marquis Cornwallis 144, 548
Marquis de Seignelay 567
Marquis of Hastings 74, 430, 178(2)
Marquis of Huntley 214
Marquis of Wellington 247, 327, 327(C), 110(2), 142(2), 256(2), 291(2), 292(2)
Marshal Wellington 359
Martha 127, 312(2)
Mary 249, 269, 422, 523, 134(2), 214(2), 263(2), 291(2), 292(2), 313(2), 490(2), 499(2), 596(2)
Mary & Elizabeth 37(2)
Mary & Sally 36(2), 374(2)
Mary Ann 6, 104, 235, 355, 404, 407, 503, 24(2), 426(2), 618(2)
Mary Anne 137
Mary Anne (Marian) 36(2)
Mary White 270(2)
Matilda 231, 358, 101(2), 163(2)
Mauritius 13(2)
Mediator 573(2)
Medina 66, 250, 272
Medway 23(2), 387(2), 419(2), 527(2), 577(2)
Melbourne 303, 379(2)
Melville Castle 419(2)
Mercury 8, 74, 25(2), 374(2), 444(2)
Merlin 573(2)
Mermaid 8, 108, 145, 266, 61(2), 62(2), 111(2), 123(2), 248(2), 306(2), 313(2), 377(2), 390(2), 434(2), 457(2), 506(2)
Mic Mac 201
Midas 1(2), 74(2), 80(2), 539(2), 548(2)
Minerva 8, 80, 101, 127, 258, 328, 352, 421, 512, 550, 111(2), 129(2), 167(2), 183(2), 216(2), 230(2), 362(2), 371(2), 422(2), 444(2)
Minorca 240, 369(2), 552(2)
Minstrel 76, 155, 524, 306(2), 435(2)

Miranda 303
Mirny 83, 99(2)
Mississippi 363, 629(2)
Moffat 430
Mona 8(2)
Monarch 83(2)
Monmouth 118, 240
Montagu 403(2)
Montreal 190, 353(2)
Morley 268, 376(2)
Moselle 105, 484(2)
Mountaineer 493(2)
Mutine 434(2)
Namur 170
Nancy 485, 519(2), 520(2)
Napoleon 426(2)
Native Youth 224
Nautilus 65, 107, 251, 568(2)
Nelson 3
Neptune 361, 567, 154(2),
  235(2), 259(2), 279(2), 281(2),
  376(2), 493(2), 580(2), 582(2)
Nereid 47
Nereide 240
Nereus 611(2)
Niger 52
Nile 138, 215, 252, 539, 116(2),
  394(2), 401(2)
Nimrod 297, 168(2), 195(2)
Ninfa 267(2)
Nisus 539
Nonsuch 506(2)
Norfolk 65, 177, 267, 294, 389,
  521, 111(2), 410(2), 418(2),
  537(2)
Norhampton 29
North Briton 232
Northampton 12, 421, 291(2)
Northumberland 115, 243,
  72(2)
Norval 69, 417, 372(2), 466(2)
Numa 566(2)
Nymph 259(2)
Oberon 142
Ocean 134, 137, 226, 238, 240,
  260, 357, 368, 491, 66(2),
  120(2), 281(2), 336(2), 622(2)
Orelia 95
Orient 124
Orissa 287, 499
Orpheus 69(2)
Ortando 184
Orwell 25(2)
Otter 266(2)
Pacific 433(2)
Palmira 72(2)
Pandora 174
Parkfield 249, 576
Parmelia 164, 236, 325, 5(2),
  376(2), 391(2), 485(2)
Parramatta 40, 156(2), 291(2)
Parsee 128, 466
Peacock 279
Pegasus 178, 130(2)
Pelican 115(2)
Pelorus 63(2), 413(2)
Pembroke 243
Penyard Park 8(2)
Perseverance 332, 352, 36(2),
  444(2)
Perthshire 253
Peruvian 212(2), 262(2)

Pestonjee Bomanjee 179, 432,
  446(2)
Pet 197
Petrel 377
Phaeton 145
Philip Oakden 290(2), 393(2)
Phillip Dundas 333, 377(2)
Phoebe 539
Phoenix 196, 371, 99(2), 199(2),
  202(2)
Pilgrim 137
Pilote 623(2)
Pique 400(2)
Piscator 201
Pitt 39, 158, 184, 351, 488,
  334(2), 403(2), 448(2), 519(2),
  570(2), 574(2)
Plantagenet 146
Planter 525
Platina 9
Pocklington 25(2)
Polyphemus 272(2), 506(2)
Porpoise 135, 166, 170, 239,
  390, 487, 491, 498, 542, 47(2),
  111(2), 121(2), 138(2), 139(2),
  217(2), 272(2), 306(2), 309(2),
  318(2), 499(2), 538(2), 577(2),
  592(2)
Port Mahon 72(2)
Port-au-Prince 95(2)
Porteous 275
Portland 399, 472, 513, 271(2),
  573(2)
Preston 288
Pride 433(2)
Prince George 112, 33(2)
Prince Leopold 273, 486,
  433(2), 507(2), 633(2)
Prince of Wales 19(2), 427(2),
  443(2)
Prince Regent 8, 190, 455,
  163(2), 226(2), 433(2), 458(2),
  458(2), 472(2), 488(2), 612(2)
Princess Amelia 567
Princess Charlotte 310, 316(2),
  464(2), 504(2)
Princess Royal 350(2), 506(2)
Prothee 145
Providence 56, 119, 218, 343,
  435, 267(2), 337(2), 375(2)
Pyramus 58
Queen 12, 36(2), 66(2)
Queen Charlotte 104, 252, 568,
  439(2)
Rainbow 348, 413, 400(2),
  446(2)
Raison, 574(2)
Rajasthan 301(2)
Randolph 386, 90(2)
Rangoon 564(2)
Rapadora 92
Rapid 540, 116(2), 117(2)
Rattler 357, 74(2), 247(2)
Rattlesnake 115, 187, 485, 545,
  577, 578, 125(2), 167(2),
  471(2)
Raven 469, 373(2)
Rebecca 68, 69, 208, 369
Recovery 268, 418
Regalia 356, 105(2), 359(2),
  395(2), 396(2), 433(2)
Regent Fox 258

Regia 425
Reliance 64, 85, 389, 536, 568,
  46(2), 443(2), 450(2), 573(2)
Rembang 174
Renard 465(2)
Renown 51(2), 56(2), 60(2),
  65(2)
Repulse 400(2)
Resolution 53, 118, 243, 244,
  486, 57(2), 67(2), 259(2)
Resource 348, 439, 72(2),
  223(2), 479(2)
Retribution 552(2)
Revenge 66(2)
Richmond 309(2), 612(2)
Richmond Packet 302(2)
Ringdove 83(2)
Rippon 145, 390(2)
Risdon Queen 230
Robert Quayle 49(2)
Rockingham 321(2)
Roebuck 277
Rolla 320, 487
Rose 105, 156, 344
Rosebud 544
Rosetta 485
Roslyn Castle 2(2)
Rover's Bride 611(2)
Royal Admiral 170, 252, 352,
  498, 558, 10(2), 96(2), 218(2),
  373(2), 420(2), 438(2), 452(2),
  574(2), 608(2), 632(2)
Royal Ann 567
Royal Charlotte 66, 123(2)
Royal Charter 440
Royal George 61, 127, 277, 567,
  128(2), 620(2)
Royal Saxon 160(2)
Royal Sovereign 353(2)
Royal Standard 564(2)
Royal William 400(2)
Royalist 148
Rubicon 487
Ruby 86, 107
Runnymede 412(2)
Saerdam 323(2)
St Albans 398(2)
St George 333(2)
St Michael 95(2), 614(2)
Saint George 353(2)
Salacia 164
Salamander 78
Sally 101, 102, 517(2)
Salsette 137, 55(2)
Samarang 465(2)
Sampson 484(2)
Samson 265(2)
Samuel 25(2)
San Domingo Colibri 105
San Pedrico 536(2)
Santa Anna 546(2)
Sappho 27(2)
Saracen 42, 212, 16(2), 25(2)
Sarah 48(2), 234(2), 389(2),
  615(2)
Scarborough 2, 242, 354, 360,
  485, 517, 4(2), 86(2), 139(2),
  154(2), 362(2), 397(2), 404(2),
  536(2)
Sceptre 398(2)
Schah 359(2)
Schomberg 564(2)

Scottish Knight 23
Scylla 539
Seahorse 141
Seppings 540(2)
Seringapatam 178, 406, 548(2)
Sesotris 331
Shah Hormuzear 31, 32
Shamrock 109, 344, 8(2),
  392(2), 601(2)
Sheerwater 66(2)
Shipley 140(2)
Siam 198(2)
Simon Cock 156
Simon Taylor 577
Sinbad 564(2)
Sinclair 380
Sir Charles Forbes 327, 281(2)
Sir Edward Hughes 316, 189(2)
Sir Edward Paget 102(2)
Sir Edward Parry 221
Sir George Arthur 325(2)
Sir George Osborne 555, 380(2)
Sir George Seymour 192
Sir Godfrey Webster 170(2)
Sir John Rae Reid 213, 409(2)
Sir William Bensley 459(2),
  576(2)
Sir William Wallace 376
Sirius 31, 50, 101, 145, 150, 226,
  237, 297, 351, 353, 487, 497,
  548, 567, 4(2), 12(2), 56(2),
  85(2), 229(2), 309(2), 312(2),
  363(2), 398(2), 420(2), 443(2),
  462(2), 573(2), 575(2), 623(2)
Skelton 144(2), 216(2), 429(2)
Skjold 33(2)
Slains Castle 222
Slaney 571(2), 578(2)
Snapper 93
Sobraon 373(2)
Socrates 340, 371(2), 372(2)
Sophia 104, 273, 392, 37(2),
  159(2), 365(2)
Sophia Jane 490, 202(2)
South Australian 177(2)
Southampton 236
Southern Cross 433(2)
Southworth 337(2)
Sovereign 438, 490, 536, 555,
  324(2), 435(2)
Sparrowhawk 47(2)
Speculator 448(2)
Speedwell 519(2)
Speedy 194, 357, 359, 485,
  53(2), 57(2)
Speke 13, 45(2), 306(2)
Spencer 538
Sphinx 508
Spitfire 567
Spring 157, 3(2)
Spring Grove 469
Spy 545
Squirrel 443(2)
Stag 553
Standard 368(2)
Steam Packet 94(2)
Sterlingshire 409(2)
Stewart Elphinstone 169
Stirling 230
Stirling Castle 145, 210, 468
Success 577, 123(2), 433(2),
  485(2), 500(2)

Sullimany 7
Sulphur 236, 5(2), 446(2),
  485(2)
Sultan 20(2)
Superb 105, 337
Supply 31, 50, 145, 173, 264,
  468, 567, 568, 46(2), 56(2),
  139(2), 229(2), 363(2), 364(2),
  442(2), 453(2), 469(2), 573(2)
Surprize 3, 126, 519, 573,
  206(2), 266(2), 312(2), 443(2),
  449(2), 451(2), 582(2), 580(2)
Surry 5, 169, 265, 275, 555,
  45(2), 187(2), 193(2), 204(2),
  205(2), 359(2), 360(2), 361(2),
  369(2), 507(2), 547(2), 548(2),
  599(2)
Susan 558(2)
Sussex 433(2)
Sutil 267(2)
Suvorov 99(2)
Swallow 56(2), 573(2)
Swift 217(2), 294(2)
Switzerland 353(2)
Sybille 66(2)
Sydney 205, 527
Sydney Cove 64, 107, 203,
  129(2), 546(2), 547(2), 547(2),
  548(2), 598(2)
Sydney Griffiths 487
Sydney Packet 204, 464(2)
Talbot 27(2)
Tam O'Shanter 378
Tamar 148, 94(2), 391(2),
  611(2), 623(2)
Tasman 303
Tasmanian 163(2)
Temeraire 66(2)
Terror 492, 34(2), 471(2)
Thalia 209, 137(2), 359(2),
  361(2), 577(2)
Thames 193, 71(2), 365(2)
The Brothers 486
Theseus 47(2)
Thistle 340, 344, 531
Thomas 376
Thomas Harrison 23(2)
Thomas Lawrie 456, 83(2),
  316(2)
Thomas Lowry 61, 500(2)
Thomson 214(2)
Thracian 469
Three Bees 369(2)
Tiger 137(2), 308(2), 371(2)
Tigress 263(2), 426(2)
Tobago 364(2)
Tom Thumb 64
Tongariro 572
Tonnant 184, 400(2)
Tortoise 169
Tottenham 569(2)
Trafalgar 420
Tranby 510
Tranmere 270
Traveller 192(2), 256(2), 550(2)
Trial 485, 130(2), 393(2)
Trident 50
Triton 59, 188, 197, 464, 513,
  143(2), 281(2), 385(2), 426(2)
Trompeuse 443(2)
Truro 233
Trusty 372

Tryall 143(2)
Tula 105, 357
Tweed 567
Tyne 562
Undaunted 111
Unicorn 506(2)
Union 127, 170, 567, 47(2),
  72(2), 121(2), 129(2), 235(2)
Urania 271(2), 577(2)
Velocity 140
Venerable 572, 305(2)
Vengeance 288
Venus 65, 108, 178, 208, 602(2)
Vesper 124
Vibilia 323
Victoria 202(2), 412(2), 464(2)
Victory 29, 539, 567, 382(2)
Vixen 272
Vostok 83, 99(2)
Waaksamheyd 50, 145, 173,
  568, 363(2), 463(2), 623(2)
Walter Hood 402
Wanderer 140, 142
Wanstead 417, 83(2), 618(2)
Waratah 525
Warbey 377
Warrior 119, 180, 189, 348,
  72(2), 231(2), 245(2), 379(2),
  483(2)
Warspite 310, 484(2)
Wasp 594(2)
Waterlily 233
Waterloo 553(2)
Waterwitch 363
Wave 275, 107(2), 505(2)
Waverley 221
Weazle 503
Wellington 178, 260(2)
Westmoreland 106, 181, 309,
  513
Weymouth 83(2)
Whaler 433(2)
William 172, 486, 208(2), 433(2)
William & Ann 178
William & Anne 383
William Barrass 498
William Glen Anderson 458(2)
William Hyde 61
William IV 302(2)
William Jardine 418(2)
William Metcalfe 115(2), 133(2)
William Penn 547
William Pitt 116, 487
William Shand 515(2)
William the Fourth 490, 137(2),
  202(2)
Wilmot 448(2)
Windham 143(2), 162(2)
Woodbridge 134
Woodford 65
Woodlark 488, 314(2)
Yarra 303
York 178, 299
Young William 78, 537(2)
Zealand 50, 66(2)
Zebra 236, 33(2)
Slavery:
  see also Laws
  Abolition of 15, 474(2)
  South Africa 45
Smuggling 127(2), 159(2)
Social Welfare 221, 53(2)

Societies: see Organisations
Songs 280(2)
South Africa:
  see also Places Index: South
    Africa
  see also Organisations: South
    Africa
  Bourke Administration 129
  Hottentots 130
  Kaffir War 455
  Slavery 45
  South Africa 548
South Australia:
  see: Cemeteries — SA
  see: Churches — SA
  see: Houses etc. — SA
  see: Newspapers — SA
  see: Organisations — SA
  see: Places Index — SA
  see: Politics — SA
  see: Religion — SA
  see: Schools — SA
  see: Universities — SA
Soviet Union: see Places Index:
  Russia
Spain: see Places Index: Spain
Spiritualism 420, 474(2)
Sport 197(2)
Sporting organisations: see
  Organisations
Squatters 4, 22, 448, 449, 480,
  481, 102(2), 135(2), 151(2),
  162(2), 168(2), 244(2), 293(2),
  339(2), 412(2), 415(2), 421(2)
Squatting 124, 132, 139, 152, 201,
  247, 330, 350, 370, 385, 481,
  543, 97(2), 101(2), 102(2),
  135(2), 165(2), 242(2), 252(2),
  257(2), 275(2), 293(2), 500(2),
  587(2), 617(2)
Stage coach 359(2)
Steam:
  boats 522(2)
  engine 224, 38(2), 359(2),
    379(2)
  mill 246(2)
  ships 137(2)
  yacht 181(2)
Stocks (punishment) 175(2)
Streets and Roads: see Places
  Index
Suicide 7, 528-9
Survey coastal 577(2)
Survey expedition 597(2)
Surveying 194, 230, 250, 282
Tariffs 246, 483, 525(2) see also
  Customs Duty
Tasmania:
  see: Cemeteries — TAS
  see: Churches — TAS
  see: Houses etc. — TAS
  see: Newspapers — TAS
  see: Organisations — TAS
  see: Places Index — TAS
  see: Politics — TAS
  see: Religion — TAS
  see: Schools — TAS
  see: Universities — TAS
Telegraph communications 295,
  502
Temperance 77(2), 85(2), 165(2),
  204(2)

Theatre 562, 67(2), 195(2), 432(2)
Theatre: England
  Covent Garden 568(2)
  Drury Lane 568(2)
  Princess Theatre, LND 298(2),
    299(2)
  Royal Circus 528(2)
  Royal Theatre 355
  Royalty Theatre 528(2)
Theatre: Ireland
  Theatre Royal 567(2)
Theatre: New South Wales
  Misc: 444(2)
  City Theatre 68(2), 98(2),
    161(2), 356(2), 446(2), 626(2)
  Olympic Theatre 68(2), 298(2),
    354(2), 446(2)
  Prince of Wales Theatre 626(2)
  Royal Victoria Theatre 161(2),
    298(2), 354(2)
  Sydney Victoria Theatre 161(2)
  Theatre Royal, Sydney 301,
    67(2), 98(2), 109(2), 298(2),
    304(2), 445(2), 626(2)
  Victoria Theatre, Sydney 68(2),
    98(2), 161(2), 280(2), 346(2),
    446(2), 626(2)
Theatre: South Australia
  New Queen's Theatre, Adelaide
    98(2)
  Queen's Theatre, Adelaide
    98(2)
  Royal Victoria Theatre,
    Adelaide 98(2)
Theatre: Tasmania
  Cameron Company 516(2)
  Royal 37(2)
  Royal Victoria Theatre 161(2)
  Theatre Royal 303, 445(2),
    516(2)
  Theatre Royal Olympic 161(2)
Theatre: Victoria
  Melbourne Pavilion and
    Queen's Theatre 161(2)
Theological controversy, NSW
  136
Theology 136
Third Fleet 178, 357, 329(2),
  594(2)
Toll Bridges & Houses 75(2),
  371(2), 401(2), 519(2) see also
  Turnpike
Tolpuddle martyrs 132(2)
Topography 212(2)
Trade: see Industry, Free Trade
Trade unions 13, 479, 131(2),
  132(2)
Trading enterprises: see
  Organisations; Companies;
  Industries
Transportation of Convicts:
  see also: Convicts
  see also: Penal Settlements
  see also: Politics
  Misc: 45, 152, 454, 165(2),
    185(2), 408(2), 418(2), 490(2)
  abolition of 420, 483
  Anti-transportation, NSW
    452(2)
  Arthur administration 32 to 38
  chain gangs 34
  convict mutiny 13

corporal punishment 13
  Molesworth Committee on
    Transportation 398, 545(2)
  Norfolk Island 13, 483(2)
  political offenders 13
  Select Committee on
    Transportation 450(2)
  Tasmania 8, 32 to 38, 414,
    138(2), 336(2), 590(2), 593(2)
  Victoria 90(2)
  Western Australia 576, 577,
    440(2)
  NSW 386, 483, 72(2), 135(2),
    151(2), 191(2), 193(2), 206(2),
    407(2), 483(2), 524(2), 587(2)
Treason 512, 156(2), 352(2)
Trials: see Convicts: Places of
  Trials. see also Court Cases;
  Law.
Trigonometrical survey 378, 418,
  117(2), 348(2), 467(2), 543(2)
Turnpike road 191(2), 210(2),
  401(2), 520(2) see also Toll
  Bridges.
Unemployment 136(2) see also
  Depressions
Unions: see Trade Unionism;
  Tolpuddle Martyrs
United States of America:
  see: Churches — USA
  see: Houses etc. — USA
  see: Newspapers — USA
  see: Organisations — USA
  see: Places Index — USA
  see: Religion — USA
  see: Universities — Misc.
Universities (miscellaneous)
  ACT — Australian National
    University 254(2)
  Austria — Vienna University
    537(2)
  Denmark — Copenhagen
    University 537(2)
  France — see below
  Germany — see below
  Italy — Pisa, University of
    376(2)
  Poland — University of Vilna
    (Poland) 403
  Russia — Kazan University 83
  Russia — Russian Naval
    Academy 99(2)
  Sweden — Uppsala University
    456(2), 537(2)
  Switzerland — Geneva
    University 206(2)
  University of Olinda 79(2)
  USA — St Louis 128
  USA — Yale College 279
Universities: England
  Cambridge University: 158,
    196, 212, 256, 286, 398, 29(2),
    38(2), 272(2), 285(2), 476(2),
    584(2), 630(2)
  Cambridge University Colleges:
  — Caius College, Cambridge
    66(2)
  — Christ's College 286, 550(2),
    619(2)
  — Corpus Christi College 361,
    368(2)
  — Gonville and Caius College

CAM 10
— Jesus College, Cambridge 111
— Magdalene College 455, 17(2), 208(2)
— Pembroke College 256, 574
— Pembroke Hall 158
— Peterhouse 87, 584(2)
— Queen's College 312(2)
— St John's College 169, 456, 198(2), 226(2), 466(2), 613(2)
— Sydney Sussex College 417
— Trinity College 89, 139, 196, 355, 407, 436, 453, 464, 480, 485, 530, 174(2), 182(2), 294(2), 311(2), 475(2), 570(2), 627(2)
— Trinity Hall 319(2), 603(2)
Oxford University: 31, 52, 154, 211, 249, 311, 345, 347, 240(2), 245(2), 285(2), 388(2), 431(2), 456(2), 406(2), 470(2)
Oxford University Colleges:
— Alban Hall 368(2)
— Brasenose College 351(2), 424(2), 618(2)
— Christ Church College 52, 99, 526, 554, 377(2), 470(2)
— Exeter College 534(2)
— Lincoln College 468(2)
— Magdalen College 371, 372, 134(2), 417(2), 437(2)
— Oriel College 207(2)
— Pembroke College 210
— Queen's College 55
— St Alban's Hall 431(2)
— St Edmund Hall 211
— St John's College 372, 285(2)
— University College 29, 134(2)
London University 21, 192, 136(2), 185(2)
Universities: France
Irish College, Paris 302(2)
Montpellier 69(2)
Paris Medical School 323(2)
Paris University 361(2)
Universities: Germany
Berlin University 102(2), 421(2)
Breslau University 33(2)
Erlangen, Bavaria 544, 88(2)
Gottingen University 102(2), 537(2)
Halle University 404, 421(2)
Universities: Ireland
Belfast College 55(2)
Catholic University, Dublin 31
Dublin University 12(2), 406(2)
Dublin University: see Trinity College 516(2)
Royal University of Ireland 31
Trinity College, Dublin 48, 168, 195, 251, 291, 314, 420, 421, 557, 14(2), 15(2), 51(2), 216(2), 234(2), 252(2), 278(2), 337(2), 392(2), 406(2), 512(2)
University College, Dublin 31
Universities: New South Wales
University of Sydney: 6, 11, 58, 86, 113, 163, 293, 315, 557, 578, 41(2), 44(2), 55(2), 82(2), 110(2), 120(2), 153(2), 180(2), 181(2), 183(2), 199(2), 241(2), 255(2), 276(2), 284(2), 285(2), 340(2), 344(2), 357(2), 415(2), 512(2), 514(2), 524(2), 526(2), 588(2), 589(2), 600(2), 614(2)
Museum of Antiquities 284(2)
University of Sydney Colleges
— St Andrew's College 82(2)
— St John's College 337, 535, 44(2), 199(2), 340(2), 344(2), 512(2)
— St Paul's College 11, 163, 255, 41(2), 237(2), 570(2)
Universities: Scotland
Aberdeen University 167(2), 399, 472, 567
Edinburgh University 51, 92, 151, 219, 232, 242, 268, 272, 286, 335, 372, 457, 499, 519, 119(2), 144(2), 172(2), 266(2), 270(2), 283(2), 285(2), 361(2), 362(2), 407(2), 418(2), 427(2), 449(2), 551(2), 624(2)
Edinburgh University Medical College 169
Glasgow University 253, 327, 335, 428, 492, 76(2), 118(2), 266(2), 357(2), 466(2)
Glasgow, Divinity Hall 327
St Andrew's University 92, 210, 232, 291, 10(2), 515(2)
Universities: South Australia
University of Adelaide 175
Universities: Tasmania
University of Tasmania 258, 330
Universities: Victoria
University of Melbourne 29(2), 93(2), 244(2), 352(2), 515(2)
Vaccination 419(2) see also Health
Vegetarianism 73(2)
Victoria:
see: Cemeteries — VIC
see: Churches — VIC
see: Houses etc. — VIC
see: Newspapers — VIC
see: Organisations — VIC
see: Places Index — VIC
see: Politics — VIC
see: Religion — VIC
see: Schools — VIC
see: Universities — VIC
Viticulture 103(2)
Wales:
see: Cemeteries — WALES
see: Churches — WALES
see: Houses etc. — WALES
see: Newspapers — WALES
see: Organisations — WALES
see: Places Index — WALES
see: Politics — WALES
see: Religion — WALES
see: Schools — WALES
see: Universities — WALES
Wars: see Army: Wars, battles etc.
Water mill 449(2), 507(2) see Wind mill
Water police 335(2)
Water supply: 90(2), 100(2), 414(2), 528(2)
Melbourne 109
Sydney 188
Western Australia:
see: Cemeteries — WA
see: Churches — WA
see: Houses etc. — WA
see: Newspapers — WA
see: Organisations — WA
see: Places Index — WA
see: Politics — WA
see: Religion — WA
see: Schools — WA
see: Universities — WA
Windmills 57, 61, 115, 356, 358, 497, 510, 108(2), 139(2), 309(2), 395(2) see also Water mill
Women 173, 181, 215, 221, 226, 330, 331, 370, 411, 465, 19(2), 52(2), 65(2), 144(2), 186(2), 259(2), 298(2), 373(2), 555(2)
Yachting 247(2)
Zoology 249, 466, 470, 167(2)